Best regards,

J. Milton Yinger

Religion, Society and the Individual

Religion, Societ

The Macmillan Comp

J. MILTON YINGER

PROFESSSOR OF SOCIOLOGY AND ANTHROPOLOGY
OBERLIN COLLEGE

and the Individual

AN INTRODUCTION TO
THE SOCIOLOGY OF RELIGION

New York

ACKNOWLEDGMENTS

ACKNOWLEDGMENT IS MADE TO THE FOLLOWING PUBLISHERS AND AUTHORS FOR PERMISSION TO REPRINT SELECTIONS FROM COPYRIGHTED MATERIAL:

ABINGTON PRESS—*The Small Sects in America,* Revised edition, by Elmer T. Clark, copyright, 1949, by Pierce & Smith.

GEORGE ALLEN & UNWIN LTD.—*The Social Teaching of the Christian Churches,* Ernst Troeltsch; *The Protestant Ethic and the Spirit of Capitalism,* by Max Weber.

THE AMERICAN ACADEMY OF POLITICAL AND SOCIAL SCIENCE—"Characteristics of American Organized Religion," by Winfred E. Garrison, *The Annals,* March, 1948.

AMERICAN ANTHROPOLOGICAL ASSOCIATION—"A Socio-Cultural Interpretation of the Peyote Cult," by Bernard Barber, *American Anthropologist,* October–December, 1941; "Cultural Significance of the Ghost Dance," by Alexander Lesser, *American Anthropologist,* January–March, 1933.

THE AMERICAN SOCIOLOGICAL SOCIETY—"Role Conflicts of Military Chaplains," by Waldo W. Burchard, *American Sociological Review,* October, 1954; "Church-Sect Dichotomy and Socio-Economic Status," by Russell Dynes, *American Sociological Review,* October, 1955; "Holiness Religion: Cultural Shock and Social Reorganization," by John B. Holt, *American Sociological*

Review, October, 1940; "A Comparative Study of Values in Social Action in Two Southwestern Communities," by Evon Z. Vogt and Thomas F. O'Dea, *American Sociological Review*, December, 1953.

CAMBRIDGE UNIV. PRESS—*Religion in America*, by Willard L. Sperry.

CHRISTIAN CENTURY FOUNDATION—"The New Look in American Piety," by Roy A. Eckhardt, reprinted by permission of *The Christian Century* from the issue of November 17, 1954; "Co-Existence or Total War?" by Reinhold Niebuhr, reprinted by permission of *The Christian Century* from the issue of August 18, 1954.

DOUBLEDAY & COMPANY, INC.—*Protestant-Catholic-Jew*, by Will Herberg, copyright, 1955, by Will Herberg, reprinted by permission of Doubleday & Company, Inc.; *The Heathens*, by W. W. Howells, copyright, 1948, by William Howells, reprinted by permission of Doubleday & Company, Inc.

DUKE UNIV. PRESS—*Religion in the Struggle for Power*, by J. Milton Yinger, copyright, 1946, by Duke Univ. Press.

THE FREE PRESS—*The Elementary Forms of the Religious Life*, by Emile Durkheim, copyright, 1947, by The Free Press; *Religion Among the Primitives*, by William J. Goode, copyright, 1951, by William J. Goode; *Conservative Judaism: An American Religious Movement*, by Marshall Sklare, copyright, 1955, by The Free Press.

VICTOR GOLLANCZ, LTD.—*The Heathens*, by W. W. Howells; *Left-Wing Democracy in the English Civil War*, by David W. Petegorsky.

HARPER & BROS.—*Protestant Churches and Industrial America*, by Henry F. May, copyright, 1949, by Harper & Bros.

HARVARD UNIV. PRESS—"The Protestant Churches and Totalitarianism (Germany, 1933–1945)," by Franklin H. Littell from *Totalitarianism*, edited by Carl J. Friedrich, Cambridge, Mass.: Harvard University Press, copyright, 1954, by The President and Fellows of Harvard College, reprinted by permission of the publishers; *Religion in 20th Century America*, by Herbert Wallace Schneider, Cambridge, Mass.: Harvard University Press, copyright, 1952, by The President and Fellows of Harvard College, reprinted by permission of the publishers.

THE EDWARD W. HAZEN FOUNDATION—*Religious Perspectives of College Teaching in Sociology and Social Psychology*, by Talcott Parsons.

HENRY HOLT AND COMPANY, INC.—*The Age of the Reformation*, by Preserved Smith, copyright, 1920, by Henry Holt and Company, Inc.

HOUGHTON-MIFFLIN COMPANY—*Patterns of Culture*, by Ruth Benedict, copyright, 1934, by Ruth Benedict.

ALFRED A. KNOPF, INC.—*American Society*, by Robin Williams, copyright, 1951, by Alfred A. Knopf, Inc., reprinted by permission of Alfred A. Knopf, Inc.

J. B. LIPPINCOTT COMPANY—*Religion and the Modern World*, by J. H. Randall and J. H. Randall, Jr., copyright, 1929, by Frederick A. Stokes Co.

LONGMANS, GREEN & CO., INC.—*The Town Labourer, 1760–1832*, by J. L. Hammond and Barbara Hammond.

THE MACMILLAN CO.—*Human Society*, by Kingsley Davis, copyright, 1949, by The Macmillan Co.; *The Social Teaching of the Christian Churches*, by Ernst Troeltsch, copyright, 1931, by The Macmillan Co.

OXFORD UNIV. PRESS, INC.—*From Max Weber*, edited by Hans H. Gerth and Charles W. Mills, copyright, 1946, by Oxford Univ. Press.

PAPERS OF THE PEABODY MUSEUM OF AMERICAN ARCHAEOLOGY AND ETHNOLOGY —*Navaho Witchcraft*, by Clyde Kluckhohn, from Vol. XXII, No. 2 of the *Papers*, 1944, by The President and Fellows of Harvard College.

TALCOTT PARSONS—*The Theory of Social and Economic Organization*, by Max Weber, edited by Talcott Parsons, copyright, 1947, by Talcott Parsons.

PUBLIC AFFAIRS PRESS—*Messiahs, Their Role in Civilization*, by Wilson D. Wallis, copyright, 1943, by The Am. Council on Public Affairs.

PAUL R. REYNOLDS & SON—*The Varieties of Religious Experience*, by William James, copyright, 1902, by William James, permission to reprint granted by Paul R. Reynolds & Son, 599 Fifth Avenue, New York 17, N. Y.

RINEHART & COMPANY, INC.—*Escape from Freedom*, by Erich Fromm, copyright, 1941, by Erich Fromm, reprinted by permission of Rinehart & Company, Inc., New York, Publishers; *Society: An Introductory Analysis*, by R. M. MacIver and Charles H. Page, copyright, 1949, by Robert M. MacIver and Charles H. Page, reprinted by permission of Rinehart & Company, Inc., New York, Publishers.

THE ROYAL INSTITUTE OF INTERNATIONAL AFFAIRS—"Religious Opposition to Nationalism in the Middle East," by Emil Marmorstein, *International Affairs*, July, 1952.

CHARLES SCRIBNER'S SONS—*The Protestant Ethic and the Spirit of Capitalism*, by Max Weber, reprinted with the permission of Charles Scribner's Sons.

SHOESTRING PRESS—*The Social Sources of Denominationalism*, by H. Richard Niebuhr, copyright, 1954, by Shoestring Press.

SOCIAL FORCES—"The Marginal Catholic: An Institutional Approach," by Joseph H. Fichter, December, 1953; "Values, Positivism, and the Functional Theory of Religion: The Growth of a Moral Dilemma," by William L. Kolb, May, 1953; "The Ras Tafari Movement in Jamaica," by George E. Simpson, December, 1955.

SOCIETY FOR THE PROMOTION OF CHRISTIAN KNOWLEDGE—"Magic, Science, and Religion," by Bronislaw Malinowski, in *Science, Religion, and Reality*, edited by Joseph Needham.

THE UNIV. OF CHICAGO PRESS—"A Contribution to the Sociology of Religion," *American Journal of Sociology*, reprinted May, 1955; *Sociology of Religion*, by Joachim Wach, copyright, 1944, by the Univ. of Chicago; *American Life: Dream and Reality*, by W. Lloyd Warner, copyright, 1953, by the Univ. of Chicago.

UNIV. OF PENNSYLVANIA PRESS—*Black Gods of the Metropolis*, by Arthur Fauset, Vol. III of the Publications of Philadelphia Anthropological Society, 1944, copyright by the Univ. of Pennsylvania Press.

ACKNOWLEDGMENTS   vii

UNIV. OF TORONTO PRESS—*Church and Sect in Canada,* by S. D. Clark.

THE UNITED STATES CONFERENCE FOR THE WORLD COUNCIL OF CHURCHES—
"From Sect to Church," by Walter Muelder, *Christendom,* Autumn, 1945.

WILLIAMS & NORGATE LTD.—*Religion and the Modern World,* by J. H. Randall
and J. H. Randall, Jr.

YALE UNIV. PRESS—*A Common Faith,* by John Dewey, copyright, 1934, by
Yale Univ. Press; *Psychoanalysis and Religion,* by Erich Fromm, copyright,
1950, by Erich Fromm; *Millhands and Preachers,* by Liston Pope, copyright,
1942, by Yale Univ. Press.

To Susan, John, and Nancy

Preface

This book is an expression of the belief that the student of society must be a student of religion. Wherever one looks—in a preliterate village, in a commercial town, in a modern metropolis—he finds religion woven into the fabric of social life. Beliefs, rituals, group structures are enormously various, but no society lacks them. To neglect the study of religion is to miss one of the most fruitful ways of studying the life of man.

This was well understood by the founders of sociology and anthropology. Although they differed widely in personal conviction, each understood that the student of human life had to set as one of his central tasks the exploration of religion. Despite the excellent beginnings, however, the sociology of religion has developed only slowly. For a generation it has been fairly remote from the most vital concerns of social scientists. Only among anthropologists, with their attention to the whole range of culture, has a vigorous interest in religion been consistently maintained.

In the last ten or fifteen years, however, this situation has begun to change. The "return to religion" is at least partially matched by a "return to the study of religion." Many psychologists and sociologists, and at least a few economists, are discovering that the analysis of religion

xi

is fundamental to a number of their most significant questions. Empirical studies and interpretive essays are appearing in increasing numbers. It is my hope that this attempt to prepare a systematic analysis of religion from the point of view of sociology may give some impetus to this development.

It is useful to draw a distinction between the sociology of religion and the sociological analysis of particular religions. The former is an attempt to discover general principles concerning the relationship of religion to society; the latter seeks to apply these principles to specific situations. One of these approaches shades off into the other, of course, and neither could be developed without the other. Yet they can be distinguished. This study is a search for general principles. There is no effort to develop a complete sociological analysis of several religions or even of one religion. The historical or "case" materials used are brought in to illustrate and to test the usefulness of general propositions. I have no doubt that many of the generalizations will have to be revised and supplemented, or discarded, as they are used in the analysis of additional situations. But if they serve to encourage further observation of human behavior and to promote the systematic study of religion, they will prove to be of value.

A systematic treatise of this kind is a product of the work of scores of writers, whose ideas are here imperfectly distilled. My indebtedness to them can only be suggested by footnote references and bibliography. Several persons have been of great help to me in the preparation of this volume. George E. Simpson has been a source of continuous encouragement and stimulation at every stage of its development. I can only inadequately express my thanks to him. I am grateful to Robin M. Williams, Jr. for a very careful and helpful reading of the entire essay. They are not responsible, of course, for any errors that may be found or for the interpretations. I should like to thank Oberlin College for a leave of absence that gave me the several quiet months needed to bring the scattered thoughts of a decade into sharper focus. Mrs. Margaret Streicher and Miss June Wright prepared the manuscript not only with speed and skill, but with unfailing good humor. Most of all, my thanks go to Winnie McHenry Yinger, my wife, for bearing so graciously the difficulties that descend upon a household when a book is in the making. By her unfailing support she expressed a quiet confidence that the product would be worth the effort. If the book has any value, her support is a major cause.

J. MILTON YINGER
Oberlin, Ohio

Contents

xiii

PART 2

Readings in the Sociology of Religion

PART 1

The Sociology
of Religion

CHAPTER 1

Introduction

It is the conviction of many thoughtful men that the objective study of religion is at best impossible, and at worst dangerous. How is it possible, they may ask, to "see" a stained-glass window from the outside? Its whole meaning is apparent only as the light shines through, just as the true meaning of religion is visible only to one on the inside. What can be the consequences, moreover, of an objective study of religion, based as religion is on faith, but the weakening of that faith? And many would add: At a time when mankind so desperately needs courage to face the crises that beset us, is not the weakening of faith disastrous?

For generations, many social scientists have either disregarded these questions or treated them lightly. It has often been assumed that everything of importance about religion could ultimately be known by objective study. And "weakening of faith" was variously regarded as desirable, unnecessary, or of no concern to the scientist.

In the contemporary scene, however, easy assumptions concerning the problems that are associated with the objective study of religion are gradually being dispelled. Social scientists are less prone to assert that all that is important about religion is available to the objective observer. This is, after all, an extra-scientific *assumption*, not itself demonstrable by scien-

3

tific study. Not many would claim that the analysis of paint, painter, and patron exhausts the meaning of art; and we are less prone now than formerly to make equivalent claims for the analysis of religion. Let the scientist realize that his propositions, derived from objective study, do not exhaust the meaning of things.

In the writer's judgment, the scientific study of religion will gain by the adoption of this more modest conception of its role. This decidedly does not mean, however, that the objective study of religion is unimportant. Nor does it mean that the scientist should refrain from the complete explanation of his topic. Indeed, it is a part truth to say that one can see a stained-glass window only from the inside. One can see the inside of the window only from the inside; but we can press the analogy a little further: From the outside one can see the outside, and one can find out who built it, who put it in, who keeps it in repair, and who goes inside to see it from that perspective. Judgments will vary concerning the importance of these questions and similar questions about religion. Though the writer thinks they are very important, for reasons which this essay may help to make clear, this is not a position that can be demonstrated or argued meaningfully with one who disagrees.

He believes it to be an error to assert that "only someone who knows religion because he practices some form of it can be expected to say something meaningful about it." [1] This is similar to the obscurantist claim of some psychoanalysts that only those who have been psychoanalyzed have any right to comment on the validity of the classic Freudian theory. Some things can be said about a religion only by the practitioner, other kinds of observations can be made by one who shares another faith, and still further study can be made by the doubter. The scientist will not prejudge any of these observations, for each approach may furnish him with data valuable for the development of his theory of religion.

The question of the desirability of an objective study of religion is even more controversial than the question of its possibility. There are few major subjects about which men know so little, yet feel so certain. The educated man is often more provincial in his religious views than in almost any other part of his thinking. It is widely held, if not often expressed, that one's received religion has all the necessary thinking already embodied in it. The writer has the strong impression—he can scarcely document it precisely—that even church historians and theologians, many of whom in the fifty years prior to the first World War strongly supported the growth of the objective study of religion, have tended now to reemphasize faith

[1] Joachim Wach, in a review of Joseph Fichter's *Southern Parish*, Vol. I, *Journal of Religion*, April, 1952, p. 139.

in *opposition to* analysis. The comparative study of religion is less of a purely intellectual activity with them and more of a means for "purifying" belief. This is not so much an anti-scientific trend as a much more qualified support of the development of a science of religion.

The writer does not want to dismiss this question lightly. He is scarcely in a position to demonstrate that the analysis of religion by science is beneficial in its consequences for all people in all times and places. His own position is a *belief*—and probably part of his religion, as we shall define the term below—that the total, long-run consequences of scientific study are beneficial. In the words of Ducasse: "To inform one's self, however, and to exercise intelligence, is a risky business—for skeptics, let it be noted, no less than for bigots. But then, risky too and probably more so, are conceit of ignorance and allegiance to bias." [2]

It may be appropriate to come back to this topic briefly at the end of the essay. Having explored some aspects of the sociology of religion, we may be in a better position to judge its consequences. Some social scientists will look upon the concern for this question as an unduly apologetic and defensive attitude, as it may be. Perhaps the writer has been too much impressed by the hydrogen bomb. Yet it may be that part of the knowledge that men of science should seek is knowledge of the consequences of their own work. Let us turn then to the analysis of religion without timidity or hesitation, but with full regard for its significance in the total human enterprise.

THE PROBLEM OF DEFINITION

Many studies of religion stumble over the first hurdle: the problem of definition. The writer is by no means certain that he can leap over this difficulty, but he has some hope, based on the conviction that the problem is less one of communication than a matter of disagreement over the nature and functions of definition. The disagreement, to be sure, is often a substantial one, based both on different values and on different conceptions of the nature of the universe in which we live. If this is recognized, disagreements will not be eliminated, but they will no longer rest on a failure of communication. One may be able at least to say: I can understand how a person, starting from those particular premises, would define religion in that way.

What are some of the disagreements over value and premise that have complicated the definition of religion? A devotee of a particular faith is likely to believe that a definition *ought* to describe the "true quality"

[2] C. J. Ducasse, *A Philosophical Scrutiny of Religion*, p. 16.

of religion. He is not happy with the concept that a definition is a heuristic device, a tool of analysis, useful for one purpose, but of no value for another. He knows what religion *is* (it is belief in and activities toward the supernatural, for example) and is impatient with a definition that may seem to be a subtle evasion of an obvious fact. A related difficulty stems from the fact that some people divide the phenomena of the world into sharply distinct categories, mistaking their labels for things and events for the things and events themselves. The scientist is more likely to look upon the world as a flowing continuum. He considers his definitions to be arbitrary dividing marks among phenomena that cannot be sharply distinguished. Thus religion-nonreligion is a continuum; we must recognize that there are some patterns that are marginally religious, according to any criteria that one may select.

  Definitions, then, are tools; they are to some degree arbitrary; they lay stress on similarities *within* a delimited area and on the differences *outside* it, thus to give emphasis to one aspect of reality. They are abstract, which is to say that they are oversimplifications. In dealing with a subject so complex and concerned with a range of data so broad as religion, a topic approached for many different purposes, one must give up the idea that there is *one* definition that is "correct" and satisfactory for all. We readily grant that the definitions of a "tree" offered by a botanist, a lumberman, and an artist might vary widely, yet each definition would be appropriate to a specific interest. Such variety is no less appropriate in definitions of religion.

  Types of Definitions. For our purposes, we need only to distinguish briefly three kinds of definitions of religion, and need not undertake a history or a catalogue of definitions. (One can gather a hundred or more in a few hours time.) Many definitions are valuative; they describe what, in the given writer's judgment, religion *ought* to be, often expressed as what it "really" or "basically" *is*. Clearly such definitions are inappropriate for the tasks of science. Other definitions are descriptive or substantive. They designate certain kinds of beliefs and practices as religion, without, on the one hand, evaluating them, or, on the other, indicating their function or seeking to discover whether other beliefs and practices perform similar functions. Thus, in Tylor's words, religion is "belief in Spiritual Beings." This kind of definition has the advantage of being clear-cut and reasonably easy to apply. One can proceed from it to a classification of the kinds of Spiritual Beings and the kinds of practices and organizations that are found in various societies. By such a definition, attention is naturally drawn to the differences among religions as distinct historical entities. The emphasis is primarily on religions as *cultural* systems. Their doctrines, rites, sacred texts, typical group structures, and the like, are described, contrasted, and compared. This is what religion *is*, such definitions say, and these particular patterns indicate what Buddhism, Judaism, and the religion of the Arunta *are*.

Substantive definitions can be of great value, particularly for those who are concerned with religions as historical and cultural facts, not with religion as a pan-human phenomenon. They are of greater value in the study of stable societies, where distinctive and coherent religious systems are more likely to develop, than they are in the study of changing societies; for in the latter, religion itself also changes, continually complicating any effort to define what it is, but suggesting efforts to study what it does.

A FUNCTIONAL DEFINITION

For many problems, it is the functional kind of definition suggested in the previous sentence that is most useful. One need not quarrel with those who prefer to define religion in terms of value or in terms of essence, but for analytic purposes the need is for a definition that focuses on process. A comparative science of religion, interested not only in the vast range of differences in belief and practice, but also in the similarities that justify the use of a common term to refer to the whole range, must be concerned with function. This is particularly true if the kinds of questions one is interested in refer not only to religion as a cultural fact, but to religion as a manifestation of personality and as one aspect of society. It is widely held today that for many purposes it is a mistake to separate the analysis of culture (the system of norms and usages designating "right" behavior to the members of a society) from the analysis of personality (the organized system of tendencies of an individual); and it is equally a mistake to separate these from the analysis of social systems ("networks of interactive relationships," as Parsons calls them). Special studies of culture, personality, and society are appropriate, of course; but their theories must remain on a highly abstract level. To come nearer to the understanding of concrete action we must study their mutual influence.

It is paradoxical that in order to focus attention more nearly on religion as concrete behavior, a definition must be more abstract. To define religion, for example, simply as "belief in God" (a definition that can be seen as either valuative or substantive or both) is to give it a fairly sharp referent; but such a definition suggests no question of the relationship between personal anxiety or concern for one's salvation, for

example, and belief in God; and it poses no problems of the relationship
between the efforts to maintain social order and religion as defined. The
more abstract definition that we shall develop below carries implicit
within it a concern for the analysis of actual behavior. It points to major
questions of human action; and thus, in our judgment, is more fruitful
for a science of human behavior. One does not say that it is more "true,"
but only that it will serve the needs of current scientific work more
fully than valuative or substantive definitions. Those who think of definitions as attempts to capture the "essence" of something look with disfavor
on this experimental approach; those who think of definitions as tools
of analysis accept it.

The person who seeks to define religion in functional terms, to be
sure, faces a number of difficulties. He must avoid a definition that is
tied only to his own religious experience or to cultures similar to his own.
He must recognize that the intense specialization of modern societies
gives one a different perspective on religion than one gets in less highly
differentiated societies, where the infusion of religious elements into all
phases of life is more obvious. Perhaps the most serious difficulty is
related to the ease with which one drifts into a valuative position in
his definition without intending to. If religion is defined by what are
thought to be its functions, then one should not be surprised to find it
"functional." And this may lead, in turn, to a circularity of reasoning:
If it can be shown that a given system of beliefs and practices that is
generally thought to be a religion is not performing the functions by
which religion has been defined, then one declares that such a system is
not "really" religion at all. This error can be avoided by indicating that
religion is an *effort* to perform certain functions for man. This does not
imply the value position that it always succeeds, nor that systems which
do not succeed are therefore not religions. And it does not necessarily
imply that one desires those functions to be performed.

To solve or reduce this problem, however, may only serve to create
another. Is every effort to perform certain functions, however wide the
range of differences—in content of belief, in number of persons involved,
in degree of historical continuity, etc.—to be called religion? Is there
no place, in other words, for functional alternatives, because every
possible "alternative" must, by definition, also be considered a religion?
We shall deal with this question at several points in this essay, and need
say here only that we shall define religion as a certain kind of effort to
perform various functions. We shall identify it by the intensity or
"ultimate" quality of the attempt, and by the interconnection of several
related functions. Thus there is a great deal of room for functional alter-

natives. Since we are dealing with several continuous variables, the problem of more or less inevitably arises, and we shall be concerned to describe some systems of belief and action that are marginally religious, in our sense, to indicate that there is no sharp dividing line.

What, then, are the functions that distinguish religion as a human activity? To try to answer this question is essentially the task of this book; hence the highly condensed statement appropriate to a definition can only hint at problems that receive fuller treatment in later chapters. Paul Tillich has said that religion is that which concerns us ultimately. This can be a good starting point for a functional definition. While there are important disagreements concerning the "ultimate" problems for man, a great many would accept the following as among the fundamental concerns of human societies and individuals: How shall we respond to the fact of death? Does life have some central meaning despite the suffering, the succession of frustrations and tragedies? How can we deal with the forces that press in on us, endangering our livelihood, our health, the survival and smooth operation of the groups in which we live—forces that our empirical knowledge is inadequate to handle? How can we bring our capacity for hostility and our egocentricity sufficiently under control that the groups within which we live, without which, indeed, life would be impossible, can be kept together?

Put in this way, these questions appear to be self-conscious and rational. They are more appropriately seen as deep-seated emotional needs, springing from the very nature of man as an individual and as a member of society. The questions appear first of all because they are felt—the death of a loved one wrenches our emotions, the failure to achieve that for which we yearn saddens and bewilders us; the hostility between ourselves and those around us infuses our social contacts with tension and prevents the achievement of mutual values. Religion may develop an intellectual system to interpret and deal with these questions, but they express first of all an underlying emotional need, not a group of rationally conceived problems.

Religion, then, can be defined as a system of beliefs and practices by means of which a group of people struggles with these ultimate problems of human life. It is the refusal to capitulate to death, to give up in the face of frustration, to allow hostility to tear apart one's human associations.

All men experience these wrenching difficulties to some degree. For some persons, however, they stand out as the most significant experiences of life. These individuals are impelled to try to discover some meaning in what seems to be senseless suffering, some road to salvation through the obstacles of human life. The beliefs and rites that make up a religion are the expressions of those who have felt the problems most intensively, who have been most acutely sensitive to the tragedies of death, the burdens of frustration, the sense of failure, the disruptive effects of hostility. Powered by the strength of their feelings, such religious innovators have created "solutions" appropriate to the enormity of the problems—solutions that frequently have burst the bonds of man's senses and of nature, but have brought their adherents some relief. Thus religions are built to carry the "peak load" of human emotional need.

Defined in this way, religion is—and seems likely to remain—an inevitable part of human life. Although the ways of struggling with these ultimate problems are enormously diverse, and seem destined for continuous change, the problems themselves are universal. A society that did not furnish its members with beliefs and practices that sought to deal with these ultimate problems would struggle along with an enormous burden of tragedy unallayed and hostility unrestrained—if indeed it could survive at all. This is only to say that some effort to deal with these questions is essential to human life as we know it, and not to say that any given religious system adequately answers these questions.

Religion, of course, is not alone in attempting to deal with the ultimate problems of human life. Rational efforts are important in all societies. Moreover, there are many individual emotional responses to insecurity and the problem of evil in addition to religion. Even in the healthiest and wealthiest and most rational of societies, however, secular responses cannot eliminate the problems of suffering, evil, and hostility. Realizing the gap between their hopes and the realities of their existence, men everywhere seek *closure* by a leap of faith that says: this need not, this will not, be true. Some time, some place, some how, suffering and evil will be defeated. (The enormous variation in conceptions of time, place, and method measures the range of religious expressions.)

The Persistent Functions of Religion. In this sense, religion can be thought of as a kind of residual means of response and adjustment. It is an attempt to explain what cannot otherwise be explained; to achieve power, all other powers having failed us; to establish poise and serenity in the face of evil and suffering that other efforts have failed to eliminate. "When other helpers fail, when comforts flee," man can give himself over to despair, or he can seek relief by the leap of faith. Most people have chosen the latter, and have preferred, in Reinhold Niebuhr's words, "a citadel of hope built on the edge of despair," to acceptance of ultimate defeat.

Dunlap uses the concept of "residual" in his definition of religion,

Hence if Unitarianism is concerned only to glorify an already glorious human animal it becomes naught but social code of rationalization that is smug but not challenging nor aw...

which he describes as ". . . the institution, or feature of culture, which undertakes, in the service of mankind, those functions for which there is no other institution or for the undertaking of which no other institution is as yet adequately prepared." [3] This definition, although it is helpful, seems to the present writer to require further attention to the *persistent* functions of religion. Is there no core of functions that seems likely to be a continuing source of religious activity? Or are science, philosophy, art, government, medicine, and the like, chiseling steadily away at religion so that it is a "suicidal institution" as Dunlap calls it? The present writer finds it difficult to envisage a society in which major unresolved problems of the "ultimate" variety we have discussed do not remain. He suspects—and here he runs the danger of an attempt to prove by definition, a very unsatisfactory kind of proof—that the belief that man can devise secular processes for performing the functions now served by religion is in itself a "citadel of hope," and not an empirically validated proposition. It is an emotional and intellectual closure more congenial to the cultural training and personality tendencies of many people today, and thus serves at least a quasi-religion function for them.

The word "residual" need not carry the connotation of "unimportant final item" or "gradually disappearing." It might better be thought of as "that which always remains." Malinowski writes:

To us the most essential point about magic and religious ritual is that it steps in only where knowledge fails. Supernaturally founded ceremonial grows out of life, but it never stultifies the practical efforts of man. In his ritual of magic or religion, man attempts to enact miracles, not because he ignores the limitations of his mental powers, but, on the contrary, because he is fully cognizant of them. To go one step further, the recognition of this seems to me indispensable if we want once and for ever to establish the truth that religion has its own subject-matter, its own legitimate field of development; that this must never encroach on the domain where science, reason, and experience ought to remain supreme. [4]

This is not a wholly satisfactory statement, from the point of view of science. It is subject to grave doubt that religion "never stultifies the practical efforts of man." Malinowski shifts easily into a value assertion when he declares that there is an area "where science, reason, and experience ought to remain supreme." But Malinowski implies, as opposed to Dunlap, that religion, as a residual mode of adjustment, is unlikely to disappear. This is an empirical question, for which we have only inadequate evidence. What evidence we have inclines the writer toward

---

[3] Knight Dunlap, *Religion: Its Function in Human Life*, p. 321.
[4] Bronislaw Malinowski, *The Foundations of Faith and Morals*, p. 34.

the view that religion as defined by the functionalist is a permanent aspect of human society, no more likely to disappear than "the family" (however much it may change) or "government" (despite the enormous range of variation).

William James, in one of his acute observations, notes that in those responses to life which "fall short of religion" we may come to accept the suffering and frustrations of life, but we regard them as impositions of necessity, and at best we accept them without complaint. In religious life, however, surrender and sacrifice are positively espoused; and in this attempt to conquer our problems, we may even add "unnecessary givings-up" in order to increase our happiness. "Religion thus makes easy and felicitous what in any case is necessary. . . ." [5] If we may tamper with James' statement a bit, to add that "religion is an *attempt* to . . . ," we might be led to another definition of some value: Religion is an organized effort to make virtue of our ultimate necessities.

Are Individual Systems of Belief to Be Called Religion?   A primary difficulty with a functional definition is that there is no obvious point at which one may draw a line and say: "Here religion ends and non-religion begins." In a religiously-heterogeneous and changing society, the question of "private" systems of belief and practice arises. Are they to be called religions? Are they not attempts to fulfill the same functions that shared and historically identified faiths seek to perform? In our view, one should answer this question in the negative. There is, to be sure, some truth in the statement that, "his work is his religion," or "he has dedicated himself to the discovery of a cure for cancer," with the implication that this is "his religion." There can be religious aspects of private systems of belief and action. A complete religion, however, is a social phenomenon; it is shared; it takes on many of its most significant aspects only in the interaction of the group. Both the feelings from which it springs and the "solutions" it offers are social, they arise from the fact that man is a group-living animal. The "ultimate questions" which we have identified as the center of the religious quest are ultimate primarily because of their impact on human association. Even death is not fundamentally an individual crisis, but a group crisis, threatening to tear the fabric of family and community.

Joachim Wach holds that all religions, despite their wide variations, are characterized by three universal expressions: the theoretical, or a system of beliefs, the practical, a system of worship, and the sociological, a system of social relationships. Until all of these are found, one may have religious tendencies, religious elements, but not a full religion,

[5] William James, *The Varieties of Religious Experience*, p. 51.

struggling with all the interrelated functions to which we have referred. Although the first of these expressions—the system of belief—is the one that modern man is most likely to think of as the heart of religion, both ethnological and etymological evidence suggests that religion as worship and religion as a system of social relationships may be the more basic aspects, belief coming in as an attempt to give coherence and meaning to worship and associations that have developed out of deeply felt needs. The word religion may have derived from the Latin *religare*, to bind together, or from *religere*, to rehearse, to execute painstakingly, suggesting both group identity and ritual. The testimony of most anthropologists gives support to the proposition that it is the acts of religion, and the associations, more than the beliefs, that give it a vital place in the life of preliterate societies. This may be less true in a literate society where the practice of seeking out explanations is more fully established and where religious specialists seek to relate religion to a complex and changing society.

The growing importance of the "belief" aspects of religion, however, should not lead us to misinterpret the nature of a religious intellectual system. It is a group of "mighty hypotheses," of "over-beliefs," of deductions that leap beyond those admissable by a calm appraisal of the facts. Man is not calm in face of the needs from which religion springs. As Durkheim says: "Science is fragmentary and incomplete; it advances but slowly and is never finished; but life cannot wait. The theories which are destined to make men live and act are therefore obliged to pass science and complete it prematurely." [6]

Are Non-theistic Systems of Belief to Be Called Religion? If the functional approach to the definition and analysis of religion is taken, it is not the nature of the *belief*, but the nature of the *believing* that requires study. Even a quick glance over the vast range of phenomena that we call religion reveals an enormous variety. The only justification for referring to such diversity of belief, of worship, and of organization by one term is the assumption that the many forms represent different attempts to deal with the same problems. In Paul Tillich's words: "We are all laboring under the yoke of religion; we all, sometimes, try to throw away old or new doctrines or dogmas, but after a little while we return, again enslaving ourselves and others in their servitude." [7] Many "non-religious" persons object to such a statement. They explicitly reject beliefs, forms of worship, and group associations that they identify as religious. It is unwise to argue this point, for from the perspective of

[6] Emile Durkheim, *The Elementary Forms of the Religious Life*, p. 431.
[7] Paul Tillich, *The Shaking of the Foundations*, p. 98.

the definition they use, they are correct in claiming to be "non-religious." The functionalist affirms simply that it is highly likely that such individuals, having left some traditional religion, will nevertheless affirm their faith in some "over-beliefs," will get emotional support from various symbols, acts, and ceremonies (worship), and will join with others in groups that seek to sustain and realize the shared beliefs. This point of view is seldom argued when it refers to some of the intense political movements of our time. Communism is now generally considered to have a religious quality.[8] Few deny the religious element in nationalism. In multi-religious societies (in the traditional sense) or in societies where an established religion has lost much of its appeal, nationalism as a religious force is particularly likely to appear. Faith, symbols, worshipful acts, and organizations built around the nation all appear. This is not simply the nationalization of religion (*Gott mit uns*), but the religionization of nation (*Vaterland über alles*).

Many modern intellectuals, perhaps particularly among the writer's fellow social scientists, will agree that many modern political and other "secular" movements might appropriately be regarded as religions, but they see no parallel in their own lives. A supernatural view of the world has become meaningless to them, they are repelled by a boastful and worshipful nationalism; they feel comfortable with a quiet kind of scientific secularism, motivated by idle curiosity with perhaps a nudge from a desire to help solve some human problem. Certainly a functional definition of religion that attempts to include such phenomena strains our imaginations. Yet a term that already includes, by common consent, the contemplations of a Buddhist monk and the ecstatic visions of a revivalist cult member, human sacrifice and ethical monotheism, may have room in it for science *as a way of life* (not as a method or as a group of tested propositions about nature). Not all scientists, in the methodological sense, accept science as a way of life. Many feel that the answers to man's ultimate problems are to be found in the traditional religions. But some turn to science even for this. If they do not require the ritualistic trappings and elaborate organization of a Comte, with his "positivistic religion," they certainly manifest many over-beliefs that, to repeat Durkheim's words, are "obliged to pass science and complete it prematurely." Few scientists doubt that the best way to grapple with human problems is to extend our knowledge of nature.

[8] This view is expressed, for example by Tillich, *ibid.*; by Erich Fromm, *Man for Himself*; by Reinhold Niebuhr, *Christianity and Power Politics*; by Jacques Maritain, *True Humanism*. See also the discussion of "functional alternatives" in Chapter 5, below.

Hydrogen bombs and the mass manipulation of people by propaganda may have given us pause, but they have not destroyed our "faith." That the gap between knowledge and action can be closed by knowledge itself is a mighty hypothesis that few of us would care to deny, but a careful reading of the story of man in the era of science would scarcely lead to the conclusion that the evidence is all in on that question. It is doubtless true that emotion-evoking symbols, rituals, elaborate group organizations for the purposes of reenforcing "science as a way of life" are rudimentary; but anyone who has attended a convention of scientists will hesitate to say that they are entirely lacking.

These sentences are not written to criticize science. Many of the author's own over-beliefs stem from science, and he finds them rich and satisfying. They are written rather to show that few men can avoid the problem of struggling with questions of "salvation" (how can man be saved from his most difficult problems), of the nature of reality, of evil (why do men suffer), and the like. Science as a way of life is an effort to deal with these questions.

Nor should this point of view be taken as a support for "religion in general." Some writers are happy about the recent trend toward a functionalist theory, as contrasted with earlier studies of religious origins, because they somehow find in this development support for a belief that *religion* is true, and often also a belief that the traditional religions have won scientific support. The problem is more complicated than they recognize.

Important problems of value inevitably arise from the functional approach. If almost any system of beliefs and actions can be religious, it is clear that one cannot regard religion in general as a "good thing." There are questions of choice. From the perspective of certain stated values, a given religion may be good, or it may be evil, or it may be a mixture of good and evil. The idea widely current in the United States that one ought "to be religious," with no reference to the nature or the consequences of various religions, is not a logical inference from the functionalist position.

We have looked at the problem of definition from several points of view. Perhaps our approach can be summed up in these words: The human individual, blessed (and sometimes cursed) with the power of language, capable, therefore, of anticipating the future, including a foreknowledge of his own death, able to verbalize ideal states, to create standards, is continually threatened with failure, with frustration, with his conception of justice unfulfilled. These problems tend to loom up as overwhelming or "absolute evils." Religion is man's attempt to "relativize" them by interpreting them as part of some larger good, some conception of the absolute that puts the individual's problems into new perspective, thus to remove or reduce their crushing impact. At the same time, man's social relations, his societies, are threatened by these same problems. Fear and frustration can lead to disrupting hostilities, unless they can be reinterpreted as part of a shared experience. In addition to that, there is the tendency of each individual to think only of himself, to make his joys, his desires into "absolute goods," threatening the patterns of mutual adjustment that social life requires. Religion is the attempt to "relativize" the individual's desires, as well as his fears, by subordinating them to a conception of absolute good more in harmony with the shared and often mutually contradictory needs and desires of human groups.

Certain kinds of belief and action very commonly, if not universally, develop from this double root of religion—the fundamental individual and group needs. First, failure and frustration are symbolically reinterpreted: failure is only apparent, death is not what it seems. Second, religion brings one into a fellowship which emphasizes shared experiences. This has two aspects: it "spreads the burdens" of one's fears and frustrations, and thus is a kind of "psychic insurance policy"; and it lays emphasis on shared and universally available values—the scheme of salvation—rather than the scarce values, thus to make the inevitable failures with regard to the latter seem less important. This leads to a third element in religion. At least some of the values which it upholds are super-empirical. This does not necessarily mean that they are supernatural, but they are beyond the reach of constant refutation by the facts of immediate experience.[9] It is a likely hypothesis that the more punishing the actual experience of a society—the more uncertain the food supply, for example, and the heavier the hand of death—the greater is the likelihood that its religion will emphasize supernatural means and/or supernatural goals. Members of a society more favorably situated, or a group in such a society, may make their leap of faith by projecting the trends they see around them in the natural world. In either event, men believe "more than the facts would allow," in an effort to sustain life and hope and to give more meaning to existence.

Such a definition of religion is, of course, highly abstract. It is an attempt to isolate, by analysis, a common factor that is embedded in enormously diverse religious systems. A different point of view would isolate different common elements that we have overlooked and obscured. Moreover, an abstract definition must be seen as a starting point for the study of religion, a point from which religions, as concrete systems of

---

[9] See Kingsley Davis, *Human Society,* pp. 518–531.

belief and action, depart in varying degrees and in many directions. These departures, as we shall see, and the forces behind them, must be of vital concern to the student of religion.

THE SOCIOLOGY OF RELIGION

Although the definition of religion which we have proposed has been developed from a scientific orientation, it can be used from various perspectives. It does not contain within it a definition of the sociology of religion. Here again, one is tempted to avoid brief denotation and to say: this book is the author's attempt to define the sociology of religion. As a starting point, however, we may sketch its mode of approach.

Sociology is variously defined in such terms as "the study of man in society," or "the study of human societies and their cultures," or "the science of social behavior." In the words of Max Weber, sociology is the search for the causes of social action. Action is behavior to which the individual attaches meaning, and social action is meaningful in that it takes account of the behavior of others.

Several facts of importance to our topic stand out as one studies human behavior in societies. The first is that behavior is heavily influenced, although not determined, by the system of norms, the prescriptions and proscriptions that characterize every human society. No society is without a culture. Nor can there be a culture, of course, independently of the individuals who sustain it in their actions. Culture as a system of norms is inferred from the patterned actions of the members of the society. Behavior in conformity with culture is secured, not so much by external social controls as by internal personality tendencies that are the result of socialization. Personality, however, is not simply the *result* of culture: the needs and tendencies of individuals have played a part in the development and change of culture; moreover, deviations from the norms are important to study.

A second fact that emerges from the study of human behavior is that a society is a complex system, not a collection of unrelated parts. There is, to be sure, incoherence and inconsistency, especially in times of rapid change; but this should not lead us to overlook the interconnections. The element of system, in fact, is often made apparent as a result of change: it can readily be observed that changes in the economy of a society, for example, are accompanied by changes in politics, in family patterns, and, as we shall see, in religion. The sociological conception of system is particularly important for the student of religion. If one tries to study religion apart from the social and cultural systems in which it is embedded, one will miss most of the sociologically important points.

Thirdly, it is widely held by students of society that there are certain "functional prerequisites" without which a society could not continue to exist. At first glance, this seems to be obvious—scarcely more than to say that an automobile engine could not exist, as a going "system," without a carburetor. No one will quarrel with the fact that a human society cannot exist that does not provide for the reproduction and protection of infants, for the satisfaction of economic necessities, etc. What is not so self-evident is that these functions are everywhere normatively governed. The processes followed for the satisfaction of these prerequisites of human life are culturally patterned. Mating is a necessity for biological survival of a group, but the family, according to this view, is necessary for its survival as a society. The family must fulfill, as a minimum, the functions of protection and socialization of the young and the reduction and control of sexual jealousies. Most writers list religion among the functional prerequisites.[10] The kind of religion, like the kind of family, can vary within extremely wide limits; but the absence of any religion, or the presence of sharply conflicting religions, imposes severe strains that a society cannot long sustain.

Three Phases of the Sociology of Religion. If this basic proposition concerning the "functional prerequisites of society" is correct, as the present writer believes it to be, the sociology of religion must be recognized as one of the central areas of sociology. In delimiting its sphere of interest we shall take the position, best developed in the work of Professor Parsons, that complete analysis of human action requires the study of social, cultural, and personality facts, both as separate systems capable of independent analysis and as mutually influencing parts of a larger system. It is perhaps justifiable to regard the study of religion as a social system (the nature of its groups, the patterns of interaction with which it is connected, its relationship to the rest of society, and the like) as the major focus of the sociology of religion. This must be closely bordered, however, by the study of religion as a cultural fact and the study of its relationship to personality tendencies.

In using the term "sociology," therefore, we have adopted a shorthand way of writing "anthropology-social psychology-sociology," in the conviction that these three fields so thoroughly interpenetrate that a theory based on one of them alone, even if it could be worked out, would be too abstract to be of value. Problems of academic structure and competition for status advantages have kept these three fields from the close interaction that adequate research and theoretical work demand. The

[10] See David Aberle, *et al.,* "The Functional Prerequisites of Society," *Ethics,* Vol. LX, No. 2 (1950), pp. 100–111.

distinction frequently drawn, for example, between anthropology, as the study of culture, and sociology, as the study of society, seems to the present writer to have a limited usefulness. It is difficult to study a society (an interacting group of human beings) without continuous reference to their culture (the system of norms and usages) by which their interaction is so strongly affected. (Even their departures from the cultural norms are highly significant.) And it is equally difficult to study a culture without constant attention to the people who are its bearers, the groups through which it is communicated, the societal processes by which it is changed. That is not to say that an analytic distinction cannot be drawn between society and culture. Indeed it is a necessary distinction. But a theory of religion that does not encompass both societal and cultural facts is very partial and likely to be misunderstood.

Professor Kroeber, while indicating that anthropology and sociology are very close, points to the emphasis on culture by anthropologists and the emphasis on society by sociologists. In the study of churches, for example, sociology is concerned with them primarily "as operating systems of interacting people," while anthropology is concerned *also* (n.b.) with their culture. Are there trinitarian, unitarian, or dualistic beliefs; what are the types of baptism? The precise doctrines and details of ritual, Kroeber writes, are not very important if one is studying the structure and function of religion as a social institution (the sociological task, in his view).

The relations of the communicants to one another are likely to be the same whether they are all trinitarians or all unitarians. On the contrary, if it is the doctrines or rituals or other cultural features, and the changes going on in them, that are the specific subject of study, the organization of the church somehow cannot properly and permanently be left out of consideration. At any rate, anthropologists so feel.[11]

To the present writer it seems very unlikely indeed that the "relations of the communicants" are independent of the beliefs they share in common. What Kroeber admits for the anthropologist—that he must study social systems to understand cultural systems—is equally true for the sociologist—he cannot comprehend society without analysis of the facts of culture. There can profitably be a difference in emphasis (and this essay will incline toward an emphasis on interaction); but we must avoid theoretical separation.

It is equally true that a theory of religion as an expression of personality needs and tendencies (the social psychological question) is less likely to be misunderstood if it is part of a larger theoretical scheme

[11] A. L. Kroeber, *Anthropology* (new edition, revised), pp. 846–847.

that encompasses social and cultural facts as well. Personality tendencies are in part a product of social processes and cultural norms; they, in turn, condition social interaction and affect the ways in which cultural requirements are carried out and are changed. We need, therefore, to pay attention to personality tendencies as they relate to a theory of religious behavior.[12] It is a matter of empirical observation that most, if not all, religions combine group and individual elements. They are generally concerned with both individual salvation and group integration. This dual reference may derive from the fact that each of these functions of religion is carried on more effectively within a religious system that contains the other also. Individual needs may be more adequately met by a *shared* system of beliefs, by a religion that furnishes some measure of the integration of society necessary for individual life. And the group functions may be adequately performed only by a religious system that seems to satisfy at least some measure of the needs of individual adherents. To be sure, the various functions will not always be found together within a single religious tradition. Confucianism paid scant heed to questions of individual "salvation," for example; but this may account for the spread of Taoism and Buddhism, with which Confucianism learned to live in a somewhat uneasy combination. If the tendency toward a duality of functions, either in a complex of religions or in a more unified pattern, is the rule, we have an additional reason for a theory of religion that is simultaneously sociological and social-psychological.

Even such a broadening of the way in which we shall ask the questions still leaves us with an abstraction. Our theory will explain religious behavior only insofar as that behavior is related to social, cultural, and personality facts. We shall need to be on our guard to avoid "the fallacy of misplaced concreteness." General psychological questions (how one learns religious ways of behaving or the effects of man's inherited nature on religious tendencies, for example) will for the most part be disregarded, except as they are involved in discussions of personality. We shall doubtless intrude occasionally, without due notice, into the psychological field, but in general psychological facts will be treated as limiting conditions.

Broadly speaking, then, the sociology of religion is the scientific study of the ways in which society, culture, and personality (or, in another sense, societies, cultures, and personalities), influence religion—influence

---

[12] On the interpenetration of social, cultural, and personality systems, see Talcott Parsons, *The Social System;* and Talcott Parsons and Edward Shils, editors, *Toward a General Theory of Action*, pp. 47–275.

its origin, its doctrines, its practices, the types of groups which express it, the kinds of leadership, etc. And, oppositely, it is the study of the ways in which religion affects society, culture, and personality—the processes of social conservation and social change, the structure of normative systems, the satisfaction or frustration of personality needs, etc. One must keep continuously in mind the interactive nature of these various elements.

Objections can well be raised to such a broad definition of the field. It is sometimes contended that a distinction should be drawn between the sociology of religion and the sociology of churches and religious institutions. The difficulty with this distinction is not simply that the one shades off imperceptibly into the other, but also that the sociology of religion, thus delimited, tends to become an ideology. Religion is defined as a cultural system only, and its "effects" spelled out, free from the influences of its institutional development, or, from a different value perspective, free from the various "distortions" or inadequate expressions with which it may become associated. From our point of view, we must be concerned with the whole range of structures and functions that become associated, under various circumstances, with the religious core. The elaborations, or if one will, the "distortions" of religion defined in cultural terms are part and parcel of religion as it is lived and used, and are essential to its comprehension. The sociology of "democracy" may be an interesting exercise, but the sociology of democratic societies is a far more important task. So it is also with the study of religion. We need to be alert to the distinction between what a religion, ideally or culturally conceived, *might* do, and what religious systems, embedded in societies and in personalities, *actually* do. Not only theologically oriented scholars, but many functional theorists, fail to make this distinction, with consequent injury to their analyses.

A further problem in the delineation of the field of the sociology of religion concerns the level of abstraction most useful for a science of religion. On the most abstract level, the theoretical propositions of the sociology of religion will apply to all societies. There are obvious difficulties and scientific dangers, however, in trying to develop a theory that will apply to religions and societies of widely different types—from those in which supernaturalism pervades almost everything, to others where much of life is given natural explanation; from those threatened continually with hunger, drought, or pestilence, to those where these dangers have been brought substantially under control; from small, relatively stable and homogenous societies, bound in "the cake of custom," to large, mobile, heterogeneous, and rapidly changing societies. What we need are generic propositions, applicable to all religions, and specific propositions, applicable to religious systems under certain stated conditions. We need a sociology of religion, but also a sociology of the Ghost Dance, of the Moslem Tijani order, of Norman Vincent Peale. Needless to say, propositions on each level of analysis should be consistent with those on other levels.

CHAPTER 2

The Relation of Religion to Morals, Science, and Magic

In the description and analysis of religion, one is inevitably confronted with the task of stating its relationship to other modes of belief and action. Its connections with the moral codes of a society, with science, and with magic are especially important. In each case there are innumerable views, many of them part of a general philosophy of religion or expressions of a particular theological orientation. It would be an oversimplification to state that there are two types of conceptions, one stating what the relationships between religion, morals, science, and magic ought to be, and the other attempting to describe what the relationships actually are; for the "is" and the "ought" are usually found together in each conception. It is possible, however, to differentiate between those descriptions of the relationship which start from a value position, although they may bring many empirical observations to support it, and those which start with the hope of objective statement, although value propositions may be mixed with it. For the purposes of this essay, the need is clearly for an objective analysis. We shall not, therefore, undertake a survey or critique of the many different views, but shall simply point out a few approaches, by way of comparison and contrast with an approach that seems consonant with the sociology of religion.

23

RELIGION AND MORALS

There are four logically possible relationships between religion and morals. Although these are seldom propounded in pure form, they can be described separately for purposes of study.

1. To a great many theologians and probably to the majority of the adherents of the "world religions," morality is an inseparable part of religion. That the Ten Commandments, for example, most of which are moral prescriptions and proscriptions, or the Golden Rule are "part of my religion" would seem to be obvious to most Jews and Christians. They are part of the laws of God, and therefore absolute and unchanging. To some who take this view, morality is only a part, and often a small part, of religion. Correct belief and correct performance of ritual mark the religious man more certainly than does correct conduct. Religion is fundamentally the relation of man to God, and if moral behavior—the right relation of man to man—is religiously significant, it is only as a sign of the relation of man to God. In the history of Christianity, this assertion that morality is merely a subsidiary part of religion has often been made in reaction against the overinvolvement of the church in secular affairs. It is a protest against the "loss of religion," the loss of primary concern for man's salvation, which is felt by many acutely religious people to be the central problem of existence. One phase of Luther's protest, for example, was the emphasis on "justification by faith alone." Logically and consistently developed, this not only had implications for the entanglements of the Roman Catholic Church with the feudal social structure, but it also led to the belief that concern with the affairs of this world, attention to good works and problems of justice, were not fundamental religious questions. The moral aspect of Christianity was not repudiated, but it was made wholly subsidiary. One could hope that justice would be the *result* of a religious life, but it was scarcely a direct religious concern.

Kierkegaard made something of the same response to what he considered the drift of the churches away from the basic religious task. It was not so much that they had lost their focus by direct involvement in almost every aspect of secular life, as was the case in Luther's day. But in their growing optimism and concern for making this life a happy one, the churches had forgotten the fundamental tragedy of human existence, a tragedy from which man could be rescued only by God, by a purely religious, not a moral, effort. To Kierkegaard, faith came first, morality second; and yet it must be added, it was "a real second," for if religion dethrones morality, it does not eliminate it.

2. This position shades off into a second conception of the relation of religion and morals. This is the belief that the two are not only inseparable, but in a very real sense, identical, that the effort to draw a distinction between a moral life and a religious life is in error. To some interpreters, Luther is nearer this position than the first. His work is seen as a protest against the separation of the concerns of this world from religious questions. Many would consider this to be the classic Christian view, contending that Jesus sought to eliminate any dualistic approach to life: "Inasmuch as ye have done it unto the least of these"; and particularly his declaration, following the statement of the first Commandment, that "the second Commandment is like unto it." On the contemporary scene, Jacques Maritain and John MacMurray are able proponents of this view. Many would place Reinhold Niebuhr at the forefront of this group, especially on the basis of his own intensive moral concerns. On the basis of his writings, he would perhaps be more closely identified with Kierkegaard in this broad categorization.

3. A third belief concerning the relation of religion and morals holds them to be separate and quite unrelated. This position can be taken by persons with widely different orientations. To some, the religious quest, in the sense of union with God or eternal salvation or nirvana, may so dominate their lives that moral questions—what happens to man on earth—are utterly unimportant. To relate them to the religious effort is to obscure it, to prevent its development in purest form. There are others who protest against moral emphasis in religion because they do not want religious sanctions to become involved in the secular struggles of the day. Usually these are persons who are fairly well satisfied with the existing social structures. They are fearful that if the conflicts become defined as religious questions, they could not possibly gain, and might well lose. Many American clergymen who have become concerned over questions of race relations or industrial conflict or poverty have been told that they ought to mind "their business," which presumably does not include attention to such moral problems. Much of the current "return to religion," which we shall discuss in various connections, has only slight moral implications, particularly with regard to the complex and impersonal contacts of human beings in a mobile society—contacts that are increasingly important and raise many new moral questions. Although over ninety per cent of American adults identify themselves with one of the major religious groups, a majority of them believe that their religion does not affect their ideas of politics and business. Interviewers for the American Institute of Public Opinion asked those who considered religion to be something "very important" in their lives, "Would you say your religious

beliefs have any effect on your ideas of politics and business?" Fifty-four
per cent said no.[1]

These two groups, what one might call the "pure religionist" and the
"comfortable layman," despite their wide differences, are often religious
colleagues, because each finds some support in the other in their common
belief that religion must be purged of "merely moral" interests. The comfortable layman, however, actually holds a very different position. His
desire to "keep religion out of politics and business," which seems to be a
call for sharp separation of morality and religion, may usually be interpreted as a desire to maintain religious sanction for his particular moral
views.

Still another group agrees that religion and morality are—or at least
ought to be—entirely separate, but for a very different reason. To the
"secular moralist," powerful and absolute religious sanctions can only
serve to make rigid and nonrational what needs to be flexible and rational.
Morality requires, in their view, continuous adaptation to a changing
situation on the basis of constant study and knowledge of consequences.
Their lament is not that concern over moral questions obscures the religious quest, but rather that a connection with religion obscures the moral
quest.

4. Those who take a fourth position agree with the proponents of the
first two that religion and morality are closely related, but they differ in
their emphasis on morality as the "senior partner." Those who take this
orientation, as well as the others, frequently mix their conceptions of what
is, with their beliefs concerning what ought to be. When Kant interprets
religious observances simply as means for directing the will toward the
achievement of moral law, it is not clear whether he is asserting that this
is indeed the case or declaring that it ought to be true.

The adherents of this view differ among themselves. Some believe that
even if religion is to be defined, with Carlyle, simply as "morality touched
by emotion," it is a necessary component of a moral system because of
the motivational force it supplies. Some contend that a supernatural religious sanction is required, to get a changeless frame of reference that
cannot be upset by variable human experience. Others believe that eventually, morality may be quite free of religion, at least of the traditional
varieties, and will find its motivation and sanctions in the expanding
knowledge of the consequences of human behavior. In this they move
toward what we have called the "secular moralist" position.

Despite these differences, there is agreement among the various pro-

[1] American Institute of Public Opinion, "Public Opinion News Service," March
20, 1955.

ponents of this view in their tendency to apply a pragmatic criterion to religion: its consequences for the moral life are the central test to which it should be put. This approach finds its most complete expression in the religious philosophy of Confucianism, which holds that the quality of a religion is to be judged, in the words of Latourette, "by its power to produce worthy character and a just social order." There are other interpretations of Confucianism, of course. It is a complex movement, with a long history, making diverse emphases inevitable; but there is little disagreement concerning the dominant theme. As Hu Shih, contemporary Chinese scholar and diplomat, says: "Teaching a moral life is the essential thing; and the ways of the gods are merely one of the possible means of sanctioning the teaching. That is in substance the Chinese concept of religion." [2]

In the history of Christianity, it has usually been marginal movements of various kinds that have upheld the position that ethical questions were the central questions. One thinks of Comte's positivistic religion or of contemporary "Ethical Culture" and "Humanist" groups more as offshoots from, than as manifestations of, the Judaic-Christian tradition. Yet their relationship to that tradition is close. Even in the main stream of Christian movements, the contention that religion is mainly to be judged by its contributions to the moral life is not without vigorous defenders. They are found not only in such sectarian developments as those led by Winstanley and the Anabaptists, but in some of the classic doctrinal and theological struggles, including those led by the monk Pelagius in the fifth century and by Arminius, an early Dutch Protestant.

The history of a religion is sometimes written as a struggle between "the priestly and the prophetic tendencies," usually by those who believe that moral questions, which should be central, are too easily obscured. They see the controlling power of religion being used by a priestly class, in their own behalf or to serve the ruling elite, the emphasis being placed on ritual and dogma to protect secular structures. Into this scene come "prophets," who declare that "true religion" is concerned with justice and righteousness, not with rite and belief. They may accomplish a reformation that gives fresh emphasis to morals, until the pendulum swings back toward priestly religion. Some view the process as one in which the moral concerns are gradually, even if waveringly, winning out. [3]

From one perspective, the history of Christianity can be read as the interplay of these four points of view concerning the possible and the

[2] Quoted by Wing-tsit Chan, *Religious Trends in Modern China*, p. 246.
[3] See for example, L. T. Hobhouse, *Morals in Evolution* and L. L. Bernard, *Social Control in Its Sociological Aspects*, p. 483 ff.

desirable relationships between religion and morality. In the struggles among them until the time of Luther and probably until the eighteenth century (perhaps one ought to say, even up to the present), the first position has won most of the official victories, with strong emphasis on some aspects of the third position. The view can perhaps be summed up in these words: moral questions, insofar as they are religious questions at all, are part of revealed religion. The second and fourth positions have had eloquent spokesmen, but have never become the established and dominant doctrines. At several points, in the chapters that follow, we shall try to discover some of the social forces that help to explain the predominance of one view of the relation of religion and morals over the other approaches.

A SOCIOLOGICAL VIEW OF RELIGION AND MORALS

Each of the preceding conceptions mixes statements of value with statements of fact. In the development of a scientific theory of religion, however, the need is for an examination of cross-cultural data to describe what the various patterns of relationship between religion and morals are, and then for an exploration of the conditions under which the various patterns occur. The first requirement is much easier to fulfill than the second. We have extensive materials on many different societies that permit us to outline some of the diverse connections of religion and morality. As we deal with various questions in the sociology of religion, we shall hope as well to untangle some of the variables that influence the relationship.

From the perspective of science, several generalizations emerge in the study of the relationship of religion and morality. It is possible and desirable to define them in independent terms and to separate them analytically. Their origins, their causes, their internal variations, and their relationships to society and culture can be studied separately. At the same time, it is vastly clear that they are interdependent in most times and places. There are many types of relationship, with widely varying consequences. There is no clear-cut line between moral codes and religious prescriptions, for they may be identical, mutually reenforcing, entirely distinct, or antithetical. The religious idea of "sin" is not synonymous with the moral idea of "wrong," for the former implies a supra-social norm (as well, perhaps, as a social norm) while the latter implies only evil social results.[4] Yet a given act may fall under both proscriptions.

One cannot clearly establish an evolutionary line from a religion without

---

[4] See MacIver and Page, *Society: An Introductory Analysis*, pp. 169–170.

moral concern, to one where moral questions are found, although subsidiary, to a situation where morality is the central question of religion, to a supposed final situation where religion has vanished and only a moral system remains. This pattern overlooks their separate quality, stemming from distinctive needs and problems. In theological terms, religion is concerned with "is-ness," morality with "ought-ness." Morality seeks, for example, to control conditions that lead to death—to prohibit cruelty and murder, to reduce sources of illness and hunger. Religion seeks to help one to adjust to the fact of death. Morality is concerned with the relationship of man to man; religion is concerned with the relationship of man to some higher power or idea, sometimes, but not always, in addition to the moral concern. Even a purely naturalistic and humanistic religion is not to be equated with a moral code, although it doubtless will have fewer norms that are unrelated or antithetical to existing moral codes, for it is still basically concerned with the development of a satisfying response to that which *is* in human existence.

These statements are largely, of course, matters of definition. It is the contention of the author that such analytic separation of religion and morals, however much they may be empirically related, is necessary to adequate study and particularly to the explanation of the wide variety of relationships. The distinction cannot be based on differences in prescribed rules of conduct, for religion, morality, and law may require the same acts; although some deeds may involve only one of the sanctions. The distinction is in terms of the authority and the sanctions that are attached to the codes.[5]

Disagreements concerning the relationship of morality and religion have arisen from the failure to see that we need not choose between two opposite theories. It is not necessary to say, either that they are aspects of one system, or that they are entirely separate. The evolutionary theorists, in their belief that there was a progressive development toward ethical monotheism, tended to describe the religious and moral codes of primitive societies in separate terms. As knowledge of primitive religions grew, it became clear that there were many types of relationship with morals. In particular, the belief that they were sharply distinct, that only the "higher religions" had an ethical content, was shown to be inadequate. Benedict writes:

Nor are all the cultures that use religion as a sanction for ethical conduct found upon the plane of complex civilization. The Manus people of the Bismarck Archipelago have an ethical religion, and it would be hard to imagine a cul-

[5] See *ibid.*, p. 168.

ture that more consistently used all their supernatural concepts to back a puritanical code of morals.[6]

Malinowski and other functionalists have swung the pendulum to the other extreme from the conception that morality and religion are separate. Speaking of the Trobriand Islanders in particular, but seeking for conclusions concerning "the nature of religion in general," Malinowski declares:

Myth, ritual, and ethics are definitely but three facets of the same essential fact. . . . Take away from the natives the belief in the reality of their sacred lore, destroy their sense of the spirit world as it exists and acts upon them, and you will undermine their whole moral outlook.[7]

It is highly desirable to call attention to the functional interconnections of morals and religion, but the evidence does not support the proposition that one type of relationship is characteristic of "the nature of religion in general." In a broad sense, since they are aspects of a socio-cultural *system,* they can be thought of as "facets of the same essential fact." They cannot exist together in society without mutually influencing each other. The morals of a society are often reenforced by the claim that they are supported by divine sanctions; and the conceptions of the gods are frequently affected by associating them with the moral qualities most admired. This should not obscure, however, the separate needs, patterns, and functions that may be involved.

TWO ILLUSTRATIONS OF THE RELATION OF RELIGION AND MORALS

A glance at ancient Greece and Judaism reveals the possibilities of different patterns of relationship. The law of Moses, in early Hebraic religion, is a combination of rules of ritual, prescribed beliefs, and moral requirements. In this tradition, religion is a source and a sustainer of morality. "We see that even in its rudest form Religion was a moral force, the powers that men revered were on the side of social order and moral law; and the fear of the gods was a motive to enforce the laws of society, which were also the laws of morality." [8] This relationship became ever closer in the later development of Judaism. In the work of the eighth century prophets, and after, the dualism was reduced to a minimum. The religious life and the moral life became as nearly identical as in any

---

[6] In *General Anthropology*, edited by Franz Boas, p. 663.
[7] *The Foundations of Faith and Morals*, pp. 25–26.
[8] W. Robertson Smith, *Religion of the Semites*, p. 53.

major religion. This is, of course, the primary source of the Christian approach to this question.

Judaism became so consistently and thoroughly a communal affair that it was less capable of struggling with more personal needs. In the words of Robertson Smith:

> It was a national not a personal providence that was taught by ancient religion. So much was this the case that in purely personal concerns the ancients were very apt to turn, not to the recognised religion of the family or of the state, but to magical superstititions. . . . There was therefore a whole region of possible needs and desires for which religion could and would do nothing.[9]

It is perhaps fair to say that Christianity, faced with this problem, has incorporated far more attention to individual "salvation." In most times and places it has brought personal needs into the religious system more thoroughly than Judaism. This reintroduces the tendency toward a dualism; and it increases the likelihood that magical elements will become entangled with religion. At the same time, as a somewhat more complicated religio-moral system than Judaism, it has often been concerned with a broader range of human needs.

In Ancient Greece, there was a sharper separation of morality and religion. When Socrates, Plato, Aristotle, and most of the other philosophers sought to discover the nature of moral obligation, the source of the distinction between right and wrong, they did not relate their answer to a religious system. The differences among them are less important in this connection than the common perspective that morality is to be discussed in human and social terms. Greek religion, on the other hand, was primarily concerned with the frightening aspects of individual life and death, not with moral obligation and community need. This is seen in the sacrifice at the Diasia, for example. This was a holocaust, in the original meaning of that word: every shred of the victim was burned. As Gilbert Murray says:

> We know quite well the meaning of that form of sacrifice: it is a sacrifice to placate or appease the powers below, the Chthonioi, the dead and the lords of death. It was performed, as our authorities tell us . . . with shuddering or repulsion. . . . The Diasia was a ritual of placation, that is, of casting away various elements of pollution or danger and appeasing the unknown wraths of the surrounding darkness.[10]

One might find similar sacrifices and ceremonies among the ancient Hebrews, purges and incantation formulas by which they sought cleansing

[9] *Ibid.*, pp. 263–264.
[10] Murray, *Five Stages of Greek Religion*, p. 29.

from sin. By the eighth century, however, these had been sharply reduced. Yahweh had become a God of righteousness more than of wrath. "Yea, though ye offer Me your burnt offerings and meal offerings, I will not accept them: neither will I regard the peace offerings of your fat beasts. . . . But let judgment roll down as waters, and righteousness as a mighty stream." Greek religion, to be sure, underwent some of this same transformation. In its early stages, it pictures the world as one of caprice and terror. This is well described in Murray's account of the Anthesteria, said to be the oldest of the feasts to the Olympian Dionysus:

On the surface there is a touch of the wine-god, and he is given due official prominence; but as soon as we penetrate anywhere near the heart of the festival, Dionysus and his brother gods are quite forgotten, and all that remains is a great ritual for appeasing the dead. All the days of the Feast were *nefaste*, ill omen. . . . On it the Wine Jars which were also Seed and Funeral Jars were opened and the spirits of the Dead let loose in the world. Nameless and innumerable, the ghosts are summoned out of their tombs, and are duly feasted, each man summoning his own ghosts to his own house, and carefully abstaining from any act that would affect his neighbours. And then, when they are properly appeased and made gentle, they are swept back again out of this world to the place where they properly belong, and the streets and the houses cleaned from the presence of death.[11]

Only gradually into this setting of dread and appeasement do the Olympian gods become prominent. The overwhelmingly fearsome quality of Greek religion takes on a new appearance. In the "reformation," led perhaps by Homer, the great mass of rites concerned with the food-supply and human fertility was swept away. Much of the worship of the dead was eliminated; and the confused pattern of spirits and deities was gradually fused into a pantheon. At least these trends could be seen in the thinking of those who lived in the centers of culture contact. The great bulk of people, isolated from the urban and commercial developments, moved much less far down this road. And in the last analysis, the "Homeric reformation" failed. In Murray's judgment, the isolation of most of the people, the inertia of the ancient traditions, the inability to remove the personal, human qualities from the gods of the pantheon, and the confusion associated with the collapse of the Greek city-state were among the forces involved in "the failure of nerve."

The response of the philosophers to culture contact and to the collapse of the *polis* was a group of brilliant intellectual systems. They saw the situation, not so much in terms of individual tragedy as of social disor-

[11] *Ibid.*, pp. 31–32.

ganization, and were led, correspondingly, to the search for ethical propositions more than to religion. Plato, for example, dismayed by the confusion and disorganization of his time, held that there were transcendental and universal norms of right which could be discovered by philosophical study, if only the disorder of life could be reduced by a rationally ordered society. He would achieve that order by cutting off the disrupting influences of outside cultures, of commerce and riches, by isolating one's group from the world, from the "bitter and corrupting sea." Aristotle was far less nostalgic. A life guided by reason and virtue would lead to happiness, which is the true aim. The philosophers who followed saw disorganization lead to collapse. They often maintained their faith in reason, but it was a kind of negative faith: it can help one to adjust to the world, but scarcely to solve the problems of the world.

None of these systems of thought was able to take hold of the imaginations of the great majority of people. When the Olympian gods fell, fate, unpredictable and overwhelming Destiny, came in to take their place. This religious successor to the pantheon gave no higher place to moral questions than had the earlier stages of religion.

Thus the Greek situation developed very differently from the Hebrew. In some measure, Christianity may be seen as an attempt to blend the two. It shares the Judaic concern for the community, for problems of morality as religiously significant; but it is also a response to the overwhelmingly fearful problems of the individual, with which the mystery cults and religions of Greece were largely concerned. One does not imply by this that it is a successful blend. An informed value judgment on this intricate question would have to be made with respect to specific times and places and would be scarcely meaningful "in general." Judaism clearly suffered, perhaps because of its very lack of magic and mystery, from an inability to appeal to the great majority of distraught individuals, more concerned with their own salvation than with ethics. Once it moved beyond the borders of a small and fairly unified society, this was a barrier to its growth. Greece, for all its intellectual achievements, its brilliant ethical theories, failed to develop a system of belief that grappled simultaneously with morals and salvation. The sharp separation tended to allow the search for salvation to march unrestrained down a road of mystery and superstition and to leave the ethical codes unsupported. Christianity, maintaining the two in an uneasy alliance, has often exhibited a rigid and parochial adherence to the customs and morals of one's own group—part of a heritage that Judaism has never been able completely to eliminate. This is one of the fruits of a close identity of morality and religion.

Equally often Christianity has followed the "Greek" line, with problems
of morality becoming obscured in the search for individual salvation.
This is one of the fruits of sharp separation of morality and religion.

Altogether, what we see is a wide variety of possible relationships between morality and religion. The task of sociology is to describe the
range, to attempt to isolate the conditions under which the various patterns emerge, and to analyze the consequences. Some attempts to deal
with small segments of this task will be found in the chapters that follow.

RELIGION AND SCIENCE

The wide variety of views concerning the existent and the desirable relationship of religion and morals is matched by the conceptions of the relationship between religion and science—or more broadly, religion and
the intellectual life. There are the same four logical possibilities: They
may be considered harmonious, or, indeed, ultimately identical; they may
be thought to be entirely distinct, and thus not engaged in any fundamental conflict; religion may be considered a "higher truth," superior to
science in any area where they may conflict; or science may be considered
the only certain road to truth, thus refuting any religious proposition
which its evidence contradicts.

From the examination of these views, the sociologist of religion is confronted with a number of questions: What are the conditions of society
and culture under which these various interpretations of the relationship
between science and religion emerge and become dominant? How has
science affected religious beliefs? Does it prove or disprove such beliefs?
Do religions vary in the degree to which they inhibit or promote the appearance and growth of science? Is there a sense in which science itself is
believed in as a "faith," with functions similar to those of religious faiths?
If so, are its own ultimate values and allegiances established by the
processes of empirical research? That is, can science determine not only
the efficiency of means but also the validity of ends? Or are the basic
premises of science as a faith super-empirical, no more to be confirmed
or refuted by scientific study than are the ultimate values and premises
of "other religions"?

All of the logically possible relationships between science and religion
can be illustrated in the history of Christianity. The view that religion
and science are fundamentally harmonious, that they are dual roads to
truth, or indeed an identical road, is an ancient one. To St. Thomas, there
could be no contradiction between religion and science, if man knew

enough, because both stem from God. A similar position is taken in modern terms by MacMurray, when he writes: "We may say that in Jesus the Jewish religious consciousness has reached the point in its development at which the law of human history has been formulated and *prediction, on a basis of knowledge,* becomes possible." [12] At least since the eighteenth century, many persons have come to this same conclusion, that science and religion are harmonious, from a position opposite to that of MacMurray. To them, it is not that religion is good science, but science is good religion. The rational religion of the enlightenment, Comte's positivism, and contemporary views that science is not only a method but a way of life all express this view.

Those who take this position, whether they approach it through religion or through science, are not unaware of the sharp conflicts between science and religion. But they can explain these conflicts, with St. Thomas, on the grounds that we do not know enough; or they can contend that it is only in incidental and unimportant matters that conflict arises. Thus Andrew Dickson White declared, in *A History of the Warfare of Science with Theology in Christendom* that the conflict was not between science and religion, but between science and dogmatic theology. Science, he contended, inevitably contributed to the health of religion.

Another way to try to resolve the conflict between science and religion is to hold that they are quite unrelated, that science is based on reason while religion is based on faith. Or one may declare that the grounds for proof of religious knowledge are entirely distinct from the processes of validation of non-religious knowledge. Religious proof comes from "inner experience." Or, as Pascal said, "The heart has reasons which reason does not know." Some would even hold, with William of Occam, that it is foolish to try to establish the "truth" of religion, for if one fails, the foundation of religion is broken. Science cannot, of course, refute this position. It is quite possible, however, that in a society where science had become crucial in the life perspective of many persons, such a view would become irrelevant and meaningless. This statement is put in the conditional, for such a society is certainly not yet to be found.

For a great many people, any conflict between science and religion is resolved in favor of religion, which is conceived to be a higher truth. If scientists contend that the earth is round, or that man is an ancient and changing species, or that miracles can be explained by natural laws, refutation comes, not from an appeal to evidence, but by reference to estab-

[12] John MacMurray, *The Clue to History,* p. 59. Italics mine.

lished religious doctrines.[13] Among the world religions, it is doubtless in Christianity that this kind of conflict is most likely to arise. Precisely because the dominant tradition in Christianity seeks to encompass the whole of life, because, therefore, it contains an intellectual system, it cannot be indifferent to changes in scientific views. Those who hold that religious truth is of a different order of truth from science are less disturbed by changes in the scientific view of the world. This dualistic view, however, is not commonly held, particularly in a society where science is highly developed. Allport writes: "For most people, even for primitives, it is not hard to assign to science that which is science's and to religion that which is religion's." [14] He might better have written, "particularly for primitives," for a frank dualism is much more congenial to societies in which there has been only a small development of science and technology than it is to a society in which increasing knowledge has led to the belief that the world is of one piece. In fact, there is a great deal of doubt whether Allport is correct when he says that "most people" find it not hard to separate religious from scientific questions. He refers to Weber's conceptions that science is concerned with problems of empirical causation while religion is concerned with problems of meaning. But these are the conceptions of a scientist. Data from one of Allport's own studies indicate that a large minority of 386 Harvard students believe that there is substantial conflict between science and religion. When asked, "How do you feel about the frequently mentioned conflict between the findings of science and the principal (basic) contentions of religion?" they answered: [15]

	%
Religion and science clearly support one another	21
Conflict is negligible (more apparent than real)	32
Conflict is considerable but probably not irreconcilable	17
Conflict is considerable, perhaps irreconcilable	14
Conflict is definitely irreconcilable	16

It would be unwise to assume that the conflict is thought to be less severe by those with less education, yet a dualistic view of the world may be more acceptable to them.

The fourth position, that science is the road to truth, that its propositions refute any religious doctrines with which they may conflict, is also

[13] On the history of the conflict of science and religion see, in addition to White, mentioned above, Clifford Kirkpatrick, *Religion in Human Affairs*, Chapters 12 and 13; Homer Smith, *Man and His Gods*.

[14] Gordon Allport, *The Individual and His Religion*, p. 20.

[15] Gordon Allport, James M. Gillespie, and Jacqueline Young, "The Religion of the Post-War College Student," *The Journal of Psychology*, January, 1948, p. 18.

held by persons with widely differing value stands. Some, seeing specific religious beliefs brought into serious question by scientific developments, have projected this trend and concluded that all of religion will one day be proved to be false. This is likely to be the conclusion of those who adopt a substantive definition of religion. Professor Howells, for example, despite a basically functional approach, is not content to dispense with a substantive definition entirely, with the result that he sees a sharp conflict between science and religion:

. . . everything religious has been founded upon the supernatural, the unseen. Now our whole culture fights tooth and nail every weekday to see the unseen, to drive the supernatural and the mystical back at every point. This can have only one effect, which is to gnaw away religious belief. Philosophers and others try desperately to hush up this conflict of science and religion, and suggest various kinds of adjustments and refurbishments of belief, but these are not promising because they are generally reduced to a set of ethics and a highly abstract idea of the divine, and could hardly serve as a religion that people at large could get their teeth into.

There is the dilemma. Can civilization retain enough of the supernatural to constitute a base for religion? [16]

Others, observing these same trends but seeing them in the perspective of a functional definition, believe there is no dilemma. The impact of science is to require drastic changes in religion to be sure. There is a "strain toward consistency" in society which makes it impossible for a religion that developed in a pre-scientific situation to remain unaffected by the growth of science. Specific beliefs and practices inevitably lose their appeal. In a functional view, however, this is no more a destruction of religion than the transition from an absolute monarchy to a limited monarchy to a democracy is the destruction of government.

DOES SCIENCE DISPROVE RELIGIOUS BELIEFS?

What is the position of the sociology of religion concerning these four ways of responding to the question of the relation of religion and science? The answer emerges from three propositions, each supported by a wealth of empirical observations: 1. There has, in fact, been a long series of sharp conflicts between science and specific religious beliefs and practices. 2. The result of these conflicts has been the drastic and continuous modification of religious systems of belief and practice. One is tempted to write that in the long run one hunded per cent of the adjustment has been made by religion. This would result, however, in a dispute over the mean-

[16] William Howells, *The Heathens, Primitive Man and His Religions*, p. 287.

ing of "the long run," for certainly religion has prevented, and is preventing, the spread of scientific propositions for substantial periods of time.
Let us be content, therefore, with the statement that most of the adjustment is made by religion. 3. Despite these drastic and continuous changes,
religion remains a vital part of the life of human societies.

If each of these propositions is correct, the answer to our question is
clear: Science disproves specific religious beliefs, but it does not disprove
religion. There may be conflict between science and a given religion, if
part of its total system is a series of propositions about the nature of the
world, but there is no general conflict between science and religion defined in functional terms. A particular religion may be destroyed by science, because the speed of change and the sharpness of the conflicts with
its beliefs and practices may be too great to permit the necessary adjustment; or the interpreters of the religion may for various reasons prevent
the adjustment. If the religion of a society is seriously weakened or destroyed, however, new religious and quasi-religious movements tend to
appear. Indeed, if the functionalist view is correct, such movements must
appear if the society is to survive. We shall hold in the next chapter that
a society that does not furnish its members a system of beliefs and actions
for handling the endemic anxieties of human existence and a system for
modifying its inter-human conflicts will collapse from the load of personal
anxiety and group tension.

In taking this position, however, the sociologist of religion does not
contend that the lack of any basic or ultimate conflict is the only important fact. Indeed, the presence of continuous and pervasive conflict between science and religion, in terms of specific beliefs, is highly significant
in its influence on human behavior. This is undoubtedly a point at which
modern societies are not of a piece. Change has been too rapid to allow
the "strain toward consistency" to work itself out, to produce an integration between science and religion. The student of religion who disregards
this fact in favor of emphasis on the absence of *ultimate* conflict, is unable
to understand a great deal of modern life. When a particular belief is
brought into question by a scientific discovery, the person whose system
of faith includes that belief as one of its sustaining elements is not likely
to be made comfortable by the proposition that in the long run, religious
systems have absorbed a great many scientific ideas without being
weakened. Even in societies where science and religion have developed
side by side for many generations, the conflicts may be sharp. They are
vastly more sharp in societies, or among those groups in a society, which
feel the impact of modern science abruptly. When the growth of science
is rapid and pervasive, several responses are possible: a given religious

system may deteriorate rapidly, a rigorous dualism may develop or be reenforced, or a strange hybrid may appear in which a superficial integration of science and religion is accomplished which hides deeper conflicts. Each of these responses may be seen in contemporary America.

Thus there is no simple answer to the questions: "Does science disprove religious beliefs?" On the one hand, modern social science emphasizes the functional importance of *some* religious system for society. It also grants that a great part of religion has to do with non-empirical propositions that are not subject to scientific proof or disproof. Science can neither validate nor refute them. On the other hand, specific religious beliefs about the world may be refuted by science. More importantly, tension between religion and the life of the intellect may be persistent because of a fundamental clash of perspectives. Much has been made of the observation that scientific discoveries are less easily adjusted to by Christianity than, for example, by Buddhism. This may be true. Christianity has not been content to leave questions of truth concerning the world of nature to secular thinkers. Yet there may well be a sense in which all religions hold to the belief that they stand for the highest truth and the conviction that their beliefs can be proved. Without this belief it is difficult to fulfill the function of giving meaning to an existence that is burdened with frustration, injustice, unequal rewards, and puzzling contradictions. Weber writes that sharp tension between religion and the intellectual sphere comes to the fore whenever rational and empirical knowledge has

consistently worked through to the disenchantment of the world and its transformation into a causal mechanism. For then science encounters the claims of the ethical postulate that the world is a God-ordained, and hence somehow *meaningfully* and ethically oriented, cosmos. . . . For the tension rests on the unavoidable disparity among ultimate forms of images of the world.

There is absolutely no "unbroken" religion working as a vital force which is not compelled at *some* point to demand the *credo non quod, sed quia absurdum*—the "sacrifice of the intellect." [17]

Even if one holds, however, that there is a basic clash between science and religion, because of the disparity in their images of the world, this need not be seen as an unhappy fact. One can see it with Alfred North Whitehead as an opportunity, not a disaster. He would look upon religion, not as a rule of safety, but as an adventure of the spirit. Part of this adventure, certainly, is the continuing tension between science and reli-

[17] *From Max Weber: Essays in Sociology,* edited by Hans Gerth and C. Wright Mills, pp. 350–352.

gion, a tension that challenges religion to try to achieve a more adequate view of nature, and challenges science to try to achieve more relevant and valid knowledge concerning the total human situation.

INFLUENCES OF RELIGION ON SCIENCE

It is scarcely necessary to document the fact that in many times and places, religions have opposed the discoveries of science, have censored its conclusions, exhorting the faithful to hold fast to the established beliefs. One must also point out, however, that religion may promote science, both directly and as an indirect consequence of its influences on society. In many societies, men of learning are also men of religion. Their learning may be narrowly circumscribed by religious tradition, but the boundaries are difficult to maintain. Having encouraged a contemplative life, a religious order may set in motion a process of observation and study that leads far beyond the existing traditional views.

Religions that are concerned not only with salvation, but with the quality of human life on earth, may give encouragement to science to support that concern. Those who observe that there have been many sharp conflicts between Christianity and scientific discoveries, might observe also that science has developed most rapidly in Christian societies. The cause-effect sequence is not clear. It may be that science has developed in spite of Christianity, due to an otherwise favorable situation. It seems more likely, however, that Christianity, and Judaism to an even greater degree, is driven to try to understand the world in order to control it, to a degree not found in many other religions. Science is doubtless primarily a product of non-religious forces; the religious approach to it is ambivalent; but it would be a mistake to consider them wholly antithetical.

In indirect and unintended ways, moreover, religion may help to stimulate scientific work. The influence of Protestanism illustrates this situation well. The Reformation certainly did not directly sponsor a situation of religious tolerance and openmindedness; but the momentum of the protest against the medieval patterns of authority and the conflicts among the Protestant churches helped to break the cake of custom and facilitated thought. Preserved Smith describes this latent function well:

. . . the chain of authority was broken and each Christian taught to acknowledge no interpreter of Scripture but his own conscience. This led, rather as a consequence than as a design, to toleration, to indifference and to skepticism.[18]

[18] *The Age of the Reformation,* p. 711; see also Ernst Troeltsch, *Protestantism and Progress,* pp. 155–161; and Robert Merton, *Social Theory and Social Structure,* chap. xiv.

Protestantism helped to break the intellectual monopoly of the clergy, it encouraged the masses to read, it established colleges and universities in greater abundance, and thus, in Smith's phrase, "made way for greater emancipations than its own."

RELIGION AND MAGIC

In the development of a theory of religion, its relationship to magic has been a major question. Some writers have emphasized the similarities, others have stressed the differences. This disagreement stems in part from the tendency to describe the numerous connections between magic and religion in actual cultural and social systems, on the one hand, and the tendency, on the other hand, to define them in analytically separate terms. To the present writer, it seems necessary to do both of these things. It is well, in the first place, to define religion and magic separately, and then to describe their relationship in concrete social systems—the religio-magical complexes of various societies. Both of these tasks are necessary because the patterns of relationship vary widely. Only by analytically separate definitions can we describe the wide variety of relationships adequately. Perhaps this point can be illustrated by an analogy: if a chemist were so impressed by the frequency of the "hydrogen-oxygen complex" that he failed to define the two elements independently, he would be unable to deal with them when they occurred separately in pure form, or, more commonly, when they appeared in compound with other elements. To define them separately, however, would in no sense be a denial of the phenomenon "water." It is, to be sure, quite unusual for magic or religion to appear in "pure" form; but it is very common for them to be found in "compound" with other systems. Magic and technology, for example, and religion and politics are frequently interrelated in complex systems. For an adequate theory of religion, therefore, one must define it separately, yet must be thoroughly alert to its frequent close tie to magic.

Even on the level of abstract definition, one must recognize similarities between religion and magic. Most important is the fact that both are "non-empirical," based on faith in processes and powers whose efficacy cannot be established simply by observation. Both are attempts to struggle with the frustrations, the fears, the imponderables of life, and to achieve a larger share of the positive values. They can be distinguished, however, both by the kinds of goals which are primary and by the attitudes associated with the efforts to achieve these goals. In Malinowski's words, "religion refers to the fundamental issues of human existence,

while magic always turns round specific, concrete, and detailed problems." [19] Religion is concerned with salvation, with death, with the meaning of existence. Magic is concerned with immediate goals—control of
the weather, assurance of a good crop, victory in battle, good health. The
devotees of magic and of religion tend to differ in their attitude toward
the non-empirical or the supernatural. The religionist prays and sacrifices,
the magician manipulates and controls. The utility of this distinction,
however, even for abstract definitions, breaks down if it is pressed very
far. The modern theory will go only part way with Frazer when he holds
that religion emphasizes a belief in the elasticity of nature, because of
the power of a personal supernatural, while magic believes in impersonal
law, or in personal forces subject to impersonal law.[20] Prayer for rain in
the midst of a disastrous drought, a supplication for help, can certainly
be distinguished from a rain-making ceremony, in which it is believed
that the proper incantations and formulas can produce the desired result.
Despite the difference in attitude, however, one must recognize that there
may be an element of coercion in the religious approach and a continuing
feeling that the world is full of caprice in the magical approach.

When one turns from definitions to empirical systems, he finds that
magic and religion are often very closely tied together. The degree to
which magical elements are found in close relationship to a religious
complex varies widely, of course, in time and place; but there is scarcely
a religion that does not have some magical aspects mixed with it. It is in
this empirical sense that we can agree with Herskovits that "magic . . .
is actually an integral part of religion."

MAGIC AND SCIENCE

An examination of the relationships of magic to science can help us to
understand its connection with religion. Here again, the early concepts
of Tylor and especially of Frazer can be instructive, even though they
are inadequate. They came to their view that magic was "primitive science" or pseudo-science on the basis of a particular conception of magic.
They held that it was rooted in the belief that man could control nature
by supernatural means if he used the proper formulas. The formulas of
magic were not empirically derived, of course, but Tylor and Frazer held
that primitive men drew no clear-cut distinction between procedures that
were based on observation and those derived from tradition. Magic, like
science, is governed by a body of "principles" that indicate how one should
proceed if he wishes to accomplish a given result.

[19] *A Scientific Theory of Culture and Other Essays,* p. 200.
[20] *The Golden Bough,* pp. 48–60.

Such a similarity, however, cannot hide the far more important differences. Magic is sustained by belief and emotion; science rests on experience and reason. When the formula of the scientist does not "work"—when it fails to give him control and prediction, he willingly revises it; the magician adduces counter-magic or error in the sanctified routine to explain his failure. In Malinowski's words:

. . . similar as they appear, science and magic differ yet radically. Science is born of experience, magic made by tradition. Science is guided by reason and corrected by observation, magic, impervious to both, lives in an atmosphere of mysticism. Science is open to all, a common good of the whole community, magic is occult, taught through mysterious initiations, handed on in a hereditary or at least in very exclusive filiation. While science is based on the conception of natural forces, magic springs from the idea of a certain mystic, impersonal power, which is believed in by most primitive peoples.[21]

Malinowski insisted that primitive peoples were well aware of the distinction between their magical practices and their technology (they can scarcely be said to have a science). Magic was no substitute for technology, but a supplement, a kind of second line of defense to protect them from dangers for which their knowledge was inadequate. He found a clear-cut distinction in the minds of the Trobriand Islanders between natural causes and other events for which there seems to be no accounting. "They know quite well what effects can be produced by careful tilling of the soil and these effects they try to produce by competent and industrious labour. They equally know that certain evils, such as pests, blights, bush-pigs, drought or rain, cannot be overcome by human work however hard and consistent." [22] They see gardens thriving despite expectations of failure, and other gardens fail despite the application of techniques on which they had come to count. It is to control these mysterious variations that they resort to magic.

It always appears in those phases of human action where knowledge fails man. Primitive man cannot manipulate the weather. Experience teaches him that rain and sunshine, wind, heat and cold, cannot be produced by his own hand, however much he might think about or observe such phenomena. He therefore deals with them magically.[23]

Malinowski has made a major contribution by correcting the picture of primitive man as a magic-ridden, pre-logical person, with no true knowledge of the world around him, quite unable to distinguish between a natural cause and a magical one. Without a great deal of empirically

[21] In Joseph Needham, editor, *Science, Magic and Reality,* p. 23.
[22] Malinowski, *Coral Gardens and Their Magic,* p. 77.
[23] Malinowski, *A Scientific Theory of Culture and Other Essays,* p. 198.

tested knowledge—of techniques, materials, foods, implements—he could scarcely exist. Yet Malinowski may have carried his argument too far in emphasizing the distinction in men's minds between their technology and their magic. It is one thing to say that every human society possesses a great deal of knowledge that derives from experience; it is something else to hold that this knowledge is readily disentangled from magical beliefs in their minds. In a study of the responses to an epidemic in "West Town," China, Hsu observed that there were rational responses and there were magical responses; but they were so closely linked together that it was only in the mind of an outside observer that they appeared to be separate.

Hsu contends that this kind of mixing of responses is characteristic of all societies. One who lives in a society where science is highly developed will be science-oriented; but his approach to it, his use of it, will not be sharply different from the magic-orientation of one from a society in which magic is widely used.

But in either case there is hardly any question of rationality, for a science-oriented people do not always differentiate magic with a pseudo-scientific wrapping from science, just as magic-oriented people mix real knowledge in their magic. In either instance there can be correct as well as erroneous belief. . . .

It is not fantastic to say that, to achieve popular acceptance, magic has to be dressed like science in America, while science has to be cloaked by magic in West Town, [China.] [24]

To this writer it seems likely that one would find, with Malinowski, some clear-cut distinctions between technology and magic in every society, and that one would find, with Hsu, other situations in which they appeared almost as a unit. One might further expect to find variations in the degree to which these tendencies occurred.

THE FUNCTIONS OF MAGIC

To the scientific observer, the magical way of thinking is invalid and ineffective. Based as it is on crude analogies and false inference, magic certainly does not "work." Why, then, is it not quickly dismissed because of its failure? The answer to that is two-fold: To the believer it *seems* to work; and to some degree, in an indirect sense, it does work. This question is interesting to the student of religion, not only because of the frequency with which magical elements are found in religious systems, but also because some of the same reasoning applies to religion.

[24] Francis L. K. Hsu. *Religion, Science and Human Crises*, p. 8 and p. 114.

To the believer, magic often seems to work. It is well known that what one perceives, the observations that he considers to be evidence, the premises on which his logical processes are based, and other cognitive acts are not independent of his personal tendencies and his cultural training. A person trained to believe in magic, can "see" its success. One instance of a positive correlation between the aims of a magical process and the results may outweigh many negative instances. This is particularly true when failures can be explained by counter-magic or by inexpert use of the formula. Moreover, many kinds of magical practice have an impressive record of "success": most medical cures "work," thanks to the recuperative powers of the human body; a rain-making ceremony that is performed when it is most needed—at the end of a long dry period— is likely to precede a rainy season.

The most ardent rationalist can accept such an argument to explain the efficacy of magic. Those who take a functionalist view, however, have made a more dramatic claim: magic does work, in a sense. It appears in human societies as one way of struggling with disruptive emotional forces that arise as a result of man's helplessness in certain situations. In the magical rite, man feels that he is doing something, not succumbing to a paralysis of fear. When he reaches an impasse, when knowledge fails him, man responds with spontaneous gestures and rudimentary beliefs. In Malinowski's well-known words:

Magic fixes upon these beliefs and rudimentary rites and standardizes them into permanent traditional forms. Thus magic supplies primitive man with a number of ready-made ritual acts and beliefs, with a definite mental and practical technique which serves to bridge over the dangerous gaps in every important pursuit or critical situation. It enables man to carry out with confidence his important tasks, to maintain his poise and his mental integrity in fits of anger, in the throes of hate, of unrequited love, of despair and anxiety. The function of magic is to ritualize man's optimism, to enhance his faith in the victory of hope over fear. Magic expresses the greater value for man of confidence over doubt, of steadfastness over vacillation, of optimism over pessimism.[25]

This rather extreme functionalist view has raised many questions: If magic is used to defeat a rival, it may bring hope to one but despair to another. How, then, does it help to establish optimism over pessimism? If at one time it gives an emotional release and a sense of confidence, does it not at other times promote delusions of fear that can lead to a paralysis of effort? There are few to argue, any longer, with Malinowski's point that magic is not an unimportant and aberrant item in a culture, but

[25] In Needham, *op. cit.*, p. 83.

a functioning part of a complex system. This does not, however, entitle one to slip easily into the position that accepts it as "functional" in a value sense, with little attention to all of its long-run consequences, many of which may be dysfunctional for the achievement of stated ends. If magic becomes established as a mechanism of adjustment to situations where knowledge is inadequate, it may become a barrier to the acceptance of new knowledge, thus entrenching a problem that might be reduced.

Radcliffe-Brown, while accepting the functionalist view, has criticized Malinowski for his excessively individualistic emphasis. A magical rite performed at the occasion of a child birth, for example, is not necessarily a way of gaining confidence in a situation fraught with danger. Without the rite, the individual might feel no anxiety: the rite is the cause, not the result of the anxiety. Its function, according to Radcliffe-Brown, might more appropriately be seen, not as a device to maintain the poise of the individual, but as an effort to ease the group through a crisis situation, to contribute to the survival of the society, by reenforcing the sense of group identity and making a solemn occasion of an important event.

Although we must avoid an extreme and uncritical functionalism, it is equally an error to study the question from the perspective of one's own cultural situation and then to generalize to other situations. The concept that magic may have some positive functions for the individual is less likely, in fact, to be exaggerated by the educated member of an urban society than it is to be disregarded. The key to the analysis is the question of available alternatives. Those among whom magic is most deeply embedded are caught in a situation for which their knowledge is wholly inadequate. The choice is not between magic and a tested medical or agricultural technology, for example, but perhaps between magic and complete resignation. Magic is a culturally furnished defense against fear and the sense of powerlessness. It may be, as Kluckhohn says of witchcraft, a channel for otherwise disruptive aggression and an affirmation of the solidarity of the group "by dramatically defining what is bad."

Witchcraft belief allows the verbalization of anxiety in a framework that is understandable and which implies the possibility of doing something. Witches (who are living individuals) are potentially controllable by the society; the caprices of the environment are not. Likewise, it is important for the adjustment of the individual that witchcraft is a focus of anxiety which the culture recognizes as valid.[26]

Kluckhohn is well aware that there are dysfunctional elements in Navaho witchcraft. "The informant's remark, 'If the white people hadn't

[26] Clyde Kluckhohn, *Navaho Witchcraft*, pp. 60–61.

stopped us, we'd have killed each other off' has more than a grain of truth in it." [27] By interpreting witchcraft in the context of the total Navaho situation, however, he is also able to see it as an effort to struggle with severe problems for which other mechanisms of adjustment are lacking.

At several points in the chapters to follow, we shall refer to problems of interpretation connected with a functional approach to religion and magic. As a formula for rigid interpretation it can lead to many errors; as a flexible group of concepts, functionalism can contribute a great deal to our understanding.

MAGICAL BELIEFS IN MODERN SOCIETY

Cultures vary widely in the degree to which magic is found. If the functionalist approach is correct, one of the reasons for this variation (not, however, the only reason), is the difference in control over life events. In a society in which scientific agriculture has greatly increased the yield and reduced the fortuitous and unpredictable aspects of farming, magical practices lose much of their meaning. Those who are in closest touch with scientific medicine are usually least likely to resort to magical cures. Those who, for economic, educational, or personal reasons are "alienated" from modern medicine, however, continue to rely on magical practices in part. This is particularly likely to occur in connection with those diseases about which scientific knowledge is least adequate. The magical treatment may, as Hsu has noted, be blurred with science, little distinction being drawn between the use of a doctor's prescription and a patent "medicine." Attempts to control the world by analogy—a prime characteristic of magic among primitives—is matched to some degree by what we might call "word analogy" today. Millions of dollars are spent annually in the United States for completely untested mixtures that carry the *word* "medicine." The religious systems of modern urban people have doubtless lost many magical elements, but some remain. The efficacy that is felt to reside in sacred objects, the feeling of well-being that comes from a rite, duly and correctly performed, are close to a magical view.

Many anthropologists have stressed the continuing importance of magic in modern societies. They have pointed out that although beliefs may be repeatedly contradicted by objective results, we may continue to accept their validity. The "formulas" don't work, they have scarcely ever been tested, but we rely on them. In international diplomacy, in the punishment of criminals, in education modern men carry out activities which may allay their fears and feelings of helplessness, but which can scarcely

[27] *Ibid.*, p. 62.

be shown to be technically competent to achieve their avowed aims. Ruth Benedict writes:

The traditional American scheme of education is distinctly magical; it does not attempt to draw up a program of what the child will need as an adult and direct its attention to the specific necessary techniques. Its method can be justified only by a faith in a magical oneness in the intellectual world; education is regarded as a power in the non-naturalistic sense.[28]

There is always the danger that we will define magic as a superstitious idea in which I do not believe. It is someone else's false inference or untested formula. The functional view tries to remove this error, by paying attention to the conditions under which magic thrives. This point has been difficult to convey for two reasons: It has often been exaggerated, to make it appear that magic was as much a part of the world-view of the contemporary urban society as of the Dobu. Yet the functionalist approach itself must lead us to realize that the increasing control that man has over many aspects of the world reduces the importance of magic. A more important problem is that much of modern "magic," in the functionalist sense, is not supernaturalistic. It is of the same genus, perhaps, but of a different species from the magical views of those who are much more completely imbedded in a supernaturalistic world-view. In the analysis of magical elements in modern societies, it is a mistake either to forget the differences or to overlook the similarities.

Summary. Perhaps our discussion of the relationship of religion to morals, to science, and to magic, can be summed up in these brief propositions: 1. They can profitably be defined in separate terms. 2. They are usually mixed in empirically complicated socio-cultural systems. 3. The patterns of relationship vary widely, depending on the religious tradition and the whole social situation in which it is found.

[28] *Encyclopedia of Social Sciences,* Vol. 10, p. 41.

CHAPTER 3

A Sociological Theory of Religion

There is a close connection between the problems of definition, with which we have been concerned in the first two chapters, and the development of a theory. The task of definition and the task of stating a systematic theory must, indeed, be carried on together. Having raised or hinted at a number of theoretical questions in our attempts at definition, we must now examine them with greater care.

One need scarcely point out that no one theory of religion is adequate for all purposes. Every theory starts from certain basic assumptions, useful for the purposes of the theorist, which are not demonstrable or provable. A scientist starts from the point of view that something interesting and useful (for the tasks of science) can be said about religion if one assumes that it is part of the world of nature, subject to the laws of causation, capable of analysis according to the methods of science. The adequacy of his statement is to be judged by its contribution to the systematic analysis of observations of an empirical, objective sort, and by the degree to which it aids further such observations. Persons asking theological, aesthetic, or moral questions may find the scientific statements irrelevant (or perhaps impudent). This need not be the case, however, if they do not try to use those statements for purposes of non-scientific investigations. It is equally incumbent on the scientist to avoid "intellectual imperialism": he should not mistake his theories for a theology, a philosophy, an ethical or an aesthetic study of religion.

Scientific theories are most frequently confused with philosophies of religion, with which, indeed, they have much in common. Yet it is well to recognize the differences. Philosophies of religion are usually specific expressions of a general philosophy—attempts to study reality as a whole, as well as to isolate its basic categories or structure. Philosophical observations may derive from intuition, revelation, logic, observation, and other modes of cognitive response to experience, for philosophy is not sharply limited in methodology, as science is. These two facts—the tendency toward a theoretical synthesis (not abstraction) and methodological diversity—make the philosophical approach to religion different from the scientific. That does not mean, however, that the scientists can disregard the observations of the philosophers. Indeed to do so is to forego a great wealth of hypotheses, sharp observations, fruitful discussion of concepts, and theoretical insights. Awareness of the philosophical quest can also help prevent the scientist from forgetting the nature of his abstraction—and the fact that he has abstracted—from a more complicated total reality than his theory can encompass. We shall draw on the philosophers wherever their observations would seem to help us to develop a sociological theory of religion; but we shall not try to develop a philsophy of religion.

We have been using the term "theory" in a broad sense. It is far too much to say that what follows is a scientific theory in the sense of a group of interrelated propositions, fully tested by empirical study, pertaining to the interaction of religious behavior with other phases of social life. Our "theory," instead, will combine propositions on several different levels, in the hope that a systematic statement at this time may make some contribution to the extensive research necessary before a well-tested theory is possible. Propositions will range from what we may call prehypotheses (insightful guesses about the relationship of variables which have not yet been posed in a manner that permits empirical tests), to hypotheses (propositions capable of testing, but not yet sufficiently explored), to statements that have been quite adequately tested by research. Since it is not known how some of these may stand up under further observation, we do not know how well the whole theoretical structure which is built out of them will carry the weight of continuing research and theoretical elaboration. Its adequacy is partly tied to the adequacy of the more general theories in sociology, anthropology, and social psychology, of which it is a specific application. Since these more general theories of human behavior have received more adequate testing in their application to other specific questions, there is reasonable grounds for the belief that they will be substantiated as our knowledge of religious behavior grows. This theory of religious behavior may help, on the other hand, to indicate the research necessary for further development of some of the major propositions in contemporary social science.

THEORIES OF THE ORIGIN OF RELIGION

We shall be primarily concerned with the development of a functional theory of religion. Our approach is systematic, not historical or biographical. Some attention to the history of theories, however, may help us to reach toward a systematic statement. Perhaps this can be done most effectively by stating briefly some of the theories of the origin of religion, for they indicate the way many social scientists first structured their questions about religion. These theories raised a number of fundamental problems, and some of them contained a great deal of implicit functional analysis from which valuable leads can be drawn.

It is now generally agreed that a scientific theory of the origin of religion is impossible. It seems clear that religious beliefs and practices reach back in the history of man tens of thousands of years; and the story of their origins has to be built out of the flimsiest of archeological, philological, and anthropological evidence, filled out with psychological and sociological guesses. These guesses have by no means been fruitless, however, for the development of a scientific theory of religion. As Herskovits says, commenting on various theories of religious origins:

Each of these scholars has provided more than enough evidence, on the face of it, to document his theory and to satisfy any who will read what he has written. Enough, that is, until the evidence for some other theory is studied, a cup equally filled to the brim and running over, and equally convincing. The contribution of these scholars, however, lies not in their having solved the riddle of how religion originated, or the steps by which it developed, or its social or psychological roots; but rather in the different phenomena of religion each emphasized and, by so doing, imprinted indelibly on all future discussions of the subject.[1]

The observations of the early scientific students of religion were based largely on data drawn from living preliterate societies. Although these data could scarcely support a theory of origins, since these societies had religions for thousands of years, and could not solve the problem of "how

[1] M. J. Herskovits, *Man and His Works*, pp. 349–350.

religion arose out of a life not religious at all," as T. H. Grafton puts it, they could, as a by-product of their search for origins, throw light on the nature and variety of religious behavior and on the functions it serves. It is possible that the functional approach of contemporary theory may repay the debt by furnishing interesting ideas concerning religious origins.

A further caution, not always observed by the students of the origin of religion, is necessary if we are to avoid the misuse of our data. Just as we need to withhold conclusions concerning religious origins that are drawn from the study of living societies, so too we need to be cautious not to assume that the study of preliterate societies is an adequate guide to the study of modern, complex, and literate societies. A general theory will be able to explain religion in the whole range of types of societies, but will indicate also the differences in religion and the variables related to those differences.

THREE TYPES OF EXPLANATION OF RELIGIOUS ORIGINS

In briefest outline, social scientific theories of the origin of religion may be classified into three types, each with some elements of functional analysis implicit within it or explicitly developed. We shall state them here, with a few comments on some of the major authors, and then pick up the functional aspects of their theories in our systematic statement below.

The first group emphasizes the cognitive aspects of religion, the need for an explanation of mysterious and awesome events. This theory can be characterized as basically intellectualistic, individualistic, and evolutionary. Religion, according to this interpretation, springs from the efforts of primitive men to explain the phenomena of dreams, echoes, visions, and above all of death. The key element in the explanation, in Tylor's famous formulation, is the concept of the soul. Such a concept gives to "the savage mind" an explanation of many puzzling bodily and mental conditions—they are the "effects of the departure of the soul." This animistic view of the world, the basis of religion in Tylor's view, represents a "fairly consistent and rational primitive philosophy."

This rationalistic conception of religion was easily related to the evolutionary doctrine. If animism is a primitive effort to explain the puzzling facts of a complicated world, it will undergo step by step modification as man's knowledge of the world increases. Presumably the final result will be the disappearance of religion when its basic function—explanation—is taken over by other elements of culture, particularly by science.

It is unnecessary for our purposes to undertake a lengthy critique of this conception of the origin of religion. It seems obviously inadequate as a total explanation, although the swing of the pendulum away from such rationalistic interpretations of human behavior may have carried too far. The failure to explore fully the deep-seated emotional qualities of religion makes the work of Spencer and Tylor seem strangely anachronistic today.

Let us recall how religion actually operates. Our reaction to the death of a deeply loved friend or relative is not simply one of cognition. We are not satisfied merely with knowing how he died. We want something more satisfying than this cold knowledge. Our emotional equilibrium has been upset, our hopes and desires frustrated. We need, in short, an interpretation in terms of sentiments and values.[2]

The animistic theory of religious origins is inadequate also in its disregard of the social and group elements in religious life. How can one account for the obligatory element in religious belief, and for its continuation in modern life despite the growth of knowledge of the naturalistic causes of the events on which animism presumably rested? An adequate theory must deal with the integrative, the social aspects of religion.[3]

The assumption of unilineal evolution has proved to be equally unsatisfactory. It was criticized both by those who, with Lang and Schmidt, believed that conceptions of "high-gods" can be found at very early stages in the development of religion, and by those who believed, with Codrington, Marett, and others, that belief in an impersonal supernatural force—mana—preceded the appearance of belief in spirits. These criticisms represent an increase in attention to the emotional and to the functional aspects of religion, but they accepted a great deal of the evolutionary approach. A sharper criticism, particularly of the assumption that religion was gradually being destroyed by the evolutionary increase in knowledge, stems from a fully developed functional theory.[4]

A second major approach to the question of the origin of religion places great emphasis on man's emotional needs. This view is readily translated into a concern for functions and an interest in the sources of

[2] Kingsley Davis, *Human Society,* p. 517.
[3] See W. J. Goode, *Religion Among the Primitives,* pp. 243–246.
[4] On this whole approach to a theory of the origins of religion and some of the controversy which it generated, see Sir James G. Frazer, *The Golden Bough;* Irving King, *The Development of Religion;* Andrew Lang, *The Making of Religion* and *Magic and Religion;* R. R. Marett, *The Threshold of Religion;* P. W. Schmidt, *The Origin and Growth of Religion;* Herbert Spencer, *The Principles of Sociology,* Vol. I; Edward B. Tylor, *Primitive Culture.*

the continuing influence of religion, as contrasted with efforts at historical reconstruction. We shall examine the functional interpretation of this question in some detail in the next chapter. Some of the writers, however, use this approach as the basis for a theory of the origin of religion as well. In *Totem and Taboo* and elsewhere, for example, Freud develops his version of "the elementary forms of the religious life," to use Durkheim's well-known title. It is a vastly different conception from that of Tylor. In Freud's interpretation, a primeval slaying of the father by the sons, primarily because the tyrannical father had monopolized the females of the horde, and the attendant guilt and repression, are the source of totemism. Out of this emerge the later forms of religion and the whole pattern of culture. In Chapter 4 we shall examine the way in which Freud uses the basic Oedipus conflict as the key to his theory of the functions of religion. The propositions that he develops in that connection are at least partially subject to testing, as his theory of origins is not.

Paul Radin interprets the origin of religion in a way that ties it closely to a functional theory. He asks, "What is it that originally led man to postulate the supernatural?" To answer the question, we must try to visualize the conditions under which man lived at the dawn of civilization. With wholly inadequate technological preparation, he was helpless before the powerful and capricious forces of the environment.

His mentality was still overwhelmingly dominated by definitely animal characteristics although the life-values themselves—the desire for success, for happiness, and for long life—were naturally already present. . . . No economic security could have existed, and we cannot go far wrong in assuming that, where economic security does not exist, emotional insecurity and its correlates, the sense of powerlessness and the feeling of insignificance, are bound to develop. . . .

It is but natural for the psyche, under such circumstances, to take refuge in compensation fantasies . . . . the main goal and objective of all his strivings was the canalization of his fears and feelings and the validation of his compensation dreams.[5]

Thus religion springs primarily, according to Radin, from man's emotional responses to a threatening situation. The third line of argument concerning the origin of religion differs from the individualistic emphasis of the first two. It sees religion as primarily a product of social interaction and group life. Once again, since we have no direct interest in a complete survey of origin theories, we shall be content with a brief

[5] Paul Radin, *Primitive Religion, Its Nature and Origin,* pp. 6–9.

mention of only two writers who make social factors the focus of their attention. These ideas are also easily transposed into functional terms, without attention to the question of historical origins at all. Simmel, in fact, who emphasizes the human relations source of religion, indicates that he is not trying to describe the historical origin, but what he calls its "psychological origin," as one of many sources. And Durkheim, the other writer whom we shall mention in this connection, is certainly important primarily, not for his speculations about origin, but for his functional analyis.

Simmel develops the thesis that one of the sources of religion is human relations which themselves are non-religious. "I do not believe that the religious feelings and impulses manifest themselves in religion only. . . ." [6] Religion is the heightening and abstracting from their particular content of certain human relations—of exaltation, devotion, fervency, and the like—that are found widely in social life. Faith, for example, is first of all a relation between individuals; we don't base our relations with others on what we conclusively know about them. "The social role of this faith has never been investigated; but this much is certain, that without it society would disintegrate. . . . In faith in a deity the highest development of faith has become incorporate, so to speak; has been relieved of its connection with its social counterpart." [7] Thus, in Simmel's view, religion is an outgrowth of human relations.

Durkheim's emphasis on the social origin of religion is more extreme than that of Simmel. For Durkheim, society is the object of religious veneration and the basic source of "the sacred." The primary function of religion is the preservation of social unity. "So everything leads us back to this same idea: before all, rites are means by which the social group reaffirms itself periodically." [8] Thus he calls attention to aspects of religion that had certainly been given inadequate attention—rite, cult organization, its relationship to the social structure. It is in such a context that he interprets totemic cults, which he considers "the elementary forms of the religious life."

From this, we may be able to reconstruct hypothetically the way in which the totemic cult should have arisen originally. Men who feel themselves united, partially by bonds of blood, but still more by a community of interest and tradition, assemble and become conscious of their moral unity . . . . they are led to represent this unity in the form of a very special kind of consubstan-

[6] Georg Simmel, "A Contribution to the Sociology of Religion," *American Journal of Sociology*, November, 1905, p. 360.
[7] *Ibid.*, pp. 366–367.
[8] Emile Durkheim, *The Elementary Forms of the Religious Life*, p. 387.

tiality: they think of themselves as all participating in the nature of some determined animal. Under these circumstances, there is only one way for them to affirm their collective existence: this is to affirm that they are like the animals of this species, and to do so not only in the silence of their own thoughts, but also by material acts.[9]

As a theory of the origin of religion, Durkheim's interpretation is doubtless one-sided, and like all the others, quite beyond demonstration. Its importance rests primarily on the attention it focuses on the group aspects of religion. It is basically a functional interpretation, not a study of origins. From this brief commentary on his, and other essays on the origin of religion, we can profitably turn to an examination of the functional theory.

THE FUNCTIONAL APPROACH TO RELIGION

It is a fairly short step from the question, "How did religion originate?" to, "What does it do for human societies and individuals?" We have suggested that the second question was implicit in much of the earlier work devoted to the study of origins. It is the virtue of more recent studies, however, that they have made the functional question explicit, thus being able to use it more effectively while at the same time pointing up its limitations and its hidden assumptions. As Kingsley Davis has pointed out, social theory has often been inadequate to interpret religion, because it has asked the wrong, or the relatively less important, questions. Viewing religion primarily from a cognitive standpoint, it has asked, "Do religious ideas represent reality?" This leads to questions concerning the nature of reality and the reasons for any errors that religious beliefs may be said to contain. There is value in this approach, but also a great weakness, for it tends to reduce religion to a system of beliefs or statements of purported facts. Whether religious ideas are "true" hinges on one's definition of the truth, and hence becomes a metaphysical, not a scientific problem. The virtue of functional analysis is that it avoids the metaphysical debate (which, for problems other than those of empirical study, may be an important debate), and states, instead: Religious beliefs and practices do exist; they have consequences for human behavior. How are they used?

Since every society seems to have something called religion, its presence can hardly be dismissed as a sociological accident. If, given the major conditions of human social life as known up to now, religion made no contribution to

9 *Ibid.*

societal survival or was not inextricably attached to something that did contribute to survival, one would expect that social systems and cultures would long since have evolved without it. There need be no assumption that religion is entirely adaptive, that its role is identical in all types of societies, or that in some distant future its functions might not be instrumented by some other kind of cultural structure. There is simply a good *prima facie* case for asking a question about its functions and trying to answer the question scientifically.[10]

A functional interpretation rests upon several related ideas. Perhaps most important is the conception, discussed briefly in Chapter 1, that societies are systems of interdependent parts. The religious patterns, therefore, cannot be understood in isolation from the whole structure in which they are embedded. For example, Fortes and Evans-Pritchard, in their discussion of *African Political Systems,* describe the ways in which religious symbols, rites, dogmas, and sacred places unify the social systems of which they are a part. They give the whole system a mystical value that promotes acceptance far beyond the obedience that the secular sanctions could bring.

The social system is, as it were, removed to a mystical plane, where it figures as a system of social values beyond criticism or revision. . . . The African sees these ritual observances as the supreme safeguard of the basic needs of his existence and of the basic relations that make up his social order—land, cattle, rain, bodily health, the family, the clan, the state. . . . Periodical ceremonies are necessary to affirm and consolidate these values because, in the ordinary course of events, people are pre-occupied with sectional and private interests and are apt to lose sight of the common interest and of their political interdependence.[11]

An idea that is closely linked to the concept of system is the proposition that there are some "invariant points of reference," in the nature of man as a biological type, in his psychology, in the structure of social systems, etc., which pose certain necessary conditions for the existence of any society. These are perhaps best stated in the form of questions, to indicate the tentative quality of many of the propositions: What is the significance of man's biological patterns—the long infancy, the length of the life span, the relative lack of "instinctual" responses, and the like —for human interaction? Are there pan-human responses to extreme stress and frustration that are manifest in every social system? Do groups as such have basic isolable properties that set limits to the kinds of developments possible in a society? Do these lead to certain "functional

[10] Kingsley Davis in Introduction to Goode, *op. cit.*, p. 15.
[11] M. J. Fortes and E. Evans-Pritchard, *African Political Systems*, p. 16 ff.

prerequisites" in all societies, to patterns essential for the very existence of a society? [12]

To some degree, these concepts are in opposition to the extreme relativism that characterized an earlier sociology. They do not deny the relativism in specific cultural content, but regard many of the specific forms as alternative ways of meeting functionally similar requirements of social life. Religion is thought, by most functional theorists, to be among the necessary patterns.

DIFFICULTIES IN THE FUNCTIONAL APPROACH

Functional analysis, to be sure, is not without weaknesses and difficulties. It is sometimes used to "prove" the ultimate validity, or inevitability, or changelessness of some specific practice or belief. These non-empirical propositions are unwarranted. Durkheim's famous proposition that social facts cannot be explained by psychological theories might be matched here by the formulation: do not try to support non-empirical statements (this religious practice is good and true because it is universal) by empirical generalizations (religion is universal). Some people have used Heisenberg's principle of indeterminancy in physics to support theological ideas. Others have jumped, reluctantly or enthusiastically, from "the mores can make anything right," (an overly-simple empirical generalization) to the moral—or if you prefer, immoral—conclusion that the culture of one society is as good as that of any other.

Perhaps more unfortunate than the floating back and forth between value judgments and statements of fact on the part of "laymen" has been the tendency on the part of some of the functionalists themselves to go beyond their evidence and to disregard the problem of dysfunctions. Robert Merton has shown that three interconnected postulates are often used, by the more extreme functionalists, that are not necessary to functional analysis and tend to make of it an ideology:

1. The postulate of the functional unity of a society—that every standardized activity or belief is functional, that is, necessary and useful, for the whole social system.

2. The postulate that every social form has a positive function—universal functionalism. ". . . *no* culture forms survive unless they constitute responses which are adjustive or adaptive, in some sense . . ." (quoting Clyde Kluckhohn).

---

[12] See the excellent discussion by Clyde Kluckhohn in *Anthropology Today*, edited by A. L. Kroeber, pp. 507–523. This whole question is treated with greatest care by Talcott Parsons in several recent works. See also David Aberle, *et al.*, "The Functional Prerequisites of Society," *Ethics*, Vol. LX, No. 2 (1950), pp. 100–111.

3. The postulate of indispensability—that certain functions are necessary to the survival of a society and/or that particular cultural or social forms are indispensable in carrying out these functions.[13]

So long as these postulates are assumptions, rather than propositions to be tested by empirical study, functional analysis will be inadequate. In the contrast that he draws between manifest and latent functions, in the attention to functional alternatives, and in his emphasis on the need to study dysfunctions and functionally irrelevant patterns of behavior, Merton develops concepts that help us to avoid these assumptions. It is particularly the study of latent functions (and dysfunctions) that is likely to add significantly to our knowledge of a social process, for these, by definition, are not common knowledge; their consequences are unintended and unrecognized.

. . . research which uncovers latent functions very often produces 'paradoxical' results. The seeming paradox arises from the sharp modification of a familiar popular preconception which regards a standardized practice or belief *only* in terms of its manifest functions by indicating some of its subsidiary or collateral latent functions.[14]

This is particularly true, perhaps, of the study of religion, in which the analysis is very likely to be carried on in terms of what religion "does" for society or the individual only as expressed in the prevailing ideology. Or, on the other hand, in various "debunking" studies, attention is paid only to manifest and latent dysfunctions, with little or no attention to possible latent functions. Preconceptions of either sort will block our ability to explore religion fully.

Goode summarizes the situation well by indicating the six questions that need to be raised if one is to develop an adequate functional analysis:

Positive Function		Negative Function		Irrelevant	
Manifest	Latent	Manifest	Latent	Manifest	Latent

Functional anthropologists have concentrated upon those *positive functions* which are *not usually known* to the members of the society, i.e., the positive, latent functions. The rebels and debunkers among modern economists and historians have concentrated upon the *negative latent functions*. It is clear that much exploration remains to be done among the remaining cells.[15]

One seldom noticed, and not altogether happy, consequence of the shift, in theoretical interest, from the question of the origin of religion

[13] See Robert Merton, *Social Theory and Social Structure*, pp. 27–38.
[14] *Ibid.*, p. 68.
[15] Goode, *op. cit.*, p. 33. See also Harry C. Bredemeier, "The Methodology of Functionalism," *American Sociological Review*, April, 1955, pp. 173–180.

to the problem of functions, has been a concomitant shift in emphasis in the study of the interaction of religion and society. The student of the origin of religion tended to ask: How does a society (or, as Durkheim might say, the very fact of society) influence the development of religion? Or, how do individual intellectual and emotional needs affect religious origins? Religion was treated primarily as a dependent variable. The "functionalist," taking religion as an established fact, is more likely to ask: What does religion do for societies and individuals? He tends to deal with religion as the independent variable. A theory that maintains a continuous and systematic interest in the *interaction* of religion and society seems to be difficult to develop. Just as questions concerning origins *tend toward* an ideology that religion is an archaic survival, destined gradually to be outgrown (Spencer and Tylor, for example), so questions concerning functions *tend toward* a conservative ideology. An objective science of religion can accept neither ideology, although it is perfectly willing to move toward one or the other proposition if the evidence points in that direction. A broad enough functional theory, one that includes latent and dysfunctional processes, can encompass the questions raised by the concept of interaction. To do this, however, requires that we avoid the assumption that society, or personality, or religion is always to be treated as the independent variable, with the others as dependent.

RELIGION AS AN INTEGRATOR OF SOCIETY

It is difficult to find a neutral vocabulary by means of which one can express the "function-dysfunction" of religion in its relationship to social integration. (The lack of an objective vocabulary doubtless indicates the absence of objective study of these phenomena.) To most people it is probably assumed that to integrate a society is good, purely and simply. No distinction is raised in their minds between integration as a general fact and a specific pattern of integration. Religion, in this view, as the primary source of integration, is good and necessary; and the particular religious beliefs and practices of the moment are therefore defended. To others, religion is a necessary ingredient of a well-integrated society because of the passions and lack of intelligence of the "masses," who must be protected from their own inadequacies. This is an ancient view, expressed, for example, by Polybius, the Greek historian. Commenting on the honesty of the Romans, because they feared their Gods, he admits that his own countrymen:

. . . if entrusted with a single talent, though protected by ten checking-clerks, as many seals and twice as many witnesses, yet cannot be induced to keep faith. However, the Romans have managed to forge the main bond of social order out of something which the rest of the world execrates: I mean, out of Superstition. . . . In my opinion, however, the Romans have done it with an eye to the masses. If it were possible to have an electorate that was composed exclusively of sages, this chicanery might perhaps be unnecessary; but, as a matter of fact, the masses are always unstable and always full of lawless passions, irrational temper and violent rage; and so there is nothing but to control them by 'the fear of the unknown' and play-acting of that sort.[16]

E. A. Ross gives a modern version of the same thesis:

The genius who is to impress the mind of coming generations as the hand impresses the waxen tablet, does not commend his ideal on the ground that it is good for society. He does not advertise it as a means of securing order. He knows that men will not do as they would be done by, or forgive injuries, or subject their impulses to reason, for mere utility's sake. The genius that succeeds takes high ground from the first. His way is not merely a better way of getting along together. He declares it the one possible path of life. It is the God-ordained type of living. It is prescribed by man's nature. It is the goal of history. It is the destiny of the race. So it comes to pass that the inventors of right and wrong, the authors of ideals, not only disguise their sociology as ethics, but often go farther and disguise their ethics as religion.[17]

Many others would agree with this doctrine that religion gives support to social order, but would not see it as a matter of conscious manipulation by an elite and would treat religion, as with Plato, somewhat more piously.

Other writers, starting from different value premises, while agreeing that religion may hold a society together, would call this, not integration, but rigidity. According to this view, the explosive tensions of a society are kept in check by the religious beliefs and practices, but this is done for the benefit of the dominant few, while the creative energies of the great majority are bottled up. This, of course, is the interpretation given by Marx in his proposition that "religion is the opiate of the people," but a similar critical view of traditional religion may be taken by others who strongly disagree with him in their judgment of how to meet the situation. Thus a wide diversity of proposals for new ways to achieve the integration of society, ranging from "scientific" humanism to "scientific" Marxism, has been developed. It is paradoxical that Marxism, despite the vigor of its attack on religion, can itself readily be interpreted as a religious movement. Far from destroying the idea of the need for

<hr>

[16] Quoted by Homer Smith, *Man and His Gods*, pp. 166–167.
[17] E. A. Ross, *Social Control*, pp. 358–359.

an integrating system of values, it simply offers itself as a substitute.

In studying these various approaches to the question of the integrating effects of religion, the functionalist makes a necessary distinction. He does not equate the concept that *some* integrating system of beliefs and practices is necessary to the survival of society, a proposition with strong empirical support (whether society ought to survive is itself, of course, a value judgment, but one which few care to deny), with the idea that a particular system, as it is operating, contributes to social integration. It is now coming widely to be observed that the "spaceless and timeless generalizations about the 'integrative functions of religion' are largely, although not of course entirely, derived from observations in non-literate societies." [18] But what, Merton asks, are the consequences when different religions co-exist in the same society? This need not always produce disharmony, as Merton seems to imply, but it often does. And how does religion make for integration in the larger more complex societies if it defends values that contradict other values of those societies? Can Hindu defense of caste-purity help to integrate a society in which value is gradually coming to be attached to efficient industrial production, with the accompanying demand for rational organization of the work situation? Whether one of these values is "better" than another need not concern us here. We are simply asking whether Hinduism can integrate a society into which the other value is intruding.

The Problem of Order.   Before we explore in more detail this question of relationship between religion and social integration, we need to take a brief look at a more general question concerning social "order." One need not agree entirely with Hobbes that human life, before the establishment of strong governments, was "solitary, poor, nasty, brutish, and short," to realize that man's egocentric tendencies place strong difficulties in the way of smoothly running social groups. Even the smallest and most stable of human societies faces the problem of distributing scarce values. The economic means of livelihood, power (the ability to influence others in directions one desires more than they can influence him), and prestige (comparative by its very nature, so that if one has more, another has less) are all, by definition, in scarce supply. How can a society prevent individual and sub-group pursuit of these values from disrupting the network of agreements and accommodations that social life requires? And how do social groups prevent the hostility that is generated by frustration, by a sense of injustice, by guilt, from constantly tearing the fabric of society? Pushed back further, the question becomes: How can we account for the fact that societies manage to exist at all,

[18] Merton, *op. cit.*, p. 30.

when the tendencies toward self-aggrandizement are so strong and hostile feelings so abundant?

Aristotle raised this question, and gave us the answer: "Man is by nature social" (political), a theory picked up in the twentieth century in the McDougallian idea of "gregarious instincts." In a day when man's anti-social potentialities loom so large, however, we are not much impressed by these doctrines, nor by the whole attempt to explain behavior by putting something "in" man, which is then pointed to as a simple "explanation" when questions arise. We are perhaps more likely to be persuaded by Hobbes' doleful belief in an ever-threatening "war of all against all," and its twentieth century variant, the Freudian doctrine that every individual has a reservoir of hostility, partly (and here we leave Hobbes) because of the very fact of society.

An adequate view, it would seem, must recognize that man has potentialities both for social life and for hostility and self-centered pursuit of values. How do societies manage to keep the latter at a minimum (or at least aimed in directions not likely to injure the social order) while strengthening the potentialities for social life? One may guess that those societies that did not learn to do this were simply torn apart and disappeared (and that this process continues). This does not tell us, however, what they learned.

There are doubtless several related social processes, some of them a long way from our conception of religion, which can be understood in this context: The hostility may be directed toward other societies. It may be focused on socially approved scapegoats within a society; (it is interesting here that the term scapegoat, originally with a religious meaning has now acquired a broader referent). There may be processes whereby the hostility and egocentricity are sublimated into activities that are not socially disruptive. (Sublimation is a slippery concept, capable of about as many non-scientific distortions as "instinct." We cannot discuss its weaknesses here, but use it in the minimal sense of accepting a substitute activity for a blocked one.) And finally, coming to the function of religion in these processes, intragroup hostility and egocentricism may be prevented from reaching destructive force by the organized system of rites and beliefs. This last requires more careful explanation.

If a society is to exist at all, it must find some means for distributing its scarce goods and values in such a way that the great majority accept the outcome or protest against it only by means approved by the social system itself. And it must find a way to control the expression of hostility generated by frustration, pain, and guilt. That even complex and mobile societies succeed in these tasks is a matter of daily observation. Although the violations get the headlines, the more important fact is the number of times we count on, and receive, normatively prescribed behavior, even from strangers. Most of us, most of the time, use means that are approved by our society, and do not use other means which, although perhaps more technically efficient in helping us acquire scarce values, are forbidden. We do not steal money, but work for it at a socially approved task; we do not destroy our competitor or spread malicious gossip about him, but compete against him. Even when we buy goods and services from strangers—a much more common occurance in urban societies—we generally get full measure and quality. We accept the "strait-jacket of culture," (as Freud might call it) at least on the conscious level, despite our tensions and fears. No strictly egocentric theory of man can explain these facts. How can we account for this order?

Certainly one level of explanation is the fear of punishment: fear of ridicule, isolation, and public censure in the simpler societies, and, added to those, the power of explicit political authorities to coerce and punish in "civil" societies. We abide by the normatively approved means for acquiring scarce values, we express our hostility only in socially designated ways, because violations threaten greater loss than gain. Obviously this fear of punishment or loss is only partially successful. In the larger, more mobile societies the amount of effort necessary to enforce the norms must be increased. Moreover, the problem of integration and social order is not thus solved, because there is the continuing danger that the enforcement authorities themselves—those who have been assigned the task of upholding the normative system of the society—may use the coercive means given them for their own advantage. This is the eternal political problem. Every society must have a pattern of control "beyond politics" that will reduce the necessity for coercion and keep the authorities themselves within bounds. This final basis of social order rests on what Davis calls the "common-ultimate ends," socialized into the individual members of that society as their basic values. These values are shared, non-competitive values, against which all other derivative goals are judged.

. . . these ends can refer not so much to a future state of the individual himself as to the future state of other individuals and, in the last analysis, to the group itself. . . . As between two different groups holding an entirely different set of common-ultimate ends, there is no recourse. But within the same community this type of ends constitutes the integrating feature.[19]

[19] Kingsley Davis, *Human Society*, pp. 141–143.

How does religion come into this picture? The answer is much clearer for static and isolated societies than for changing ones: Insofar as it is accepted religion, by rite and symbol, gives emotional support to the fundamental values of a society; it softens the hardness of the struggle for scarce values by emphasizing values than can be achieved by all (e.g., salvation); and it lessens the tensions of those who have failed to achieve a desired level of a society's values by approved means by emphasizing supra-mundane values. Beyond the integration that comes from socialization and social control in their secular aspects, beyond economic and political integration, beyond the focusing of disruptive hostilities onto socially designated scapegoats within the society or enemies without, every society has a transcendent system of unifying values, beyond politics and, indeed, in most cases, beyond history.

This is not to say that any particular religion is, therefore, good. The statement above is empirical, not valuational. The support it gives may be to a society based on principles one considers bad, e.g., slavery; the rites its uses may, from the value stand of the outsider, seem barbarous, e.g., human sacrifice; the lowering of the sense of frustration may, in some circumstances, cut the nerve of effort that many would regard as essential. On another level, in connection with the relations between societies which have a different kind of religious integration, strong barriers to inter-society cooperation and accommodation may be erected. One's value judgment concerning the integrative function of religion, therefore, can most profitably be based on the analysis of *all* the consequences, manifest and latent.

The concept of religion as an integrator of society is, as we have seen, an ancient one. It is at least as old as Confucius, who declared that rites bind the multitudes together and "serve as dikes against excesses to which the people are prone." Leaping across the centuries, one finds integration to be an important function of what Henri Bergson calls the static religion of the closed society. In his view, ". . . religion is then a defensive reaction of nature against the dissolvent power of intelligence." Individual intelligence, unregulated, would lead primarily, Bergson says, to egocentric behavior. "Primitive religion, taken from our first standpoint, is a precaution against the danger man runs, as soon as he thinks at all, of thinking of himself alone." [20]

Bergson also stresses, as we shall see, the function of religion in countering the fact of death. Some writers, however, have placed almost the whole emphasis on the role of religion as social integrator. Benjamin

[20] Henri Bergson, *The Two Sources of Morality and Religion*, pp. 112–113.

Kidd builds this idea into his very definition when he writes that a religion ". . . is a form of belief, providing an ultra-rational sanction for that large class of conduct in the individual where his interests and the interests of the social organism are antagonistic, and by which the former are rendered subordinate to the latter in the general interests of the evolution which the race is undergoing." [21] This statement is inadequate both as definition and as a theory of the functions of religion. Like other writers of the same period, Kidd placed too much emphasis on the "belief" aspects of religion; and as a theory of functions, the statement is a great over-simplification.

Difficulties in the Emphasis on Integration. How can this approach to religion be brought into an adequate theory? Several problems need to be solved before this long-established insight into the role of religion as "integrator of society," can take its place in a scientific theory of religion:

1. A great deal of empirical observation, in different types of societies, is still needed to discover how generally the proposition applies, to discover where, if at all, it does not apply (religion as disintegrator of society, or as unimportant in this regard), and to specify the *conditions under which* these various possibilities occur. Did religion "integrate" Russian society, 1915–1917? Would Taoism and Buddhism, independent of Confucianism, have held Chinese society together? Although this insight is perhaps three thousand years old and has taken its place in dozens of philosophies of religion, the task of isolating the conditions under which it applies has not yet adequately been carried out.

2. A statement of the integrative function must be united with statements of religion's other functions and dysfunctions, and this broader statement tested by widespread empirical observation. Is there a changeless core of functions without which one should not speak of "religion"; or are some of these functions performed primarily by other kinds of social structures in certain kinds of societies? (Here again, the problem of definition is not easily solved.) Is there an "inherently" inter-related group of functions that one finds always embodied together in religion because one cannot be carried out effectively in the absence of the other? It is a plausible hypothesis that the functions for the individual, which we shall discuss in the next chapter, are better served by a religious system that also integrates society, and that the group function is more adequately performed by a religion which also satisfies various individual needs. Oppositely, societal integration is less likely to be accomplished, according to this hypothesis, by a pattern of beliefs and practices which

[21] Benjamin Kidd, *Social Evolution,* p. 111.

fails to satisfy important needs in the lives of individual adherents (remembering how exceedingly various these needs, many of them defined by the religion itself, may be). And finally, in this regard, a religious system that for the moment satisfies individual needs but fails to hold together the society within which those satisfactions are achieved, is unlikely to be able to continue to carry out even the individual functions. Before the observation that religion contributes to social integration can become part of an adequate scientific theory of religion, this hypothesis needs further exploration.

3. The proposition also needs to be related to broader theories of society and personality. If it is true that a system of religious beliefs and practices supports, under stated conditions, social integration, what is there about the nature of society and of personality that makes this true? Is this proposition congruent with other statements about society and personality? Can it be reduced to a more general theory of human behavior, following the principle of parsimony, thus bringing it more solidly into the framework of sociology?

We are slowly making headway in answering these questions; and it is our hope that this essay, drawing on the increasingly rich resources, can contribute to the process of bringing such ancient insights as we are discussing into the framework of an adequate theory.

Variables Influencing the Integrative Function of Religion. The growth of the comparative study of religions, both of preliterate and literate societies, and the study of how a religion changes as the society in which it is embedded changes are our primary sources of information. On the basis of that material, some of which will be discussed in other connections in later chapters (empirical material will be kept at a minimum in this systematic statement), the following propositions concerning religion and social integration seem justified. These propositions are not mutually exclusive, because each one deals with part of an interacting group of forces—where one is present, several others are also likely to be found. The statements are put negatively, reversing the usual emphasis, to point up the need for indicating the conditions under which religion will tend to produce social cohesion. The integrative function of religion is at a minimum—other things being equal:

1. In societies where more than one religion is practiced.

2. When the "established expectancies" of the members of a society are frustrated. This refers, not to some absolute level of need, but to the satisfactions that the members of a society have come to expect. When these are denied, those who feel frustrated may become "more religious," in the manner of the "Old Believers" in Russia, and as it is

seen in the explosive Kitiwala movement in the Belgian Congo—a politico-religious sect built around Christian symbols—but not in the sense of embracing more strongly a unifying religious tradition. They are more likely to use religion to express their sense of separation and even as a weapon to fight for the reestablishment of their "rights." This is illustrated by the way in which nominally Christian Indians used the Ghost Dance against white Americans.

3. When social change reduces the appeal of the ritual and belief systems. What will give one generation a sense of a unifying tradition may alienate parts of another generation who have been subjected to different social and cultural influences.

4. When mobility from society to society is greatest; and the corollary, when a society is composed of members who were socialized to different patterns of behavior. Even when the mobility is among societies sharing the same basic religious system, there are bound to be local variations in the religious tradition, and the heterogeneous society will have a wider range of personality systems to integrate.

5. When a society is sharply divided into classes, or other hierarchical divisions, and this is strongly felt as an oppressive fact. Religion itself may help to *prevent* a stratification system from being felt as an oppressive fact, as in the case of classic Hinduism or medieval Christianity, but it may not be able to do so in the face of competing value systems derived from non-religious sources or from some aspects of the religion itself. If a religion cannot "explain away" the differences in income, power, and prestige on the basis of its own principles, it is less able to serve the function of integrating a society. Those who are most disadvantaged are particularly likely, under these circumstances, to desert the dominant religion and to accept some new religion, or proto-religion as the way to solve their problems. In such a situation, the religious forces are as likely to express and even to accentuate the internal tensions of a society as they are to integrate that society. Thus the lower classes were those most likely to desert the emperor worship of Rome in favor of Christianity. In the nineteenth and twentieth centuries, the lower classes and alienated members of the middle and upper classes have been the most likely to leave Christianity for the secular salvation of communism. And in India today, most converts to Christianity from Hinduism are drawn from the highly disadvantaged groups. The proponents of a religious system are likely to argue that "true" Christianity or "true" Hinduism could not thus be involved in social conflict instead of social integration. Only "corrupt" versions could do that. This is a point on which debate is likely to be fruitless. Let us say simply that, whatever may be the

basic ideology, religion as it is lived and used becomes, under certain circumstances, an important factor, as symbol and cause, of social conflict.

6. When outside pressures split a society. Perhaps this is only to say that when outside forces are strong enough or of a particular kind, the cohesive effects of religion may be inadequate to maintain the unity of a society. Thus many American Indian tribes are divided into "reactionaries" (those who want to reaffirm the validity of their original culture) and "liberals" (who would prefer recognition simply as individual Americans), with many positions in between. Religious differences usually match these differences and perhaps intensify them. We must state, of course, that under other circumstances outside pressure may have the opposite effect: It may revivify a religious system and greatly increase the internal solidarity of a society. Judaism is often cited as the classic illustration of this process. It is well to recognize that often both tendencies—the unifying and the disrupting—may be present in an ambivalent relationship. Thus there have been continual splits among Jews, showing that religion is unable to resolve all the differences that may occur as a result of the outside situation. And, oppositely, some of the religious movements among American Indians served to express their unity, as against the white man. (It is in such a situation, where opposite tendencies are found, that analysis is most complicated and where overly-simple theories are most likely to prevail. Only more intensive search for the many variables involved can reduce this difficulty.)

These are among the conditions which, when present, reduce the integrative effects of religion. This discussion perhaps serves to make clear why we cannot accept the simple assertion that "religion produces social integration." When the tendencies that we have discussed run in the opposite direction, of course, they will serve to strengthen the integrative aspects of religion. It should also be noted that we have used a "society" as our unit. When one is concerned with some subdivision of a society—a class or minority-group, for example—some of the limitations on the power of social cohesion through religion do not apply, although several of them are relevant even to the question of integration of such groups.

Many students of religion might accept these qualifications with respect to the integrative function of religion, but then ask: Is it not true that there is a *tendency* in a society, in the face of these disintegrative influences, to recover or discover a unifying religious theme? If we define religion broadly enough, the answer would seem to be yes. These tendencies, however, may not have time to work themselves out before new disintegrative influences enter the scene—thus maintaining a continuously mixed situation. Here we are in the realm of pre-hypothesis, but the speculation may be worthwhile. When religious integration is weakened, other types of integration for subdivisions of a society or the whole society tend to emerge, because of the functional necessity of a unifying system of values. Nationalism is an outstanding example in our time. (The causal sequence may, of course, be the other way around: Nationalism, as a unifying system of values, may have come about as a result of causes independent of the presence or absence of a unifying religious tradition and then *caused* the weakening of the religious view. More likely, the various influences continuously interacted.)

It may be true, however, that sub-societal religions or secular systems of value integration *tend toward* a full-fledged religious pattern, because such a pattern serves the individual and group functions more successfully. Religion may tend to spread to the boundaries of a society (and in our time, beyond), because the existence of conflicting systems weakens these functions. Most secular systems of value integration, moreover —what we may call incipient or proto-religions—tend to prove inadequate because of their inability to achieve their proclaimed goals. Religion, by making extra-empirical goals (salvation) most important (not necessarily all-important), by trans-valuing the meaning of human failure and suffering, by dealing in shared, not scarce and therefore competitive, values, may reduce this difficulty.

These propositions are to some degree illustrated by Warner's description of the half-patriotic, half-religious ceremonies of Memorial Day in the United States. In this description, one sees a complex and heterogeneous society struggling toward a group of cohering, unifying beliefs and practices, building the unifying theme out of materials from the society's own experience—the widely shared and emotionally significant experiences of death in war.

It is the thesis of this chapter that the Memorial Day ceremonies and subsidiary rites (such as those of Armistice Day) of today, yesterday, and tomorrow are rituals of a sacred symbol system which functions periodically to unify the whole community, with its conflicting symbols and its opposing, autonomous churches and associations. It is contended here that in the Memorial Day ceremonies the anxieties which man has about death are confronted with a system of sacred beliefs about death which gives the individuals involved and the collectivity of individuals a feeling of well-being. Further, the feeling of triumph over death by collective action in the Memorial Day parade is made possible by re-creating the feeling of well-being and the sense of group strength and individual strength in the group power, which is felt so intensely during the wars when the veterans' associations are created and when the feeling so necessary for the Memorial Day's symbol is originally experienced.

Memorial Day is a cult of the dead which organizes and integrates the various faiths and national and class groups into a sacred unity. It is a cult of the dead organized around the community cemeteries. Its principal themes are those of the sacrifice of the soldier dead for the living and the obligation of the living to sacrifice their individual purposes for the good of the group, so that they, too, can perform their spiritual obligations.[22]

SUMMARY OF SOCIAL INTEGRATIVE FUNCTION OF RELIGION

Our discussion of this aspect of a sociological theory of religion, and its relationship to a general theory of society, may be summarized in the following propositions:

1. Social order requires a unifying value scheme, specifying approved means and ends, to hold in check the conflict involved in the individual pursuit of scarce values and the hostility generated by the frustrations and disappointments of life.

2. This value scheme must be largely "self-enforcing"—built into the personalities of the members of the society—if it is to withstand the strains imposed by man's egocentric pursuit of his own interests.

3. Political enforcement—designation of legitimate authorities who may use force, taxation, and other coercive measures (widely variant from society to society)—becomes more and more important as societies become larger and mobility more common. This source of order, however, continues to rely on the self-enforcing source of order; and it raises the new problem of the use of political authority for individual gain.

4. Religion may, under some circumstances, help to solve the problem of order, both as a designator of goals (with particular emphasis on shared goals), and as an enforcer of means. By ritual, by symbol, by its system of beliefs, its doctrines of rewards and punishments, religion may help to produce the socialized individuals who accept the dominate values as to legitimate means and ends. This aids the political authorities, but also applies to them.

5. None of these points implies a value judgment concerning the desirability or undesirability of any *particular* system of social order. Religion may help to preserve a social order which, from stated value premises, is bad.

[22] Lloyd Warner, *American Life: Dream and Reality*, pp. 2–3.

6. Certain conditions weaken, or even reverse, the place of religion in social integration. In some times and places it becomes involved, as symbol and cause, in social conflict and the reduction of order. Again, whether this is desirable or undesirable can be stated only with reference to certain stated values and cannot be determined "in general."

CHAPTER 4

Religion and Personality

Analysis of religion that was concerned only with its group elements would certainly be inadequate. Closely associated with the "function-dysfunction" of religion in connection with social integration is the relationship between religion and the needs of the individual members of a society. This is the second major element in a functional approach to religion. Here again unexpressed value judgments sometimes disrupt analysis. Although for many purposes, such judgments are essential, it seems unwise to let them become attached to objective study. Both analysis and valuation are thereby confused. Even the value judgments can most effectively be made, not by the study of what a religion might do, or does according to the ideology of its proponents, but by the weighing of all its actual consequences—functional and dysfunctional, manifest and latent. (This is obviously much easier with respect to some other society's "superstition" than one's own "religion.") The ethnocentric bias has been overcome by most social scientific students of religion, but many of them have fallen into a more subtle bias of the opposite kind: Since "religion" in the abstract is necessary, since it performs important functions, it is good, and therefore (here the subtle shift occurs) this particular religion that I am studying is good; and further, one religion is as good as another. Value judgments, it would seem to the present writer, should be based, not on "religion," but on religions as they are lived; and this requires discrimination among the various forms.

Some writers, on the other hand, declare simply that religion is unfortunate in its consequences for personality. Just as some functionalists tend to argue from "religion in general" to a specific religion, these critics argue from their observations about a specific practice to "religion in general." Neither tendency is justified by a scientific approach.

These difficulties and errors can be avoided only if we separate clearly our analysis from our valuation, and if, in evaluating, we study the total, long-run consequences of specific systems of belief and practice.

RELIGION AND PERSONAL NEED

With these qualifications in mind, we can proceed to the discussion of the relationship between religion and various personality tendencies and needs. Virtually every human desire finds expression, at one time or another, in one individual or another, in religious belief and behavior. The complex and varying conceptions of the deity, as Allport points out, indicate the multiplicity of the human needs that become involved in religion. God is omnipotent, the embodiment of power; He is the source of security and strength; He is cosmic perfection. "When we need affection, God is love; knowledge, He is omniscient; consolation, He granteth peace that passeth understanding. When we have sinned, He is the Redeemer; when we need guidance, the Holy Spirit. Divine attributes plainly conform to the panorama of desire, although the individual is seldom aware that his approach to his deity is determined by present needs." [1]

RELIGIOUS INTERPRETATIONS OF DEATH

Doubtless the most significant of these tendencies with which religion everywhere grapples is fear of death. Bergson believes this to be the second major source of "static religion" (control of selfishness being the first). "Looked at from this second standpoint," he writes, "religion is a defensive reaction of nature against the representation, by intelligence, of the inevitability of death." [2]

---

[1] Gordon Allport, *The Individual and His Religion*, pp. 10–11. "Determined" is certainly too strong a word.

[2] Henri Bergson, *The Two Sources of Morality and Religion*, p. 121.

Malinowski, in his well-known analysis of primitive religion, brings the problem of death into his theory not only of the functions, but also of the origins of religion:

The savage is intensely afraid of death, probably as the result of some deep-seated instincts common to man and animals. He does not want to realize it as an end, he cannot face the idea of complete cessation, of annihilation. The idea of spirit and of spiritual existence is near at hand, furnished by such experiences as are discovered and described by Tylor. Grasping at it, man reaches the comforting belief in spiritual continuity and in the life after death. Yet this belief does not remain unchallenged in the complex, double-edged play of hope and fear which sets in always in the face of death. To the comforting voice of hope, to the intense desire of immortality, to the difficulty, in one's own case, almost the impossibility, of facing annihilation there are opposed powerful and terrible forebodings. The testimony of the senses, the gruesome decomposition of the corpse, the visible disappearance of the personality—certain apparently instinctive suggestions of fear and horror seem to threaten man at all stages of culture with some idea of annihilation, with some hidden fears and forebodings. And here into this play of emotional forces, into this supreme dilemma of life and final death, religion steps in, selecting the positive creed, the comforting view, the culturally valuable belief in immortality, in the spirit independent of the body, and in the continuance of life after death. In the various ceremonies at death, in commemoration and communion with the departed, and worship of ancestral ghosts, religion gives body and form to the saving beliefs.[3]

This statement is not without serious weaknesses. The use of the term "instinct" to explain the source of the fear of death is scarcely to do more than to give a name to a phenomenon that needs more careful explanation. A second difficulty is that Malinowski has given inadequate attention to the variation in concern for and fear of death among individuals, societies, and religious systems. It is doubtful that one can afford to disregard the differences between the conceptions of "Nirvana" and of heaven as a physically located place with golden streets (even if, by stretching the meaning a great deal, one defines them both as demonstrations of a belief in immortality). And thirdly, the *assumption* that belief in immortality is "positive" and "culturally valuable," needs exploration and not simply assertion. If it brings poise and serenity to some, does it not also, on occasion, arm an inquisition and justify its brutality (for who can afford to let an anti-Christ endanger the immortal souls of thousands)? Is it not possible that belief in im-

---

[3] Bronislaw Malinowski in *Science, Religion and Reality*, Joseph Needham, editor, pp. 49–50.

mortality may help to produce resignation in face of suffering and in-justice—a resignation that, according to certain stated value stands is sometimes good, sometimes bad? Once again, a clear separation of value stands from functional analysis seems necessary.

In the light of these difficulties in Malinowski's statement, it may be more accurate simply to state: Religious systems everywhere are *involved in* the way individuals and societies grapple with the problem of death. This does not imply an instinctive origin of fear of death (or even that fear of death is a universal emotion); it does not imply that a belief in immortality is universally the way in which religions meet the fact of death; it does not assume that the system of beliefs and practices of any particular religion is entirely functional for the total value system of the individuals and groups involved.

This much, then, remains: everywhere, the ways in which men meet the problem of death is in the realm of the "sacred." One of the most fundamental of the *efforts* of religion is to rescue individuals and societies from the destructive force of death. Whether these efforts are successful will depend on the degree to which they are congruent with other personality tendencies in the individuals involved and on other forces at work in the society. In a stable and homogeneous society, a coherent body of rites and beliefs may emerge which function "as well as might be expected"—in face of the stubborn fact that death remains. But in a mobile, heterogeneous society, individual personalities will be developed for whom the existing system of rites and beliefs proves to be unsatisfactory. Here one will see a continuous struggling with new solutions, new formulas that will permit one to exclaim, with St. Paul, "Death, where is thy sting."

We do not say, therefore: "One of the functions of religion is to solve the personality needs that come from the fact of death," but rather, "religions everywhere struggle, sometimes partially successfully, some-times unsuccessfully, with the problem of death." The particular religious system may not "work" for some individuals; it may tend to break down for a whole social group that has been drastically changed by some intrusive force (industrialization or great mobility or outside invasion); it may produce unintended consequences (latent functions and dysfunc-tions) that complete analysis must explore.

Our discussion has implied that the way in which a religion meets the fact of death has consequences for the society as well as for the in-dividual members. The close interaction of these effects indicates again why an adequate theory of religion must combine the analysis of societal and personality systems. Parsons indicates this when he writes:

No ritual observances will bring the deceased back to life. But precisely for this reason, the problem of emotional adjustment is all the greater in importance. The significance both practically and emotionally of a human individual is of such a magnitude that his death involves a major process of readjustment for the survivors. Malinowski shows that the death of another involves exposure to sharply conflicting emotional reactions, some of which, if given free range, would lead to action and attitudes detrimental to the social group. There is great need for patterns of action which provide occasion for the regulated expression of strong emotions, and which in such a situation of emotional conflict reinforce those reactions which are most favorable to the continued solidarity and functioning of the social group.[4]

Some writers, following Durkheim, would stress this group function of rituals and beliefs regarding death almost to the exclusion of the individual function (the countering of individual fear and dismay). Radcliffe-Brown, for example, would say that the rites create the individual anxiety, rather than growing from it and expressing it. They represent primarily an effort on the part of society to reaffirm its solidarity. To the present writer, the interaction of the individual and group aspects seems to be the fundamental fact.

The wide range in the ways in which religions interpret death can perhaps be illustrated by contrasting the traditional Christian view of personal immortality with selections from a funeral address used by the Ethical Culture Societies. If one were to ask a Christian layman to give his religious interpretation of death, he might well cite one or more of these passages from the Bible:

Yea, though I walk through the valley of the shadow of death, I will fear no evil: for thou art with me; thy rod and thy staff they comfort me. (Psalm 23:4)

For God so loved the world that he gave his only begotten Son, that whosoever believeth in him should not perish, but have everlasting life. (John 3:16)

So when this corruptible shall have put on incorruption, and this mortal shall have put on immortality, then shall be brought to pass the saying that is written, Death is swallowed up in victory. (I Corinthians 15:54)

Contrast these views, with their emphasis on the individual and his needs and fears, with brief selections from the Ethical Culture Society's funeral address, with its primary emphasis on the group and on moral problems. Yet note also that in both, despite the contrast, the effort is to make death somehow meaningful, to place it in a larger context, and to rescue the mourner from despair.

Death brings us into closer communion with each other. We are not singled out for a special judgment when we give up our dead; we but enter

[4] Talcott Parsons, *Essays in Sociological Theory Pure and Applied*, pp. 58–59.

into a common sorrow that visits the proudest and humblest, that has entered into unnumbered hearts before ours, and will enter into innumerable ones after us; a sorrow that tends to make the world one by dissolving all other feelings into sympathy and love.

. . . And when death speaks to us, what does it say? It does not speak of itself. It does not say: Fear me. It does not say: Wonder at me. It does not say: Understand me. It bids us think rather of life, of the privileges of life, of how great a thing life can be made. In the presence of death we are awakened to think of the meaning of life. And when we thus reflect, we see that there are things that are mightier than death. Honor is mightier than death, for men and women have died to escape dishonor. Justice is mightier than death, for men and women have chosen death rather than countenance or do injustice. Love is mightier than death, for men and women have ofttimes died for those they loved.

. . . Let us commit ourselves with a new consecration to living in the spirit of human love and service. For it is only thus that true peace can be won. We would that out of this our sorrow may come a deeper sense of the worth of that love which prompts to self-forgetfulness, and finds solace in doing justice and in being ever more kind in our relations one with another. . . .[5]

RELIGIOUS RESPONSES TO FRUSTRATION AND SUFFERING

The problem of death is the most difficult and serious of the personality tensions with which religions attempt to deal. It cannot be separated, however, from other tension-creating difficulties that weaken social order and threaten the unity of personalities. Men carry the constant burden of earthly frustration and failure, as defined largely by the cultural system they share. They face the fact that the highest earthly rewards manifestly do not always go to those who most closely follow the codes of a society; the just and the righteous may suffer and fail while "the ungodly" may prosper. Why do men suffer; why is there evil in the world? This is a central religious question. Tension may also arise from the need for some explanation of the mysterious, awesome, and sometimes frightening facts of nature. Early students of the origins of religions doubtless gave too much emphasis to this cognitive problem, just as they defined religion too largely in terms of belief. But it would be equally unwise to disregard the partly emotional, partly intellectual questions that press in on us from nature. If we are no longer concerned with echoes and shadows or even the awesome movement of the sun and stars, a large part of mankind is still puzzled by dreams, by visions and hallucinations, by the great mystery of how the universe, and man, came to be.

It is clear that these problems not only threaten the unity of the in-

[5] Quoted by James H. Leuba, *The Reformation of the Churches*, pp. 213–215.

dividual personality, but are also disruptive of social order. A society that does not develop some system for dealing with them places a great burden on its members and risks its own disintegration. Individuals will, of course, vary widely in the degree to which they experience these difficulties and in the meaning they attach to the difficulties they do experience. Some will have a great deal of frustration, others much less; but, in addition, some will have a higher tolerance level for frustration than others. Some will be relatively indifferent to the "injustice" in the distribution of rewards, while others will be acutely sensitive to the fact that "sinners" sometimes prosper while "saints" suffer. Few men, however, can escape "the problem of evil" entirely. Why do I suffer so? What can be the meaning of an existence in which so much suffering is found? It is to answer these questions that the religions of the world offer their roads to salvation.

Not only are there wide individual variations in frustration, tolerance for frustration, and sense of injustice, but there are also wide variations in the degree to which social systems produce these personality tendencies. For that reason, among others, there are many differences in the types of religion and the extent of religious interest in various societies. (Here again the interpenetration of social, cultural, and personality facts demands attention.) It is quite possible, for example, that in the United States between 1865 and 1914, there was a lower level of frustration than in many times and places; there was perhaps a greater chance for improvement of status than is true in most societies; and there was a cultural ideology that made these facts seem more extensive than they were. In such a situation, interest in the traditional religions was at a rather low ebb and a type of religion that James has called "the religion of healthy-mindedness" had strong appeal.

Even during this period, it must be emphasized, the problems to which we have referred continued at a high level for a great many people, although they were perhaps somewhat less acute than at other times. Social systems may reduce somewhat the individual religious needs by lowering the level of frustration and reducing the sense of injustice, but they can scarcely avoid these problems. In any society, the total reservoir of need is likely to be large. Those who feel it most acutely may struggle with it in religious terms, making articulate what others sense only dimly. These struggles will have meaning for most individuals, if not at one time, then at another; and for a few—the mystics, the ascetics, the prophets—they become the dominant preoccupation of life.

It is not simply the objective facts of suffering, of frustration, of injustice that determine the extent of an individual's sensitivity to this aspect of religion. One could scarcely in this way account for the religious interests of a Luther or a Tolstoy, whose lives were marked by far more success and power than are achieved by most men. Mystical and theological explanations are often brought in at this point: Since it is not always those who suffer most who struggle with a religious interpretation of the problem of suffering, this aspect of religion cannot be explained by a naturalistic theory of personality; mystical experience or revelation must be involved. The scientist does not boldly refute this statement. He says simply that he is concerned only with naturalistic explanations, that he will pursue them as far as the evidence will permit him to go; and that if someone else is unsatisfied with the conclusions and finds it more satisfactory to start from different (non-naturalistic) premises, he (the scientist) cannot prove him wrong.

The relationship between the sense of "sin" and suffering and religious interests is complex. An explanation that reduces this aspect of religion to some narrow idea of self-interest (as Marx and Nietzsche did, in very different ways) is entirely inadequate. Modern personality theory makes clear that a sense of guilt relates to the basic problem of security and anxiety and not simply to the objective facts as they appear to someone else. An "anxious" person (in the psychiatric sense) may carry an enormous burden of guilt over a minor infraction of the norms, while a secure person may find it much easier to be tolerant of his own deviations. The anxious person may also be intolerant of minor deviations of others, while the secure person accepts deviations without being greatly upset. Those who are familiar with the work of James, Cooley, and Mead, are not likely to define "self" in such narrow terms that they fail to see that some individuals may feel a sense of identity with a wide circle of other human beings. The frustrations and pains of others become, for such an individual, his own suffering. He may be an acutely religious person, perhaps with ethical emphasis, just as the "anxious" person may be religious with a mystic or ascetic emphasis.

For the great bulk of the *followers* of a religious system, however, the objective facts of their own experience are likely to be much more determinative of this aspect of their religious interest: Those whose desires are most blocked, those who suffer most, those who see around them most frequently the success of the "unrighteous," those who live in societies where these things are most likely to occur are most likely to have an intense interest in religion, or in some functional alternative.

The Varieties of Religious Experience. The range of religious experience was made vivid a half-century ago in William James' classic distinction between the religion of "healthy-mindedness" and the religion of "the sick soul." The weakness of his explanation was his tendency to rely on a vague concept of temperamental differences to account for the range, rather than to explore the differences in personal experience and the differences in social environment that lie behind individual variation. The healthy-minded are inclined to view life optimistically; they do not linger over the darker facts of human existence. In contrast to this deliberate minimization of evil is the tendency of "the sick soul" to maximize evil ". . . based on the persuasion that the evil aspects of life are of its very essence, and that the world's meaning most comes home to us when we lay them most to heart." [6] There are those who cannot easily throw off the burden of evil and guilt, but suffer constantly from its presence. As we have noted, the sense of failure, pain, and helplessness may come even to the successful and the powerful. Such individuals resist what they consider to be the superficiality of the "healthy-minded" view of life. Those in whom awareness of sin and sorrow and suffering is most acute reason that

To ascribe religious value to mere happy-go-lucky contentment with one's brief chance at natural good is but the very consecration of forgetfulness and superficiality. Our troubles lie indeed too deep for *that* cure. The fact that we *can* die, that we *can* be ill at all, is what perplexes us; the fact that we now for a moment live and are well is irrelevant to that perplexity. We need a life not correlated with death, a health not liable to illness, a kind of good that will not perish, a good in fact that flies beyond the Goods of nature.[7]

To those who hold this view, an individual not thoroughly aware of suffering and evil is short-sighted. If *he, now,* does not suffer, does not need their radical scheme of salvation, in time he will.

The present writer would agree with James and with the great majority of theologians who hold that a religion that does not grapple with the pessimistic aspects of life is a truncated, incomplete religious system. (This is primarily a matter of definition, although it doubtless represents in part a statement of value.) It is also likely to be a fairly short-lived religion or one that appeals to a relatively small number of people. That is not to say, however, either that there are no individual processes and social structures of a non-religious sort that are relevant to this question of adjustment, or that a religion that is alert to the problems of suffering is necessarily successful in dealing with them. Each of these statements requires a brief comment.

In order to emphasize again that there is no sharp dividing line between religion and non-religion, but only a gradual shading off from

[6] William James, *The Varieties of Religious Experience*, p. 128.
[7] *Ibid.*, p. 137.

one to the other, we need to see that secular processes are often connected with the same individual and group functions as religion. An individual may respond to frustration, for example, not (or not only) with religion, but with aggression, perhaps with a hopeless defeatism, or with a renewed effort unconnected with religious belief. An extraordinary sense of guilt or suffering may be part of a process leading to neurosis or psychosis. We cannot yet be certain whether or not this is more likely among those who have been cut off from a religious system which gave "meaning" to their guilt or suffering. An individual may seize upon a socially established system of discrimination and prejudice against minority groups to assuage his self-doubt or to try to reduce his sense of failure. Indeed, some studies have found a positive correlation between prejudice and a traditional religious view of the world. This does not prove, of course, that religion causes prejudice. Although this may be partly true, it is more likely that the correlation shows that the guilty, or self-doubting, or frustrated person grasps at *both* prejudice *and* religion to try to reduce his difficulties. In addition to individual non-religious responses, social movements of various kinds (nationalism is perhaps the best example) that may be called incipient religions, may develop as efforts to face these problems of inadequacy and frustration. We shall comment on this question of secular alternatives at greater length in the next chapter.

We must also stress again that to say that religions are *attempts* to help the individual face frustration, failure, and the injustice involved in human society, is not to say that any given religion succeeds in fulfilling this function. In rapidly changing societies, particularly, systems of belief and practice that once were effective in helping individuals face critical problems of life may prove to be ineffective. They are not thus proved to be "false," any more than they were proved to be "true" when they were effective; they simply become irrelevant, meaningless. Only new religious patterns (usually built directly on the old, for the break is not sharp) that are congruent with the new societies and the personalities developing within it are likely to be effective. Thus a doctrine of transmigration may seem to ease the suffering and explain the lowliness of a Hindu peasant in a static society. None around him climbs to new statuses and no new methods for the reduction of pain and powerlessness are to be found. Such a doctrine, however, is proving to be less satisfying to the urbanized peasant who comes in contact with ideas and facts of social mobility, who acquires new needs for this life, and who sees that various means for struggling to satisfy those needs are being used.

Under these circumstances, Hinduism tends to change, and some of its adherents leave it for other religions or for secular systems of belief and practice that seem to them to be more relevant to their needs. Thus the late Dr. B. R. Ambedkar led perhaps 300,000 untouchables in a mass conversion to Buddhism, and most of the converts from Hinduism to Christianity are drawn from the lowest castes.

Part of this emphasis on the need for study of actual consequences is the attention to *latent* functions and dysfunctions. Calvin's doctrine of predestination was essentially a religious doctrine, but it had many latent consequences. The effort to prove to one's self and to others that he was of "the elect" may, as Weber declared, have driven men on to unusual thrift and industry. (We shall discuss Weber's thesis in a later chapter.) Most people would regard this as a latent function, a desirable, but unexpected consequence of religious belief. It may also, however, have encouraged fanaticism, a desire to make certain that no "sinners" invaded the community of the elect, an arrogance, a lack of an ability to enjoy this life while proving one's self chosen for heavenly success—effects that most people would regard as dysfunctional. And under other circumstances, the doctrine of predestination leads to a defeatism that may carry undesired consequences. It is the total results that must be analyzed.

Once again, the comments of William James are highly interesting and instructive. In his discussion of "saintliness" he asks, what are its fruits? On the one hand, "The highest flights of charity, devotion, trust, patience, bravery to which the wings of human nature have spread themselves have been flown for religious ideals." [8] And yet, devoutness may lead to fanaticism; purity may lead to utter withdrawal; tenderness and charity may preserve the unfit and breed parasites; asceticism, carried to an extreme, repudiates life. It is clear that James considered these to be unhappy results. Regardless of value judgments, however, adequate analysis requires that we explore the conditions under which these various possibilities come about, before we can understand the total functions and dysfunctions of religion for personality and society. James also emphasizes, of course, what he considers to be the creative aspects of saintliness: Our soft age cannot appreciate, he writes, the hard life of the ascetic. We have become afraid to be poor, and we are thus subject to slaveries from which the poor are free. We are less able to achieve the prophetic view of the world that is grasped by the ascetic.[9]

[8] *Ibid.*, p. 254.
[9] See *ibid.*, pp. 254–369.

The task of analysis is to discover the conditions that maximize and those that minimize the various consequences of "saintliness."

With these qualifications in mind concerning the function of religion in serving personality needs, it may be well to summarize the way in which religion is an *effort* to reduce tension, allay fear, and give a sense of unity to one's life. Howells describes the situation well:

Man's life is hard, very hard. And he knows it, poor soul; that is the vital thing. He knows that he is forever confronted with the Four Horsemen—death, famine, disease, and the malice of other men. And because he can speak and so frame ideas for himself and his mercurial imagination, he is nature's great and only worrier; he can worry alone and he can worry in unison, always with justice. It is among people living a primitive existence, however, that this should be particularly true.[10]

The last sentence is perhaps open to doubt. Howells may give too much attention to the physical problems of survival, too little to the tensions that come from a sense of failure to achieve socially learned goals, a feeling of justice (as defined by a person or society) unserved. Moreover, in a day of hydrogen bombs, the power of science to grant life and health is brought into question. But his basic point is sound, and he weaves it into his very definition of religion, which he conceives to be something that is:

used to piece out the ground between what man can attend to himself and what his imagination tells him must be attended to. It is the extension of his wishes and beliefs beyond the edges of what his senses grant him; it is what lies outside the light of the campfire. It is the notions he feels he must accept if life is to be satisfactory, or even safe. In other words, religion is composed of all the serious things man feels obliged to take for granted. . . . More than anything, it seems to reflect the refusal of man's whole being, physical and psychic, to accept a block to his aspirations or a menace to his peace of mind.[11]

Few human beings are able to avoid all the things they have learned to dread or to achieve all the things they have been taught to desire. Religion is the effort to make the dreaded fact seem less dreadful, the failure less important or part of a larger, ultimate success; "for *all things* work together for good, for them that love God." Moreover, religion furnishes goals that all may share. "These are goals that transcend the world of actual experience, with the consequence that no evidence of failure to attain them can be conclusive. If the individual believes

+ this "God's will" [margin note]

[10] William W. Howells, *The Heathens, Primitive Man and His Religions*, p. 17.
[11] *Ibid.*, p. 19 and p. 293.

that he has gained them, that is sufficient. All he needs is sufficient faith, and faith feeds on subjective need." [12]

So it is that the religious person, acutely aware of man's finitude and of the tragedies and frustrations of life, may declare, with Isaiah:

> The foundations of the earth do shake.
> Earth breaks to pieces,
> Earth is split in pieces,
> Earth shakes to pieces,
> Earth reels like a drunken man,
> Earth rocks like a hammock;
> Under the weight of its transgression earth falls down
> To rise no more!

> Lift up your eyes to heaven and look upon the earth beneath:
> For the heavens shall vanish away like smoke.
> And the earth shall grow old like a robe;
> The world itself shall crumble.
> But my righteousness shall be forever,
> And my salvation knows no end. (Isaiah 24; 18–24)

THE PROBLEM OF EVIL—AND OF SALVATION

What we have been discussing becomes, in theological terms, the problem of evil and the question of religious efforts to save man from evil. In one way or another, religions declare that though the "earth breaks to pieces," "my salvation knows no end." It is the sociologist's task to inquire: How do different societies, or separate groups in a society, interpret suffering and evil? What different ways to salvation do they find meaningful and satisfying? Are these differences related to their total social situation? Since we shall be concerned with these questions in various connections in later chapters, we shall here only sketch the range of answers.

One may describe a broad continuum along which religions are ranged in their interpretation of evil. The world may be considered basically good—evil and suffering being thought of as specific problems, not the ultimate stuff of the world, with which men can hope to grapple successfully. The Homeric interpretation of Greek religion, classic Confucianism, and modern humanism are close to this position. Or, the world may be thought to be filled with evil, and yet be "sanctifiable." This is the ambivalent position of the classic Moslem and Christian

---

[12] Kingsley Davis, *Human Society*, p. 532.

traditions. They are pessimistic about the present state of the world, but the pessimism is conditional. One need not give up to despair or resignation, for with God's help man may struggle with evil and suffering with enough success to make it worthwhile, even if ultimate success is not likely on earth. The third position is more radically pessimistic. Evil and suffering are the inevitable lot of man on earth; they can be dealt with only by rejection of the world, by detachment from this life. This is the dominant view in Hinduism and more especially Buddhism.

There are various possible modes of orientation to evil and suffering in addition to religion. One might take each problem as it comes along and try to reduce it, without trying to find some ultimate meaning. One might examine it objectively, trying to find out how it came about. Religion, however, which offers itself as a road to salvation from man's ultimate problems, must try to furnish an answer to the question of *why*: Why is there evil; why do men suffer? And more than that, why is there such wide variation among men in the extent of suffering and of evil?

It is not the concern of the sociologist of religion to judge among the various answers to these questions, but to ask: In what kinds of societies and among what groups do the various interpretations of evil arise? And what are their various consequences? The evidence does not suggest any clear and easy formula that answers these questions. There is no clear development, for example, from religions that make a thoroughly pessimistic response to the question of evil and suffering, through religions that take an ambivalent position, to those that tend toward "this-worldly optimism." The religions of primitive peoples, which we assume, perhaps unwisely, to be very ancient, seldom if ever adopt a radically pessimistic view, devaluing this world, counseling resignation to suffering, projecting hopes outward to another world. The idea of heaven, if it is conceptualized at all, is likely to be thought of as a continuation of the good of this life, for the religions of primitive peoples describe no dichotomy between the evil of this world and the peace and happiness of the next.

However a given conception of the problem of evil may have developed (and we shall see in the chapters on social change that one may sometimes regard religion as the dependent and sometimes the independent variable) it has great implications for the whole social system. It is functionally interdependent with many secular values and structures. Thus a society which blocks the aspirations of many, one that is overwhelmed by pestilence and war, may nourish a religious view of the world that is highly pessimistic in its conception of evil. Oppositely, such a religion, once established, helps to shape the values which its adherents will pursue in their secular activities.

Within a society, there are often different interpretations, by those on whom suffering has fallen in unequal amounts, of the meaning of evil. When there are class differences, the successful need to feel justified in their success, and seek, by religion as well as by other means, for ways to protect themselves against the claims of the unsuccessful and against their own doubts. Thus if suffering and evil befall the poor, this is a sign of their odiousness, their unworthiness. Those on the lower status levels, on the other hand, seek support for their violated sense of justice and an assurance that their present state is a meaningful part of a total career (here and beyond) that promises ultimate success. Suffering, indeed, now becomes a mark of virtue, and lowliness of status a condition for greater rewards to come.

The religious view of a society or of a class in a society is by no means perfectly correlated with the existing level of suffering, but social circumstances are among the factors influencing the ways in which the problem of evil will be handled.

RELIGIOUS ROADS TO SALVATION

Not only do conceptions of the nature of evil vary widely, both in terms of what are man's deepest problems and how irradicable they are, but the ways of salvation are also extremely diverse. On this much, religions agree: man can be saved; suffering and injustice are not his final lot. There is wide disagreement on how and when salvation will be achieved; but every religion, by definition, offers itself as a road, and many claim to be *the* road, to salvation. Many human endeavors, of course, are concerned with salvation in some sense, again indicating that religion is not sharply cut off from other aspects of life. King expresses this well when he writes:

Art would save man from ugliness and boredom; philosophy from the unexamined life and the incoherent intellectual world; science, as the epitome of all practical disciplines, would save us from ignorant slavery to natural forces and the more severe physical threats to life and welfare; politics would provide a bulwark against social chaos, anarchy or civil war within, and against aggression from without; ethics would save us from unprincipled and unregulated conduct.[13]

Thus religion, as King says, enters a somewhat crowded field. A line can be drawn between the religious and the non-religious approaches to salvation, however, on the basis of the "ultimate" quality of the re-

[13] Winston L. King, *Introduction to Religion*, p. 122.

and How is idea of salvation a social product of any given society

ligious attempt. One may find within various religious systems, ways of protecting the believer against almost every threat—sickness, hunger, childlessness, false pride, malevolent spirits, and on through a long list. These are concerns which religions share with—and perhaps tend to turn over to—other techniques of human adjustment. The core that remains to religion, however, is the attempt to save man from meaninglessness, from despair when his partial efforts at salvation fail, from the sense of final annihilation.

The idea of salvation raises many questions for the sociologist. How do religions vary in proposed roads to salvation? When and where will man be saved according to the various conceptions? Are there systematic differences among types of societies and among individuals in terms of the approaches to salvation that they are likely to find satisfying? What are the consequences for human interaction of the adoption of different patterns? In the chapters that follow, we shall be exploring such questions as these in some detail, with reference to specific groups and situations. Here we shall simply sketch the broad outlines of the range of answers.

In response to the question, how shall man achieve salvation, there are three possible answers: By action or works, by devotion, by knowledge.[14] No religion is likely to give emphasis exclusively to one of these approaches, although particular groups and individuals may do so. Differences in status and other secular facts are often related to differences in emphasis and the attendant controversies over the best roads to salvation. Salvation through action may be of many different varieties: full and correct performance of the religious law may be considered most important—a strong element of the Moslem and Jewish traditions; partaking of sacraments may be emphasized, as in Roman Catholicism; or morality, right behavior toward one's fellows, in the manner of Puritanism, may be given primary attention.

To seek salvation through devotion is often the way of the untrained layman, the religiously "illiterate." Unskilled in the law, unmoved by the established forms of worship, he seeks salvation by the ardor of his belief. If he cannot follow the mystic's pursuit of direct "knowledge" of the universe, or win reassurance with the priest by punctillious performance of correct action, he can give a fervent and emotional demonstration of his faith in the efficacy of his religious patterns, and thus seek to insure his salvation.

To seek salvation by "knowledge" in the religious sense is not to follow the prosaic and severely limited methods of the scientist. To pursue

[14] For an excellent discussion of this topic, see *ibid.*, Part III.

knowledge through controlled observation may be accepted and even encouraged, but it is almost never considered to be the fundamental source of "truth" for religion. A much higher place is given to "intuitive" knowledge through meditation, to knowledge derived directly from God, to the insight of the mystic into the "ultimate reality." This approach to salvation is found in its most intensive form in Hinduism and Buddhism, but it is not lacking in the religious life even of "secularized" urban people in Western societies.

Religions vary not only in their conceptions of how salvation may be achieved, but in their ideas of when it will come about. These differences reflect the degree of optimism or pessimism concerning suffering and evil to which we have referred. If suffering on earth is the eternal lot of man, then the hope for salvation must be projected into another existence. If there is hope, however, that men's most difficult problems can be reduced on earth, salvation may be sought by changes in this life. When pressed to an extreme, these two positions become sharply contradictory. If one believes that some measure of salvation within the limits of human societies is possible, the projection of all hope into another existence is very unfortunate. But if one believes that the fundamental fact of human life on earth is tragedy, religious efforts to alleviate what are seen as minor ills in this life may seem to endanger the wholehearted search for salvation beyond.[15] In the Jewish, Moslem, and Christian traditions, these two positions are often found in uneasy balance. Confucianism, insofar as it is a religion, envisages salvation primarily in terms of the reduction of the ills of this world; while Hinduism and Buddhism conceive of it basically in transcendental terms.

The central task of the sociology of religion in dealing with this problem is to see what societies, what groups, and what individuals take the various views of salvation. Niebuhr suggests a thesis—although an overly-simple one:

Evolutionary millennialism is always the hope of comfortable and privileged classes, who imagine themselves too rational to accept the idea of the sudden emergence of the absolute in history. For them the ideal is in history, working its way to ultimate triumph. They identify God and nature, the real and the ideal, not because the more dualistic conceptions of classical religion are too irrational for them (though they are irrational); but because they do not suffer as much as the disinherited from the brutalities of contemporary society, and therefore do not take as catastrophic a view of contemporary history.[16]

Class position, as Niebuhr suggests, is doubtless one of the factors influencing the view of salvation that will be adopted, but its impact will vary

[15] See Talcott Parsons, *The Social System*, pp. 367–379.
[16] Reinhold Niebuhr, *Moral Man and Immoral Society*, p. 62.

with the religious tradition, with the nature of leadership, with the personal development of a given individual, with the total social situation in which class identity is experienced. There are times when the "disinherited" support religious movements that conceive of salvation in history; and members of the "privileged classes" may project their religious hopes wholly into a future life. Such circumstances do not contradict the thesis that schemes of salvation are related to social facts; but they indicate the need for exploring complicated series of social facts.

One further question concerns the *consequences* for human behavior of various approaches to salvation. Emphasis on "works" promotes the development of elaborate ecclesiastical structures for the interpretation of the laws and the administration of the sacraments. This leads to very different results for the social order than an emphasis on mysticism, the individual pursuit of religious understanding, or on devotion. A highly structured Roman Catholicism, with its emphasis on "works," is very differently related to the societies of which it is a part than Fundamentalist Protestantism, with a primary emphasis on devotion as the road to salvation. An even sharper contrast can be drawn between Catholicism and Hinduism, where the mystical approach is of great importance. The mystic's search for direct contact with the "ultimate reality" of the universe can be carried on in almost complete indifference to the situation around him. That is not to say it does not affect that situation, but it does so indirectly. Catholicism, on the other hand, becomes directly and immediately involved in the total social structure.

We must be thoroughly aware, therefore, that however the different approaches to salvation may have developed, once they become established they act back upon the social situation and must be seen as important forces influencing human life.

SOCIAL FACTORS IN RELIGIOUS INTEREST

In the preceding pages, we have been primarily concerned with the relationship between religion and several personality tendencies and needs that are found among all men or are characteristic of most of the members of a society. The fact of death, the sense of injustice and of failure, the feeling of helplessness—in sum, the problem of evil is a universal human experience in one form or another. Emphasis on this aspect of the relationship between religion and personality, however, should not lead us to forget the range of differences among individuals in the strength and direction of their religious interest. We must be concerned with the question of *variation* in personality as a factor in *variation* in religious behavior. Why do individuals in modern societies differ so widely in the strength and form of their religious interest? Is this simply a manifestation of differences in training, or does it also indicate the influence of differences in "basic character structure" and of variation in other personal tendencies? Is it related to different social roles, with their various requirements and influences? In the next chapter we shall describe some of the ways in which different personal needs are related to variation in religion. This discussion may convey the impression that a religious interest is found only among those with a high level of personal anxiety. This impression is not correct. One can learn a great deal, to be sure, about the functions of religion from the analysis of the beliefs and practices of insecure persons. But such an analysis should not obscure the close interconnection of socio-cultural influences and the personality systems of "standard" members of a society.

The sacred books, the rites, the basic beliefs of a religion doubtless spring from the intensely religious persons, from those who have felt the problems of suffering and evil most acutely. They also develop during the critical periods of history—the times of disorder and maximum stress. Thus religions are equipped to carry the "peak load" of human need. For many people, however, suffering and evil are less acute. It is a mistake to assume that only the intensive religious experience of the mystic or the ascetic or the person overwhelmed by the problem of evil needs explanation. The more casual beliefs and actions of the mildly religious are also important. This requires some attention to normal socialization and to the cultural norms that are transferred to most members of a society in the process of growing up.

There are several aspects to this question: 1. The need for religion is partly a culturally learned need and will vary, therefore, with the nature of one's training. 2. Variation in religion is partly related to different social roles; one's place in the social structure influences the extent and direction of religious interest. 3. Differences in experience beyond those that derive directly from culture and role affect personal tendencies and therefore religious inclinations. The basic attitude toward one's self, for example—a product in large measure of the experiences of the first decade of life—is an important influence on one's religious inclinations. As we turn, in the next chapter, to an examination of the social psychology of some contemporary religious developments, we will do well to keep the interplay of these various forces in mind. It is perhaps the influence of culture and of role that are most likely to be minimized.

Intensive analysis of the place of religion in the struggle for individual adjustment sometimes causes us to overlook the rather prosaic fact that those persons who are most interested in religion, who express the strongest "need" for religion are drawn largely, although not entirely, from those groups that are most concerned to train their members to be religious. The direction as well as the extent of the religious interest is to an important degree the result of training. Fundamentalist parents tend to bring up children who share the fundamentalist tradition; liberal religious views are found most often among those who have been trained to such views. Changes in religious belief and practice and variations among those brought up in the same tradition indicate, to be sure, that cultural training alone does not account for individual religious attitudes and behavior. We are indicating simply that it is important not to overlook the influence of normal socialization. This is obvious when one takes a cross-cultural view; it should be given full attention in the explanation of religious variation within a society as well.

In a study of 412 Harvard and 85 Radcliffe students, Allport, Gillespie, and Young found a marked relationship between the extent of religious influence in a person's upbringing and the feeling of need for religion. Among the men, 82 per cent of those who reported a "very marked" religious influence in their early training indicated a need for religion; only 32 per cent among those who answered "none at all" to the training question reported such a need. The percentages among the women were 96 and 44. Clearly the felt need for a religious orientation is in part a product of one's training; yet it should not be overlooked that a third or more of those who had no early religious training still expressed a need for religion.[17] And a functional theorist must inquire further whether those who declared that they felt no need for religion may not express a need for some alternative, some system of faith and devotion that does not bear the name religion but functions for them in many of the same ways.

In terms of the direction of interest, Dreger found almost no significant personality differences between religious conservatives and religious liberals.[18] This suggests that efforts to explain differences in religious belief in terms of basic character, or degree of anxiety, and similar concepts, must first take account of the normal processes of culture. The liberal and conservative may be manifesting no deep-seated personality differences; perhaps they were simply taught different religious beliefs.

The interrelationship of the personality aspects of religion with the socio-cultural influences is further shown by variation in religious interest

[17] Gordon Allport, James Gillespie, and Jacqueline Young, "The Religion of the Post-War College Student," *The Journal of Psychology*, January, 1948, p. 11.

[18] See R. M. Dreger, "Some Personality Correlates of Religious Attitudes, as Determined by Projective Techniques," *Psychological Monographs*, Vol. 66, No. 3, 1952.

among those who occupy different social roles. The concept of "role" is one of the key meeting-places of personality theory and socio-cultural theory, for it represents an internalized style of life for the individual and at the same time a cultural blueprint of approved behavior for certain designated members of a society. Although our evidence is not precise, there is little doubt that the extent and nature of religious interest varies significantly among persons occupying different social roles. One illustration may serve to make this point: Women in the United States are known to be "more religious" than men; they make up a larger proportion of church membership, take a larger part in religious-group affairs, and express more interest in religion when asked about their beliefs than men do. Allport found that 82 per cent of the women students whom he studied reported need for a religious orientation, as compared with 76 per cent of non-veteran men and 64 per cent of veterans.[19] In a sample of native-born Protestants in Indianapolis, Lenski found a highly significant difference (a probability of less than .001) in the extent of religious interest between men and women. A third of the men expressed "little" interest, but only 20 per cent of the women; 24 per cent of the men indicated "much" interest, compared with over 38 per cent of the women.[20] These items give support to the widely observed difference in religious interest between men and women in American society, a difference which should be neither exaggerated nor overlooked.

How can these facts be accounted for? They can be explained most reasonably, in our judgment, by reference to differences in social role. Women occupy a more important place in the socialization of the young. The rights and duties embodied in their role expectations in American society give them less latitude and choice. They are expected to abide more closely by the traditional standards of the culture than are men. In addition to these cultural facts—the normative influences on their behavior—there are certain effects of their place in the social structure. Women in general have narrower contacts and have therefore experienced somewhat less secularization than men. There are strains that derive from their roles in a situation where there is an equalitarian ideology, but many non-equalitarian facts—a situation that produces some "minority-group" influences on their religious behavior. Women in American society wield less secular power than men, they have fewer secular-group contacts. Religious-group associations and religious interests, therefore, seem to fill a more important place in their lives.

[19] See Gordon Allport, *The Individual and His Religion*, p. 37.
[20] Gerhard Lenski, "Social Correlates of Religious Interest," *American Sociological Review*, October, 1953, pp. 535–536.

This contrast between men and women does not apply to many societies. Due to different cultural expectations and different influences of
their place in the social structure, it is often the men who are "more
religious." The effects of roles are deeply imbedded in the patterns of
specific societies. Our brief comment here may indicate the need, in the
analysis of the relationship between personality and religion, for constant
attention to the interaction of personal tendency, cultural norm, and social
structure. It may also help us to avoid the implication, as we turn to the
analysis of the relationship between personality and some current religious movements, that religious interests are found only among the more
anxious and insecure members of a society.

CHAPTER 5

Religion and
Personality ...... *continued*

SOME CONTEMPORARY ROADS
TO SALVATION

Stable societies pass on to each generation, as part of its cultural equipment, patterns of ritual and belief that are widely accepted as the right ways to deal with problems of individual tension, guilt, and anguish. It is the fate of many members of changing societies, however, to find these patterns unsatisfactory. Mobility, culture contact, changing intellectual climate, the development of new social roles and new problems raise doubts concerning the validity and efficacy of the prevailing religious system. Even a stable religion may fail to bring "peace of mind" to many people, as the almost frantic ceremonial life and the elaborate taboos of some primitive societies demonstrate. But the religious patterns themselves will be challenged only in situations where mobility and culture contact have furnished some outside frame of reference. Under these circumstances, religious efforts take on many aspects of a "search" for something that has been lost, or for something new, or more probably for a mixture of the old and the new. The religious results of the search will vary greatly among different members of a society, for they will differ in the problems they face, in the degree to which they have been affected by change, and in their cultural preparation for different kinds of developments. Clearly the results will also vary widely among different societies.

95

Throughout the range, however, one can see individuals in search of rites and doctrines and organizations that will help them to grapple with their bewildering problems.

Material to illustrate this relationship between personality needs and religion abounds. One may find it in the development of ancient Judaism or in the proliferation of religious movements in contemporary Japan. It is found in the classic statement of Gilbert Murray, in his description of the "failure of nerve" of the Greeks in the generations after the classic period. Erich Fromm has given it a trenchant formulation in his analysis of the efforts of modern man to "escape from freedom." Lutheranism and Calvinism, from the point of view of his social psychology, can be understood as attempts to free men from many of the bonds of medieval society, which had come to be felt as heavy chains, and yet at the same time to tie men to new obligations and new patterns, for the new freedom left men feeling alone and afraid.

The compulsive quest for certainty, as we find with Luther, is not the expression of genuine faith but is rooted in the need to conquer the unbearable doubt. Luther's solution is one which we find present in many individuals today, who do not think in theological terms: namely to find certainty by elimination of the isolated individual self, by becoming an instrument in the hands of an overwhelmingly strong power outside of the individual.[1]

RELIGION AND THE LONELINESS OF MODERN SOCIETY

Contemporary events have only served to accentuate the bafflement and doubt of many people; and many current religious movements, as well as various secular activities, can be understood in part as attempts to deal with this personal confusion. A great deal has been written in recent years to describe "the modern individual's sense of isolation, his so-called spiritual homelessness, his bewilderment in the face of the seemingly impersonal forces of which he feels himself a helpless victim, his weakening sense of values."[2] Lowenthal and Guterman describe the social ground well when they write:

This malaise reflects the stresses imposed on the individual by the profound transformations taking place in our economic and social structure—the replacement of the class of small independent producers by gigantic industrial bureaucracies, the decay of the patriarchal family, the breakdown of primary personal ties between individuals in an increasingly mechanized world, the

---

[1] Erich Fromm, *Escape From Freedom*, pp. 77–78.
[2] Leo Lowenthal and Norbert Guterman, *Prophets of Deceit. A Study in the Techniques of the American Agitator*, p. 15.

compartmentalization and atomization of group life, and the substitution of mass culture for traditional patterns.[3]

One should not overlook the fact that many of the fundamental problems of modern society have their ancient counterparts. (There is something strangely contemporary about the passage from Isaiah that we quoted earlier—"the foundations of the earth do shake.") The form that these problems take, however, and doubtless also their intensity vary from society to society, from time to time. If many of us live today in "the lonely crowd," for example, we would expect to find religious themes and movements that declare: You are not alone. Even this is an ancient theme, but it has particular relevance to mobile societies. And as Paul Tillich has pointed out, the sense of our separation from others is heightened today by our growing knowledge of the hidden streams of hostility within us. We know, with Immanuel Kant, that there is something in the misfortune even of our best friends which does not displease us. "Are we not almost always ready to abuse everybody and everything, although often in a very refined way, for the pleasure of self-elevation, for an occasion for boasting, for a moment of lust?"[4] The feeling of separation is increased by ambivalence toward ourselves. It is difficult to avoid a mixture of self-love and self-hate in a time of mixed systems of social norms, in the presence of large gaps between aspirations and achievements.

The Oxford Group Movement.   In such situations, the religious theme, "You are accepted," is likely to be a dominant one. We shall see later that this is one aspect of the religious movements of minority groups and of the recently urbanized lower classes. It is an important part of the appeal of the Oxford Group Movement to some members of the middle and upper classes. The Movement is not formally a church, but an effort to revitalize religious life. Mr. Frank Buchman, the founder, came to believe that the "up-and-outers," the high status persons of modern society, were religiously neglected.[5] By its doctrine of individual "right-living," by the sharing of doubt and guilt in small, congenial groups, by its assumption that the world's ills can be solved by "getting right with God"—with no need for change in the social structures in which they have found privileged positions—in these ways the Oxford Group Movement tells its members that they are "accepted."

[3] *Ibid.*
[4] Paul Tillich, *The Shaking of the Foundations*, p. 157.
[5] See Hadley Cantril, *The Psychology of Social Movements*, Chapter Six; W. H. Clark, *The Oxford Movement: Its History and Significance*; Allan Eister, *Drawing Room Conversion. A Sociological Account of the Oxford Group Movement*; Peter Howard, *The World Rebuilt* (an uncritical, laudatory account of the work of Frank Buchman).

The fact that many adherents are drawn into the movement for a few months or years and then drift away may indicate that the prescriptions of the Oxford Group Movement are too "easy." They demand little intellectual effort, little personal sacrifice or discipline, little change in style of life. There is good evidence that in the "economy" of the personality, a system of salvation that is bought too "cheaply"—with little sacrifice or effort on the part of the adherent—soon wears out; it does not work. Somehow—the personality processes are not clear—the individual comes to believe, consciously or unconsciously, that a "solution" to his fundamental problems that requires so little of him cannot be of much value.

This need for a "difficult" religion is not equally shared by everyone, however, and is perhaps relatively unimportant with many of those attracted to the Oxford Group Movement. Its appeal has been primarily to educated, well-to-do persons whose early training typically had been in a fairly conservative Protestant church. They had become mobile, urban people without many community roots, "worldly" and somewhat sophisticated. The influence of the earlier conceptions of religion, however—the idea of sin, the belief in a personal relationship to God, and the like—was still strong. The nature of the religious appeal of the Oxford Group Movement may thus be seen as an attempt to tie together a conservative background and a partially sophisticated present that has left many persons uncertain and insecure.

The Movement illustrates Weber's conception of a "theodicy of good fortune." Its membership is largely drawn from among the "successful." But their self-confidence has been weakened by a succession of crises in the society in which they have won high status. Depression, war, and the power of communism have aroused many anxieties. The program of the Oxford Group, however, reassures them that their way of life is good. Its conservative—and sometimes reactionary, in the literal sense—political leanings correspond with their inclinations. Its emphasis on individual "moral rearmament" harmonizes with their need to find the source of their difficulties, not in a social system that has treated them well, but in individual perversity. Its "house party" approach brings them together with a congenial group which reduces their sense of alienation, reassures them concerning the validity of their status, and gives them an exciting sense of "doing something" about the world's problems in precisely the way best calculated to reduce their own self-doubts.

GUIDES TO "CONFIDENT LIVING"

We have suggested that the Oxford Group Movement is a fairly cosmopolitan and somewhat "elitist" religious development, appealing to a high status, but doubt-ridden group. It may be seen as a "guide to confident living," but one that has attraction for persons with a particular combination of needs and tendencies. Other groups appeal to those with a different constellation. There is wide variation in the degree to which the members of society feel its tensions and are equipped to deal with them. There is also great variety in the kinds of cultural preparation for various "solutions." These differences in personality are reflected in the kinds of religious movements that appeal to different people. The widespread influence of Norman Vincent Peale is found primarily among the urban middle classes who have been "tuned" to his message by their cultural training and their personal problems. He appeals to those afflicted with "fear, inferiority, tension and kindred troubles," those who want to know how they can succeed, why, indeed, they are not succeeding when success is all around. And the answer he gives is the answer that middle class Americans, trained to the optimism of a bountiful environment, but "temporarily" confused and anxious, are ready to accept: Your problems are not deep; the solutions are ready at hand, and almost as easy to apply as a mouth-wash. "Think your way to success"; "forget failures and go ahead." All that is needed is contact with God, so that his power can come into one. Fear breaks that contact, but faith restores it. Peale quotes the prescription that is sometimes given by "a young and highly trained physician" to persons suffering from fear and inferiority: "Go to church at least once a Sunday for the next three months." [6]

If you will utilize the principles of faith stated in this book, you too, can solve the difficult problems of your personality. You, too can really learn to live.[7]

Socio-cultural Sources of Belief in "Positive Thinking." It is not surprising that persons raised on claims that a change to the correct facial soap can revolutionize one's chances for marital happiness, or to implications that if you improve your vocabulary by twenty words a day you may become a big executive, should respond favorably to "the power of positive thinking." But that is only a small part of the environment which has created persons favorable to the religious views of Dr. Peale. It would be a mistake to forget the factual reenforcements of the attitude that "salvation" (the reduction of fear and inferiority feelings, an increase in worldly success) comes fairly easily. One can find all around many individuals (probably a small minority, but highly visible) who, by a combination of hard work, self-confidence, a little luck, and a little ability have achieved fame and fortune. Peale's formula, moreover, is plausible

[6] Norman Vincent Peale, *A Guide to Confident Living*, p. 1.
[7] *Ibid.*, p. 17.

to those trained to values of individual initiative. There is little reference to possible social causes of human problems, no need to criticize or tamper with the social structure—an uncongenial task to most middle class members.

His work appeals to a generation trained to think that "science" is important and a valuable aid in the solution of problems. It is doubtless fair to say that no religious movement could attract the contemporary American urban middle classes to any extent that did not try to show its harmony with "science," that did not minimize any "conflict between science and religion." The harmony may be on a fairly superficial level; there may be no intensive effort to analyze the relation of science to religion (many psychiatrists think that Dr. Peale has set their work back); but at least at the level of slogans, there must be accommodation.

There are other elements in the cultural preparation of individuals for such religious developments as those represented by Peale. His adherents have been raised in an atmosphere of the "liberal" theology, with its optimistic view of man, its relative lack of concern with tragedy and the "sinfulness of man," with little insistence upon dogma, yet with a general value that the "good man ought to be interested in religion," perhaps a kind of residue from an earlier piety. Thus Peale has no dogma or ritual, he can appeal to people "whatever your church." And he makes little of the traditional and the neo-orthodox emphasis on "sin," an emphasis that makes little sense to people brought up to optimism, to belief in moral man in moral society, as one might put it.

To persons with different personality tendencies, trained to a different pattern of cultural values, living in a different social situation, there is no power in "positive thinking" as it is preached by Peale. Some are simply unmoved by him; others are vigorously opposed. It is the latter who express themselves and thus allow some assessment of the personality factors involved in his acceptance or rejection. Some of his critics oppose him because of his theological views. They believe that his approach to "salvation" shows far too little awareness of the depth of human suffering and evil. His religious views, therefore, according to these critics' conception of life, are shallow and unsatisfying. Despite Dr. Peale's active cooperation with psychiatry, his "bootstrap" approach is also thoroughly unsatisfactory to many scientists, both in its analysis of the source of human difficulties and its attempts at therapy. He solves few problems, in their judgment, for human problems lie deeper than he knows. He harms as many as he helps when he declares that one needs only faith to solve his problems, for those who continue to suffer, accuse themselves of lack of faith, thus increasing their sense of guilt. His approach demonstrates that "the battle of the Renaissance" is still far from won. He has retarded the development of efforts to find solutions to problems of personal anxiety by the systematic application of human intelligence, by his attention to such "magic formulas" as "energy-producing thoughts," "7 simple steps," and "8 practical formulas."

Needless to say, some psychiatrists work actively with or support Dr. Peale, either because they accept his formulas, or because they believe his religious approach has pragmatic value for certain kinds of emotional disturbances. We shall comment on this larger question of the relation of religion and psychiatry below.

A Catholic Guide to Peace of Soul. Although some people are led to seek confident living by positive thinking (we have suggested that they are largely urban, middle class people, of an average educational level, with conservative political leanings, from non-liturgical Protestant backgrounds—a characterization that is impressionistic), others, with different personality tendencies, find this approach unsatisfactory. It is not too gross an over-simplification to say that Bishop Fulton Sheen represents a contemporary Catholic approach to the same constellation of problems of urban, middle class people that Dr. Peale represents for "standard" Protestants. Drawing on a different tradition, however, his guide is to "peace of soul," not "confident living," and the people to whom he appeals have had different cultural training in what constitutes an effective and valid religious adjustment to their problems. Thus, though many of the problems are the same, the religious efforts to deal with them are different. Persons of Catholic training, and some Protestants of course, have been taught to need a religious expression with a complex doctrinal and dogmatic system. The writings of Bishop Sheen have an elaborate intellectual framework and a philosophical cast completely foreign to the work of Dr. Peale. Intellectuals (of "humanistic" rather than "scientific" leanings) may be drawn to the former, but almost certainly not to the latter.

The writing of Sheen also emphasizes the traditional doctrine of the "sinfulness of man," in a way congenial to those trained to Catholicism and to "twice-born Protestants" (those in whom the sense of tragedy, sin and guilt is particularly acute). Such an emphasis only alienates those who respond favorably to an optimistic and liberal view of man.

Nice people must see themselves as nasty people before they can find peace. When they exchange their proud and diabolical belief that they never did anything wrong to hope for a Divine remedy for their mistakes, they will have attained to the condition of normality, peace, and happiness. . . . The *nasty* people are the convertible people; aware of their own imperfections, they sense within themselves an emptiness. . . . This sense of sin in them does not beget a forlorn despair, but a creative despair, when once they know that they can look beyond themselves for loving relief.[8]

Just as Peale attempts to help men escape from anxiety by affirming the optimistic Protestant creed (to an important degree the product of American middle class life), so Sheen seeks to help by affirming the classic Christian theology and dogma: There is a natural law, and feelings of guilt are inevitable when this law is broken. The solution of men's problems, if they will recognize their guilt and give up their pride, is to turn to God, who forgives and understands.

Sheen makes a substantial attack on some aspects of psychoanalysis, claiming that what is true in it has long been known by the Church, and that its efforts to remove the sense of guilt are destructive. The attack is not frivolous or shallow, but elaborate and reasoned (although not necessarily reasonable). This appeals to those who require careful argument, if not substantial evidence, who are trained to Catholic doctrine of guilt or show some residues of Calvinist feeling, and who feel alienated from a world of secular liberalism and science.

RELIGION AND HEALTH

In the preceding pages, we have made several references to the ways in which contemporary religious movements are related to the anxieties of modern men. One important aspect of the search for "peace of mind" is the search for mental health and emotional poise, thus bringing religion inevitably into contact with psychiatry either to oppose or to work with it. The relationship between religion and medical practices is, of course, primordial. From the manipulations of the "medicine man"—near the magical end of the pole—to the prayers and sacrifices and appeals to faith—near the religious end of the pole—the religio-magic complex has everywhere been concerned with problems of ill-health. We shall not undertake to review this whole complicated question, but shall explore only some phases of recent religious developments, to show how this continuing personality need for reduction of pain and anxiety is drawn into current religious trends in ways that seem appropriate to individuals living in a day of psychiatry and other elaborate medical practices.

The Social Psychology of Christian Science. The search for health looms large in the efforts of some religious groups; it is in the background of the work of others, but nowhere is it entirely lacking. Although Dr. Peale has long given attention to "psychiatry," the primary theme in his writing is that one can win success by the elimination of fear and the development of faith and self-confidence. Christian Science, another

---

[8] Fulton J. Sheen, *Peace of Soul*, p. 85.

urban, middle class movement, is more centrally concerned with problems of health. As contrasted with the development of interest in psychiatry and medicine in the established denominations, however, the approach of Christian Science is "sectarian," not "churchly." We shall define those terms at length in Chapter 7 and therefore shall distinguish them here only briefly, with reference to the immediate question: The churches attempt to absorb modern medicine into their framework, to adjust to it, and to use whatever aspects of it they can in their work. The sectarian approach of Christian Science is to challenge the claims of secular approaches to health and to offer itself as a substitute. It should be emphasized that this is becoming less and less true, that Christian Science is following the familiar road "from sect to church," and in many ways can now scarcely be distinguished in modes of worship, church organization, and even in its approach to health, from the more standard middle class denominations. The trend is illustrated by the growth in the importance of church services, as contrasted with an earlier greater emphasis on practitioners. Middle class sects, as we shall see, are particularly likely to be short-lived, to be absorbed quickly into the main-stream of the churches, with only residues of special emphasis, tradition, and a separate literature remaining.

Without trying to assess how far this process has gone in Christian Science (there is doubtless wide variation from congregation to congregation), we shall speak of its more sectarian approach to religion and health. Not only does it set itself as a substitute for secular medical practices (accepting only those aspects which harmonize with its own teaching, rather than the churchly approach of accepting what medical men affirm, and harmonizing teaching to that), but it offers a metaphysical doctrine and a mysticism in the guise of science that are more congenial to the needs of some people than a simple attempt to apply secular psychiatry under church auspices.

In the basic document of Christian Science, Mary Baker Eddy writes:

How do drugs, hygiene, and animal magnetism, heal? I venture to affirm that they do not heal; they only relieve, and exchange one disease for another. I classify disease as error, that nothing but Truth, or Mind, can heal, and this Mind must be divine, not human. Mind transcends all other power, and will ultimately supersede all other means in healing. . . . What are termed Natural Science and Material Law are laws of mortal mind. The physical universe expresses the conscious and unconscious thoughts of mortals. Physical force and mortal mind are one. Drugs and hygiene oppose the supremacy of the Divine Mind, and act against it. Drugs and inert matter are unconscious. Certain results, supposed to proceed from them, are really caused by that faith in them which human consciousness is educated to feel.[9]

[9] Mary Baker Eddy, *Science and Health*, pp. 414–415.

This passage may suggest something of the tone of the "Science of Divine Mind," in some ways a deeply fundamentalist interpretation of Christianity, but in other ways a mystical and messianic deviation that seeks to absorb the word "science" into its special theology and doctrine.

To whom does such a movement appeal? The range of persons is wide, and doubtless has become wider in recent years, as Christian Science has modified the mysticism of its founder and moved toward a "standard middle class denomination." Yet we can perhaps describe a modal type that indicates some of the functions of this religious group. R. W. England [10] has made an interesting analysis of a sample of 500 letters drawn from the columns of the *Christian Science Journal,* in various years from 1929 to 1946. Letter-writers are probably not a good sample, in the statistical sense, of readers of the *Journal,* who in turn are not a statistical sample of Christian Scientists. They are under-representative of the more casual members, over-representative of the more intense and perhaps the more disturbed members. Yet if one recognizes this, he can use the data from the letters to highlight the approach of Christian Science to illness and other problems. The letters suggest that perhaps half of the writers were drawn to Christian Science because of specific, chronic troubles: ill-health, financial problems, bereavement, family worries, or "undesirable" personal traits. The largest group of adherents are urban, middle class, married women with bodily disorders. Many of their letters are testimonials to remarkable cures, often from vague and emotionally toned illnesses, that promote and sustain interest.

Like every other system of medicine, from that of the primitive witch-doctor to modern scientific practice, Christian Science profits from the self-validation that follows from the fact that most illnesses "cure themselves." There are very few other fields in which one may have such a good "batting average" just by not making too many mistakes. This is one of the reasons why it is difficult to prove the inadequacy of many approaches to health: almost any method "works" for a great many people. And only secular science lacks an additional advantage: if a cure is not forthcoming, one can attribute the failure to improper application of the formula or to lack of faith. Secular medicine imposes upon itself the requirement that the formula itself be continually investigated.

England well summarizes the basic doctrine of Christian Science:

Briefly, Christian Science teaches that the power of Divine Mind can manifest itself at the behest of believers by curing ills, harmonizing interpersonal relationships, providing material needs, and by otherwise ameliorating one's lot upon the moral plane of existence. The only "reality" is the reality of God; all

[10] "Some Aspects of Christian Science as Reflected in Letters of Testimony," *American Journal of Sociology,* March, 1954, pp. 448–453.

else is illusion. Traditional Christian virtues are identified with God. Inharmony, such as sickness, poverty, war, is the illusory product of mortal mind and error.[11]

As a phase of the contemporary religious search for "peace of mind," Christian Science shares some tendencies with such religious developments as those epitomized by Dr. Peale and it differs in other respects. They are similar in appealing primarily to persons of the middle class who respond favorably to the "individual" approach. This requires no examination of the fact that some human ills may find their source in the structure of society. Most of *their* ills, indeed, are not in society, at least in a direct sense, for they are persons of moderate or even large success. The adherents of both groups have come largely from what might be called "standard Protestant" backgrounds, but they had lost interest in the traditional churches. Both appeal to those with a smattering of knowledge of modern science. Those in whom the orientation of science has become a crucial life perspective—whether for good or ill—can scarcely be attracted to either movement.

There are other ways in which Christian Science differs rather sharply in its social psychological meaning from a religion of confident living. We have suggested that it is a sect more than a church, or was, at any rate, in its earlier days. As a sect it involves a great deal of the thought and energy of its members, penetrating into many areas of their lives. It appeals to people with mystical tendencies, those who might be discontent with the fairly pat and unimaginative formulas of Peale, but who are drawn to the fairly elaborate and mysterious formulas of Mary Baker Eddy. These require that one be able to set himself somewhat apart from traditional American views, for many "hard-headed, practical," middle class people feel little attraction to doctrines of the power of "Divine Mind." And finally, as contrasted with the *use* of modern medicine that Peale attempts to make, Christian Science opposes many of its premises. It attracts many people who, for different reasons, distrust doctors—perhaps because the vague, emotional difficulties that they so frequently face are at present substantially beyond the reach of medicine.

It is perhaps not too wide of the mark to suggest that the doctrines of Peale represent an absorption of Christian Science into the framework of the "church," as many another sectarian movement has been absorbed. In the transition, many aspects have been changed, particularly those that represent separation from society; but many of the personality needs from which Christian Science springs are expressed in such churchly developments as those of Peale.

[11] *Ibid.*, p. 449.

For lower-class, poorly-educated people, close to the fundamentalist Christian tradition, there is little need, in the search for health through religion, to try to adjust to science and to use it, as Peale does, or to prove that one's doctrines are a kind of superior science, as Christian Science does. Heirs of a tradition that includes miraculous cures, closer to the ancient stream of medical magic, they can appeal more frankly to the religio-magical complex in their search for health. The distinction is not sharp, of course, for it is a question whether their approach is essentially less scientific than many of the middle class movements. It is more openly non-scientific, however, for the training of its adherents has not presented them with so many problems of reconciliation between science and religion. There are fewer inhibitions placed by their own personality tendencies to the use of the magical healing cults and formulas. This does not prevent them from using scientific remedies as well, for they can be thought of as alternative means to the same end—a kind of dualistic thinking that is characteristic not simply of the Trobriand Islanders, but probably of most of mankind.

RELIGIOUS RESPONSES TO PSYCHIATRY

For some religious leaders, problems of reconciliation between religion and medicine, particularly psychiatry, have become acute. They cannot disregard the scientific approach to health, with the cultists, nor be content with adding the *word* "science" to the name of their group. As religious leaders, they are heirs of a tradition that contains a good deal of insight into the nature of mental anguish, rooted in sorrow, guilt, hostility, and a sense of aloneness. From the point of view of modern science, these insights, concerning both diagnosis and therapy, are mixed with magic and a miraculous view of the universe that is unacceptable; yet the insights should not be underemphasized. These religious leaders are also strongly affected by the developments of modern science. Many are highly educated men who are aware of the ways in which psychiatry is struggling with the emotional problems with which religion has so long been concerned. How can the efforts of religion and science be united? That is the question they are asking.

The answers that they give range over a long continuum, from a few easy propositions drawn from psychiatry added to the traditional insights (which themselves are variously understood), to serious study of psychiatry, including a recognition of the conflicts in theory and in premises as well as the harmony between religion and psychiatry. The majority of ministers probably incline toward the former end of the continuum, since few of them have more than a minimal training in the various disciplines relevant to psychiatry. There are also some deep conflicts between the two traditions that are generally resolved in favor of their primary training. Yet it would be a mistake to overlook the growing interest and training of many religious leaders in psychiatry.

Some psychiatrists and clinical psychologists, in turn, are reaching toward religion. Only a little observation reveals that many deeply religious people have a poise and an ability to withstand emotional strain that must command the psychiatrists' professional admiration. It inevitably occurs to some to ask: Can I, by giving my patient a "dose of religion," develop in him some of that poise? The question is put in this rather impudent fashion to indicate the utilitarian and pragmatic interest in religion that frequently characterizes the medical man. He, too, is likely to make use of a few pat formulas. The fact that the religious leader is likely to have an equally pragmatic view of psychiatry reveals the basic differences in assumptions and first premises from which men in the two traditions often proceed.

Our interest here is to show how the personality tendencies of some contemporary religious leaders pose for them serious problems of adjustment or of reconciliation with science. We shall not explore the very extensive literature, along the whole continuum, which represents the many efforts to relate religion to psychiatry.[12] We shall note only briefly that the efforts range from statements that what is true in secular psychotherapy has long been religious knowledge, to the development of clinics and seminary courses for the training of ministers in psychotherapy.

Those who emphasize the traditional role of religion in psychotherapy hold that modern medicine is refining and rediscovering truths that are part of the religious view of man. Effective therapy, they hold, requires the development of a religious faith. They do not oppose the secular developments, though they often criticize their premises, but contend that these developments are true insofar as they harmonize with religious conceptions. This is the view taken by Misiak, with special reference to psychosomatic medicine:

The value of religion in psychosomatic medicine becomes evident when we consider the following points: 1. Religion furnishes man with a philosophy of life and gives to his intellect the necessary enlightenment. It becomes to a

[12] See A. T. Boisen, *The Exploration of the Inner World;* Joshua Liebman, *Peace of Mind;* Albert C. Outler, *Psychotherapy and the Christian Message; Review of Religion* (Horace L. Friess, editor) issues of May, 1946 and March, 1949 on "Religion and Health"; David E. Roberts, *Psychotherapy and a Christian View of Man;* James H. Van der Veldt and R. P. Odenwald, *Psychiatry and Catholicism.*

man what a mariner's compass is to a ship, offers him direction and guidance on the sea of life. 2. Religion assists the will of man, strengthens it, and helps him to carry out the orders of the intellect. 3. Religion fulfills the most basic spiritual needs and yearnings of man, especially that for love and immortality.[13]

From these contributions, Misiak holds, come "peace of mind," internal harmony, and the ability to resist moral dangers. Some psychiatrists agree with this appraisal in a general way, but their utilitarian view of religion leads many of them to see it as one of various alternative modes of adjustment—a position that the dedicated religious person cannot accept. Allport points out that religion and therapy are alike in stressing the need for unity and order in personality.

But from the point of view of psychotherapy sentiments dealing with family, art, sports, business, would be equally good if they succeeded in marshaling energy and bestowing order in the life. Religion is bound to disagree at this point, asking whether such sentiments are adequate to sustain personality. Can a person ever really attain integration until he has likewise signed and sealed a treaty of peace with the cosmos? [14]

Many medical men may answer "no" to this question, and thus support religion as fundamentally related to emotional health. The extent of the agreement should not be exaggerated, however, for virtually all psychiatrists take a very tolerant and undogmatic view of religion that is not likely to be satisfactory to those who defend specific religious beliefs and practices as the fundamentally valid ones—however much they may tolerate the "partial insights" of other religions. Thus Christian ministers who turn enthusiastically to Jung (as they may not to "Jünger") perhaps do not see the full implications of his views. His support of religion is well known:

Among all my patients in the second half of life . . . there has not been one whose problem in the last resort was not that of finding a religious outlook on life. It is safe to say that every one of them fell ill because he had lost that which the living religions of every age have given to their followers, and none of them has been really healed who did not regain his religious outlook.[15]

Religious liberals, who incline toward a functional view and look upon the continuous modification of ritual and doctrine as a natural and desirable process, can find strong support in Jung. Those who "know" un-

[13] Henry Misiak, "Psychosomatic Medicine and Religion," *Catholic World*, February, 1953, p. 343.
    [14] Gordon Allport, *The Individual and His Religion*, p. 79.
    [15] Carl G. Jung, *Modern Man in Search of a Soul*, p. 284; see also his *Psychology and Religion*.

changing religious truths, however, can find in him little defense of *the* way.

Those who stress the extent to which modern psychotherapy reaffirms religion often refer, not only to the agreement on the need in the individual for a unifying scheme of values, but also to similarities in therapy. William Roberts, for example, points to several common aspects: psychotherapy reenacts the process of justification by faith; both religion and psychoanalysis stress the "sinful" powers of man; clinicians perform many priestly functions—ministering to suffering, the awakening of hope.[16] Those who have seen the way in which a recently analyzed person defends his "faith," and uses it for explanation and adjustment, will not doubt that psychoanalysis has a religious quality for him. One might add that the current attention to "group therapy" builds on, or at least matches, a religious pattern of long standing. Indeed, organized religious worship is easily regarded, from the perspective of traditional religion, as a "healing of the soul." And some current religious practices, the Oxford Group Movement, for example, make explicit use of small groups for mutual confession and support—a development that has probably been virtually unaffected by secular group therapy. Needless to say, any emphasis on the similarities of psychotherapy to religion must pay full attention to the differences. Both may emphasize man's capacity for "sin," for example, but the concept fits into their total schemes in very different ways.

Toward the other end of the continuum are those who are not so concerned to prove that modern psychiatry is only an adaptation of ancient religious theories and methods as they are to learn from psychiatry all they can, recognizing in it something at least partially new. They look upon psychotherapy as a valuable ally in the struggle to deal with man's age-old problems of anxiety. Some of these religious leaders pay little attention to possible points of contention between the allies, while others are more alert to the conflicts in premises and in theories, despite the consensus on many aims. Rabbi Liebman's popular *Peace of Mind* illustrates the former position and Outler's *Psychotherapy and the Christian Message* the latter. Such writers agree, however, that the cooperation of religion and science is valuable and necessary in the search for harmonious individual lives. The extent of the agreement with this idea is seen in the great increase in emphasis on "pastoral psychology"; some ministers look upon this as their central function today, and few escape "clinical" demands upon their time. It is shown in the flood of writings concerning

---

[16] See "Analysis and Faith," *New Republic,* May 16, 1955, pp. 16–22, where the statement by Roberts is followed by replies from several psychiatrists and clergymen.

religion and psychotherapy, in the development of specialized periodicals, in the increase in seminary curricula of courses in the psychology of religion and counseling. It is shown most dramatically perhaps by the fact that hundreds of clergymen have been given clinical training, in the last few years, in hospital centers where special institutes have been established for them.

Thus on the contemporary religious scene we can see a wide range, from "faith healing" to active cooperation between religious leaders and psychiatrists. The search for health and for peace of mind continues to be a vital part of the religious complex, pursued by various people in ways that reflect the differences in the urgency of their needs, their educational level, the extent of their acceptance of the *ethos* of modern science, the nature of their religious training, and the many other aspects of their "personality systems."

PSYCHOANALYSIS AND RELIGION

When one looks at the religion-personality complex from the point of view of the clinician, the question raised is not, how can the efforts of religion and science be united (a question that assumes that they can be), but, does religion contribute to mental health. Among the various aspects of psychiatry, psychoanalysis has been most influential in exploring this question. Both directly, as an effort to develop a complete system of theory and therapy, and indirectly, by its impact on other personality theories and clinical practice, psychoanalysis has strongly affected the social psychology of religion. From a brief examination of psychoanalytic ideas—both of the Freudian school and other approaches—one can learn a great deal about the ways in which religion and personality are related. Both the errors, from the point of view of the theory we are developing, and the insights of psychoanalysis can be instructive. The various schools of psychoanalysis are likely to be very sensitive to their differences; but we must be equally alert to the similarities—particularly the agreement on the way in which the question should be posed: What is the function of religion in the total "economy" of the individual? How is it related to his search for happiness? From what needs does it spring? Does it help to satisfy or does it block the satisfaction of those needs?

The Freudian Theory of Religion. We shall be primarily concerned with Freud, whose sharp propositions can be very instructive, even when they are most in error.[17] It is paradoxical that Freud is attacked for his

---

[17] See particularly the following works of Freud: *Civilization and Its Discontents; The Future of an Illusion; Moses and Monotheism; Totem and Taboo.*

view that religion is an "illusion," and yet his analysis of the nature of man is sometimes cited to support conservative religious doctrines.[18] A brief examination of his theory of religion may help to explain the paradox.

Freud never relinquished his view that the norms of culture were somehow "unnatural." The proscriptions and prescriptions that everywhere accompany communal life have to be imposed on the majority of men; they are built upon coercion and instinctual renunciation; they stand in opposition to the destructive anti-social tendencies in all men. Most men "accept" culture, despite its required renunciations, because of the narcissistic satisfactions it brings, based primarily on the right to despise outsiders. "True, one is a miserable plebian, tormented by obligations and military service, but withal one is a Roman citizen, one has one's share in the task of ruling other nations and dictating their laws." [19] If the prohibitions of society were removed, one would take his instinctual pleasures as he wished—killing, robbing, sexual satisfactions without confine. That is, one would until he discovered that others acted in the same way (a kind of Kantian categorical imperative, it would seem, that Freud implies would lead men back to the restrictions of culture). "Indeed, it is the principal task of culture, its real *raison d'être*, to defend us against nature." [20]

Needless to say, this is scarcely an adequate view of culture, from the perspective of modern sociology and anthropology. Culture creates and expresses needs, does not simply repress "nature." Group life is also "natural," and the manifestations of society and culture in the personality cannot adequately be interpreted as intrusions from outside. Yet the attention to the inhibitive aspects of culture is legitimate, if one avoids trying to build a total theory from them. How does religion become involved in this "defense against nature"? It is, says Freud, a key cultural tool: "The gods retain their threefold task: they must exorcise the terrors of nature, they must reconcile one to the cruelty of fate, particularly as shown in death, and they must make amends for the sufferings and privations that the communal life of culture has imposed on man." [21]

Such a statement brings Freud close to a functional theory—which, indeed, he helped to build. Had he brought the phenomena of society (culture in particular) into his analysis of nature, and had he conceived of the individual needs with which religion is connected in less narrow

---

[18] See David Riesman, *Individualism Reconsidered*, pp. 388–408.
[19] Sigmund Freud, *The Future of an Illusion*, p. 22.
[20] *Ibid.*, p. 26.
[21] *Ibid.*, p. 30.

terms, he would have been less inclined to interpret religion simply as an attempt to build an illusionary shield against the severe blows of individual fate. Few scientists will quarrel with his proposition that to understand religion, one must understand man and his total situation. The controversies concern his interpretation of the nature of man and of group life.

The strength of religion, according to Freud, derives from the power of the wishes which it reflects. It is impossible to establish the truth of the illusions on which religion is built, but these illusions grow from man's most persistent wishes, and ". . . the secret of their strength is the strength of these wishes." [22] Helplessness, demands for justice unfulfilled by culture, the desire for the prolongation of life—these are the forces out of which religion is built. It may or may not be true, for illusion is not demonstrably error, but it is always tied to a wish.

Freud interprets religion as one of several ways in which men seek to avoid the pains of life and to increase its pleasures. To avoid pain—and it is significant that Freud emphasizes this negative view of the problem —one may create powerful diversions, which lead to caring little about his misery, he may seek substitute satisfactions, which lessen misery, or he may take intoxicating substances, which make him insensitive to it. This suggestion of "functional alternatives" is a very important lead which, unfortunately, Freud did not follow up. Nowhere does he adequately discuss the conditions under which one or another of the roads to happiness will be taken; but without that analysis, he cannot develop a theory of the interrelationship of personality tendencies and religion. Freud suggests that one may seek happiness by voluntary loneliness to avoid the unhappiness that comes from human relations, by intoxication to ward off misery, by "annihilation of instincts," by sublimation in mental work, by a positive search for pleasure (especially for love, but we are defenseless against suffering when love is not returned), by flight into neurotic illness, and by the "illusions" of art and religion.[23]

When will one or another of these paths be taken, and what are their various consequences? Although Freud gives little attention to the former question, he is not hesitant about giving his judgment concerning the latter: Religion has not done its job; it has performed some services for men, but not enough. It is comparable to a childhood neurosis, built on the admiration and fear of one's father. Freud expresses a very guarded optimism that man may outgrow this childhood phase and develop responses to his situation that are based on reason, not illusion.

[22] *Ibid.*, p. 52.
[23] See *Civilization and Its Discontents*, pp. 23–42.

Religion circumscribes these measures of choice and adaptation by urging upon everyone alike its single way of achieving happiness and guarding against pain. Its method consists in decrying the value of life and promulgating a view of the real world that is distorted like a delusion, and both of these imply a preliminary intimidating influence upon intelligence. At such a cost—by the forcible imposition of mental infantilism and inducing a mass-delusion— religion succeeds in saving many people from individual neuroses. But little more. There are, as we have said, many paths by which the happiness attainable for man can be reached, but none which is certain to take him to it. Nor can religion keep her promises either. When the faithful find themselves reduced in the end to speaking of God's "inscrutable decree," they thereby avow that all that is left to them in their sufferings is unconditional submission as a last-remaining consolation and source of happiness. And if man is willing to come to this, he could probably arrive there by a shorter road.[24]

This severe judgment was rooted in a theory of the origin of religion which blocked the development of an adequate functional theory toward which Freud was moving, almost in spite of himself. His ingenious attempt at anthropological reconstruction, however plausible and convincing to the "faithful," cannot be the basis for a scientific theory of religion; yet it set the framework within which his later conceptions were formulated. Fortunately, his acute powers of observation prevented his analysis of the function of religion in personality from being quite as bad, from a scientific point of view, as his attempts to reconstruct the origin of religion. It is the Oedipus myth, of course, which he uses as his version of the Garden of Eden. Man's "fall" occurred when the brothers, who had been expelled from the "primal horde" in which the father monopolized all the females, joined forces, "slew and ate the father, and thus put an end to the father horde." But after they had satisfied their hate "the suppressed tender impulses had to assert themselves." Remorse and a sense of guilt made the dead father more powerful over them than he had been when alive. The slaying of the father and the remorse that followed are specifically, to Freud, the source of totemism. (The totem animal is a father substitute, who may not be killed; and the men deny themselves the women of the totem group, a further recognition of their guilt.)

The totemic system was a kind of agreement with the father in which the latter granted everything that the child's phantasy could expect from him, protection, care, and forbearance, in return for which the pledge was given to honor his life, that is to say, not to repeat the act against the totem through which the real father had perished.[25]

[24] *Ibid.*, p. 42.
[25] Sigmund Freud, *Totem and Taboo*, p. 238.

This imaginative account of the origins of totemism could be set down more readily as interesting speculation if Freud had not used it as a general theory of the origin of religion.

All later religions prove to be attempts to solve the same problem, varying only in accordance with the stage of culture in which they are attempted and according to the paths which they take; they are all, however, reactions aiming at the same great event with which culture began and which ever since has not let mankind come to rest.[26]

This kind of historical and psychological reductionism serves only to obscure the complex of forces that lead to religion. Few, aside from convinced Freudians, will be persuaded of the validity of these observations by the claim that they "harmonize" with the conception of personality that emerges from psychoanalytic treatment. Most will demand firmer evidence. One can imagine that Freud himself was not entirely happy with his solution. He came back to the Oedipus relationship in *Moses and Monotheism* and opens the door, at least a crack, to some other kind of explanation than "racial memory." The primeval experience of family conflict, he writes, was such an important one that " . . . I cannot help thinking, it must have left some permanent trace in the human soul— something comparable to a tradition." [27]

Despite its weaknesses the Freudian analysis of religion can contribute a great deal to a functional theory. Even the Oedipus account, if not taken literally, can lead one to a study of the ambivalent feelings, the aggressive impulses, the sense of guilt, the helplessness that are among the forces that sustain the religious quest. The serious weaknesses of Freud's interpretation derive from the narrowness of his general theory and the selective nature of his evidence. His description of the consequences of religion (that it sustained inadequate institutions, prohibited critical thinking, prevented the continuing development of an adequate morality, and fostered an infantile fixation) is based primarily on the religious expressions of neurotic people. This duplicated his tendency to elaborate a total psychological theory on the basis of evidences drawn from the study of upper-middle class, neurotic, Viennese women in 1900 —to state the case a little too severely. He tended to assume that all religions were alike in their consequences, hence he could leap from a fanciful anthropological reconstruction to a contemporary religion without being concerned with major social and cultural differences.

Modifications of the Freudian View of Religion. Several writers who

[26] *Ibid.,* p. 239.
[27] *Moses and Monotheism,* p. 167.

have been strongly influenced by Freud have sharply modified his negative judgment of the effects of religion. We have mentioned Jung, who is
much more inclined to stress the positive functions of religion in helping
one to achieve "individuation" or self-realization. He declares that man
stands in need of mystery and symbols, that he has a natural desire to
submit to powers higher than himself. Such submission may lead to the
infantilism and uncritical thinking that Freud describes, but it can also,
Jung holds, contribute to self-realization.

Among the "neo-Freudians," Erich Fromm is outstanding for his interest
in religion and his contributions to a functional theory. Unlike Freud, he
differentiates sharply among varieties of religion, in terms of their relationship to what he calls full self-realization. And from the point of view
of contemporary social science, his analysis is much more adequate than
that of Jung, because he explores the kinds of socio-cultural conditions
in which various types of religious patterns are most likely to appear.
Fromm defines religion in very broad terms: "I understand by religion
any system of thought and action shared by a group which gives the
individual a frame of orientation and an object of devotion." [28] The very
conditions of human existence, he believes, create in man a need for a
common system of orientation and an object of devotion. Religion, therefore, is an inevitable aspect of any culture. The question for Fromm as a
therapist is not, shall there be a religion, but what kind of religion shall
man have and with what consequences for human life. Many traditional
religionists will applaud this statement. They may not agree, however,
with his instrumental approach, nor with his comments on the kind of
religion that he considers necessary for the full realization of human
potentialities (a goal, indeed, which they may not accept as the primary
one). Fromm, to be sure, indicates that there are aspects of the major
world religions which contribute to full human development; but he
stresses the ease with which they regress toward more "primitive" forms
that are "incompatible with the essential teachings of monotheism." Ancestor worship, totemism, fetishism, compulsive ritualism, in his judgment, lie just beneath the surface of most contemporary religion, and are
frequently encouraged by institutional forms.

A religion that contributes to the full realization of human powers will,
according to Fromm, be sharply different from the traditional varieties. It
will, in his terms, be "humanistic" not "authoritarian." The analytic distinction is sharp, although particular religious complexes may contain
both tendencies. The usual conception of religion, he believes, inclines

[28] *Psychoanalysis and Religion,* p. 21.

strongly toward the "authoritarian" type. The very definition of the *Oxford Dictionary*, for example, is not of religion as such, but "is a rather accurate definition of authoritarian religion." It states that religion is the "recognition on the part of man of some higher unseen power as having control of his destiny, and as being entitled to obedience, reverence, and worship." It is not alone the emphasis on a controlling, higher power outside of man that makes this an authoritarian conception, according to Fromm.

What makes it so is the idea that this power, because of the control it exercises, is *entitled* to "obedience, reverence and worship." I italicize the word "entitled" because it shows that the reason for worship, obedience and reverence lies not in the moral qualities of the deity, not in love or justice, but in the fact that it has control, that is, has power over man. Furthermore it shows that the higher power has a right to force man to worship him and that lack of reverence and obedience constitutes sin.[29]

Why is authoritarian religion dysfunctional, according to Fromm's analysis of personality? Because it alienates man from himself. In humanistic religion, God is the image of man's higher self, a symbol of what he ought or might be; "in authoritarian religion God becomes the sole possessor of what was originally man's: of his reason and his love. The more perfect God becomes, the more imperfect becomes man. He *projects* the best he has onto God and thus impoverishes himself." [30]

Religion can serve man, only when it encourages love and the assertion of one's own powers, not fear and submission. Fromm declares that early Christianity and the mystic thinking in many religions are strongly "humanistic." "Jesus' precept that 'the kingdom of God is within you' is the simple and clear expression of non-authoritarian thinking." [31] In emphasizing this aspect of early Christianity, Fromm doubtless minimizes the paradoxes and the complexities, indeed even the contradictions, which it contained. His tendency to make of Jesus a kind of early-day neo-Freudian and a full supporter of "humanistic" religion seems wide of the mark. It does emphasize in a dramatic way, however, the insights into personality that Christianity contains. The Oedipus complex, Fromm declares, can be understood in its full significance only when it is translated from the sphere of sex into that of interpersonal relations. The "incestuous" craving for the parents is not sexual, as Freud believed, but is an expression of the "much more profound" desire to remain a child, to remain attached to protecting figures.

[29] *Ibid.*, p. 35.
[30] *Ibid.*, pp. 49–50.
[31] *Ibid.*, p. 48.

When Jesus said, "For I am come to set a man at variance against his father, and the daughter against her mother, and the daughter in law against her mother in law," he did not mean to teach hatred of parents but to express in the most unequivocal and drastic form the principle that man must break incestuous ties and become free in order to become human.[32]

One can imagine the many responses to this interpretation. Our concern is only to describe it as part of Fromm's attempt to define a religion which in his view is positively functional for human personality. The attachment to parents, although it is the most fundamental form of "incest," is not the only form. The tribe, the nation, the race, the class may serve as protecting "homes." "Here are the roots of nationalism and racism, which in turn are symptoms of man's inability to experience himself and others as free human beings." [33]

Thus Fromm does not share Freud's categorical judgment that religion is an infantile fixation which man may hopefully someday be able to afford to discard. While stressing the ease with which it serves selfish interests and neurotic trends in the individual, Fromm also declares that religion can help men to achieve their highest potentialities. Under what conditions is this most likely to occur? Although Fromm gives no detailed answer to this question, he shows his full awareness of the fact that the kind of personality capable of "humanistic religion" will emerge in certain kinds of socio-cultural situations. He who would make man religious, in Fromm's sense, must work to create the kind of conditions in which character structures capable of mature religious experience will develop.

What people think and feel is rooted in their character and their character is molded by the total configuration of their practice of life—more precisely, by the socio-economic and political structure of their society. In societies ruled by a powerful minority which holds the masses in subjection, the individual will be so imbued with fear, so incapable of feeling strong or independent, that his religious experience will be authoritarian. . . . On the other hand, where the individual feels free and responsible for his own fate, or among minorities striving for freedom and independence, humanistic religious experience develops.[34]

Such an hypothesis—one can scarcely say that it has been fully demonstrated—is pertinent only to an instrumentalist approach to religion which asks: How does religion affect the quality of human life? To those who seek to establish or defend "the truth" and to those for whom the relevance of religion to the quality of adjustment to this life is quite unim-

[32] *Ibid.*, p. 81.
[33] *Ibid.*, p. 81.
[34] *Ibid.*, p. 52.

portant, Fromm's observations have little significance. To those who share
his orientation, the key question remains: Does "humanistic religion"
merely reflect mature personalities, which in turn are the product of
favorable socio-cultural conditions? Or does such a religion, once established, help to create mature persons and a non-authoritarian society?
Fromm strongly implies that the latter is true, but does not adequately
describe the process by which the influence is conveyed. The ease with
which religions become "authoritarian" shows that man has not yet
learned how to prevent religion from becoming an accumulating reservoir
of his projected needs. But there are also evidences of close connections
between religion and personal growth and "individuation," to use Jung's
term. The full picture must include both tendencies.

SECULAR ALTERNATIVES TO RELIGIOUS ACTION

From a functional point of view, religion-non-religion is a continuum.
There is no sharp break that distinguishes religious behavior from other
kinds of behavior, but only a shading off as various criteria in one's definition become less and less applicable. It is possible, of course, to pay
so much attention to a few similarities among phenomena that the large
differences are obscured. Neurosis may be described as a "private form
of religion," or a man's job may be called "his religion." These are not so
much wrong as they are intriguing part truths that require careful qualification. The opposite difficulty, however, is perhaps more common:
Differences among phenomena are so heavily stressed that the important
similarities, in terms of function, are overlooked. At the extreme is the
assertion that nothing is religion except my own system of beliefs and
practices. In a day of widespread culture contact, this is less likely than
the contention that, although there may be many forms of religion, no
phenomenon should be admitted to this category unless it bears the *name*
religion. Functional theory, however, is not concerned with names but
with processes. If nationalism, for example, performs some of the same
individual and group functions as "religion," this is an important fact that
must be explored, despite differences in name.

There are two primary questions to keep in mind in the analysis of
"functional alternatives": What are the conditions under which one alternative rather than another will be followed? And what are the similarities
and differences in their consequences? These are difficult questions, to
which we shall refer at various points in the chapters that follow, in connection with specific situations. In a general answer, one may only say
that social, cultural, and personality facts set limits to the kinds of alterna-

tives that may be selected. A contemporary American may develop such a faith in the power of science, may make it so much an object of devotion, that it can fairly be said that "science is his religion." Clearly this would not be an available alternative in many other socio-cultural situations. Nor is it "available" to persons of different personality tendencies. Those in whom a love of mystery is strong; those who have been taught to distrust reason; the "twice-born" torn by doubt and a sense of sin—these are unlikely to adopt such an alternative.

The consequences of having adopted one alternative rather than another also vary from situation to situation and from individual to individual. One cannot say that the results of infusing nationalism with a religious fervor will be everywhere the same. To respond to a sense of powerlessness by joining a nazi movement does not have the same consequences as a universalist religious response to the same feeling. Clearly there are important value questions involved, as well as problems of analysis, for one response may be far less effective in achieving stated goals than another and may produce more unintended dysfunctions.

Almost every personality need that we have mentioned in connection with religion finds expression in a wide variety of secular movements. This is particularly true in modern society in which the process of secularization has gone so far—that is, in which traditional religious symbols and forms have lost force and appeal. The needs with which religion is connected are still with us. If we are not trained to look to a religious system in our attempts to satisfy them, we will tend to infuse secular patterns with a "religious" quality. We may seek to overcome a sense of aloneness by joining a lodge, rather than (or in addition to) joining a church congregation. We may struggle with a feeling of powerlessness by imbuing our nation with an absolute quality, rather than identifying with an all-powerful God. We may attempt to rid ourselves of guilt by projecting our weakness onto a minority group, instead of by taking confessional. We may try to reduce a sense of confusion and doubt by adopting rigid "all-knowing" secular formulas to explain the world's ills, holding to them with a desperation born more of uncertainty than of conviction. We may attempt to reduce the sense of meaninglessness in life, of boredom on our job, by avid pursuit of entertainment or by alcohol, trying to capture on a week-end what is denied us in the course of our work. (It is in such a situation that "the lost week-end" takes on a tragic quality, for if the week-end is lost, what remains to a man alienated from his job?)

Such secular attempts to reduce our problems do not necessarily stand in the way of religious efforts. A person with a strong sense of guilt, for example, may be drawn to religion and at the same time express strong racial prejudices, as a result of a tendency toward projection. This does not necessarily show a causal connection between the two patterns of behavior, although they may be causally interrelated. On the other hand, a secular alternative may be quite incompatible with certain kinds of religious attempts to deal with the same problem. The chauvinist who exalts the state into a God may also support a parochial religion, but he can scarcely give full allegiance to a universalist religion.

Those on whom the pressures of life fall most heavily (either because of individual circumstance or because of the times in which they live) *and* for whom an established religious system is lacking, are the most likely candidates for a secular movement of a proto-religious variety. These are the discontented, alienated people who follow the *Prophets of Deceit,* as Lowenthal and Guterman call them.

Movements that are very different in ideology or in proclaimed goals may satisfy many of the same needs—needs for direction, for a sense of belonging to a vital and significant group, for projection and displacement of one's guilt and doubt, for answers to the meaning of life. Since few social movements accomplish more than a minimum of what they promise, there is a restless moving in and out, propelled by the unsatisfied needs. Eric Hoffer describes "the interchangeability of mass movements":

In pre-Hitlerian Germany it was often a tossup whether a restless youth would join the Communists or the Nazis. In the over-crowded pale of Czarist Russia the simmering Jewish population was ripe both for revolution and Zionism. In the same family, one member would join the revolutionaries and the other the Zionists. Dr. Chaim Weizmann quotes a saying of his mother in those days: "Whatever happens, I shall be well off. If Shemuel [the revolutionary son] is right, we shall all be happy in Russia; and if Chaim [the Zionist] is right, then I shall go to live in Palestine." [35]

Religious Aspects of Communism. The search for an "over-whelmingly strong power" on which to rely may lead one person to give himself to God while another may give himself to "the party." It is a mistake to disregard the differences which these choices indicate, but equally a mistake to overlook important personality similarities. There is ample evidence that some of the recruits to the Communist Party have been highly sensitive people, bewildered by the confusions of modern society, idealistic, and needing a clear-cut program that claimed to be able to solve the problems they felt so deeply. They found in the authoritative program of communism and in its seeming dedication to justice an "escape from

[35] Eric Hoffer, *The True Believer,* pp. 16–17.

freedom" that gave them both a sense of belonging and a sense of power. They were no longer the alienated; they had a "home" and a program. For many of them, of course, communism became "the God that failed," able to give them a sense of identity with an exciting movement, but scarcely able to satisfy their idealism. As they became disenchanted with communism, they turned to other programs, propelled by the same burning needs for a way to struggle with their bewilderment and sense of powerlessness. Some turned to vigorous anti-communism, investing it with the same energy and dedication they had formerly shown for communism. Others turned to classical religion, in several celebrated cases to Roman Catholicism. Such a dramatic change doubtless indicates a strong reaction against communism; but it also shows some personality continuity, for the Catholic Church, more than any other in Christianity today, furnishes its members a fixed dogma, definitive rites, and an unchallenged structure of power that can bring a sense of certainty to those torn by doubt—something of the same appeal that communism had for some.[36]

Arthur Koestler describes the religious quality that communism had for him in vivid words:

By the time I had finished with *Feuerbach* and *State and Revolution,* something had clicked in my brain which shook me like a mental explosion. To say that one had 'seen the light' is a poor description of the mental rapture which only the convert knows (regardless of what faith he has been converted to). The new light seems to pour from all directions across the skull; the whole universe falls into pattern like the stray pieces of a jigsaw puzzle assembled by magic at one stroke. There is now an answer to every question, doubts and conflicts are a matter of the tortured past—a past already remote, when one had lived in dismal ignorance in the tasteless, colorless world of those who *don't know.*[37]

Among the 221 former communists studied by Almond, almost half came from homes where religious interests were important. He interprets their opposition to the religion of their parents, not simply as anti-religious development, but often as a redirection of interest to a movement that was embraced with religious fervor.

The way in which communism functions as a religion in some situations can be seen not only in the responses of some of its adherents, but in its own structure and "theology." Problems of the present are inter-

[36] See Whittaker Chambers, *Witness;* and the highly insightful accounts in *The God that Failed,* edited by Richard Crossman; see also Arthur Koestler's *The Yogi and the Commissar.* For attempts to explore some of the social psychological factors in adherence to communism, see Gabriel Almond, *The Appeals of Communism* and Morris L. Ernst and David Loth, *Report on the American Communist.*

[37] In *The God that Failed,* p. 23.

preted in terms of a glorious future that gives those problems meaning. There are appeals to faith. A writer in *The New Masses* declared: "The loss of religious faith is good only if we can put in its place a faith in life so real and driving that it endows men's acts with an equal validity. . . ." [38] Many despotic movements of the past have sought to use religion to reenforce their power, but in societies in which distinctive religious institutions have developed, despots have seldom been able to bring the religious forces completely under their control. Some element of restraint, some limit on their power was imposed by a partially competing religious system. Waldemar Gurian has distinguished such despotisms from modern totalitarianisms by the fact that the latter are not content simply to use or control the religious forces: they supplant them with their own creed, thus absorbing and using the religious interest to support their cause.

The totalitarian movements and their power replace God and religious institutions such as the Church; the leaders are deified; the public mass-meetings are regarded and celebrated as sacred actions; the history of the movement becomes a holy history of the advance of salvation, which the enemies and betrayers try to prevent in the same way as the devil tries to undermine and destroy the work of those who are in the service of the City of God.[39]

There seems little doubt that from the point of view of a functional theory of religion, modern totalitarian systems serve as religions for many people. They attempt to make the grave problems of life more bearable by reference to a happier future, thus sharing the cosmic optimism of religion. The dictator becomes a living embodiment of a "supernatural" power, scarcely limited by the forces that have prevented other men from solving overwhelming problems. History is on the side of "the elect." Ritual, emotionally evocative music, pageantry are used to heighten support for the cause. Sacred writings and official doctrines are recited and republished endlessly. (In Hitler's time, a copy of *Mein Kampf* was given to every newly-wed couple.) Before the totalitarian parties have achieved power, there are many "sectarian" elements (in terms of a typology we shall develop in the next chapter) in their approach. After they have come to power, they become "churchlike." Altogether, the religious aspects of communism and other totalitarian movements are important elements to the person interested in understanding their influence.

Neurosis as a "Secular Alternative." The alternative to religion may be, not some social movement with which one can identify, but a private

---

[38] Quoted by Reinhold Niebuhr, *Christianity and Power Politics,* p. 192.
[39] Waldemar Gurian in *Totalitarianism,* Carl J. Friedrich, editor, p. 122.

pattern of belief and ritual used by an unhappy individual in his attempts to counter personal failure and isolation. In extreme cases, this private system will be identified by others as a neurosis. Many writers have noted the thin line that separates a moving religious experience from neurotic illness. James developed this point in his classic work. Freud, of course, tended to identify all religion as an expression of neurotic trends. Fromm adds that neurosis can be seen as a private form of religion—an attempt to struggle with the isolation and powerlessness that overwhelms one. If reality is too painful to bear, one can redefine it with the schizophrenic, stand in opposition to it, with the paranoic, or alternately run past it and hide from it, with the manicdepressive. That each of these responses has its religious equivalent can readily be seen. In his detailed study of 173 seriously disturbed patients, Boisen observes the similarities between their efforts to struggle with their pains and religious behavior. He notes that many great religious leaders—George Fox, John Bunyan, St. Paul, for example—had emotional disturbances comparable to acutely disturbed patients. Yet they were not simply neurotic individuals; ". . . the correct contrast is not between the pathological and the normal in religious experience but between spiritual defeat and spiritual victory." [40] Unfortunately, even if we accept his value judgment, Boisen does not explore the conditions under which one may hope for the visions of a Fox instead of the illusions and delusions of a disturbed person. The scientist must try to discover the social, cultural, and personality factors that incline one toward a religious effort in dealing with his anxieties rather than toward a neurotic effort.

In any discussion of alternatives, important value questions inevitably arise. The scientist cannot say simply, this is a better alternative than that; but he can declare: If this be one's aim, then choice A is better than choice B. Even Freud was willing to grant that in most cases, religion was better than neurosis, because it was a shared "illusion." The religious person, because he deals with others, finds his way to some part of reality—which to Freud was a basic goal. The neurotic is an isolated person; indeed, the most painful and difficult part of every neurosis is the overwhelming sense of isolation. Freud thus grants very little, however. The religious person is likely to assert, not only that religion will rescue man from the despair and isolation of neurosis, but will harness man's energies for positive achievements. Taking a leaf from the functionalist's notebook, he asks: If man cannot live without a "frame of orientation and an object of devotion," is not classical re-

[40] A. T. Boisen, *The Exploration of the Inner World*, p. 79.

ligion better than communism, or nazism, or parochial nationalism? Would we not have fewer social movements with narrow and limited goals, yet armed with convictions of absolute validity, and would we not have fewer distraught and bewildered persons, if men were to "return to religion"? Others, granting the force of this argument, will say: But classical religion is too loaded with the superstitions of the past and itself too easily twisted to support the aims of limited groups—of classes and nations—to make it clearly superior to its secular alternatives. What is needed is a "new universalism," fully harmonious with modern science and the modern world.[41] Still others believe that at least some of the functions formerly undertaken by religion are as well or better performed by secular alternatives. Few people now oppose secular medical practice, for example. Why should this development not fully include emotional disturbances as well as physical ailments?

It is not our purpose in this essay to explore these highly significant value questions. It is our task to note the functional interconnections of different social and personal facts, secular and religious. But one need not deny the hope that a scientific statement may contribute to effective study and action in terms relevant to the facts of contemporary life.

[41] See, for example, in addition to Fromm, *op. cit.*, John Dewey, *A Common Faith*, and John Herman Randall and John Herman Randall, Jr., *Religion and the Modern World*.

CHAPTER 6

Religion and Variation Among Societies

Frequently, in the preceding chapters, we have referred to the fact that systems of religious belief and practice vary greatly from society to society. If one starts from the premise that the nature of a religion is intricately tied up with the society, the culture, and the personality tendencies and needs of the individuals who practice it, the conclusion follows that no one of these can vary without the others being affected.

Anthropological investigations, studies in religious history, the "higher criticism" of sacred writings, sociological study of societal integration have all made it clear that we cannot understand a religion scientifically without relating it to society and culture. There are many scholars, of course, who contend that the most significant aspects of religion are divinely ordained and have been revealed to man by God, and are not to be regarded simply as parts of a social process. This is also the view taken by most of those for whom religion is something to be lived and not simply analyzed. All but the most conservative among these groups, however, are ready to agree that society plays some part in the nature and development of religion.

It is now a commonplace to note that details of religious belief and practice vary with the size and mobility of a society, the nature of its

125

economy, the type of stratification system, the kinds of contact it has had with other societies, etc. There is an intricate connection between religion and morals and a powerful mutual influence between religion and intellectual pursuits as we have seen. No account of economic activities, political problems, kinship systems, aesthetic expressions, or medical practices would be complete without a description of the ways they affect and are affected by religion. Even the religious innovator—the prophet or "charismatic leader," the ascetic, the mystic—although he is often thought to be a spontaneous new force in history, does not escape the imprint of his society and culture. When social patterns change or when a religion is transplanted into a new society, the changes it undergoes further indicate the close interconnection of religion and society. Most of these propositions will be discussed in some detail in later chapters. Although we separate them into different topics, for purposes of analysis, we shall find them highly interrelated and will need to refer frequently to their close connection. In this chapter, we shall be concerned with some of the general questions which arise from the interdependence of religion and society, using as our chief illustration the relationship between social stratification and religious differentiation.

Major culture patterns and values, as well as the nature of society, are closely related to religion. Ruth Benedict's typology of culture "patterns" is doubtless overly rigid and simple, but her description of the interpenetration of religious values and other cultural elements is supported by evidence from other societies. "Disharmonies" between religious beliefs and other value systems are more likely to be found in mobile, urban societies than in the preliterate societies described by Benedict. In fact, some variations in values, some range in the interpretation of culture norms, may be necessary to the successful functioning of urban societies.[1] Even in the more complex societies, however, there is a "strain toward consistency," a *tendency*, however incompletely carried through, for religious values and other values to support each other. Thus in classic Chinese society, a strong kinship system, patriarchal authority, filial piety, and ancestor worship form an interlocking group of values. In a contemporary democracy, the doctrine of predestination is likely to lose much of its hold and tends to be replaced with such a doctrine as the Methodist "grace abounding to all." Nevertheless, it is in static and relatively more simple societies that the congruence of religious and other cultural values is closest and these may be used as a kind of limiting case to describe the relationship.

---

[1] See R. M. Williams, Jr., *American Society*, Chapter 10; and Talcott Parsons and E. A. Shils, *Toward a General Theory of Action*, p. 179.

Benedict points out that the relaxed, non-competitive Zuni reject, in their religious life, the pursuit of ecstatic visions, torture, self-torture, the frenzy of the Ghost Dance, or the hallucinations of the Peyote cult. Although the Zuni pueblos were near the Mexican plateau where the peyote button was obtained and were in contact with the Apache, who were peyote-eaters, the practices of the cult made very little headway among them.

Whether by the use of drugs, of alcohol, of fasting, of torture, or of the dance, no experiences are sought or tolerated among the Pueblos that are outside of ordinary sensory routine. The Pueblos will have nothing to do with disruptive individual experiences of this type. The love of moderation to which their civilization is committed has no place for them. Therefore they have no shamans.

Shamanism is one of the most general human institutions. The shaman is the religious practitioner who, by whatever kind of personal experience is recognized as supernatural in his tribe, gets his power directly from the gods. He is often, like Cassandra and others of those who spoke with tongues, a person whose instability has marked him out for his profession. In North America shamans are characteristically those who have the experience of the vision. The priest, on the other hand, is the depository of ritual and the administrator of cult activities. The Pueblos have no shamans; they have only priests.[2]

We may contrast this with the religion-magic complex among the Dobu, with their very different cultural values. "The violence of Dobuan regard for ownership and the degree to which it involves the victimizing of others and their reciprocating suspicion and ill-will are grossly reflected in their religion." [3] This religion is strongly infused with magic, for in Dobu "there is no propitiation of supernatural beings, no gifts or sacrifices to cement cooperation between gods and petitioners. The supernatural beings that are known in Dobu are a few secret magical names, the knowledge of which . . . gives the power of command." [4] These magical names and the incantations in which they are used are not common property; they are held in secret and fiercely fought over. "The incantations are remarkable for their malevolence and for the degree to which they embody the Dobuan belief that any man's gain is another's loss." [5]

It is perhaps useful, once again, to insert a warning against the assump-

---

[2] Ruth Benedict, *Patterns of Culture,* pagination from Penguin Books edition, pp. 87–88.
[3] *Ibid.,* p. 131. We shall comment below on the assumption that religion is primarily a dependent variable, as indicated in the phrase "reflected in their religion."
[4] *Ibid.*
[5] *Ibid.,* p. 134. For another valuable description of the close interconnections between religion and other social structures, see Ruth Underhill, *Papago Indian Religion.*

tion that religion is always the independent variable, "causing" certain developments in society and culture, or that it is wholly a dependent variable, reflecting its social environment. We *have* assumed that religion is a natural expression of man as an individual and as a member of society. (For other than scientific purposes, this may be an irrelevant or unhappy assumption.) But religious forces, once set in motion, become part of a complex system of interaction. The requirements of a cult ceremony may lead to efforts to get a more accurate calendar; a priestly hierarchy may prevent the breaking-up of a feudal land-tenure system; trade may be stimulated by religious festivals; intense and almost ascetic economic activity may result from a desire to prove one's self of the elect; religious emotion may strongly affect an artistic style. For such questions as these, it is often useful to treat religion as the independent variable, keeping fully in mind the nature of one's abstraction. The influence of religion is sometimes facilitating, sometimes inhibitive; its functions may be manifest or latent and unanticipated; its effects may be good or ill from the point of view of a stated value. However these may be, the scientist cannot disregard the influence of religion anymore than he can overlook the ways in which religion is shaped and reshaped by its social environment.

RELIGION AND TYPE OF SOCIETY

The nature of the relationship between society and religion varies with the type of society—with its size, the degree of mobility, the kind of technology, the extent of internal differentiation, and other variables. There are imperative factors in a social system that set limits within which the religious development will take place. This is equally true, of course, of other social patterns. A tightly-knit consanguine kinship system, for example, with close ties between generations, strong parental authority, choice of marriage partner by parents, etc., is almost certain to disappear in a society where there is a great deal of spacial mobility, emphasis on improvement of status, occupational specialization, and urbanization. Similarly, in such a society, a tightly-integrated religious system, with a strong other-worldly emphasis is unlikely to survive. "The pattern of religious toleration and a diversity of denominations as in the American case seems to be the least disruptive structure." [6] Whether this is a happy or unhappy fact, we need not try to determine, but there is strong support for it as an empirically valid statement.

[6] Talcott Parsons, *The Social System,* p. 189.

Through the largest part of man's history, the boundaries of a religious system were identical with the boundaries of a society or tribe.

Each social group had its own divine beings who were its founders and protectors. Its rites of sacrifice, purification, and communion were manifestations of organized civic life. The temple was a public institution, the focus of the worship of the community; the influence of its practices extended to all the customs of the community, domestic, economic, and political. Even wars between groups were usually conflicts of their respective deities.

An individual did not join a church. He was born and reared in a community whose social unity, organization and traditions were symbolized and celebrated in the rites, cults and beliefs of a collective religion.[7]

Contrast that situation with the one that prevails in differentiated societies, where different religions may be found, where specialized religious practices and leaders emerge, where there is a measure of individual choice in matters of belief. Even if there is an established church that seems to unify the society religiously, that establishment, as Dewey observes, is constituted by the state and can be unmade by the state.

Joachim Wach emphasizes the need for a distinction between a religion that is conterminus with a "natural group"—a society or tribe or kinship group—and what he calls "specifically religious groups." Although the correlation is not perfect, for there are some specifically religious groups to be found in primitive societies, the predominant tendency as societies become more complex is to move from an identity of social and religious groupings to specifically religious groups. The latter can be illustrated by "a special cultic group within a larger social or political unit (tribe or nation) or by a religion professed by ethnically or politically disparate adherents."[8] Thus the religiously specialized groups can separate members of one society or religiously bind together members of different societies. In either case, the identity of the religious and the social boundary is broken.

As Wach points out, it is not only the growing differentiation in the secular structure of a society that produces this transition, for changes in the religious experience itself are also involved. These changes are perhaps not "autonomous," as Wach calls them, for they are set in motion in part by changes in the societal and cultural situation and concomitant changes in personality tendencies; but once underway, as a result of a complex of causes, they develop in ways that cannot be understood simply by referring back to the secular environment. Particularly after the appearance of religious specialists and specifically designated religious

[7] John Dewey, *A Common Faith*, p. 60.
[8] Joachim Wach, *Sociology of Religion*, p. 57; see pp. 56–205.

practices, the religious system begins to undergo its own "inner dialectic," as Troeltsch calls it, which can profitably be studied as a closed system, if one does not forget the nature of his abstraction. The religious development then reacts back upon the society from which it grew.

Robert Redfield has shown how the functions and the management of religion change when folk society changes into civilization. In the first, classes are not separated by differences in knowledge or faith; there is no skepticism, no sense of a need to defend or to modify the basic ideals of the society. These things change as the society becomes larger and more differentiated. Among the Mayans, after about 320 A.D., there was a growth of shrine cities. Priests acquired the authority to manage the principal ceremonies on behalf of the whole community. They became specialists—writers, calculators, thinkers—separated from the mental world of the rural farmer to a significant degree. Reflection and systematization brought new dimensions into the religious system. Thus civilization is not simply the development of the technical order; it destroys some moral and religious orders and creates others—for some ideas cannot be imagined until societies become complex and come into contact with each other. A religious conception of universal human brotherhood is possible only in civilization. Indian tribes that had known each other only as enemies are brought together, they get a sense of common Indianness, under the attacks of the dominant whites.[9]

Thus any analysis of the relationship of society and religion must ask, "what kind of society?" Is it small and homogeneous or large and diverse; is it isolated or in contact with other societies with different systems of value? Is it authoritarian in the distribution of power or based on democratic principles? Have religious specialists appeared who have developed an articulate system of beliefs, a tendency toward coherence and order in rite, and a specialized institution whose prestige and power they are eager to maintain and increase? This last can be a source, as well as a result, of religious and social change, for it can set in motion competition for the title of true interpreter or for control of the institutional structure. How far has the technical development of the society allowed it to bring hunger and disease under control? The great increase in the competence of the Western world to solve these difficulties has helped to create the idea that we can have "a brave, new world."

When man depends obviously and inescapably on forces outside himself, as he does in a primitive agricultural society, the Christian doctrine that pain and perplexity are sent by a loving Father at least makes sense. But when man begins to feel himself the master of his physical environment, and his awareness

[9] See Robert Redfield, *The Primitive World and Its Transformations*, pp. 63–83.

of a transcendent order becomes dim, then he begins to regard evil and suffering either as a technical problem (like the conquest of malaria) or as a political problem (like the defeat of the Communist Party).[10]

In the light of current religious trends, this statement requires qualification. The reduction of problems of hunger and ill-health does not mean that modern societies have reduced the sum of the difficulties with which men must deal. They may have aggravated the questions: Do I belong? Have I done right? Can I count on my neighbor? Many theologians regard human problems as perennial and inevitable, however they may seem to vary in their particular expression. In a day of intense international problems, one is inclined to agree with this view and to grant that there is a great deal of force to the critique that Reinhold Niebuhr and others make of "progressive" theories of history. This is not the kind of question which one can answer definitively, however, for who can say that the weight of basic difficulties is the same or heavier or lighter for modern man than for his predecessors? And even if the perennial nature of human problems be assumed, it does not necessarily follow (a) that Niebuhr's explanation of the cause—man's fundamental egoism, a kind of "original sin"—is a meaningful statement of the problem for a scientist, (b) that the differences in form that human problems take are unimportant for society or religion (man's struggle for "acceptance" may prove to have very different consequences from his struggle for bread), or (c) that his theological solution must be accepted. The scientist, obviously, cannot answer the last question at all, nor is he under any obligation to accept the theological consequences that Niebuhr believes flow from the original proposition. To the sociologist, it is sufficient to note that the ways in which religions empirically *do* struggle with individual and group problems, the ways, indeed, that they *may* struggle (not in a value sense, but in the sense of limits imposed by the social, cultural, and personality systems within which they work) in fact vary. An objective study of religion, therefore, must give careful attention to the variations.

RELIGIOUS DIFFERENTIATION AND SOCIAL DIFFERENTIATION

The significance of the way in which religion varies from one type of society to another can well be explored by describing the nature of the religious situation in highly differentiated societies. The wide variations

[10] K. S. Collier in *Religious Faith and World Culture*, A. W. Loos, editor, p. 25.

of belief and practice among various groups within a society, even among those who share the same basic religious tradition, is a leading clue to the need for a functional analysis. We now have a rich body of evidence that regional groups, classes, occupations, majority and minority groups, educational levels, persons of different ages, men and women, individuals of differing personality tendencies—to mention some of the ways in which a society may be divided—often show different religious inclinations and express themselves religiously in different ways. The analysis of only one of these divisions—classes, for example—is clearly inadequate, for in a multiple-variable situation, there is always the likelihood that the variables may offset each other to a greater or lesser degree. Persons of different class status may be religiously quite similar because of similar residence, educational level, and some shared personality needs. The fact that they are somewhat alike in their religious inclinations does not prove that class is unimportant, but only that it is one of several factors. The influence of the variables may, of course, be cumulative, with the result that religious differences become large: a well-educated, urban, white professional man can be sharply distinguished, in religious tendencies, from a Negro farmhand.

The degree to which religion is involved as a factor in the *reduction* of social differentiation is much less adequately explored. To some degree this problem is implicit in the question of the integrative function of religion; but a new factor is added here, because there can be integration in a highly differentiated society. That persons who are socially very different, but who share a basic religious tradition in common, may have some similar beliefs, worship together, and embrace some elements of a common moral code can be amply demonstrated. This observation, however, does not establish the power of religion to reduce social differentiation. Even a concept of "equality before God" may prosper in a very inequalitarian society (indeed, some would say, precisely in such a society). It is clear that the degree to which, and the processes through which, the sharing of religion reduces social differentiation requires much more careful attention than it has had until now. The related question, does religious differentiation, once established, reenforce the lines of the social divisions out of which it grew, is also inadequately answered. We know that when some of the social factors involved in a religious division have disappeared, there may be a reunion (as, for example, in American Methodism). But has the process by which the social differentiation was reduced been slowed down by the religious split? Might Methodists of similar class and occupation in the South and in the North be somewhat more alike (in politics and in attitudes toward race relations, for example) if they had shared the same religious communion in the century after 1844? That the Episcopalians, who were much less sharply split by the problem of slavery than were the Methodists, seem to be more unified today than the Methodists in their attitudes toward race relations gives us a hint—but only a hint—of the possible effects of religious division. (Class and educational differences between the two groups and the fact that a much higher proportion of Methodists were in the South are variables that prevent one from making any easy generalization.)

With regard to this same question, one might ask, Does the experience of being brought up in touch with a "lower-class" religious group give one values, levels of aspiration, motives, political and economic beliefs, etc. that tend to fix one in lower-class status? It was once thought that the sect-to-church transition disproved this; that, as John Wesley declared, the virtues that went along with sectarian religious fervor helped one to climb the class ladder; that piety led to riches. (Wesley was not at all certain that the reverse of this was true, and so regarded the situation as a serious dilemma.) The history of the Quakers in the United States is also often cited as evidence that religious differentiation does not fix the lines of class division. There is some evidence, however, on the other side. The transition from sect to church may be characteristic of the institutional structure only and may not be indicative of what is happening to the status of individual members. If churches become middle-class in values, doctrine, and ritual, lower-class members tend to drop out and to look for some other religious (or secular) expression more in keeping with their desires.[11]

Although the following discussion, and the material of the next several chapters, may throw some light on this question of the impact of religious differentiation on social differentiation, we shall be primarily concerned with the question posed in the opposite way: To what degree are the functions of religion revealed by the development of religious variation in socially heterogeneous societies?

THE CAUSES OF RELIGIOUS DIVISIONS

There is no reason to suppose that the breaking-up of a religious organization into various groups is *only* a result of social differences among its members. We shall see that wherever religious specialists are found their "intrinsically religious" elaboration of the questions with which they are professionally concerned can lead to differentiation in doctrine,

[11] See Liston Pope, *Millhands and Preachers.*

ritual, and institutional structure. This point needs to be made along with the refutation of the common assumption that religious differences are *wholly* an expression of disagreements over dogma or ritual. Religious professionals are themselves strongly conditioned, of course, by their status, their audiences, the secular problems and splits of their time. The ways in which their religious observations are received and used are even more strongly conditioned by such forces. We shall pay some attention, however, following Weber, Troeltsch, Wach, and others, to that aspect of their thought which can profitably be viewed as the internal development of a religious system.

The secular impact on the differentiation of religious-group structure will be more apparent under some circumstances than others. It is commonly observed, for example, that the proliferation of religious divisions is far more extensive under Protestantism than under Catholicism. This does not mean simply that Catholicism shapes the religious needs of its members into a common mold, although this may be partly true, but it shows also that the structure of the Church permits a vast range of different needs and interests to be satisfied within it. Protestantism, with its greater emphasis on individual religious experience (and its greater development in mobile and individualistic societies—we cannot here explore the causal problems involved), encouraged the development of different religious structures. Catholicism reflects the variations in religious needs *within* its pattern: There are Catholic trade unions and support for large estate owners; monasteries and church supported festivals and bingo games; Catholic sociology and magical relics. Where Protestant polity is dominant, the wide range of personal inclinations is far more likely to be reflected in the proliferation of separate religious structures.

Religious Divisions in Christendom.   Most of the studies of the relationship between social differentiation and religious differentiation have been concerned with Christianity. Variation in Hinduism, the several divisions of sectarian Shinto, contrasts between the crude peasant god Thor and Odin, the refined god of the nobility, the wide differences between the intellectualized beliefs of the upper classes of Ancient Greece and the mystery cults of the masses, the development of orthodox, conservative, and liberal branches of Judaism, etc., have all been explored. The most extensive work, however, has been done on the materials dealing with Christianity. Like all the major religions, primitive Christianity was capable of many diverse interpretations. In fact, its success in becoming the dominant religion of the Roman Empire was to an important degree based on the potentialities it had for being so many things to so many different kinds of people. This very diversity of appeal, however, made it vulnerable to schism, for as Christianity became more highly institutionalized, it began to give more weight to one emphasis rather than another, and thus encouraged the protest and perhaps the withdrawal of those who believed that the neglected aspect was the right one.

One well-known illustration of this tension concerns the relevance of Christianity for "social reform." It seems likely that a few of the immediate followers of Jesus looked upon him as a social reformer—or at least hoped that he would be—an emphasis that finds expression in Luke, as contrasted with the "spiritual" emphasis in Matthew. The dominant theme of the new religion, however, was certainly not social reform. The religious crisis which marked the close of the ancient world was part of the vast social crisis—the destruction of the *polis,* the extinction of freedom under the military and bureaucratic power of the Empire—in which, as Troeltsch shows, it had become clear that the social ideal of the Hebrew people was not to be realized by human thought and effort. The belief that the kingdom of God was to be of this world began to give way. This did not occur rapidly, nor was the process carried to completion in Christianity. Nevertheless, out of the centuries of frustrations and disappointments, culminating in the oppressions of Rome, religious thought lost much of its optimism concerning the possibilities of reordering the affairs of this world. The order established by the Roman Empire came to be accepted.

. . . henceforth the conduct of external affairs was left to the rulers, while men sought and cultivated individual and spiritual freedom. This applies to the later development of Platonism and Stoicism; it applies to countless new religious movements, and in particular it applies to the establishment of Christianity as well as to the preparation for it within Judaism.[12]

Yet the implications of Christianity for the life of this world were there; the continuing hopes of man for justice and happiness and success on earth were not smothered. Tied together in primitive Christianity, as Troeltsch observes, is a thoroughgoing religious asceticism and an ethical-prophetic strain. They are not easily distinguished in the teachings of Jesus and the other sources of Christianity which tended to view life monastically.[13] But followers could read into the teachings a reference to their own particular needs. Throughout the history of Christianity, one can see the emphasis, now on one, now on the other of these two themes. Hammond and Hammond describe the situation clearly:

[12] Ernst Troeltsch, *The Social Teaching of the Christian Churches,* p. 47.
[13] See Paul Tillich, *The Shaking of the Foundations,* pp. 24–28, on "The Paradox of the Beatitudes."

The devout Christian, confronted with the spectacle of wrong and injustice, may draw either of two contrary conclusions. In the eyes of his religion the miner or weaver is just as important as the landlord or the cotton lord. Clearly then, one will argue, it is the duty of a Christian State to prevent any class, however obscure and trivial its place in the world may seem to be, from sinking into degrading conditions of life. Every soul is immortal, and the consequences of ill-treatment and neglect in the brief day of its life on earth will be unending. If, therefore, society is so organised as to impose such conditions on any class, the Christian will demand the reform of its institutions. For such minds Christianity provides a standard by which to judge government, the industrial and economic order, the life of society, the way in which it distributes wealth and opportunities. This was the general standpoint of such a man as Shaftesbury. But some minds drew a different moral from the equality that Christianity teaches. Every human soul is a reality, but the important thing about a human soul is its final destiny, and that destiny does not depend on the circumstances of this life. The world has been created on a plan of apparent injustice by a Providence that combined infinite power with infinite compassion. The arrangements that seem so capricious are really the work of that Power. But the same Power has given to the men and women who seem to live in such bitter and degrading surroundings, an escape from its cares by the exercise of their spiritual faculties. It is those faculties that make all men equal. Here they stand, in Marcus Aurelius's phrase, for a brief space between the two eternities, and no misery or poverty can prevent a soul from winning happiness in the world to come. Thus whereas one man looking out on the chaos of the world calls for reform, the other calls for contemplation: one says, Who could tolerate such injustice? the other says, Who would not rejoice that there is another world? One says, Give these people the conditions of a decent life; the other says, Teach them to read the Bible.[14]

These two differing interpretations are, indeed, possible. Our concern is to ask, who will make the one and who the other? What are the circumstances that will cause the one to be emphasized and not the other? What organizational forms will the different expressions take? Our task, in other words, is to discover the social sources of religious differentiation.

The Sources of Schism. In a recent study of "schism in the early church," Greenslade discusses the causes of the splits that occurred frequently in the ranks of Christianity in the first few centuries. His research gives support to the thesis of Richard Niebuhr that variations in the ethics, polity, and theology among various denominations, have their roots

. . . in the relationship of the religious life to the cultural and political conditions prevailing in any group of Christians. . . . The exigencies of church discipline, the demands of the national psychology, the effect of social tradition, the influence of cultural heritage, and the weight of economic interest play their role in the definition of religious truth.[15]

[14] J. L. and Barbara Hammond, *The Town Labourer, 1760–1832*, pp. 223–224.
[15] H. Richard Niebuhr, *The Social Sources of Denominationalism*, pp. 16–17.

Greenslade gives somewhat more emphasis than does Niebuhr to the differences that develop as a result of personal conflicts among leaders; and he stresses the disputes that arise from the internal elaboration, by specialists, of the religious system. Both of these emphases can be related, in our judgment, to the personality factors of the leaders and to their social settings. It is useful, however, to see them on another level as well, for once set in motion, they become proximate causes of religious differentiation that it would be unwise to ignore.[16] Greenslade discusses five causes of schism in the early church, appropriately treating them as interactive and mutually reenforcing:

1. *Personal.* This category includes the pursuit of individual power, personal rancour, etc. Seldom were these the predominant cause of schism. (This influence may be seen today most clearly in the continual splitting up of the insecure cult movements of minority group members.)

2. *National, Social and Economic Influences.* This is the major emphasis of Richard Niebuhr's important work and will receive a great deal of documentation below.

3. *The Rivalry of Sees.* As a cause of schism, this is often difficult to distinguish from national and economic rivalries; but wherever separate ecclesiastical bureaucracies develop, the distinction is useful.

4. *Liturgical Disputes.* This category includes tensions between the opposing ideals of liturgical uniformity and freedom. Religious leaders, searching for the most effective ways of conveying their message, come to these different conclusions about liturgy. We may explain this on the basis of their differing social experiences and individual personality tendencies; but the possibility of this relationship should not be allowed to obscure the further meaning that the disputes are the result of internal elaborations of a religious system. Liturgical disputes are not, in Greenslade's use of the term, serious doctrinal quarrels, in which theological differences lie behind a schism. They are seldom, in his judgment, sufficiently powerful to be the single cause of schism, but may combine with more powerful causes and often perpetuate separation after it has occurred.

5. *Problems of Discipline and the Puritan Idea of the Church.* The

[16] Note the remark of Paul Hutchinson concerning the 1954 meeting of the World Council of Churches: "Evanston, we dare hope, could thus come to be remembered as the place where the World Council discovered how quickly the impulse to Christian unity in action could be sidetracked and reduced to impotence by a demand for prior theological agreement." *Christian Century,* September 22, 1954, p. 1125. Sociologists, who are often careful students of the internal forces in bureaucracies or of the patterns of control and development *within* an industrial plant or a university, sometimes fail to see the same processes at work in religious structures. Such developments are of no less interest to sociology than are external forces that shape the patterns of religious groups.

puritan spirit—with its emphasis on perfection and individual religious experience—has often caused men to break off from the main ecclesiastical group to set up a "congregation of saints." Reaction against the disciplines imposed by the hierarchy were a major source of such early schisms as Montanism, Novatianism, and Donatism. Intensification of the patristic doctrine of the church was, in turn, a response to these schisms.

. . , the tendency of Montanism was to repudiate the existing hierarchy altogether, and—by its emphasis on prophets under immediate inspiration—to deny the whole principle of order and authority which the bulk of the Church had welcomed, as well as the particular idea of apostolic succession which was at this time coming into prominence as the basis of episcopal authority.[17]

We must stress again that these causes are interactive and that they may be studied on different levels of analysis. For the sociologist of religion it is necessary to pursue farther than Greenslade does, particularly with reference to points four and five above, *why* some take this side in a liturgical dispute, some another, *who* defends most vigorously the need for church discipline and who the opposing doctrine of prophetic inspiration. Although these may partly be understood in terms of efforts to make a religious system as effective as possible, they must also be seen as manifestations of secular conflicts. Whenever the institutional and authoritarian elements in the church have become predominant and the validity of its claim to religious leadership and holiness has been held "not to rest upon the achieved saintliness of its members," schismatic protests have arisen. Rigid insistence on the authority of the established structure and the exclusive validity of its system of rites and beliefs weakens the ability of the religious organization to fulfill the functions of religion for the weak and powerless, because, as we shall see, the highly institutionalized structure becomes adjusted to the needs and interests of the dominant elements in society. The "disinherited" are not simply those who are cut off from the predominant religious institution by economic and political differences. They are also alienated by the differences in belief, in form of worship, and in moral emphasis that their different needs demand.

It is significant for a functional analysis that the protests of the early schismatics, as expressed for example in Donatism, have recurred again and again, in much the same terms, in the religious movements of the "disinherited."

[17] S. L. Greenslade, *Schism in the Early Church*, p. 110; for his discussion of the causes of schism, see pp. 37–124; see also G. R. Cragg, "Disunities Created by Differing Patterns of Church Life," *Ecumenical Review*, April, 1952, pp. 276–281; and Reinhold Niebuhr, *The Nature and Destiny of Man*, Vol. I, pp. 49–53.

They preferred enthusiastic movements of the spirit to humdrum official Christianity; they believed that the Holy Spirit can make His own ministers where he wills, apart from the authorised methods of the Church; they repudiated the ministrations of unworthy clergy; they held to the notion of the gathered congregation, the communion of saints, exercising a discipline which casts out the unworthy, and they believed that the Church can be infected by unworthy members to the point of corruption and death.[18]

For our purposes, these comments on the causes of schism can be brought into a larger system of concepts which summarize the causes of religious differentiation. These are highly interactive and often mutually reenforcing:

1. Variations in personal religious needs and interests, due to differences in basic personality tendencies, in the strength of feelings of frustration and guilt, in level of intellectual development, in capacity for certain kinds of religious experience, etc.

2. Variations in economic and political interests.

3. Nationality differences.

4. Social mobility and social change.

5. Differences that derive from the internal development of the religious system. Since we shall be concerned repeatedly in this essay with the first four points, we shall not discuss them here; but a brief explanation of this last point may be helpful. It is akin to Greenslade argument that liturgical disputes and disagreements over the desirable amount of religious "discipline" are sources of schism independent of what are usually called the "social sources." Certainly the elaboration of theological ideas, inventiveness in the field of ritual, and differences in judgment among religious leaders concerning the problems of continuity and authority can be productive of sharp cleavages among the "professionals." These are not sources of religious differences that are outside the interests of a sociology and social psychology of religion, for they too can be seen as the results of the interaction of social, cultural and personality factors. But it is well to remember that however caused, these variations become part of the cycle of interaction. It is not enough simply to reduce them to a supposed "original" cause.

Whether or not religious "inventions" lead to different religious groups is a question that leads us back to the other causes of schism, for this depends in part upon the way in which laymen react to the variations. These reactions are much more dependent upon the differences outlined in the first four points, above, upon the way in which new religious ideas and rites can be used to grapple with varying human needs, than upon

---

[18] Greenslade, op. cit., pp. 114–115.

some inevitable consequence of the new religious forces themselves. There is a level of analysis on which it is appropriate to study religious innovations as starting points of a series of events. The degree of acceptance of those innovations, however, and the direction of their spread, is vitally dependent on the needs and desires of potential "audiences." In Weber's term, there is an "elective affinity" between certain religious ideas and the social circumstances of particular groups. Complete analysis must pay attention, not only to the fact that a given group accepted a stated religious innovation—as if it forced itself upon them independently, without connection with their inclinations—but must seek to discover the functions which they believed the religious idea served.

The Dilemma of Religious Leaders as a Source of Religious Differentiation. Another aspect of this question of the importance of internal religious development requires some attention. A religion almost inevitably requires many actions of its adherents that they would not perform without the religious motivation. These actions would have no meaning in the context of purely egocentric, or economic, or hedonistic criteria. Certain ascetic restraints, taboos, self-torture, sacrifice, etc., can be understood only with relation to religiously motivated desires. They are tied, in the religious system, to the supposed achievement of the ultimate satisfactions, to the accomplishment of the greatest values, and thus are accepted or even enthusiastically espoused. To the non-believer of a given religion, however, many of these acts may seem "irrational," "immoral," and "unpleasurable," as well as irreligious. Many modern Christians are revolted by the human sacrifices of the Aztecs, annoyed by the caste taboos of the Hindus, unconvinced that any value can come from eternal vows of chastity. They are baffled by the large-scale destruction of economic goods that is religiously prescribed in some societies; they cannot understand the devaluing of this life that is common in many religions. Yet these actions seem, or have seemed, absolutely essential to those who looked at them from the perspective of the believer.

Now we must ask: What happens when doubts begin to arise, when the efficacy of the religious restraints and sacrifices to achieve supposed higher values is brought into question, when the egocentric tendencies of man—never far away—begin to push for immediate satisfaction? Suppose that social change sets in motion various forces that undermine faith in the religious system, increase the desire for the satisfaction of immediate interests and needs, make the rewards of religion seem uncertain, less important, and distant. Then those who still believe intensively in the religious system as the road to the supreme values, and are eager for others also to believe, are confronted with a difficult dilemma. If these religious leaders, as we may call them (those in whom the religious interest is high and who are concerned about its meaning for others), demand too close allegiance to those aspects of the religious ideal that require the sacrifice of other values that have come into importance or reasserted themselves, they run the risk of being persecuted or neglected. On the other hand, if they do not insist on close allegiance to the religious values, if they compromise drastically with the secular interests, they also promote the neglect of the religious values.

Variation in how religious movements and leaders respond to this dilemma is one of the important sources of religious differentiation. Responses vary according to many factors: the nature of a particular religious tradition, the personality tendencies and needs of the leadership, the strength and nature of the secular values of the persons to whom the religion appeals, or is attempting to appeal. Interacting with the other causes of religious divisions that we have listed, they produce the various types of religious organizations that we shall discuss below. Some react to this conflict between the demands of the religious ideal and the claims of secular interests by making strong concessions to the latter. This we shall call the church-type reaction. It is supported by strong secular interests; but on our present level of analysis, it can be seen in part as the result of a religiously motivated "strategic" decision: Not to compromise is to alienate completely the people whom we hope to win or hold, says the churchman; to fail to recognize the impervious quality of man's secular interests is not to conquer them, but to be defeated by them. By accepting what in any event has to be accepted (war or slavery, or great inequalities of station, for example) we can remain in a position of influence where we can gradually undermine their causes. Not so, says the sectarian. Compromise is a one-way street down which the church moves, concession after concession, until it finally has arrived at the place where the secular values are completely dominant. The only solution is to maintain the purity of the religious system of values in an uncompromised community of believers, hoping it may become a beacon to the wayward.

Thus a religious strategic decision may promote differences in religious group structure. This cause, however, is never found in isolation from the other causes of religious differentiation. Since efforts to achieve the values of a religion require some kind of power over often recalcitrant human beings, organizations are developed. These organizations take on compulsions of their own, relative to their own order, control, and continuation, which are irrelevant to the religious quest. Moreover, other secular interests "invade" the religious organization, using it to support

their claims for national independence or imperial dominance, land reform or preservation of slavery, legitimization of their complaints against
society or legitimization of their right to rule. Faced with these secular
interests, which cannot simply be dismissed or overcome, the religious
leader makes the religious strategic decision, with varying consequences
for the relationship of his group to "the world." Those in whom the
secular interests are dominant may support him and his group, but as the
result of asking a different question: What religious approach makes my
view of the world, my claims and complaints, seem legitimate and right?
The question is seldom if ever asked as baldly as that, of course; it is
simply a matter of feeling the "rightness" of an approach that does justice
to one's own view. A church that accepts the basic structure of a society,
that has compromised with the secular powers, is likely to be the group
that is supported by those who have fared relatively well in the distribution of goods and power in their society. They are likely to believe that
the compromises are in any event not crucial, since they believe that there
is nothing *basically* evil about a society that has treated them so well.
There are, of course, important exceptions to this, for the needs of men
are diverse, and the need to maintain power and station may be relatively
unimportant for some. A sect that is based on a conviction that there are
basic evils in society with which one must not compromise, is most likely
to be supported by the least privileged groups. An arrangement that
treats them so poorly is clearly not one with which their most exalted
aims can compromise; consequently they oppose or withdraw from "the
world." They support the religious leader who holds that the religious
idea can be maintained only in freedom from the impact of the secular
powers, in a "pure" religious community of believers. Thus the various
causes of "schism" interpenetrate.

TYPES OF RELIGIOUS ORGANIZATIONS

One of the effects of the variations in religious interests and needs
among the members of a differentiated society is the development of
different religious group structures. These vary widely, but a number of
attempts to classify them have proved helpful in the study of the relationship between society and religion. Classifications are arbitrary, of course;
they "oversimplify" the data by disregarding what are held to be minor
differences in order to emphasize what are thought to be major similarities; they are constructs in the student's mind, not descriptions of total
"reality." Classifications are specialized instruments, appropriate only to
a particular task. If one tries to use them for a different purpose, he will

find the schemes wholly inadequate. Illnesses, for example, might be classified according to the length of time they persisted and the financial costs of treatment, if one were studying the economic consequences of ill-health. Such a scheme would be virtually useless, however, if one were concerned with the causes of sickness.

Our system of classification of religious groups is an effort to describe typical relationships between religion and society. It will cut across the lines of division that other typologies would make, on the basis, for example, of kinds of aesthetic activities or extent of supernaturalism. It will be completely inappropriate for classifications based on valuational criteria. In the discussion that follows we shall build on and extend the analysis of the causes of religious differentiation given above and relate the variations in religious structure to the question of the functions of religion.

Virtually all attempts to develop a typology of religious groups have been concerned with Christian materials; their applicability to other religions has yet to be tested adequately. Most of the classifications start from the basic distinction, first fully developed by Ernst Troeltsch, between the "church" and the "sect," a distinction derived from an early one between "priest" and "prophet," but used with more methodological sophistication and with reference primarily to group structure, not to leadership. The development of this instrument of analysis inevitably gives emphasis to the differences between church and sect, minimizing the similarities that all of the religious organizations within a particular socio-cultural system share in common. The Jehovah's Witnesses and the Catholic Church, for example, appear to be very different when they are viewed from close range. On the basis of a wide culturally comparative study, however, their many similarities become apparent. Murray makes this point with regard to a temporal comparison:

Take three orthodox Christians, enlightened according to the standards of their time, in the fourth, the sixteenth, and the twentieth centuries respectively, I think you will find more profound differences of religion between them than between a Methodist, a Catholic, a Freethinker, and even perhaps a well-educated Buddhist or Brahmin at the present day, provided you take the most generally enlightened representatives of each class.[19]

In constructing our typology, we will do well to keep clearly in mind that it represents a deliberate stress on distinctions, in order to highlight various functions of religious groups.

The two-fold scheme of classification developed by Troeltsch has

[19] Gilbert Murray, *Five Stages of Greek Religion*, p. 212.

proved to be a very useful concept, but it suffers from two primary weaknesses, which later discussions have attempted to reduce: It is difficult, in any dichotomous typology, to give an adequate picture of the full range of the data. The empirical world is filled with many mixtures and variations of degree which a system of classification must try to describe. If "church" and "sect" are designated as end points on a continuum, the description of intermediate positions can prevent misunderstanding. By the addition of the concept of "mysticism," Troeltsch broadened the typology, but this served to point up the second difficulty in his classification: the failure to give an adequate discussion of the conditions under which the various types of religious organizations were most likely to occur. He notes that they all stem from fundamental Christian ideas and describes their relationship to social crises and historical movements; but he is more concerned with their variations as religious systems than in specifying sharply the social and personality factors involved in the various religious-group types.

The Church.   Keeping these difficulties in mind, we may profitably describe the church and the sect in Troeltsch's terms, relate them to our theory of religion, and then see what extensions may give a more adequate picture of the range of types of religious groups. The church as a type is a religious body which recognizes the strength of the secular world and, rather than either deserting the attempt to influence it or losing its position by contradicting the secular powers directly, accepts the main elements in the social structure as proximate goods. (As we shall see, some churches have defended an existing power arrangement not simply as a proximate good, but almost as though it were an absolute good.) It is built therefore on compromise; it is mobile and adaptive; "it dominates the world and is therefore dominated by the world." An individual is born into the church, which claims universality, in contrast with the voluntary membership of a select group in the sect. The church supports the existing powers in peace and war. It ". . . utilizes the State and the ruling classes, and weaves these elements into her own life; she then becomes an integral part of the existing social order; from this standpoint, then, the Church both stabilizes and determines the social order; in so doing, however, she becomes dependent upon the upper classes, and upon their development." [20]

The emphasis of the church is on sacrament and creed, while that of the sect is on "right" behavior. Of the two primary functions of religion that we have discussed, the one stressed by the church is the effort to insure social cohesion and order. The church must thus strive to be co-

[20] Troeltsch, *op. cit.*, p. 331.

extensive with society, to bring everyone within its "means of grace." To do this, however, requires a willingness to compromise with the wide ranges of behavior that may be found in a society. "The moral demands are relaxed because salvation depends not upon ethical achievement but upon the reception of the sacraments and acquiescence in the creeds. . . . Discipline tends to be moderate and the ban may be more readily used to exclude those who question the faith than those who fail to realize the ethical standards." [21]

This "function-dysfunction" of social integration is likely to be latent in the church, for its manifest intentions are more likely to be the assurance of individual salvation. The fact that the support to "social order" is latent, however, makes it no less real or powerful. It creates the continuing possibility—indeed likelihood—that a religious system in which the church-type organization is predominate will serve to reenforce the power situation of the dominant classes of a society. In the logical extreme, the church-type lends itself to the support of an authoritarian pattern of order. This is the product of the compromises forced on a church when it tries to organize the whole of society.

A church, thus defined, is almost impossible in a mobile and heterogeneous society, particularly one based on democratic values. It can be thought of as a limiting case which actual situations more or less closely approximate. More empirically possible churchlike types will be described in our elaboration of this typology below.

The Sect. Astute religious leaders are aware of the possibility of capitulation to secular powers, of course; they realize the dilemma we have discussed above, and seek to reduce its sharpness by incorporating within the religious pattern some attention to the needs of the individual. But if some of these needs are—or are thought to be—a product of the very society which the religious system also supports, they are unlikely to be successful with those who feel those needs most strongly. When, due to compromises with the secular powers, rigidity of ecclesiastical structure, the failure of doctrine and ritual to change as prevailing personality inclinations change (what are appealing symbols to one generation may lack meaning to another), when, that is, the religious system loses some of its ability to satisfy various individual and group needs, it promotes sectarian developments.

As we shall see, the kinds of needs with which sectarian movements are related vary widely, as do the types of ways in which the needs are served. Our attention was first drawn to the sectarian movements of the

[21] Roland H. Bainton, "The Sectarian Theory of the Church," *Christendom*, Summer, 1946, p. 382.

lower classes—protests against the failures of the church to satisfy them emotionally, to give them a sense of dignity, to challenge those aspects of society which the sectarians felt were unjust and sinful. Thus they rejected the church and frequently the society they identified with it. This is the primary emphasis in Troeltsch's discussion of the sect. It is a group that repudiates the compromises of the church, preferring "isolation to compromise"; in the Christian tradition it stresses literal obedience to the Synoptic Gospels. There is a small, voluntary membership, stressing individual perfection and asceticism, usually associated with the lower classes.[22] It is either hostile or indifferent to the state, and opposes the ecclesiastical order. The sect is lay religion, free from worldly authority, able therefore on one hand to forget the world in asceticism, or on the other to fight it in radicalism. Troeltsch thus lists its traits:

. . . lay Christianity, personal achievement in ethics and in religion, the radical fellowship of love, religious equality and brotherly love, indifference toward the authority of the State and the ruling classes, dislike of technical law and of the oath, the separation of the religious life from the economic struggle by means of the ideal of poverty and frugality . . . , the directness of the personal religious relationship, criticism of official spiritual guides and theologians, the appeal to the New Testament and the Primitive Church.[23]

We shall broaden the meaning of the term sect somewhat to refer to any religious protest against a system in which attention to the various individual functions of religion has been obscured and made ineffective by the extreme emphasis on social and ecclesiastical order. This emphasis often takes the form of primary attention to rite and dogma, with strong latent implications for the question of order. There can be no doubt that the need for some adjustment to the problems of poverty and powerlessness (age-old problems in every religion) should be given, as Troeltsch gives them, primary attention. This analysis does not explain, however, such middle and upper class developments as Christian Science or the Oxford Group Movement, religious groups that represent protests against the failure of established churches to deal successfully with feelings of inadequacy, confusion, ennui, pain, and guilt. If these are included in the same concept, we may define a sect as a movement in which the primary emphasis is the attempt to satisfy, by religious means, various basic individual needs. It is usually seen as a revolt against a religious system in which these needs have been inadequately dealt with. *What* these needs are will vary from group to group. *How* they are treated in the

    [22] See Russell R. Dynes, "Church-Sect Typology and Socio-Economic Status," *American Sociological Review*, October, 1955, pp. 555–560.
    [23] Troeltsch, *op. cit.*, p. 336.

sect will also vary, creating the necessity for sub-classifying sectarian movements into types.

In the logical extreme, the sect emphasis on religious beliefs and practices that are efforts to deal with individual needs—with a minimum attention to the function of social integration—leads to anarchy. The sectarian associates order with the disliked order of the church and society in which he feels his needs are smothered. This may lead to the avoidance of any political claims over him, the rejection of some of the moral standards of the society (note the various experiments, of extreme sectarians, with new patterns of sexual morals or forms of marriage), and the repudiation of other aspects of the supposed wicked society—learning and art, for example. Seldom is this potentiality for anarchy carried to the extreme, but the tendencies are there, just as the tendencies for authoritarian rigidity are present in the church.

The sect cannot, however, avoid the problem of order. The problem begins immediately to reassert itself even in the isolated communities into which the sectarians sometimes withdraw. Moreover, the needs of the members may change—their socio-economic level may improve, for example. The leadership tends to become established and to look for ways of assuring continuity of power. With the coming of a second generation, the problem of voluntary membership becomes acute, for parents are not willing or able to postpone the training of their children. Thus the sect moves back toward the church.[24] In mobile societies, where problems of order and the nature of human needs are undergoing continuous change, the dialectic between church and sect seems likely to continue. Even the syntheses of a St. Thomas and a Calvin were highly unstable, and there have been no approximations to a synthesis in the last three centuries. It may be that like the proverbial lament of man (I cannot live with her and I cannot live without her), the church cannot live with the sect, in a mobile society, but cannot live without it either. This need not be a lament, however, for, if the author may insert a value judgment, it may be that in the effort to maintain a moving equilibrium between the two emphases, man finds one of his greatest challenges.

Refinements of the Typology. Although the church-sect dichotomy can be a highly informative concept, it is not adequate to describe the full range of the data. On the basis of two criteria—the degree of inclusiveness of the members of a society and the degree of attention to the function of social integration as contrasted with the function of per-

[24] See Walter G. Muelder, "From Sect to Church," *Christendom*, Autumn, 1945, pp. 450–462; H. Richard Niebuhr, *op. cit.*, pp. 19–21 and throughout; Liston Pope, *Millhands and Preachers*; and J. Milton Yinger, *Religion in the Struggle for Power*, pp. 31–34.

sonal need—a six-step classification can be described that may prove to be helpful.

1. The Universal Church. This is a religious structure that is relatively successful in supporting the integration of a society, while at the same time satisfying, by its pattern of beliefs and observances, many of the personality needs of individuals on all levels of the society. It combines both church and sect tendencies in a systematic and effective way. It is thus universal both in the sense that it includes all the members of a society and in the fact that the two major functions of religion are closely interrelated. In heterogeneous societies, this balance is likely to be achieved only very rarely and is not likely to be maintained very long: the lack of flexibility of the system itself, the insistent demands of the ruling groups that the order favorable to them be maintained without the adjustments that are inevitable in a changing society, the variations in personality needs—these all lead to the "tendency toward schism" so common in the religions of complex societies. The Catholic Church of the thirteenth century is perhaps the best illustration of a universal church in Western civilization. It was relatively successful in finding a place (primarily the monasteries) for the individualizing tendencies in Christianity, its system of beliefs and rites was satisfactory to large numbers of people on all levels, and it reflected and helped to maintain a fairly well-integrated social structure. Even the most thoroughly universal church, however, can be described only as relatively capable of fulfilling these various functions, for the intense problem of order, the continuing intrusions of man's selfish tendencies, the pervasiveness of the problems of suffering are not difficulties easily to be solved.

One needs to be aware, moreover, of the continuing possibility of dysfunctions. In this regard it is perhaps well to indicate again that a judgment concerning the church's ability to maintain itself as a "moving equilibrium" and to hold the allegiance of most of the members of a society is not at the same time a value judgment—a distinction that is difficult to maintain in functional analysis.

2. The Ecclesia. We have borrowed here a term from Howard Becker's adaptation of the systematic work of Wiese. Like the universal church, the ecclesia reaches out to the boundaries of the society; formal identification with the group is found on all levels of society. But the ecclesia is less successful than the universal church in incorporating the sect tendencies. It has become so well adjusted to the dominant elements that the needs of many of its adherents, particularly from the lower classes, are frustrated. It is more successful in reenforcing the existing pattern of social integration than in fulfilling the many personality functions of religion.

There tend, therefore, to be widespread indifference, sectarian protests, and secular opposition. The ecclesia, as we are using the term, might be called a universal church in a state of rigidification. Established national churches tend toward the ecclesiastical type, although they vary widely in the degree to which they incorporate sectarian elements. (Compare the contemporary state churches in the Scandinavian countries, which are in the direction of the universal type, with the Russian Orthodox Church of 1915, which, when confronted with both religious and secular "schism" only embraced the established order the more closely. This suggests again the close relationship between type of religion and type of society.) Becker describes the ecclesia in these terms:

The social structure known as the ecclesia is a predominantly conservative body, not in open conflict with the secular aspects of social life, and professedly universal in its aims. . . . The fully developed ecclesia attempts to amalgamate with the state and the dominant classes, and strives to exercise control over every person in the population. Members are *born into* the ecclesia; they do not have to *join* it. It is therefore a social structure somewhat akin to the nation or the state, and is in no sense elective. . . . The ecclesia naturally attaches a high importance to the means of grace which it administers, to the system of doctrine which it has formulated, and to the official administration of sacraments and teaching by official clergy. . . . The ecclesia as an inclusive social structure is closely allied with national and economic interests; as a plurality pattern its very nature commits it to adjustment of its ethics to the ethics of the secular world; it must represent the morality of the respectable majority.[25]

3. The Class Church or Denomination. This religious-group type is still less successful in achieving universality than the ecclesia, because it not only minimizes the sectarian tendency to criticize or withdraw from the social order, but it is also limited by class, racial, and sometimes regional boundaries. It may still be called a church, because it is in substantial—not perfect—harmony with the secular power structure. Few churches are of a "pure" type—there are sectarian elements in all of them and all class levels tend to be represented in their membership (although unequally, and to a lesser degree in positions of leadership). This is partly due to the fact that many denominations started out as sects and have not completely escaped their origins. One must also note the range within this type, in American society, for example, from Congregational-

---

[25] Leopold von Wiese, *Systematic Sociology*, adapted and amplified by Howard Becker, pp. 624–625; see pp. 624–628 of this work for a four-fold classification scheme; see also Harold W. Pfautz, "The Sociology of Secularization: Religious Groups," *American Journal of Sociology*, September, 1955, pp. 121–128, for a five-class typology based on the degree of secularization.

ism, with fairly persistent sectarian tendencies, to Lutheranism, which is more thoroughly accommodated to the secular powers. In general, however, the denomination is conventional and respectable; it has gone rather far along the road of compromise. This is partly due to the fact that in a society of religious divisions, in contrast with the relative unity of the Middle Ages, the sect elements are much more likely to form their own institutions, instead of being incorporated into a universal church. Even during the Middle Ages, of course, sectarian and theological protests signified the pressures toward religious diversity.

4. *The Established Sect.* The next three types ought, perhaps, to be read in reverse order, for the established sect is an outgrowth of types five and six. They are written in this order to maintain the continuum relative to the two criteria, the degree of universality and degree of emphasis on social integration as compared with personal needs, that we indicated above. The small, uncompromising religious groups that we have described as sects are, by their very nature, unstable. Either the group disintegrates when the members die, or it has been molded into a more formal structure with techniques for admitting new members and preserving their common interests. Professional leaders emerge, because the intense enthusiasm of the first generation which sustained the lay character of the movement tends to decline. The needs of "birthright" members are frequently different and their class status may be improved. Direct challenge or opposition to the social order subsides. Nevertheless, the full transition into a class or national church may not take place. Certainly one cannot fully equate Methodism and Quakerism today, although both started out as sectarian protests and both have changed a great deal through the generations. Methodism has evolved into a denomination, as we have defined it, while Quakerism has developed into an established sect. An adequate theory must account for the difference. It does not seem that differences in status improvement can explain the contrast, because both Methodists and Quakers moved up the class ladder. Quakers were much more vigorously opposed and persecuted, developing in them a stronger feeling of isolation and more intense group morale. But this, in part, is only a proximate cause: Why were they more strongly persecuted? This seems to lead back to the nature of the sect in terms of its original protests. Those sects will tend to develop into denominations which, in the first instance, emphasized problems of individual anxiety and sin, those that are primarily efforts to reduce burdens of confusion and guilt. Middle class sectarian developments usually fall into this group. They develop rather quickly into denominations. On the other hand, sects will tend to develop into estab-

lished sects whose original concern was predominantly with the evils of society. Such groups make demands for social justice and reform, as did the Anabaptists and Levellers and to a lesser degree the Quakers; or they withdraw from the society by refusing certain obligations or by establishing isolated communities. The contrast between the two types of sects is well described by Richard Niebuhr:

. . . Methodism was far removed in its moral temper from the churches of the disinherited in the sixteenth and seventeenth century. Briefly, the difference lay in the substitution of individual ethics and philanthropism for social ethics and millenarianism . . . . the Methodist movement remained throughout its history in the control of men who had been born and bred in the middle class and who were impressed not so much by the social evils from which the poor suffered as by the vices to which they had succumbed.[26]

Niebuhr suggests that leaderships is an important variable in setting the direction of a movement. One must add to that the process of selectivity that takes place in membership of different sects, as a result of varying emphases. Individuals who believe that the reform of the evils of a society are the primary problems will be drawn into the ethical-protest sects. Those who feel most strongly the burden of individual doubt and suffering will be drawn into sects that emphasize individual regeneration. This selectivity will, in turn, condition the development of doctrine.

Actual religious organizations seldom correspond precisely to the types we are defining, but the type pictures should make comparison more accurate. Certainly there are many denominational elements in contemporary Quakerism: its opposition to the state has strongly subsided, professional leadership is common among some branches, most members have been "born into" the group. Methodism is also a mixed case, as it has been from the beginning, for, despite the middle-class and educated status of its top leaders, it was predominantly a lower-class movement with substantial lay leadership. Sectarian elements remain: pacifism among a small, but significant, minority; and a persistent interest in social reform. Yet the two must still be differentiated in terms of the degree of their accommodation to the secular world.

A sharper contrast can be drawn between a strictly middle class sect that rapidly became a denomination and a sectarian movement that was even more pessimistic than the Quakers in their view of the world, that, even after three centuries, has not developed into a denomination. We refer to Christian Science on the one hand and the Mennonites,

[26] *Op. cit.*, pp. 65–67.

an outgrowth of the Anabaptists, on the other. The difficulties which are expressed in the emergence of a middle class sect are not primarily economic hardship or a sense of injustice in the secular world. They are more likely to be a feeling of inadequacy, confusion of standards in a highly mobile world, guilt, and physical pain. A religious movement that attempts to meet these difficulties has no need to make a sharp challenge to the society and the established churches; the pendulum swing away from them is much shorter and the return much quicker. This kind of sect represents a protest against the lack of attention to these needs in the churches; but since the churches can begin to pay more attention to these needs without raising any serious questions about the structure of society, without any need for a basic reorganization of their views of the world, they can quickly absorb these new emphases from the sect. Thus churches "steal the thunder" of such sects very easily. This is part of the meaning of the development of "pastoral psychology," of attention to "peace of soul," of advice on "confident living." This too is christian science if not Christian Science. The sect, in its turn, goes through the familiar process of institutionalization. We may say, then, that a sect will become a denomination instead of an established sect if the protest it represents can readily be absorbed into the dominant religious stream without a serious challenge to the secular social structure and without the necessity for a reorganization of the religious pattern.

The challenge of the Anabaptists was sharp: the society which makes us suffer and the churches which sanctify it are evil. Bear no arms, swear no oaths, accept the religious fellowship only of those who have proved themselves. Such doctrines set a group on a different road from that traveled by the less uncompromising sects. Once set in motion, these influences may resist for many generations the disintegrating effects of improved economic status, mobility, persecution, and education.

5. *The Sect.* After this lengthy discussion of the established sect as a type and some of the processes by which it emerges, we need say little more about the sect. It can be described substantially in Troeltsch's terms, given in the basic dichotomy with which we started. We need only make more explicit the sub-divisions of this type that result from the differences in need from which they spring and the differences in response. This can be done in terms of the three possible responses to an undesired situation: One can accept it, one can aggressively oppose it, or one can seek ways to avoid it. All three of these responses are usually found in a sect movement, but one is likely to predominate.

A. ACCEPTANCE. Middle class sects are likely to accept the social pattern without much challenge. Although the members feel confronted with serious problems which the dominant churches are not helping them to solve, they do not interpret these in social terms. Society, on the whole, has been good to them and those with whom they associate. The key difficulties, they believe, are lack of faith, selfishness, and isolation, not an evil society. Therefore, have faith, show the hand of friendship, come together in a congenial group. The Oxford Group Movement illustrates this type of sect.

B. AGGRESSION. As we have seen, some lower-class sects express most strongly the problems of poverty and powerlessness. In Christianity, they interpret the teachings of Jesus in radical-ethical terms: His was a program of social reform. Society which treats us so badly is evil and true religion, therefore, must reorganize the social order. Such a group runs into strong opposition and, it would seem, pretty certain failure. It is likely, as a result, to disappear or to be transformed into type C. Again we may cite the Anabaptists as illustrative of this type.

C. AVOIDANCE. If one cannot accept society with type A or have hope of reforming it with type B, one can devalue the significance of this life, project one's hopes into the supernatural world, and meanwhile reduce one's problems by forming into a communion of like-minded fellows. This is the most common sectarian protest, particularly in the contemporary world where aggressive protests are more likely to be secular than religious in nature. It faces the hard facts of life for the lower classes, as the first type does not (poverty and suffering and injustice and powerlessness are persistent); it cannot so easily be broken by failure as can the second type, for who can prove, to those who believe, that another life will not redress the ills of this world; it grows easily out of the church which, for all its failure to adjust to new problems as they emerge, has never been able to disregard the problem of evil. The avoidance reaction is similar to what Elmer Clark calls the pessimistic or adventist sects. They have reached a final despair of satisfying their needs in society.

They see no good in the world and no hope of improvement, it is rushing speedily to hell, according to the will and plan of God. The adherents of such sects magnify millenarianism and see the imminent end of the present world-order by means of a cosmic catastrophe. They have turned on the world, and they seek escape through a cataclysm which will cast down those who have been elevated, and secure to the faithful important places in a new temporal kingdom as well as eternal bliss in heaven.[27]

This type of sect, like the first, is more likely to develop into a denomination than into an established sect, for it is less in conflict with society

[27] Elmer T. Clark, *The Small Sects in America*, p. 22.

than indifferent to it, so that accommodation to its major patterns is fairly easy. The various "holiness" groups in the United States represent the "avoidance" response. We shall explore some of their functions in our discussion of "class and religion" in the next chapter.

There are, of course, other ways to classify sects.[28] Clark, whom we have cited above, divides the small sects of America into seven classes, primarily on the basis of cultural differences—variations in beliefs, rituals, taboos, etc.—although some functional elements intrude into his principle of classification. Important questions concerning cultural systems and personality systems arise from his typology. Persons with what kinds of tendencies, in what kinds of cultural contexts will, for example, build their religious adjustment primarily out of the belief in the second-coming of Christ as compared with those who are primarily concerned with trances, visions, "speaking with tongues," and the "spirit of prophecy" (the charismatic or pentecostal sects, in Clark's terminology)? To whom is perfectionism likely to appeal as the right way to meet the problems of human existence? There has as yet been little study to help us answer questions of this kind, so that "cultural" classifications have been largely on the descriptive level. For our purposes, the adventist, pentecostal, and to a lesser degree the perfectionist sects can be classified together as "avoidance" groups, and their varying beliefs and practices can be understood in terms of a common function— to struggle with life's problems by transforming the meaning of life, by substituting "religious status for social status," in Liston Pope's meaningful phrase.

6. *The Cult*. The term cult is used in many different ways, usually with the connotations of small size, search for a mystical experience, lack of an organizational structure, and presence of a charismatic leader. Some of these criteria (mysticism, for example) emphasize cultural characteristics that are inappropriate in our classification scheme; yet there seems to be the need for a term that will describe groups that are similar to sects, but represent a sharper break, in religious terms, from the dominant religious tradition of a society. By a cult, therefore, we will mean a group that is at the farthest extreme from the "universal church" with which we started. It is small, short-lived, often local, frequently built around a dominant leader (as compared with the greater tendency toward widespread lay participation in the sect). Both because its beliefs and rites deviate quite widely from those that are traditional in a society (there is less of a tendency to appeal to

---

[28] See *ibid.* and Reinhold Neibuhr, *The Nature and Destiny of Man*, Vol. II, pp. 169–180.

"primitive Christianity," for example) and because the problems of succession following the death of a charismatic leader are often difficult, the cult tends to be small, to break up easily, and is relatively unlikely to develop into an established sect or a denomination. The cult is concerned almost wholly with problems of the individual, with little regard for questions of social order; the implications for anarchy are even stronger than in the case of the sect, which is led by its interest in "right behavior" (whether the avoidance of individual sin or the establishment of social justice) back to the problem of social integration. The cults are religious "mutants," extreme variations on the dominant themes by means of which men try to solve their problems. Pure type cults are not common in Western society; most groups that might be called cults are fairly close to the sect type. Perhaps the best examples are the various Spiritualist groups and some of the "Moslem" groups among American Negroes.

CHAPTER 7

Religion and Social Status

With the concepts and typology of Chapter 6 in mind, we can explore some of the ways in which the divisions of a society are reflected in and interact with its religious system. We shall be more concerned in this discussion with empirical materials, in order to test the usefulness of the theoretical approach outlined in the preceding chapters. The number of ways in which a society may be divided, in ways relevant to differences in religious behavior, is very large. Men and women, persons of different ages, those with varying amounts of education, individuals of different family backgrounds in terms of consequences for "basic character structure"—these and other lines of demarcation might profitably be studied. Because we have too little reliable evidence on some of these questions, however, and because some of them can be at least partially explored under other topics, we shall give our attention to other lines of division. There has been a great deal of research on the relationship between lines of religious divisions, on the one hand, and class, occupational, and racial divisions, on the other. These three topics are closely allied. They are indicative not simply of social differentiation, but of that kind of differentiation that implies ranking into higher and lower, i.e., social stratification. This particular kind of differentiation is

156

vitally involved in the religious systems of complex societies and must, therefore, receive careful attention from the sociologist of religion.

We need not be concerned here with general theoretical questions concerning social stratification—whether this is a universal social phenomenon, why societies are stratified, the consequences for non-religious aspects of a society, factors that make for mobility or rigidity in a stratification system, and the like. These are extremely important questions; but for our purposes we may take stratification as a given fact, and ask: How does religious behavior vary among the different strata of a society? If the functional approach to religion is useful, it should guide us in the study of the ways in which differences in personal needs, on different levels of society, are manifest in religion. It should help us explore the ways in which efforts at sub-group integration, as contrasted with societal integration, employ religious themes. We shall have to inquire to what degree this is dysfunctional for the integration of the whole society.

RELIGION AND CLASS

There is a great deal of overlapping in the categories of class, occupation, and race, so that to discuss the relation of one of them to religion is to suggest relevant material for the others. We shall not discuss occupation separately, but shall make reference to its interaction with religion in our examination of class influences. Every aspect of religion can vary from class to class: beliefs, rites, aesthetic expressions of religious emotion, the structure and leadership of the religious organizations, and every other phase of the process of "being religious," may be very different in one class from another. One must be careful to avoid easy hypotheses to explain the details of these differences. Propositions that the beliefs of the upper classes are more "rational" or the rites of the underprivileged more austere may seem "obvious," but the evidence is not all in their favor. Wach points out that Puritan motives may restrain the ritual of aristocratic groups and lower classes may insist on "as lavish a service to the deity as they can possibly afford." [1] This does not demonstrate a lack of variation in religious behavior according to class, but only that the variation requires careful study, for the relationship is complicated and other lines of division may obscure its effects. If a functional analysis is fruitful, it will certainly point up the ways in which differences in needs, variations in life style and experiences, different development of facility with language and other modes of ex-

[1] Joachim Wach, *Sociology of Religion*, pp. 234–235.

pression, variation in claims and requirements—all of which vary from class to class and among other social divisions—manifest themselves in religious behavior.

Max Weber has shown how the religious meaning of suffering and of salvation has varied from class to class. Nietzsche had developed a kind of class-determined theory of religion in his doctrine of "resentment": Religion is an expression of the repressed resentments of the powerless; it is their attempt to enchain their masters by symbolic means in face of the failures of other methods to break their control. Weber declares, however, that it is not primarily resentment, but suffering, with which religion has dealt, and goes beyond Nietzsche to show the differences in the meaning of suffering. On the one hand there is the "theodicy of good fortune," which justifies the well-placed in their fortune by treating suffering as a sign of odiousness in the eyes of the gods and as a sign of secret guilt. On the other hand is the glorification of suffering—even the seeking out of suffering to achieve salvation— on the part of the powerless, rescuing a religious victory from earthly defeat. Differences in religious interpretation of suffering do not always or necessarily show a class character, but that is frequently the case.[2]

The effects of class may be manifest by variations within one religious tradition or they may be revealed in the dominant themes of a total religious system. In making this point, Weber indicates that religious behavior is not a mere reflection of class, for having originated in the context of one class—and being shaped by its style of life—a religion may strongly influence persons in other classes in the societies through which it spreads. Weber thus describes the stratum of the special carriers and interpreters of the world religions:

Confucianism was the status ethic of prebendaries, of men with literary educations who were characterized by a secular rationalism. If one did not belong to this *cultured* stratum he did not count. . . .

Early Hinduism was borne by a hereditary caste of cultured literati, who, being remote from any office, functioned as a kind of ritualist and spiritual advisers for individuals and communities. . . .

Buddhism was propagated by strictly contemplative, mendicant monks, who rejected the world and, having no homes, migrated. . . .

During its first period, Islamism was a religion of world-conquering warriors, a knight order of disciplined crusaders. . . .

Since the Exile, Judaism has been the religion of a civic "pariah people." . . .

Christianity, finally, began its course as a doctrine of itinerant artisan jour-

[2] See H. H. Gerth and C. W. Mills, editors, *From Max Weber: Essays in Sociology*, chapter 11.

neymen. During all periods of its mighty external and internal development it has been a quite specifically urban, and above all a civic, religion.[3]

Occupational and educational as well as class variables are involved in this analysis by Weber; but it serves well to illustrate the point that a religion is strongly influenced by the style of life of the stratum which is its special carrier and interpreter. If one looks upon a religion as something which has been created in all its essentials by one great founder or suddenly revealed, this analysis has little meaning. But if one sees it as a cumulative product of many persons, making their religious interpretations in a specific social and cultural environment, then the shaping influence of the values and needs of the stratum which develops it is highly important. Once the "tone," the basic view of the nature of man and the problem of evil, is fixed in a religious system, under the selective emphases of one stratum, that tone strongly influences other strata who come within the religious tradition.

One must note very carefully, however, that if a religion spreads from one class to others, it absorbs many elements from these new strata. Under a process of selective adaptation, building on earlier potentialities, it is influenced by the needs and values, the style of life, of the new classes. By such a process the world religions have become multiple systems of ways for dealing with the fundamental problems of life, systems from which the different strata may select the emphases most congenial to them at the same time that they share some common views. Thus as societies become more complicated, more highly stratified, and affected by mobility and social change, their dominant religions become loosely-jointed congeries of systems of belief and practice. While using many common symbols and sharing some doctrines and rites, the classes will vary greatly in their definitions of what is evil and their conceptions of how one should deal with the problem of evil. This can be illustrated in many ways:

Louis Finklestein interprets the differences and struggles within Judaism in its early development, between the prophetic and pharisaic elements, to be a result of the economic and cultural conflicts between the semi-nomadic shepherds and the settled farmers, the unlanded groups and the great landowners, and, in the cities, between the artisans and the nobles.[4]

It is a mistake to overlook the ways in which Judaism cuts across

---

[3] *Ibid.*, pp. 268–269.
[4] See Louis Finklestein, *The Pharisees: The Sociological Background of Their Faith.*

class and occupational lines or to ignore the influences that the religious views of one group had on the lives of the others; but it is also necessary to see the ways in which it contains the varying needs and interpretations of different strata. An even wider range may be found among the diverse interpretations of Hinduism on different social levels, among the twenty or more sects in Japanese Buddhism, and among the variant developments of Christianity.

If, as Weber says, Christianity was first borne by itinerant artisan journeymen, it nevertheless became, in the course of a few centuries, the religion of peasant and nobleman, of warrior and monk, of artisan and merchant. In its very beginnings it was a complicated hybrid, building not only on Judaism, but on classic Greek "humanism," and on the very different mystery cults. It drew together many different groups who were united only by their opposition to the ancient world and their discontent with the prevailing religious attempts to deal with life's problems. It developed a conception of equality which bound them together, and yet left the differences that separated them close beneath the surface, for under the guidance of Paul, the equality that was essential to Christianity was religiously interpreted.

. . . Christianity, along with all the radical equalizing of men in the sight of God and with all the penetration of this idea in the whole life of the soul, and in all personal relations of men to one another, is yet at the same time very cautious towards any attempt to carry over this equality into the sphere of secular relationships and institutions, which have nothing to do with the real religious basis of this equality.[5]

Christianity did not, indeed could not, eliminate the status differences, with their influences on religious need and behavior. The medieval synthesis of Thomism was achieved under the favorable circumstances of a relatively stable society that had little trade and lacked a money economy. Yet even that relatively unified view was opposed by the radical individualism of mysticism, by sectarian movements, as well as by such theological protests as Nominalism.

At various times in the history of Christianity, different status groups have been drawn together in a joint effort, only to break apart when their different needs and values proved incompatible. Luther, for a few years, united several movements that were held together largely by their common opposition to the Church and the society it reenforced. Those who, like Luther himself, were primarily concerned with a re-

[5] Ernst Troeltsch, *The Social Teaching of the Christian Churches*, p. 75.

shaping of the religious view of the world, were joined by humanists, German nationalists, and peasants. Because some of these hoped to use the Lutheran movement for secular purposes, however, and because the kinds of religious formulations that could seem meaningful and satisfying varied among these groups, there were soon widespread defections. The humanists discovered that their grounds for opposition to the Church—its support of superstition and its intellectual tyranny, as they saw it—were not Luther's grounds. Many of the German nationalists were uninterested in the specifically religious problems that were central with Luther. When the political circumstances were favorable, they were easily "reconverted" by the counter-Reformation. And some of the peasants, when they found that Luther's doctrines had no reference to the land-tenure system under which they suffered, when they felt the harshness of his opposition to the means they used to redress their grievances, turned to other religious movements. They were the source of the radical sects, that other important part of the Reformation, which played their role in the religious life of several societies.[6] Those who thus left the Lutheran movement were not simply expressing secular conflicts. For many, there were religious issues involved; but differences in secular position affected the way they viewed the religious questions.

RELIGIOUS DIVISIONS IN THE ENGLISH CIVIL WAR PERIOD

A similar story of the union of diverse forces in opposition to a common enemy, and then their break-up, can be seen in the development of the religious situation during the period of the English Civil War. An industrial and commercial revolution in the century after 1540 had created powerful new classes who found that their development was blocked by the Stuart government. At the same time, the revolution had enlarged the group of merchants and businessmen, had intensified the land problem of the peasants, and had created the beginnings of an urban proletariat. All of these groups had reason to be unhappy with the existing political situation and discontented with a religious establishment which supported it. By the time of the death of Elizabeth, the nation was sharply divided, with the King and the Church on one side and Parliament and the Puritans (using that term in its broadest meaning) on the other. The Established Church, bound to the sovereign by statutes and oaths, was a stanch supporter of the crown and the landed gentry. It taught, in the

[6] See Roland H. Bainton, "The Left Wing of the Reformation," *Journal of Religion,* January, 1941, pp. 124–134; Arthur C. M'Giffert, *Protestant Thought Before Kant;* Preserved Smith, *The Age of the Reformation.*

Homilies, ". . . that the King's power was from God alone; that, as it was
a perilous thing to commit to subjects the judgment which prince was
godly and his government good and which otherwise, as though the foot
should judge the head, it was in no case lawful to resist, wicked though
he might be." [7] It is clear that such a doctrine could not be accepted by
powerful new classes who opposed the feudal authority of the king. They
turned away from the Church that denied their right to acquire power
and became the dominant element among the Puritans.

We are primarily concerned, however, not with the split between
Church and Puritan, but with the diversity of classes, with their various
religious needs and views, to be found within Puritanism itself. Religiously,
the republican forces combined Presbyterians, Independents, and radical
sectarians. They united to carry through successfully the Civil War,
but their different status positions broke them apart politically and accentuated their religious differences; ". . . the different directions in which
Puritan thought developed were dependent on the economic conditions
and interests of the various classes which advanced and supported the
new developments." [8] As Weber frequently pointed out, the followers of a
religious movement, those who develop it after the first surge of enthusiasm, are much more likely to demonstrate by their interpretations the
effects of class status on religion than are the founders.

The Presbyterians, the right-wing of the Puritan coalition, found their
chief support among the aristocrats who had joined the parliamentary
cause and among the wealthy merchants. They wanted ". . . to limit the
objectives of the revolution: to assert the effectual sovereignty not of the
people but of Parliament, and to preserve at all costs the sanctity of property, whether real, personal, or political (the historic rights of the Crown
and the material possessions of the Church alone excepted)." [9] At the
beginning of the Civil War, the various groups under the parliamentary
banner were united in their opposition to the claims of the monarch and
in their fear of Catholicism.

But when the grounds for their fears had been removed by the destruction of
prelacy and they were forced to give positive expression to their convictions
in a system of ecclesiastical government, they were riven by profound differences that would admit of no compromise. Whatever purely religious considerations might have been involved, the rich merchants of the City had no
intentions of relaxing an ecclesiastical discipline that enabled them to control
effectively the classes they wanted to exploit and to prevent the propagation

[7] G. P. Gooch, *English Democratic Ideas in the Seventeenth Century*, p. 54.
[8] R. B. Schlatter, "The Problem of Historical Causation in Some Recent Studies of
the English Revolution," *Journal of the History of Ideas*, June, 1943, p. 363.
[9] A. S. P. Woodhouse, *Puritanism and Liberty*, p. 15.

of ideas they considered dangerous or subversive. The lesser gentry, the smaller merchants, the tradesmen, frightened by the avenues of oppression a system of central control opened up and aware of the drastic limitation on social criticism Presbyterianism imposed, insisted on a broader freedom than those who dominated Parliament were prepared to extend.[10]

The Independents, drawn from "the lesser gentry, the smaller merchants, the tradesmen" mentioned above, the center party of the Puritan coalition, were themselves too uncertain of their place in the new society, too mindful still of the struggle to win the rights of free religious choice and unrestricted economic activity, to agree fully with the Presbyterians. For a time, many of the sectarian protests of the English lower classes found some expression in Independency. The sectarians and the Independents agreed on the separation of church and state and particularly on the need for complete liberty of conscience. But the center group, along with the Presbyterians, moved toward a church-type accommodation to the society in which they were winning an important place.

The various sectarians, the left-wing of the Puritan coalition, supported the parliamentary group in the hopes of alleviating their economic distress and powerlessness. When they discovered, however, that the leaders of the parliamentary forces were scarcely more interested than the Royalists in helping them to solve their economic problems, in distributing political power throughout the population, or in establishing religious liberty, they broke away from the Puritan group in both political and religious movements.

These diverse strata, although they were united in their opposition to Catholicism and developed in common from the Reformation, could not be held together either in politics or religion. Their needs, the problems with which they struggled, were too different. They all might point to the teachings of Calvin to defend very different conclusions, for as one Puritan put it, "We can pick and choose from a Reformer what fits to the standard of our own light and reformation, and cast the other by. . . ." [11] Wide differences in doctrine, in church organization, in ethical emphasis, in style of worship, in relationship to the state were exhibited by the various Puritan groups.

The Presbyterians gave the doctrine of predestination a fundamental place. This inegalitarian doctrine harmonized well with their demonstrated success in this world and armed them with proof that they need not be concerned with the poor—for were they not obviously among the

---

[10] David W. Petegorsky, *Left-Wing Democracy in the English Civil War*, p. 61.
[11] Quoted by Woodhouse, *op. cit.*, p. 62.

damned; ". . . the restriction of salvation in the hereafter to a limited number of souls chosen out of all the rest by God alone, whatever one may choose to think of it as theology, was certainly sound political psychology." [12] Here is Weber's "theodicy of good fortune," the interpretation of suffering as a sign of guilt, of non-election. Puritans who took the doctrine of predestination seriously, however, were not entirely convinced, even by their own worldly success, that they were among the chosen. Accomplishments on earth were at best only a portent, not a proof. This lingering doubt may help to account for some of their rigidity of doctrine and the severity of their restrictions on worldly pleasure; for thus they sought to prove, more to themselves than to others, that they were truly elected.

To this doctrine of predestination, the lower classes raised strong religious protest. Drawing partly on the tradition of Wycliffe, but affected more by the more radical and humanistic ideas of Winstanley and others, the sectarians broke with the dominant Puritan group. Their answer to predestination was to declare the equality of all persons before God. With many persons of this group, equality had a specifically political and secular meaning, particularly during the struggles of mid-seventeenth century. This was gradually transformed—although never fully—by the Quakers and other pietistic groups to have largely a religious meaning.

The Puritans claimed that knowledge of God came only through the study and understanding of the Bible, thus removing the direction of religious affairs from the prelates only to put it in the hands of a literate, educated class. The sects replied by declaring that an inner spiritual inspiration was the source of religious knowledge—a source open to the illiterate and poor, a way available to any man, no matter how humble his station.[13]

Cromwell was able to block the political efforts of the lower classes, but he could not destroy the awareness of their problems that had been aroused by the conflicts of the Civil War period. Petegorsky writes:

After 1649 and 1650 that social consciousness could no longer be given direct political expression. Instead, it found its voice in the tremendous revival of mystical enthusiasm and millenary fervour that dates from those years. If the price of political agitation was persecution and imprisonment, it was much more convenient to shift the initiative for social change to the Lord who could risk with impunity the wrath of the dictators. And if the practical efforts of mortals had failed to achieve the desired results, surely God, in His time, would bring the eagerly awaited millennium.[14]

[12] William Haller, *The Rise of Puritanism*, p. 169.
[13] See Petegorsky, *op. cit.*, p. 65.
[14] *Ibid.*, p. 235.

This is doubtless to make religious movements too directly and completely the reflections of class position, to make them seem almost consciously chosen strategic efforts. Yet one can scarcely avoid the conclusion that the religious differences that sprang from Puritanism demonstrate how religion is attached to the whole of life, how it expresses differences in need and value among various strata, how it is used as one of the instruments by means of which man attempts to meet those needs and satisfy those values. Differences among classes are not simply economic, of course. There are wide variations in modes of expressing emotion, in the extent of hope, in the aesthetic symbols to which they respond.

The Restoration even more than the rule of Cromwell made clear that the lower classes were not going to have their problems solved by the emerging new society. "The Civil War had made it certain," as Petegorsky says, "that neither an absolute king nor an absolute Church would ever again impede economic progress." That having been accomplished, the old aristocracy and the newly powerful middle classes found that they had more in common than they had supposed. Their quarrels made them less able to oppose the demands from the lower classes that the parliamentary government for which they fought should give them some of the promised rewards—some relief from poverty, some political influence. "The Restoration was essentially a compromise between the aristocracy and the middle classes for the exploitation of the economic opportunities an expanding society presented." [15] Anglican and "rightwing" Puritan alike accepted the basic structure of the new social order, seeking primarily to assure individual goodness and salvation within that order. As the richest merchants and industrialists became more sharply distinguished from the lesser men of business, they felt closer to the landed gentry. By the eighteenth century, wealthy non-conformists were joining the Anglican Church. Just as their earlier class differences were matched by religious differences, so now the converging political and economic interests of the landed aristocracy and the most powerful of the new bourgeoisie were matched by converging religious inclinations.[16]

Opposed by such a united front, the sects turned further away from the hopes of a Winstanley for immediate reform by the union of political and military means with religion. They turned to quiet waiting for the millennium or patient non-resistance, and to more specifically religious interpretations of life.

It is interesting to note that in the case of the English sects as in that of the German the method of non-resistance was not espoused until efforts toward a violent revolution had been found unavailing in the face of the superior power

---

[15] *Ibid.*, pp. 240–241.
[16] See R. B. Schlatter, *The Social Ideas of Religious Leaders, 1660–1688.*

of the ruling classes, while, at the same time, the ideal of a new social order was abandoned in favor of a sectarian organization of mutual aid and brotherhood.[17]

Thus religious efforts change when attempts to solve the intrusive problems of life have been found to be inadequate. This same transformation can be seen to some degree in the development of Jewish hopes for an earthly kingdom into a conception of the kingdom of God; it is found in the "failure of nerve" of many of the Greeks after the third century B.C. and their "retreat" to the mystery cults;[18] it is important in the declining emphasis of early Christianity on the reformist hopes that at least some few had seen in it. These movements vary greatly, of course, in the extent of the shift. And in none of them is the hope for solutions of problems of this world simply given up. That is partly true, for the values of life on earth may be sharply discounted. Another aspect of the shift, however, is the adoption of religious means to replace the frustrated political, military, or economic efforts. Apocalyptic views, a literal interpretation of "he that loseth his life shall find it," an emphasis on personal goodness and righteousness may have reference to this life as well as to eternal salvation.

THE DEVELOPMENT OF SECTS IN THE AMERICAN SETTING

Turning to the American scene, one can see many ways in which religious differences correspond to status differences. In the early years, status differences were correlated, to a degree, with geography, so that one could contrast the religious tendencies of the East with those of the frontier.

The religion of the urban, commercial East tended to take on or to retain the typical features of all bourgeois or national religion—a polity corresponding to the order and character of class organized society, an intellectual conception of the content of faith, an ethics reflecting the needs and evaluations of a stable and commercial citizenry, a sober, ritualistic type of religious expression. The religion of the West, on the other hand, accepted or produced anew many of the characteristics of the faith of the disinherited, for the psychology of the frontier corresponds in many respects to the psychology of the revolutionary poor. This is especially true of the emotional character of religious experience, which seems to be required in the one case as in the other. The isolation of frontier life fostered craving for companionship, suppressed the gregarious

---

[17] H. Richard Niebuhr, *The Social Sources of Denominationalism*, pp. 52–53.
[18] One should note that "failure of nerve," as Gilbert Murray described it, was a Western concept with an implied value, not simply a descriptive statement. Few Buddhists, for example, would look upon a mystical religious development as a failure of nerve, but might see it rather as a courageous and intelligent response to the facts of the universe.

tendency and so subjected the lonely settler to the temptations of crowd suggestions to an unusual degree.[19]

This contrast combines the effects of many variables—degree of isolation, level of education, occupation, etc., as well as class—thus pointing to the need for avoiding an over-simplified view of the effects of class differences.

A number of studies in recent years have described the religious developments on our new "frontier"—the city—showing that many of the tendencies of the earlier days reappear. Although there are many sources of sectarian growth today, it is primarily among the recent migrants to the city, the urban "peasants," that sects are forming.[20] And in these sects, the class element is clearly apparent. These groups differ widely from the denominations around them in theology, style of worship, ethical emphasis, and church organization. It is relevant to ask: What are some of the causes of the rise of these sects; how do they differ in religious behavior, and what are the consequences of their beliefs and practices?

When a lower-class person moves from a rural area into a city, to work in mill or factory, he is confronted with a number of difficult problems of adjustment. He is forced to accept an enormous change in his style of life —the rhythm of his work, the nature of his associations, his place in a neighborhood. He is likely to be almost wholly lacking in organized social contacts, because he enters the new society at its most poorly organized level. And his sense of isolation is increased by the way in which he is looked down upon by the established urban groups.[21] This is the kind of problem with which religion might be expected to deal: You are not alone; you belong; your problems are not everlasting, or at least they have meaning in a transcendental context. But the established churches of the city are poorly equipped to give these assurances to a lower class migrant from a rural area. For the most part they are fully accommodated to the middle and upper classes of the city—the forms of their services of worship, the content of the preaching, the programs and leadership of the various groups in the church are all adjusted to the urban members of long-standing. The lower-class sect movement, then, is in this situation an attempt to grapple with the problems faced by the migrant, a response to what Holt calls the "cultural shock" that comes from the shift to an

[19] H. R. Niebuhr, op. cit., p. 141.
[20] See H. P. Douglass, "Cultural Differences and Recent Religious Divisions," Christendom, Winter, 1945, pp. 89–105.
[21] See John B. Holt, "Holiness Religion: Cultural Shock and Social Reorganization," American Sociological Review, October, 1940, pp. 740–747. See also W. Lawson Jones, "Some Psychological Conditions of the Development of Methodism up to 1850," British Journal of Psychology, November, 1951, pp. 345–354, for an interesting parallel in the British scene.

urban life, an attempt to heal the distress caused by isolation and insecurity. It is not likely to be an economic protest, at least in any direct sense. The migrant may be better off financially in the city. He is almost certainly ill-equipped by earlier training to protest against his economic status. The established churches, in fact, are probably more liberal on economic issues than are the lower class sects. Far more than an economic protest, the urban sect demonstrates the widely different personality needs and modes of expression that one finds among status levels. The religious forms that have been accommodated to one status group are felt to be inadequate by another.

If the need for stable and secure social relations is one cause for the rise of the holiness and pentecostal sects, poverty itself is another. There was a rapid increase in such sects during the depression of the nineteen-thirties.[22] Most of the churches with which the unemployed and the poverty-stricken had been associated—for many of them were members of established denominations—had little to say about this problem. They neither pressed for secular solutions or gave serious attention to a religious interpretation of the meaning of want. The small sects which sprang up among the poor, however, were diligently trying to give an interpretation of the economic distress of the members. Almost none of them, to be sure, gave—or give—any attention to the economic and political situation around them. The Winstanleys of our time seldom use religious terms; direct protests against secular institutions come from secular groups almost entirely, from labor unions, political movements, etc. As in Luther's Germany and pre-Cromwellian England, it is those with some hope of success who make direct protests—whether in religious or secular terms—against the ruling powers of their society. When these hopes are persistently frustrated, spiritual solutions are given more emphasis. So it is that among America's lower classes, those who are poorest off, those who have little chance to improve their lot by secular instruments, turn to religious interpretations of the meaning of poverty.

Closely related to isolation and poverty, is a third factor in the recent rise of sects in the United States: the need for an emotional expressiveness that is lacking in the dignified and ritualistic services of most of the churches. Clark calls the sects "refugees of the emotionally starved." The poor ". . . cannot afford, or do not have access to the recreations, associations, social functions, and cultural activities wherein the prosperous find outlets for their emotions." [23] More than that, the *need* for emotional re-

---

[22] See A. T. Boisen, "Religion and Hard Times. A Study of the Holy Rollers," *Social Action*, March 15, 1939, pp. 8–35; and E. T. Clark, *The Small Sects in America*.
[23] Clark, *op. cit.*, p. 220.

lease may be greater among the lower classes, because of more frustrations and the monotony of many of their jobs. Liston Pope notes, with respect to a southern mill town, that life is monotonous and dull; production methods in the mills are largely mechanical; the worker has little opportunity for choice or control over the forces that influence his life.[24] In the small religious group, the members can set their own schedule and determine their own modes of expression.

If these are indicative of the needs that foster the growth of class-differentiated sects in American society, we may now ask: How do the sects attempt to meet these needs? To those who feel isolated in the older churches, the new, small groups are their own, to lead, to organize as they like. (That the members may like very different things and compete for leadership is shown by the frequent splits that occur.) The sects are orthodox—according to their own standards—to the point of fanaticism. At first glance, this does not seem to be an adaptation to the problems of the religiously disinherited; but it becomes meaningful as a way of saying: we belong to a very highly selected and exclusive association. New members are admitted only after having given evidence of a religious experience and showing that they will abide by the group's norms. There is rigid enforcement of certain standards of behavior, a kind of modern asceticism that assures the members that they deserve to belong to the exclusive group and will share the rewards it promises. Pope indicates that the sects are very quick to expel members who violate their code (for such violations tear the fabric of their solutions to life's problems): "In 1938 one Free-Will Baptist Holiness Church in Gastonia received 33 new members and expelled 24 persons, of a total membership of 88. A Church of God with 143 members has expelled 30 in the last two years; another with 95 members has expelled 40; a third with 101 members has expelled 20 in the last four years." [25] For a person to be expelled from a church in our time is a rare occurrence. The exclusiveness and insistence upon "Puritan morality" of the sect is not simply ". . . elevating the manners they cannot well escape into moral virtues established by the will of God," as Clark describes it. It is, beyond that, the expression of the psychology of the sacrifice: We deserve religious success for our purity, for what we have given up. Anything or anybody who endangers that assurance must be cast out and repudiated.

Within the sect, the desires of the members for leadership, for status, for expression, for assurance that their difficult lot has some ultimate significance are dealt with. They can give free rein to their emotions

[24] See Liston Pope, *Millhands and Preachers*, pp. 133–134.
[25] *Ibid.*, p. 138.

and, as Clark says, "attribute the pleasant thrills thereof to a divine agency."

There is little direct challenge to the economic and political order within which they fare so poorly, although the "comfortable" people may be criticized for their "immorality." Most of the sects in American society today accept the basic secular institutions. Their members look for their reward in heaven or in some apocalyptic transformation of the world. According to the dominant theology, man is depraved. Only by the second-coming of Jesus will the world escape its ills. Other groups, such as the Jehovah's Witnesses, emphasize the withdrawal theme more strongly: since this is a world of sin, we must not only be indifferent to it, but withdraw from it and refuse its commands over us. This is a somewhat less pessimistic response to the secular world, for it carries the implication—although often very obscurely—that some of the world's problems might be solved within a pure community of believers. But whether the acceptance or the avoidance theme is stronger—and both are almost always found—the sects deal with the economic problems of their members primarily by redefining them, not by offering ways in which they might be solved in terms of the "world's" definitions. Their solution of economic distress is a collective look to the future, beyond history. As Boison points out, this "solution" carries certain implications: It requires the coming to terms with God, as the doctrines of the sect interpret God; hence there is strong emphasis on confessions and the strict enforcement of rules. The strong realization that the sectarians have that their problems will not readily be solved precludes any "easy" religious solution. Their own experience has been so hard that they would not at all be convinced by easy formulas and doctrines.

Thus the sects strive to deal with the many needs of their members in terms that harmonize with their past training, their level of education, and their experiences in life. Pope summarizes this situation well when he writes:

The sects substitute religious status for social status, a fact which may help to account for their emphasis on varying degrees of Grace. This emphasis, indeed, forms their most distinctive theological tenet. As over against the lack of religious differentiation within older denominations, the newer sects divide their members, and people in general, into several religious classifications: saved, sanctified, baptized with the Holy Ghost, baptized with water, recipient of the first, second, or third blessing and the like. What matters it, then, if a Methodist has more money but has never been baptized with the Holy Ghost? As over against segregation from the community, the newer sects affirm separation from the world; in the face of exclusion on educational, economic, and religious grounds, they affirm exclusion from their own fellowship of those

who engage in mixed bathing, dancing, card playing, bobbing the hair, gamb-
ling, baseball, county fairs, drinking, and using tobacco. Because they have no
jewelry to wear, they make refusal to wear jewelry, including wedding rings,
a religious requirement. They transmute poverty into a symptom of Grace.
Having no money, they redeem their economic status by rigid tithing of the
small income they do possess, and thus far surpass members of churches of
any other type or denomination in per capita contributions, despite the fact
that they stand at the bottom of the economic scale.[26]

The universal human skill of making virtue of necessity is nowhere
put to more extensive use.

Functional Consequences of Sectarian Movements. In addition to
stating some of the causes of the rise of contemporary sects and describing
their various manifestations, we may ask further: What are the consequences of these beliefs and practices? If the manifest functions are to
furnish the members with ways of handling enormously difficult problems, what are the latent functions and dysfunctions? Unfortunately, we
have little evidence on this question. One of two extremes is often easily
assumed, without the difficult study necessary to test it. Some middle
class observers who themselves would be entirely unsatisfied by the
sectarian religious views assume that they must be equally unrewarding
to others, not realizing the differences in needs, accustomed modes of
expression, and available alternatives that distinguish them from the
lower class sectarians. Others take a kind of tolerant functional view, with
circular reasoning that guarantees "proof": It *must* be an effective and
satisfying kind of religion, or they wouldn't accept it. Neither of these
extremes does justice to the complexity of the functional-dysfunctional
situation. One can judge the "success" of a sect, of course, only in terms
of certain stated objectives. If one applies a specifically religious criterion,
as the sect leaders are likely to do, he asks simply: Do the members
accept the doctrines and carry on the proscribed practices of the group?
If they do, the movement is a success. If one asks, as the sociologist of
religion is likely to do: What are the total, long-run consequences, for
mental health, for economic security, and the like? he is faced with a
more difficult question. Its answer would require a comparative study
of two groups that were just alike in economic status, personality tendencies and needs, etc., one of which embraced a sectarian religious movement while the other attempted to solve its problems by other means—
perhaps by economic or political action. Lacking this, we can only offer
the informed guesses and hypotheses of the students of sect movements.

Holt observes that many of the beliefs and ethical practices of the

[26] *Ibid.*, pp. 137–138.

recently urbanized "peasants" are drawn from a disintegrating agricultural tradition and may be much less adequate in the urban environment. Neighborliness, for example, has an important meaning in a fairly stable rural community; but it may have far different consequences when applied to the complicated relationships of industrial workers to an absentee management. The sect may have a latent function for the high status groups, because of its ability to funnel the attention and energy of the lower classes away from this world's problems onto the problems of the hereafter. Better to hate the devil than the boss—certainly from the point of view of the boss, who can sometimes be found among the financial supporters of revival services that encourage the appropriate transfer. It is not surprising, looking at the situation from the opposite side, that the boss should often believe that labor unions or others who bring him back into the focus of opposition are most certainly in the employ of the devil—however the devil may be conceived.

On the other hand, the sect may inspire hope in the migrant and encourage a type of behavior that will raise his status above his class by developing a seriousness of purpose.[27] Boisen takes a position that might be called "psychiatric functionalism" in his statement that the holiness sects show nature's power to heal:

They are the spontaneous attempts of the common people to deal constructively with the stresses and trials which fall with peculiar severity upon them. Their unconcern with economic and social conditions which they are powerless to change and their turning to problems for which they are directly responsible is not entirely an unwholesome reaction. . . . In any case these "holy rollers" are bringing to many distressed individuals release from the burden of guilt. They are giving them hope and courage and strength to keep going in the face of difficulties. In so far as they succeed in doing this, their economic and social status is likely to be raised.[28]

S. D. Clark arrives at a somewhat different conclusion from his study of sectarian movements in Canada. Implicit in his statement is the thesis that some attention to the organization of society, and not just to the improvement of the status of individuals, is necessary to deal effectively with the needs which the sect movements express.

In the long run, perhaps, the effect of the influence of such a movement as the Salvation Army was to arrest the development of a stable urban order. People's attentions were diverted from the real problems of an industrial so-

[27] See Holt, op. cit.
[28] A. T. Boisen, "Economic Distress and Religious Experience," Psychiatry, May, 1939, p. 194.

ciety; the Army following tended to be held in a state of political and economic illiteracy. The effect was particularly evident in retarding the development of working-class organizations. It may be questioned, however, whether stable secular institutions would have developed much greater strength if the Salvation Army had not emerged. Another form of fanaticism almost certainly would have grown up in place of the religious. The sort of people to whom the Army appealed in the Canadian city in the closing years of the past century were the sort of people looking for a form of social participation on the most elementary level. The task of social building required building from the bottom, and it was on the bottom that the Army built strongly and securely.[29]

These differing judgments may show the difficulty in measuring the consequences of the sect movements. It is very easy to have one's attention drawn to one particular function or dysfunction, without regard for the many other results. The present writer would offer the following very tentative propositions as a summary of the consequences of contemporary sects, entirely apart from any question of the "validity" of their views:

1. They have demonstrated their ability to relieve the immediate "pain" that many people feel as a result of their highly disprivileged position.

2. For those on the bottom of a status system, the sects are not usually dysfunctional in terms of economic and political institutions, because their adherents are not in any event equipped by training and inclination to challenge those institutions by other means. For those who are in a slightly more favorable position, however, a sectarian religion that discourages efforts to respond to deprivation by secular or religious challenges to the social situation may help to preserve that situation.

3. Many individual adherents are helped, by the self-disciplines that the sect encourages, to improve their own status; while at the same time the sect is irrelevant to the social and cultural causes that continue to create such disprivileged individuals.

4. The sect is inadequate, and perhaps completely irrelevant, to the basic societal problem of freedom-and-order, with which mankind has continually to struggle. The "accepting" and "avoiding" sects are completely unable to deal with "society as the patient"; and the "aggressive" sects, with their inclinations toward a perfectionist view of man, are too unmindful of the difficult problems of freedom-*and*-order to make a large contribution to the reconstruction of a society. We shall see in other connections that a churchlike response, by itself, is equally inadequate to this task.

[29] S. D. Clark, *Church and Sect in Canada*, p. 424.

RELIGION AND MINORITY-GROUP STATUS

Looking upon religion as one of the ways that individuals and groups use to try to achieve life's values, one is not surprised to discover important religious differences between minority-group members and majority-group members. The principles involved in the explanation of those differences are the same as those we have developed in the analysis of class status. Much of our analysis of the functions of lower-class sects is therefore appropriate here as well. Certain additional concepts, however, can aid us in the interpretation of a large and interesting mass of data. These further concepts are necessary because members of a minority-group are not simply persons in a disprivileged status. They are *categorically* assigned to that status on the basis of prejudgments by members of the dominant group, using such criteria as nationality, race, and religion itself. Thus there is a degree of rigidity of status and often a sense of belonging to a group of similarly disprivileged persons that are not necessarily true of a class position. This is not a sharp distinction, of course, and there is a tendency toward convergence of the two statuses of class and minority-group. The analysis of minority status and religion, therefore, must build on our earlier discussion.

In the typology of religious groups that was developed in Chapter 6, a distinction was drawn among three kinds of sects, based on the degree to which an acceptance, avoidance, or aggressive theme was predominant in their response to the social patterns. These same three responses have been widely used to classify the kinds of reactions that minority-group members make to their status in society.[30] And nowhere are the differences more clearly apparent than in their various religious movements. Some minority-group religious movements passively accept the disprivileged status, emphasizing only the importance of the achievement of religious values. Other sects implicitly criticize, but do not explicitly attack, the dominant social order, by their emphasis on withdrawal. The important thing for them is to "live right" in a pure religious communion, avoiding so far as possible an evil society that one cannot change. Still others protest, on religious grounds, against the society that treats them so badly; these are the aggressive religious movements.

Variables Influencing Type of Sect. The degree to which one or another of these tendencies will be predominant—they are probably never found in pure form—depends upon several variables:

1. The degree of hope that the group feels regarding the chances for

[30] See George E. Simpson and J. Milton Yinger, *Racial and Cultural Minorities: An Analysis of Prejudice and Discrimination.*

improvement in their status in the secular scheme of things affects the type of sect they will support. The more hopeful, the more likely they are to express themselves aggressively; the more their aspirations have been blocked and the more overwhelming the power of the dominant group seems, the greater the likelihood that avoidance and acceptance themes will be used. The degree of hopefulness is affected by, but not precisely determined by, the actual facts of the power situation. Due to its cultural traditions, the nature of its leadership, and other variables, a group may be more optimistic about the chances for improving its situation than the facts would warrant. This may be the case with some of the American Indian religious movements, as we shall see. Such an excess of optimism, however, is not likely to prevail for very long. The opposite kind of "mis-evaluation" of the situation is also possible of course. This "excessive resignation" in religious expressions is likely to promote, or at least to be found in the same situation with, *secular* movements which try to take advantage of the opportunities for improvement. This is to some degree true among American Negroes.

2. The nature of the religious and the total cultural tradition of a group influences the use of the acceptance, avoidance, and aggressive themes. A Hindu sect that challenged the social order is far less likely than such a protest by a Christian sect, for the importance of the doctrines of karma and reincarnation in Hinduism make direct attacks on the social order by some reinterpretation of the Hindu tradition very difficult. Christianity, however, contains the potentialities for such attacks, even though they are usually curtailed by more dominant themes.

3. The availability of secular movements of various kinds affects and is affected by religious movements. Sometimes an aggressive secular movement, for example, seems to drain off those who, because of their cultural tradition, degree of hope, etc., might have supported an aggressive religious sect. Occasionally the two may come together, but the actual difficulties that minority-group members and other relatively powerless people face are so great that an "optimistic" religious view of the world is likely to be short-lived. A "pessimistic" view—withdrawal or accept-ance—may well express a more accurate understanding of the existing situation. Even the optimistic liberal Christianity of American middle and upper class Protestantism, a view that characterized the nineteenth and the first part of the twentieth century, has been sharply curtailed in its influence by pessimistic "neoorthodoxy." War, tyranny, and depres-sion tend to be problems common to powerful and powerless alike, and obscure their religious differences. The religious theme that man is a "sinner," capable of sanctification only by God, that his fond hopes for peace and brotherhood will not be realized on this earth, may be ex-

pressed in very different terms by a Reinhold Niebuhr and a "holiness" evangelist, but they represent similar religious responses to the human situation. If religious "optimism" is an unstable view even among the fortunate, how much less likely is it to prevail among the powerless and disprivileged.

It is frequently helpful to study the secular and the religious expressions of minority-group members within the same framework, for they can be seen in various circumstances not only as alternatives but also as supplementary modes of adjustment. Among northern urban Negroes in the United States, for example, their religious movements can be seen almost as a "second line of defense." They protest against their status by political activity, by support of the National Association for the Advancement of Colored People, by labor union activity; but their religious life has very little of this protest theme. This contrast, to be sure, may not be true of individuals, for only a small proportion take part in the secular protests; these same individuals may be the ones most likely to support religious movements that demand social reform and improvement of the status of the Negro. Those Negroes whose religious expressions are most "escapist" are also least likely to make secular demands.

Whichever of the various possible relationships between secular and religious movements prevails, it is useful to see them together. One can thus better understand religion as one of several types of efforts to struggle with the problems of life.

4. The degree of acculturation to the values of the dominant society also influences the nature of the religious life of a minority-group. The more a group has embraced the values of the majority and the more it aspires to share those values, the less likely it is, other things being equal, to sustain a religious movement that simply accepts low status or devalues society. George E. Simpson found that in Jamaica, those among the disprivileged who were least acculturated to European values were the most likely to participate in escapist cults, while the more acculturated groups began to express some aggressive themes. Even the most aggressive cults, however, had a great many escapist elements—a reflection of their powerlessness. Interestingly enough, the "escapism" of the Ras Tafari (Haille Selassie) cult was a "this-worldly escapism," a back to Africa movement that represented an unwillingness to give up the hope of success in this world and yet made a very pessimistic appraisal of the chances of improvement of their status in Jamaica.[31] This may be a kind of half-way station between the complete projection of one's hopes into a heaven and the hopes of reforming one's own society.

[31] See George E. Simpson, "The Ras Tafari Movement in Jamaica: A Study of Race and Class Conflict," *Social Forces,* December, 1955, pp. 167–170.

A similar range of types of religious responses can be seen among American Negroes. The folk Negro of the rural South tends to accept his role as defined by the dominant group. His religion may be seen as an attempt to help him adjust to his station. As Negroes have absorbed more and more of the aspirations of other Americans, withdrawal themes, implicit protests, and finally to a small degree explicit reform efforts have come into their religious life. The last development can be seen in some of the urban Negro churches especially, where concern for the political and economic welfare of the members is given some attention. We shall explore these various types of Negro religious expressions below.

The situation among minorities that are pridefully resisting acculturation is somewhat different. In this circumstance, the minority is a separate social group with a separate culture, reacting against the encroachments of a dominant group. It is not a stratum within a larger society. To the degree that the members feel an intrusion and are disorganized by it, they tend to develop religious movements that aggressively oppose the dominant group. It is the *least* acculturated, the "old-timers" who are likely to lead such movements. When some of their members absorb the values and aspirations of the majority, they begin to struggle religiously with their problems as disprivileged persons more in escapist terms. We shall see below that this describes to some degree the religious protests of American Indians against the white man. The difference between their situation and that of the American Negro, for example, is that the Indians had a sustaining culture—or at least the tradition of a very recent one—of their own, while this is only slightly true of the Negroes, who share the dominant culture. A corollary of this is that many of the Indians did not want acculturation, while most of the Negroes want nothing more than to be treated as Americans. Thus it is not simply the *degree* of acculturation that influences the type of religious movement, but the presence or absence of a sustaining culture of its own among the minority and the degree of desire for acculturation. The form of the religious movement, of course—its symbols, its beliefs, its rituals—will vary widely from culture to culture.

5. The influence of leaders must be taken into account in the study of the probable type of a religious movement. We shall not discuss a theory of leadership here more than to make this brief statement: Although the kind of leader who will rise to the surface and achieve power is sharply limited by all the other variables, the exact nature of his program is not set by these influences. The unfocused needs and tendencies of a group may be drawn together by a leader who is inclined toward one kind of religious response, which might have been pointed toward a somewhat different religious expression or toward a political

or economic response, had a leader with different inclinations appeared earlier. One should not exaggerate the range of possibilities: a person who tries, for example, to develop an aggressive economic and political movement among a group who have very little hope and power is certain to be a voice crying in the wilderness. Yet there is a little "play" left in the limits set by the various conditions faced by a would-be leader. His tendencies and needs, then, help to determine the final outcome. One doubts very much if the organizer of a separate Negro political movement might just as readily have acquired influence as Father Divine, had he appeared at the same time and place. The limits of history are not so tolerant. But a Father Divine a little less interested in economic boycotts or a little more interested in organized political action might have prospered equally well, had he chanced to appear.[32]

6. The personality systems—the whole complex of tendencies to act in various ways—must also be taken into account in trying to determine the kinds of adjustment, religious or otherwise, that will be made to the problems of life. Two persons, with equal opportunities for secular action, heirs of the same tradition, similarly acculturated, may make different adjustments because of different personality tendencies. One of them may, because of his early training, be particularly burdened by self-doubt, by guilt, by anxiety. Against this background, the tragedies and frustrations of life will strike him with special poignancy. The other may have been brought up under circumstances that enable him to face frustration and disappointment, his own errors and those of others, without great torment. Feeling more secure, he has a higher level of tolerance for tragedy and guilt and doubt. The first is likely to be a strong candidate for what William James has called the religion of the twice-born. The second will be drawn to a more optimistic religion or join a hopeful secular movement.

Thus the nature of religion among minorities, as among others, is the result of the interplay of many forces. This complicates the task of analysis; but any attempt to understand religion as a consequence of one or two factors alone will be inadequate.

The variables we have been discussing may be summarized in the following proposition: The more a minority group does share and wants to share in the dominant culture of a society, the greater its power, the stronger its hope, the more its religious tradition encourages an emphasis on the values of this life, the more aggressive its leadership, the more

---

[32] "Chanced," not because he was uncaused, but because the influences that brought him to his particular inclinations can be seen as independent of the situation with which he came in contact.

the personality tendencies of the members encourage them to confront life directly, rather than inventing symbolic solutions—under these circumstances, the farther the religious response to its status will move down the road of acceptance-avoidance-aggression, and the more it will develop secular themes to supplement or replace the religious sectarian movements.

Keeping these variables in mind, we can illustrate the religious movements among minority groups by an examination of some of the developments among American Indians and Negroes.

RELIGIOUS MOVEMENTS AMONG AMERICAN INDIANS

If the view of religion that we have adopted has any validity, we would expect to find among American Indians, as a result of the enormous disorganizing pressures to which they have been subjected, a series of religious adjustments and movements, alongside many other types of response. We are not here concerned with a functional analysis of their aboriginal religions, but with a few of the religious reactions, springing generally from a hybrid Indian-Christian situation, to white domination. The form of these religious movements was partly conditioned by the fact that the Indians had a widespread myth that a culture hero would appear to lead them to a terrestrial paradise. A large number of messianic movements have developed from this myth, growing in the context of personal deprivation and cultural confusion. Sometimes the Indian prophets helped to bring together normally warring tribes against their common enemy, the white intruder, promising them that it was now the Indian's turn to conquer.

The Ghost Dance was the most dramatic and widespread of these Indian religious protests.[33] In its development and spread, one can see religion being used in an effort to overcome personal confusion and frustration, to reestablish the validity of Indian cultures, and to oppose the overwhelming power of the white man. It spread first in the early 1870's among the tribes of the Far West, stemming from the vision of a Paiute shaman, Wodziwob. He prophesied that all the dead Indians would come back, brought to life by the dance. His own tribe did not become very excited, but his message was amplified and spread by other missionaries: those who believed, who danced, would see their relatives in a very few years and the white people would disappear. Some tribes

---

[33] See W. W. Howells, *The Heathens;* Bernard Barber, "Acculturation and Messianic Movements," *American Sociological Review,* October, 1941, pp. 663–669; Alexander Lesser, "Cultural Significance of the Ghost Dance," *American Anthropologist,* January–March, 1933, pp. 108–115.

were unconvinced by Wodziwob or his followers. "But elsewhere the doctrine seemed better at third hand than at first hand, and it ran like a powder train." In 1871 it spread through several tribes in California, Oregon and Nevada, receiving fresh interpretations and variations as it moved. "As it traveled, it appears that the tribes which took up the cult most hungrily were those suffering the greatest deterioration in their former ways of life, while those which were lukewarm or flatly rejected the dance were the ones who had had the least disturbance." [34]

After a few years, the Ghost Dance began to decline, for its promise of an immediate reestablishment of the Indian to his old place was not fulfilled. In 1890, however, another Paiute, Wovoka, a shaman whose father had been associated with Wodziwob, received a vision that was the starting point for another wave of the dance. The nature of the vision is not entirely clear, for Wovoka proclaimed some Christian ethical views (live in peace with one another and the whites, avoid lying, stealling, and war); and yet in a letter to the Arapaho and Cheyenne he repeated the idea that there would be a reunion on earth with the dead Indians, that the dance which God had given him would prevent the whites from interfering with the Indians any more.[35]

The dance spread quickly, not through the tribes that had taken it up twenty years earlier, nor among the then prosperous Navahos or the self-contained Pueblos, but across the Rockies among the Plains Indians—the Cheyenne and Arapaho, the Pawnee and Sioux. Here it is to be understood only against the background of white domination, cultural confusion among the Indians, the loss of the buffalo with all that it meant for the Indian economy and way of life, the inability to carry out the old rituals. The Ghost Dance represented a renaissance of Indian culture to the Pawnee, "the very flame of new hope to the Sioux."

Into this situation of cultural decay and gradual darkness, the Ghost Dance doctrine shown like a bright light. Indian ways were not gone, never to be recovered. Indian ways were coming back. Those who had lived before in the 'golden age' were still carrying on the old ceremonies, old dances, old performances, and old games in the beyond. They were coming back; they were bringing the old ways and the buffalo. Dance, dance, dance. The white man would be destroyed by a great wind. The Indian would be left with the buffalo, with his ancestors, with his old friends and his old enemies. Cast aside the white man's ways like an old garment; put on the clothes of the Indian again. Get ready for the new day and the old times.[36]

[34] Howells, op. cit., p. 270.
[35] See ibid., pp. 269–273.
[36] Lesser, op. cit., p. 112.

The Ghost Dance was a last desperate attempt to reestablish the native values, to recover a sense of the worthwhileness and meaning of life. Among the Sioux it led to tragedy, for it precipitated the complicated series of events that brought about the battle of Wounded Knee where over two hundred Indians and sixty white soldiers were killed.[37] And with them died the Dance among the Sioux.

Can we interpret this vigorous religious protest in terms of some of the variables we have discussed above? First, hope among the Indians that they could reestablish the supremacy of their way of life ran fairly high, despite the enormous defeats they had suffered. During the eighteenth and early nineteenth centuries, the Plains Indians had known great prosperity and success—and this was still a living memory among them in 1890; they were proud of their cultures and not ready to accept the possibility of their extinction. This hope may seem wholly unrealistic to the outsider, but it stemmed from the Indian experience. The failures of the Ghost Dance and the continued reduction in their power soon cut away the roots of hope—and aggressive religious movements became less likely.

Second, the Ghost Dance was built out of the cultural materials of the Indians—shamanism, the strong belief in visions, efficacy of the dance, with a mixture of Christian beliefs and ethical elements that had spread among the tribes.

Third, effective secular protests were lacking or had proved entirely inadequate. The Indians, to be sure, had protested militarily against the continuing intrusions into their territories and the destruction of their way of life; they had negotiated politically; but these had not stopped the white man nor reestablished the old ways. The Ghost Dance can be seen as another attempt to do what war and negotiation had not done.

Fourth, the vigorous protest not only against their own deprivation and suffering but against the ways of the white man was a sign of low acculturation. The Indians were not fighting simply for a higher status within a white society, but for the reaffirmation of their own cultures. Among those who do not want a distinct cultural identity, aggressive religious movements are more likely among the most acculturated; but when the goal is a separate culture, it is the least acculturated who support aggressive religious—and other—movements.

Fifth, the Ghost Dance was encouraged by some of the powerful and irreconcilable Indian leaders. There were other types of leaders as well who gained power when the situation changed. But for a period, the

[37] See Howells, op. cit., pp. 274–278.

protest theme was encouraged by aggressive religious and political-military leaders.

When hope began to fade, when the white culture had intruded further into the life of the tribes, avoidance and escapist themes came more frequently into the religious movements among the Indians. The Peyote cult, which is non-violent, not-threatening to whites, has frequently followed the Ghost Dance. Here one finds passive acceptance and resignation in the face of deprivation, combined with an assertion of Indian solidarity in a situation where extreme individualism threatened the foundations of community life. The Peyote cult has been able to survive, its appeal not depending on what must be counted an impossible victory.[38] Among some of the California tribes, another non-aggressive religious movement followed the Ghost Dance. In 1872, the Bole-Maru cult, also originating in dreams and built around the dance, showed a much larger mixture of Christian elements. It did not attack white society, but represented an absorption of some of its elements and a projection of hopes into a life hereafter.

The reward of belief was heaven, and not the return of the dead. Now, when the millennium failed to appear the Ghost Dance and the Earth Lodge petered out, but the Bole-Maru still exists (or did in 1934). The other two cults were anguished protests against the falling apart of Indian life, but the Bole-Maru was a first compromise, to keep what could be kept. Starting as something mainly Indian, it became gradually more like American cults, so that in the end it brought together shamanism and Christian revivalism, and made it possible for such churches as the Indian Shakers, the Four Square Gospel, and the Pentecostal to come in and take its place.[39]

Thus the type of religious protest varies with the situation. It will be interesting to see if the desire for acculturation and assimilation becomes stronger and if the hope for improvement of their status *within* the larger society grows, whether these "escapist" religious movements among American Indians will be replaced or supplemented by a new kind of religious protest, expressing not the reactionary dreams of the Ghost Dance but the reformist hopes of a modern Anabaptism. This would complete, in the experience of American Indians, the full range of sectarian religious movements found among minority groups.

[38] See Barber, *op. cit.* and Barber, "A Socio-Cultural Interpretation of the Peyote Cult," *American Anthropologist*, October–December, 1941, pp. 673–675. See also Charles Brand, "Peyotism Among the Kiowa-Apache and Neighboring Tribes," *Southwestern Journal of Anthropology*, Vol. 6 (1950), pp. 212–222.

[39] Howells, *op. cit.*, p. 271; see also Philleo Nash, "The Place of Religious Revivalism in the Formation of the Intercultural Community on Klamath Reservation," in *Social Anthropology of North American Tribes*, Fred Eggan, editor, pp. 375–442.

RELIGIOUS MOVEMENTS AMONG AMERICAN NEGROES

Negro sectarianism is a product of the same fundamental causes as sectarianism in general, but there are some special factors that have affected it. It can be understood only in the total context of the Negro's place in American society. With reference to its cultural content if not its functions, some attention must be paid to the persistence of at least a few African religious elements. Exploration of these questions would take us too far afield from our main interest, so that we must be content with this brief remark: The minority status of the Negro has a rigidity that gives it some aspects of a caste situation; and yet at the same time most Negroes identify fully with the main themes of American culture, have more and more absorbed its aspirations, and have begun to see a lessening of the restrictions that bind them. This contrast produces tensions that are to some degree different from those of a pure caste situation on the one hand or of a less rigid lower-class status on the other. With regard to the persistence of African religious practices and beliefs among American Negroes, there is wide disagreement. This "minimum" statement would perhaps be accepted by most writers: The beliefs and rites of American Negroes, particularly of the rural and more isolated groups, contain some African elements; but the functions of these survivals are to be understood only by reference to the contemporary situations that they face. The survivals, insofar as they exist, do not explain the working of Negro sects as attempts to struggle with life's problems; they simply help to explain the symbolic expression of those problems.[40]

Most Negroes in the United States attend segregated churches.[41] This is not to be understood solely as a manifestation of the discriminatory patterns of the dominant whites, although that is part of the explanation. Co-attendance at religious services would call constant attention to what many regard as the greatest weakness in the armor that protects the privileged position of whites—their moral ambivalence. Just as many

[40] For some questions—e.g., the description of the history of culture contact or the degree of acculturation—the details of the surviving elements are very important and would require systematic exploration. For a range of views on the persistence of Africanisms in America, see M. J. Herskovits, *The Myth of the Negro Past,* Harper and Brothers, 1941, where the importance of survivals is argued and A. H. Fauset, *Black Gods of the Metropolis* and E. F. Frazier, *The Negro in the United States,* The Macmillan Company, 1949, where their importance is minimized.

[41] See Liston Pope, "Caste in the Church," *Survey Graphic,* January, 1947, pp. 59–60 ff.; F. S. Loescher, *The Protestant Church and the Negro;* W. W. Alexander, *Racial Segregation in the American Protestant Church;* Dwight Culver, *Negro Segregation in the Methodist Church.*

whites do not want Negroes in their schools, their offices, their neighborhoods, so they want them excluded from their churches. Before the Civil War, to be sure, common worship was the rule, but this was not at all a sign of equality. It was rather an effort on the part of planters better to be able to control their slaves. At first they had opposed Negro members in their churches, for an old unwritten law declared that a Christian could not hold a fellow believer in bondage. Most churches, however, relaxed this doctrine by the development of the comforting thought, often expressed in the history of Christianity, that equality before God had no reference to earthly status. Thus they were able to conciliate the consciences of the slave-holders and win more power in the mission field. If some planters feared that Christianity would encourage the kind of revolution that shook Haiti or a Nat Turner rebellion, they were shown that the Gospel, properly taught, could encourage submission and peace. Thus, says Richard Niebuhr, the union of Negro and white in churches before the Civil War was ". . . in most instances designed to enlist the forces of religion in the task of preserving the civil relationship between masters and slaves." [42]

The appearance of more segregated churches after the Civil War is not simply a new assertion of white discrimination. It is also to be understood in terms of the different religious needs and interests that result from the different experiences of Negroes and whites, the desire of Negroes to use religion more effectively to protest against or adjust to their status, and the desire for organizations of their own which they can control. These causes, of course, would scarcely have come into being had it not been for the prior cause of discrimination which produced these various tendencies among Negroes. Niebuhr is undoubtedly right when he states that, although Negroes have frequently taken the initiative in forming separate churches, white men have furnished the motivating force. "Their unquestioned assumption of superior privileges, their unconscious wounding of Negro self-respect, their complacent acceptance of the morality of the world as fitting for the church, have once more divided the body of Christ along the lines of social class." [43]

Types of Negro Churches. It is impossible, of course, to speak of "the" Negro church, for there is a wide variety of types. One can think of a kind of continuum ranging from the churches of the plantation South, to the less isolated village, to the lower-class urban migrant, to the "native" urbanite of lower-class status, and finally to the churches of the middle and upper-class Negroes. In general, as one moves along this

[42] H. R. Niebuhr, *op. cit.*, pp. 252–253; see also pp. 236–263.
[43] *Ibid.*, p. 260.

continuum, he finds among the members an increase in education, a larger amount of assimilation to the values of the dominant group, a greater hope in the possibilities of improvement of status, more secularization of outlook, and an increase in secular alternatives for expression and for the achievement of one's goals. These all affect the personality tendencies, the needs, and the religious forms to be found among the various groups of Negroes.[44]

The plantation church expresses the religious needs of a group almost completely cut off from "the American dream" of equality and improvement of status. It accepts the social order as it finds it, furnishing its small and powerless congregation with the compensations of heaven. The members are given emotional release and relief from the tensions of their difficult lives by the music and shouting and dancing in the services. There is little of the asceticism and moral emphasis that begins to appear in other Negro churches as part of the effort to prove one's right to improvement of status—an improvement that is too unlikely to be imagined by this isolated group; ". . . instead of stressing self-control and bringing pressure toward impulse renunciation, they aid the individual in increasing his daily satisfaction in life by the ceremonials which relieve his guilt." [45] This kind of adjustment has become less and less common as a result both of the migration of Negroes from the plantation areas and the intrusion of urban influences into those areas.

The rural church in the non-plantation areas and in small villages has taken on additional functions. The increased expectancy of recreation, in a group that is still blocked completely from any share of the recreational life of the larger community, finds somewhat more expression in the program of the church. The entrance of hope for some improvement of individual status is reflected in an increasing attention to personal conduct, an emphasis on the need for abiding by the standards of the dominant society. Greater opportunities for leadership are found in the more complicated organizational structure of the group. The other-worldly element in their doctrines is still overwhelmingly important; but an indirect note of criticism against the white man may be sounded

---

[44] The following discussion attempts to systematize materials found in a large number of empirical studies. Among them, the following are of particular value: St. C. Drake and H. R. Cayton, *Black Metropolis;* V. E. Daniel, "Ritual and Stratification in Chicago Negro Churches," *American Sociological Review,* June, 1942, pp. 352–358; A. H. Fauset, *Black Gods of the Metropolis;* John Dollard, *Caste and Class in a Southern Town;* Charles S. Johnson, *Growing Up in the Black Belt;* Hortense Powdermaker, *After Freedom;* B. E. Mays and J. W. Nicholson, *The Negro's Church;* A. W. Davis, B. B. Gardner, and M. R. Gardner, *Deep South;* E. F. Frazier, *Negro Youth at the Crossways.* See also George E. Simpson and J. Milton Yinger, *op. cit.,* Chapter 18.

[45] John Dollard, *op. cit.,* p. 249.

by the suggestion that there may be a reversal of statuses in heaven, where the last shall be first. Hortense Powdermaker makes the interesting observation that the meekness of the rural and village Negro disguises strong aggressive feelings. Humbleness is an attempt to rescue victory from defeat; suffering is only a prelude to ultimate reward; one gets power from suffering.[46]

This idea that Christian virtue will be rewarded in "the sweet by-and-by," that ultimate victory will be given to the faithful, not the powerful, is similar in function to the Hindu conception of reincarnation. In both instances, the doctrines are tied to the belief that one's status in this world is not the important thing and that, in any event, one's status is not to be explained by evil social institutions, but by personal failures (whether in an earlier life, as with the Hindus, or in this life, as with the village Negroes). In this situation of relative powerlessness, acceptance and avoidance themes predominate. Religion does not challenge what it cannot hope to change. During the depression of the 1930's, the Negro church in the rural South did not blame the plantation system or other economic institutions for the poverty of the tenants, but attributed it to the thriftlessness and sinfulness of individuals. In Natchez, ". . . no preacher in either the rural or urban county was ever heard to complain in his pulpit against the plantation system. The dogma concerning economic behavior was always that the members should be hard and faithful workers." [47]

When the Negro peasant moves to the city, he acquires new problems, new aspirations, and new possibilities for the satisfaction of some of his needs. These all affect the nature of his religious life. He brings with him his rural training, of course; he is still poorly educated, still used to vivid emotional expressions in religion, still unable to formulate a critique of the society which keeps him in low status. He is also still segregated, and even more painfully aware of his inability to participate in many aspects of the life of the dominant society. The old and new influences combine to shape the nature of his religious life.

Although the city furnishes many opportunities for recreation and entertainment, they are often unavailable to the migrant, because of segregation, because they are not his accustomed modes of expression, or because he cannot afford them. His church continues, under these circumstances, to be a center for many aspects of his life, a quasi-community center where clubs may meet, dances held, music, plays, and

[46] "The Channeling of Negro Aggression by the Cultural Process," *American Journal of Sociology*, May, 1943, pp. 750–758.

[47] A. W. Davis, B. B. Gardner, and M. R. Gardner, *op. cit.*, pp. 416–417.

visiting enjoyed. The church services themselves, with their attention to "good music" and "good speaking," are recreational events in part. The migrant faces a difficult task of adjustment to the life of the city.

In the North, much of the old accustomed way of life has been shattered. Not only is the erstwhile southern Negro embarrassed by the presence of thousands of "sophisticated" Negroes who want no reminders of "back-home" ways, but the infinitely more baffling problem of making a new adjustment to life as a relatively free man, and consequently having to meet free competition (instead of the paternalistic regard so commonly manifested towards Negroes by white people in the South) are more than this type of Negro is able to cope with easily, after the experience of many years in the South.[48]

To the migrant, his religious group, which is most often a small, store-front sect, is a place where he tries to allay his sense of strangeness in the company of others similarly confused. He is taught new modes of responding to the dominant whites—a reduction in the acceptance theme, an increase in emphasis on avoidance (self-reliance and race consciousness) and some increase in open opposition.

The ecstatic services of many of the groups enable the members of the congregation to escape, for a few moments, the hardships and humiliations of life. The congeniality of the meetings of what Daniel has called the "semi-demonstrative cults," "affords fellowship, personal recognition, and tension release, so consoling to the former ruralite in the urban situation." [49] There continues to be a strong supernatural emphasis in the doctrines of these groups. The deprivations of this life are interpreted as unimportant or as preludes to the rewards in heaven for those who are faithful.

The various religious organizations of lower class, urban Negroes share many tendencies in common, but there are also important differences among them. They range from fairly standard Protestant sects to esoteric cults on the margins of the Christian tradition. The latter appeared in large numbers during the economic depression of the 1930's, offering "solutions" to the difficult problems of poverty, illness, discouragement, and discrimination. The cults shade off into the organizations of the charlatans and racketeers who consciously exploit human misery for gain and power. Negro cults share the tendencies which we used in our definition in Chapter 6: They are usually small, "store-front" groups, relatively short-lived, dominated by the leader, and often at sharp variance with the stream of Christian influence from which most of them

[48] Fauset, *op. cit.*, p. 80.
[49] V. E. Daniel, *op. cit.*, p. 358.

stem. Drake and Cayton report that the number of "Spiritualist" groups in the Negro community of Chicago increased from 17 to 51 between 1928 and 1938. Their description of some of the activities of such a group shows the way in which it combines several traditions and is affected by the other influences on the persons to whom it attempts to appeal:

It borrows its hymns from the Baptists and Methodists, and appropriates altar, candles, and statues from the Catholics. It offers healing, advice, and "good luck" for a prayer and the price of a candle or holy flower. It provides colorful robes for its preachers and "mediums," but despite its name it rarely offers messages from the dead. Its "mediums" claim direct contact with the sources of wisdom. And, most important, the Spiritualist church in Bronzeville has no unkind words for card-playing, dancing, policy, ward politics, or the "sporting life." [50]

In his description of a "Voodoo Cult" in Detroit, Benyon gives us a picture of the appeal of an esoteric religious movement to the recent Negro migrant. The cult was started by a "prophet" who usually went by the name of W. D. Fard. He claimed that he had come from Mecca to teach that the black men of North America are not Negroes, but members of the lost tribe of Shebazz who had been stolen by traders from Mecca 379 years ago. Fard came to restore the true language, nation, literature and religion of this lost tribe. Caucasians are colored persons who have lost their color. To solve their problems, the cult followers must obey the prophet of Allah, change their names (Fard usually received ten dollars for each new name), and accept the self-disciplines and mild asceticism of the group. Most of the 8,000 persons who Benyon estimates joined the Voodoo Cult, were recent migrants from the South. Shocked by the discovery that the North was not the great land of hope, disillusioned when they discovered that the whites who mistreated them worshipped the same God, caught in poverty and unemployment, crowded into slum areas, they found an appeal in this drastic redefinition of their situation.[51]

Such cult tendencies are not limited to Negroes, of course. They experience in accentuated form many of the pressures that some white persons also feel.[52] Nor are cultist movements the dominant ones among Negroes, many of whom find it uncongenial to depart so widely from the Christian heritage with which they feel closely identified.

[50] Drake and Cayton, op. cit., p. 642.

[51] See E. D. Benyon, "The Voodoo Cult Among Negro Migrants to Detroit," American Journal of Sociology, May, 1938, pp. 894–907.

[52] See Charles S. Braden, "Why are the Cults Growing," Christian Century, January 12, January 19, January 26, and February 2, 1944.

Thus the problems of the Negro migrant are manifest in the nature of his religious life: His emotional needs are reflected in the ecstatic services of worship and in the congeniality of the small groups; the need for a feeling of dignity and importance, to counter the crushing facts of segregation and low status, is shown in the widespread participation in the life of the church, in the very pattern of church organization; the desperate difficulties of his earthly status are related to a heavenly bliss; and his recreational and social needs as a member of a disprivileged community are demonstrated in the larger pattern of the church organization as a kind of community center. Whether these are "good" adjustments for the members, whether they do what it is generally supposed they are intended to do, is a very difficult question. We shall be concerned with that question briefly below; but we need to warn ourselves that the intended or supposed functions are not necessarily the actual, or the only, functions.

Those Negroes who have become adjusted to city life to some degree, those who are native urbanites, develop somewhat different tendencies and needs which affect their religious behavior. The break is not sharp, but new forces gradually come into play. There remain for most Negroes, of course, the overwhelmingly important facts of deprivation, of frustrated hopes, of segregation. These are modified somewhat, however, and are seen in a different light. The level of education is raised; occupational and income levels are improved for some; race consciousness (a sense of a common identity and in some measure a common fate) takes on a growing importance; more of the goals of the dominant group are absorbed, so that frustrations take on an added sharpness; forms of economic and political protest are nearer at hand, making the escapist doctrines of some of the religious groups seem less attractive; secular recreation and entertainment are more readily available, partly because of improved income, partly by the development of specifically Negro recreational ventures, partly by the growth in participation in voluntary associations. All of these developments inevitably affect the religious life of the urbanized Negro.

Although our data are not at all adequate for a precise statement, it seems clear that there is a decline in the participation in religious groups among the more thoroughly urbanized Negroes. With the increase in alternative ways of satisfying recreational interests, the growth in labor union memberships, the acquisition of some political power, and the like, some of the functions of the religious groups are reduced. The theologically inclined person is likely to say at this point: The fundamental religious problem remains: How is man, the sinner, able to achieve salvation? Whether one is lower or middle class, white or Negro, with or without political power, able to go to the movies or not are all marginal questions that become associated with religious groups under certain circumstances; but they should not be confused with the central religious question. The sociologist can profitably study this remark. There is a danger that if everything connected with a religious organization, from basketball games in the church gymnasium to Easter services, is taken into account in the analysis of religious behavior, the definition of the phenomenon of our interest may become vague indeed. Yet the sociologist must risk this danger. He must be concerned with the total range of the social and cultural systems that appear in connection with man's efforts to deal with the ultimate frustrations of life, with the coercive facts of death and pain, egocentricity and group tyranny, anxiety and bafflement. He must, in fact, be concerned precisely with the ways in which a vast variety of beliefs and activities become associated with what a religious leader might call the fundamental religious quest. He wants to be able to predict the kind of relationships that will occur between certain social, cultural, and personality facts on the one hand, and certain doctrines, rites, and religious group structures on the other. For persons with other interests, a different conception of the nature of religion, and perhaps a far narrower one, may be appropriate.

With this brief restatement of our point of view in mind, we can return to the examination of the slowly changing nature of religious life among urban Negroes. We find that the other-worldly emphasis remains dominant—as it does, indeed, among most of the churches even of the more prosperous whites. But moral questions receive more attention—not simply the questions of individual morality, but some concern with the problems of society. With the slow improvement in their economic status, an increase in their political power, and a growing hope for a better life, urban Negroes are less willing to accept the declaration that "the meek shall inherit the earth," or the belief that "when I get to heaven, gwine put on my shoes . . . and robe . . . and crown." There is an increasing hope—and demand—that they have shoes on earth; and a religion that does not sustain and work for that hope is left behind. Whether one considers "my home is over Jordan" a deep spiritual insight and brilliant adjustive achievement or a hopeless mirage, one must recognize that it is now being supplemented by a demand for at least a temporary cottage in Bronzeville. Some Negro sects have adjusted very slowly to this change, with a consequent loss of support; others have responded only by an anti-white sentiment that does not come to grips with the roots of the difficulties faced by Negroes; still others offer palliatives that relieve some of the temporary economic difficulties, for example, but leave the major problems unexplored. Secular organizations express most of the rising hope of Negroes. Despite a few protest themes in contemporary religion, an aggressive sect has yet to appear.

In the face of all this, one must say, however, that concern for the economic and political situation as it concerns Negroes is becoming more important in the churches that appeal to the urbanized groups, particularly those who have experienced some economic improvement. In such groups, ministers are expected to be "race men." They often encourage the support of Negro business and professional men and preach the doctrine of "the double-duty dollar." Religious leaders may help to organize boycotts against firms that discriminate against colored workers or customers. The 1955–1956 Montgomery, Alabama bus boycott is a nationally prominent example of this, but is by no means the first. A religious group may support, as does the Father Divine Peace Mission Movement, a chain of hotels (heavens) in which the members can find inexpensive meals and lodging. Because of widespread segregation, this has far more than an economic meaning. As Fauset says:

White Americans look forward to travel as one of life's richest boons; but the American Negro contemplates travel in the United States with a degree of misgiving amounting to dread. A Negro when setting out on a trip, either must have every stopover very carefully arranged in advance, or he must see to it that he does not arrive at an unknown place too late in the evening to shop around for accommodations; otherwise he is likely to be compelled to spend the night out of doors and without anything to eat.[53]

The more stable Negro churches have developed extensive programs, not only on the local level, but in their state and national organizations, thus increasing the opportunities for participation and leadership. Drake and Cayton believe this chance for self-expression is the main attraction of the Negro church.

With the increase in literacy, in adjustment to urban life, in self-confidence, Negroes require changes in form of worship, as well as in doctrine and church organization. There is a growth of what Daniel has called the Deliberative and Liturgical Denominations, a reduction in the vivid emotional expressions of the rural Negro and the migrant, an increased formality about the service. This is precisely the shift that occurs in the religious practices of whites, of course, as they have moved from

[53] Fauset, *op. cit.*, pp. 92–93.

isolated, rural areas and climbed up the class and educational ladders.

Turning to the churches of the Negro middle and upper classes—the last step on the continuum we are describing—we find no important new factors, only a further development of the trends we have described. This is a small group, with a fairly large proportion that is "unchurched," both because some of its members identify religion with the earlier "escapist" doctrines and emotionalism, and because the improvement of status has opened up other ways for trying to achieve life's values. For those who continue to participate in religious groups, the doctrines and rites that they find meaningful are scarcely to be distinguished from those of their white brethren. They differ, however, in making explicit the protest against discrimination and segregation.

Some Functional Consequences of Negro Religious Trends. We can conclude this discussion of Negro churches by asking again the question: What, in sum, are the consequences of the kinds of religious activity we have described? Referring particularly to the escapist and emotional forms of the rural and urban lower classes, can we discover in them clear-cut functions and/or dysfunctions? It is not difficult to find opinions on this question. Fauset writes:

> It *must* come [italics mine] as a great relief as well as release to such people to enter into the spirit of a group like one of the holiness cults, with its offer of assurance through grace and sanctification, and the knowledge that they will be aided not only in their efforts to support their customary burdens, but that in addition they will be equipped to measure arms with the white man, something they scarcely dreamed of doing previous to their advent into the North.[54]

On the other hand, Sperry points out:

> Way back in the 1830's Harriet Martineau noted the advertisements in the New Orleans papers of the sales of occasional lots of "pious negroes" as being an especially good bargain. They would give no trouble here and now. The modern radical Negro agitator regards his pious brothers as one of his liabilities; they are an obstacle to the full and final freedom of the race.[55]

These two supposed results of Negro religion—making a terribly difficult status bearable at the same time that it makes it more likely —are not mutually exclusive; in fact, the second may flow from the first. Whether they are functional or dysfunctional depends, of course, on the value premises from which one starts. To a white man who wants to

---

[54] *Ibid.,* p. 81.
[55] Willard L. Sperry, *Religion in America,* pp. 195–196.

keep the Negro in subservience, the second is functional and therefore the first is also, if it helps to assure the second. To a person, white or colored, who opposes racial discrimination, the reenforcement of low status by religious beliefs and practices is a dysfunction; and the effect of making a difficult status bearable, although desirable by itself, may also be tied to a chain of dysfunction.

Within the Negro group, a religious pattern may be functional for some, dysfunctional for others. A Negro preacher, for example, may find his various needs for leadership, for financial support from influential white persons, and the like, well served by a segregated church and the beliefs that support it. These are almost certain to be latent functions, not mentioned in any ideology by which he defends the segregated pattern. Members of his congregation may have some of their important desires frustrated by this same pattern. Needless to say, some Negro ministers set the highest value on Christian brotherhood and the elimination of discrimination; for them, both the latent and manifest consequences of segregated churches may be undesirable. Those Negroes who are most seriously disprivileged may be well served by religious beliefs and practices that help them to bear a status which in any event they are powerless to change, while those who live in a situation where there is some chance for improvement of status may be poorly served by the same beliefs and practices.

This last point raises again the question of functional alternatives. There are many ways in which men respond to the difficult problems they face. Not only are there various kinds of religious expressions, but these seen together are only one of a number of possibilities. Individuals may respond by utter personal demoralization, a loss of any will to act or even to live. This has happened to some American Indians and to members of other societies that have been overwhelmed by a powerful invading group; and it is the response of some Negroes. Mental illness may be interpreted as a form of adjustment, or escape from problems that are too difficult for the individual to face on a realistic basis. William James long ago pointed out the narrow line that separates some mental illness from various kinds of religious expressions. One can struggle with his problems by political as well as religious "escapism"—whether it be the Garveyite "back-to-Africa" movement among Negroes or a more sophisticated utopia. Or political and economic action may be the method chosen to deal with one's difficulties.

The objective student of religion still cannot describe adequately the combination of forces that determines the development of one response or adjustment rather than another. He can, however, specify some of the variables that enter into that determination. We have discussed above six variables that affect the possibilities of various kinds of religious response (the amount of hope, the nature of the religious tradition, the availability of secular movements, the degree of acculturation, the type of leadership, and the range of basic personality tendencies). These same variables also affect the likelihood that some of the other responses we have mentioned will be chosen, either supplementing or supplanting the religious adjustments.

Just as we know too little to predict with precision which of the various responses will be chosen by a particular individual or group, so we are not certain which ones are objectively possible, granted all the forces at work in a specific situation. It is unwise to complain that an "escapist" religion rigidifies the status pattern, if the only other adjustments available to individuals are utter demoralization and mental illness. But oppositely, it is unwise to say that religion helps a group to bear the enormous burdens of low status, if that very religion obscures the real possibilities of other kinds of action that could reduce those burdens. In the writer's judgment, there is *a tendency for* the religious movements of minority groups to be functional in the general sense (the satisfaction of the maximum possible needs of the individuals and group). That is, they slowly and partially demonstrate an adjustment to the actual limiting conditions and possibilities of life. It is in the *lag*, however, the slowness to respond to changes in the conditions and possibilities, that critics of religion (friendly or otherwise) are likely to find the most useful point of departure and the analyst of religion some of his most difficult problems.

CHAPTER 8

Religion and Economics

In the preceding chapter we have shown how religious doctrines, rites, and group structures vary among various strata of a society. Although we have been primarily concerned with the description of the differences in religious life, we have suggested at several points the way in which these differences are involved in economic and political questions. In this chapter and the next we shall explore these questions directly, building on the earlier discussion.

The central problems of economics, as an objective science, are the determination of the way in which value is ascribed to goods and services, the description of how a society distributes its income, and the study of the organizations and the processes through which the various scarce resources are combined to produce the desired values. This last shades off into the study of technology, to which, strictly speaking, the problem of the scarcity of the resources is irrelevant. A plant manager asks a technological question when he considers how he can produce a given object; he asks an economic question when he wonders whether it is worthwhile for him to produce that object (instead of using labor, materials, plant in alternative ways). Although economic and technological questions can be clearly distinguished, they mutually affect

195

each other in important ways: The costs of the various resources are among the factors that determine a technological decision on *how* to produce; and the available technical processes of production are among the factors determining an economic decision on *whether* to produce.

Religion is involved in both the strictly economic and in the technological questions. We shall be primarily concerned with the former, which has through the course of history become the more significant relationship, but will deal briefly first with the latter problem.

RELIGION AND TECHNOLOGY

It would be an over-simplification to state, without qualification, that the more primitive the technology and the more precarious and uncertain the results from one's efforts to obtain food and other goods, the more religion is used to bolster man's efforts. Yet the correlation is undoubtedly high. Religion is very widely used as one of the techniques by which success in the hunt, productivity of the garden, protection for the flocks is sought in primitive societies. Some writers describe the desire to re-enforce a desperately inadequate technology as one of the complex of forces that lie at the very origin of religion. Radin writes:

> To understand the beginnings of religion we must try to visualize as accurately as we can the conditions under which man lived at the dawn of civilization. Manifestly he lived in a variable and essentially inimical physical environment and possessed a most inadequate technological preparation for defending himself against this environment. . . . His methods of food production were of the simplest kind—the gathering of grubs and berries and the most elementary type of fishing and hunting. He had no fixed dwellings, living in caves or natural shelters. No economic security could have existed, and we cannot go far wrong in assuming that, where economic security does not exist, emotional insecurity and its correlates, the sense of powerlessness and the feeling of insignificance, are bound to develop.[1]

Out of this context, says Radin, came the beliefs and rites of primitive religion.

Whether or not the inadequacy of the technical resources of man was involved in the origin of religion, it certainly was involved in many of its expressions. It is not surprising that in societies where survival itself depended upon the annual rains that their most sacred beliefs and most devout rites should be appeals for rain—as among the Zuni, the Lovedu, or the aboriginal Australians. In a society where agricultural production

---

[1] Paul Radin, *Primitive Religion: Its Nature and Origin,* pp. 6–7.

has been vastly improved, where ever-normal granaries and rapid transportation virtually eliminate the threat of starvation, rain-making becomes, not a matter of religio-magic ceremony, but of airplanes and silver iodide. Even in the societies that have achieved a great deal of technical efficiency, however, food production is sometimes threatened by drought. The welfare of a region and the livelihood, if not the survival, of thousands of families may be endangered. Religious beliefs (this is punishment for evil or a test of faith) and practices (prayers that the drought may be broken) may then return as marginal, if not basic, activities in connection with food production.

The relationship between technology and religion is a complicated one requiring attention to several qualifications: Some societies with fairly proficient techniques of production nevertheless have developed an intricate connection between their technology and religion; some religious beliefs and practices which are clearly antithetical to efficient production, are devoutly defended anyway, because they are religiously right; and many of the observances to assure productivity are more nearly magical (as we have defined that term) than religious. These qualifications, which we will keep in mind as we discuss and illustrate the connections between religion and technology, should prevent us from making any easy technological explanation of religion. They do not, however, eliminate the fact of a broad pattern of relationship.

Societies with pantheistic religions generally are well supplied with gods and goddesses who are the patrons of crafts, protectors of flocks, guarantors of fertility. Ceremonial detail is interwoven with technical act; sacrifice and petition to the deities are considered essential to success; holy days and festivals are devoted to praise of the protecting deities. Concerning the Zuni, Benedict writes:

If they are asked the purpose of any religious observance, they have a ready answer. It is for rain. This is of course a more or less conventional answer. But it reflects a deep-seated Zuni attitude. Fertility is above all else the blessing within the bestowal of the gods, and in the desert country of the Zuni plateau, rain is the prime requisite for the growth of crops. The retreats of the priests, the dances of the masked gods, even many of the activities of the medicine societies are judged by whether or not there has been rain. To "bless with water" is the synonym of all blessing. Thus, in the prayers, the fixed epithet the gods apply in blessing to the rooms in Zuni to which they come, is "water-filled," their ladders are "water-ladders," and the scalp taken in warfare is the "water-filled covering." The dead, too, come back in rain clouds, bringing the universal blessing. People say to the children when the summer afternoon rain clouds come up the sky, "Your grandfathers are coming," and the reference is not to the individual dead relatives, but applies impersonally to all forbears. The masked gods also are the rain and when they dance they constrain their own being—rain—to descend upon the people. The priests, again, in their retreat before their altars sit motionless and withdrawn for eight days, summoning the rain. . . . Rain, however, is only one of the aspects of fertility for which prayers are constantly made in Zuni. Increase in gardens and increase in the tribe are thought of together.[2]

Malinowski found, among the Trobriand Islanders, an interesting contrast that points up the way in which magical practice supplements technological activity, particularly in societies that live a precarious existence. In the situation he describes, more than in the case of the Zuni, the beliefs and rites that are connected with technology incline toward magic rather than toward religion. The reference is to a specific goal more than to general social welfare. The practices are not thought to be ends in themselves, but means to ends. But as we have seen, one cannot readily assign the complexes of belief and ritual simply to magic or to religion. Malinowski found that two closely related tribes approached their common task of fishing quite differently. One tribe, which fished largely in protected inland waters and lagoons where there was little danger and little chance of failure, carried on their work quite matter-of-factly. There was no room for precautionary rituals aimed at protecting the men and insuring a good catch. The other tribe fished in the open sea, where the catch was much less certain and the hazards far greater. Around their work they had developed an elaborate system of rites, in an effort to placate the unknown forces that constantly threatened their success and to rid themselves of the sense of insecurity.[3]

Such practices are not, as Malinowski makes abundantly clear, simply a mistaken or crude kind of technology, a kind of "primitive science," rooted in complete lack of knowledge of the real causes of events. Primitive man follows his technology as far as it will take him—and he often manifests an extensive understanding of the technical facts. But he knows also that no matter how carefully he does his work he may, for reasons beyond his control and usually beyond his comprehension, fail to get a good catch or harvest a good crop. It is at this point that he grasps for the assurance of magical and religious practices.[4]

In some societies, the relationship between religion and technology is exceedingly close even though they have developed a fairly abundant and stable source of food. This is true, for example, of the Todas of South India, whose economy is built around dairying activities. A large share

---

[2] Ruth Benedict, *Patterns of Culture*, pp. 58–59.
[3] See Bronislaw Malinowski, *Argonauts of the Western Pacific*.
[4] See Malinowski's paper "Magic, Science, and Religion," in *Science Religion and Reality*, Joseph Needham, editor, pp. 30–32.

of the work in caring for the cattle is carried on in accordance with the prescribed ceremonial forms by dairymen-priests.[5] These are not desperate attempts to bolster a shaky technology by supernatural means, for the Todas have a fairly adequate and secure food supply. Some may assume that the intricate connection between religion and technology demonstrates the survival of beliefs and rites that originated in more difficult times; but this assumption requires more careful proof than the data now permit. It is possible, in fact, that the relationship was the other way around: the religiously prescribed value assigned to cattle and to their care may have helped to bolster the economy. Or the relationship may have been interactive.

This qualification suggests the further comment that religious requirements may be clearly opposed to the efficient production and use of economic goods. They may be recognized as such, and defended on religious grounds, or they may be held to be subtle aids to technology. The actual effects would be, under such circumstances, latent dysfunctions. Taboos on the consumption of certain foods—ritualistic restriction on the use of totem animals to certain periods of the year, for example—may sometimes help to protect a food supply; but at other times, taboos permanently remove an available food from human use. Ceremonial restrictions on techniques of production may prevent the development of efficient processes. The observance of holy days and festivals or the carrying out of the requirements of mourning rituals may prevent work for significant periods of time. These are in part strictly economic influences on production—determining how the members of a society shall use scarce goods or scarce time; but they are in part also technological influences, for they affect the work processes themselves.

On the other hand, religious observance may increase productivity. As Goode says, "the very cooperation expected by ritual conformity may actually increase efficiency at the time." Religious demands for particular care of gardens or animals may increase the supply of food. Craftsmen may be religiously motivated to develop a higher skill in their work. These are primarily technological effects. It is more likely, however, that the religious encouragement to production will be economic, rather than technological. It is not so likely to affect the actual techniques of work as it is to influence the use of time and material: Religious requirements may motivate the members of a society to productive activity rather than to some alternate use of time, just as they may do the opposite. Thrift may be religiously obligatory. "In order to please the gods one must save or acquire enough food or wealth for the payments,

---

[5] See W. H. R. Rivers, *The Todas.*

gifts, or offerings needed." [6] Weber has argued, as we shall see later, that the religious prescriptions of Calvinism have strongly influenced the productivity of capitalist societies. The relationship is perhaps more complicated than he made it out to be, but freed of its exaggerations, his thesis is a clear demonstration of the significance of religion for technological and economic matters.

Whether one concludes that religion basically contributes to or interferes with technological efficiency—and it would seem that the latter is the predominant effect—it is a mistake to assume that the members of a society, in following the religious norms, think of themselves simply as using an efficient process to increase production. The technological relevance of religion is distinctly secondary to the basic problems of group integration and individual salvation. There are *implications* for technology in religious belief and action, but seldom direct concern. The relationship is well analyzed by Goode, in his discussion of the Manus, a society that stresses the importance of shrewd economic calculation. Their religious life centers around a personal deity, Sir Ghost; but the Manus do not regard their deities simply as powerful forces who can bring them food, prestige, health, and so on, if they are properly manipulated. Such a secular and rational attitude would deny the religious relationship.

The strongly rationalistic element in the Manus economic system displays itself in a cool calculation of the profits to be made from various enterprises, and the exploitation of one's kin in various ways. Since the religious system includes, as do other religions, requests for favors on the part of the worshipper, as well as giving favors to the spirits, one might expect a strong contractualistic bias in the Manus pattern of religious activity. To some extent this exists. . . .

However, this relationship between economic contract and the religious pattern does not turn out to be one of identity. . . . rational calculation cannot alone constitute any basis for the continued existence of a society. Each society follows certain values, among which are religious ideas and practices, and these are not subject to logico-empirical proof or disproof. These partly furnish the motivation to action for the members of that society. However, if a religious system were found in which the individual merely manipulated the sacred forces for personal advantage, in a cooly shrewd and impersonal manner, that general contention would have to be modified basically. Specifically, if the Manus actually do think of their Sir Ghosts only in terms of what the Sir Ghost can bring them in the form of food, health, wealth, and so forth, then this theory could not be accepted as it has been presented.

In general terms, the answer is clear. The attitude of the Manus toward the favors performed for Sir Ghost is that they express his solicitude for Sir

[6] See William J. Goode, *Religion Among the Primitives*, pp. 135–137.

Ghost. Also, he does not think of his relationship to Sir Ghost as merely a contractual one, worth only what it might bring in an "open market." The relationship must rather be considered a covenant. . . .

Its functions are different from those of the Manus contract, which is individualistic and nonmoral. For what seems at first to be a mere trade of good fishing and health for some respect and a food offering to a skull or spirit is, on closer examination, a public and moral connection and an important factor in maintaining public morality. . . .

Sir Ghost in turn is not merely the helper of the Manus, but insists on the other hand that the individual accept and live up to the demands of various economic obligations, by husbanding his resources, by allocating his wealth to the proper channels instead of using it selfishly or shortsightedly, and by producing energetically so as to make his payments when they are required.[7]

Thus religion, struggling with the fundamental problems of human existence, inevitably reaches out to affect technology, as it affects all other aspects of life, in the effort to solve these problems. It is, in turn, affected by the technological facts and requirements of society. The nature of the influence of religion on technology varies widely, as we have seen. The fact that its "solutions" are largely symbolic means that a wide range of possibilities may be tried. There are only a certain number of ways to plant and care for a garden that will yield a crop. But there are infinite possibilities for variations in religious rituals that are calculated to assure a good harvest. The religious influence on technology is particularly likely to be strong in those societies that have least successfully solved the problems of production, because it is in just such societies that the individual and group functions of religion are persistently affected by low productivity. If a religious system is to carry out these functions, it must solve the problems (intra-group tension, individual anxiety, more illness and death, etc.) that derive from inadequate technology. And so it tries. In technically efficient societies, other problems are more likely to press in on religion for solution.

RELIGION AND THE DISTRIBUTION OF WEALTH

In the preceding discussion, some aspects of the relationship of religion to economic questions were raised, particularly those associated with production, because of their inevitably close association with technology. We have noted that the ways in which scarce time, skill, and resources are used are often affected by religiously motivated decisions. The structure of work groups and situations may be influenced by religion. Thus

[7] *Ibid.*, pp. 99–105.

the study of a Hindu caste, or a medieval manor, or some labor unions reveals that economic questions concerning the production of goods and services are conditioned by religious values.

A second economic question—the description of the way in which comparative values are ascribed to the products of society—is also influenced, at least to a small degree, by religious considerations. Some goods and services are worth more, have a higher economic value, because they have a religious value, and others are worth less because religion places a negative value upon them. A primitive man may invest a great deal of time and skill—an economic decision—to carve the appropriate symbols or designs on a sacred drum, because they contribute to its religious efficacy. Were it not for their religious meaning, he would not value them so highly and would be unwilling to spend so much for them. Similarly, a church may invest a great deal of money in a stained-glass window, because of the meaning it has for the members. Thus religion affects the demand side of the familiar supply-demand equation. On the other hand, it may influence the supply side, if the values it upholds encourage or discourage the production of various goods and services.

These are rather specific economic problems, and we shall not, therefore, give them further attention. It is in the influences on the distribution of wealth and income that religion has its most significant economic effects; and it is also at this point that the economic consequences of religion are most important for society, culture, and personality. Hence the sociologist of religion must explore this question carefully.

In the first place, religious activity everywhere receives a certain share —often a fairly large share—of the wealth of a society. Even those groups that live on the edge of subsistence devote part of their substance to the maintenance of holy places, sacrifices, ceremonial feasts, sacred objects, and the like. Indeed, if there is any correlation between the amount of wealth of a society and the proportion of its wealth that is spent for religion, it may be an inverse one: the poorer the society or group, the higher the proportion of its wealth that is devoted to religious activity.

Part of this expenditure, in societies where religious specialists have appeared, is used to support the priestly class. This adds a new dimension to the question of the economic significance of religion, especially where there is no clear-cut determination by the religious values themselves of the appropriate share of the income that should go to the religious professionals. The traditions may encourage mendicancy, as with the early Buddhists or some Christian monastics. But more commonly the religious norms encourage, or at least permit, the priestly group to strive for a larger share of the wealth. The religious views may then combine with secular ambitions among the clergy, who in most instances have secular as well as religious interests, to bring them substantial incomes. As mediators, if not as dispensers, of salvation, they are often in a commanding position. If their religious authority is combined, by a churchly decision, with the power of secular authorities, they may dominate or share in the ruling of the society and even acquire substantial wealth.

Some will say at this point: This is not a description of the economic power of religion, but of the transformation of religion into a secular quest, under religious guise. Perhaps so. But it is precisely in the possibilities of such transformation, in the frequency with which religious institutions take on secular power, that many of the implications of religion for society reside. Sometimes it is the religious professionals themselves who gain wealth and power; sometimes it is a secular group who acquire religious sponsorship for their claims to hold, or to win, wealth and power; often it is both.

Analysis of the conditions under which these various possibilities occur is an important task. The following variables seem to be involved, and we shall have them in mind as we discuss some of the evidence relating to religion and the distribution of wealth.

1. *The Degree of Secularization.* Where most of the questions of life have a religious aspect, the importance of religion for economics is likely to be large, and the priestly class likely to be well supported. Where many important questions—e.g., health, technology—are thought of primarily in secular terms, as in the United States today, the economic influence of religion is reduced.

2. *The Nature of the Religious Traditions and Organizations.* Religions in which ethical questions are least important, those in which the means to salvation are most thoroughly institutionalized, most under the domination of one ecclesiastical group, and least under the control of the individual believer, are those that aid the acquisition of power by the professional religious leaders.

3. *The Nature of Power Distribution in the Secular Aspects of Society.* When economic and political power are highly concentrated in the hands of a small ruling group, the higher clergy are likely to occupy positions of influence and to share generously in the income of a society. Under such circumstances, churchly compromise with "the world" is carried very far; the rulers and their practices are upheld and defended with a minimum of criticism. This is partly because the dilemma of religious leaders which we have discussed is particularly sharp in authoritarian societies;

and it is partly because the secular gains for the clergy, if they will support the ruling group, are large in such societies. In democratic situations, where power is diffused, the dominant group is less willing to share influence and income with religious leaders if they will sanctify their dominant position. Powerful secular groups have little to gain thereby, because the lower strata of society have other means—political action, labor unions, etc.—of making their claims in any event. It is of little value to block one hole in a sieve, of little value to inhibit the claims to a greater share of life's goods under religious auspices if they are going to have other auspices anyway. Moreover, the lower classes, in a democratic society, are less likely to accept a religious system that has accommodated itself thoroughly to the dominant groups, because they have other means of working for their goals.

These three variables are closely interrelated. Their combined effect can be to influence strongly the wealth of the churches and the income of the clergy. In the United States, for example, religious professionals are not, on the average, well paid. Their income is below that of industrial workers. Each of the variables contributes to this result: Many questions that formerly had a strong religious aspect have been substantially secularized; there is a strong emphasis on religious toleration and the right of an individual to be his own religious interpreter—the opposite of a monopoly on the means of salvation; and secular power is quite extensively diffused.

When such a situation is compared with that of medieval Europe, the importance of the three factors in affecting the wealth of the church and the income of the clergy is well shown. In medieval times, the interpretation of medical, agricultural, astronomical, and other kinds of events was far less secularized. One church, organized into an elaborate hierarchy with a monopoly over sacraments, using a language unknown to the masses of people, dominated the religious scene. Individual initiative in religious matters, the expression of the belief that the layman could have dealings directly with God, without the need for the intercession of the church, were heretical acts, justifying severe punishment. Finally, the secular setting was one in which power was highly concentrated in the hands of the hereditary nobility. Under these circumstances, the churches and the clergy commanded a great deal of wealth. It was very unequally distributed, to be sure; the majority of priests were far from affluent; but the total wealth, especially in land, was great. Preserved Smith writes:

The wealth of the church was enormous, though exaggerated by those contemporaries who estimated it at one-third of the total real estate of Western

Europe. In addition to revenue from her own land, the church collected tithes and taxes . . . . the clergy paid dues to the curia . . . . the priests recouped themselves by charging high fees for their ministrations. At a time when the Christian ideal was one of 'apostolic poverty' the riches of the clergy were often felt as a scandal to the pious.[8]

In the analysis of the influence of religion and religious institutions on the distribution of wealth, however, it is not the effects on the priestly class that have received most attention or are most important, for they are generally a fairly small proportion of the population. The use of religion to hold or to acquire a greater share of the wealth by *secular* classes and groups, from all levels of society, is the more fundamental phenomenon. The analysis of the factors affecting the income of professional religious leaders can be brought within this larger question, for it is the nature of their association with the secular groups that is largely responsible for their income position. In our further discussion of religion and the distribution of wealth, therefore, we shall deal with these two aspects together.

Description of the use of religion by secular groups to hold or acquire scarce values is very closely related to the topic of religion and social stratification, with which we dealt in the last chapter. Our concern here, however, is not so much with the variations in beliefs, rites, and religious-group structure among social strata and the several reasons for these variations. It is more with the processes of interaction by means of which religion is used to justify specifically economic claims. This will require that we explore, more fully than we have up until now, the churches of the middle and upper classes, as we have already studied the sects of the lower classes. The sects have seldom, at least for long, made direct economic claims on the basis of religion. The actual facts of the situation have too persistently frustrated their desires for improving their status by appeals to religion to permit them much hope. Their religious expressions, therefore, have been more inclined to redefine the meaning of their economic status (poverty is a sign of virtue; this life is scarcely significant anyway) than to attack it. The consequences of their religious beliefs for economic matters have been more indirect than direct, latent rather than manifest functions. This is true whether those consequences have been to make their status more rigid, by reducing motivation to change, or to make it less rigid, by encouraging frugality and industry.

It is otherwise with the middle and upper classes. They face many serious difficulties, to be sure, but their economic hopes have been substan-

[8] *The Age of the Reformation*, pp. 21–22.

tially rewarded, not frustrated. Their task is not to adjust to poverty and powerlessness, but to feel justified in their good fortune. This too can be a difficult problem, particularly among those who share a religious tradition that embodies a large measure of the insights and responses of persons who were dealing with ill-fortune. This is true of all major religions. They are substantially the products of suffering, of a sense of evil, of unhappiness, often as these problems have been developed in the minds of people peculiarly sensitive to them. The well-to-do share these religions because they are brought up in societies where they prevail, but more importantly because they too, in the last analysis, face the problems of suffering and evil, even if in somewhat different ways. So they embrace religions that help them struggle with these difficulties. But they do not suffer from poverty. Can they get religious sponsorship for this *lack* of suffering? They succeed in doing so in the churches; but this cannot be done without transforming them, to a greater or lesser degree, into secular institutions, reducing their ability to help other classes, and, in the long run, weakening their ability to deal with the particularly religious problems of the dominant classes themselves.

RELIGION AND THE ECONOMIC CLAIMS OF PRIVILEGED CLASSES

We can test the usefulness of these propositions by describing a few specific situations in which churches gave substantial support to the dominant groups and to the institutions through which they maintained their position, furnishing the privileged persons with a justification for their good fortune. Because of the richness of the sources, this can perhaps best be done by analyzing the interaction between the bourgeoisie (the industrial and commercial classes that came slowly into power from the late medieval period on) and the religious leaders and groups of their societies. This will require that we bring in various aspects of the relationship between religion and social change—anticipating some of the discussion of a later chapter.

SOME ECONOMIC ASPECTS OF THE REFORMATION

We can begin this discussion with the Reformation.[9] Our concern will not be with a description of all phases of this religious movement, but

---

[9] Among the large number of studies of the Reformation, the following works are particularly helpful in the analysis of its economic and political significance: H. B. Workman, *The Dawn of the Reformation;* T. N. Lindsay, *A History of the Reformation;* Preserved Smith, *The Age of the Reformation;* G. G. Coulton, *Five Centuries*

only with the way in which it was involved, as cause and/or effect, in the gradual development of power among the middle classes. There are several possible explanations of the significance of the Reformation for the rise of the middle classes: 1. It may be claimed that the Reformation, particularly its Calvinist phase, is primarily an invention of the new classes to justify their new vocations and claims to power. 2. Oppositely, it may be declared that the Reformation is a strictly religious movement, with no implications for the economic situation of the time. 3. It may be held that it is substantially religious in its origins, but that the ways in which it dealt with the problems of evil and salvation were peculiarly influential in shaping motivational and ethical approaches to economic questions. 4. Finally, it may be argued that the Reformation was a complex movement with many different possibilities within it, a product of developments in intrinsic religious thought, of continuity with the medieval church, and of the problems of the emerging new society; and from this complexity, different groups with different economic needs, selected and shaped beliefs and practices that were meaningful to them.

The first two of these explanations seem to the writer to be clearly inadequate. The latter two offer far better possibilities for a valid theory, particularly if they are combined in such a way as to emphasize the *interaction* of the economic requirements of the new classes and the religious requirements of the new movements. We shall approach the subject primarily from the perspective of the fourth statement, but with the addition of some aspects of the third. The *origins* of a religious movement cannot be explained simply in terms of the economic and other needs of the groups who may later embrace it, although it is in part a product of economic and other secular problems. *In the beginning,* it intrudes into an economic situation with some force of its own, setting the direction of economic change to some degree, even though through the course of the years and generations the religious movement will itself be reshaped by various classes in ways that support their various claims and needs.

It is no accident that the Reformation occurred during a period of political upheaval and economic change. It was, in fact, one of several developments—and by no means the first—which protested against the religious, political, and economic situation of the late medieval and early modern periods. Territorial and national churches, designed to buttress

---

of Religion, Vol. 3; A. C. McGiffert, *Protestant Thought Before Kant;* Ernst Troeltsch, *The Social Teaching of the Christian Churches,* Vol. 2; Max Weber, *The Protestant Ethic and the Spirit of Capitalism;* R. H. Tawney, *Religion and the Rise of Capitalism;* Wilhelm Pauck, *The Heritage of the Reformation.* Several paragraphs in this and the following chapter have been taken from the writer's *Religion in the Struggle for Power,* with the permission of the Duke University Press.

the emerging nations against the claims of the papacy, are part of the history of England, France, Germany, and elsewhere. Several sect movements—Cathars, Waldenses, Lollards, Hussites—preceded Luther and to some degree prepared the ground for the Reformation. Peasant uprisings expressed discontent; a secular literature, such as the work of Marsiglio of Padua, called for the dominance of the state, with the church limited to religious functions. The Conciliar Movement sought to reduce the power of the papacy and to decentralize the authority of the church. Such developments as these expressed the widespread discontent with the religious and secular patterns of the time.

Part of the protest against the church was secular. The ecclesiastical system was not simply a religious organization, but a government, controlling vast lands and collecting large sums of money. The history of the papacy itself up to the Reformation had been a story of increasing secularization.

At Rome the popes came to occupy the position of princes of one of the Italian states, and were elected, like the doges of Venice, by a small oligarchy. Within seventy years the families of Borgia, Piccolomini, Rovere, and Medici were each represented by more than one pontiff, and a majority of the others were nearly related by blood or marriage to one of these great stocks. The cardinals were appointed from the pontiff's sons or nephews, and the numerous other offices in their patronage, save as they were sold, were distributed to personal or political friends.[10]

The political murders of Sixtus IV (1471–1484), the bribes paid by Innocent VIII for his election, the intrigue associated with Alexander VI and his son Caesar Borgia and his daughter Lucretia all testify to the secularization of the papacy.

The significance of this development is increased by the fact that through the course of centuries, the participation of laymen in the affairs of the church had been sharply curtailed. Salvation was available only through the ministrations of the priests. And this monopolization of the means of salvation was used as an instrument of political power and a source of extensive wealth. Income from land holdings, tithes, and taxes, was very great. In addition, many church offices were filled by sale, and dues were often levied on the first year's income from an ecclesiastical appointment. These charges were passed on to the constituents of the parish. It is easy to suppose that such practices weakened the "faith" of those who were becoming more and more involved in the expanding commercial economy and of the more traditionally religious peasants and

[10] Preserved Smith, *op. cit.*, pp. 15–16.

artisans. As Smith says, "The common man's conscience was wounded by the smart in his purse."

The sale of indulgences was another rich source of revenue which became more and more an ordinary means of raising money for the ecclesiastical powers.

How thoroughly commercialized the business of selling grace and remission of the penalties of sin had become is shown by the fact that the agents of the pope were often bankers who organized the sales on purely business lines in return for a percentage of the net receipts plus the indirect profits accruing to those who handle large sums. Of the net receipts the financiers usually got about ten per cent.; an equal amount was given to the emperor or other civil ruler for permitting the pardoners to enter his territory, commissions were also paid to the local bishop and clergy, and of course the pedlars of the pardons received a proportion of the profits in order to stimulate their zeal. On the average from thirty to forty-five per cent. of the gross receipts were turned into the Roman treasury.[11]

Thus the territories were drained of vast resources. It is not difficult to see in this situation the seeds of revolt. Two classes shared a common grievance against the church: "the lower class, earlier in the field, struggling for existence, and the middle class, struggling for power." [12]

It would be a mistake, of course, to suppose that the Reformation was simply an economic and political revolt, disguised in religious symbols. Concomitant with the secularization of the ecclesiastical structure and its position as a secular power was the decline of its ability to satisfy the religious needs of many people. A religion that "integrates" society only on the basis of the relationships of an agrarian and feudal system, can only help to "disintegrate" a society that is coming more and more to involve urban, commercial, and industrial groups; for this societal function of religion can be carried out only if these new groups are given a place in the social order and if the new problems that urban life brings are given attention. A religion that deals fairly successfully with the personal needs of an illiterate peasantry and a self-confident nobility may find that its system of beliefs, rites, and church structure is quite inadequate for a more mobile and secularized urban proletariat. It will be even less adequate for commercial classes who have been affected by a Renaissance, by the intellectual climate that produced a Petrarch, a Boccaccio, an Erasmus, by a growing spirit of individualism, as well as by the need for a conviction that their new occupations are legitimate. The ecclesiastical

[11] *Ibid.*, p. 24.
[12] E. S. Bates, *American Faith*, p. 26.

institutions preceding the Reformation were also very unsatisfactory to those priests and monks and others whose primary concern continued to be with religion. In 1372 the monasteries of the Rhineland entered into a compact to resist the levy of Gregory XI, who was demanding a tithe of their revenues. They wrote:

In consequence . . . of the exactions with which the Papal Court burdens the clergy, the Apostolic See has fallen into such contempt that the Catholic faith in these parts seems to be seriously imperilled. The laity speak slightingly of the Church, because, departing from the custom of former days, she hardly ever sends forth preachers or reformers, but rather ostentatious men, cunning, selfish and greedy. Things have come to such a pass that few are Christians more than in name.[13]

Societal Factors in Lutheranism. The prophets, the reformers themselves cannot be understood outside of their secular context, but it is their concern for the inadequacies of the medieval church as a religious institution that represents the center of the Reformation as they developed it. Their work was then embraced, and changed, by many groups who saw in it the possibilities for solutions of their secular and religious problems. Luther's propositions had relevance immediately for several of these problems, particularly those of the groups who were rising to power. Their secular interests were related to the emergence of independent states, freed from the domination of Rome. Germany had had, before Luther, a long history of opposition to the dominance of the Pope. The economic interests of individuals on almost every level of society would be affected by a reduction in papal authority. We need not undertake an analysis of the complexities of Luther's thought except to point out ways in which the doctrines which he emphasized are relevant to the topic of this chapter.

Perhaps most significant in this regard is the emphasis he gave to the doctrine that salvation comes, not by works, but from faith only. Not the acceptance of proper sacraments, but faith is the mark of the Christian. This was a revolutionary challenge to the church.

In view of the fact that in the Catholic Church all avenues of salvation are controlled by the priest, the elimination of a professional priesthood, as Luther recommended, implied the end of the Church itself. At an early stage Wycliffe had championed the ideal of a priestless church, but he had been unable to transform this ideal into reality. Luther, however, ruling out the conventional forms of mediation between God and man, succeeded in establishing the

[13] Quoted by H. B. Workman, *op. cit.*, Vol. I, pp. 36–37.

autonomous parish with a vicar elected and if necessary deposed by the parishioners.[14]

In his later years, to be sure, Luther came to disagree with Wycliffe and Huss and other more complete protestants in seeing the church as an indispensable means of salvation—not because, as with the Catholics, it dispenses grace, but because it teaches the gospel.

In this we see a second significant element of his protest—the shift from the claim that religious truth was revealed in church doctrines and traditions and the interpretations of the hierarchy, to the declaration that the Bible was the fountain of truth. Luther supported this declaration by his translation of the Bible which made its study available to the layman. Religious thought and interpretation were thus, to a far larger degree, democratized and individualized.

As one aspect of his protest against the selling of indulgences, Luther accepted the doctrine of predestination, a belief that supported his attack on the church as the mediator of salvation and harmonized with his conception of justification by faith alone. We shall be concerned later with the way in which predestinarianism may have influenced the behavior of the middle classes. It can affect individuals in very different ways, so that it is important to discover why one person or group interprets it one way, while others interpret it differently. To an intensively religious person, it may permit the development of a disinterestedness in his own needs, a selflessness in charity—for if one is already saved, his concern for others need not disguise a deeper concern for himself. "No one can give himself in self-forgetful love to the service of his neighbour so long as he is anxious and troubled about his own fate." [15] The effects of the doctrine of predestination, however, may be different with others. It may encourage a passive resignation—for why should one try to change a situation, or even to act, when one's lot is determined even before he is born? This is likely to be the reaction of those who are already, because of the discouraging outlook of their lives, inclined toward resignation. On the other hand, there may be those who are encouraged for other reasons (expanding economic opportunity, for example) to act vigorously, who will be persuaded by predestinarianism to act even more energetically in order to convince themselves and others that they are of the elect. Just as the same wind can blow two boats in opposite directions, so one doctrine can influence people who are already inclined in different ways to

[14] Walther Köhler, *Encyclopedia of Social Sciences*, Vol. 13, p. 189.
[15] A. C. McGiffert, *op. cit.*, p. 37.

respond very differently. Thus a predestinarianism that was given a place of importance by Luther (and even more emphasis by Calvin) had one meaning for the religious leaders and very different (latent) consequences for various groups who accepted it.

The beliefs and activities of Luther that we have discussed had implicit within them forces that supported the rising urban and commercial society. Luther's influence, however, was more negative than positive in this regard; it helped to clear the ground, but it did not build a modern edifice. Luther contributed to the destruction of the hold of the papacy, supported the development of nation-states, and gave some support to individualism. Yet Luther was no modern. The emphasis on lay religion, the attacks on ecclesiastical monopoly that he made in his famous early essays, *Address to the Christian Nobility of the German Nation* and *Concerning Christian Liberty*, gave way in his later years to a new emphasis on the church system, with purity (rigidity) of doctrine, supported and dominated by the state. As Milton expressed it later on, "New presbyter was but old priest writ large." Luther could scarcely have written in his later years what he said in his *Address to the Christian Nobility*: "It is not my intention here to judge John Huss's belief and to defend his errors, although my understanding has not been able to find any error in him. . . ." Huss' sectarianism and his attacks on the secular order were in sharp contrast to developed Lutheranism.

Luther's enormous respect for authority and the growth of a church-type organization well accommodated to the powerful classes destroyed the appeal that his attack on the papacy and his emphasis on personal religious experience had had for many members of the lower classes. "Luther accepted the social hierarchy, with its principles of status and subordination, though he knocked away the ecclesiastical rungs in the ladder." [16] He repudiated the radical implications of sectarian Christianity which called for good works, and not faith alone. "Divine grace is only obscured by human effort."

The way in which Lutheranism developed and changed, even within the lifetime and in the writings of the founder, make it impossible to accept without qualification the thesis that in its early years, the influence of a religious movement is primarily the result of its own internally developed religious ideas, relatively uninfluenced by the secular situation. This is the position taken by Weber and Troeltsch with respect to Calvinism, as we shall see. It needs to be qualified by a recognition (a) that even the origin of religious ideas is affected by the whole circle of social

[16] Tawney, *op. cit.*, p. 93.

forces by which the religious thinker and leader is surrounded, (b) that his own development will be subtly affected by the secular and religious interests of the people (the audience) to whom he tries to appeal, and (c) that the audience will select and emphasize those aspects of the religious innovator that serve their particular needs and correspond with their interests. These are qualifications of the thesis—rather severe ones, to be sure—but they do not refute it. The religious material is not completely malleable. Having accepted a religious system, perhaps because it seemed to harmonize with their needs, a group is influenced by the inner compulsions of the religion.

The composition of the group that supported Luther gradually changed. The intellectuals who were with him at Worms, later found him to be quite medieval, an opponent of learning, and more and more narrowly dogmatic. Restless peasants and radical urban groups were told by Luther to accept their lot and to obey the authorities: "There ought to be no serfs because Christ has set us all free. What then is that? This means that Christian freedom would be quite carnal—did not Abraham and other patriarchs and prophets also have bondmen?" Luther was opposed to the whole economic development of his age, attacked large-scale commerce, opposed usury even more vigorously than the Catholic Church of his time. He described as the ideal society, the traditionally stratified rural society, with a natural rather than a money economy and with personal, face-to-face economic dealings.

I do not see many good manners that have ever come into a land through commerce . . . . without doubt the greatest misfortune of the Germans is buying on usury. . . . The system has not been in force for more than one hundred years, and has already brought poverty, misery, and destruction on almost all princes, foundations, cities, nobles, and heirs. If it continues for another hundred years Germany will be left without a farthing, and we shall be reduced to eating one another. . . . All I know is that it were much more godly to encourage agriculture and lessen commerce; and they do the best who, according to the Scriptures, till the ground to get their living. . . .[17]

To understand Luther's position with respect to trade, however, one must remember that the economic setting in which he lived was far from modern. There were only the beginnings of capitalism, and these did more to disrupt the "natural economy" than to bring wealth to most people. Production was for a small market, money was unimportant in the traditional rural economy, commerce and finance were incidents rather

[17] *Address to the Christian Nobility.*

than central elements in the economic system.[18] The restless competition for gain which was beginning to appear upset the stability of the existing order and left confusion, while its possible achievements within a new order could not yet be seen. Luther sought, therefore, to solidify the old order against the disorganizing effects of the new developments.

With the loss of many of the intellectuals and the sectarians, and the low appeal to commercial middle-classes, ". . . official Lutheranism became an established church, predominantly an aristocratic and middle-class party of vested interest and privilege."[19] The individualism, the challenges to authority, the opposition to an established church that were found in early Lutheranism were destroyed or sharply curtailed; the quietism, the support to nationalism, the support to the aristocracy of a semi-feudal society were emphasized. It became an instrument of power for a basically conservative ruling group, justifying their power while it sought to moralize and restrain it. Gradually it adapted itself to the commercial and industrial classes who came more and more into prominence. It succeeded only poorly in incorporating doctrines that appealed to the lower classes, particularly of the cities. Hence the force of the Anabaptist movement in Germany (and in part perhaps even of the secular protests that sprang from German soil centuries later).

CALVINISM AND THE RISE OF COMMERCE

Calvin was strongly influenced by the Lutheran movement; but he appeared in a somewhat different situation, and from the start gave emphasis to different religious concepts. Gradually his teachings, and those of his followers particularly, came to harmonize more and more with the requirements of the new commercial and industrial groups. How did this development take place?

The relationship between "the Protestant ethic and the spirit of capitalism" has undoubtedly received more intensive examination than any other question in the sociology of religion. In the half century since Max Weber published his famous study, dozens of scholars have studied the problem, only to arrive at very diverse conclusions.[20] Some have taken

[18] See R. H. Tawney, "Religious Thought on Social and Economic Questions in the Sixteenth and Seventeenth Centuries. III. The Social Ethics of Puritanism," *Journal of Political Economy*, 1923, p. 805.

[19] Smith, *op. cit.*, p. 100.

[20] In addition to Weber's, *The Protestant Ethic and the Spirit of Capitalism*, a partial list of the books that deal with this question includes R. H. Tawney, *Religion and the Rise of Capitalism*; H. M. Robertson, *Aspects of the Rise of Economic Individualism*; Talcott Parsons, *Structure of Social Action*; Werner Sombart, *The Jews and Modern Capitalism*; Amintore Fanfani, *Catholicism, Protestantism, and Capitalism*; Ernst Troeltsch, *The Social Teaching of the Christian Churches*; H. R.

Weber's thesis—that Protestantism, particularly its Calvinist phase, was *one important factor* in the development of the spirit of capitalism—and, disregarding his qualifications, used it to "prove" the primary force of religion in secular affairs. Others contend that religious change was only symbolic of more basic changes in the economic and political situation, that Calvinism simply indicates that new classes develop new religious tendencies harmonious with their interests and needs. Some hold that religious factors were important in the development of capitalism, but that Weber should have given greater attention to Catholicism or Judaism. And many have given some support to Weber's thesis, but believe that he was insufficiently alert to the *selective* development of Calvinism through many generations, as a result of its constant interaction with the many forces involved in the emergence of the modern world.

The present writer takes this last position. An approach to the sociology of religion that stresses the ways in which religious developments are embedded in the total social situation must be alert to the ways in which religion and society interact. In terms of the topic of this chapter, one might state the proposition in this way: The emergence of a society in which business and industrial interests are becoming progressively more important will strongly influence the *churches* of that society in the direction of doctrines, rituals, and organizational patterns satisfying and acceptable to the newly powerful groups. Oppositely, the religious organizations of that society, partly as a result of their own "inner development" at the hands of religious specialists will affect and set limits to the types of developments possible in economic matters.

Weber runs the risk, in consciously choosing to explore only one phase of this interaction, of seeming to disregard the ways in which Calvinism was shaped and interpreted in ways that were harmonious with the inclinations of its adherents. There was, in his own phrase, an "elective affinity" between certain interpretations of the complex doctrines of Calvin and the secular concerns of its middle class adherents. In the work of Calvin there is retained a strong element of Catholicism as well as of Lutheranism. These were reduced in influence in later Calvinism. Calvin gives emphasis to the idea that the purpose of the universe is to glorify God, that man has reason only that he may more fittingly glorify God. This doctrine might as readily lead to mysticism or to an ascetic denial of the importance of this world as to vigorous pursuit of a worldly calling —this last being the actual consequence in Weber's judgment. Calvinism

---

Niebuhr, *The Social Sources of Denominationalism;* Albert Hyma, *Christianity, Capitalism and Communism;* J. M. Yinger, *Religion in the Struggle for Power.*

did not create the spirit of capitalism, but the needs and tendencies of capitalists were involved in the process which selected from the various possibilities of interpretation of Calvinism. Once those possibilities were chosen, however, they imposed on their adherents certain limitations and obligations.

The important place Calvin gave to the doctrine of predestination, similarly, need not have had the consequences which Weber describes, had it been developed by persons in a different social situation. With Calvin, it demonstrated that pure, unmerited grace comes from God, because man, by his "fall" has lost the ability to achieve grace. Calvin had no trust either in works or in sacramental forms and rites. This might easily lead to mysticism and quietism. If it encouraged "worldly asceticism" among the commercial groups that embraced Calvinism, it is because such an interpretation had some meaning to those who were winning positions of influence in a dynamic society. Having accepted such an interpretation, however, they were bound to some degree by its implications—thrift, hard work, self-denial.

It is well to remember that Weber's analysis of the impact of Protestantism on the spirit of capitalism was part of a series of monographs in which he explored the significance of religion for economic matters. In studies of Confucianism and Taoism, Hinduism and Buddhism, and Ancient Judaism, he sought to discover the ways in which religious ideas blocked or encouraged the appearance of rational business enterprise.[21] In each case, he took account of the political, economic, and other social forces at work, thus sketching a broader picture than in his essay on Protestantism, in which he described only one side of the causal chain.

Weber found that Confucianism, for example, contained a great deal of the rationalism characteristic of Western business ethics; it was quite definitely utilitarian; it had a positive evaluation of wealth. Despite all this, however, Confucianism was limited by a fundamental traditionalism. The ideal of the Confucian gentleman was a static idea—the assimilation of the established body of literary culture expressed in the classics. Tradition was not only accepted but sanctified. Moreover, the specialization of Western bureaucratic structure was thoroughly opposed in the classical education of the Confucian gentleman, who was to become a well-rounded harmonious work of art. Again, the Western ethic rests on universalism and on far-reaching mutual confidence even among strangers; Confucian-

---

[21] See *Gesammelte Aufsätze zur Religionssoziologie*. Most of this series has now appeared in English translation. In addition to *The Protestant Ethic*, see *Ancient Judaism, The Hindu Social System*, and *The Religion of China*.

ism, on the contrary, was primarily concerned with a "particularistic" structure of relationships. Finally, the basic metaphysical foundation of Confucianism, says Weber, the concept of Tao, the principle of Order, is in contrast to the evolutionism, the idea of development in Judaeo-Christian thought.[22]

As an interpretation of the relationship between religious influences and economic affairs, this essay raises two fundamental problems. Why is it that China continued to be bound by Confucian traditionalism, while Europe was gradually freed from the equally or more restrictive influence of the Christian traditionalism? If one answers, as Weber does, that Christianity was reinterpreted by the Protestant "prophecy," the question immediately arises: Why did the prophets appear in Europe? Why did Confucianism not have a Reformation? The natural congeniality of Christianity for prophecy is probably a legitimate part of the explanation. (The cause of this congeniality can be disregarded for Weber's immediate problem, although it is of the utmost importance for other questions in the sociology of religion.) That conditions in sixteenth-century Europe were ripe, however, for all kinds of "prophecy" is proved by the series of revolutions—commercial, legal, political—that was going on. This limits his conception of the immanence of the religious developments.

Related to this is a second problem: To demonstrate that a religious ethic can *restrict* the appearance of a new economic form and to claim that a religious ethic can *precipitate* a new economic form are two different things. All of Weber's essays, except *The Protestant Ethic*, seek to show how the appearance of capitalism was greatly restricted by a religious system. Very few will deny, except in points of detail, the thoroughness of his demonstration. The most rabid historical materialist is the one who insists that "religion is the opiate of the people"—an admission that it has a telling effect on their behavior. A religion *once established* (and whatever the cause of its own doctrine) certainly becomes in its turn a "cause" of succeeding events. But in *The Protestant Ethic*, Weber argues precisely that the congeniality of Calvinism for capitalism preceded the major development of capitalism and was greatly responsible for its peculiar spirit. Moreover, he held that this Calvinistic doctrine emerged—although not entirely—out of a religious dialectic, and became conjoined with emerging capitalism only by a "historical accident." That this claim is on an entirely different level from that of the others is immediately apparent. We have suggested that such a claim takes insufficient account of the selective development of religious movements, of the "elective

[22] See *The Religion of China*.

affinity" which Weber himself is alert to in other connections. We can explore this problem by an examination of some more recent manifestations of the interconnections of religion and economics.

PROTESTANTISM AND THE AMERICAN MIDDLE CLASSES

If Luther, Calvin, Wesley, and other religious leaders sought each in his own way, to bring the life of the world under religious control, this was scarcely the preoccupation of most of their followers. Through the generations, their doctrines were gradually reshaped, more to support than to restrain the claims of their adherents. These groups, having won their way to great influence in the dominant nations of the world, had lost a great deal of the sense of tragedy and depravity and of God's saving grace that the "reformers" never escaped. Luther's keen awareness of the evil of life, Calvin's concern lest the glory of God be obscured by self-glorification, even Wesley's more "middle class" conception of the "stewardship of wealth," with its implications of radical sharing, were highly incompatible with the self-confident and optimistic view of the world of the successful commercial and industrial groups. An examination of the religious perspectives of some of the heirs of the Reformation can shed a great deal of light on the relationship of economic forces and religion.

In the United States, by the latter half of the nineteenth century, there was scarcely a doubt in the established Protestant churches that the "Gilded Age" was solving most of man's problems, that the economic theories of the middle and upper classes were religiously valid—and that those who opposed the prevailing distribution of power and wealth, therefore, were anti-Christian. Adam Smith (at least the Smith of the *Wealth of Nations,* if not of the *Theory of Moral Sentiments*) became a church father. During the 1880's, students of ethics in American colleges were familiar with D. S. Gregory's *Christian Ethics,* where it was argued:

By the proper use of wealth man may greatly elevate and extend his moral work. It is therefore his duty to seek to secure wealth for this high end, and to make a diligent use of what the Moral Governor may bestow upon him for the same end. . . . The Moral Governor has placed the power of acquisitiveness in man for a good and noble purpose.[23]

And a few years later, Bishop Lawrence of Massachusetts declared:

In the long run, it is only to the man of morality that wealth comes. We believe in the harmony of God's universe. We know that it is only by working along His laws natural and spiritual that we can work with efficiency. . . .

[23] Quoted by Walter G. Muelder, *Religion and Economic Responsibility,* p. 69.

Godliness is in league with riches. . . . Material prosperity is helping to make the national character sweeter, more joyous, more unselfish, more Christlike. That is my answer to the question as to the relation of material prosperity to morality.[24]

Workingmen did not always appreciate the harmony in God's universe, nor agree that godliness was in league with riches. By the 1870's they were expressing their discontents in mass meetings, in strikes, and sometimes in violence. They found little support for their protests among the churchmen. During the strikes of 1877, the *Christian Union* wrote: "What a sorry set of ignoramuses they must be who imagine that they are fighting for the rights of labor in combining together to prevent other men from working for low wages because, forsooth, they are discontented with them." And the *Congregationalist* called for drastic measures:

Bring on then the troops—the armed police—in over-whelming numbers. Bring out the Gattling guns. Let there by no fooling with blank cartridges. But let the mob know, everywhere, that for it to stand one moment after it has been ordered by proper authorities to disperse, will be to be shot down in its tracks. . . . A little of the vigor of the first Napoleon is the thing we now need. Compromise would simply sow the wind for 'future whirlwind-reaping.' [25]

Henry Ward Beecher, who had achieved considerable wealth as a preacher and writer, and liked to display that wealth, denounced the strikers for not bearing their poverty more nobly:

It is said that a dollar a day is not enough for a wife and five or six children. No, not if the man smokes or drinks beer. It is not enough if they are to live as he would be glad to have them live. It is not enough to enable them to live as perhaps they would have a right to live in prosperous times. But is not a dollar a day enough to buy bread with? Water costs nothing; and a man who cannot live on bread is not fit to live. What is the use of civilization that simply makes men incompetent to live under the conditions which exist. . . .[26]

A few years later, when Governor Altgeld of Illinois pardoned two of the men convicted after the Haymarket riot, Lyman Abbott denounced him from the pulpit as "the crowned hero and worshipped deity of the anarchists of the northwest." And the *Congregationalist* rejoiced that the governor had been hung in effigy "by the indignant citizens of Illinois." [27]

The significance of this attitude toward economic conflicts among the

---

[24] Quoted in *ibid.*, p. 70.
[25] Quoted by Henry F. May, *Protestant Churches and Industrial America*, p. 93.
[26] *Christian Union*, August 1, 1877, p. 93; quoted in May, *op. cit.*, pp. 93–94.
[27] See Arthur E. Holt, "Organized Religion as a Pressure Group," *Annals of the American Academy of Political and Social Science*, May, 1935, pp. 47–48.

religious leaders can be understood only in the context of the changes
that were taking place in society. Commerce, industrial specialization,
the development of larger and larger factories with their costly machine-
tools and equipment, rapid urbanization—these and other changes were
forcing the reorganization of the lives of ever-increasing numbers of people. The relatively self-sufficient and independent farmer and handicrafts-
man lost control of the tools with which they worked and the skills which
had given them some independence. In large numbers they were becoming unskilled and semi-skilled factory workers. The whole society became
vastly more interdependent, creating moral problems that were unknown
to stable, agricultural societies. Along with the technical changes, there
was a great increase in the power of the owners, financiers, and managers
of the industrial and commercial enterprises. Like many dominant groups
in the first upsurge of their power, they had little sense of *noblesse oblige;*
they were impatient of any restraints on their demands. The kinds of civi-
lizing checks and "countervailing powers" that develop in a democratic
society had not yet had time to gather much strength, with the result
that power tended to become more concentrated in the hands of the new
elite. Between 1860 and 1890, national wealth in the United States increased by almost 500 per cent, but the increase was not universally
shared. In the decade of the seventies, real wages, which had always been
at the subsistence level, declined from an average of four hundred dollars
to three hundred dollars. "The American industrial revolution, in the process of creating wealth such as the world had never seen or dreamed of, produced also a sullen proletariat resentful of the poverty it had obtained as
its share of the bounty. . . ." [28] Labor unions began to gain strength, some
of them under the leadership of emigré German socialists. Their strikes
were bitter and harshly suppressed. Between 1881 and 1894 there were
fourteen thousand strikes and lockouts in the United States, involving
four million workers. Many of these conflicts have achieved notoriety as
a thinly veiled industrial war.

This is the setting in which church support of the dominant groups, the
praise of wealth, the vigorous protests against strikes must be understood.
It is not surprising that many workmen lost interest in the religion of these
churches, and turned either to secular movements or to religious groups
of their own. Powderly, head of the Knights of Labor, made the statement that if the Sermon on the Mount were preached without reference
to its author, the preacher would be warned not to repeat such utopian

[28] C. H. Hopkins, *The Rise of the Social Gospel in American Protestantism 1865–
1915*, pp. 79–80.

ravings, and "the fashionable pews would be emptied." Samuel Gompers wrote in 1898: "My associates have come to look upon the church and the ministry as the apologists and defenders of the wrong committed against the interests of the people. . . ." [29]

Gradually, as we shall see, some concern for the problems of an industrial society began to appear in American churches; but the large majority continued to accept the values and to support the claims of the middle and upper classes, seeking only to "Christianize" those claims. This is implicit in the very definition of a church. Liston Pope, in his careful study of the churches in a mill town in the South, describes the way in which the ministers and churches responded to sharp economic conflict in these words:

To sum up, for emphasis, in statements too sharply put: in the cultural crisis of 1929 Gastonia ministers revealed that their economic ethicways were products of the economic system in which they lived, with no serious modfication by any transcendent economic or religious standard. They were willing to allow the power of religious institutions to be used against those who challenged this economic system, and themselves assisted in such use. At no important point did they stand in opposition to the prevailing economic arrangements or to drastic methods employed for their preservation. In no significant respect was their role productive of change in economic life. By and large, they contributed unqualified and effective sanction to their economic culture, insofar as their words and deeds make it possible to judge. [30]

Value positions with regard to the situation we have been describing range all the way from thankfulness that the majority of churches have stood for the right (and Right) to condemnation because they have been mere agents of the powerful classes. Either extreme is liable to obscure objective analysis of the two basic reasons for the transformation of the religious formulations of the Protestant innovators into institutional supports for the middle and upper classes. These are the two reasons we have discussed in Chapter 6 in our definition of "church." From the point of view of the laymen, only if the church supported the main outlines of the society in which they were dominant would they give it allegiance. Religion was only one of their interests, and probably not the most powerful one for most of them. If the beliefs and practices of the churches had obstructed their search for power, made no place for their new occupations, denied their claims to authority, they would not have accepted those beliefs and practices to turn their backs on the society in which

[29] *Ibid.*, p. 85.
[30] See Liston Pope, *Millhands and Preachers*, pp. 330–331.

success—as they defined it—was being won. They would, rather, have turned their backs on the church and looked for other religious sponsorship.

Religious leaders felt some of these same influences, but their support of the churchlike decision is to be explained, insofar as they were primarily interested in religion, by the second reason for religious differentiation: the dilemma of religious leaders. For them to have denied the claims to power and income of the dominant groups would have been to give up the effort to "Christianize" those groups. It is unlikely that they would have persuaded many of the laymen of the middle and upper classes, usually characterized by a less than urgent religious concern, to abdicate their positions of authority. The clergy chose rather (it was hardly a conscious decision, of course) to accept and defend the social structure. This had important implications for their religion, setting limits within which it must develop: For example, they had inevitably to continue to emphasize eternal salvation, not the elimination of problems on earth, for the latter might have required an examination of the secular institutions which their congregations thoroughly supported. For the same reasons, it inevitably led, in ethical questions, to the concern for personal good conduct—generosity, honesty, neighborliness—and not to an exploration of the ethical questions implicit in the social structure itself. The limits imposed on the directions which churchlike religious institutions can take are reflected in the remark by Walter Rauschenbusch that ". . . the older brethren told us that the true function of the ministry was not to 'serve tables,' but to save the immortal souls of men. One told me that these were 'mere questions of mine and thine,' and had nothing to do with the Gospel. A young missionary going to Africa to an early death implored me almost with tears to dismiss these social questions and give myself to 'Christian work.'" [31]

Some American churchmen carried the accommodation to the dominant groups to such great lengths that it became not simply an acceptance, but a positive acclamation of support. In *The Man Nobody Knows,* Bruce Barton made Jesus into an astute businessman (The Man Whom Nobody but Bruce Barton Knows, as someone has retitled it). This is more than a modern variation of the eighteenth century *Navigation Spiritualized* or *The Religious Weaver,* for these earlier attempts to formulate the religious problems of an occupation were less concerned to give religious sanction to an occupation than to restrain its excessive secular interests. In the next chapter we shall see how far this accommodation may be carried with reference to the political order.

[31] Walter Rauschenbusch, *Christianizing the Social Order,* p. 92.

If churchmen accepted the social structure, however, most of them did not give up the effort to impose religious restraints on the secular activities of powerful people. They were concerned with suffering and injustice; but, as churchmen, they were inclined to deal with these problems by an appeal to "character," not by attempts to change institutional patterns. This approach is shown by the highly popular novel of Charles M. Sheldon, *In His Steps* (1898), a book that sold twenty-three million copies in English editions, was translated into twenty-one other languages, and made into a movie. In the story, a "dusty, worn, shabby-looking young man" arose in church one morning and told his story of privation and suffering, and then collapsed in the aisle. A few days later he died. Moved by this story, and with the encouragement of the minister, fifty members of the congregation—including an heiress, a college president, a railroad executive, a newspaper editor, a merchant—resolved never to do anything without first asking themselves the question, "What would Jesus do?" Needless to say, their lives underwent an abrupt change. By means of this novel, millions of people found to their satisfaction that the alleviation of suffering required only the personal conversion of persons in high places. "Moral Rearmament" was anticipated.

SOCIAL FACTORS IN THE RISE OF THE "SOCIAL GOSPEL"

Accommodation to a society dominated by the middle and upper classes and appeals to personal morality do not tell the whole story of the relationship between Protestant churches and the secular powers in the United States. They are not so closely tied to class interests as the discussion heretofore might seem to indicate. Even though it is true that an important latent function of the churches has been to legitimatize the power situation, their primary direct concern has been with the trans-human problems that are at the heart of religion.

Moreover, a small minority within the churches has criticized and sought to reorganize some aspects of the social structure. They have assumed that Christianity had direct relevance for society. Although their criticisms of secular institutions share some things in common with sects, these religious leaders are not sectarians, for they work within the framework of the churches. An overly-simplified economic interpretation of religious movements finds it difficult to explain these developments within the established churches. These tendencies began to be a significant part of the religious situation in the latter part of the nineteenth century and became progressively more important during the next several decades. If "social Christianity" is less prominent today than it was a few decades ago, this is not simply because of the decline of this manifestation of the religious interest. That may be part of the story, for the enormous political and economic tensions of our time have persuaded some religious leaders that they would be wise to turn away from these "mere questions of mine and thine" to more "spiritual" problems. The explanation rests in part, however, on the gradual absorption of "social Christianity" into the whole body of the church, on the partial accomplishment of its aims, on the secular movements which have taken over its tasks.

Before turning to an examination of the causes of this "unchurchlike" behavior in the churches, let us describe very briefly some of its manifestations. Its roots are to be found in the very nature of the synthesis of Christianity which, as we have seen, is capable of being interpreted in ways that make of it a program of reform. This interpretation has been sustained primarily in the sects, which, if they were successful in making an appeal to a significant number, forced any church that was interested in encompassing the whole of a society to heed their doctrines. But there have been few such sects in the United States. Ideals kept alive in secular institutions and the competition of secular movements have been more important than sectarian prophets in reminding the churches of this aspect of Christianity.

Before the Civil War, there were a few strains of criticism of society to be found in the established churches. The abolition movement may seem like a good example; but it was strong only in that part of the society where the owning groups had given up slavery anyway. Most of the churchmen of the South made a vigorous scriptural defense of slavery. A better early example is perhaps to be found in Transcendentalism, an offshoot of the Unitarian movement, which was somewhat hospitable to socialism. And the liberal writings of Maurice and Kingsley had some influence in this country by way of the Protestant Episcopal Church. It was near the end of the century, however, that the "social gospel" movement began to get more extensive attention. We shall not here try to trace its development in courses in "social ethics" in many seminaries; in the writing and preaching of several nationally famous religious leaders; in the formation of social-service boards or commissions in most of the large denominations; in the declaration of social creeds that indicated the interest of the churches in problems of the industrial worker; in the organization in 1908 of the Federal Council of Churches of Christ in America (now the National Council); in the ecumenical movement which has, as one of its aspects, a concern for the way in which class divisions and economic conflict divide "the church"; and, most recently, in the growing concern for the way in which Negroes are segregated, economically, educationally, and religiously.[32]

No one will deny that these represent, in American Protestant churches,[33] an extensive growth of interest in the institutional problems of modern industrial society. How is this growth to be explained? Is it an intrinsic religious development, a reaffirmation of some of the ethical concerns of "primitive" Christianity stimulated by the new problems created by urbanization? Is it the manifestation of the religious force of a few leaders—modern prophets? Is it the instrument of disprivileged groups, trying to employ religious beliefs and practices to improve their lot in the world? Is it simply churchlike recognition of new forces in the world, of changes already partly accomplished by secular pressures, to which the churches had to give some recognition or relinquish completely their claim and hope for a universal brotherhood?

Although all four of these factors, and others, are doubtless involved, it is the judgment of the present writer that the last one mentioned is most important in getting the "social Christianity" movement underway. The other factors then began to give it force and direction. Churchmen, whose strategic situation is not unlike that of politicians, understand the advice of Sir Robert Peel: "If you see a move coming . . . *head* it." American religious leaders did not succeed in heading the movements to improve the working conditions and income of the lower classes, reduce child labor, eliminate racial discrimination, etc.; but some of them, when they saw important secular movements struggling with these problems, at least jogged up to the head of the column to give the leaders "moral support." A few actively participated in the campaigns.

That the "social gospel" is primarily a churchlike accommodation to new forces, and not a demonstration that churches easily transcended the class lines that limit their appeal and their sphere of action, is indicated by the following facts: 1. The problems that social Christianity became seriously aware of only in the late nineteenth century had been long in existence. 2. Secular movements—political agitation, labor unions, associations for the advancement of colored people—preceded any extensive religious protests by about a generation. 3. Some business leaders, politicians, editors, and scholars were discovering, from a secular point of view, that in a mass

---

[32] See Hopkins, *op. cit.;* May, *op. cit.;* Charles Stelzle, *The Church and Labor;* Federal Council of Churches of Christ in America, *The Social Ideals of the Churches.*

[33] Although we are using Protestantism as our illustrative "case study," equally instructive material is to be found in the story of American Catholicism. Because of its closer tie to the lower classes in the United States, however, the Catholic Church has had a different pattern of development of "social gospel" themes.

production economy, the interests and power of the middle and upper classes were *not* injured by such things as higher wages, social security, and non-discrimination in hiring policy. 4. Extensive concern with "social questions" has continued to characterize the work of only a minority of churchmen; and these have been more largely represented in seminaries, religious publications, "institutional" downtown churches with predominantly lower-class congregations (being, therefore, largely sectarian), and various boards and agencies that are somewhat separated, as national organizations, from continuous contact with most laymen, than they have been found in local pulpits where any deviations from "respectable" religious views would be readily apparent to the middle and upper class congregations.

This is not to dismiss the "social gospel" movement as meaningless. Even though their own class identity and outlook and the dilemma they face may force churchmen to support class oriented religious practices, there can scarcely be any doubt that those who give serious thought to their religious situation must and do resist this tendency. Such serious thought may be stimulated, however, only by crisis, and the direction of the "solutions" that emerge from that thought will be strongly affected by the whole secular context. Industrial conflict, depression, war, and the bitter fruits of prejudice have dealt a severe blow to the complacency and easy optimism about society that characterized most American churches a few decades ago. It is not so easy to be certain, with Russell Conwell, that there are "Acres of Diamonds" all around us. For decades, churchmen had been relatively indifferent to the ways in which unrestrained pursuit of wealth can destroy religious interest, as they themselves defined it. But repeated crises forced them to reexamine that problem, to consider whether or not Wesley was right when he declared that "if I leave behind me £ 10, . . . I bear witness against me that I lived and died a thief and a robber." No American churchman agreed with that, but some of them began, at least, to consider the problems of modern society and to reframe their religious responses to that society.

The religiously thoughtful person, facing the difficulties of our time, can say, with Walter Rauschenbusch, there must be something wrong with a society that can manifest such unChristian tensions; or he can say, with Karl Barth, that we have not comprehended the depth of the tragedy of earthly existence, that we have been wrong in giving ourselves to the hope that the evil in man can be reduced by human organizations instead of by a transcendental gift of grace from God; or one can, with Reinhold Niebuhr, maintain both of these positions, in a kind of uneasy coexistence. But a church that talks of human brotherhood, of a Christ who knows no rich or poor, in whom there is "no East or West," must say some of these things, or in some other way deal with the intrusive crises of our time. It is obvious that a complacent middle class church was not going to be able to attract workingmen who felt the brunt of industrial crisis nor hold the allegiance of those members of the dominant classes who felt the confusions and tragedies of the day in acute form. Religious leaders could see many workers looking for some "profane salvation," or leaving their churches for more satisfactory religious expressions; they could also see that the workingman was winning a measure of economic and political power. Under these circumstances, more and more church-men "discovered" that strikes, when properly qualified, were sometimes justified, that hours of labor should be shortened, that child labor was a menace, rather than a brace, to character. This was not the triumph of a radical Christianity, forcing society to justice, but the emergence of new forces to which the churches had to adjust—as they adjusted to the rising commercial classes of the seventeenth century—if they were not to lose what influence they yet maintained over a large group of people and give up the belief in a universally valid Christianity.

On the basis of his careful study of the evidence, May writes:

In 1876 Protestantism presented a massive, almost unbroken front in its de-fense of the social status quo. Two decades later social criticism had penetrated deeply into each major church. Some of the most prominent Protestant leaders were calling for social reform; Christian radicals, not unheard, were demanding complete reorganization of society. The immediate cause of this important change lay neither in theological innovation nor in the world "climate of opinion" but in the resistless intrusion of social crisis, and particularly in a series of large-scale, violent labor conflicts. For a generation slums and de-pressions, farmer protests and labor parties had been pictured by church theorists as necessary, incidental flaws in the inevitable improvement of society. The events of 1877, of 1886, and of 1892–94 were, however, impossible to ignore and difficult to explain away. Optimistic theory had to be reconsidered in the light of burning freight cars. Spokesmen of religion were forced, like editors and professors, to answer the question why, in the home of Christian progress, desperate men were refusing well-meant advice, defying authority, organizing and battling with the determination of despair.[34]

To say that it was primarily the great secular problems and crises that caused some churches and religious leaders to reexamine their views of society is not to say that the process and results of this reexamination are merely symptomatic. Once set in motion, they became part of the causal stream that brought about various responses to these problems. When a

[34] May, *op. cit.*, p. 91.

Methodist bishop supports unionism, it is more difficult to dismiss it as an ungodly attack on democracy and freedom. When the National Council of Churches publishes an interracial news service and works for racial equality, it becomes more difficult to defend segregation and discrimination on religious grounds. One may consider these developments, as Veblen might say, "salutory or the reverse," but he cannot in either case dismiss them simply as effects. May writes:

At a crucial time, the social Christian movement gave encouragement to developing American progressivism. To attack the undiluted individualism which had, in America, the prestige of historical success, social critics of the late nineteenth century had to call to their aid the equally powerful tradition of equality. Yet in the tradition of the Enlightenment, individualism and equality were almost inseparably linked. Only in the Christian doctrine of brotherhood could men of this period find a belief universally recognized which at once proclaimed equality and condemned selfish individualism in telling terms.[35]

Although Norman Vincent Peale and Billy Graham get the headlines, there are today substantial groups and leaders in American Protestantism giving effective support to the "social gospel." The theological perspectives are different, some of the earlier questions have become relatively less important because they are now largely non-controversial (social security), but the desire to make Christianity relevant to the problems of an urban society continues to receive support.[36] Forty years after the NAACP and twenty years after the CIO, American churches are giving substantial attention to the efforts to reduce racial discrimination and segregation. It was inevitable that as "churches" they would not lead this movement. But now that it is underway, churches can affect its pace and aid the transition. (And it should be added that a substantial proportion of the opponents of segregation in the South have strong religious connections and concerns. They must be accounted sectarians, not churchmen; but they sprang from the church.)

In assessing the influence of the social gospel, it would be a mistake to forget the limitations imposed on a church by its very nature, or to

---

[35] *Ibid.*, p. 265.
[36] The literature giving expression to this concern is very large. See, for example, John C. Bennett, *Christian Ethics and Social Policy;* John A. Hutchinson, editor, *Christian Faith and Social Action;* Walter Muelder, *op. cit.;* J. Richard Spann, editor, *The Church and Social Responsibility;* Reinhold Niebuhr, *Christian Realism and Political Problems; Six Ecumenical Surveys,* a document prepared for the Second Assembly of the World Council of Churches, 1954; a six volume series on "Christian Ethics and Economic Life" prepared for the National Council of Churches, 1953; an interpretation and commentary on these volumes by Marquis Childs and Douglas Cater, *Ethics in a Business Society;* and frequent articles in such journals as *Christianity and Crisis* and *Christian Century.*

forget the dilemma of religious leaders. Despite the apparent resurgence of interest in religion on the contemporary scene, Christianity is a minority movement. Many church leaders today echo Kierkegaard's lament: how to find Christians in Christendom. To disregard this limitation is to misunderstand the nature of the religious influence in the social movements of the twentieth century. If the last few decades have witnessed a somewhat strengthened effort on the part of churchmen to bring the whole society into one religious framework, it has not seen—and will not see—the majority of churchmen supporting a society in which the claims of all groups are held to be equally valid. The church cannot change basic secular institutions; it will sponsor modification of them only when important groups have already moved in that directiton.

Nevertheless, it can have an indirect influence on the distribution of economic and political power. If the appeal to "Christian motivation" does not change the class situation, it can at least soften some of the harshness of the conflicts in that situation. It can help to maintain some sense, among all classes, of a common identity. This is vital, for all history shows that the inevitable processes of change are made most brutal and violent when classes are most sharply divided. When the groups within a society feel no sense of common destiny, when even their religious life sets different aspirations and beliefs, the mutual adjustments that human life demands are made far more difficult. For a church, as we have defined it, to help to integrate a complex modern society is a supremely difficult task; but there has been some reaching out toward this goal which the student of religion, as well as the practitioner, cannot afford to disregard.

CHAPTER 9

Religion and Political Institutions

Many of the principles which we have discussed in the preceding chapter are applicable to the study of the relationship between religion and political institutions, but several new questions also arise. Because many of the values for which human beings strive—power, prestige, income—are in scarce supply, every society is faced with disruptive tensions. If everyone were permitted to pursue these values by means of his own choosing, an organized society would be impossible. In every society, therefore, certain means (differing widely from society to society) are approved as ways of maintaining or securing scarce values. Political institutions are the norms that designate how the ultimate coercive power—even to the extreme of administration of death—shall be used, and by whom, to enforce the approved ways of achieving life's values.

The existence of a political system—and it will be explicit only in the more complex societies—does not solve the problem of order; it does not guarantee that the approved means for achieving scarce values will be employed. If the norms were not substantially self-enforcing, as a result of the socialization of the members of the society, the level of coercion would have to be very high, with an increase in disruptive

230

tensions. Moreover, the political authorities themselves, those who have the culturally established right to use coercive power, may violate the approved means to their own advantage.

TYPES OF RELATIONSHIP BETWEEN RELIGION AND POLITICS

Religion may become involved in this political problem in many different ways:

1. Religious beliefs and practices may help to create the socialized individuals who will substantially abide by the norms of the society; and by its rewards and punishments, religion may inhibit the violations of those who have been inadequately socialized. The religious system may also help to set and enforce the limits on the use of coercive power by those who possess it. And by emphasizing common values, religion may reduce the sharpness of the tensions that result from the pursuit of scarce values. Although these relationships between religion and politics are present even in mobile and complex societies, they are seen in their purest form in stable, sacred societies. On this level, religious community and political community are virtually identical. As we have seen in Chapter 3, these patterns are what one usually has in mind when he refers to "the integrative function of religion."

2. In societies where social differentiation and social change are important, other modes of relationship between religion and politics appear, supplementing and often contradicting the "integrative" relationship. On the one hand, the political authorities may become so powerful that, rather than having their use of coercive means limited and governed by religious values, they may succeed in transforming the religious institutions precisely into another instrument of coercion. To the degree that this happens (and nowhere is this tendency carried to its logical extreme, both because the rulers are themselves limited by the instrument they employ and because the less powerful members of a society would not long accept a religion that was *merely* a political agent), religious beliefs and practices become simply one manifestation of the political situation, and their control one phase of *the* political problem (preventing authorities from using their power to their own advantage). This development implies a change in the religious tradition and organization, a *selective* application of its doctrines, rites, and structures, emphasizing those that enhance the power of the rulers, denying or obscuring those that might restrain it.

3. On the other hand, there may develop a sharp tension between

religion and the political system. The founders and developers of the world religions, struggling with the problems of evil and suffering, have propounded "radical" solutions that make no reference to political boundaries. They may devalue, or even oppose, political institutions and the claims for the allegiance of individuals that are made by the state. The religious requirements may contradict political requirements.

The key task of the sociology of religion in its examination of religion and politics is to discover the conditions under which these various relationships occur and their consequences for society. One pattern is seldom found in "pure" form, of course, so that the task is complicated by the need to study various combinations, to analyze the effects of the interaction of these patterns. We need to measure, for example, the effects of the interaction of a religion of world-brotherhood, with its supra-political claims, with a political order in which the authorities are trying to forge religion into another instrument of power.

Identity of Religious-group and Political-group Membership. The first mode of relationship—religion as a factor in the integration of society—relatively uncomplicated by the other two modes is most likely to occur in isolated, preliterate societies, especially where religious specialists have not appeared to an important degree. The boundaries of the tribe or society and the boundaries of the religious system are identical. The gods of the group guarantee or represent its values; they fight its opponents. The beliefs and rites of the group express the sharing of a common fate. No religious system has been "invented," in such settings, that could challenge the validity of the group's norms or give them a merely relative position, for this requires that individuals be given some point of reference outside the tribe from which to see and judge its standards. With fewer religious specialists, there has been less development of a separate religious structure, a center of power which might compete with the political structures. And political authorities, without such a system to manipulate, are themselves fully circumscribed in their views by the beliefs of their own society. Thus they are unlikely to be able to use the religious patterns to reenforce their own power beyond the limits of the established norms.

In primitive societies it is impossible to draw sharp distinctions among the institutional patterns of religion, kinship, economics, government, and education. They are part of a closely articulated social whole. This does not mean that the members of "sacred" societies make no distinction between religious acts and other acts, nor that members of "secular" societies sharply differentiate religion from the rest of life. The contrast is not so sharp. Even in highly secularized societies, as we shall see, a sense of common purpose between religion and politics, particularly in times of crisis, is by no means lacking. This is vastly more true, however, in relatively stable and isolated situations, even where a universalistic religious creed is accepted. As Robertson Smith writes: "The Spanish peasants who insult the Madonna of the neighbouring village, and come to blows over the merits of rival local saints, still do homage to the same antique conception of religion which in Egypt animated the feuds of Ombos and Tentyra, and made hatred for each other's gods the formula that summed up all the local jealousies of the two towns." [1]

This tendency toward an identity of religious communion and civil community is clearly shown in the early history of Israel. "Separation of church and state" was, of course, utterly inconceivable. To change nationality was to change religion. Smith expresses it well:

When David in the bitterness of his heart complains of those who "have driven him out from connection with the heritage of Jehovah," he represents them as saying to him, "Go, serve other gods." In driving him to seek refuge in another land and another nationality, they compel him to change his religion, for a man's religion is part of his political connection. "Thy sister," says Naomi to Ruth, "is gone back unto her people and unto her gods"; and Ruth replies, "Thy people shall be my people, and thy God my God": the change of nationality involves a change of cult. [2]

The Use of Religion by Political Powers.   The relationship between religion and politics becomes more complicated in societies that are more highly stratified and have developed religious specialists. This is often accompanied by some culture contact and social change—and the opportunity, therefore, for some groups to see that their values are not universally shared. This loosens the hold of the social norms; it raises the possibility that some members of the society will get an instrumental attitude toward religion—seeing in it an instrument of power—an attitude that is unlikely so long as religion is seen and experienced only within the confines of one stable society. The ruling class is now able to see in religion a means of preserving order—an order that places them at the apex. It is probably seldom that they simply cynically manipulate a religious system: They too believe in it—in fact they find it very easy to believe in a religion that helps to preserve the social patterns which reward them so richly; and they are therefore likely to be very zealous.

It is difficult to distinguish between a situation in which religion re-

[1] W. Robertson Smith, *Lectures on the Religion of the Semites,* p. 32.
[2] *Ibid.,* p. 36.

enforces a stable social order and one in which religion is used by those who possess political power to their own advantage in violation of the norms of that order. Most outsiders might agree that the Russian Orthodox Church of 1915 was not simply "integrating" Russian society, but was clearly an instrument of power in the hands of the aristocracy. Or it might perhaps be shown that the fairly explicit and organized effort to revive Shinto in Japan in the nineteenth century was rooted in the desire of the ruling classes to increase their power and to oppose the tradition-breaking effects of industrialization. Can one be so certain, however, of the relationship between religion and the political authority in Ancient Egypt? There is a grave danger that one will claim that religion is simply another coercive force used by the ruling class when he is referring to a social order that he does not like, and will hold that it is "integrative of social order" in referring to a social system of which he approves or about which he is indifferent. An objective solution of this problem is impossible so long as "order" and "integration" are implicitly assumed to be normal and good. Perhaps we can reduce this hazard if we remind ourselves again that a social order may be evil, from the perspective of a given value. We can also get an important clue to the distinction between the integrative and the political function of religion by observing the *selective* development of the religious system. If these elements that might challenge the power of the ruling group are denied or even forcibly suppressed (as in the case of many Christian sectarian movements), there is a clear sign of the political use of religion.

Religious Challenges to Political Authority. The third type of relationship between religion and politics has its beginning in the development of religious specialists, although other factors must be added before it can develop fully. When religious life is simply part of the daily activity of "laymen" it will not be separated from the economic, political, and other questions with which they are concerned. The kinds of "solutions" to life's great problems which religion will develop under these circumstances will be tied very closely to the rest of the culture of the society. Ritual may be fairly elaborate, but theology and religious-group structure will be far more simple. Even where the management of the religious system moves away from the whole group into the hands of the chief or ruler, the conception of a universal religion is still impossible. The political structure and the religious structure are identical; their conceptions are mutually harmonious. The political manipulation of religion to enhance the power of the rulers may come in at this point, although it is unlikely until culture contact has pointed up the variations in social norms among societies—including the norms of religion. A conception of religion that reaches beyond the boundaries of society, however, a view that is not tied completely to the social system, will not be developed by non-specialists practicing a received religion or by a priest-king ruling over a stable society.

Whenever specialists appear, however, new forces are set in motion. Even if these specialists are functionaries of the ruler, their organization will begin to take on some measure of autonomy, for they will be the experts in managing the approved rites, the authorities in matters of dogma. Because they give full time to religion, they can develop more elaborate systems to deal with the problems with which religion is concerned. The stage is set for personal struggles for power between religious and political leaders, for clashes in principle, for conflicts between the ecclesiastical and political organizations. These struggles may be entirely political, involving only disagreements over the use or distribution of secular power. But they may represent the appearance of religious ideas that are not harmonious with the secular institutions, that contradict their claims or values. This marks the appearance of a new stage in the relationship of religion to society. Religion seems to transcend society.

How is this development to be explained? Some writers believe that great religious leaders cannot be explained simply in terms of their own societies and their cultures, that, indeed, an objective interpretation of their appearance is impossible. Joachim Wach writes:

Now we must concentrate our attention on one of the most significant phenomena in religion and one that has repeated itself often enough to have tremendous historical importance—the emergence of a *new faith* prepared for by the protest against the rejection of the traditional cult. The change affects all fields of expression of religious experience—theology, cult, and organization. . . . It is generally agreed that the emergence of a great new religious faith is one of the inexplicable mysteries which have accompanied the ascent of man and bears the most convincing testimony to the contingency and spontaneity of his spiritual history. We have reviewed the origin of the great founded religions from this point of view and have stressed the fact that no prior preparation and path-breaking could alone explain the emergence of the new inspiration and its effect.[3]

This is the kind of question about which debate is likely to be particularly fruitless, because of differences in basic assumptions. The scientist cannot afford to be dogmatic, for he certainly cannot show empirically that Professor Wach is in error. He can only say: *If my assumptions are correct*, or, to the degree that they are correct, the emergence of a great new faith is not "one of the inexplicable mysteries," but the inevitable

<hr>

[3] Joachim Wach, *Sociology of Religion,* p. 307.

product of certain interacting forces. And he must try to go as far as he can from that starting point, unsatisfactory as it will be to those who prefer a different starting point. For the scientist to give up his fundamental premises when confronted by the enormously difficult questions pertaining to the appearance of the world religions or in face of the sacred attitudes that surround contemporary faiths, is only to become a poor theologian. Better than this, in the writer's judgment, is to be consistent in one's interpretation, however unimportant a science of religion may be considered by some to be.

From this point of view, then, we shall hold that the development of religions that seem to transcend the social systems from which they come is the result of creative religious leaders, struggling with the problems with which religion is basically concerned. Social change and culture contact have made them discontented with the traditional solutions. They propound or invent partially new interpretations of suffering and roads to salvation. The believer is likely to give his primary attention to the "new" elements, while the objective student must also point out the continuity with tradition and the borrowing. Arnold Toynbee lists eighty-seven correspondences between the story of Jesus' life and the accounts of various Hellenic "saviors." The recent discoveries of the "Dead Sea Scrolls" only seem to confirm the idea that there was substantial continuity between Christianity and earlier religious developments. (See Chapter 10.) Yet the founders of the universalist religions must also be recognized as important turning points in religious development. They appear in settings where the social systems have been peculiarly unable to fill the needs with which religion deals. Suffering—not simply physical deprivation—has been acute, and the religious imagination leaps the bounds of the society which has caused that suffering. It refuses to accept the answer which the pains of earthly existence within a society seem to require. The world religions, moreover, have appeared at world-crossroads, at points where the limitations not simply of a society, but of society, might be observed and felt. Such a setting also accounts for the blending of diverse elements and for the inventiveness which so frequently springs from culture contact. One who follows such a train of thought is not among those who "generally agree" that the founded religions are inexplicable mysteries.

What are the implications of universalist religions for politics? These religions create tensions with the political order; they encourage loyalties that are larger than the tribe or nation. A unified God for the entire world, particularly a God of love, brings a demand for brotherliness that may sharply contradict the requirements of citizenship. As Weber points out, the ultimate appeal of a political group is to force; it is concerned with power, and "reasons of state" may require action that is repugnant to or meaningless to religion:

The state's absolute end is to safeguard (or to change) the external and internal distribution of power; ultimately, this end must seem meaningless to any universalist religion of salvation. This fact has held and still holds, even more so, for foreign policy. It is absolutely essential for every political association to appeal to the naked violence of coercive means in the face of outsiders as well as in the face of internal enemies. It is only this very appeal to violence that constitutes a political association in our terminology. The state is an association that claims the monopoly of the *legitimate use of violence*, and cannot be defined in any other manner.

The Sermon on the Mount says "resist no evil." In opposition, the state asserts: "You *shall* help right to triumph by the use of *force*, otherwise you too may be responsible for injustice." [4]

Such a conflict could not occur between a tribal religion and the political processes of that tribe. A religion that is confined to one stable society is an instrument in the pursuit of its individual and group values and a compensation for the failure to achieve them; but it is never a repudiation of those values. The universal religions, however, represent a certain amount of disillusionment. The absolute level of suffering has probably not been greater in the settings where they developed than that experienced by many other groups, but it was suffering in the context of greater aspirations. The growing complexity of culture and the increased inter-culture contact encouraged dreams of change and accomplishment. Frustration and disappointment took on an added poignancy in the setting of the tribal conflicts and religious confusion of the Arabian peoples, or in face of the repeated denials of the Jewish hope for national independence and greatness, or as a result of the rigidity of an orthodox Hinduism that led to Buddha's "sectarian" protest. Only an enormously vivid and radical religious formula seemed to yield satisfaction in such situations as these. Particularly among those in whom the religious interest was strongest, but also to some degree among their followers, the quest for earthly success and the hope for alleviation of suffering through secular processes, seemed vain. It is in this context that Wach is right (although he might not have agreed with this interpretation) when he says:

[4] Max Weber, *From Max Weber*, edited by H. H. Gerth and C. W. Mills, p. 334.

. . . it is the *intensity* of the religious experience which determines the religious attitude toward the state in the new religious communities. . . . The
intensified religious experience which caused the emergence and growth of
the universal religions necessarily produces a transformed attitude toward
reality in all its aspects. It is rather difficult to generalize upon this changed
attitude. Speaking broadly, it implies a less optimistic acceptance of the world,
a certain amount of critical reserve and alienation from it. In extreme cases
it results in renunciation, withdrawal, and self-mortification. . . .[5]

This conflict between the universal religions and "the world" is only
one tendency among several, of course, and is constantly obscured and
modified by the other modes of relationship we have discussed. It gets
fairly full institutional embodiment only in sects which, by definition,
are relatively powerless minority movements. Yet the conflict is there,
even in the churches, which are accommodated to society and its political
institutions but never fully in agreement with them. In the last analysis,
a universalist religion, consistently carried through, *must* conflict at various points with the political activity of a society, with its concern for only
a segment of mankind and its ultimate appeal to force. Under some circumstances, the conflict may be very rudimentary, almost lost in the
shaping of the religious institutions into political instruments, but unless
the religious system around which the institutions have been built is
completely destroyed, an implicit conflict will remain. Despite the enormous pressures toward the nationalization of religion in the modern
world, it seems highly unlikely to the present writer that the universalist
element in the world religions will ever be lost, however much those religions may change in theology, ritual, or organization. Indeed, as the
world grows smaller and more interdependent, it would seem that *only*
a universalist religion can offer a road to salvation that will be meaningful to those who recognize this interdependence.

Weber has brilliantly described how politics may enter into direct competition with religion at decisive points, particularly in the requirements
of modern war for "an unconditionally devoted and sacrificial community among the combatants . . . ," a community that is nation-wide, not
a universal brotherhood.

Moreover, war does something to the warrior which, in its concrete meaning,
is unique: it makes him experience a consecrated meaning of death which is
characteristic only of death in war. . . . Death on the field of battle differs
from death that is only man's common lot. . . . As the values of culture increasingly unfold and are sublimated to immeasurable heights, such ordinary
death marks an end where only a beginning seems to make sense. Death on

[5] Wach, *op. cit.*, pp. 309–310.

the field of battle differs from this merely unavoidable dying in that in war, and in this massiveness *only* in war, the individual can *believe* that he knows he is dying "for" something. The why and the wherefore of his facing death can, as a rule, be so indubitable to him that the problem of the "meaning" of death does not even occur to him. . . .

This location of death within a series of meaningful and consecrated events ultimately lies as the base of all endeavors to support the autonomous dignity of the polity resting on force. Yet the way in which death can be conceived as meaningful in such endeavors points in directions that differ radically from the direction in which the theodicy of death in a religion of brotherliness may point. The brotherliness of a group of men bound together in war must appear devalued in such brotherly religions. It must be seen as a mere reflection of the technically sophisticated brutality of the struggle. And the inner-worldly consecration of death in war must appear as a glorification of fratricide.[6]

That the churches of the world religions frequently support the national interpretation of death does not contradict Weber's point, but it does show the limits of its application. The universalist theme is often driven into the background by the "social integration" and the "political" themes, in the relationship between religion and nations. What kinds of responses can religion make to these tensions with politics? The nature and the degree of the conflict which Weber describes will vary with the religious tradition and with the structure of power in society. The responses are affected by the same influences. The religious institutions may themselves employ violence to establish the supremacy of their claims over what they consider to be merely political claims. This is not uncommon, particularly in the history of Christianity and Islam. This is one of the two "solutions" that Weber holds are consistent with the universalist views of the world religions in their dealings with the counter-claims of politics. He calls them puritanism and mysticism. "Puritanism, with its particularism of grace and vocational asceticism, believes in the fixed and revealed commandments of a God who is otherwise quite incomprehensible. It interprets God's will to mean that these commandments should be imposed upon the creatural world by the means of this world, namely, violence—for the world is subject to violence and ethical barbarism."[7] It is not difficult to see how such a response, even if it starts out as primarily a religious protest against limiting secular claims, might readily be transformed into a secular and political movement itself, thinly disguised as a universalist religion.

On the other hand, the mystic's "solution" to the conflict between the claims of religion and politics, is an extreme anti-political attitude: "re-

[6] Weber, *op. cit.*, pp. 335–336.
[7] *Ibid.*, p. 336.

sist not evil," "turn the other cheek." "It withdraws from the pragma of
violence which no political action can escape." [8] This entails as many risks
for an ethic of brotherliness as does puritanism, for in disregarding the
hard tasks of politics, it does not eliminate them. Only a few are privileged or condemned—as you wish—to become mystics, while the rest of
mankind continues to pursue scarce values. So long as that is true, the
political problem of order remains, and a religious response which for-
gets this leaves the solution to other forces.

Neither puritanism or mysticism, then, escapes the dilemma of religion, rooted in the fact that religion is only one of man's interests and the
predominant one for only a few. The universalist religions have brought
a new factor into the interaction of politics and religion, but they have
not transformed that interaction; the two earlier modes of relationship
continue to prevail.

CHURCH AND STATE

The principles we have been discussing can perhaps be clarified by the
analysis of some aspects of the relationship between church and state, or
more appropriately religion and citizenship, in modern Christendom.[9]
We will be particularly concerned with the responses of churches to
war—an issue which puts the relationship of religion to politics into very
sharp focus. We shall see that all three of the modes of relationship which
we have described are involved in an intricate pattern.

The frustrating political history of the Jews had made painfully clear
to them that the political communities into which they were forced were
not the religious community of their hopes. Despite the intricate union
of religion and citizenship in their early history, "church" and "state"
came to mean clearly separate facts. There was no danger that the Jews
would mistake the Assyrian or Babylonian empires which held political
power over them for their religious community. It is in such contexts that
universalist, non-parochial religious concepts develop. This was, of course,
a major element in the early period of Christianity. After Constantine,
however, the Christian Church was directly involved in the political
situation. As a small and persecuted sect, the Christian community had
opposed emperor worship, but it had been more indifferent than hostile
to the state. As a church, however, becoming more and more involved in

---

[8] *Ibid.*

[9] See Heinrich Geffken, *Church and State,* for a basic historical treatment; Luigi
Sturzo, *Church and State* is a scholarly Catholic work; Anson Phelps Stokes, *Church
and State in the United States* and Leo Pfeffer, *Church, State and Freedom* are
valuable recent works with emphasis on the United States.

secular affairs, it could be neither hostile nor indifferent; yet it was confronted with the tensions that are inevitably generated between a universalist religion and the requirements of politics. It sought to resolve this difficulty by balancing two statements from scripture: "The powers that be are ordained by God," but if those powers require action that is contrary to religious belief, "We must obey God rather than man." This gradually developed into the doctrine, closely akin to the thinking of the Stoics, of "relative natural law": The state, along with other secular institutions, is part of the natural law; it is inevitable and God-ordained. Yet it embodies the weaknesses of men, the cloudiness of reason that resulted from the "fall," and hence is only relative. As the church developed in power and wealth, it became more and more highly identified with the secular institutions, and thus less and less able to assert that they were relative. For the most part it was only in some of the monasteries that the relative quality of the state was stressed; and even there, it was largely by implication.

With the church so closely identified with the Empire, it was inevitable that when the Empire began to break up, so would the church, first in the great schism that divided the East and West, reflecting the growth of Byzantine power, and later in Western Europe, with the growth of nationalism in that area. These conflicts were not primarily an expression of the tension between a universalist religion and national political leaders seeking to use religion for political purposes: they were conflicts between rival political structures. The medieval church, accommodated to, and indeed a part of, the political and economic system of the Empire, opposed the rising power of the national kings and princes. But church and empire could not stand against the growing national consciousness in those areas favored by lingual and cultural unity and a certain geographical identity; nor could they defeat the growing power of commerce (which required an end to localism in matters of money, tariffs, commerical law, and economic self-sufficiency).

Varieties of Relationship between Church and State. It is not our purpose to develop further the complicated story of the relationship between religion and citizenship in pre-Reformation Europe, although one can discover in that story a great deal of information of value to the sociology of religion. We turn rather to the modern scene, because the development of distinctly secular states and of religious institutions partially separate, if not actually independent, from the state has created a situation that points up in a clear way the various modes of relationship between church and state.

The presence of a monotheistic, universalist religion that stresses allegiance to God above all other loyalties does not resolve the problems of "church and state"; it does not establish a clear-cut hierarchy of values. Conflicting demands and competing values lead to many different patterns of relationship. To declare that one should "render unto Caesar the things that are Caesar's and unto God the things that are God's" is only to pose the question. The nature of the reconciliation will vary widely, depending on the location of political power, the structure of the ecclesiastical organization, the needs of the individuals involved, the distribution of economic power. In the writer's judgment, the actual separation of church and state, or, to put it in another way, the effective presence of a universalist element in religion, capable, at times, of challenging, modifying, or denying the claims of politics, is possible only where power is diffused. Those forces that give to "the average man" some measure of economic freedom, political instruments for expressing his individual judgment, unhampered sources of information on which to base his opinions, and the like, create a setting in which religious challenges to the secular power structure are most likely to occur. Where these are lacking, church and state are not likely to be effectively separate, whatever the formal institutional structures may be. The ecclesiastical structure may be the dominant one, or, more commonly, the political authorities will dominate the church; but in either case "church and state" will not be separate. Put in sociological terms, this is to say that the relationships between religion and politics are imbedded in a whole social structure and will vary with variations in that structure.

There can be a great variety of connections between "church and state" even among those situations which exhibit formal union. Does the state nominate important church officials and otherwise influence clerical recruitment and training; does it control religious publications, and sharply limit the freedom of non-official churches (Spain)? Or does it accept simply a broadly defined "established church," granting it a great deal of autonomy, and allowing freedom of action to other churches (Great Britain)? These reflect wide differences in the total social structure, and in their turn affect the societal developments in different ways.

Anson Phelps Stokes has given us a useful summary of the types of relation between church and state in Christian societies. Among the early patterns attempted, he distinguishes: 1. imperial domination (subordination and often persecution of the church until 313 A.D.); 2. church-state alliance (St. Augustine, *De Civitate Dei*); 3. ecclesiastical domination (Gregory the Great, 540–604); 4. the ecclesiastical state or theocracy (the papal states, and later, Calvin's Geneva). Among the modern solutions attempted, Stokes distinguishes: 1. the Erastian plan (the state determined the policy of the church and virtually controlled its conduct, as in Czarist Russia); 2. state-church plan (in which the official church is given much autonomy and other "sects" are allowed freedom, as in Great Britain); 3. the jurisdictional plan (equal status for several confessions, all supervised by the state, the pattern of the Peace of Westphalia); 4. the separation plan (this may be benevolent, as in the United States, or hostile, as in Mexico in the first decades after the revolution).[10]

The task of the sociology of religion is to try to discover the conditions under which these various patterns of relationship between church and state develop. We have noted above some of the variables involved, with the suggestion that the range from most to least autonomy for religious organizations was very strongly dependent upon the degree of diffusion of power. It should be made clear that the autonomy to which we refer is the independent power to challenge the state—its war pattern, its demands on the citizen, its influence on the distribution of economic values, and the like. Freedom to preach a universalism that has only other-worldly significance may be found—and even encouraged—in situations where secular power is highly concentrated. Even here, the secular authorities may be ambivalent, for the line between other-worldly and this-worldly influence is not clear. The complexities of the situation are well shown in the variety of patterns in the United States.

CHURCH AND STATE IN THE UNITED STATES

In the United States, all three of the modes of relationship between religion and politics that we have discussed can be found in complicated interaction. Although the society is highly secularized, religious values are an important part of the value core which holds it together as a society, giving it the minimum consensus necessary to a common life. Bates declares that the roots of democracy

. . . are to be found in the attempted revival of primitive Christianity by the radical lower-class sects of the Protestant Reformation, those peasants and yeomen who were our own ancestors, and who initiated the Reformation and eventually carried out its basic principles—especially in America—to conclusions undreamt of in the beginning. . . . Democracy was envisaged in religious terms long before it assumed a political terminology.[11]

[10] See Stokes, *op. cit.*, pp. 37–49.
[11] E. S. Bates, *American Faith*, p. 9; see also Ralph Barton Perry, *Puritanism and Democracy*.

Bates doubtless overstates the case. Both the French and American Revolutions were carried on without, and to a strong degree against, the churches. Many of the leaders were inspired by the rationalism of the Enlightenment. Important secular forces were involved in the whole process of the development of democratic societies. There is widespread agreement, however, on the less specific claim that Christianity furnishes many of the "first premises" by which Americans make their value decisions. Whether this is objectively true or not—it would seem to the writer to be substantially true—is perhaps less important for our purposes than that it is widely accepted as true, and is acted upon and used in societal interaction. An editorial in *Fortune* illustrates the situation well.

As the leading democracy of the world, therefore, the United States is perforce the leading practical exponent of Christianity. The U. S. is not Christian in any formal religious sense; its churches are not full on Sundays and its citizens transgress the precepts freely. But it is Christian in the sense of absorption. The basic teachings of Christianity are in its blood stream. . . . Christian idealism is manifest in the culture and habits of the people, in the arguments that orators and politicians use to gain their ends; in the popular ideas of good taste, which control advertising, movies, radio, and all forms of public opinion; in the laws, the manners, and the standards of our people.[12]

To the careful student of American mass media of communication, of American manners and morals, this too must seem to be an overstatement; but its very use indicates the kind of *final* appeal on value questions that is likely to be used. The Supreme Court has given it an official sanction by declaring (in 1892 and at other times) that the United States is a Christian nation, in the broad sense that Christian principles underlie its laws and values.

On the second level, we find the widespread use of religious values and symbols to try to win various kinds of political struggles. Thus we have such groups as the Christian Front and Spiritual Mobilization on the right and the Fellowship of Christian Socialists on the left, each claiming a religious mandate for various political policies. The roster of lobbyists in Washington working for churches and other religious organizations is an extensive one.[13] Political candidates and parties not infrequently encourage the belief that their election will strengthen religious values. And in international affairs, many Americans find it difficult to distinguish between a political struggle and a religious crusade. This is not to sug-

[12] *Fortune*, January, 1940, p. 26.
[13] See Luke E. Ebersole, *Church Lobbying in the Nation's Capitol;* Ralph L. Roy, *Apostles of Discord;* George Younger, "Protestant Piety and the Right Wing," *Social Action*, May 15, 1951, pp. 5–35.

gest, be it noted, that in these various political conflicts, no religious issues are involved, nor that all claims are equally to be accepted, or denied. It is only to note that mutually contradictory claims—each in the name of the same religious tradition—can scarcely all be valid. America well illustrates the principle that in a heterogeneous society, religious symbols will be used by competing interests to support their various demands and values.

THE SEPARATION OF CHURCH AND STATE IN THE UNITED STATES

It is the third mode of relationship between religion and politics, however, that is usually thought to be most expressive of the American pattern. Relatively few societies have developed so distinctly the formal principle of "the separation of church and state" as has the United States. The sociologist is concerned to ask: Under what conditions does this principle develop? Do the informal patterns of relationship between the two institutions reenforce or modify the principle of separation? Does it mean also the separation of religion and citizenship? What are the conditions under which this mode of relationship is changed? What are its consequences?

The original constitutional statement is an expression of the combined influence of several forces working in American society in the late eighteenth century. Leanings toward an Established Church—and they were not entirely lacking among Puritans and Episcopalians—were blocked, because there could have been no agreement on a single church. This was probably not the major factor, however. There was, as part of the total struggle for liberty, widespread opposition to any Establishment. Even among the Calvinist clergy, there had begun what might be called the "Americanization" of their theology. This process became much more explicit in the development of Unitarianism in the nineteenth century, but it was implicit in the writing of the liberal group of pre-Revolutionary ministers. As Sperry says:

The laymen of Massachusetts who went to the second Continental Congress and the Constitutional Convention, first to declare American Independence and then to fashion the Constitution, were of the liberal rather than the conservative party, theologically. They would have had no interest in trying to foist the passing theocracy of an earlier time upon the country as a whole. If the Episcopal Church in Virginia was weakened by the exodus of its loyal clergy, the Puritan Church in New England was weakened by theological controversies within its own borders.[14]

[14] Willard L. Sperry, *Religion in America*, p. 52.

A further influence in the development of the principle of the separation of church and state has sometimes been overlooked in the context
of recent discussions which emphasize America's religious background.
Anti-clericalism and rationalism were vigorous at the time the Constitution was written. Sperry's judicious words well express their influence:

. . . the prevalence of enlightened deistic ideas among educated classes was
in part responsible for the studied silences of the document as to the existence
of God, and its unwillingness to commit itself, even in the most general terms,
to any Christian ideas. One can only say that, given the prior history of
colonial times and the subsequent record, the framers of the Constitution must
be credited with religious understatement, rather than with overstatement.
There had been and there was to be more religion in American life than the
Constitution would seem to suggest. But it is probably true that the deliberate
silences of the document upon the whole matter, and its understatements, were
the price which had then to be paid for a vindication of the principles of
toleration and liberty in matters religious.[15]

Modifications of the Principle of Separation of Church and State.
That the Constitution understates the mutual influence of religion and
government in the United States can be shown by a simple listing of some
of the ways in which they affect each other: church interest and influence
in marriage and divorce laws and in birth control legislation; the concern of many church groups with "social legislation"—child labor, social
security, etc.; the interest of some churches with·processes in the courts
and prisons; government chaplaincies and religious services in the armed
forces; required oaths; blasphemy laws; Sunday observance laws; government observance of special religious days and occasions; concern of the
churches over the "Bill of Rights," which includes religious freedom and
involves the problem of censorship; church interest in radio and television, the protection of religion in programming and the granting of time
to religious groups, in part by legal requirement.[16]

Only a very few persons in the United States contend that such mutual influences as these represent violations of the Constitutional principle
of the separation of church and state.

The great majority of presumably religious Americans allowed these encroachments on the strict "neutrality" of the state to accumulate with relatively little
concern or with ineffective opposition. There were always minor complaints
arising from the introduction of religious materials in the public schools: Jews
protested at being taught Christmas carols, Catholics protested against the
use of the King James version of the Bible, atheists protested against the use

[15] *Ibid.*, p. 58.
[16] See Stokes, *op. cit.*, Vol. III, chap. 20.

of prayers in legislatures and the presence of sectarian religious workers and teachers on state university campuses.[17]

The present legal and constitutional situation (as interpreted by the Supreme Court) reflects the shifting balance among many forces, with their various positions on the question of the relationship of church to state. Just as there are few who openly avow and work for the complete separation of religion and government, so there are few who support a formal union, an Establishment. In between, however, is a wide range of opinion indicative of the heterogeneity of American society. There are those who want government support and encouragement for religious values, but who oppose any direct government support to churches as organizations, even if they are all treated alike. This distinction is often a difficult one to draw. Virtually no one in this group, for example, opposes the tax-exempt status of churches; many of them support "released time" from schools for religious education.[18] In the religiously heterogeneous situation of the United States, however, enthusiastic support for such government encouragements to religion is hindered, not only by the belief in the "separation of church and state," but also, especially for the dominant Protestant groups, by the realization that government encouragement is likely to yield a *comparative* advantage to "minority" religious organizations, particularly Catholicism and the Protestant sects, precisely because it puts them all on an equal level. This realization is made the clearer by the more vigorous use often made of such government encouragement as "released time from schools" by the "minority" churches.

The Roman Catholic bishops of the United States have shown more concern over secularism and indifference to religion in government than in any weakening of constitutional separation. They have suggested the formula, "the cooperation of church and state," and call for government support not only of religious values, but also of churches, so long as all preferential treatment is avoided. They claim—as do the defenders of each of the other positions—constitutional support for their interpretation. It is a monopolistic Establishment that is prohibited, in their judgment, not government support of the work of the churches.

We feel with deep conviction that for the sake of both good citizenship and religion there should be a reaffirmation of our original American tradition of free cooperation between government and religious bodies—cooperation in-

[17] H. W. Schneider, *Religion in 20th Century America*, pp. 31–32.
[18] Several recent books affirm this position. In addition to the cited works of Pfeffer and Stokes, see C. H. Moehlman, *The Wall of Separation Between Church and State* and J. H. Nichols, *Democracy and the Churches*.

volving no special privilege to any group and no restriction on the religious liberty of any citizen. We solemnly disclaim any intent or desire to alter this prudent and fair American policy of government in dealing with the delicate problems that have their source in the divided religious allegiance of our citizens. . . .

We stand ready to cooperate in fairness and charity with all who believe in God and are devoted to freedom under God to avert the impending danger of a judicial "establishment of secularism" that would ban God from public life. For secularism is threatening the religious foundations of our national life and preparing the way for the advent of the omnipotent state.[19]

Thus a diversified society, with a somewhat ambiguous constitutional principle, exhibits a wide range of opinions concerning the proper relationship between church and state. There is an almost equally wide range of action. In the writer's judgment, there has been a trend in the direction of what might be called—to change the phrase of the Catholic bishops slightly—"the cooperation of churches and state." In a time of crisis, particularly from 1917 until the early twenties and from 1940 until the present, one of the aspects of the search for unity and consensus in American society has been a stress on religion and the religious foundations of the nation—all in the context of much reaffirmation of the "principle of the separation of church and state." Decisions by the Supreme Court have registered this hesitant trend. In *Everson v. Board of Education*, 1947, the Court allowed transportation expenses out of public funds to be given to parochial schools because, and insofar as, these schools met the state's secular education needs. To what other expenses this principle is applicable is a continuing subject of debate. In 1948, in the *McCollum* case, the Supreme Court invalidated a state statute permitting the release of children from public school time to take religious instruction on the school premises. But in the *Zorach* case, 1952, a New York City law allowing released time away from the school was upheld. The Court held that no absolute separation of church and state is required by the Constitution. It is required only that there be no interference with the free exercise of religion and that there be no Establishment. The many ways in which the state does indeed deal with religion were noted in the decision.[20]

We shall see below how the relationship between religion and government has been affected by war. "Both President Wilson and President Roosevelt did not hesitate to include religious appeals and sentiments in

[19] From the manifesto of the American Roman Catholic Bishops, November 20, 1948; see *The National Catholic Almanac*, 1949, pp. 86–91.
[20] See Pfeffer, *op. cit.* and F. Ernest Johnson, *American Education and Religion. The Problem of Religion in the Schools.*

their public utterances and documents during wartime. The use of such phrases as 'this nation under God' was intended to give a general religious solemnity to the struggles and to suggest officially that 'in God we trust.' " [21] Congress has added the words "under God" to the pledge of allegiance to the flag. Among many conservatively inclined citizens, non-religious or anti-religious beliefs and actions are synonymous with un-American activity: church and state may be separate, but religion and citizenship are identical. When asked to define a "communist," some say that it is a person against religion or one who teaches things contrary to the *Bible.* Thus political and national conflicts become identified with religious controversies. Samuel Stouffer writes: "It has perhaps not been adequately appreciated that a considerable element in the opposition to a free market in ideas in America is religious in origin." [22]

Effects of the American Pattern of Relationship between Church and State. From the point of view of the central problem of this chapter, these developments raise the question: What are the influences of the principle of separation and its modification on the three modes of relationship between religion and politics? One can speak here only in a most tentative way; but the sociological perspective offers at least some hypotheses.

Consider first the effects of the emphasis on the separation of church and state. This can scarcely be said to promote an integrating system of values rooted in religion—the first mode of relationship—but it at least prevents the aggravation of differences. A high level of coercion, not integration, would be the result of a politically sponsored religious unity in a religiously heterogeneous society. The political manipulation of religion --the second mode of relationship—is made less likely by the separation of church and state. In a religiously diverse society, where each church has equal political rights, one can scarcely make unambiguous claims that his political views are religiously sustained. Equally powerful religious claims for different political views can be offered. That is the reason that those who seek to prove that their political program has God's blessing must first try to prove that their religious views are the truly American ones—an established religious ideology if not an Established Church.

The development of religious institutions free to, and capable of, effective criticism of the established political pattern—the mode of relationship we have called universalism—is in some ways encouraged and in some ways blocked by the separation of church and state. The central thesis

[21] Schneider, *op. cit.,* p. 32.
[22] *Communists, Conformity, and Civil Liberties,* New York, Doubleday and Co., 1955.

of Stokes, Pfeffer, and others is that separation (without antagonism) has fostered the growth of freedom in the United States and has increased the influence of religion on many aspects of American society, as contrasted with a state-church situation. Separation is supported because it allows greater freedom to both the churches and the state. Where the religious leaders lack direct political influence, they also escape direct political domination, are freer to criticize political processes and the structure of power, are less invaded by political demands. The state, in turn, is given greater flexibility when it is not tied to an ecclesiastical structure.

The evidence does not, however, wholly support this view. Freedom from the structures of power raises the question of powerlessness. "The dilemma of the churches" is clear at this point, for to claim separation from the state is to reduce one's ability to influence the decisions of the state; while institutional union raises the likelihood that a church which seems to have a voice in political decisions is actually only an echo of decisions made on political grounds. There is no easy way to avoid this dilemma in the search for an anchorage for an effectively autonomous religious influence in politics. Even the concepts of a monotheistic and universalistic religion run the risk of political irrelevancy if they are tied to a thorough-going separation of church and state and the opposite risk of being twisted to the purposes of the nation-state (in the name of universalism) if the institutional connection is close.

How to be simultaneously in politics (thus to influence it) and beyond politics (thus to challenge it) is an ancient problem among the world religions. Islam has tended strongly toward the former pole, although some mystical sectarian movements challenge this position, and has thus frequently served only to reenforce the political power of the ruling classes of Islamic societies. Buddhism has tended toward the latter pole, although not without exceptions, particularly in recent decades, and thus has often been irrelevant to political problems—a position that is equally likely to reenforce the power of the ruling groups. The situation in Christianity has been more complicated. There has been a more explicit recognition of the dilemma, stemming in an important degree from the Judaic background of Christianity. It has been formulated in a skilled way in such concepts as St. Thomas' "relative natural law." Recognition of a dilemma is not synonymous, however, with its resolution. The history of Christian societies is filled with illustrations of religious movements that have (always with qualifications) "joined the state" in "Islamic" fashion (e.g., Spain today) and of other movements that have disregarded the problems of politics in "Buddhist" fashion. (It is sociologically interesting that this latter approach is most commonly found among the extremely disprivileged members of a society whose status makes the pessimistic view of this world congenial.)

To avoid both horns of the dilemma requires, not so much skilled maneuvering by religious leaders (though this is not unimportant) as a favorable socio-cultural context. In broadest terms we have defined this context as one of diffused power, based on economic, political, educational, technical, and other social structures.

It is perhaps the recognition of this dilemma that has been partly responsible for recent reduction in the sharpness of separation of churches and state in the United States. There is, of course, no question of a formal connection; but as we have seen, political leaders have been more likely to use the language of religion, and religious organizations in recent decades have become much more concerned with "social action," and "the bases of a just and durable peace." They have sought to influence political decisions by organized effort, by carefully worked out pronouncements from national councils, by lobbying. How has this modification of the sharper separation of church and state that characterized the earlier period of America affected the balance of the three modes of relationship with which we are concerned?

Religious concern for political decisions can promote the value integration of a society only to the degree that diverse religious groups emphasize common values. If they enter the political arena in competition with each other, creedal differences will be emphasized and the tensions of the society increased. Integration is scarcely served when religious leaders become concerned with political and economic questions, only to take such diverse views as the following:

The election was a great surprise and was for me a great disappointment. I had no special brief for Dewey and Warren, but felt it was important that there be a change to avoid the collectivist doom of communism or some other totalitarianism.[23]

The ethical result is inherent in the competitive, private property system regardless of the motives of its managers. . . . Yes, "God works in wonderous ways His marvels to perform." [24]

. . . it is perhaps another instance of the indirect consequences of the economic factor in religion that there should be more alarm among preachers over the atheism and metaphysical materialism of the Communists than there is over the denial by capitalism of the supremacy of the spirit in the life of man.[25]

[23] James W. Fifield, Jr. in his church bulletin, November 11, 1948.
[24] Samuel Pettingill in Christian Economics; quoted by R. L. Shinn, in Christian Faith and Social Action, edited by John A. Hutchison, p. 25.
[25] Harry F. Ward, Our Economic Morality and the Ethic of Jesus, p. 304.

These are, of course, extreme instances. There is substantially more value agreement in the views of large numbers of religious spokesmen on the requisites of a just and good society. Witness the convergence of views, and to some degree the active cooperation, among the National Catholic Welfare Conference, the Central Conference of American Rabbis, and the Protestant National Council of Churches.[26] Their cumulative influence is to underline a dominant, if not a universally shared, value core. They represent an adaptation of a religiously heterogeneous society seeking to maintain at least a minimum value concensus. There is no evidence that universal agreement on this value core is necessary—or from some perspectives desirable—for the continuation of a changing, modern society; but if the conception of society that we have adopted is correct, some strong central tendency is required. The *balance* of contemporary religious developments in the United States would seem to be contributing to the maintenance of this central core of values.

It should be noted, however, that in a society of diverse religious connections, the reenforcements of ritual and the supports of dogma are "not available," for they accentuate the differences within the society, not its unity. The religious influence in the traditional sense is reduced to a kind of least common denominator. It is partly for this reason that symbols of nation, rather than of creed, are most expressive of the unity of a modern, complex society.

The second mode of relationship between religion and politics—the use of religious symbols for the political purposes of part of the society—has probably been increased by the reduction of the sharpness of separation of church and state in the United States. Political claims in the name of religion are given more credence in a situation in which the two spheres are thought to be mutually significant.

To understand the effects of the reduction in sharpness of separation of church and state on the third mode of relationship—a universalist religious emphasis capable of imposing restraints on the state—we must refer again to the dilemma of the churches. When prominent church leaders, denominational boards, and interdenominational conferences give more vigorous attention to questions of racial or labor or international relations, seeking to influence and guide the government, they reduce the likelihood of powerlessness, but at the same time they run the risk, both of mistaking their various parochial views with universal judgments and of a reduction in the full flexibility of action. "The state" will listen to "the church" only if there is agreement on certain basic premises—and it is often precisely these premises that a universal perspective

[26] See Stokes, *op. cit.*, Vol. III, pp. 3–32.

might bring most sharply under criticism. At a time when instruments of destruction of incalculable power have shattered the adequacy of existing political structures, when we know—if expert testimony is accepted —that a few bombs can kill tens of millions, and that a shift in the wind may determine who the tens of millions will be, in such a time, one might expect a universalist religion to bring dramatic and persistent challenges to secular structures that divide the world. But one finds little of this on the local level, in the writer's judgment. Even in the National Council of Churches and the World Council of Churches, as they have sought to influence the course of action in international relations in the last decade, one senses a tendency to proclaim their approval of peace and disarmament, but some reticence in relating their concerns directly to the existing patterns and the basic premises of governmental policy. From various value perspectives this may be looked upon as a happy or an unhappy development; but it indicates the dilemma of the churches, seeking influence in a world with many powers and many values besides their own.

RELIGION AND WAR

The various forms of relationship between religion and the political aspects of society are revealed sharply in the analysis of religious attitudes toward war. Our primary attention will be given to situations in which a universal religion confronts the problem of war, with its inevitable divisive impact; for it is in such situations that the full complexity of the relationship is found. We can indicate the other patterns briefly.

In those situations where religious membership and social membership are identical, war is scarcely a problem. If the society is at war, the gods give their support; religion is used unambiguously to sustain the society's claim; ritual and prayer and sacrifice are devoted to the cause of victory. The enemies of Jehovah, in the earliest days, were simply the enemies of Israel; Asshur gave strength in battle to Assyria; the Guardian Spirit of a Dakota Indian was at his side in battle. Thus religion was used to weld the society together and to give individual courage, in order to bring victory and to help the adherents to face the risks and sacrifices of war.

Where a growing social complexity has produced a differentiation between the political and religious structures—with the possibility of clashes of policy and competition for power, and the greater likelihood of differences in interest among the members of the society—the relationship between religion and war is not so unambiguous. There is still no question of war as such being a problem, for religious views are still society-bound, but there are questions of when and where and how war should be employed, based on differences of interest and value. Under these circumstances, a religious ideology may be manipulated by those in power to support a war that is opposed or given only reluctant backing by large segments of society.

The modern Japanese situation illustrates this mode of relationship, although not without complicating aspects. The West tended to look upon Japan preceding and during the second World War as a nation of wholly dedicated belligerents. But this was scarcely an accurate picture. "Only the common people," said a Japanese writer in 1939, "know the bitterness of war." The ruling group exploited the powerful symbols of National Shinto to tie the nation together in unified support of its war program. According to the ideology of Shinto, "The sacred quality of the divine emperor attaches to a Japanese war. All the wars of Japan are holy wars since they are under the supreme command of an emperor who can do nothing wrong." [27] Shinto made the Japanese state, not merely a secular power, but a sacred church as well, ". . . founded on the arrogation that in the last analysis the validity of its decisions was superhuman or supernatural." [28] Although this shares some elements of a simple tribal religion lending support to the nation in its external conflicts, the situation is actually far more complicated than that. It is a great mistake to think of the ceremonies and ideologies of National Shinto as one would think of the religious war dances and beliefs of a small, relatively homogeneous tribal society. A nation of eighty millions, with its diverse classes and interests, its various hopes, its widely different outlooks on the world, indeed its variety of religions, develops the degree of unity necessary for modern war only by great effort. The explicit *revival* of Shinto in the last third of the nineteenth century, in the face of a strong Buddhist and some Christian influence—with their theoretical opposition to war—is the clearest sign of the manipulative aspect which is the basic element in the second mode of relationship between religion and government.

In societies where religions with a universalist emphasis are predominant, war itself has become a problem, for it clearly represents a sharp split in the universal brotherhood of man that these religions support. But if war is a problem, so is defeat and the possibility of domination for the nation. In no case, therefore, do we find the churches of such societies dwelling solely on the universal theme, opposing war and refusing to cooperate with the government. The themes of "tribal unity," the manipulation of religion by partial interests, and universalism mingle in

---

[27] D. C. Holtom, *Modern Japan and Shinto Nationalism*, p. 54; see also Robert O. Ballou, *Shinto, the Unconquered Enemy*.

[28] Holtom, *op. cit.*, p. 176.

complicated interaction. The task of the sociology of "religion and war" is to try to discover the conditions under which various balances among these themes occur.

RESPONSES OF CHRISTIAN CHURCHES TO WAR

Some reference to the responses of Christian churches to war will be of value in helping to find these conditions. During the first centuries, when Christianity was a small and persecuted sect, pacifism was the dominant theme. This is not surprising, for the sect had neither the responsibilities nor the coercive possibilities of power. By the time of St. Augustine, however, Christianity had become a powerful secular as well as religious force. The pacifist position was gradually given up as the church became involved in problems of coercion and conflict. St. Augustine drew on an accumulating doctrine of justification for Christian participation in war to formulate what is still the essential pattern of the Catholic, and to a substantial degree the Lutheran and Anglican, doctrine of war: the Church can give its support to a war only if the cause of one side is manifestly just and only if it is fought without vindictiveness, a kind of reluctant participation in a "just and mournful war." On either side of this policy there remained pacifism (largely in the Christian sects) and the crusade—at first a holy cause fought under the authority of the church, but of late a national cause fought with the blessing of the church.[29]

The changes in attitude of religious spokesmen toward war are well known. Sometimes within a few months, the dominant attitude can shift from sharp condemnation of war mixed with pacifism to vigorous support of a government in the prosecution of a war. The sociological meaning of "church" as a religious institution thoroughly integrated with a society and the concept of "the dilemma of the churches" can help us to interpret this shift. It is inconceivable that a church—by its very definition—should fail to support a nation in a major war. Church leaders could scarcely hope to be effective in a society if they turned away completely from a basic struggle in which that society was engaged. They accept the reality of much that is inevitable, so far as their own power is concerned, in order to be able to exert a qualified influence. This does not necessarily mean that they have relinquished the universalist theme of their religion—although it may signify that. It may demonstrate only the recognition of the dilemma that they face. This is well illustrated by

[29] See Roland H. Bainton, "The Churches Shift on War," *Religion in Life,* Summer, 1943, pp. 323–335.

Margaret Fuller, writing from Rome during the Revolution of 1848. She was trying to explain her attitude to organized friends of peace in the United States who had condemned the struggle for liberty which she was supporting by work in a hospital for the insurgents:

What you say about the Peace way is deeply true; if any one sees clearly how to work in that way, let him, in God's name! Only, if he abstain from fighting giant wrongs, let him be sure he is really and ardently at work undermining them, or better still, sustaining the rights that are to supplant them. Meanwhile, I am not sure that I can keep my hands free from blood.[30]

The degree to which war will be supported by churches only as part of the *"relative* natural law," that is, the degree to which war will continue to be criticized for its destruction of universality at the same time it is being supported, varies greatly, even in the course of a few years. American churches during the first World War, for example, were very strongly inclined, with few exceptions, to give the war unqualified support.[31] During World War II, however, there was much more restraint, a more frequent expression of America's responsibilities in the sequence of events that led to the war, a stronger insistence that victory be used as an opportunity for promoting world brotherhood. Early in 1942, for example, the editors of *Christianity and Crisis* stated their aims for the year to be: (1) to recognize responsibilities as citizens of a belligerent nation, (2) to "resist tyranny and help to establish justice without hatred or bitterness. This can only be done if we avoid self-righteousness . . . ," (3) to develop the resources of the church for service to both civilians and men in the armed forces, (4) to keep the consciousness of the universal church alive, (5) to deal at length with the problems of postwar reconstruction.[32] Here is certainly a modern version of St. Augustine's just and mournful war, by men who had insisted that America should join the war several months before hostilities actually began, but who continued to stress its dangers and weaknesses as an instrument of justice. Shortly after Pearl Harbor, the executive committee of the Federal Council of Churches, while condemning "the calculated treachery of recent aggressions," also pointed to America's involvement in the events that led up to the conflict, emphasized the separate tasks of the church, as distinct from the government, during war, declared that "the church must be in the vanguard of

[30] Quoted by Merle Curti, *Peace or War, The American Struggle, 1636–1936,* p. 45.
[31] See Ray Abrams, *Preachers Present Arms;* Stokes, *op. cit.,* Vol. III, chapter 21; J. Milton Yinger, *Religion in the Struggle for Power,* chapter 5.
[32] *Christianity and Crisis,* January 12, 1942, pp. 1–2.

preparation for a just and durable peace," and underlined the universalist theme:

As members of the world-wide church which transcends all differences of race and nation, we have obligations which reach beyond our own country. We must preserve at all costs the world-wide Christian fellowship without which no free world order of justice and peace can be achieved.[33]

To point to such data is not to prove that the churches *effectively* promoted a universalist program in the midst of war. This is not to disparage the efforts, but to point to the serious question of power. It would be difficult to uphold the proposition that in the decade after the second World War there was a smaller harvest of bitterness, a less divided world than after the first World War. This does not prove the ineffectiveness of the efforts of the churches to promote universalism, of course, for the second war was much more divisive and destructive than the first: the world might be even more divided were it not for religious efforts. It does, however, warn us not to mistake church pronouncements for effective political action. It is well to remember several things in this connection: probably only a minority of churchmen took part in these actions; a great many secular groups (not without religious motivation in part) were also concerned with problems of peace and international justice; a verbal bow to a universal ideology is a very common accompaniment of war in the modern world (even National Shinto declared that Japanese victory would bring "the whole world under one roof")—such a bow is perhaps a necessity to relieve the sense of guilt of peoples to whom war has become a social problem; and the churches found it easier to agree on aims than on procedures, without which the aims remain unfulfilled.

Yet even conferences and declarations show that a religion with a universal ethic may, under some circumstances, resist many of the pressures that would make it simply a symbolic arm of a government in conflict.

That an emphasis on the part of churches that reaches beyond national aims is subject to a rather delicate balance of forces in the secular environment may be indicated further by the responses to the "Cold War" since 1948. In the writer's very tentative judgment—his exploration of the data on this question has not been adequate—the churches of America have done very little to confront the average layman in the local situation with a universalist critique of the policies of government during

---

[33] *Christian Century*, January 14, 1942, p. 60.

this period. The enormity of the holocaust—in the literal meaning of the word—that would result from an atomic and hydrogen bomb war, rather than prompting them to intense effort to state and implement the universalist idea, seems to have partially paralyzed their efforts—as it has the efforts of many who are not identified with the churches.

Sects and War. The least ambiguous assertion of a universalist ethic (but not necessarily, therefore, the most powerful) in the face of the divisions of war is found in sectarian pacifism. Here is direct opposition to the policies of government. This is always the position of a minority; but the size even of the minority varies widely from situation to situation. During peace time, pacifism may have substantial support, even in the churches; but during war, the conflicting loyalties and the dilemmas of influence persuade all but a small number to change their positions. This was especially true during the first World War.[34] During the second World War, however, there were many more pacifist churchmen, just as there was more insistence, on the part of churchmen who supported the war, on a continuous pursuit of just war aims. The pacifists included a number of the country's most prominent ministers. The most common position among them can perhaps be summarized in these words: The church does not obstruct the work of the government, but it has a different task—to reduce hate, to plan continuously for peace, to defend civil liberties, to improve race relations, to carry on all those tasks that can minimize the division of the world and keep alive the sense of community necessary for the postwar world.

Although there is pacifism in the churches, showing the inaccuracy of any scheme of classification, it is found in largest proportions in the sects. Here again, the number of actual opponents of war was greater during the second World War than during the first. This follows the trend toward more restrained judgments among secular and church leaders that we have already remarked and doubtless reflects also a more favorable legal situation. Perhaps the most accurate index of the extent of pacifism is the number of conscientious objectors. (We need not here explore various distinctions that are sometimes drawn between pacifism and conscientious objection.) The data are by no means accurate—it seems likely, in fact, that there was a persistent effort on the part of Selective Service officials to minimize the number who claimed exemption from military service on conscientious grounds—but a very careful appraisal by Sibley and Jacob arrives at the number 100,000 as the total number of conscientious objectors in the United States between 1940 and 1947.[35]

---

[34] See Abrams, *op. cit.*
[35] See Mulford Sibley and Philip Jacob, *Conscription of Conscience*, pp. 83–84.

Of this total number, about 12,000 were assigned to "Civilian Public Service" camps and over 6,000 were sentenced to prison for refusal, at various points, to accept the draft. A large proportion of these most vigorous objectors came from sectarian religious groups. Over sixty per cent were members of the three "historic peace churches" (Mennonites, Brethren, and Quakers) and the Jehovah's Witnesses. Among these groups there is a wide range in the types of opposition to the claims of the state in war. The opposition of many of the Jehovah's Witnesses has expressed itself not only in unwillingness to participate in war, but in a much more complete withdrawal from the "world of sin." Many refused to register in the draft; for this and other reasons, some 5,000 of them served time in prison. Mennonites tended toward non-resistance, as contrasted with non-violent resistence; while many Quakers shared Gandhi's idea of *satyagraha*—an active struggle for peace, using non-violent means. (In Gandhi's case, of course, this meant the actual pursuit of political power, the use of boycott, civil disobedience, and other vigorous measures of protest, so long as they were non-violent.) Somewhat different from this, although still far removed from the sectarian withdrawal of the Jehovah's Witnesses, is the concept of "vocational Christian pacifism." This describes a role very similar to that of the pacifist churchmen that we have described above. Pacifists are thought of as a small minority whose task it is to keep before the majority, who are caught in the midst of a conflict, a different picture of how the world may be ordered. This concept is well expressed by Elton Trueblood:

The pacifist who keeps alive this different conception is contributing to the future welfare of his people by providing a balance to the extremes of hatred which arise, and by holding aloft the principles of ultimate peace which might otherwise be forgotten. He is keeping a humble fire burning, to light the new fires which must burn again after the storm is over. If he understands his position rightly he accords his government the same courtesies which he expects. That is, the government grants him a measure of recognition of his conscientious objection and he, in turn, does not try to embarrass the government. It is for this reason that some of the recognized leaders of English Quakerdom have refused to sign a petition asking the government to sue for peace now.[36]

Members of withdrawal sects contend that this involves so much compromise that the fundamental condemnation of war is lost. Others have

---

This is probably less than half the ratio of Great Britain, whose legal pattern was more tolerant of the conscientious objector. There were four times as many objectors in Great Britain during World War II as in World War I. See *ibid.*, pp. 2–7.

[36] Elton Trueblood, "Vocational Christian Pacifism," *Christianity and Crisis,* November 3, 1941, pp. 2–5.

called it a return to monasticism—where a small group maintained the religious principles in relatively pure form and lived them vicariously for the whole society. From the point of view of the sociology of religion, it would seem to be an attempt to reduce the sharpness of the dilemma of religious influence by criticizing the pattern of war but not withdrawing from the problems of the society. Active attention to those problems has taken not only the familiar form of relief and rehabilitation, but more recently the pattern of an attempt to keep open the channels of informal communication among diplomats. This has been done, for example, by maintenance of Quaker House beside the United Nations buildings in New York, where representatives of all nations may meet in informal conversations, and by sponsorship of informal seminars for diplomats in Europe.[37]

Just as some churchmen have avoided the sharp reduction in influence that comes from accepting completely the aims and methods of the secular society, so some sectarians have won a measure of influence by avoiding the extremes of "withdrawal."

Political Domination of the Universalist Theme. Any account of religion and war that did not give fuller attention than we have until now to the frequency with which a universalist religious doctrine has been twisted to national and class purposes would be very inadequate. Time and distance make it seem clear that universalist claims for a "holy war," are often disguises for limited aims. We are likely to be more myopic in judging situations that are closer to us in time and space. An adequate sociology of religion must specify variables so precisely that trained observers on both sides of a conflict would agree on the degree to which the belligerents were using the symbols of a universalist religion to justify limited goals and the degree to which religion was concerned with genuinely human-wide problems. It need scarcely be noted that this is now very unlikely, at least for the analysis of any conflict contemporary with the observers. When a Japanese Buddhist writes that, "Japan is a lover of peace, so even if she goes to war, it is always a war for peace," [38] American sociologists have no difficulty in recognizing this as inaccurate. Presumably Japanese observers were equally persuaded that any claims by American churchmen that victory for the United States in the second World War was vital for the cause of world brotherhood were not accurate. It was clear, outside of Germany, in 1917, that *Gott mit Uns* was pretension; but it was probably equally clear inside of Germany that there were many inaccuracies in the statement by the Federal

---

[37] See Elmore Jackson, *Meeting of Minds.*
[38] Quoted by Holtom, *op. cit.*, pp. 149–150.

Council of Churches of Christ in America that America was fighting "to vindicate the principles of righteousness. . . ."

This is not to imply that all these claims are equally valid (or invalid) —the writer cannot so easily escape his own myopea—but only to suggest that their relative validity can be determined only by a very careful specification of "criteria of universality." The following criteria seem to be useful in distinguishing between the fact and the pretense of claims to a universal emphasis made by religious leaders and churches during war; or, to put it more accurately, to determine the *degree* of accuracy of the claims, for it is doubtless always a continuum:

1. The degree to which the *full range* of the religious ideology is emphasized. When a Japanese Christian stresses the contribution of Christianity to the code of *Bushido*—the way of the warrior—by its emphasis on self-sacrifice, loyalty, courage, discipline,[39] but pays little regard to the different elements in the Christian ideology ("resist not evil," all men are brothers), we have an example of the distortion of a universalist religion for limited aims.

2. The degree to which a conflict is described in "all and none" terms. If religious spokesmen describe the enemy as absolute beasts, if there is no recognition of the interactional sources and the mutual involvement of nations in the generation of conflicts, no appreciation of one's own errors, then claims to universality are likely to be invalid. This is based on the premise that the causes of conflict are reciprocal and cumulative—that the Smoot-Hawley tariff had something to do with Japanese foreign policy after 1930—and are not simply the evil of one side.

3. The degree to which churches—even though giving basic support to a government during war—continue to criticize specific acts and policies of the government as incompatible with universalist aims. An age of "total war" presents especially sharp problems of this kind. "Saturation bombing," "unconditional surrender," "massive retaliation," "anticipatory defense" raise important questions for the world religions. Problems of civil liberties, the rights of conscientious objectors, the treatment of enemy captives, responsibilities for refugees, and the like are likely to be seen in military terms by a nation at war. Do the churches continue to insist on a broader interpretation?

4. The degree to which churches take direct part in military and supporting activities, as contrasted with emphasis on separate (even though complementary) tasks. The ability to emphasize universalist goals is obscured if the churches do not maintain a sharp sense of organizational

[39] See Arimichi Ebisawa, "The Relation Between the Ethics of *Bushido* and Christianity," *Cultural Nippon*, December, 1939, p. 27.

separation from the state. (This, incidentally, is compatible with the status of Established Church.) When churches sell war bonds or recruit soldiers from the pulpit (as some American churches did during the first World War), as contrasted with giving care for bombed-out civilians or giving attention to the problems of war-boom communities (tasks which are equally important for a nation at war), the likelihood that they will maintain a universalist perspective is reduced.

5. The degree to which the churches carry on *action* that continues to emphasize their conception of universality. This is closely related to the previous criterion. Verbal reaffirmation of world brotherhood by itself is as often related to limited actions as it is to actions with a universal concern. Virtually every national participant in war in the modern world, in fact, contends that it fights for a cause of world significance. Churches, for their part, validate this claim only by actions that have more than national import.

These criteria have scarcely been put to an adequate test. The most that can be said for them is that the writer has found them useful in trying to answer the question: How can one measure the degree to which the world religions have maintained a universal perspective in the face of the limiting pressures of a nation at war? Their validation requires that other persons, preferably with very different value stands, apply them to the same data that we have referred to in this chapter, and arrive at similar conclusions.

THE SOCIO-CULTURAL CONTEXT OF UNIVERSALISM

Even were the usefulness of these criteria established, we would not have an answer to the more basic question: What are the conditions under which universalism will be most strongly affirmed? The criteria we have listed are an index of measurement, but only indirectly a statement of causes. At various points in this chapter we have referred to causal factors. It may be well now to try to draw them together.

1. We have suggested, in the first place, that a universal religion will be invented only in a particular socio-cultural context. There must be extensive social differentiation, religious specialists, culture contact, and a long period of frustration of major needs and aspirations. The culture must be one in which the values encourage religious struggles with these problems, as contrasted with (or in addition to) economic, political, military, and other struggles with them. There is a need for individuals peculiarly sensitive to these influences and qualified, by personal make-up, to

deal with them in religious terms. Frequently one individual will stand out in this regard (Buddha, Jesus, Mohammed); but this is not necessarily the case, as the development of Judaism shows. Moreover, it is important not to disregard the cumulative development that led up to "the founder," so clear in the case of Christianity and Islam. We know too little about the situation in India preceding Buddha to judge the cumulative element in his case. Nor should we forget the influence of followers, as well as predecessors in "creating" a founder. St. Paul, St. Augustine, and Luther, for example shaped Christianity in vital ways.

2. The socio-cultural factors in the origin of universalism in religion must be distinguished from the factors involved in its influence in particular situations. It has been our thesis that the effective presence of a universalist theme, challenging and contradicting limited political claims, varies most significantly with the degree of the diffusion of power. Where secular power is most heavily concentrated, the universal theme is most completely obscured.

3. Sectarian movements emphasizing a universal theme will be most common in a society where major groups feel frustrated in their basic hopes and thus feel no real stake in the society to which they belong. Drawing on their religious tradition, they criticize that society in the name of universal values. At first glance this may seem to be a contradiction of the previous point, for certainly frustration and secular powerlessness will be most common in societies where power is not diffused. We need to refer again to the various types of sects to eliminate this apparent contradiction. Sects in situations where power is least diffused, where hope and aspirations for this world are lowest, will tend to be of the "withdrawal" variety. Their universalism is other-worldly. Only in situations where hopes for improvement on earth loom large, where the disinherited, though weak, are not indeed powerless, do we find sects aggressively working for a universalism relevant to this world.

4. Universalism will vary with the immediate historical context. Situations vary in the amount of international communication, the degree of awareness of the lives and problems of persons in other nations, races, or classes, and particularly in the degree of actual interdependence. All of these have increased in the modern world, so that thoughtful religious people are continuously confronted with problems that the existing political structures may be incompetent to handle, or may be handling in ways contradictory to the theme of universalism. Another aspect of the immediate historical situation concerns the swings in emphasis in a complicated religious tradition. If one part of that tradition is given predominant attention, a movement to emphasize other parts is likely to appear—

sponsored both by religious specialists, who professionally seek to encompass the whole tradition, and by those laymen who find their own needs and values unsatisfied by the existing balance of emphases. This may account for the stronger awareness of universal values in American churches during the second World War than during the first: there was a revulsion away from the enormous enthusiasm for unqualified support of government policy that many churches had shown.

5. The patterns of group relationship are not of primary significance, yet they play some part in affecting the degree of universalism. An Established Church, for example, may demonstrate a great deal of autonomy, while churches sharply separate from the state in the formal sense may be subservient to its commands or incapable of influencing its policies. Whatever the formal relationship, that pattern of church-state connection which allows independent judgments and actions and at the same time encourages religious groups to be concerned with problems of politics—in the broadest sense—is most likely to promote the universalist emphasis.

6. Finally, we may mention leadership. Weber's concept of "charisma" —leadership that is a specifically revolutionary new force in human affairs—is scarcely adequate until it too has been explained. Religious leadership, whether charismatic or of a more prosaic variety, must be referred, by the sociologist of religion, to its socio-cultural setting. On the most general level, this means that certain contexts help, both to create persons with certain personality tendencies, and to draw them into positions of influence. The leaders, in turn, react back upon that situation and take their part in the stream of influences at work.

These several variables, and doubtless the many others that might be added, interacting together, shape the degree to which the universalist theme in a religion will be emphasized or obscured.

CHAPTER 10

Religious Change and Social Change

In coming to the analysis of the mutual influence of religious change and social change, we approach what is doubtless the central question in the sociology of religion, a question that has inevitably been involved in each of the previous chapters but now requires more explicit treatment. The discussion of the relationship between religious change and social change can serve as a kind of summary of many of the concepts of the sociology of religion. Is religion a prime mover in history, or perhaps, as some contend *the* prime mover, "the clue to history"? If this is true, how does one explain changes in religion itself? Oppositely, is religious change a mere reflection of other changes, a symbol, but not a part of the causal interaction? Or is religion one of several "levels of causation," a force that once set in motion is part of a complex of causes that mutually condition each other? If this last is the most adequate position, as we shall contend, it is likely that the influence of religion will vary from situation to situation. It may be an important part of the explanation of social change in one setting and inconsequential in another. We need to try to discover, therefore, the conditions which maximize and those that minimize its influence. We have held that the general condition which maximizes the ability of religion to affect the processes of social change is the existence of some degree of autonomy in the religious institution.

In the previous chapter we have indicated some of the variables that influence the degree of autonomy in religions with a universalist ideology. Since our primary interest in this chapter will be with such religions, it will be well to keep those variables in mind.

Varous writers have emphasized three modes of relationship between religious and social change, each of which requires some attention: religious change as a result of social change; religion as a barrier to change; religion as an initiator of change. The first of these is the subject of this chapter.

RELIGIOUS CHANGE AS THE RESULT OF SOCIAL CHANGE

No clearer indication of the functional interdependence of religion with society can be found than the changes which religions undergo when their social settings change. Only those who hold that religions, in all their complexity, are the products of one flash of inspiration or revelation are likely to deny that religious systems develop and grow in various directions because of changes in the society in which they are found. Virtually all theologians and church historians today will readily grant that beliefs, rites, and religious group structure are affected by social changes, although most of them would contend that the *fundamental* elements in their faith (and perhaps in other world religions, if not in all religions) are ultimately fixed, rooted in the nature of "being," and not, therefore subject to modification by society.

SOCIAL CHANGE AND THE DEVELOPMENT OF EARLY JUDAISM

In preceding chapters we have indicated how the appearance of religious movements among American Indians, the rise of sects, the developments within Calvinism, and other religious changes could be explained, in part, as responses to fundamental changes in the social situation. Certainly the gradual transformation of Judaism from a tribal religion, infused with magic, with a god of "hosts" (battles) who insists on the total destruction of the Canaanites, into a monotheistic, universalist religion, with a god of justice and love, is a process that can best be understood by studying it in the context of the social forces affecting the Jewish people.[1] Before the changes accomplished by the prophets, through the

[1] See W. Robertson Smith, *Lectures on the Religion of the Semites;* L. T. Hobhouse, *Morals in Evolution;* Louis Finklestein, *The Pharisees: The Sociological Background of Their Faith;* Max Weber, *Ancient Judaism;* Louis Wallis, *Sociological Study of the Bible;* Homer W. Smith, *Man and His Gods.*

course of several generations, the religion of Yahweh had contained the common beliefs that suffering was the result of sin and that sacrifice could win atonement. In the face of acute and prolonged suffering, however, these beliefs are likely to be very unsatisfying; they are patently "false"; they do not "work." A new conception of God begins to emerge. Sacrifice has clearly not atoned for sin; what then does God require: that one put away evil and walk justly. "I hate, I despise your feasts. . . . But let judgment roll down as waters, and righteousness as a mighty stream." God has been transformed from an anthropomorphic being, delighting in gifts and homage, into a spirit, "and they who worship him must worship him in spirit and in truth." This was the prevailing message of the early prophets who transformed Yahweh worship, with its burnt offerings and sacrifices and its tribal limitations, into a monotheistic religion, emphasizing repentance.

Yet the suffering continued. Living at the crossroads of empires, the Jews were overrun by powerful neighbors, carried into captivity, and their hopes for power and success destroyed. One could say that this was punishment for evil, that Israel had not put away its evil ways, that the cities were corrupt, and that faith had been placed in false gods. Or one could give the prolonged suffering a new meaning, find a place for it in God's scheme of things, a place that would remove the religious beliefs from the constant doubt that is felt when a faith is considered to be more or less directly a way of solving life's immediate problems. The later Jewish prophets did both of these things. They continued to call for righteousness and justice, but they began to declare that suffering had a meaning and a value of its own. Israel became the suffering servant, "despised, and rejected of men, a man of sorrows and acquainted with grief." The Jewish victory was to be a spiritual victory; God had chosen them to bring righteousness to the world.

Growing social differentiation within Israel, as well as external attacks, influenced the development of Judaism. The clear-cut monotheism of Amos appeared in the context of sharp protests against the great contrast of wealth and poverty that he found in the cities. These religious inventions were not, of course, the inevitable products of the social changes experienced by the Jewish people. There were other possible "solutions" to their difficulties: They might have concluded that their continued suffering proved the inferiority of their god and deserted him for the gods of Babylon, as some doubtless did. They might have met their difficulties with a renewed nationalism; and despite the continued frustration of their national ambitions, this theme was never completely obliterated. Many religious interpretations of the meaning of life were doubtless tried, but most were to be found unsatisfying in the face of the persistent difficulties that overwhelmed them. An explanation of the development of Judaism must leave full room for the role of the religious innovator. Yet the social situation set definite limits to the kind of religious development that could be functionally adequate for individuals and the group. It is interesting that the combination of emphasis on individual righteousness, eschatological hope, faith in ultimate vindication, and a belief that they must keep the true faith alive for others—all important in Judaism—are central in the religious movements of many contemporary Christians who suffer most: the sects of minority groups and lower classes. Many of these elements appear, in fact, in other religions, among those who have had to face deprivation and continuous suffering. As Hobhouse says, in commenting on the development of Judaism: ". . . by a very different road and with much difference of implied meaning, we are reaching the Buddhist doctrine of renunciation and humility—those cardinal points of spiritualized religion." [2]

EARLY CHRISTIANITY AND SOCIAL CHANGE

Developments in Christianity, even during its earliest years, can scarcely be understood without relating them to the Jewish background that we have discussed briefly, and to the social situation in which it appeared. The picture of a religion, founded in all of its complexity by Jesus, with the whole range of its teachings embodied in a sacred and changeless literature, has been supplanted—not least of all by biblical scholars and church historians—by the story of a religious synthesis from many societies. Christianity was strongly influenced by the setting in which it developed; it changed and adapted itself to the different situations with which it was confronted. (It perhaps should be said, to avoid misunderstanding, that most biblical scholars and church historians believe that the central elements in Christianity are revelations through the son of God. Scholarship may reveal the instruments, but not the basic source. They show how these revelations, in their view, are variously recorded in the Bible; they show how the church, as the carrier of Jesus' teachings, has been influenced by the social changes going on around it; but many of them would be unwilling to accept any attempt to interpret the whole of religion on an objective basis.)

Historical research has shown that many of the elements of Christianity that were long thought by its adherents to be unique were common ideas, practices, and myths in the Ancient world. Some of its doctrines and practices were added, during the course of several generations, as it developed

[2] Hobhouse, *op. cit.*, p. 495.

from a small Jewish cult into a dominant religion. Resurrected gods had been worshipped in many societies for several centuries before the appearance of Christianity. The doctrine of virgin birth was familiar to pagans; and it is significant that the doctrine was not used by Paul nor by Mark, author of the earliest gospel, who said nothing about the early years of Jesus' life. A kind of eucharist meal was found in many pagan cults. And belief in miraculous powers was virtually universal in the Ancient world. "Jesus turned water into wine, as did Dionysus on January sixth of every year; and multiplied loaves of bread as did Elisha. He walked on water like Orion, Poseidon's son. He raised men from the dead, as did Elijah and Elisha—this feat had once been so common that Aristophanes in *The Frogs* (ca. 405 B.C.) made Dionysus say of Hermes and Hermes's father, that performing resurrections was a family profession." [3] That there is no mention of Jesus' miraculous powers in Paul's Epistles gives support to Smith's contention that the miraculous elements were added to Christianity in an effort to convert the pagans and to convince the Jews that Jesus was the true messiah.

Many of the Christian holy days were blended with celebrations of ancient origin. The death and resurrection of Attis, the God of vegetation, had been celebrated in Rome on March twenty-fourth and twenty-fifth, the spring equinox being the appropriate time for his revival. It seems certain that the official dates for the commemoration of the death and resurrection of Christ were assimilated into this established custom; and the nativity of Christ was placed at the winter solstice in December—the date that was widely celebrated as the birth date of the Sun.

There is little doubt that Christianity drew from ancient mystery cults, from Greek philosophy (especially Stoicism), as well as from Judaism. The recent discoveries of the "Dead Sea Scrolls" tend to give support to this conception of the pre-Christian existence of many Christian ideas. There is much scholarly work yet to be done before the full significance of the Scrolls can be ascertained. It is now generally accepted, if not proved, that they are authentic documents of a Jewish sect—perhaps the Essenes—dated about 100 B.C. Insofar as they are Biblical texts, they tend to confirm the authenticity of other texts. The new documents among the Scrolls present a picture of a sect that in many ways is similar to the earliest Christian groups.

The controversies surrounding the Dead Sea Scrolls have gone beyond those of scholarship and have become partly matters of faith. It is interesting to inquire why this latest indication of the ways in which Christianity was embedded in the situation of the ancient world should arouse de-

[3] Homer Smith, *op. cit.*, p. 202.

bate. Biblical criticism is many centuries old, even its modern approaches dating back two hundred years. It may be that the existence of many actual documents brings a sharper challenge to the conceptions of revelation and the uniqueness of Jesus than earlier studies did. The Scrolls have also received wider publicity than did earlier research, thus seeming to pose a greater threat to those who look upon Jesus as a starting point. This conception of a starting point is certainly a central thesis in Pauline Christianity, which lies at the foundation of most branches of Christian interpretation today. It is conceivable that the fact that nowhere in the Bible are the Essenes mentioned, despite their similarity to Christians, is an indication of the effort to establish the uniqueness of Jesus.[4]

Even the most liberal interpretation of the Scrolls does not establish a historical connection between Jesus and the Essenes. These documents do, however, add weight to the accumulating evidence that in the very building of Christianity, elements were assimilated from many sources, that it changed and developed as it reached out to many different cultures. Without this process, it could not have appealed to the Roman masses and to their rulers and to the "barbarians" of Northern Europe. "This Christian synthesis was marvelously inclusive; everything in the Roman world seems to have found a place, from Greek rationalism and humanism to the ideas and ideals of Egyptian and Babylonian priests, already old before the Greeks discovered Greece." [5] And as the experiences, values, and problems of its adherents have changed, Christianity has continued to change, continued to absorb new elements.

Not all aspects of a religious system are changed with equal speed or ease, but the process of development can be seen in every phase of religious life, from forms of worship and aesthetic symbolism, to group organization and polity, to theology and doctrine. A religion will not long hold the allegiance of a group of people who have acquired, as a result of non-religious causes, new aesthetic tastes, new intellectual perspectives, new occupational interests, new moral conceptions—unless that religion adjusts to those changes. *Semper idem,* the motto of the Catholic Church, is a valid claim only in a stable society, as the history of the Church itself shows, for Catholicism has shown itself to be marvelously adaptable to changing circumstance. Always the same—except that it drops its defense of medieval cosmology, after decades of opposition to the astronomers; it reverses its opposition to trade unions, in environ-

---

[4] See Millar Burrows, *The Dead Sea Scrolls;* Millar Burrows, *et al.,* "The Dead Sea Scrolls," *The New Republic,* April 9, 1956, pp. 12–25; and Edmund Wilson, *The Scrolls from the Dead Sea.*

[5] See J. H. Randall and J. H. Randall, Jr., *Religion and the Modern World,* pp. 16–17.

ments where Catholic workers are finding unions helpful; it supports the integration of church and state, except in the United States and other countries where such a doctrine is frowned upon; it opposes usury, except when the development of a commercial and industrial economy changes the significance of lending money at interest. These changes are cited, not to show the "inconsistency" of the Catholic Church, but to illustrate how a religious organization, seeking to be effective in a changed situation, adapts itself. Protestantism has undoubtedly changed even more. One need only mention the decline of the doctrine of predestination, the assimilation of the idea of evolution, the qualified acceptance of divorce to suggest the variety of changes.

Perhaps the most obvious changes in religion occur in the process of adjustment to major intellectual developments. The Randalls point out how strongly Christianity has been affected in this way:

On three separate occasions Christianity was confronted by imposing bodies of belief, great systems of carefully worked out and articulated ideas. Each time able thinkers arose to fit the Christian faith into those bodies of science. The simple gospel of the early Christians met the great Platonic philosophy of the Hellenistic age. The outcome was not disintegration; it was the formulation of Christian theology by the Alexandrian Fathers of the Church, Clement and Origen and Athanasius, and the marvelously rich system of Augustine. The crude and primitive religious life of the early Middle Ages was confronted by the scientific thought of Aristotle. The result was not the abandonment of faith; it was the intellectual synthesis of the Scholastics, now hailed as orthodoxy by the Catholic Church. Profoundly shaken by the humanism of the Renaissance and the mysticism of the Reformation, Christianity was brought face to face with the negative rationalism of 17th century physics. The culmination of a long struggle was, intellectually, the religious philosophies of the idealistic movement, and practically, the mass revivals of the early 19th century. Need we imagine that the fourth great set of scientific ideas, the biological and social sciences of the last two generations, will destroy man's faith at last because it throws such a flood of light upon it? [6]

If our conception of religion is correct, the answer to the question in the previous sentence is no; but the content of faith will continue to change. And this change will not proceed only until some vital center is reached, it will continue indefinitely. Proponents of a faith are likely to contend that changes in their religion have taken place only in the "outer layers," that the inner core remains unmodified. Every religious system certainly contains a group of fundamental beliefs and rites that are highly resistant to modification. In face of basic changes in society, however, even these may be revised so drastically that the old is scarcely

[6] *Ibid.*, pp. 14–15.

visible beneath the new. Then controversies are likely to arise between those who claim that anyone who accepts the new doctrines or practices has deserted the faith and those who contend that the new formulations are necessary and logical developments. Those who embrace the new religious elements will be those who have experienced the changes in society in the most complete way. If they modify the old faith, rather than accepting a new one, they will do so gradually, through "reinterpretations," through the discovery that beliefs which formerly were accepted as literally true are simply symbolic representations.

RELIGIOUS CHANGES IN THE UNITED STATES

This brief statement of a perspective and the illustrative references to early Judaism and the founding period of Christianity may serve to introduce the problem of the relation between social change and religious change in more recent times. If the approach that this discussion has suggested is useful, the topic should have special relevance for the modern world, in which social and cultural change are so dramatically rapid. In a day of strong nationalistic aspirations, Buddhism develops a more vigorous concern for political struggles, or it loses ground to secular and religious competitors.[7] As India becomes more industrialized and in more extensive contact with the West, her religious views show some increase in this-worldly emphasis.[8] When Europe began to feel the impact of growing trade, more extensive culture contact, urbanization, growth of knowledge, nationalism, and the many other aspects of "the modern world," her religious life inevitably changed. The Protestant Reformation is one dramatic indication of this relationship; but the change was not so abrupt as we sometimes suppose. There was a great deal of continuity with the past (St. Augustine would not have felt uncomfortable with most of the ideas of Luther or Calvin); and religious change in the post-Reformation period continued unabated. In Chapter 6 we explored some aspects of the fact that religious developments in England in the seventeenth and eighteenth centuries had to be interpreted in the context of the changes and struggles of English society. Roman Catholicism, Calvinism, Anabaptism and other continental religious influences were there, but all were strongly reshaped.

[7] See Wing-tsit Chan, *Religious Trends in Modern China;* C. S. Braden, *War, Communism and World Religions;* D. C. Holtom, *Modern Japan and Shinto Nationalism.*

[8] See Hajime Nakamura, "The Changing Value of Man in Modern India," in *Symbols and Values,* Conference on Science, Philosophy and Religion, 1954, pp. 701–731.

When Puritanism, one of the complex religious movements that were developed in England, was brought to America, it too was drastically modified. Rites, theology, and church polity that had developed in thirteenth century Italy, sixteenth century Germany and Geneva, and seventeenth century England (to oversimplify the case) were not likely to go unmodified in eighteenth century America. The stern doctrine of election, the tightly controlled church system of Puritanism, the emphasis on man's sinfulness, from which he can be rescued only by the grace of God—such patterns as these were not likely to be congenial to many people in the "New World." It was not difficult to accept the Cromwellian idea of a Holy Commonwealth, but its meaning was drastically changed. The earliest religious writers in America, the heirs of the "right-wing" of European Protestantism, accepted most of the traditional Puritan framework. By the middle of the eighteenth century, however, and particularly by the time independence was won, important religious leaders had reshaped that tradition in significant ways. "The expectation of a Holy Commonwealth to be brought into being on these shores by an act of God was restated as a vote of political confidence in the average man and his corporate ability to achieve a democratic Utopia." [9] Or, as Laski wrote:

. . . by the time of Jonathan Edwards the sense of this world as a vale of tears and the acceptance of the doctrines of grace and election were speedily losing ground before the conviction, so evident in the rise of innumerable socialist communities and in the Emersonian doctrine of self-reliance, that man saves himself by his own effort and that he accomplishes his salvation in the world of here and now.[10]

There is little doubt that "God himself became republican" in America, particularly in the religion of the middle and upper classes and in the thinking of most of our writers. Certainly Emerson's "self-reliance" is closer to this aspect of America than is "saved by God's election." There is a danger here, however, as there is so often when one judges past events by the thoughts of well-known people, that the less articulate members of a society will be forgotten. Much of the traditional theology survived in the religious life of the lower classes especially. The other-worldliness, the strong conviction of the sinfulness of man, the reliance on God's help were by no means eliminated. They were mingled, to be sure, with ideas of individual responsibility, of equality before God (as opposed to predestination), and with conceptions of church polity that emphasized the

---

[9] Willard L. Sperry, *Religion in America*, p. 250.
[10] Harold J. Laski, *The American Democracy*, p. 729.

role of laymen and freedom of religious choice. Thus "fundamentalism" and "liberalism" both are to be found in the American environment, sharing together some of the influences of that environment, but demonstrating also different religious backgrounds and needs.

What are some of the socio-cultural factors involved in these trends in the direction of the "Americanization of Christianity"? Perhaps most important was the fact that in a land where status assignments were not rigid, where new land and new economic opportunities were extensive, where population was sparse, it was easy to develop a theory—nourished by many facts—that men could shape their own destiny. A pessimistic theology was not likely to survive in a situation where so much hope and optimism prevailed (always remembering the strong qualifications on this statement when one refers to the large number for whom hope continued to be distant). A doctrine of predestination was scarcely likely to be congenial to people who saw all around them a social mobility unprecedented in European societies.

A Calvinist theory of the church found equally poor soil. Many of the migrants to America, particularly outside New England and Virginia, were from the lower classes. In Europe they had been in closer touch with Anabaptist movements or other phases of the "left-wing," of the Reformation than with Puritanism. Thus a concept of a "free church," with strong lay influence, emphasizing religion as an intensely personal matter was already important for them. This was strengthened by pioneering conditions, which cut them off from most connections with ecclesiastical organizations. Puritanism itself contained an inner contradiction that continually challenged ecclesiastical structure—inner religion, purity of doctrine, direct contact with God were held in high esteem. It has frequently been stated that the highly disciplined and restrained services of early Puritanism were entirely inadequate to the emotional needs and patterns of expression of the isolated, poorly-educated people on the frontier. This is a plausible hypothesis, but the personality processes involved have scarcely been adequately described.

In the preceding chapter we have described some of the factors that created the constitutional guarantees of religious freedom and the separation of church and state in the United States. The competition among church organizations, but more importantly, the opposition to ecclesiastical authority as part of the larger struggle for freedom, were important in creating the American pattern of religious organization. One of the most significant consequences of this situation was the ease with which new religious groups could be formed, reflecting large or small variations in religious interpretation, social circumstance, or personal need—a kind of free enterprise in religion to match the pattern in business (for we should not forget the matching ideology of "separation of business and state" and the matching modifications of the last half-century). This pattern of diversity was encouraged by the heterogeneity of the immigrant groups, regional differences, industrialization, and the general fact of the speed of social changes.[11]

To speak in terms of a broad generalization, the religious situation in the United States in the nineteenth century can be described as an extension of the trends we have outlined. Among the middle and upper classes an optimistic view of human possibilities and a strong emphasis on self-reliance were matched by theological liberalism and religious individualism. The society around them was to their liking, so there was little need for a "social gospel," and their own careers were filled with success and hope, so theirs was largely the religion of the "once-born." A contemporary critic is likely to declare that their theology was superficial, insufficiently aware of the tragedy and evil in life, too naively reliant on human enterprise. The liberal school of American religious thinkers, for their part, was likely to dismiss orthodox theology for its pessimism, its dark picture of human nature, its irrelevance to a democratic society. The sociologist of religion is interested in the way these various interpretations have been affected by the social and cultural forces around them.

The nineteenth century was not without its fundamentalism of course. It lingered in the larger denominations, particularly those which, like the Baptists and Methodists, had won many of their adherents from the lower classes. And it was the predominant doctrine of the sects. There was a lively sense of evil and sin in the camp meeting and the revival and in the fervent services of the sects. "The second-coming" was a firm belief, mingled in a complex way with other-worldliness—a messianic hope for the dramatic improvement of this world by God's intervention alongside doctrines that devalued this world, as a kind of second line of defense.

New religious groups continued to appear, encouraged by immigration, migration to the West, urbanization, and other forces. There was little tendency to modify the separation of church and state or the separation of religion and economics that characterized a situation that emphasized individual salvation so strongly.

[11] On the early American religious situation, see Thomas C. Hall, *The Religious Background of American Culture*, H. R. Niebuhr, *The Social Sources of Denominationalism*; Winfred E. Garrison, "Social and Cultural Factors in our Divisions," *Ecumenical Review*, October, 1952, pp. 43–51; Sperry, *op. cit.*; John M. Mecklin, *The Story of American Dissent*; and the several works of W. W. Sweet, including *The American Churches. An Interpretation* and *The Story of Religion in America*.

AMERICAN RELIGIOUS TRENDS IN THE
TWENTIETH CENTURY

After the Civil War, and particularly by the beginning of the twentieth century, the social and cultural environment of American religious movements changed with great speed. Theology, church organization, patterns of worship, and conceptions of the right relationship of religion to government and economic problems have all shown some of the marks of that change. We have already discussed several aspects of this process. In Chapter 8 we traced briefly the development of the "social gospel" as one manifestation of religious response to the new problems of the industrial age; and in the next chapter we noted some of the developments of the concept "separation of church and state." At this point we shall only call attention to those movements as clear illustrations of the way in which social changes precipitate religious changes.

Some Theological Changes.   Probably the most important theological development has been the rise of "neo-orthodoxy" to a position of great prominence in American Protestantism. One can scarcely speak with confidence concerning the extent of its influence today. How far it has affected the laymen it is particularly difficult to know. One is doubtless correct in stating, however, that among the younger seminary-trained Protestant clergy it has been the most influential theological development of the last twenty years.[12]

Neo-orthodoxy is a complex movement with many shades of meaning, which we need not explore for our purposes. It is not simply a reassertion of fundamentalism, although it shares some of its views. (And in some of its less intellectually inclined exponents the distinction is not easy to draw. As the doctrines move from Broadway to Main Street they are reshaped by the different setting. Clergymen who had never lived happily with "modernism" and liberalism, enthusiastically accepted the "new" trends, happy for their intellectual respectability and brilliant sponsors, but unmindful of the new thinking they involve.) Neo-orthodoxy is an attempt to develop a theology for a democratic and urban situation, alert to the impact of "the social gospel and concerned with political problems," yet seeking to reemphasize what it considers to be the insights of historic theology—the incapacity of man to grapple alone with evil and

---

[12] Thomas Hamilton gives some empirical support to this. In a sample of sermons published in the *Christian Century Pulpit*, 1929 to 1940, he found a decline in the optimistic and "social gospel" emphasis from 95 per cent to 36 per cent; and an increase in "pessimistic" sermons, emphasizing the sinfulness of man and the need for faith, from 5 per cent to 64 per cent. *Public Opinion Quarterly*, Summer, 1942, pp. 280–283.

tragedy, the tendency he has of mistaking his partially successful efforts for fundamental solutions. The proponents of this view hold, not only that the optimism of liberal theology and its secular counterparts is an inaccurate interpretation of the human situation, but also that it leads to unhappy consequences. Reinhold Niebuhr expresses this point clearly when he writes:

When we were tempted to isolationism, the Christian and the secular idealism which sanctified this attitude was intent on proving our nation more moral than other nations because it did not become involved in their "quarrels." Now that we are tempted to imperialistic domination of the weak nations by our strength, another form of heedless idealism tries to sanctify our position. We equate rigorous opposition to Communism at all costs with "morality" and accuse our allies of "expediency."

Both types of idealists, who captured the imagination of our nation successively, are blind to the endless complexities in the moral issues of politics, whether on the national or the international level. They do not understand that it is not possible to be both pure and responsible. If we define purity as being untainted with conflict, we deliver our fellowmen into the hands of tyrants for lack of resistance to their power. If we define purity as being untainted with comradeship with tyranny, we reject every form of coexistence, and are in peril of falling into the abyss of total war.[13]

Neo-orthodoxy calls for responsible political and social action in the context of full recognition of how easy it is for man to fail. Critics of this view are likely to contend that this is a basically unstable union of two ideas. They can point to the frequency with which the renewed emphasis on the pessimistic picture of man is quite unaccompanied by interest in political and social questions. Catholic critics are likely to hold that insofar as "neo"-orthodoxy has relevance, it is scarcely different from Thomist orthodoxy—an affirmation of the need to work with the "relative" values of this world, while being fully aware of their relativity (the evil they contain as human products) from the perspective of religious absolutes. The proponents of neo-orthodoxy might be expected to reply to the one critic that the two ideas, far from being in unstable alliance, are an essentially correct view of the human situation (or perhaps that the instability derives from a failure to grasp the total system); and to the other they might reply that the Thomist system, in its attempt to organize the whole of life, fell constantly into the error of confusing the "relative" with the "absolute," and of an excessive pessimism concerning politics.

What are some of the social and cultural changes that help us to understand the appearance of a theological emphasis so different in

[13] *Christian Century*, August 18, 1954, p. 973.

many ways from the prevailing theology (at least of the middle and
upper classes) of a century and a half? The immediate sources of the
emphases of neo-orthodoxy are the tragedies and crises of our time—depression, war, tyranny—that have so clearly revealed the enormous obstacles in the way of the realization of the liberal dreams of modern man.

Another source of change in theological emphasis was the internal
development of religious thought. The liberal theology which neo-orthodoxy has put on the defensive, although by no means eliminated, is
certainly an unsatisfying view of man's lot to those who are particularly
sensitive to the succession of tragedies and conflicts of modern life.
Liberalism, of course, has many diverse elements within it. The various
perspectives perhaps stem in common from the opposition to fatalism, to
extreme other-worldliness, to literal interpretations of the Bible. To many
intellectuals, these were impressive protests. But in a day of repeated
catastrophes liberalism seems less impressive, because of its lack of concern with the whole range of human life—its darker aspects as well as
the more hopeful ones.[14] To many theologians, the liberal tendencies in
religion that brought man and his welfare to the forefront of concern ran
the risk of making man himself the object of worship. In less theological
terms, this is to increase the danger, as opponents saw it, of parochialism
—of putting one's faith in the partial, the temporary, the customs and
forms of a time and place. This, of course, is the perennial problem of
all religion. The present writer is not at all certain that orthodoxy or
neo-orthodoxy any more successfully escapes it than did the rather shallow and perhaps excessively optimistic theology of a few decades ago.

Neo-orthodoxy is the heir of the long stream of Christian theology; it
has been in close touch with religious thought in Europe (where pessimism came earlier and deeper than in the United States); it has sought
to give a religious interpretation to the enormous tragedies of our time,
to which it has been particularly sensitive; and yet it has also been
affected by liberalism and democracy. One ought perhaps to add in a
description of its origins that its disillusionment with man, its pessimism
with regard to the claims of inevitable progress in democratic societies,
were anticipated and accompanied by developments in science, literature, and criticism. The theologians write—as they would readily agree
—in a context in which biological science, from Darwin to Freud and

---

[14] To avoid misunderstanding, perhaps the author may be permitted to say that
were he to attempt an amateur theology, he would be much more inclined in a
"neo-liberal" direction than in any other. There is no logical incompatibility between
central concern with problems of this life and faith in rational efforts on the one
hand and full recognition of the "evil" in man, the enormity of the problem, on
the other. See J. Milton Yinger, *Religion in the Struggle for Power*, footnote 43,
pp. 232–234.

after, has emphasized man's hostile potentialities. "If not Adam, then the ape and the tiger live on in us, to say nothing, as Bishop Creighton used to add, of that much more intractable animal, the donkey." [15] Kierkegaard, Nietzsche, and Kafka, each in his own way, helped to set the tone for many current theological developments. Social science has stressed, indeed perhaps exaggerated, the place of violence and conflict within and between societies. The realism and naturalism of William Dean Howells, Frank Norris, Theodore Dreiser, Sinclair Lewis; the muck-raking of Lincoln Steffens and others; the repudiation of an unqualified acceptance of American economic, political, and cultural life by such writers as Henry Adams and Ludwig Lewisohn—all of these represent a degree of pessimism and disillusionment that are part of the situation in which neo-orthodoxy developed.

The "Return to Religion." The widespread interest that the neo-orthodox theology has aroused in intellectual circles can be seen in a larger context as part of a "return to religion" that has been pointed to frequently in the last decade or more. The growing membership lists of the churches, the rise of many religious books to the "best-seller" lists, the numerous articles in mass-circulation magazines, the popularity of movies involving religious themes, the frequent affirmation by political leaders of our religious heritage, the increase in favorable attitudes toward the church and the reality of God among college students,[16] and other evidences are cited to prove the strength of the movement. Paul Hutchinson writes:

. . . there are so many prayer meetings for the mighty along the Potomac that the subject is beginning to attract derisive comment . . . . conspicuous devotion is by no means confined to official circles. In the Southwest Conference they start football games with prayer; I happened to be in Dallas when the selection of a bathing beauty queen was begun under the same evangelical auspices.[17]

The American Institute of Public Opinion reports that 97 per cent of Americans identify themselves with one of the major religious groups.[18] Eighty per cent of adult Americans say they believe the Bible to be the "revealed word of God."

One can easily "explain" current religious interest by pointing to the frustrated hopes that many had placed in science, in humanism, in radical

---

[15] Sperry, *op. cit.*, p. 254.
[16] See A. R. Gilliland, "Changes in Religious Beliefs of College Students," *Journal of Social Psychology*, February, 1953, pp. 113–116.
[17] *Life*, April 11, 1955, p. 138.
[18] Public Opinion News Service, March 20, 1955.

political movements. Having over-played the power of science, having rested too much hope in secular political movements, one returns to the religious road to salvation. The great personal confusion and anxiety and suffering of our time encourage this trend. Societies fumbling for a coherent value scheme give it further impetus. And "the bomb"—that frightful proof of man's self-destructive power—causes even the least sensitive to pause and to wonder.

Despite such evidences, one must speak with caution in interpreting the present situation as one characterized by a "return to religion." The Bible may be acclaimed as the revealed word of God, but 53% of those who thus acclaimed it could not name even one of the first four books of the New Testament. "Every aspect of contemporary religious life reflects this paradox—pervasive secularism amid mounting religiosity, 'the strengthening of the religious structure in spite of increasing secularization.' " [19] The "return to religion" can be understood only by noting the simultaneous secularization of the church. What one returns to is an institution that makes few creedal demands. It has been so secularized that to join many middle class churches is not sharply different from joining Kiwanis. As Robin Williams has pointed out, Americans are not irreligious, but there has been a withdrawal of "affect," of pervasive emotional involvement with traditional religions. Religious organizations are unusually separate from other structures. There is a tendency to think that religion is good because it is useful for *other* major values, thus reversing the means-end relationship in which religion is thought to be the ultimate value. This is related to the fact that many of the key values of American society are not couched in religious terms, but in secular, particularly national, terms.[20] The very tolerance of Americans in religious matters is an indication that their key values, the first premises from which they start, are not found in their religious patterns.

It is the American Way of Life that supplies American society with an "over-arching sense of unity" amid conflict. It is the American Way of Life about which Americans are admittedly and unashamedly "intolerant!" It is the American Way of Life that provides the framework in terms of which the crucial values of American existence are couched. By every realistic criterion the American Way of Life is the operative faith of the American people.[21]

As Herberg well realizes, this is to overstate the case. For many members of ethnic-immigrant churches, for some Lutheran and Reformed groups, for some sections of Catholicism, for sects of the disinherited, for

---

[19] Will Herberg, *Protestant—Catholic—Jew*, p. 14.
[20] See Robin Williams, *American Society*, chapter nine.
[21] Herberg, *op. cit.*, p. 88.

neo-orthodox and other theologians, for many religious liberals, the "operative faith" could scarcely be limited to the system of values, beliefs, and practices that can be identified with the American way of life.

Moreover, "Americanism" has many religious roots. In many ways it is a common denominator for Protestant, Catholic, and Jew—a relatively creedless and formless "national church" that obscures differences while furnishing a common value frame. In this sense, it is an emergent religious movement in a society of heterogeneous religious traditions and of pervasive secularism. When President Eisenhower declares that our system of government makes no sense without religious faith, "and I don't care what it is," stanch churchmen may shudder at the lack of standards. Does it make no difference what one believes?

Every American could understand, first, that Mr. Eisenhower's apparent indifferentism ("and I don't care what it is") was not indifferentism at all, but the expression of the conviction that at bottom the "three great faiths" were really "saying the same thing" in affirming the "spiritual ideals" and "moral values" of the American Way of Life. Every American, moreover, could understand that what Mr. Eisenhower was emphasizing so vehemently was the indispensability of religion as the foundation of society.[22]

In this sense, many Americans are stanchly religious; they have an extraordinary "faith in faith" as a kind of miracle drug of the spirit. It may take, as Herberg observes, the introverted form of "peace of mind" or the extroverted form of "positive thinking"; but in any case, it is good to believe.[23]

With such various facts before us, it would probably be impossible to prove or disprove the thesis that the United States is more "religious" in general than it was a generation ago. There are some who would contend that many of the evidences we have cited are indications of a deterioration of religion, while others regard them as proof of renewed vitality in religious interests. Without entering that argument, we can explore some aspects of specific developments, in an effort to discover the social factors involved in their appearance.

Although neo-orthodoxy has received a great deal of attention in some of the seminaries and aroused great interest among "the intellectuals," it probably has influenced many fewer people than various religious doctrines of a far less intellectual sort. These are doctrines almost completely lacking in systematic theological concern, but speaking more to the immediate problems of individuals in terms that harmonize with many deep-

---

[22] *Ibid.*, p. 98.
[23] See also William Lee Miller, "Piety Along the Potomac," *The Reporter*, August 17, 1954, pp. 25–28.

seated attitudes. Indeed, the writer has a strong impression—although he could scarcely defend it with adequate data—that the emphasis on the evil in man, the insistence on his incapacity to deal alone with a history inevitably filled with tragedy, has not really persuaded the respectable and successful members of the congregations in which these doctrines are now being preached. The laymen are, to be sure, deeply disturbed by the enormous difficulties of our time; they are at least ready to listen to this "new" theology; their easy optimism in an inevitable progress has been shattered. But their belief in individualism is too deep-seated, the habit of asking secular questions about the problems they face too well-established, their own relative success—despite the world's problems—too real to them in terms of the values they place high, to permit them to accept whole-heartedly the neo-orthodox view.

Confronted with a chaotic world, faced by individual problems of anxiety and guilt, many contemporary Americans, particularly in the middle classes, are likely to turn to a religious version of "how to win friends and influence people" or a psychotherapy clothed in religious terms that promises solutions that seem to be within their grasp. Few are inclined to embrace a difficult theology that contradicts much of what they have been taught about the power and perfectability of man. The "power of positive thinking" is a religion for boom times, for those who are climbing, but still find themselves anxious and unhappy. It was difficult enough in an earlier day to keep up with the Joneses—but now everybody has become Jones. This is part of the context of current religious movements.[24] We have explored these developments in Chapter 5, where we dealt with some aspects of the social-psychology of religion. We need only mention here that well over a million people have bought Peale's The Power of Positive Thinking. Although the writer does not know how many copies of Niebuhr's The Nature and Destiny of Man have been sold, he suspects that if it is over one per cent of the previous figure, all concerned with it are pleased. That is not to suggest that this gross statistic measures the comparative influence, but only to hint that the distinction between the "religion of the intellectuals" and "the religion of the masses" is relevant in the United States as it is in so many other societies. "The masses" refers here, of course, to the broad stratum of the middle classes. We ought perhaps to add the further statistic, again for gross comparative purposes, that the Jehovah's Witnesses circulate some fifty million magazines, pamphlets, and books a year.

Certainly any description of religious trends in the United States that did not refer to the strength of the "holiness" sects, using that term in a

<hr>

[24] See Russell Lynes, "Take Back Your Sable," Harper's, June, 1956, pp. 35–39.

broad sense, and the currents of revivalism would be incomplete. The
sects are probably growing at a more rapid rate than the middle class
churches. Since we have interpreted their growth from a sociological
point of view at some length in Chapter 7, we need indicate here only
the way in which they demonstrate the impact of social change on religion. A strong emphasis on other-worldliness, fundamentalism in doctrine, and the pattern of revivalism are by no means new, of course. They
represent continuity in the Christian tradition and in American experience. From the "Great Awakening," to the Western Revival in the early
part of the nineteenth century, to Dwight L. Moody, to Billy Sunday, to
Billy Graham is a path that involves many turnings but no basic change
in direction. Yet revivalism also demonstrates the influence of changes in
the social setting. There are obvious differences in the types of worship
—compare a frontier camp meeting with an elaborate revival in the
Hollywood Bowl. The impact of radio and television has been felt among
the holiness groups, as it has among other religious organizations. The
decline in revivalism in the larger evangelical churches, especially Methodist and Baptist, has reduced the appeal of these groups to some members of the lower classes, who have therefore been drawn toward the
holiness sects.

Perhaps most importantly, however, the strength of these groups has
been drawn from the same basic social situation as has neo-orthodoxy
and the middle-class religious movements we have mentioned—a situation of major tragedies, of personal anxiety, and of confusion. Each group
has experienced this situation in different ways and reacted to it differently. To the theologian, who sees it in largest dimension, it is a religio-
intellectual problem, requiring an interpretation that will bring meaning
to the total "community of suffering." To many of the middle classes, and
their religious spokesmen, the crisis of our time has come in the form of
personal frustration and tragedy, individual doubt and anxiety. They are
prepared by cultural training primarily for an individual solution, not
involving analysis of the social structure or complicated problems of
"universal tragedy." The solutions should come, in terms of their cultural
preparation, fairly easily, in small congenial groups, by faithfulness to
duty, and by the manipulation of appropriate slogans—as one would
buck up a lagging business. "Forget Failure and Go Ahead." To many
members of the lower classes, the great problems of our time have been
felt, not only as personal tragedy and the frustration of hope, but also as
bewilderment. They are less well prepared, by their early experience, to
deal with the changes of modern life. They turn to a religious movement
that will give them a sense of identity and of anchorage. Thus it is in the
cities that we see many of the holiness groups prospering. Although

statistics are not entirely adequate, they seem to be more urban than the total population.[25] People living in congested areas of low security turn to the sects for a feeling of well-being and of significance, to deal with the "cultural shock," as Holt has called it, that migrants from the rural areas particularly feel.

Persons of very different values may agree on the increase in interest in religion in the United States that we have briefly sketched. They disagree sharply, however, in their interpretations of its meaning. On the one hand, religious leaders are likely to declare that it demonstrates the failure of secularism and excessive self-reliance. Enormous tragedies had to come to man—stemming from this very secularism—before he could comprehend the significance of religion. On the other hand are those who declare that the "return to religion," at least in most of the forms it has taken, is an unhappy sign of a "new failure of nerve." They will agree with the religious writers that the revival has taken place in the face of the crises and tragedies of the last generation and that it has been strongly motivated by them. These writers argue, however, that the tragedies of modern man do not stem from his humanism and secularism, but from his lack of knowledge and his lack of nerve—his inability to carry through on his secularism and humanism.[26] It is the task of the sociologist, wherever he falls personally along this value range, to try to describe its many manifestations and the conditions with which they are associated.

The Americanization of Catholicism.   A further development in American religious patterns deserves careful analysis. Our brief mention of it here can serve only to point to it as a significant problem for the sociology of religion: To what degree have Catholicism and Judaism been affected by the American environment? The material on which we have drawn for our discussion of the impact of social change on religion in the United States has been concerned almost wholly with Protestantism. Yet one would assume, on a priori grounds, that the same principles apply to all religious groups—paying full attention to unique elements in their traditions, constituencies, and institutional connections.

In a conflict situation, antagonists often assume that an opponent is incapable of change and unaffected by the situation in which he is found. Thus some Americans believe they can predict the day-by-day policy of the Kremlin by reading the *Communist Manifesto*. Paul Blanshard and others give something of this same impression in their analyses of Ameri-

[25] See Charles S. Braden, "The Sects," *Annals of the American Academy of Political and Social Science,* March, 1948, pp. 53–62; and H. Paul Douglass, "Cultural Differences and Recent Religious Divisions," *Christendom,* Winter, 1945, pp. 89–105.
[26] See the series of articles on "Religion and the Intellectuals," in the *Partisan Review,* 1950, the Feb., March, April, and May–June issues.

can Catholicism. In a chapter entitled "The Catholic Plan for America," Blanshard makes it appear that were the Catholic Church to become dominant in the United States, it would scarcely differ in its program from the present situation in Spain or Portugal.[27] A sociologist is likely to inquire about the way in which the total setting of a church system affects its program.

There can be no doubt that the long European experience of the Catholic Church and its elaborate international organization, which holds the national churches in a common framework, have created tendencies that resist the "Americanization" of the Catholic Church in the United States. These influences are accentuated by the recency of much of the immigration of Catholics to this country. At the time of the Revolution, they constituted only one per cent of the population. Even the large Irish migration of the mid-nineteenth century has been exceeded by the Italian and Polish migration of the late nineteenth and early twentieth centuries. The emphasis from the beginning of the United States, on religious freedom and equality may have retarded the "Americanization" of the religions of immigrants. Some pressure has been brought on them to change "their foreign ways" in most areas of life, but because of freedom of religion, this has been least apparent in the religious field. This point must not be weighed too heavily, however, because it can be argued that under some conditions, the *lack* of pressure is most conducive to rapid assimilation.

It would certainly be a mistake to argue on sociological grounds that the Catholic Church in the United States will soon become "simply another denomination." The weight of its ideology and the organization of its hierarchy on an international basis argue against this. Those who defend the thesis that Catholicism is fundamentally out of harmony with the traditional American pattern of cooperation and mutual tolerance among denominations, the separation of church and state, the supremacy of public schools, and the like are not lacking in evidence. Occasionally an influential Catholic will indicate that he believes the present separation of church and state, with all denominations treated equally, is not an ideal arrangement, but a necessary *modus vivendi* under the present circumstances.[28] The hierarchy often stands in the way of inter-faith cooperation or blocks contacts that would seem to put other churches on an equal plane with the Catholic Church.[29] On July 8, 1954, on the eve of the

---

[27] See Paul Blanshard, *American Freedom and Catholic Power.*

[28] See *ibid.*, p. 49.

[29] Because of the controversial nature of this problem, it may be well to note that from one value stand these appear to be intelligent and courageous acts, from another, they are regarded as bad.

assembly of the World Council of Churches in Evanston, Samuel Cardinal Stritch, Archbishop of Chicago, warned Catholics that they cannot join persons of other faiths in religious assemblies, because theirs is "the one and only church of Christ" (as reported by the United Press).

Such data do not tell the whole story, however. Indeed the thesis of this book, that religions are imbedded in the society of which they are a part, would be seriously weakened if there were not evidences of the "Americanization of Catholicism." The Catholic Church is a large and complex organization, with a wide range of opinions within it, making it possible to prove by careful selection of material that many different trends are the "essential" Catholic position.

A useful hyopthesis is that as one moves from the top hierarchy to the parish priest to the laymen, other things being equal, one finds a progressively larger American element in the phenomenon of "being Catholic." One would expect this on the basis of training, organizational connections, roles, and values. (This broad generalization is qualified, of course, by the variety of perspectives on each level.) As Catholics become increasingly "old American," as a larger proportion of the priesthood and hierarchy are native born, as the American branch of the Church grows in influence in the international organization, as its members are spread throughout the class and occupational structure of the United States in a pattern matching that of the majority—thus sharing secular values, roles, organizations—in short, as Catholicism gets deeper involved in American culture and society, we can expect extensive changes. These changes have already begun, of course.[30] We should not forget that they are dependent on such trends as we have mentioned nor disregard the forces blocking Americanization.

These trends have not yet been carried so far that the differences between Protestants and Catholics—in the sense that each is equally at home in the American setting—have been eliminated. Samuel Lubell argues cogently that the powerful pull of the "red issue" on Catholics is an indirect indication of their desire to prove what good Americans they are. On many issues, they feel somewhat at a disadvantage in proving that they are one hundred per cent American. On the communist question, however, prompted by their religious training, they can assert their full identity with the nation. (Some, of course, have "over-compensated" and have helped to sustain an hysterical anti-communism that the present writer considers to be very *un*American.) Lubell writes: ". . . the Communist issue is almost the first political cause which has given Catholics

---

[30] See Anson Phelps Stokes, *Church and State in the United States*, Vol. III, pp. 480–483.

generally the chance to feel more American than other Americans. In the past, the social and economic status of Catholics was hurt by their religion. In terms of the present cold war, however, Catholicism and the American struggle against Russia merge as one." [31]

Herberg develops the thesis that Catholicism, and Judaism, while being strongly affected by the American environment are nevertheless maintaining their distinctive patterns. We have, not a single, but a "triple melting pot," somewhat separate sub-cultures among Protestants, Catholics, and Jews with one of which the vast majority of the population identifies. This is not a sign, however, that Catholicism has been unaffected by the American situation. Indeed, it is a manifestation of the American pattern of religious freedom, of a pervasive secularization that makes it less important what one's religious identity is, of an underlying shared belief in "the American way." It also represents a need, in a heterogeneous and very mobile society, to find one's identity, to find a group to which one can indubitably belong, to establish one's "brand name." [32] The effect of these forces is to preserve and perhaps to strengthen the separate identity of Catholicism in the very midst of a situation where that identity is less important. The American creed has become the operative and shared religion of the nation to a substantial degree. [33]

One further fact ought to be mentioned. In recent years there has been some controversy concerning the extent of mutual conversion of Catholics and Protestants. Several highly publicized conversions to Catholicism have given the impression of a dramatic shift in that direction. The very newsworthiness of these incidents, however, may indicate that they are unusual, as contrasted with a quiet drift toward the religious organizations of the majority, with their somewhat more secure status positions. They may indicate also, not the extent of the departure

---

[31] "The Politics of Revenge," *Harper's Magazine,* April, 1956, p. 31.

[32] See Herberg, *op. cit.,* especially chapters 2 and 3.

[33] A number of Catholic scholars have shown a lively interest in the sociology of religion, but relatively little of their work has gone beyond the descriptive level to raise such theoretical questions as those suggested above. What are the effects of "freedom of religion" on Catholicism? In what different ways does it develop in different economic and political contexts? What are the results of being a "minority" as contrasted with being the dominant church? Questions of this kind are only infrequently raised.

The descriptive work is often of high quality. Much of it has been concerned with "the parish" as the unit of study. See Joseph H. Fichter, *Dynamics of a City Church* and *Social Relations in the Urban Parish;* Gabriel LeBras, *Études de sociologie religieuse;* C. J. Nuesse and Thomas J. Harte, editors, *The Sociology of the Parish.* Unhappily, one often finds a "Catholic sociology," rather than sociological analysis by Catholics. The essays edited by Nuesse and Harte are substantially affected by their Catholic orientation. In a scientific treatment, this is as unwarranted as "Episcopalian chemistry."

of these individuals from previous views, but the extent of the Americanization of some branches of the Catholic Church. It is easy to exaggerate the degree to which such a change requires a shift in belief, in values, in styles of worship.

The precise statistics of mutual conversion are not available. The *Christian Herald* claimed in 1954 that over four million Catholics had become Protestants in the last decade, while one million Protestants had become Catholics. In a study done for the *Catholic Digest*, a market research company came to the conclusion that in the last twenty years, fewer than a million and a half Catholics had become Protestants and about two and one-third million Protestants had become Catholics. In still a third study, the Public Opinion News Service estimated that about 1,400,000 persons had moved in each direction. Whatever the exact data, most observers agree that the number of shifts is fairly large, although the percentages are small. According to the Public Opinion News Service data about two per cent of Protestants have become Catholics and about six per cent of Catholics have become Protestants. The transfer would seem to the writer to be a sign of relatively small differences between some branches of the churches, for one does not readily step across a religious gap that is wide.

The Americanization of Judaism. Equally interesting questions for the sociology of religion are involved in the study of the degree to which there has been an "Americanization" of Judaism. Here too is the pull of opposite forces. On the one side is the long, self-conscious history of Jews as a distinct people, with a vital religious and cultural tradition; there is the renewed sense of a common weal and a common fate brought about by prejudice, by recent persecutions, by the reestablishment of Israel; there is the recency of migration of most Jews to the United States. On the other side is the speed with which many Jews have penetrated to the middle and upper strata of American society, thus giving them a strong sense of identity with that society; there is freedom of religion, public education, and the relative absence of barriers to economic and political activity; there is the increase in congregational church polity, with strong influence from the laymen; there are the different national origins, that throw up barriers to a sense of common Jewishness.

Under the influence of these various forces, Judaism has changed in the United States, yet it has retained its identity. Using an overly-simple formula, but one that is basically correct, one can say that Reform Judaism represents the predominance of the pressures toward change, a continuation of the trend toward assimilation to a modern, urban society that was begun in Germany, France, and elsewhere. Orthodoxy represents the predominance of the forces of conservation, an island of security and familiarity for the more recent immigrants. Conservative Judaism is an attempt to mediate between these two forces—to preserve all that is basic to Judaism, in the thought of its supporters, yet to encourage beliefs and practices in harmony with the American environment. The very title of a recent book by Marshall Sklare captures this idea, *Conservative Judaism, An American Religious Movement*. He describes the changes and the continuity. "Since Conservatism is a response to the process of embourgeoisement, it is the change to the *style of life* and worship characteristic of the new peer group which has been the chief concern. This holds true because ideologies and philosophical orientations change more slowly than less basic matters such as manners, dress, and aesthetic sensibilities." [34]

A sociological study of American Judaism can profitably make use of the concepts of "the social sources of denominationalism," and "the dilemma of the churches"—a dilemma that requires changes if a religious organization is to survive or have influence in a new environment. Changes in Judaism did not begin in the United States, of course. Reform Judaism, for example, might first be thought of in terms of the "Europeanization" of Jews. It was a movement of those Jews who were most successful in winning a place in Western European societies and wanted to insure full cultural, economic, and political participation. Yet they wanted also to maintain their historical connection with Judaism. To work for both of these ends required drastic modification of Orthodox views and practices, many of which had lost their meaning to persons fully assimilated to western societies. Judaism was no longer considered to be a national religion; it was not a complete way of life, with cultural and political implications, but a universalist religion.

At first, Reform Judaism in the United States continued the trends that had developed in Germany. But the new environment, in which Jews were a small minority, created even stronger pressures toward change. The lack of any history of political or economic disability, the freedom of religion, the expanding economic situation, and other forces all tended to dissolve the sense of membership in a unique religious community. As Handlin says: "The new views compelled the Jews radically to revise their own conceptions of themselves and of the nature of their culture." [35] Some Jewish leaders felt that without drastic changes to adjust to the new environment, Judaism would disappear in the United States. Building on the doctrinal and theological developments of the German Reform

---

[34] Marshall Sklare, *Conservative Judaism: An American Religious Movement*, p. 118.
[35] Oscar Handlin, *Adventures in Freedom*, p. 73.

movement, American Jews in mid-nineteenth century began a rapid change in synagogue procedures and forms of worship.

. . . there was a call for more decorum, for the revisions of the liturgy to permit shorter and more intelligible services, for the replacement of "German and Slavonic dialects" by English, for family pews to eliminate the segregation of women, for sermons in the American style, for mixed choirs and organs. Later, demands for the "simplification" of *kashrut* (dietary) and Sabbath prohibitions were heard.[36]

These changes had been extensively adopted when the immigration of Eastern European Jews began in large numbers. Of the two million Jews who entered the United States between 1870 and 1914, over sixty per cent were from Russia. For the most part, they had lived in Orthodox Jewish communities; they had suffered serious political and economic disprivilege and violent persecution. Having little sense of identity with the Russian state and society, they felt a vital connection with the conception of a Jewish homeland and Judaism as a total way of life. It is not surprising that the Jews in the United States, many of whom were "Old American," should have received the new flood of immigration with mixed feelings. There was a sense of common religious allegiance, yet also the fear of being "Russified" and of losing the gains of a century. Religious perspectives themselves varied widely, of course—the Reform Jew being as close to liberal Protestantism, perhaps, as to Orthodox Judaism. Thus by 1880, American Jews entered upon a period of change, and indeed of internal conflict, that was to last for two generations.

We shall not undertake to tell the complicated story of the changes and the tensions of this period.[37] The most significant new development, for our concern, was the appearance of Conservative Judaism. Sociologically speaking, this movement did for the large number of Eastern European migrants, particularly in the second and third generations in the United States, what the Reform movement had done for the earlier migrants from Western Europe: it formed a link between the total Jewish culture of the past and the requirements and possibilities of the American present. It did not duplicate Reform Judaism in the size and direction of its changes for several reasons: America's tradition of freedom of religion required that it "give up" fewer of its distinctive patterns; the greatly increased size of the Jewish population encouraged the maintenance of some of the older forms, because contact with non-Jews was

---

[36] Herberg, *op. cit.*, p. 189.

[37] See the works of Handlin, Herberg, and Sklare cited above; see also, Rufus Learsi, *The Jews in America* and Joseph Zeitlin, *Disciples of the Wise: The Religious and Social Opinions of American Rabbis.*

often limited; the lively memories of persecution were not readily dismissed; the continuing immigration of Orthodox Jews from Europe renewed the established ways; support for a Zionist cause—not for themselves, but for European co-religionists—helped to sustain a strong sense of identity with Judaism as they had known it; and finally, the new eruptions of anti-Semitism, from the Dreyfus Affair to the ghastly genocide of Hitler's New Order, revitalized the meaning of Judaism as a religious response to the tragedies of life.

Despite such forces as these which retarded the "Americanization" of Judaism, powerful influences have been at work on the other side to shape the religious beliefs and practices of American Jews. As they were absorbed into the secular structure of American society, it was inevitable that their religious needs, the kinds of doctrine, ritual, and church organization that would appeal to them, would change. The impact of public, secular schools, job diversification, status improvement, political freedom and participation, and increasing contact with the members of other religious groups has been to modify Judaism in many ways. In the Conservative branch, there is still a strong tie to traditional Jewish beliefs. Forms of worship and of congregational polity have been more likely to change than systems of belief. The total effect, however, of location in a society so different from those in which Orthodox Judaism developed has been to produce major transformations in the course of two generations. Sklare states clearly the functional interpretation of these changes:

> The greatest contribution of the German Reform movement may be said to be its function as the provider of a cushion for the disintegrative effects of emancipation. It helped to indicate a *modus vivendi* between assimilation and a no-longer acceptable Orthodoxy. In the same tradition, American Conservatism has cushioned the effects of the dissolution of Judaism as an integrated and highly traditional sacred system. It too has offered a *modus vivendi* for the alienated. True, its public has been different from that of German-Jewish Reform, and the conditions under which it has developed have also been radically different. Thus, while both movements have taken divergent paths, they do express the same need. In summary, the signal contribution of Conservatism would seem to be that of offering an acceptable pattern of adjustment to the American environment for many East-European-derived Jews.[38]

This is perhaps to assume the "functionalist" position, in a narrow sense, too quickly. That Conservatism has actually served to produce some desired balance between an overly-rapid de-culturization, with attendant personal confusion, and an overly-slow assimilation, with attendant alienation, is a proposition that seems to have a great deal of merit. Its full

---

[38] Sklare, *op. cit.*, p. 249.

validation, however, must await more comparative research into all the functional consequences for those who adopted different patterns of adaptation to the American scene. The need is for comparative study, not only of the functions and dysfunctions of membership in the various branches of Judaism, but also of other religious decisions and secular alternatives that some Jews have selected. This is a subject of great complexity. The present writer points to it only to suggest the need for tentative generalizations at the present stage of functional analysis.

A sociological study of American Judaism cannot stop with the brief examination of the Orthodox-Conservative-Reform pattern. Recent developments, arbitrarily we may say since 1940, have set other forces in motion that are strongly affecting Judaism. Broadly speaking, we may say that there has been a renewal of interest in religion and a blurring of the lines of distinction among the three denominations of American Jews. Orthodoxy continues to change, but perhaps more surprisingly, there is some return to traditional patterns among the Reform groups. This expresses in part the general "return to religion" that we have discussed; many of the forces affecting a "neo-orthodoxy" in Christianity are also influential among Jews. There are, however, some additional factors: The tragedies of the Hitlerian period undoubtedly gave vitality and a sense of common identity to all branches of Judaism. Economic distinctions have been reduced, so that the picture—always an overly-simple one—of the German employer and the Russian employee is less and less accurate. Residential migration into mixed suburbs, where one's Jewishness cannot be taken for granted, where one's children are more likely to ask, "what is a Jew," has led many to rethink their religious origins. During thirty years in which immigration has been much reduced, the association of Jewishness with foreignness and with the "strange" ways of unmodified Orthodoxy has been greatly diminished.

The results of these forces on Judaism can be understood only in terms of the American environment which discourages many aspects of "ethnic-group" survival, but which permits religious differentiation. Those who would like to see a continuation of Jewish identity, therefore, are led more and more to emphasize its strictly religious meaning.[39] At least in this generation, the lines among Catholic, Protestant, and Jew remain sharp, despite the reduction in secular differences among the constituent groups. This may well express the tensions of a society in which we seek to "escape from freedom" by embracing a partially traditional system of answers; it may be a manifestation of "the lonely crowd," in which we

---

[39] See Nathan Glazer, "The Jewish Revival in America," *Commentary*, December, 1955, pp. 493–499 and January, 1956, pp. 17–24.

seek a feeling of identity by relating ourselves more closely with an established group; and these may be possible because close identity with a religious group does not alienate us from the total society. Religion has become somewhat marginal—a brand name—while our basic allegiance is given to "the American Way of Life." [40] If this argument is valid—and it can be offered only as a hypothesis—then the renewal of interest in Judaism and the reduction of differences among its various denominations are not signs of the slowing down of "Americanization" of Jews. They are, indeed, the signs of how deeply involved Jews are in the total pattern of American society.[41]

Other Religious Changes. We have dealt with only a few of the changes in religious belief and practice that one can observe in contemporary America. Just a brief listing, with very little commentary, of other changes will indicate the extent to which religious life is influenced by changes in the social situation of which it is a part.

The reduction of the congregationalism of congregational churches, by the growth of state and national organizations; the trend toward church union (several Methodist churches or the Congregational-Christian-Evangelical and Reformed, for example); the growth of interdenominational organizations (the National Council of Churches); interfaith cooperation (the National Conference of Christians and Jews); and the ecumenical movement (the World Council of Churches) are indications of a common tendency to coordinate religious efforts. In a day when poultrymen, engineers, and physicians have joined together in their various organizations for a more effective pursuit of their interests, it is not surprising to find religious groups following the same pattern. In a large and complicated society, the individual voice is likely not to be heard. The reduction of some of the differences that underlay separation is another reason for closer organizational connections. And perhaps most important has been the increased sense of common purpose and common problem ("the huddling together of Christians into an ecumenical movement," Schneider has called it) that has grown from the religious examination of the critical issues of modern society. "The social sources of denominationalism" are still operative; dogmatic and theological differences loom large; but there are counter trends.

One of the interesting developments, reflecting a changing environment, is the growth of "institutional churches" in the cities. Confronted by constituents with more leisure, with new interests, with problems

---

[40] See Herberg, *op. cit.*

[41] See Herbert J. Gans, "American Jewry: Present and Future," *Commentary*, May, 1956, pp. 422–430; and "The Future of American Jewry," *Commentary*, June, 1956, pp. 555–563.

peculiar to urban society (housing, unemployment, rapid mobility), and faced with vigorous secular competitors for the time and enthusiasm of the population, many churches have extended their programs into recreation, nursery schools, discussion groups, psychotherapy, race relations, and many other activities.[42] In view of these developments, the sharp separation of religion and of religious institutions from the rest of society —a separation that sociologists have sometimes contended was characteristic of modern society—can scarcely be considered an unambiguous and inevitable trend. Queen and Carpenter have pointed out that when a church is declining, its members moving away, its area being "invaded" as a result of ecological changes, there may be a number of different responses: The church may adapt its program to the changing character of the district; it may seek a new location; it may disband and sell the property; it may gradually grow smaller, with a faithful few holding on in the hopes that something will happen to allow them to preserve the organization; or it may develop into a metropolitan church.[43] Sociologists of religion have scarcely explored this situation enough to specify the variables that influence which of these various responses will be made. The type and speed of the "invasion," the class status of the constituency, the denominational connections, the nature of leadership are perhaps important factors.

We can summarize the ways in which religious organizations, in various ways and in different degrees, have responded to changes in the American environment in the words of Schneider:

Noteworthy are better educated clergymen, more secular content in sermons, very secularized evening "services" (practically entertainments), theatrical effects, reviews of current fiction, discussion of secular public problems, vaguely "religious" education in place of "Bible schools," and a broader religious press. In many and subtle ways . . . religion itself has accepted the ways of modern life. That is to say, much of what in 1900 would have been recognized as "worldliness" is now embodied in the conventional forms and habits of "liberal" religion. And I am not now speaking of theological modernism. I mean that even apart from profound change of doctrine or faith, there has been an accommodation in religious conduct and activities to the forces and inventions of secular life to such a degree that the practical meaning and influence of religion has been revolutionized.[44]

---

[42] See Ross W. Sanderson, *The Church Serves the Changing City;* H. P. Douglass and Edmund de S. Brunner, *The Protestant Church as a Social Institution.*

[43] See Stuart A. Queen and David B. Carpenter, *The American City.*

[44] H. W. Schneider, *Religion in 20th Century America,* p. 12.

CHAPTER 11

Religious Change and Social Change .... continued

RELIGION AS CAUSE

There is no more controversial area in the study of religion than the analysis of its "independent" influence. Viewing the question of social change from the opposite perspective of Chapter 10, we can examine religion as a barrier to change or, from a different perspective, as a conserver of values and can inquire into the degree to which it initiates change. When one discusses religion as a conserver of values or a barrier to change (it is indicative of the lack of objective study in this area that we have no neutral vocabulary to subsume these two value perspectives), one scarcely looks upon it as a thoroughly independent variable, but rather as part of a causal complex. The cause-effect, independent-dependent dichotomies, it should be noted, are exceedingly dangerous in social science, as compared with concepts of interaction and of "levels of causation," so that we should use them carefully, fully aware of their heuristic quality. It is clear that when one speaks of religion as a barrier to change, he implies an instrumental quality. It is being *used,* and is therefore regarded as causal only on a very "low level." This is less obvious in the thinking of many of those who regard religion favorably as a conserver of the best. In their thinking it is likely to be taken as a "given," to be regarded as

295

an independent variable, or at the least to be placed at a "high level" of causation—more effective than affected by the cycles of interaction.

THE INTERACTION OF IDEAS AND SOCIAL ACTION

In its broadest terms, the problem of the influence of religious concepts is clearly not limited to the sociology of religion, but is basic to the whole of social science and philosophy. What is the role of ideas in history? One's answer to the question put in this way is more likely to take the form of a methodological proposition or a philosophical assumption than of an empirically demonstrated relationship. This does not mean that the answers are wholly arbitrary, from the point of view of science, for some methodological propositions are far more fruitful of research and theory than others, and some philosophical assumptions more harmonious with the scientific perspective than others. We have proceeded on the basis of interaction and functional interdependence, repudiating the idea that science must look for *the* cause, or the prime cause, whether it be thought to reside in ideas or in "material conditions."

One might sketch the range of possible views concerning the place of ideas, and arbitrarily locate certain important thinkers, along a continuum in the following way:

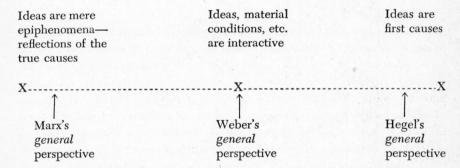

Ideas are mere epiphenomena— reflections of the true causes	Ideas, material conditions, etc. are interactive	Ideas are first causes

X--------------------------------------X--------------------------------------X

↑	↑	↑
Marx's *general* perspective	Weber's *general* perspective	Hegel's *general* perspective

In our view no general perspective is adequate, because the situations that require interpretation do not exist "in general." An adequate scientific perspective will seek out the conditions under which the interaction of the several forces approaches one or the other end of the continuum. Each situation, then, will be interpreted according to the degree to which these various conditions are present. And for some purposes it is scientifically legitimate to concentrate on one phase of an interacting situation, taking some force or forces as "givens," provided that one does not forget that in his abstraction he cannot explain the whole sequence of events.

An instrumental approach to ideas and values refers, not to their content, but to their function. There are wide differences, however, in the ways in which this approach to ideas may be developed. These ways vary greatly in the amount of "immanence" assigned to ideas. Marx and Nietzsche, for example, in very different ways, see ideas as manifestations of interests. The former interpreted ideas in terms of their functions in the struggles among classes, the latter primarily in terms of their psychological function for individuals.[1] It had been observed long before Marx and Nietzsche, of course, that ideas are a function of interests. One need only mention the names of Machiavelli, Bacon, and Hume to illustrate this point. Only at a time of intensive culture contact and great change, however, could this observation become a central concern. In the twentieth century, the relationship of ideas, of the life of consciousness, to the total self and its social roles has been even more thoroughly explored in the work of Freud, Mannheim, and others. Gradually, the observations are going beyond the unmasking of the pretensions of one's opponents or "exposing" the thought of strange and inferior people, to systematic and empirical study. This development required a social theory of self and explicit formulation of the concepts of society and culture. Out of these developments we are getting a sociology and psychology of knowledge that is of great importance to the sociology of religion.

There is a tendency on the part of Marx and Nietzsche to treat all ideas in the same manner, to assume that they all have the same relationship to interests and to action. The kind of distinction that Parsons draws between "existential ideas" (the description and analysis of things as they exist, or are thought to exist) and "normative ideas" (conceptions about the way things ought to be) is essential to the study of the relationship between ideas and action.[2] This distinction is rooted deep in the history of this problem; but for all that, it has not been effectively used, even by Mannheim, who has contributed so much to the sociological study of thought.[3]

One class of existential ideas, those based on empirical study, verifiable by others, clearly has a measure of autonomy and of initiatory power. The mathematical and physical study that led to $E = MC^2$ can clearly be understood as an important cause of later events, whatever its own ori-

---

[1] See Max Weber, *From Max Weber,* introduction by Hans Gerth and C. Wright Mills, pp. 61–62.

[2] Talcott Parsons, "The Role of Ideas in Social Action," *American Sociological Review,* October, 1938; reprinted in *Essays in Sociological Theory Pure and Applied,* pp. 151–165.

[3] See Karl Mannheim, *Ideology and Utopia* and *Essays on the Sociology of Knowledge.*

gins may be. Only a *faithful* materialist will find it meaningful to claim that nevertheless, in the last analysis, these ideas can be explained as an effect of the conditions out of which they came. This kind of reductionism to some supposed ultimate starting point is meaningless to science. It is more pertinent to observe, with Parsons that

The very processes of technological change to which many of our 'materialists' assign so fundamental a role are in part a function of knowledge, i.e., of ideas, in exactly the same sense in which economic processes are. And there, far more than in the narrowly economic realm, knowledge has become a variable which we think of as to a high degree autonomous.[4]

More important for our purposes is the question of the degree of autonomy in normative ideas and in a second class of "existential" ideas, those propositions about nature or existence that are unverifiable, that are posed in such a way that scientific criteria are inapplicable. Parsons warns against the "positivistic bias" that assumes that these latter propositions could be tested, if our evidence were adequate, by scientific methods. They are *non*-scientific, rather than *un*scientific; in Pareto's phrase, they "surpass experience." Belief in the doctrine of reincarnation or a concept of predestination can scarcely be shown to be true or false by empirical research. Are such ideas, in the first instance, merely a reflection of the "material" situation, becoming, when once established, a barrier to social change? Or do they enter actively into the process of social change?

Even Marx, and more particularly Engels, recognized that there was some autonomy in the idea sphere, particularly in the field of natural science, but to some degree in the normative sphere and among the non-empirical, existential ideas of Parsons' classification. Engels pointed out that when professional lawyers appeared, for example, an independent source of ideas was created, for they began to elaborate a system, built around such values as "justice," that sought consistency in itself. ". . . in order to achieve this, the faithful reflection of economic conditions is more and more infringed upon."[5] This internal development is true also of religious and philosophical ideas.

To indicate that ideas may originate out of the internal elaborations of a religious system is not to claim, however, that they enter directly into the processes of social action and social change. To Marx and Engels, only those ideas that had relevance to the struggles of classes and parties would survive or enter effectively into social interaction. Thus ideas are

---

[4] Parsons, *op. cit.*, p. 155.

[5] Engels, quoted by Robert K. Merton in "The Sociology of Knowledge," chapter 13 of *Twentieth Century Sociology*, Georges Gurvitch and Wilbert Moore, editors; see especially pp. 380–382 of this excellent essay.

instruments more than causes, in their view. This anticipates a concept developed more fully by Weber, especially in his phrase "elective affinity." Having admitted some degree of autonomy to the origin of ideas, however, Weber does not then deny their continuing influence by his use of this concept. He goes on to stress the continuing influence of ideas—the mutual modifiability of ideas and interests, the possibility of tensions between them. Ideas are not completely plastic, to be selected and molded according to individual need and desire or according to group interests. Once developed and accepted, they make demands of their own.

Gerth and Mills well express Weber's conception of the origin of ideas, when they write:

For Weber, there is hardly ever a close connection between the interests or the social origin of the speaker or of his following with the content of the idea during its inception. The ancient Hebrew prophets, the leaders of the Reformation, or the revolutionary vanguard of modern class movements were not necessarily recruited from the strata which in due course became the prime bearers of their respective ideas. Only during the process of routinization do the followers "elect" those features of the idea with which they have an "affinity," a "point of coincidence" or "convergence." [6]

In their next statement Gerth and Mills may exaggerate the degree to which Weber moves back toward a Marxian position. This is an exaggeration, however, which is invited by Weber's own development of the concept of "elective affinity." They write:

. . . in time, ideas are discredited in the face of history unless they point in the direction of conduct that various interests promote. Ideas, selected and reinterpreted from the original doctrine, do gain an affinity with the interests of certain members of special strata; if they do not gain such an affinity, they are abandoned. Thus by distinguishing the phases of the personal and charismatic origin of ideas and their routinization and social impact, Weber is able to take into account a number of complications, which are reflected in changing shades of meaning. Both the ideas and their publics are seen as independent; by a selective process elements in both find their affinity.[7]

The last sentence seems to describe most accurately Weber's thought, for it indicates the *continuing* place that he gives to ideas in social interaction. Thus Calvinism had important elements of immanent religious development within it, in Weber's view; these were shaped and selected by the emerging capitalist classes; but they in turn were shaped by it— by its concept of salvation and its ethical requirements, for example.

[6] *From Max Weber,* pp. 62–63.
[7] *Ibid.,* p. 63.

The concept of an immanent quality to ideas does not imply that they are spontaneous generations, not themselves requiring explanation. Why are men interested in religious ideas in the first place? To Weber, the driving force was a "religious interest," but he was not content to posit this as an "explanation," after the fashion of the "four wishes" or "six basic interests" that were fashionable a generation ago. (Such curiosity-stoppers are no more useful than "instincts" in scientific explanations.) He made some effort to account for this interest in the nature of individual and social life. "A typical example is the interest in salvation, an interest which has in turn a complex derivation from, among other things, certain stresses and strains to which individuals are sometimes subjected in social situations where frustration of the worldly ends seems inevitable and founded in the nature of things." [8] This is, of course, no final explanation, but using it as a starting point, the key question, from the point of view of the problem with which we are dealing, becomes: Do different conceptions of salvation have different consequences for human action?

Weber, as we have seen, answered yes to this question. His whole series of studies that sought to discover the relationship between economic developments and religious beliefs led to the conclusion that different conceptions of salvation strongly influenced economic behavior. The doctrine of transmigration, for example, makes any effort to seek salvation by intensive worldly effort meaningless; while a doctrine of "calling" in the Calvinist sense, encourages one to seek salvation by vigorous activity. We have explored this problem in Chapter 8, where we noted that it was one thing to declare that a religious belief blocked economic development and other changes, as do the doctrines of Karma and transmigration, and another thing to hold that a belief motivated one to economic activity, as Weber held that the doctrine of the "elect" and the idea of a "calling" did. Virtually no one will disagree with the former position. Here is religion as the conserver or the barrier. The latter must be explored in light of Weber's own conception of elective affinity. There are many shades of meaning that may be given to "election" or "predestination," with widely different implications for action. A doctrine of a "calling" can be associated with quiet acceptance of one's status and traditional activity; predestination can lead to quietism. Until one describes more fully than Weber did the process whereby they developed into supports for energetic worldly endeavor, claims for the autonomy of religious ideas, growing out of their own "inner dialectic," are not entirely supported.

All but the most ardent defenders of religion agree that it is more likely

[8] Parsons, op. cit., p. 159.

to be a conserver of old values than a creator of new. Religious values and requirements compete, in the lives of most men, with other powerful interests and claims. He who seeks, through religion, to change individuals or society must recognize and respond to that fact. As an institution that is adjusted to the secular claims and requirements of a society, the church is a recognition of these powerful competing interests. The churches of a society represent the values, the needs, the interests of the people involved in them. As Arthur Swift has said, one cannot expect them to be ahead of themselves. This conserving aspect of religion is increased by the nature of religious expression. Reliance on symbols, on tradition, on sacred writings, on the cultivation of emotional feelings of identity or harmony with sacred values turns one to the past far more than to the future.

The conservation of values and social patterns by religion may be considered a happy or an unhappy fact. To the ruler of an Islamic society, it may seem only obvious that the religious reenforcement of the patterns of that society—including the legitimacy of his own authority—is a good thing. To those who oppose his rule as the leader of government, it may seem to be an unhappy fact that to attack the caliphate is to demand religious reform. In fact, they may be far less able to oppose him, both because they share the religious ideology which legitimates his rule, and because, even if they do not, if the majority of the society do, the caliph can maintain support by appeal to religious sanctions.

This is not to say that religion prevents change, but only that it may be used in an attempt to prevent change. The final result may be only to slow down changes that are being promoted by powerful developments in society, thus helping to guarantee that the changes, when they do occur, will be more drastic and accompanied by more violence. The experience of Czarist Russia well illustrates this situation. If the pressures toward change are not powerful, the religious sanctions for the existing order (along with the other sanctions available) may be adequate to prevent change for long periods. This has been substantially the case in many of the Islamic countries through the last several generations; but one would be rash to predict that the present rulers of these Moslem societies can continue to control change, in part by the appeal to religious symbols. They may only insure that more rapid change, when it does come, will be explosive and extreme.

If this interpretation of the place of religious ideas in a causal complex is valid, it would seem that Weber—and how much more most other writers—paid too little attention to the conditions under which "charismatic ideas" will appear, their routinization will be rapid or slow, and the shaping and interpretation of ideas to put them into service for individual or group interests will be extensive or slight. Religion cannot be understood simply as a force that blocks or retards change—whether for good or ill. The extent of its "independent" influence as compared with the extent to which it simply expresses other influences can be measured only when we give up the attempt to arrive at a *general* formula. At several points, especially in Chapter 9, we have referred to some of the specific variables that influence the relationship between religion and social change. Only by more careful attention to such variables in scientific research can we hope to specify with more precision the place of religion in social change.

TYPES OF RELIGIOUS LEADERS

One of the ways of approaching this question of religion and social change is to examine the roles of religious leaders, a topic we have introduced briefly in other connections but have not examined with care. There is, of course, a wide range of general interpretations of the influence of leaders. To some, they are the prime movers of history; to others, "leaders" are only the symbolic manifestations of social forces. An analytic view requires that we not attempt to arrive at any such general proposition. The task is to specify the conditions that affect the degree of leadership influence; or, to put the matter somewhat differently, the need is to describe types of leaders, indicating the kinds of situations in which they appear and the variations in their influence.

There are many typologies of religious leaders, most of them primarily descriptive. They indicate different patterns of relationship between leaders and the religious organizations and followers with which they are connected, using various principles of classification. Some systems of classification are primarily interested in patterns of authority in a religious system as a whole; others are concerned with types of leaders on the local or congregational level.

The first variety is well illustrated by Joachim Wach's list of nine types of religious authority: the founder, reformer, prophet, seer, magician, diviner, saint, priest, and "religiosus" (a plain man who lives a highly religious life). Wach's careful definitions of these types help in the systematic ordering of the wide variety of leaders to be found in a complex religious pattern. To some degree—although he is less helpful here—he explores the social factors involved in the appearance of these types of authority and the nature of their influence.[9]

[9] See Joachim Wach, *Sociology of Religion*, pp. 331–383.

Classifications concerned with the local religious group are perhaps more likely to describe types of functions than types of leaders. The functions may all be performed by one man, or there may be some division of labor. Drawing on a typology worked out by the "University Seminar in the Professions in Modern Society" at Columbia University, Sklare describes eight functions of contemporary church leaders: priest (conductor of public worship), preacher, cleric (a functionary of the state, empowered to perform certain ceremonies), rector (administrator of an organization), pastor (counsellor), father (head of a congregation in a psychological sense), parson (representative of the church to the community), and rabbi (teacher and interpreter of religious doctrines). Sklare's specific interest is in the way that forces in the American environment have modified the traditional Rabbi role, adding the several functions more familiar to Christian priests and ministers.[10] The typology is also useful, however, for more general questions concerning the functions of religious leaders. The study of changes in emphasis, of additions to and subtractions from the functions of ministers, is an important guide to the interaction of religion and society.

Other typologies of religious leaders are directly concerned with the question of social change. This problem is implicit in the distinction between the "prophet" and the "priest" that has been widely used. The former, whose own origin is often left unexplained, is thought of as a dramatic new force, challenging the existing patterns and, if successful, changing the lives of his followers by the impact of his message or example. The latter is part of a functioning system, one who carries out established patterns (often with the implication that they have become outmoded) without influencing them. Max Weber has sought to bring the concept of prophet-priest into the framework of a sociological analysis by more careful definition of terms and by exploration of the social contexts with which leaders interact. A prophet, in his terms, is a religious manifestation of charismatic leadership. "The term 'charisma' will be applied to a certain quality of an individual personality by virtue of which he is set apart from ordinary men and treated as endowed with supernatural, superhuman, or at least specifically exceptional powers or qualities." [11] The charisma is validated only by the free acceptance of it by those subject to the leader's influence, such recognition being a sign of personal devotion and trust, not of traditional patterns or institutional power.

In Weber's view, charismatic leadership brings a new force onto the scene:

[10] See Marshall Sklare, *Conservative Judaism*, pp. 177–180.
[11] Max Weber, *The Theory of Social and Economic Organization*, p. 358.

The genuine prophet, like the genuine military leader and every true leader in this sense, preaches, creates, or demands *new* obligations. . . . Charismatic authority is thus specifically outside the realm of everyday routine and the profane sphere. In this respect, it is sharply opposed both to rational, and particularly bureaucratic, authority, and to traditional authority. . . . Within the sphere of its claims, charismatic authority repudiates the past, and is in this sense a specifically revolutionary force. . . . Pure charisma is specifically foreign to economic considerations. . . . In traditionally stereotyped periods, charisma is the greatest revolutionary force. The equally revolutionary force of "reason" works from without by altering the situations of action. . . . Charisma, on the other hand, may involve a subjective or internal reorientation born out of suffering, conflicts, or enthusiasm. It may then result in a radical alteration of the central system of attitudes and directions of action with a completely new orientation of all attitudes toward the different problems and structures of the "world." [12]

As a proposition concerning the influence of religious leaders on social change, Weber's concept of charisma raises two difficult questions. What is the context out of which charismatic leaders come? (Even a "specifically revolutionary force" has to be explained.) And what happens to their demands for new obligations; who follows them, for how long, and in what ways are they modified? Weber furnishes a much more satisfactory answer to the second than to the first question. He relied heavily on the statement that men are very differently qualified for religious experience, a fact that "stands at the beginning of the history of religion." To state such a fact is to make clear the need for social-psychological and cultural study to explain it. The degree to which charisma is a "revolutionary force" can be meaningfully interpreted only when its own origins are more thoroughly explored. Although Weber seems insufficiently aware of this problem, he did not disregard it entirely. In *Ancient Judaism,* for example, he writes: "The prophecy of doom can largely be traced to the psychic dispositions of the prophets, as conditioned by constitution and experience. It is no less certain that it was indeed the historical fate of Israel, which provided this prophecy with its position in the religious development." [13] Weber's awareness of the societal and cultural factors involved in conditioning charisma is shown by the distinction he draws between exemplary and emissary prophecy, the former leading toward a contemplative and perhaps even an apathetic response to the world, the latter addressing its demands precisely to the world. Whether a religious virtuoso will be an exemplary or an emissary prophet is strongly affected by the religious tradition and the social stratum from which he springs.[14]

[12] *Ibid.,* pp. 361–363.
[13] Weber, *Ancient Judaism,* p. 307.
[14] See *From Max Weber,* pp. 285–290.

Thus the sources of charisma itself require explanation. This is not to deny, however, that once set in motion prophetic leadership may "result in a radical alteration of the central system of attitudes and directions of action." Surely one may define Vinoba Bhave as a prophet. The new demands which he is making in India today are based on the old Hindu ideal of *tapas* (renunciation); but the precise nature of the demands is new. He has persuaded Indian landlords, at last report, to give nearly four million acres to landless peasants. Here is a religiously generated motivation and goal effecting an important social change. (Perhaps it should be remarked that he is much more nearly an emissary than an exemplary prophet, in Weber's terms, indicating the need for avoiding an identification of one or the other type with various world religions.)

It is at the beginning of his challenge, Weber believes, that a prophetic leader is most influential. Gradually there is a cooling off of the ardor which he had generated and an institutionalization of his followers. As his message spreads through a group, the diverse interests and needs of the members act upon it—selecting, interpreting, forgetting. "Indeed, in its pure form charismatic authority may be said to exist only in the process of originating." [15] Rather quickly, the process of "routinization of charisma" begins. [16] Those for whom the prophet's demands have an "elective affinity" continue to "follow" him, but in the process, his specifically religious thought is assimilated to their economic, political, and social, as well as their religious, needs. In such a situation, he is a "cause" of the developments and changes only in a very limited sense. Indeed, many unintended consequences may flow from the interpretations that his followers place upon his teachings. It is unlikely that Calvin wholly anticipated all the results that were related to his emphasis on "this-worldly asceticism."

In sum, a religious leader is part of a complicated causal nexus. He cannot be understood without a knowledge of his social and cultural environment, including information concerning culture contact and borrowing. His impact is intricately related to the needs and tendencies of the people who come in contact with him. Some who hear him will be unaffected and those who do respond will respond each in his own way. For the explanation of certain problems—the abstraction of a limited piece of time and circumstance which the scientist may wish to explain —the religious leader may profitably be regarded as a "cause," as a starting point for some sequence of interaction. For another problem, he must be seen as a product of other forces, an effect, a carrier of influence but

---

[15] Weber, *The Theory of Social and Economic Organization*, p. 364.
[16] See *ibid.*, pp. 363–386.

not its source. There is little warrant in science for a more general conception.

RELIGION INITIATES CHANGE

Almost all that we can say on the degree to which religion is an initiator of social change has been said in the previous sections or in other parts of this essay. It remains only to make a brief summary statement. The whole weight of the evidences of contemporary "behavioral science" makes it appear certain that the life of the mind is shaped by individual needs and interests and by social roles and group structures. Religious beliefs, from this perspective, cannot be seen as intrusive forces from outside; they spring from human life and are shaped by its imperatives. It is equally clear, however, that ideas and beliefs enter into life. They organize experience and influence that *selective* response to the environment that characterizes human behavior. Perception is affected by what one believes is there, by what one has been taught to see and hear, by what one wants to perceive, by the groups within which one perceives. There is no reason to suppose that religious beliefs, religiously defined needs, and religious groups fall outside this rule; they shape our perception of the world. Motivation is equally influenced by what one believes and by one's group identities. Machine operators may work slowly or show a high rate of absenteeism, if they define a situation as unjust or dull or of only marginal interest to them. The norms of the groups to which they belong will strongly influence their levels of achievement and aspiration. If the work situation corresponds with their sense of justice, if they feel involved in its planning, if their group encourages vigorous activity, production levels will rise and absenteeism fall.

Again, there is no reason to suppose that the influence of religious beliefs and religious groups falls outside this social psychology and sociology of motivation. One of the main efforts of this study has been to show that an adequate sociology of religion must be brought into the framework of a general theory of human behavior. Religious beliefs and group patterns may contribute to a "slowdown" of effort, to "absenteeism from this world," or to vigorous activity and intensive efforts to change the world.

To try to change the world, of course, is not synonymous with changing it, although effort is an essential ingredient. And even the origin of the beliefs and groups that lead to the desire to try has to be explained. We have tried to show that it is related to the individual, social, and cultural facts of a given situation. Once started, religious ideas and structures are continuously involved in the interactions of human life. A Mormon community is different, not only in the days of the charismatic leadership of Joseph Smith, but today. The course of its development is shaped, in part, by religiously defined patterns.

Let us observe once again that the force of religion may be chained to economically or politically defined goals, to the injury or defeat of the religiously defined goals—the quest for human brotherhood in the "universal religions," for example. And it may be well to repeat that such initiatory or causal influence as religion has is not intrinsically good or bad. If communism shares many of the characteristics of a religion, its power to initiate social change is seen to be very unfortunate by contemporary Americans. The dedication of a kamikazi pilot, inspired by the ceremonies and beliefs of National Shinto, was not looked upon with equal enthusiasm by all whose lives he changed. The influence of some parts of the Calvinist ethic is not regarded in the same light by a psychoanalyst and a fundamentalist minister.

Apart from these value questions—which are, of course, of enormous importance—what may one say about the initiatory power of religion, not in any primary sense, but in the sense of one of the levels of causation? Our argument can perhaps be summarized in this statement: Religious influence on the course of social change will be greatest when the strategic decisions of religious individuals are made with clearest recognition of "the dilemma of the churches," when prophetic or charismatic leadership is most abundant, when religious institutions are most effectively autonomous from the secular institutions of power. Strategy, prophecy, and autonomy are highly interactive, of course. And they too require explanation by the sociology of religion—an explanation which we have attempted in part, at various points in our discussion. Moreover, they apply almost wholly to universal religions, not to tribal or societal religions, for in situations of which the latter are a part, it is almost meaningless to isolate a specifically religious influence on social change.

The observation that the influence of religion varies is rooted deep in the thought and action of "the average man" and in the more sophisticated ideas of philosophers and theologians. The task of science is not only to test the validity of this general observation, but more particularly to discover the conditions that underlie the variations. Bergson's interesting philosophical ideas contribute little to a science of religion when he asserts—even if he demonstrates its truth—that a fresh religious impulse may break into society with revolutionary force. Under what influences does this occur and in what situations does the institutionalization of the "creative impulse" proceed? Troeltsch poses a key problem for science, but is less concerned to solve it, when he describes a great antinomy running through Christianity—a quiescent "aesthetic-ritualistic piety" and an "ethical-prophetic piety." Science must try to discover in whom the one and the other will predominate. MacMurray states what is in effect an hypothesis in the sociology of religion, when he writes: ". . . the main evidence that Christianity is a real creative force in history is the pressure and the struggle to realize, by reform and revolution, a society based on the principles of freedom and equality." [17] But his evidences are largely propositions of faith. Niebuhr recognizes the variations in religious influence:

Traditional and institutional religion . . . tend to impart the aura of the absolute to the existing order of things. . . . Religion in its quintessential character is devotion to the absolute and a yearning after value and truth which transcends the partial, the relative and the historical. Since the absolute must always be symbolized in terms of the relative it leads naturally to the absolutizing of. the relative, so that devotion to God comes to mean loyalty to "holy Russia" or obedience to the Jewish law, or acceptance of the prejudices of western civilization, or conformity to puritan moral standards or mainte-nance of a capitalistic civilization. Yet religion is never exhausted in these corruptions.[18]

A scientific study would avoid the adjectives, for what is one man's quintessence is another's corruption. And it would ask: What are the circumstances that cause religion to accept the existing order or to "transcend the partial"?

Conclusion

The relentless search for causes, for conditions, for variables may seem to many to "take the heart out of religion." One can argue that if religion can be undermined by analysis, so be it. But it is possible that growing knowledge of the nature of religion can only add to its contribution to the quality of man's adjustment to the universe of which he is a part. The author subscribes to the latter view. This, to be sure, is an affirmation and not a statement of fact. One is scarcely able to prove it. Some explora-tion of the reasoning and feeling behind it, however, may help in the understanding of its meaning. Thus we come back to a question raised

[17] John MacMurray, *The Clue to History*, p. 69.
[18] Reinhold Niebuhr, *Reflections on the End of an Era*, pp. 183–184.

in the first pages of this volume in the hope that we can now examine it more fruitfully. These last paragraphs are not "sociology of religion"; they are estimates and projections and affirmations. But they express what the author believes to be judgments that flow naturally from the study of religion and society.

Effects of the Scientific Study of Religion. The initial impact of the sociology of religion, and of other scientific studies, on religion may be different from the long-run effects. "A little learning is a dangerous thing." Yet a little ignorance may be even more dangerous. What are some of the immediate effects of the scientific study of religion? It makes a naive, simple, unquestioning belief in some changeless religious view less likely. The emphasis on functions, the attention to religious institutions, with their involvement in all aspects of the secular society, the development of a comparative view of many religions—these require that one pull back from his faith to see it at a distance. For many people, religion is accepted without thought, by habit or perhaps by fear; many aspects of it are believed that contradict other conceptions which they accept. Such contradictions are less likely to be noticed if religion is not studied. Scientific examination may "weaken the faith" of persons thus inclined.

Sociology inevitably takes a naturalistic view of religion. This is a necessary *assumption,* not a demonstrated truth, from which all science proceeds. Religion is in man; it is to be understood by the analysis of his needs, tendencies, and potentialities. The scientist presses forward from this starting point as far as his evidence will carry him. Insofar as sociology has any effect on religious starting points, it will probably be to encourage naturalism. This will not be because it has proved its "ultimate validity"—an impossibility—but because the capacity of human beings for compartmentalized thinking is limited. There is a tendency, however slowly it may develop, for a person to accept harmonious premises. For those who identify religion with supernatural views of the world, it must appear that scientific analysis may weaken religion.

Those who define religion functionally do not regard the loss of belief in specific items of a traditional faith or the increased likelihood of naturalistic premises as forces that weaken religion. Moreover, there are other influences set in motion by serious scientific study that may, in the long run, strengthen religion and help to renew it in the modern world:

First, scientific study has revealed the great functional significance of religion for individuals and for groups, leading to the conclusion that religion is a permanent, necessary, and inevitable part of human life. Man is "incurably religious." If a well-integrated and acceptable system of beliefs and practices is not available, he invents one, joins a movement, follows a leader. The implication to be drawn from scientific study is not simply that religion is important in human affairs, but also that the *kind* of religion is vital. Simply to "believe" is not enough. We shall come back to this question below.

Second, the distinction that functional analysis draws between the changing content and the basic functions of religion may help to create a situation in which a religion adjusted to the contemporary world, and therefore more effective in it, can more readily develop. If one identifies religion with a system of established beliefs and rites, he opposes a developmental approach. But failure to change can only alienate from religion the people whose whole life situation is undergoing rapid transformation. They may become indifferent to or reject completely a religion that contains a great many insights into human life—insights won through centuries of tragedy and struggle—only to embrace a proto-religion whose road to salvation seems shorter but whose detours have been quite uncharted. The sociologist, by noting that religion is a product of societies, by his attention to its cultural sources, by his examination of social change and culture lags, may help to facilitate the process whereby a religion adequate to this dynamic situation may be strengthened.

Third, a scientific study of religion can make an important contribution to the understanding of the relationship of religion to morality. In Chapter 2 we have suggested that there are many types of relationship between them. Not all of these are equally appropriate—in terms of the achievement of stated values—to a changing, heterogeneous society. In a "sacred" society, the tradition building process has time to embody guide lines to action that have relatively foreseeable consequences. One does not need to be a philosopher and a scientist to "know" the consequences of his actions—these can be embedded in moral rules that emerge out of the repetitions of human experience. This is not true of a rapidly changing social situation. Today it is far more difficult to be moral, because the results of our actions are far more difficult to predict. Our behavior now affects persons far removed from us in time and space. The vast interdependence of the world means that we affect strangers as often as friends. The decisions of the rulers of China affect a farm boy in Iowa; the actions of the American Congress influence the trends in Egypt. A few moral formulas learned as a child cannot adequately guide the contemporary man; there is no easy way out of the difficult task of trying to discover the probable consequences of various actions. *How* does one love his neighbor today? Do we continue to press the building of a large stockpile of atomic and hydrogen bombs? Do we bring German troops into the forces of NATO? These are new problems. If one thinks of a changeless religious system embodying a moral code adequate to the needs of men today, he can only hinder the search for answers to such questions. A sociological study that explores the functional interdependence of religion and society points to the conclusion that our type of society needs a highly flexible, undogmatic religion, one dedicated to the free study of society, if it is to contribute to the solution of our major moral problems.

What Religious Perspective for the Modern World?   Not all kinds of religion fit equally well into the complex framework of contemporary societies. Some men have gloried in the opposition of their faith to reason. Their faith was something fixed and final. This, in a diverse and changing world, is a guarantor of conflict, for systems of faith continually meet and sharply conflict; and man's changing situation requires new religious thought. This does not mean that a great deal cannot be drawn from the religious efforts of those who preceded us; but each generation must struggle with its own religious situation. In the words of Wilhelm Pauck (though we would not attribute to him the implications carried here): "The church must always be reformed."

If some men have gloried in the opposition of faith and reason, others require the use of reason to the fullest extent, the constant search for truth, in order that faith may not prove ephemeral. "Faith is the substance of things hoped for," the projection of a society's most fundamental aspirations outward in time and into areas where science is inapplicable —the realm of ideals and value-choices. That the author of the book of *Hebrews* should complete the sentence by stating that faith is "the evidence of things not seen" is an indication of the deep antinomy running through Christianity. If faith is "evidence" it can lead to sharp conflicts with reason and can result in doctrinal rigidity.[19] These are religious tendencies, in the writer's judgment, that make extremely difficult the religious quest of modern societies. No effective "return to religion" can be of a thirteenth or sixteenth century variety. The present enthusiasm for the churches seems relatively superficial; while the true situation is more accurately marked by Kierkegaard's call, echoed by many contemporary theologians and church leaders, where are the Christians in Christendom. Their scarcity is partly to be accounted for by the weakness of the continuing reformation, the failure to develop a religion whose symbols and problems are meaningful to men today. The result is a hasty return to the church while a great deal of the operating faith resides in national creeds. These creeds are not sharp departures from the religious

[19] See J. H. Randall and J. H. Randall, Jr., *Religion and the Modern World*, chapter eleven.

traditions to which they are related, of course, but they give weight to the limited and parochial views of those religions—in a day when the universalism of man has been transformed from an exciting vision to a vital necessity.

If sociological analysis tends to lead one to the conclusion that a religious system is necessary for human life, it also suggests that an effective religion must be fully sensitive to the training, the perspectives, the problems, the total life situation of the contemporary generation. Concern for this question led John Stuart Mill to suggest the need for *lack* of agreement in religious matters, to prevent the growth of hierarchical institutions that might block the necessary changes in a dynamic society. There is a part truth in this observation. It is sensitive to the dangers of rigidity and is aware of the diversity of religious needs. But it fails to recognize that if the explicit religious patterns lack a unifying theme, this theme will get support in some other social pattern—often one more limited and rigid than the religion it replaced.

We are fully aware of the great difficulties in a continuing reformation. The task is similar to the rebuilding of Grand Central Station while keeping the trains running. One must avoid waiting so long that the building collapses, yet build so skillfully that traffic may continue. In religious matters, for fear of "stopping traffic" many people resist the building process; others, dismayed at the shakiness of the ancient structure, try to halt all traffic until a new structure can be built. (This cannot be done; the customers buy a ticket on some other road to salvation.) Beyond some contribution to the intrinsic tasks of science, one may hope that this difficult struggle with the analysis of religion may suggest some reconciliation between those who are dedicated to keeping the trains running and those who are convinced that the structure must be rebuilt. If the present writer is inclined to emphasize the latter, it is only out of conviction that the need for continuous rebuilding is more likely to be forgotten than the need for the leap of faith.

PART 2

Readings in
the Sociology of
Religion

Introduction

The selection of a group of readings to accompany the essay which makes up Part 1 of this volume is in many ways a frustrating task. Not only must one choose from among a long list of valuable studies, but having made the choice, one is faced with the additional problem of abbreviating many of the selections. This is especially difficult, of course, in the case of books which have one central theme.

These difficulties, however, are small compared with the advantages that may be gained from the study of the wide range of authors that can be included in a collection of readings. It is my hope to put into the readers' hands a small "working library" that will permit him and encourage him to explore the topic of this volume at greater length. Several criteria have guided my choices: There is an attempt to bring in some of the "classics," to allow the authors of key volumes to speak for themselves; several of the selections are included because they give primary attention to empirical studies, and thus furnish documentation for the systematic statement of Part 1; a number of the papers explore in greater detail, and often from a different perspective, questions that have been raised in the essay above.

Not all of the selections that follow can be called sociology of religion, strictly defined; but each of them, in the present writer's judgment, presents data or suggests hypotheses from which the sociologist of religion can profit. Several of the papers include value stands and interpretations that derive from a theological perspective. One who approaches the subject from a different perspective may feel it necessary to "translate" into a different frame of reference; yet he can derive a great deal of insight from these discussions.

No attempt has been made to include a reading for each of the topics discussed in Part 1, although most of the major questions are explored in one or more of the selections. Frequently a paper is relevant to more than one problem and can profitably be studied in connection with several different parts of the preceding essay. Broadly speaking, however, the selections in Section 1 of the Readings deal with issues that have been developed in Chapters 1 and 2, Section 2 deals with Chapter 3, Section 3 with Chapters 4 and 5, Section 4 with Chapter 6, Section 5 with Chapter 7, Section 6 with Chapters 8 and 9, and Section 7 with Chapters 10 and 11.

Religion, Morals, and Magic

In the selections that follow, two questions are explored that we have discussed in Chapter 2. MacIver and Page indicate that, from a sociological point of view, religious codes and sanctions can best be understood by studying them as one variety among the several to be found in society. They note the need for distinguishing between religion and morals, while recognizing the close connection between them. In the second paper of this section, Goode systematizes in a useful way the similarities and the differences between magic and religion.

1. Religion and Morals

R. M. MACIVER AND CHARLES H. PAGE *

THE DISTINCTION OF THE RELIGIOUS FROM THE MORAL CODE

Religion and morals are very closely interwoven. If we are to draw a proper distinction between them it must be in terms of the authority and sanction attached to their respective prescriptions rather than in terms of the contents of the codes themselves. (Note "Contrast A" in Chart.) Religion prescribes rules of conduct, and in so doing tends to identify these with moral conduct. On the other hand, some ethical cults, such as Auguste Comte's creed of "positivism" or the contemporary Ethical Culture Society, claim to be also religious. There are again what we may call "substitute religions," where the emotional characteristic of religious observance is associated with nonreligious or even antireligious elements, as in certain expressions of communism or some other "social gospel." Those who profess no religion have, nonetheless, their own moral codes—indeed amorality is a rare phenomenon. A clear distinction between the two is therefore necessary.

[1] THE SUPRASOCIAL SANCTION OF RELIGION

Religion, as we understand the term, implies a relationship not merely between man and man but also between man and some higher power. Hence it normally invokes a sanction which may be called *suprasocial,* whether it be primitive ghost fear or the present "wrath of God" or the penalties of an afterlife of torture in hell or merely the sense of being "out of tune with the infinite" when its supposed laws are disobeyed. Any ordinance is likewise part of a religious code which emanates from an authority accepted on religious grounds as the interpreter of a creed or the deputy or "vice-regent of God." Religion prescribes also the relation of man to man, but in so far as the sanction of this prescription is thought of as suprasocial, its code is religious rather than strictly moral. It envisages "God's purpose" for man as distinct from man's own purposes, and generally regards the church as an agency for the fulfillment of this "divine end."

* From *Society, An Introductory Analysis,* pp. 168–174.

DOMINANT INTERRELATIONSHIPS OF MAJOR CODES AND SANCTIONS

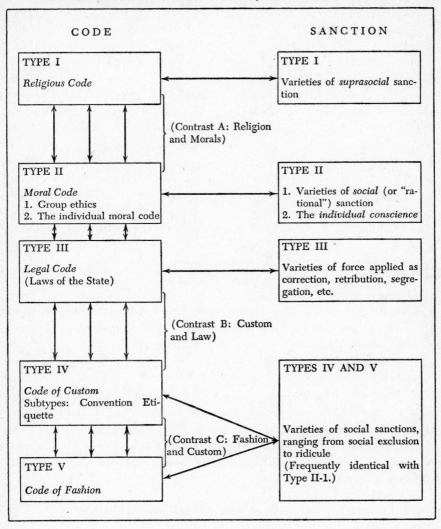

CODE

SANCTION

TYPE I

Religious Code

TYPE I

Varieties of *suprasocial* sanction

(Contrast A: Religion and Morals)

TYPE II

Moral Code
1. Group ethics
2. The individual moral code

TYPE II

1. Varieties of *social* (or "rational") sanction
2. The *individual conscience*

TYPE III

Legal Code
(Laws of the State)

TYPE III

Varieties of force applied as correction, retribution, segregation, etc.

(Contrast B: Custom and Law)

TYPE IV

Code of Custom
Subtypes: Convention Etiquette

(Contrast C: Fashion and Custom)

TYPE V

Code of Fashion

TYPES IV AND V

Varieties of social sanctions, ranging from social exclusion to ridicule
(Frequently identical with Type II-1.)

[2] THE SOCIAL SANCTION OF MORALS, RELIGION, AND SOCIAL RELATIONS

A code cannot strictly be called "moral" except in so far as the sanction comes from the apprehension of evil social results directly accruing from the conduct the code forbids. Here we have the distinction between the religious idea of "sin" and the moral idea of "wrong." The two ideas are naturally blended or associated in many minds, but we cannot understand the difference between religion and morals unless we distinguish them. The one may still remain as the support of the other, and some writers, such as Benjamin Kidd or the contemporary philosopher C. S. Lewis, assume that a moral code cannot endure without the support of religion.[1] Other thinkers, like Herbert Spencer and Thomas Huxley and various modern "naturalists" and "humanists," maintain that a moral code can never become pure and wholly responsive to the needs of a changing society unless it is dissociated from the special sanctions of religion.[2] It is significant, by the way, that representatives of both these schools of thought have characterized the moral sanction, in contrast to the religious, as a "rational" one.

All social norms, however derived, whether they be the reputed revelation of the gods or the inherited wisdom of the past or the ordinances of the present, reveal the ideas prevailing in the group concerning the *social relations* and the *modes of living* they hold desirable. The chief difference between religious norms and all others, including the strictly moral codes, is that the religious are addressed *indirectly* to the social situation. The code of a religious creed expresses an orientation of conduct and attitude toward a reality conceived of as transcending human life and human aims. It seeks to establish social relationships in which human purposes are linked up with, and frequently subordinated to, the assumed will of superhuman powers regarded as benign or demonic or even as indifferent to humanity.

[3] THE PROBLEM OF RECONCILING SOCIAL NEEDS AND THE RELIGIOUS CODES

Since man, especially in prescientific ages and circles, has conceived supernatural powers according to his fears and in ignorance and misin-

---

[1] B. Kidd, *Social Evolution* (new ed., New York, 1920); C. S. Lewis, *The Case for Christianity* (New York, 1944). For a more extensive discussion of this problem and related ones, see J. Wach, *Sociology of Religion* (Chicago, 1944), Chap. III; and for an elaboration of the distinction between morals and religion by an outstanding student of the latter, see R. Otto, *Das Heilige* (Gotha, 1927).

[2] Spencer, *Principles of Sociology*, III, Chap. XIV; Huxley, *Evolution and Ethics*

terpretation of the phenomena of nature, his religious codes could scarcely be a true reflection of his social needs. They often perverted social relationships and admitted or inspired conduct detrimental to social interests. To such older and more primitive examples as taboos against useful foods, human sacrifice, religious prostitution, maiming initiation rites, and stultifying superstitions may be added such modern religiously sanctioned prescriptions as that against planned parenthood or against proper medical care of the ill or injured. The religious codes often emerge as powerful engines of control to maintain the interests of the established order against the processes of change, as when the Greek Orthodox Church became a bulwark of the tyranny of the Russian Tsars.[3] Yet in the interpretation and promulgation of religious codes the social ideals of the group inevitably find a place. A *partial* accommodation is made to social needs, though the bias of the interpreters, the medicine men, or the priests, tends to check the process. In any event, the reconciliation of religious code and social need can never be complete so long as the code is based on dogmatically false conceptions of the laws of nature and of society.

Precepts incorporated in a religious code, as in the Ten Commandments, may be inspired more by social than by religious considerations, since in the formative stage it is easy to make the "word of the Lord" the expression of a sense of social need. But the formal distinction between the two types of precept remains. A code is *religious*—no matter whether its precepts are concerned with the relation of man to God, as in the first four commandments, or with the relation of man to man, as in the last six—when its source is presented as divine authority and its sanction is supernatural, or when the penalty is exacted in the name of religion. A code is *moral* when it promulgates standards of conduct that directly derive their sufficient justification from the human interpretation of good and evil.

[4] *THE QUESTION OF PRIORITY*

Many writers have discussed the questions as to which of the two codes was the original one and as to which of them was derived from the other. Some have held, like Auguste Comte in his account of the evolution of

---

(New York, 1905). For a discussion of various modern representatives of the humanist and naturalist viewpoints, see E. A. Burtt, *Types of Religious Philosophy* (New York, 1939), Chaps. IX and X; and for two pertinent essays by students of naturalism, see Chaps. II and XV by S. P. Lamprecht and J. H. Randall, Jr., in *Naturalism and the Human Spirit* (Y. H. Krikorian, ed., New York, 1944).

[3] For numerous other examples see Wach, *op. cit.*, Chap. VI.

mankind from the theological to moral or "positivist" conceptions, that religion was the matrix of morals. Others, like Ferdinand Tönnies and Émile Durkheim, have taken the view that religion arose as a projection or sanctification of social or moral ideas. Tönnies held that the mores of the group became gradually reinforced by the religious sanction, gaining through tradition and the authority of the elders that aura of reverence and awe which led on the one hand to the worship of ancestors and on the other to the suprasocial sanction of the established ways. Durkheim regarded religious ideas as arising out of social situations and the religious life as "the concentrated expression of the whole collective life." [4]

The distinction between religion and morals has arisen in the course of social evolution. As we shall see later, we cannot say that either the religious or the moral mode came first. Religion incorporates elements derived from social and moral reflection, and the latter in turn has been greatly influenced by religious conceptions. The distinction of these elements was largely concealed in the primitive outlook upon life, even as it is partially concealed in the outlook of the less educated minds among ourselves. Herbert Spencer thought that the earliest forms of religion contained no moral element, pointing out that they were intended to propitiate evil rather than good spirits and that they were characterized by cruel and atrocious observances.[5] But this situation (not always present among primitive peoples) does not prove his point, since a moral code, too, may be misguided and may make what seems to us atrocious demands. The morals of a primitive tribe are no more the morals of Spencer than its religion is his religion. It would be more correct to say that in primitive religions were contained, in solution, as it were, religious and moral and other elements.

CONFLICTS BETWEEN RELIGION AND MORALS

Ever since man has distinguished between moral and religious codes they have had a great influence on each other. Moral codes, with such prescriptions as the duty of humility or obedience or respect for elders, have prepared the way for the perpetuation of religious beliefs. Religious codes have strongly reinforced with their supernatural sanctions the prevailing morals of the group. But the equilibrium of their joint control over conduct has been subject to many strains.

[4] See Tönnies, *Die Sitte*, and Durkheim, *Elementary Forms of the Religious Life* (J. W. Swaine, tr., New York, 1926).
[5] Spencer, *op. cit.*, III, 152.

[1] THE CONSERVATISM OF RELIGION AND HISTORICAL ADJUSTMENTS

The religious code, as the more conservative of the two, has come into frequent conflict with the moral discernments responsive to changing social needs. And sanctioned by its "higher authority," it has frequently menaced the autonomy of judgment which is the prime condition of an enlightened adult morality. The more conservative religions have resisted the fresh moral insights and the social applications derived from advancing science. They have opposed, for example, the quest for the truth concerning human origins, the first employment of anaesthetics for the alleviation of pain, the admission of divorce where marriage was a living death because of the insanity or cruelty of either partner, and the practice of birth control. At one time witches were burned in the name of the religious code and at another national campaigns against venereal disease were opposed on the same basis—the conservatism of religion has a large and well-known record.[6]

However, this rupture between religion and morals has been partly disguised, and often partly healed, by the consequent transformations of religion itself and the appearance of new religious creeds in response to moral demands. In general terms, religion seeks to confirm established moralities, and new moralities seek to modify religion. In the long run, and particularly in modern societies where the divisions of religion itself prevent any one form from dominating the mores and where the sense of definite and dread types of supernatural sanction has dwindled, both religion and morals tend to be brought into *relative* harmony with social needs.

As a major illustration of the adjustment of religion to changing moral and social conceptions we may cite the development of Protestantism. One acute writer on the subject, Max Weber in his *Sociology of Religion* developed a theory previously suggested by various novelists and historians, that the ethics of Calvinism, in contrast to the religious teachings of the preceding age, were not only in conformity with, but an important preparation for, the growth of capitalism. For the Protestant ethic underscored those virtues of thrift, discipline, personal responsibility, self-help, and unremitting toil which were congenial to the capitalist spirit. While Weber's theory has been subject to certain modifications, he and other writers provide ample evidence of the close relationship between the

---

[6] See, for example, J. M. Yinger, *Religion in the Struggle for Power* (Durham, N. C., 1946), Chap. V.

Protestant and capitalistic developments and of the adjustment of the religious code to the changing moral code.[7]

[2] THE "HUMANISTIC" TREND TODAY

When religion is strongly dogmatic, as in the case of pre-Protestant Christianity, there is a serious problem of reconciling the religious and the more changeful moral code. Social welfare, when not made subordinate, is viewed in the light of a suprasocial principle. The conflict is clearly seen in the distinction between "faith" (adherence to a creed) and "works" (social conduct) and in the Protestant controversy as to their relative importance; and it is worth remembering that the *religious* problem is their relative importance in the "sight of God." Another instructive indication is "the system of concessions, tolerances, mitigations and reprieves which the Catholic Church with its official supernatural morality has devised for the multitude," thereby seeking to adjust the rigor of the religious code to the common temper of the age.[8]

Within the major religions of the Western world the growing interest in "works" and in social morality in recent decades has shown itself in a definite trend away from supernaturalism and toward a promulgation of social ethics. The trend has many forms, most of which have certain elements of modern "humanism." "Man's major religious ideas, humanists hold, are everywhere functions of the dominant needs and values of the people holding them. God, far from being the creator of man, is always himself created by man; he is the result of the play of man's idealizing imagination over the quest for the appealing goods that life appears to render possible."[9] "Humanism," in this sense, rejects supernaturalistic notions of creation, heaven and hell, inherent sin, and so on, and strives to unite people on the basis of a code of social morality rather than on the basis of creed or denomination or "belief." It generally welcomes the discoveries of science, physical and social.

[3] GROUP-CENTERED RELIGION AND THE LARGER MORALITY

A solution of the conflict between religion and morals is found *in so far as* religion comes to transcend the egoisms of tribe and nation and, puri-

---

[7] See Weber, *The Protestant Ethic and the Spirit of Capitalism* (T. Parsons, tr., New York, 1930). For appraisals of Weber's thesis, see R. H. Tawney's Introduction, *ibid.*, and his *Religion and the Rise of Capitalism* (New York, 1926); and Yinger, *op. cit.*, Chap. IV.

[8] Quoted from the Introduction to John Dewey's *Human Nature and Conduct* (New York, 1922).

[9] Burtt, *op. cit.*, p. 375.

fied by science of its stubborn misinterpretations of reality, grows world-conscious or cosmos-conscious. Under these conditions it loses the fierce compulsive power which unites the faithful in strong social bonds against the infidel, and sends a nation forth to conquest with the promise, *In hoc signo vinces*—"under this sign thou shalt conquer." It becomes, instead, the emotional integrating sense of the whole, whose range of immensity and power is beyond man's understanding, so that he can only *feel* his communion with it and dimly sense his tiny purposeful life as a moment in its eternal being. Then it no longer divides people from people, and within a people the orthodox from those who "go awhoring after strange gods." It loses that immoral intolerance which only the exclusive vision-ary possession of an unreasoned faith can inspire.

The great religions that originated in the Western world and have spread in modern times, Judaism and Christianity and Mohammedanism, and at least one of the Oriental religions, Shintoism, have rarely achieved such breadth and tolerance. On the contrary, they have often been as-sociated with tribal and national aspirations, with intolerance of one an-other, at times with bloody conflict. Perhaps we have much to learn, as one philosopher has recently argued,[10] from the more flexible and more inclusive "religious philosophies" of the East.

Religion, growing world-conscious, may well sustain the nearer sense of our community with one another and thus fall into consistency with a purely moral code. But it can no longer dictate an authoritative morality, since thus sublimated it is no longer capable of defining moral precepts for the particular occasions of life. No longer do most men expect a church, as in the Middle Ages, to lay down precise rules touching the morality of monopoly and usury; and if this limitation is true of the more conservative religions in the modern world, it is still more true of the wider faiths. If in this way morality has lost an anchorage, though one that moored it too fixedly to the past, at least there is the compensation that a freer morality, springing from the consciousness and sheer experi-ence of social good and evil, has become possible.

[10] F. S. C. Northrop, *The Meeting of East and West* (New York, 1946), especially Chaps. IX and X.

2. Religion and Magic

WILLIAM J. GOODE *

The traditional distinction between magic and religion has gradually assumed conceptual clarity in anthropological literature during the past three decades. The present discussion centers on that distinction and the implications of it for a better understanding of primitive society.

This theoretical clarity has emerged slowly because of concrete similarities in the phenomena, and the consequent conceptual difficulty of cleaving through such apparent similarities.

SIMILARITIES

The rather close similarities to be observed in the concrete phenomena stem, naturally, from their relationship to the supernatural. They are (1) both *concerned with the nonempirical.* They refer to a realm beyond that of the "logico-experimental," to the nonmeasurable, the intangible, where the nonbeliever "cannot see" those elements which are real enough to the faithful. Thus, (2) they both stand in somewhat the *same relationship to Western science,* which itself has imposed this distinction on the primitive. To the primitive society, of course, such a distinction is impossible: the supernatural is as real as what we call the empirical, and the world does not stop at the borderline of the Western scientist's senses.

Further, (3) both are pervasively *symbolic.* That is, objects which may be ordinary in one situation are endowed with religious or magical significance in another: they *stand* for something else, such as a magical force, an idea, an occurrence; etc. This suggests another similarity: (4) they both deal with nonhuman forces, sometimes called the sacred.

A systematic symbolism suggests, (5) however, a *ritual system,* and this, too, is common to both, the rituals frequently functioning as external representations of the supernatural. As to the things or forces symbolized in the rituals, both systems (6) contain many "anthropopsychic" entities. That is, the entities are dealt with frequently as though they had mentalities like the members of the society: they can be threatened, cajoled, or addressed; they may be whimsical, moody, or vain; their definition of who is worthy to approach is similar, etc. Now, as to practitioners,

* From *Religion Among the Primitives,* pp. 50–54.

(7) there is usually a specialized (a) *set of skills,* and (b) *a select group* holding those skills, for dealing with such forces.

In spite of such similarities, however, anthropologists have been working toward a distinction based upon a number of characteristics. Part of this distinction goes back to Tylor's idea that magic is a pseudoscience based on an inaccurate association of ideas, divination being a "sincere but fallacious system of philosophy." From this notion, several other characteristics emerge. One, naturally, is the instrumental nature of magic, meaning that it can be used for either good or evil. Malinowski and his student Ian Hogbin have both pointed to this use of sorcery in the Trobriands and in Ontong Java. There is thus an implicit acceptance of the impersonality of magic.

This instrumental and impersonal nature of magic suggests an emphasis on *personal* ends, not *groupal* ends. Reasoning from this, it would seem likely that there might be fewer cult activities in the case of magic, and thus a simpler structure, than in religion. "As a general rule," this may not be far wrong. However, under conditions which have been generalized as hypotheses, a complex cult development seems to be possible.

Lowie has qualified somewhat the notion of impersonality, and the attitude of control, presumed to be held by the magician. In his discussion, Lowie agrees that this "roughly" describes the "more or less prevalent character of individual reactions." Nevertheless, he suggests that this is not at all a universal reaction. Even in the religious situation, one may find the Winnebago practitioner "compelling" the spirits (following Radin), in spite of reverence. Malinowski, in his treatment of the "origin" of magic (almost in biological terms, in the "primal situation"), emphasizes the emotional nature of the magical situation, and of course there may be respect, if not reverence, for the magical apparatus and formulas. Nevertheless, both in his earlier and later treatments, Malinowski adheres in his descriptions to the conception of magic as prosaic, without humility or reverence for the most part. Evans-Pritchard, who also notes that there may be emotion in the magical situation when the disease is serious, follows this conception of "ordering" the magical forces, calmly, "just as he would tell a boy were he dispatching him on an errand."

Yet the magician clearly has more than a craftsman's attitudes toward his apparatus and beliefs. For this reason, Lowie, seconded later by Radin, suggests that we should expect some overlapping between magic and religion. Little change in the one would be required to convert it to the other. Marett, Goldenweiser, and others express ideas close to this. Herskovits goes further, claiming that "magic is regarded as an integral part of the Dahomean religious system." Warner, similarly, maintains that

". . . the essential nature of magic and ritual is the same . . . at least in Murngin society." In Firth's Tikopia, the magical and religious practitioner are the same.

Such a brief discussion suggests several propositions: A. A distinction between magic and religion has generally been made in anthropological literature; B. The distinction seems to be based on several concrete criteria; C. There is rough agreement on these criteria; and D. There is no sharp concrete line to be drawn between the two.

The corollary of these propositions is that magic and religion can be distinguished through the use of a theoretical tool, the polar ideal type concept. Such a conceptual device is widespread in the social sciences, and in some form occurs in all anthropological generalization, whether consciously or not. In its application one accepts the idea that any given magical or religious system is concretely not to be found at either extreme, theoretical pole, but somewhere between the two. If the conceptual "exaggerations" constituting the poles are useful, such systems will fall near one or the other of the two. This is, of course, always an approximation, as the application of any scientific concept to concrete situations will be: the unique situation or phenomenon rarely, if ever, equates with the conceptual description or theoretical formulation of any science. Further, the decision as toward which pole a supernatural system falls requires *several* characteristics, each of which is a variable running between two opposing or antithetical forms. . . .

The characteristics most prominently emerging in anthropological writings as theoretical aids in distinguishing these two complexes seem to be the following:

1. *Concrete specificity of goal* relates most closely to the magical complex. This overlaps toward the religious goal more than most characteristics, since religious rewards are usually to be found in this world. However, religious goals do lean more heavily in the direction of "general welfare," "health," "good weather," and eschatological occurrences.

2. The *manipulative attitude* is to be found most strongly at the magical pole, as against the supplicative, propitiatory, or cajoling, at the religious pole.

3. The *professional-client relationship* is ideally-theoretically to be found in the magical complex. The shepherd-flock, or prophet-follower, is more likely in the religious.

4. *Individual ends* are more frequently to be found toward the magical end of this continuum, as against groupal ends toward the other.

5. The magical practitioner or his "customer" *goes through his activities as a private individual,* or individuals, functioning much less as groups.

At the religious extreme pole, groups carry them out, or representatives of groups.

6. With regard to the process of achieving the goal, in case of magical failure, there is more likely to be a *substitution or introduction of other techniques*. Stronger magic will be used, or magic to offset the counter-magic of enemies, or even a different magician. Since much of religious activity is less specifically instrumental, is concerned more with the intrinsic meaning of the ritual, and is expected to achieve concrete goals indirectly, by maintaining the proper continuing relationship with the gods, such a substitution is far rarer in the area of the religious pole.

7. Although the practitioner may feel cautious in handling such powerful forces, *a lesser degree of emotion* is expected at the magical end of this continuum. This may be described as *impersonality*. At the religious end, one expects a greater degree of emotion, possibly awe or worship.

8. The *practitioner decides whether* the process is to start at all, toward the magical pole. Toward the religious, the ritual *must* be carried out. That it must be done is part of the structure of the universe.

9. Similarly, the *practitioner decides when* the process is to start, in the case of magic, more often than in the case of religion. Toward the latter end of the continuum, the time relationships of rituals are fairly fixed, within rough limits, even when not calendrical.

10. Defined as instrumental by the society, magic is thought of as at least *potentially directed against the society*, or a major accepted group within it, or a respected individual in good repute with the gods. Religious rituals are not thought of as even potentially directed against the society or such respected people.

11. As a final, ideally distinguishing characteristic, magic is *used only instrumentally, i.e., for goals*. The religious complex may be used for goals, but at its ideal pole, the practices are ends in themselves.

Such a set of ideal-typical criteria is sufficient to set apart the extreme poles, and it seems likely that a given magical or religious complex will fall fairly definitely toward one pole or the other, although of course no such concrete complex will be found exactly at either extreme.

Approaches to a Functional Theory of Religion

The papers that follow, despite their wide differences, converge in their interest in discussing religion, and several other social patterns, from the point of view of functionalism. How is religion embedded in the social situation and in the individual needs of its adherents? Simmel and Durkheim give this question a strongly sociologistic answer: religion is a product and an expression of social life. Malinowski, while granting the "public and tribal character" of religion, introduces the needs of individual personalities into his analysis. The papers by Kluckhohn and Warner help us to see the need for careful attention to patterns of thought and action that are not defined as religion if we are to understand religion itself.

3. A Contribution to the Sociology of Religion

GEORG SIMMEL *

The ambiguity which surrounds the origin and nature of religion will never be removed so long as we insist upon approaching the problem as one for which a single word will be the "open sesame." Thus far, no one has been able to offer a definition which, without vagueness and yet with sufficient comprehensiveness, has told once for all what religion is in its essence, in that which is common alike to the religion of Christians and South Sea islanders, to Buddhism and Mexican idolatry. Thus far it has not been distinguished, on the one hand, from mere metaphysical speculation, nor, on the other, from the credulity which believes in "ghosts." Its purest and highest manifestations are not yet proof against comparison with these. And the multiplicity of psychological causes to which religion is ascribed corresponds to this indefinite conception as to its nature. It matters not whether fear or love, ancestor-worship or self-deification, the moral instincts or the feeling of dependence, be regarded as the subjective root of religion; a theory is only then entirely erroneous when it assumes to be the sole explanation, and then only correct when it claims to point out merely one of the sources of religion. Hence the solution of the problem will be approached only when all the impulses, ideas, and conditions operating in this domain are inventoried, and that with the express determination that the significance of known particular motives is not to be arbitrarily expanded into general laws. Nor is this the only reservation that must be made in an attempt to determine the religious significance of the phenomena of social life which preceded all religion in the order of time. It must also be emphatically insisted upon that, no matter how mundanely and empirically the origin of ideas about the super-mundane and transcendental is explained, neither the subjective emotional value of these ideas, nor their objective value as matters of fact, is at all in question. Both of these values lie beyond the limits which our merely genetic, psychological inquiry aims to reach.

In attempting to find the beginnings of religion in human relations which are in themselves non-religious, we merely follow a well-known method. It has long been admitted that science is merely a heightening,

* Abridged from *The American Journal of Sociology*, November, 1905, pp. 359–376. Reprinted, May, 1955. Translated by W. W. Elwang.

a refinement, a completion, of those means of knowledge which, in lower and dimmer degree, assist us in forming our judgments and experiences in daily, practical life. We only then arrive at a genetic explanation of art when we have analyzed those aesthetic experiences of life, in speech, in the emotions, in business, in social affairs, which are not in themselves artistic. All high and pure forms existed at first experimentally, as it were, in the germ, in connection with other forms; but in order to comprehend them in their highest and independent forms, we must look for them in their undeveloped states. Their significance, psychologically, will depend upon the determination of their proper places in a series which develops, as if by an organic growth, through a variety of stages, so that the new and differentiated in each appears as the unfolding of a germ contained in that which had preceded it. Thus it may help us to an insight into the origin and nature of religion, if we can discover in all kinds of non-religious conditions and interests certain religious momenta, the beginnings of what later came to be religion, definitely and independently. I do not believe that the religious feelings and impulses manifest themselves in religion only; rather, that they are to be found in many connections, a co-operating element in various situations, whose extreme development and differentiation is religion as an independent content of life. In order, now, to find the points at which, in the shifting conditions of human life, the momenta of religion originated, it will be necessary to digress to what may seem to be entirely foreign phenomena.

It has long been known that custom is the chief form of social control in the lower culture conditions. Those life-conditions which, on the one hand, are subsequently codified as laws and enforced by the police power of the state, and, on the other hand, are remitted to the free consent of the cultivated and trained individual *socius*, are, in narrower and primitive circles, guaranteed by that peculiar, immediate control of the individual by his environment which we call custom. Custom, law, and the voluntary morality of the individual are different unifying elements of the social structure which can carry the same obligations as their content, and, as a matter of fact, have had them among different peoples at different times. Many of the norms and practices of public life are supported both by the free play of competing forces and by the control of the lower elements by higher ones. Many social interests were at first protected by the family organization, but later, or in other places, were taken under the care of purely voluntary associations or by the state. It can, in general, be asserted that the differentiations which characterize the social structure are always due to definite ends, causes, and interests; and so long as these continue, the social life, and the forms in which it expresses itself, may be exceedingly diverse, just as, on the other hand, this differentiation may itself have the most varied content. It seems to me that among these forms which human relations assume, and which may have the most diverse contents, there is one which cannot be otherwise described than as religious, even though this designation of it, to be sure, anticipates the name of the complete structure for its mere beginning and conditioning. For the coloring, so to speak, which justifies this description must not be a reflection from already existing religion; rather, human contact, in the purely psychological aspect of its interaction, develops that definite tendency which, heightened, and differentiated to independence, is known as religion.

We can safely assume that many human relations harbor a religious element. The relation of a devoted child to its parent, of an enthusiastic patriot to his country, of the fervent cosmopolite toward humanity; the relation of the laboring-man to his struggling fellows, or of the proud feudal lord to his class; the relation of the subject to the ruler under whose control he is, and of the true soldier to his army—all these relations, with their infinite variety of content, looked at from the psychological side, may have a common tone which can be described only as religious. All religion contains a peculiar admixture of unselfish surrender and fervent desire, of humility and exaltation, of sensual concreteness and spiritual abstraction, which occasion a certain degree of emotional tension, a specific ardor and certainty of the subjective conditions, an inclusion of the subject experiencing them in a higher order—an order which is at the same time felt to be something subjective and personal. This religious quality is contained, it seems to me, in many other relations, and gives them a note which distinguishes them from relations based upon pure egoism, or pure suggestion, or even purely moral forces. As a matter of course, this quality is present with more or less strength, now appearing merely like a light overtone, and again as a quite distinct coloring. In many and important instances the developing period of these relations is thus characterized; that is to say, the same content which previously or at some subsequent period was borne by other forms of human relation, assumes a religious form in other periods. All this is best illustrated by those laws which at certain times or places reveal a theocratic character, are completely under religious sanctions, but which, at other times and places, are guaranteed either by the state or by custom. It would even seem as if the indispensable requirements of society frequently emerged from an entirely undifferentiated form in which moral, religious, and juridical sanctions were still indiscriminately mingled, like the Dharma of the Hindus, the Themis of the Greeks, and the *fas* of the Latins, and that finally, as historical conditions varied, now one and now the other of these sanctions developed into the "bearer" of such requirements. In the relation of the individual to the group also these changes can be observed; in times when patriotism is aroused, this relation assumes a devotion, a fervor, and a readiness of self-surrender which can be described only as religious; while at other times it is controlled by conventionality or the law of the land. For us the important thing is that it is, in every case, a question of human relations, and that it is merely a change, as it were, in the aggregate condition of these relations when, instead of purely conventional, it becomes religious, and instead of religious, legal, and then, in turn, voluntary, as a matter of fact, many socially injurious immoralities first found a place in the criminal code because of the resentment of the church; or, as illustrated by anti-Semitism, because a social-economic or racial relation between certain groups within a group can be transferred to the religious category, without, however, really becoming anything else than a social relation; or, as some suppose, that religious prostitution was merely a development of sexual life which was earlier or elsewhere controlled by pure convention.

In view of these examples, a previously indicated error must be more definitely guarded against. The theory here set forth is not intended to prove that certain social interests and occurrences were controlled by an already independently existing religious system. That, certainly, occurs often enough, brings about combinations of the greatest historical importance, and is very significant also in the examples cited. But what I mean is precisely the reverse of this, and, it must be admitted, of much less apparent connection, and one more difficult to discover; namely, that in those social relations the quality which we afterward, on account of its analogy with other existing religiosity, call religious, comes into being spontaneously, as a pure socio-psychological constellation, one of the possible relations of man to man. In contrast to this, religion, as an independent phenomenon, is a derivative thing, almost like the state in the Roman and modern sense, as an objective and self-sufficient existence, is secondary in contrast to the original causes, relations, and customs which immediately controlled the social elements, and which only gradually projected upon or abrogated to the state the conservation and execution of their contents. The entire history of social life is permeated by this process: the positively antagonistic motives of individuals, with which their social life begins, grow up into separate and independent organisms. Thus, from the regulations for preserving the group-life there arise, on the one hand, the law which codifies them, and, on the other, the judge whose business it is to apply them. Thus, from socially necessary tasks, first performed with the co-operation of all, and according to the rude empiricism of the times, there develop, on the one hand, a technology, as an ideal system of knowledge and rules, and, on the other hand, the laborer as the differentiated means for accomplishing those tasks. In a similar manner, although in these infinitely complex affairs the analogy constantly breaks down, it may have happened in things religious. The individual in a group is related to others, or to all, in the way above described; that is to say, his relations to them partake of a certain degree of exaltation, devotion, and fervency. From this there develops an ideal content, on the one hand, or gods, who protect those who sustain these relations; who brought the emotions which they experience into being; who, by their very existence, then bring into sharp relief—as an independent entity, so to speak—what had hitherto only existed as a form of human relation, and more or less blended with more actual lifeforms. And this complex of ideas or phantasies finds an executive representation in the priesthood, like law in the person of the judge, or learning in a scholarly class. When this identification or substantialization of religion has been accomplished, it, in turn, has its effect upon the direct psychical relations of men among themselves, giving them the now well-known and so-called quality of *religiosity*. But in so doing it merely gives back what it had originally received. And it may, perhaps, be asserted that the so often wonderful and abstruse religious ideas could never have obtained their influence upon men if they had not been the formulæ or embodiments of previously existing relations for which consciousness had not yet found a more appropriate expression. . . .

The faith which has come to be regarded as the essential, the substance, of religion, is first a relation between individuals; for it is a question of practical faith, which is by no means merely a lower form or attenuation of theoretical belief. When I say, "I believe in God," the assertion means something entirely different from the statement, "I believe in the existence of ether waves;" or, "The moon is inhabited;" or, "Human nature is always the same." It means not only that I accept the existence of God, even though it be not fully demonstrable, but it implies also a certain subjective relation to him, a going out of the affections to him, an attitude of life; in all of which there is a peculiar mixture of faith as a kind of method of knowledge with practical impulses and feelings. And now, as to the analogy of all this in human socialization. We do not base our mutual relations by any means upon what we conclusively know about each other. Rather, our feelings and suggestions express themselves in certain representations which can be described only as matters of faith, and which, in turn, have a reflex effect upon practical conditions. It is a specific psychological fact, hard to define, which we illustrate when we "believe in someone"—the child in its parents, the subordinate in his superior, friend in friend, the individual in the nation, and the subject in his sovereign. The social rôle of this faith has never been investigated; but this much is certain, that without it society would disintegrate. Obedience, for example, is largely based upon it. In innumerable instances it depends neither upon a definite recognition of law and force, nor upon affection, or suggestion, but upon that psychical intermediate thing which we call faith in a person or a group of persons. It has often been remarked that it is an incomprehensible thing that individuals, and entire classes, allow themselves to be oppressed and exploited, even though they possess ample power to secure immunity. But this is precisely the result of an easy-going, uncritical faith in the power, value, superiority, and goodness of those in authority—a faith which is by no means an uncertain, theoretical assumption, but a unique thing, compounded of knowledge, instinct, and feeling, which is concisely and simply described as faith in them. That, in the face of reasonable proof to the contrary, we still can retain our faith in an individual is one of the strongest of the ties that bind society. This faith, now, is of a most positive religious character. I do not mean that the religion was first, and that the sociological relations borrowed their attribute from it. I believe, rather, that the sociological significance arises without any regard for the religious data at all as a purely inter-individual, psychological relation, which later exhibits itself abstractly in religious faith. In faith in a deity the highest development of faith has become incorporate, so to speak; has been relieved of its connection with its social counterpart. Out of the subjective faith-process there develops, contrariwise, an object for that faith. The faith in human relations which exists as a social necessity now becomes an independent, typical function of humanity which spontaneously authenticates itself from within; just as it is no rare phenomenon for a certain object to produce a certain psychical process in us, and afterward for this process, having become independent, to create a corresponding object for itself. Human intercourse, in its ordinary as well as in its highest content, reveals in so many ways the psychological form of faith as its warrant that the necessity for "believing" develops spontaneously, and in so doing creates objects for its justification, much as the impulses of love or veneration can fasten themselves upon objects which in themselves could by no means evoke such sentiments, but whose qualifications for so doing are reflected upon them from the needs of the subject, or, as

looked at from the other side, God as creator has been described as the
product of the causal necessity in man. This last assertion by no means
denies that this conception also has objective reality; only the motive out
of which it grew subjectively into an idea is in question. The assumption
is that the infinitely frequent application of the causal idea in the realm of
its origin, the empiric-relative, finally made the need for it a dominating
one, so that it found satisfaction, which was really denied it in the realm
of the absolute, in the idea of an Absolute Being as the cause of the world.
A similar process may project belief beyond the confines of its social
origin, develop it into a similar organic need, and beget for it the idea of
deity as an absolute object.

Another side of the social life which develops into a corresponding one
within the religious life is found in the concept of unity. That we do not
simply accept the disconnected manifoldness of our impressions of things,
but look for the connections and relations which bind them into a unity;
yes, that we everywhere presuppose the presence of higher unities and
centers for the seemingly separate phenomena, in order that we may orient
ourselves aright amid the confusion with which they come to us, is
assuredly one of the important characteristics of social realities and
necessities. Nowhere do we find, so directly and appreciably, a whole
made up of separate elements; nowhere is their separation and free movement so energetically controlled by the center, as in the genes, the family,
the state, in every purposive organization. When primitive associations
are so often found organized in tens, it means, clearly, that the group-
relationship is similar to that of the fingers of the hand—relative freedom
and independent movement of the individual, and, at the same time,
unity of purpose and inseparableness of existence from others. The fact
that all social life is a relationship at once defines it as a unity; for what
does unity signify but that many are mutually related, and that the fate
of each is felt by all? The fact that this unity of society is occasionally attacked, that the freedom of the individual prompts him to break away
from it, and that it is not absolutely true of the closest and most naïve
relations, like the unity of the constituent parts of an organism—all this
is precisely what must have driven it home to human consciousness as a
particular form and special value of existence. The unity of things and
interests which first impresses us in the social realm finds its highest
representation—and one, as it were, separated from all material considerations—in the idea of the divine; most completely, of course, in the
monotheistic, but relatively also in the lower, religions. It is the deepest
significance of the God-idea that the manifoldness and contradictoriness
of things find in it their relation and unity, it matters not whether it be

the absolute unity of the one God, or the partial unities of polytheism. Thus, for example, the social life of the ancient Arabians, with the all-controlling influence of its tribal unity, foreshadowed monotheism; among Semitic peoples, like the Jews, Phœnicians, and Canaanites, the method of their social unification and its transformations was plainly reflected in the character of their gods. So long as family unity was the controlling form, Baal signified only a father, whose children were the people. In proportion as the social aggregate included foreign branches not related by blood, he became a ruler objectively enthroned above. So soon as the social unity loses the character of blood-relationship, the religious unity also loses it, so that the latter appears as the purely derived form of the former. Even the unification which rises superior to the sex-differentiation forms a particular religious type. The psychological obliteration of the sex-contrast, found so conspicuously in the social life of the Syrians, Assyrians, and Lydians, terminated in the conception of divinities which combined the two—the half-masculine Astarte, the man-woman Sandon, the sun-god Melkarth, who exchanges the sex-symbols with the moon-goddess. It is not a question about the trivial proposition that mankind is reflected in its gods—a general truth which needs no proof. The question is, rather, to find those particular human characteristics whose development and extension beyond the human create the gods. And it must also be borne in mind that the gods do not exist as the idealization of individual characteristics, of the power, or moral or immoral characteristics, or the inclinations and needs of individuals; but that it is the inter-individual forms of life which often give their content to religious ideas. In that certain phases and intensities of social functions assume their purest, most abstract, and, at the same time, incorporate forms, they form the objects of religions, so that it can be said that religion, whatever else it may be, consists of forms of social relationships which, separated from their empirical content, become independent and have substances of their own attributed to them.

Two further considerations will illustrate how much the unity of the group belongs to the functions that have developed into religion. The unity of the group is brought about and conserved, especially in primitive times, by the absence of war or competition within the group, in sharp contrast to the relations sustained to all outsiders. Now, there is probably no other single domain in which this non-competitive form of existence, this identity of aim and interest, is so clearly and completely represented as in religion. The peaceful character of the group-life just referred to is only relative. With the majority of the efforts put forth within the group there is also implied an attempt to exclude others from the same goal; to reduce as much as possible the disproportion between desire and satisfaction, even if it be at some cost to others; at least to find a criterion for doing and enjoying in the corresponding activities of others. It is almost solely in religion that the energies of individuals can find fullest development without coming into competition with each other, because, as Jesus so beautifully expresses it, there is room for all in God's house. Although the goal is common to all, it is possible for all to achieve it, not only without mutual exclusion, but by mutual co-operation. I call attention to the profound way in which the Lord's Supper expresses the truth that the same goal is for all, and to be reached by the same means; and also to the feasts which objectify the union of those who are moved by the same religious emotions, from the rude feasts of primitive religions, in which the union finally degenerated into sexual orgies, to its purest expression, the *pax hominibus*, which extended far beyond any single group. That absence of competition which conditions unity as the life-form of the group, but which always reigns only relatively and partially in it, has found absolute and intensest realization in the religious realm. It might actually be said of religion, as of faith, that it represents in substance—yes, to a certain extent consists of the substantialization of—that which, as form and function, regulates the group-life. And this, in turn, assumes a personal form in a priesthood which, despite its historic connection with certain classes, stands, in its fundamental idea, above all classes, and precisely on that account represents the focus and unity of the ideal life-content for all individuals. Thus the celibacy of the Catholic priesthood frees them from every special relation to any element or group of elements, and makes possible a uniform relation to each; just as "society" or the "state" stands above individuals as the abstract unity which represents all their relationships in itself. And, to mention a thoroughly concrete instance, throughout the Middle Ages the church afforded every benevolent impulse the great convenience of a central reservoir into which every benefaction could flow unchallenged. He who desired to rid himself of his wealth for the benefit of others did not have to bother about the ways and means, because there existed for this very purpose a universal central organ between the giver and the needy. Thus benevolence, a form of social relation within the group, secured, in the church, an organization and unity above the individual.

In like manner the reverse of this relation, with, however, the same germ, is seen in the attitude toward heretics. That which arrays great masses in hatred and moral condemnation against heretics is certainly not the difference in the dogmatic content of teaching, which, in most instances, is really not at all understood. It is rather the fact of the opposition of the one against the many. The persecution of heretics and dissenters springs from the instinct which recognizes the necessity for group-unity. Now, it is especially significant that in many instances of this kind religious variation could very well exist in conjunction with the unity of the group in all vital matters. But in religion the social instinct for unity has assumed such a pure, abstract, and, at the same time, substantial form that it no longer requires a union with real interests; while non-conformity seems to threaten the unity—that is to say, the very life-form—of the group. Just as an attack upon a palladium or other symbol of group-unity will evoke the most violent reaction, even though it may have no direct connection with it at all, so religion is the purest form of unity in society, raised high above all concrete individualities. This is demonstrated by the energy with which every heresy, no matter how irrelevant, is still combated.

And, finally, those internal relations between the individual and the group which we characterize as moral offer such deep analogies to the individual's relations to his God that they would seem almost to be nothing more than their condensation and transformation. The whole wonderful fulness of the former is reflected in the many ways in which we "sense" the divine. The compelling and punitive gods, the loving God, the God of Spinoza who cannot return our love, the God who both bestows and deprives us of the inclination and ability to act—these are precisely the tokens by which the ethical relation between the group and its members unfolds its energies and oppositions. I call attention to the feeling of dependence, in which the essence of all religion has been found. The individual feels himself bound to a universal, to something higher, out of which he came, and into which he will return, and from which he also expects assistance and salvation, from which he differs and is yet identical with it. All these emotions, which meet as in a focus in the idea of God, can be traced back to the relation which the individual sustains to his species; on the one hand, to the past generations which have supplied him with the principal forms and contents of his being, on the other, to his contemporaries, who condition the manner and extent of its development. If the theory is correct which asserts that all religion is derived from ancestor-worship, from the worship and conciliation of the immortal soul of a forbear, especially of a hero and leader, it will confirm this connection; for we are, as a matter of fact, dependent upon what has been before us, and which was most directly concentrated in the authority of the fathers over their descendants. The deification of ancestors, especially of the ablest and most successful, is, as it were, the most appropriate expression of the dependence of the individual upon the previous life of the group, even though consciousness may reveal other motives for it. Thus the humility with which the pious person acknowledges that all that he is and has comes from God, and recognizes in him the source of his existence and ability, is properly traced to the relation of the individual to the whole. For man is not absolutely nothing in contrast to God, but only a rust-mote; a weak, but not entirely vain, force; a vessel, but yet adapted to its contents. . . .

This arrangement of religious and ethical-social ideas is supported by the fact that God is conceived as the personification of those virtues which he himself demands from the people. He is goodness, justice, patience, etc., rather than the possessor of these attributes; he is, as it is sometimes expressed, perfection in substance; he is goodness itself, and love itself, etc. Morality, the imperatives that control human conduct, has, so to speak, become immutable in him. As practical belief is a relation between persons which fashions an absolute over and above the form of relation; as unity is a form of relation between a group of persons which raises itself to that personification of the unity of things in which the divine is represented; so morality contains those forms of relation between man and man which the interests of the group has sanctioned, so that the God who exhibits the relative contents in absolute form, on the one hand, represents the claims and benefits of the group, as against the individual, and, on the other, divests those ethical-social duties which the individual must perform of their relativity, and presents them in himself in an absolutely substantial form. The relations of persons to each other, which have grown out of the most manifold interests, have been supported by the most opposite forces, and have been cast into the most diverse forms, also attain a condition in the aggregate whose identification with and relation to a Being above and beyond them we call religion—in that they become both abstract and concrete, a dual development which gives religion the strength with which it again, reflexively, influences those relations. The old idea that God is the Absolute, while that which is human is relative, here assumes a new meaning: it is the relations between men which find their substantial and ideal expression in the idea of the divine.

If investigations like this, touching the fundamentals of being, are usually accompanied by the hope that their significance should be understood sufficiently comprehensively, the reverse must here be the case, and the wish expressed that the arguments here set forth must not be permitted to intrude upon neighboring domains, beyond their own limited boundaries. They are not intended to describe the historical course of the origin of religion, but only to point out one of its many sources, quite irrespective of the fact whether this source, in conjunction with others, also from the domain of the non-religious, gave birth to religion, or whether religion had already come into being when the sources here discussed added their quota to its content—their effectiveness is not dependent upon any particular historical occasion. It must also be borne in mind that religion, as a spiritual experience, is not a finished product, but a vital process which each soul must beget for itself, no matter how stable the traditional content may be; and it is precisely here that the power and depth of religion are found, namely, in its persistent ability to draw a given content of religion into the flow of the emotions, whose movements must constantly renew it, like the perpetually changing drops of water which beget the stable picture of the rainbow. Hence the genetic explanation of religion must not only embrace the historical origin of its tradition, but its present energies also which allow us to acquire what has come down to us from the fathers; so that in this sense there are really "origins" of religion whose appearance and effectiveness lie long after the "origin" of religion.

But, more important even than to deny that we offer here a theory of the historical origin of religion, is it to insist that the objective truth of religion has nothing whatever to do with this investigation. Even if we have succeeded in the attempt to understand religion as a product of the subjective conditions of human life, we have not at all impinged upon the problem whether the objective reality which lies outside of human thought contains the counterpart and confirmation of the psychical reality which we have here discussed. Thus the psychology of cognition seeks to explain how the mind conceives the world to be spatial, and of three dimensions, but is content to have other disciplines undertake to prove whether beyond our mental world there is a world of things in themselves of like forms. It is true, there may be a limit beyond which the explanation of subjective facts from purely subjective conditions may not be sufficient. The chain of causes may have to terminate somewhere in an objective reality. But this possibility or necessity can concern only him who has in view the complete elucidation of the origin and nature of religion, but it does not affect our attempt to trace only a single one of the rays that are focused in religion.

Finally, the most important consideration remains. The emotional value of religion—that is to say, the most subjective reflexive effect of the idea of God—is entirely independent of all assumption about the manner in which the idea originated. We here touch upon the most serious misconception to which the attempt to trace ideal values historically and psychologically is exposed. There are still many who feel that an ideal is deprived of its greatest charm, that the dignity of an emotion is degraded, if its origin can no longer be thought of as an incomprehensible miracle, a creation out of nothing—as if the comprehension of its development affected the value of a thing, as if lowliness of origin could affect the already achieved loftiness of the goal, and as if the simplicity of its several elements could destroy the importance of a product. Such is the foolish and confused notion that the dignity of humanity is profaned by tracing man's origin to the lower animals, as if that dignity did not depend upon what man really is, no matter what his origin. Persons entertaining such notions will always resist the attempt to understand religion by deriving it from elements not in themselves religious. But precisely such persons, who hope to preserve the dignity of religion by denying its historical-psychological origin, must be reproached with weakness of religious consciousness. Their subjective certainty and emotional depth must assuredly be of little moment, if the knowledge of their origin and development endangers or even touches their validity and worth. For, just as genuine and deepest love for a human being is not disturbed by subsequent evidence concerning its causes—yes, as its triumphant strength is revealed by its survival of the passing of those causes—so the strength of the subjective religious emotion is revealed only by the assurance which it has in itself, and with which it grounds its depth and intensity entirely beyond all the causes to which investigation may trace it.

4. The Elementary Forms of the Religious Life

EMILE DURKHEIM *

The general conclusion of the book which the reader has before him is that religion is something eminently social. Religious representations are collective representations which express collective realities; the rites are a manner of acting which take rise in the midst of the assembled groups and which are destined to excite, maintain or recreate certain mental states in these groups. So if the categories are of religious origin, they ought to participate in this nature common to all religious facts; they too

* Excerpts from *The Elementary Forms of the Religious Life*, pp. 10, 37 ff., 416 ff.

should be social affairs and the product of collective thought. At least—
for in the actual condition of our knowledge of these matters, one should
be careful to avoid all radical and exclusive statements—it is allowable
to suppose that they are rich in social elements. . . .

All known religious beliefs, whether simple or complex, present one
common characteristic: they presuppose a classification of all the things,
real and ideal, of which men think, into two classes or opposed groups,
generally designated by two distinct terms which are translated well
enough by the words *profane* and *sacred* (*profane, sacré*). This division
of the world into two domains, the one containing all that is sacred, the
other all that is profane, is the distinctive trait of religious thought; the
beliefs, myths, dogmas and legends are either representations or systems
of representations which express the nature of sacred things, the virtues
and powers which are attributed to them, or their relations with each
other and with profane things. But by sacred things one must not understand simply those personal beings which are called gods or spirits; a
rock, a tree, a spring, a pebble, a piece of wood, a house, in a word, anything can be sacred. A rite can have this character; in fact, the rite does
not exist which does not have it to a certain degree. There are words,
expressions and formulae which can be pronounced only by the mouths
of consecrated persons; there are gestures and movements which everybody cannot perform. If the Vedic sacrifice has had such an efficacy that,
according to mythology, it was the creator of the gods, and not merely a
means of winning their favour, it is because it possessed a virtue comparable to that of the most sacred beings. The circle of sacred objects
cannot be determined, then, once for all. Its extent varies infinitely, according to the different religions. That is how Buddhism is a religion: in
default of gods, it admits the existence of sacred things, namely, the four
noble truths and the practices derived from them. . . .

The really religious beliefs are always common to a determined group,
which makes profession of adhering to them and of practising the rites
connected with them. They are not merely received individually by all
the members of this group; they are something belonging to the group,
and they make its unity. The individuals which compose it feel themselves united to each other by the simple fact that they have a common
faith. A society whose members are united by the fact that they think in
the same way in regard to the sacred world and its relations with the
profane world, and by the fact that they translate these common ideas
into common practices, is what is called a Church. In all history, we do
not find a single religion without a Church. Sometimes the Church is
strictly national, sometimes it passes the frontiers; sometimes it embraces

an entire people (Rome, Athens, the Hebrews), sometimes it embraces
only a part of them (the Christian societies since the advent of Protestantism); sometimes it is directed by a corps of priests, sometimes it is
almost completely devoid of any official directing body.[1] But wherever
we observe the religious life, we find that it has a definite group as its
foundation. . . .

Thus we arrive at the following definition: *A religion is a unified system
of beliefs and practices relative to sacred things, that is to say, things set
apart and forbidden—beliefs and practices which unite into one single
moral community called a Church, all those who adhere to them.* The
second element which thus finds a place in our definition is no less essential than the first; for by showing that the idea of religion is inseparable from that of the Church, it makes it clear that religion should
be an eminently collective thing. . . .

The theorists who have undertaken to explain religion in rational
terms have generally seen in it before all else a system of ideas, corresponding to some determined object. This object has been conceived in
a multitude of ways: nature, the infinite, the unknowable, the ideal, etc.;
but these differences matter but little. In any case, it was the conceptions
and beliefs which were considered as the essential elements of religion.
As for the rites, from this point of view they appear to be only an external
translation, contingent and material, of these internal states which alone
pass as having any intrinsic value. This conception is so commonly held
that generally the disputes of which religion is the theme turn about the
question whether it can conciliate itself with science or not, that is to say,
whether or not there is a place beside our scientific knowledge for another form of thought which would be specifically religious.

But the believers, the men who lead the religious life and have a
direct sensation of what it really is, object to this way of regarding it,
saying that it does not correspond to their daily experience. In fact, they
feel that the real function of religion is not to make us think, to enrich our
knowledge, nor to add to the conceptions which we owe to science others
of another origin and another character, but rather, it is to make us act,
to aid us to live. The believer who has communicated with his god is not
merely a man who sees new truths of which the unbeliever is ignorant;

[1] Undoubtedly it is rare that a ceremony does not have some director at the moment
when it is celebrated; even in the most crudely organized societies, there are
generally certain men whom the importance of their social position points out to
exercise a directing influence over the religious life (for example, the chiefs of the
local groups of certain Australian societies). But this attribution of functions is still
very uncertain.

he is a man who is *stronger*. He feels within him more force, either to endure the trials of existence, or to conquer them. It is as though he were raised above the miseries of the world, because he is raised above his condition as a mere man; he believes that he is saved from evil, under whatever form he may conceive this evil. The first article in every creed is the belief in salvation by faith. But it is hard to see how a mere idea could have this efficacy. An idea is in reality only a part of ourselves; then how could it confer upon us powers superior to those which we have of our own nature? Howsoever rich it might be in affective virtues, it could add nothing to our natural vitality; for it could only release the motive powers which are within us, neither creating them nor increasing them. From the mere fact that we consider an object worthy of being loved and sought after, it does not follow that we feel ourselves stronger afterwards; it is also necessary that this object set free energies superior to these which we ordinarily have at our command and also that we have some means of making these enter into us and unite themselves to our interior lives. Now for that, it is not enough that we think of them; it is also indispensable that we place ourselves within their sphere of action, and that we set ourselves where we may best feel their influence; in a word, it is necessary that we act, and that we repeat the acts thus necessary every time we feel the need of renewing their effects. From this point of view, it is readily seen how that group of regularly repeated acts which form the cult get their importance. In fact, whoever has really practised a religion knows very well that it is the cult which gives rise to these impressions of joy, of interior peace, of serenity, of enthusiasm which are, for the believer, an experimental proof of his beliefs. The cult is not simply a system of signs by which the faith is outwardly translated; it is a collection of the means by which this is created and recreated periodically. Whether it consists in material acts or mental operations, it is always this which is efficacious.

Our entire study rests upon this postulate that the unanimous sentiment of the believers of all times cannot be purely illusory. Together with a recent apologist of the faith [2] we admit that these religious beliefs rest upon a specific experience whose demonstrative value is, in one sense, not one bit inferior to that of scientific experiments, though different from them. We, too, think that "a tree is known by its fruits," [3] and that fertility is the best proof of what the roots are worth. But from the fact that a "religious experience," if we choose to call it this, does exist and that it has a certain foundation—and, by the way, is there any experience

[2] William James, *The Varieties of Religious Experience.*
[3] Quoted by James, *op. cit.*, p. 20.

which has none?—it does not follow that the reality which is its foundation conforms objectively to the idea which believers have of it. The very fact that the fashion in which it has been conceived has varied infinitely in different times is enough to prove that none of these conceptions express it adequately. . . .

. . . there is something eternal in religion which is destined to survive all the particular symbols in which religious thought has successively enveloped itself. There can be no society which does not feel the need of upholding and reaffirming at regular intervals the collective sentiments and the collective ideas which make its unity and its personality. Now this moral remaking cannot be achieved except by the means of reunions, assemblies and meetings where the individuals, being closely united to one another, reaffirm in common their common sentiments; hence come ceremonies which do not differ from regular religious ceremonies, either in their object, the results which they produce, or the processes employed to attain these results. What essential difference is there between an assembly of Christians celebrating the principal dates of the life of Christ, or of Jews remembering the exodus from Egypt or the promulgation of the decalogue, and a reunion of citizens commemorating the promulgation of a new moral or legal system or some great event in the national life? . . .

We have said that there is something eternal in religion: it is the cult and the faith. Men cannot celebrate ceremonies for which they see no reason, nor can they accept a faith which they in no way understand. To spread itself or merely to maintain itself, it must be justified, that is to say, a theory must be made of it. A theory of this sort must undoubtedly be founded upon the different sciences, from the moment when these exist; first of all, upon the social sciences, for religious faith has its origin in society; then upon psychology, for society is a synthesis of human consciousnesses; and finally upon the sciences of nature, for man and society are a part of the universe and can be abstracted from it only artificially. But howsoever important these facts taken from the constituted sciences may be, they are not enough; for faith is before all else an impetus to action, while science, no matter how far it may be pushed, always remains at a distance from this. Science is fragmentary and incomplete; it advances but slowly and is never finished; but life cannot wait. The theories which are destined to make men live and act are therefore obliged to pass science and complete it prematurely. They are possible only when the practical exigencies and the vital necessities which we feel without distinctly conceiving them push thought in advance, beyond that which science permits us to affirm. Thus religions, even the most rational and laicized, cannot and never will be able to dispense with a particular form of speculation which, though having the same subjects as science itself, cannot be really scientific: the obscure intuitions of sensation and sentiment too often take the place of logical reasons. On one side, this speculation resembles that which we meet with in the religions of the past; but on another, it is different. While claiming and exercising the right of going beyond science, it must commence by knowing this and by inspiring itself with it. Ever since the authority of science was established, it must be reckoned with; one can go farther than it under the pressure of necessity, but he must take his direction from it. He can affirm nothing that it denies, deny nothing that it affirms, and establish nothing that is not directly or indirectly founded upon principles taken from it. From now on, the faith no longer exercises the same hegemony as formerly over the system of ideas that we may continue to call religion. A rival power rises up before it which, being born of it, ever after submits it to. its criticism and control. And everything makes us foresee that this control will constantly become more extended and efficient, while no limit can be assigned to its future influence. . . .

Thus sociology appears destined to open a new way to the science of man. Up to the present, thinkers were placed before this double alternative: either explain the superior and specific faculties of men by connecting them to the inferior forms of his being, the reason to the senses, or the mind to matter, which is equivalent to denying their uniqueness; or else attach them to some super-experimental reality which was postulated, but whose existence could be established by no observation. What put them in this difficulty was the fact that the individual passed as being the *finis naturae*—the ultimate creation of nature; it seemed that there was nothing beyond him, or at least nothing that science could touch. But from the moment when it is recognized that above the individual there is society, and that this is not a nominal being created by reason, but a system of active forces, a new manner of explaining men becomes possible. To conserve his distinctive traits it is no longer necessary to put them outside experience. At least, before going to this last extremity, it would be well to see if that which surpasses the individual, though it is within him, does not come from this super-individual reality which we experience in society. To be sure, it cannot be said at present to what point these explanations may be able to reach, and whether or not they are of a nature to resolve all the problems. But it is equally impossible to mark in advance a limit beyond which they cannot go. What must be done is to try the hypothesis and submit it as methodically as possible to the control of facts. This is what we have tried to do.

5. Social and Individual Sources of Primitive Religion
BRONISLAW MALINOWSKI *

IF MALINOWSKI'S INTERPRETATION OF PRIMITIVE RELIGION SOUNDS TOO UN-CRITICALLY FUNCTIONAL IN THE VALUATIVE SENSE, AS IT DOES AT LEAST TO THE PRESENT WRITER, WE SHOULD REMEMBER THAT IT APPEARED AT A TIME WHEN MOST SOCIAL SCIENTISTS WERE INTERPRETING RELIGION ALMOST WHOLLY IN COGNITIVE TERMS. THEY ASKED, DO RELIGIOUS BELIEFS FIT REALITY; MALINOW-SKI ASKED, WHY DO PEOPLE HOLD THOSE BELIEFS, HOW DO THEY FIT INTO THE TOTAL CULTURE. THIS WAS AN ESSENTIAL REFOCUSING OF THEORY, AL-THOUGH IT HAS PROVED NECESSARY, AS WE HAVE SEEN, TO QUALIFY FUNCTIONAL ANALYSIS IN MANY WAYS.

THE PUBLIC AND TRIBAL CHARACTER OF PRIMITIVE CULTS

The festive and public character of the ceremonies of cult is a conspicuous feature of religion in general. Most sacred acts happen in a congregation; indeed, the solemn conclave of the faithful united in prayer, sacrifice, supplication, or thanksgiving is the very prototype of a religious ceremony. Religion needs the community as a whole so that its members may worship in common its sacred things and its divinities, and society needs religion for the maintenance of moral law and order.

In primitive societies the public character of worship, the give-and-take between religious faith and social organization, is at least as pronounced as in higher cultures. It is sufficient to glance over our previous inventory of religious phenomena to see that ceremonies at birth, rites of initiation, mortuary attentions to the dead, burial, the acts of mourning and commemoration, sacrifice and totemic ritual, are one and all public and collective, frequently affecting the tribe as a whole and absorbing all its energies for the time being. This public character, the gathering to-

---

* From *Science Religion and Reality*, Joseph Needham, editor, pp. 52–58, 62–64.

gether of big numbers, is especially pronounced in the annual or periodical feasts held at times of plenty, at harvest or at the height of the hunting or fishing season. Such feasts allow the people to indulge in their gay mood, to enjoy the abundance of crops and quarry, to meet their friends and relatives, to muster the whole community in full force, and to do all this in a mood of happiness and harmony. At times during such festivals visits of the departed take place: the spirits of ancestors and dead relatives return and receive offerings and sacrificial libations, mingle with the survivors in the acts of cult and in the rejoicings of the feast. Or the dead, even if they do not actually revisit the survivors, are commemorated by them, usually in the form of ancestor cult. Again, such festivities being frequently held, embody the ritual of garnered crops and other cults of vegetation. But whatever the other issues of such festivities, there can be no doubt that religion demands the existence of seasonal, periodical feasts with a big concourse of people, with rejoicings and festive apparel, with an abundance of food, and with relaxation of rules and taboos. The members of the tribe come together, and they relax the usual restrictions, especially the barriers of conventional reserve in social and in sexual intercourse. The appetites are provided for, indeed pandered to, and there is a common participation in the pleasures, a display to everyone of all that is good, the sharing of it in a universal mood of generosity. To the interest in plenty of material goods there is joined the interest in the multitude of people, in the congregation, in the tribe as a body.

With these facts of periodical festive gathering a number of other distinctly social elements must be ranged: the tribal character of almost all religious ceremonies, the social universality of moral rules, the contagion of sin, the importance of sheer convention and tradition in primitive religion and morals, above all the identification of the whole tribe as a social unit with its religion; that is, the absence of any religious sectarianism, dissention, or heterodoxy in primitive creed.

1. SOCIETY AS THE SUBSTANCE OF GOD

All these facts, especially the last one, show that religion is a tribal affair, and we are reminded of the famous dictum of Robertson Smith, that primitive religion is the concern of the community rather than of the individual. This exaggerated view contains a great deal of truth, but, in science, to recognize where the truth lies, on the one hand, and to unearth it and bring it fully to light, on the other, are by no means the same. Robertson Smith did not do much more in this matter, in fact, than set forth the important problem: why is it that primitive man performs his ceremonies in public? What is the relation between society and the truth revealed by religion and worshipped in it?

To these questions, some modern anthropologists, as we know, give a trenchant, apparently conclusive, and exceedingly simple answer. Professor Durkheim and his followers maintain that religion is social for all its entities, its God or Gods, the Stuff all things religious are made of, are nothing more nor less than Society divinized.

This theory seems very well to explain the public nature of cult, the inspiration and comfort drawn by man, the social animal, from congregation, the intolerance shown by religion, especially in its early manifestations, the cogency of morals and other similar facts. It also satisfies our modern democratic bias, which in social science appears as a tendency to explain all by "collective" rather than by "individual forces." This, the theory which makes *vox populi vox Dei* appear as a sober, scientific truth, must surely be congenial to modern man.

Yet, upon reflection, critical misgivings, and very serious ones at that, arise. Everyone who has experienced religion deeply and sincerely knows that the strongest religious moments come in solitude, in turning away from the world, in concentration and in mental detachment, and not in the distraction of a crowd. Can primitive religion be so entirely devoid of the inspiration of solitude? No one who knows savages at firsthand or from a careful study of literature will have any doubts. Such facts as the seclusion of novices at initiation, their individual, personal struggles during the ordeal, the communion with spirits, divinities, and powers in lonely spots, all these show us primitive religion frequently lived through in solitude. Again, as we have seen before, the belief in immortality cannot be explained without the consideration of the religious frame of mind of the individual, who faces his own pending death in fear and sorrow. Primitive religion does not entirely lack its prophets, seers, soothsayers and interpreters of belief. All such facts, though they certainly do not prove that religion is exclusively individual, make it difficult to understand how it can be regarded as *the Social* pure and simple.

And again, the essence of morals, as opposed to legal or customary rules, is that they are enforced by conscience. The savage does not keep his taboo for fear of social punishment or of public opinion. He abstains from breaking it partly because he fears the direct evil consequences flowing from the will of a divinity, or from the forces of the sacred, but mainly because his personal responsibility and conscience forbid him doing it. The forbidden totem animal, incestuous or forbidden intercourse, the tabooed action or food, are directly abhorrent to him. I have seen and felt savages shrink from an illicit action with the same horror and disgust with which the religious Christian will shrink from the committing of what he considers sin. Now this mental attitude is undoubtedly due in part to the influence of society, in so far as the particular prohibition is branded as horrible and disgusting by tradition. But it works in the individual and through forces of the individual mind. It is, therefore, neither exclusively social nor individual, but a mixture of both.

Professor Durkheim tries to establish his striking theory that Society is the raw material of Godhead by an analysis of primitive tribal festivities. He studies especially the seasonal ceremonies of the Central Australians. In these "the great collective effervescence during the periods of concentration" causes all the phenomena of their religion, and "the religious idea is born out of their effervescence." Professor Durkheim lays thus the emphasis on emotional ebullition, on exaltation, on the increased power which every individual feels when part of such a gathering. Yet but a little reflection is sufficient to show that even in primitive societies the heightening of emotions and the lifting of the individual out of himself are by no means restricted to gatherings and to crowd phenomena. The lover near his sweetheart, the daring adventurer conquering his fears in the face of real danger, the hunter at grips with a wild animal, the craftsman achieving a masterpiece, whether he be savage or civilized, will under such conditions feel altered, uplifted, endowed with higher forces. And there can be no doubt that from many of these solitary experiences where man feels the forebodings of death, the pangs of anxiety, the exaltation of bliss, there flows a great deal of religious inspiration. Though most ceremonies are carried out in public, much of religious revelation takes place in solitude.

On the other hand there are in primitive societies collective acts with as much effervescence and passion as any religious ceremony can possibly have, yet without the slightest religious coloring. Collective work in the gardens, as I have seen it in Melanesia, when men become carried away with emulation and zest for work, singing rhythmic songs, uttering shouts of joy and slogans of competitive challenge, is full of this "collective effervescence." But it is entirely profane, and society which "reveals itself" in this as in any other public performance assumes no divine grandeur or godlike appearance. A battle, a sailing regatta, one of the big tribal gatherings for trading purposes, an Australian lay-corrobboree, a village brawl, are all from the social as well as from the psychological point of view essentially examples of crowd effervescence. Yet no religion is generated on any of these occasions. Thus the *collective* and the *religious*, though impinging on each other, are by no means coextensive, and while a great deal of belief and religious inspiration must be traced back to solitary experiences of man, there is much concourse and effervescence which has no religious meaning or religious consequence.

If we extend yet further the definition of "society" and regard it as a permanent entity, continuous through tradition and culture, each generation brought up by its predecessor and molded into its likeness by the social heritage of civilization—can we not regard then Society as the prototype of Godhead? Even thus the facts of primitive life will remain rebellious to this theory. For tradition comprises the sum total of social norms and customs, rules of art and knowledge, injunctions, precepts, legends and myths, and part of this only is religious, while the rest is essentially profane. As we have seen in the second section of this essay, primitive man's empirical and rational knowledge of nature, which is the foundation of his arts and crafts, of his economic enterprises and of his constructive abilities, forms an autonomous domain of social tradition. Society as the keeper of lay tradition, of the profane, cannot be the religious principle or Divinity, for the place of this latter is within the domain of the sacred only. We have found, moreover, that one of the chief tasks of primitive religion, especially in the performance of initiation ceremonies and tribal mysteries, is to sacralize the religious part of tradition. It is clear, therefore, that religion cannot derive all its sanctity from that source which itself is made sacred by religion.

It is in fact only by a clever play on words and by a double-edged sophistication of the argument that "society" can be identified with the Divine and the Sacred. If, indeed, we set equal the *social* to the *moral* and widen this concept so that it covers all belief, all rules of conduct, all dictates of conscience; if, further, we personify the Moral Force and regard it as a Collective Soul, then the identification of Society with Godhead needs not much dialectical skill to be defended. But since the moral rules are only one part of the traditional heritage of man, since morality is not identical with the Power of Being from which it is believed to spring, since finally the metaphysical concept of "Collective Soul" is barren in anthropology, we have to reject the sociological theory of religion.

To sum up, the views of Durkheim and his school cannot be accepted. First of all, in primitive societies religion arises to a great extent from purely individual sources. Secondly, society as a crowd is by no means always given to the production of religious beliefs or even to religious states of mind, while collective effervescence is often of an entirely secular nature. Thirdly, tradition, the sum total of certain rules and cultural achievements, embraces, and in primitive societies keeps in a tight grip, both Profane and Sacred. Finally, the personification of society, the conception of a "Collective Soul," is without any foundation in fact, and is against the sound methods of social science.

2. THE MORAL EFFICIENCY OF SAVAGE BELIEFS

With all this, in order to do justice to Robertson Smith, Durkheim, and their school, we have to admit that they have brought out a number of relevant features of primitive religion. Above all, by the very exaggeration of the sociological aspect of primitive faith they have set forth a number of most important questions: Why are most religious acts in primitive societies performed collectively and in public? What is the part of society in the establishment of the rules of moral conduct? Why are not only morality but also belief, mythology, and all sacred tradition compulsory to all the members of a primitive tribe? In other words, why is there only one body of religious beliefs in each tribe, and why is no difference of opinion ever tolerated?

To give an answer to these questions we have to go back to our survey of religious phenomena, to recall some of our conclusions there arrived at, and especially to fix our attention upon the technique by which belief is expressed and morals established in primitive religion.

Let us start with the religious act par excellence, the ceremonial of death. Here the call to religion arises out of an individual crisis, the death which threatens man or woman. Never does an individual need the comfort of belief and ritual so much as in the sacrament of the viaticum, in the last comforts given to him at the final stage of his life's journey— acts which are well-nigh universal in all primitive religions. These acts are directed against the overwhelming fear, against the corroding doubt, from which the savage is no more free than the civilized man. These acts confirm his hope that there is a hereafter, that it is not worse than present life; indeed, better. All the ritual expresses that belief, that emotional attitude which the dying man requires, which is the greatest comfort he can have in his supreme conflict. And this affirmation has behind it weight of numbers and the pomp of solemn ritual. For in all savage societies, death, as we have seen, compels the whole community to forgather, to attend to the dying, and to carry out the duties towards him. These duties do not, of course, develop any emotional sympathy with the dying —this would lead merely to a disintegrating panic. On the contrary, the line of ritual conduct opposes and contradicts some of the strongest emotions to which the dying man might become a prey. The whole conduct of the group, in fact, expresses the hope of salvation and immortality; that is, it expresses only one among the conflicting emotions of the individual.

After death, though the main actor has made his exit, the tragedy is not at an end. There are the bereaved ones, and these, savage or civilized, suffer alike, and are thrown into a dangerous mental chaos. We have given an analysis of this already, and found that, torn between fear and piety, reverence and horror, love and disgust, they are in a state of mind which might lead to mental disintegration. Out of this, religion lifts the individual by what could be called spiritual co-operation in the sacred mortuary rites. We have seen that in these rites there is expressed the dogma of continuity after death, as well as the moral attitude towards the departed. The corpse, and with it the person of the dead one, is a potential object of horror as well as of tender love. Religion confirms the second part of this double attitude by making the dead body into an object of sacred duties. The bond of union between the recently dead and the survivors is maintained, a fact of immense importance for the continuity of culture and for the safe keeping of tradition. In all this we see that the whole community carries out the biddings of religious tradition, but that these are again enacted for the benefit of a few individuals only, the bereaved ones, that they arise from a personal conflict and are a solution of this conflict. It must also be remembered that what the survivor goes through on such an occasion prepares him for his own death. The belief in immortality, which he has lived through and practiced in the case of his mother or father, makes him realize more clearly his own future life. . . .

It is, perhaps, unnecessary to go in detail over all the other types of religious acts. Totemism, the religion of the clan, which affirms the common descent from or affinity with the totemic animal, and claims the clan's collective power to control its supply and impresses upon all the clan members a joint totemic taboo and a reverential attitude towards the totemic species, must obviously culminate in public ceremonies and have a distinctly social character. Ancestor cult, the aim of which is to unite into one band of worshippers the family, the sib or the tribe, must bring them together in public ceremonies by its very nature, or else it would fail to fulfill its function. Tutelary spirits of local groups, tribes, or cities; departmental gods; professional or local divinities must one and all—by their very definition—be worshipped by village, tribe, town, profession, or body politic.

In cults which stand on the borderline between magic and religion, such as the Intichuma ceremonies, public garden rites, ceremonies of fishing and hunting, the necessity of performance in public is obvious, for these ceremonies, clearly distinguishable from any practical activities which they inaugurate or accompany, are yet their counterpart. To the co-operation in practical enterprise there corresponds the ceremony in common. Only by uniting the group of workers in an act of worship do they fulfill their cultural function.

In fact, instead of going concretely into all the types of religious ceremony, we might have established our thesis by an abstract argument: since religion centers round vital acts, and since all these command public interest of joint co-operative groups, every religious ceremony must be public and carried out by groups. All crises of life, all important enterprises, arouse the public interest of primitive communities, and they have all their ceremonies, magical or religious. The same social body of men which unites for the enterprise or is brought together by the critical event performs also the ceremonial act. Such an abstract argument, however, correct though it be, would not have allowed us to get a real insight into the mechanism of public enactment of religious acts such as we have gained by our concrete description.

3. SOCIAL AND INDIVIDUAL CONTRIBUTIONS IN PRIMITIVE RELIGION

We are forced therefore to the conclusion that publicity is the indispensable technique of religious revelation in primitive communities, but that society is neither the author of religious truths, nor still less its self-revealed subject. The necessity of the public *mise en scène* of dogma and collective enunciation of moral truths is due to several causes. Let us sum them up.

First of all, social co-operation is needed to surround the unveiling of things sacred and of supernatural beings with solemn grandeur. The community whole-heartedly engaged in performing the forms of the ritual creates the atmosphere of homogeneous belief. In this collective action, those who at the moment least need the comfort of belief, the affirmation of the truth, help along those who are in need of it. The evil, disintegrating forces of destiny are thus distributed by a system of mutual insurance in spiritual misfortune and stress. In bereavement, at the crisis of puberty, during impending danger and evil, at times when prosperity might be used well or badly—religion standardizes the right way of thinking and acting and society takes up the verdict and repeats it in unison.

In the second place, public performance of religious dogma is indispensable for the maintenance of morals in primitive communities.

Every article of faith, as we have seen, wields a moral influence. Now morals, in order to be active at all, must be universal. The endurance of social ties, the mutuality of services and obligations, the possibility of co-operation, are based in any society on the fact that every member knows what is expected of him; that, in short, there is a universal standard of conduct. No rule of morals can work unless it is anticipated and unless it can be counted upon. In primitive societies, where law, as enforced by judgments and penalties, is almost completely absent, the automatic, self-acting moral rule is of the greatest importance for forming the very foundations of primitive organization and culture. This is possible only in a society where there is no private teaching of morals, no personal codes of conduct and honor, no ethical schools, no differences of moral opinion. The teaching of morals must be open, public, and universal.

Thirdly and finally, the transmission and the conservation of sacred tradition entails publicity, or at least collectiveness of performance. It is essential to every religion that its dogma should be considered and treated as absolutely inalterable and inviolable. The believer must be firmly convinced that what he is led to accept as truth is held in safekeeping, handed on exactly as it has been received, placed above any possibility of falsification or alteration. Every religion must have its tangible, reliable safeguards by which the authenticity of its tradition is guaranteed. In higher religions, we know the extreme importance of the authenticity of holy writings, the supreme concern about the purity of the text and the truth of interpretation. The native races have to rely on human memory. Yet, without books or inscriptions, without bodies of theologians, they are not less concerned about the purity of their texts, not less well safeguarded against alteration and misstatement. There is only one factor which can prevent the constant breaking of the sacred thread: the participation of a number of people in the safekeeping of tradition. The public enactment of myth among certain tribes, the official recitals of sacred stories on certain occasions, the embodiment of parts of belief in sacred ceremonies, the guardianship of parts of tradition given to special bodies of men: secret societies, totemic clans, highest-age grades—all these are means of safeguarding the doctrine of primitive religions. We see that wherever this doctrine is not quite public in the tribe there is a special type of social organization serving the purpose of its keeping.

These considerations explain also the orthodoxy of primitive religions, and excuse their intolerance. In a primitive community, not only the morals but also the dogmas have to be identical for all members. As long as savage creeds have been regarded as idle superstitions, as make-believe, as childish or diseased fancies, or at best crude philosophic speculations, it was difficult to understand why the savage clung to them so obstinately, so faithfully. But once we see that every canon of the savage's belief is a live force to him, that his doctrine is the very cement of social fabric—for all his morality is derived from it, all his social cohesion and his mental composure—it is easy to understand that he cannot afford to be tolerant. And it is clear also that once you begin to play ducks and drakes with his "superstitions," you destroy all his morality, without much chance of giving him another instead.

6. Functions and Dysfunctions of Navaho Witchcraft

CLYDE KLUCKHOHN *

WITCHCRAFT IS FAR NEARER TO MAGIC, AS WE HAVE DEFINED IT, THAN TO RELIGION. WITHOUT EXPLICITLY DISCUSSING THE DISTINCTION, THIS VALUABLE STUDY HELPS TO MAKE CLEAR THE EMPIRICAL BASES ON WHICH IT RESTS. ITS PARTICULAR VALUE HERE, HOWEVER, IS THE SYSTEMATIC AND FULL APPLICATION OF A FUNCTIONAL APPROACH TO THE ANALYSIS OF NAVAHO WITCHCRAFT.

Let us observe, first of all, how socialization implements the persistence of witchcraft beliefs. The child, even before he is fully responsive to verbalizations, begins to get a picture of experience as potentially menacing. He sees his parents, and other elders, confess their impotence to deal with various matters by technological or other rational means in that they resort to exoteric prayers, songs and "magical" observances and to esoteric rites. When he has been linguistically socialized, he hears the hushed gossip of witchcraft and learns that there are certain fellow tribesmen whom his family suspect and fear. One special experience of early childhood which may be of considerable importance occurs during toilet training. When the toddler goes with mother or with older sister to defecate or urinate, a certain uneasiness which they manifest (in most cases) about the concealment of the waste matter can hardly fail to become communicated to the child. The mother, who has been seen not only as a prime source of gratification but also as an almost omnipotent

* Abridged from *Navaho Witchcraft*, Part II, Section 3, pp. 45–72.

person, is now revealed as herself afraid, at the mercy of threatening forces. . . .

Other early experiences of the child help to create a soil fertile for the implanting of belief in such a phenomenon as witchcraft. What with a diet which no longer has even the advantages of being a trial and error adaptation over many generations to the peculiar conditions of Navaho life, with no skills for combatting the disease introduced by Europeans, with drafty hogans and wet clothing and other inadequate protections, it is hardly surprising that Navaho children are frequently ill. The threats to health which were characteristic of the aboriginal culture are still largely present, but additional threats arising out of unwise adoption of our dietary habits and from other European borrowings have been added. In short, it is inevitable that the Navaho child experiences discomfort and pain—without quick or satisfactory means of alleviation. The child likewise sees others ill and suffering. Hunger, too, is an early experience. Not many Navaho have attained adulthood without knowing starvation for short periods and hunger rations for long periods. Since the child soon discovers that even his mother cannot control these things and since the doings and sayings of his elders make it plain that all of these privations occur even when people work very hard and very skilfully, it is small wonder that experience has a capricious and malevolent component for most Navahos.

Thus we see, in a very general way, how a belief in witches fits with what the young Navaho very soon comes to expect of living. But as yet we have learned little as to why these particular forms of belief in *witchcraft* should be perpetuated. The learning of urine and faeces concealment may act as a conditioning mechanism specific to witchcraft belief. Otherwise, however, the only thing which seems demanded by the conditions listed is fear of *some* sort of malevolent forces. To get beyond the demonstration of a social matrix favorable to the survival of beliefs of the generic type of witchcraft, we must examine systematically the contributions which the witchcraft pattern assemblage makes to the maintenance of personal and social equilibrium. First, however, the conceptual tools which will be used in this analysis must be set forth.

MANIFEST "FUNCTIONS" AND LATENT "FUNCTIONS"

My basic postulate for the ensuing discussion is that no cultural forms survive unless they constitute responses which are adjustive or adaptive, in some sense, for the members of the society or for the society considered as a perduring unit. "Adaptive" is a purely descriptive term referring to the fact that certain types of behavior result in survival (for the individual or for society as a whole). "Adjustive" refers to those responses which bring about an adjustment of the individual, which remove the motivation stimulating the individual. Thus suicide is adjustive but not adaptive.

An analysis in terms of adaptive and adjustive responses is very similar to that which many anthropologists have termed "functional." Thus Radcliffe-Brown has recently written: ". . . I would define the social function of a socially standardized mode of activity, or mode of thought, as its relation to the social structure to the existence or continuity of which it makes some contribution." However, since, as has often been pointed out, the word "function" is used in importantly different senses in mathematics, physiology and anthropology, the introduction of the concepts "adaptive and adjustive responses" seems a means of avoiding the ambiguities which have inhered in "function" and "functional." Moreover, the concept of "adjustive response" should direct our attention to the contributions which this aspect of Navaho culture makes to the preservation of the equilibrium of individuals. Anthropological "functionalism" has too often been so interested in formulating the relations between the abstracted parts of the social structure that there has been a tendency to lose sight of the concrete organisms. The motivations and rewards felt by persons have been lost sight of in the preoccupation with the significance of a culture pattern for the social system.

In this study the terms "function" and "functional" will always be used in quotation marks—as a reminder that they are not intended as equivalents for these terms as used in either mathematics or physiology. Rather, a given bit of culture is "functional" insofar as it defines a mode of response which is adaptive from the standpoint of the society or adaptive and adjustive from the standpoint of the individual. This definition is broader than the one which has been usual in anthropology in that the relation of the culture pattern to both the total social structure and to individual organisms is envisioned. The definition also seems more rigorous: the operations by which the "function" of a culture pattern is defined consist in showing how the fulfilment of the pattern promotes the solidarity or survival of the society and the maintenance of their equilibrium on the part of individuals.

Lest a needless confusion arise, it is useful at this point to introduce Merton's helpful distinction between "manifest function" and "latent function." One can very easily point to cultural forms which lack manifest "function." For example, a cowboy (or a recent Plains Indian) will spend an hour catching a horse which he then rides for a distance considerably shorter than he covered on foot while catching the animal. Taken literalistically and superficially, this act (and the pattern of which it is a manifestation) seems distinctly "non-functional." It does have no *manifest* "*function.*" But more than one *latent* "*function*" may be pointed out. The cowboy escapes the ridicule to which he would be exposed if another cowboy saw him walking (on any other mission than that of catching a horse). He also preserves his own sense of self-respect and of the fitness of things. . . .

What, then, are the "functions," the sociological *raison d'être,* of belief in (and perhaps practice of) witchcraft by the Navaho? It will be convenient to consider this question first from the standpoint of the adjustive responses which such beliefs and practices make possible for the individual. We shall then see how they constitute, up to a point, adaptive responses for the society. Since a society is made up of individual organisms, the two categories inevitably merge, but an emphasis upon the two angles of perspective will show the "functions" in sharper focus.

MANIFEST "FUNCTIONS" OF WITCHCRAFT FOR THE INDIVIDUAL NAVAHO

The manifest "functions" are limited in number. So far as practice is concerned, witchcraft is obviously a means of attaining wealth, gaining women, disposing of enemies and "being mean." In short, witchcraft is a potential avenue to supernatural power. Power seems to be an important central theme in Navaho culture of which gaining wealth, disposing of enemies, and even, to some extent, obtaining possession of women are merely particular examples.

An inadequate memory, lack of the fees for teachers (the teacher of witchcraft needs to be paid only by the sacrifice of a sibling!), or other factors prevent some Navahos from attaining supernatural power through the socially approved route of becoming a singer. For such persons learning witchcraft is a manifest antidote to deprivation. Indeed, the presence of the witchcraft patterns must be a constant "temptation" to Navahos who lust for power but have not attained it by other means. The practice of witchcraft similarly supplies an outlet to those Navaho in whom aggressive impulses are peculiarly strong. Old Navahos often comment that the men who used to organize war parties were of a special personality type: "they were the ones that always liked to stir up trouble." One may speculate that personalities who found leading a war party an especially congenial occupation would find becoming a witch the most congenial substitute in the contemporary Navaho world.

But since most of the data evidence belief in witchcraft rather than practice of witchcraft, our major attention must be given to seeing how witchcraft "functions" in the lives of Navahos who are not witches. At the manifest level, it may be pointed out, first of all, that witchcraft stories have the obvious value of the dramatic—the exciting story. They partially fulfil the "functions" which books and magazines, plays and moving pictures carry out in our culture. In the second place, it must be realized that witchcraft ideology gives a partial answer to the problems which disturb the Navaho as well as other peoples—stubborn illness without apparent etiology, death without visible cause. One of man's peculiarities is that he requires "reasons" for the occurrence of events. One of the manifest "functions" of belief in witchcraft is that such belief supplies answers to questions which would otherwise be perplexing— and because perplexing, disturbing. More specifically, the availability of witchcraft as an explanation helps to maintain the Navaho's conviction in the efficacy of the curing ceremonials. If a chant which has been per- formed without a hitch by a singer of great reputation fails, nevertheless, to cure, the Navaho need not wonder: "Are the chants really any good? Or are we perhaps, after all, hopelessly at the mercy of the forces that cause illness?" A culturally acceptable alternative explanation is at hand: "The disease was caused by witchcraft, *that's why* the chant didn't work." This line of reasoning also gives an obvious out for the singer who has failed. . . .

But would the convenience of witchcraft as an explanation be, of itself, sufficient to ensure the survival of such beliefs at the expense of more rational modes of explanation? It must be remembered that acculturated Navahos characteristically continue to fear witches after they have lost all trust in Navaho medicine. . . . To understand fully why witchcraft belief has such survival value among the Navaho, we must look at the latent "functions" of belief in witchcraft for the individual.

LATENT "FUNCTIONS" OF WITCHCRAFT FOR THE INDIVIDUAL NAVAHO

The most obvious of these is that the individual can capitalize on the credence of his fellows in these patterns to gain the center of the stage for himself. It is difficult to know how often Navahos complain of the symp- toms of witchcraft as a device for getting attention. But close analysis of some cases where the personal context is well-known indicates that this mechanism is sometimes employed. A high proportion of those who have suddenly "fainted" or gone into a semi-trance state at "squaw dances" or other large gatherings are women or men who are somewhat neglected or occupy low status. The rich and powerful (who are usually, of course, somewhat aggressive types) tend to announce or to have it discovered by a diagnostician in the privacy of their homes that they are victims of witchcraft. But, out of 17 cases where I have the relevant facts, 11 of those who collapsed at large gatherings were women and 13 of those were persons known to receive a minimum of prestige responses in the normal run of things. These facts fit well with similar phenomena which have been reported from other cultures. It is a commonplace that European and New England witch trials were frequently started by publicity seekers, often children. It is probable that in the South frustrated women make up a considerable proportion of the accusations which get Negroes lynched. Linton points out that among the Tanala of Madagascar "most of those subject to *tromba* [a neurotic seizure indicated by an extreme desire to dance] are persons of minor importance. . . ."

A second latent "function" of the corpus of witchcraft lore for individuals is that of providing a socially recognized channel for the expression (in varying degrees of obliquity) of the culturally disallowed. Certain aberrant impulses (such as those toward incest and necrophilia) may achieve some release in phantasy . . .

Quantitatively more significant as adjustive responses are the ways in which witchcraft beliefs and practices allow the expression of direct and displaced antagonisms. . . . Witchcraft is, of course, only one of many possible ways of handling this problem and is indeed only one of a number of ways utilized by the Navaho. Fights occur; aggression is expressed against dead relatives as ghosts; there are other cultural devices for meeting the hostility problem which will be discussed in due course. But if myths and rituals provide the principal means of *sublimating* the Navaho individual's anti-social tendencies, witchcraft provides one of the principally socially understood means of *expressing* them. . . .

NAVAHO WAYS OF HANDLING HOSTILE IMPULSES

In no society is socialization attained without frustration. In every adult society socialized individuals experience some deprivations and at least occasionally find themselves in conflict situations. They feel some resentments when their attempts to satisfy biological and other needs run afoul of the prohibitions of the culture as mediated by cultural agents, and the interference of other persons competing for the same gratifications. Always and everywhere human beings have hostile impulses toward other human beings. But every society restricts and channels the expression of hostility. Intra-group killing is universally forbidden. In our society, the son who resents his father's tyranny must sharply suppress the expression of such resentment on pain of losing economic support. In most cases, when husbands and wives freely manifest their hostilities toward each other, the marriage comes to an end. Since most hostile impulses must to greater or lesser extent be suppressed or repressed, there is need in every society for hate satisfaction. But unless there are some forms of hating which are socially approved and justified, everyone will remain in an intolerable conflict situation, and neuroticism will be endemic in the population.

Aggression, whether overt or masked, is not, to be sure, the only possible adjustive response. Withdrawal, passivity, sublimation, conciliation, flight and other responses are sometimes effective in reducing the motivation of those who have been deprived or threatened. Some social systems are much more efficient than others in directing hate satisfactions into oblique and socially non-disruptive channels. It would be too much to say that all societies *must* necessarily have their "witches," i.e., persons whom it is proper to fear and hate and, under defined circumstances, to behave aggressively toward. "Witches" are not very prominent in the sentiment systems of some societies. But no culture which has yet been described leaves "witches" out of its definition of the situation for every sector of life or for every group within the society. "Witches" in this very general sense of "scapegoats" have probably played some part in all social structures since Palaeolithic times. Most contemporary European societies feature such witches quite obtrusively. These "witches" may be either a minority within the society or an external society. Thus the Nazis have had the Jews; the Fascists have their Communists and their "plutocratic democracies"; "liberals" have the Jesuits (and vice versa). For a period of time the French had the Germans.

To make the broadest possible structural comparison, Navahos blame their troubles on witches instead of upon "Jews" or "niggers." We should be putting the matter over simply but not altogether incorrectly if we said that a belief in witchcraft was Navaho culture's substitute for "race prejudice." Just as witchcraft practice has the manifest "function" of providing a channel through which direct aggression can be released, so witchcraft belief has the latent "function" of channeling displaced aggression. But in place of selecting its "scapegoats" by the color of their skin or by their separate religious tradition or by their occupation, Navaho culture chooses certain individuals who are supposed to work evil by secret supernatural techniques. . . .

One possible overt response which may be regarded as a substitute for aggression is that which some psychologists would call "leaving the field." This may take the form of social withdrawal or that of flight from reality through the use of narcotics. Both these types of response are employed by the Navaho, but there are circumstances which prevent their bringing large scale relief. Within the last five years peyote suddenly became very popular in restricted areas of the Navaho country. However, conflict with the native religion and the vigorous opposition of the Indian Service have sharply curtailed this practice. The use of alcohol is much more widespread. The compulsive (and apparently increasing) propensity of Navahos for drinking must, in part, be understood as a response which produces adjustment by deadening certain sensations and by granting release from some of the specific enactments of the culture. Here again, though, the interference of Indian and white police makes this a device which can be used only very occasionally by all save that minority of the Navaho population which lives in continued proximity to white bootleggers. . . .

LATENT "FUNCTIONS" OF WITCHCRAFT: AGGRESSION RELEASE

The two most important latent "functions" of Navaho witchcraft for the individual relate to the crucial Navaho problems of aggression and anxiety. These latent "functions" seem to be less related to individual status than to certain general pressures which affect (to varying degrees) all Navahos. Let us briefly review the picture. The intra-societal tensions which are present in every society are aggravated in the case of the Navaho by their uncushioned dependence upon a capricious physical environment, by emotional inbreeding, by insecurity consequent upon the pressure of our culture and society, by restrictions upon various methods for discharge of aggressive impulses. Non-aggressive ways of handling hostile feelings are inadequate. Most direct forms of intra-group aggression constitute too great a challenge to social solidarity and to subsistence survival. Under these circumstances the beliefs and practices related to witchcraft constitute eminently adjustive cultural solutions for Navaho individuals.

DISPLACEMENT OF AGGRESSION

There are few socially legitimated hostilities among the Navaho. The witch is the person whom the ideal patterns of the culture say it is not only proper but necessary to hate. Instead of saying all the bitter things one has felt against one's stingy and repressive father-in-law (which would threaten one's own economic security as well as bring down upon one's head unpleasant social disapproval), one can obtain some relief by venting one's spleen against a totally unrelated witch in the community. This displaced aggression does not expose one to punishment so long as one is discreet in the choice of the intimates to whom one talks. And if one rages against a witch who isn't even in the locality but lives over the mountain a safe hundred miles away one is perfectly assured against reprisals.

The fact that a high proportion of witchcraft gossip refers to *distant* witches makes Navaho witchcraft much more adaptive than most patterns which center witch activity within the group. At Zuni where everyone knows everyone else the effect appears to be much more destructive. But in a Navaho story the witch can be specified as a Navaho—with a gain to the imaginative reality of the tale—and yet never have been seen by narrator and hearers, or perhaps seen only rarely when he visited the community to conduct a ceremonial. . . .

DIRECT AGGRESSION

Witchcraft, however, not only provides "scapegoats" against whom hostile impulses may be displaced. Under some circumstances, witchcraft provides a means for attack upon the actual targets of my hostile feelings. If I am a singer and smarting under professional jealousy of another singer I can whisper accusations of witchcraft against my rival. Or I can mitigate the burning of my envy of a rich neighbor by suggesting that perhaps the way his riches were obtained would not bear too careful scrutiny. If my wife runs off with another man, I can often say to my relatives "Oh, he got her by Frenzy Witchcraft." This both permits intensified and socially justified indignation on my part and also reduces my shame: it is not that the seducer is a better man than I—*he* used magical powers. . . .

LATENT "FUNCTIONS" OF WITCHCRAFT:
HANDLING THE ANXIETY PROBLEM

It is almost inevitable, given the generalized *beta press* and the amount of hostility which has to be repressed, that Navaho life today should be anxiety ridden. But nothing is more intolerable to human beings than being persistently disturbed without being able to say why or without being able to phrase the matter in such a way that some relief or control is potentially available. It is worth noting that man not only craves reasons and explanations, but in most cases these reasons involve some form of personification, some humanlike agency either natural or supernatural. It seems that only a small minority among highly sophisticated peoples can fairly face impersonal forces and the phenomena of chance. Doubtless the explanation for this attitude is that during the years of dawning consciousness practically everything that happens is mediated by human agents—the parents or their substitutes.

Witchcraft belief allows the verbalization of anxiety in a framework that is understandable and which implies the possibility of doing something. Witches (who are living individuals) are potentially controllable by the society; the caprices of the environment are not. Likewise, it is important for the adjustment of the individual that witchcraft is a focus of anxiety which the culture recognizes as valid. The symptoms of anxiety which the members of different societies manifest under conditions of stress are characteristically different. For a Navaho, witchcraft is something in terms of which he can acceptably justify his anxiety to his fellows. It is a peculiarly adjustive response in that he can justify his anxiety without taking any blame himself. For in the case of those illnesses which are normally treated by Holy Way chants the ultimate etiology from the Navaho point of view rests in the infraction of some cultural prohibition. To some degree, it is the individual's own fault that he is sick. However, the Navaho consider the witch victim as guiltless. Thus, between various possibilities for the objectification of anxiety, witchcraft is one of those which is most wholly advantageous. But the cultural validity is the issue which concerns us immediately here.

If a Navaho merely complained or put forward an explanation which might carry weight in another culture, the reaction of his family would eventually be indifference or active irritation. For a Navaho to tell his unacculturated family that he was suffering from lack of vitamin B_1 would affect them much as we should be affected if a member of our family told us that he was ill because last year he was careless enough to look upon a cow that had been struck by lightning. But so long as a Navaho or his family or a diagnostician can suggest that a witch is responsible for uneasiness or illness social support is assured. . . .

Belief in witchcraft would not, of course, be an adjustive response for the individual if it only defined and justified anxiety. When fright is instilled sufficiently, organic sickness and death may and do result. Most organisms can stand flashes of anxiety. But, when flashes of anxiety become transformed into acute attacks, anxiety ceases to have the function of mobilizing the defenses of the organism and becomes a self-contained menace. A distinguished physiologist has recently set forth the probable bodily mechanisms involved. There can be no question of the reality of the threat to the organism's survival. Therefore, if witchcraft fear is to be at all an adjustive response, the culture must also, through the techniques of protection and cure, provide means of alleviating the distress. There must be organized, institutionalized attempts to relieve anxiety.

It is to be noted that the most powerful of these do not stop with the individual's taking a self-administered medicine. The expensive ceremonials, demanding the presence and interaction of the patient's family with practitioners who represent the general social organization, symbolically affirm that the victim is succored by the whole social structure. . . .

WITCHCRAFT AS AN ADAPTIVE STRUCTURE FOR THE LOCAL GROUP AND FOR NAVAHO SOCIETY

That most Navahos believe in witchcraft is, up to a point, a danger not merely to the solidarity but to the very existence of the society. The informant's remark, "If the white people hadn't stopped us, we'd have killed each other all off" has more than a grain of truth in it. Paradoxically, however, belief in witchcraft, so long as other forces hold the disruptive tendencies in check, is an adaptive structure of a high order. The principal manifest "function" is that witchcraft lore affirms solidarity by dramatically defining what is bad: namely, all secret and malevolent activities against the health, property and lives of fellow tribesmen. This sanction is reinforced by attributing to witches all the stigmata of evil: incest, nakedness and other kinds of forbidden knowledge and act.

But credence in witchcraft likewise has many specific latent "functions" which make for the preservation of the group's and the society's equilibrium. It tends, along with other social mechanisms, to prevent undue accumulation of wealth and tempers too rapid rise in social mobility. A rich man knows that if he is stingy with his relatives or fails to dispense generous hospitality to all and sundry he is likely to be spoken of as a witch. Individuals know also that if they accumulate wealth too rapidly the whisper will arise that they got their start by robbing the dead of their jewelry. In a society like the Navaho which is competitive and capitalistic, on the one hand, and still familistic on the other, any ideology which has the effect of slowing down economic mobility is decidedly adaptive. . . .

WITCHCRAFT AS A TECHNIQUE OF SOCIAL CONTROL

Accusation of witchcraft is, indeed, a threat which Navaho social organization uses to keep all "agitators," all individuals who threaten to disrupt the smooth functioning of the community, in check. When Manuelito in 1884 brought about the execution of more than forty "witches," there is good evidence that this was a very astute way of silencing leaders throughout the Navaho country who were beginning to advocate another armed resistance to the whites. Manuelito was convinced that the only hope for his tribe lay in peace. He knew that if he caused the trouble-makers to be arrested and turned over to the United States government his own prestige would suffer and possibly be destroyed. But they could be tried and killed as witches with full social approval. I may here be attributing undue prescience to Manuelito, but the interpretation has the support both of Navaho informants and qualified white observers. . . .

DISCUSSION AND SUMMARY

After presenting patterned cultural theory and practice relating to one sector of Navaho culture which may be referred to in English by the one word "witchcraft," an attempt at "explanation" has been made. That is, I have tried to show that certain available data bear a determinate relationship to other data and to generalized propositions. In particular, we have seen that the data did not bear a haphazard relationship to the physical environment, economic problems, health conditions, the concrete situation of the individual and to such other sectors of culture as the forms of habit training and general social organization.

The study of Navaho witchcraft does not stop, then, with the bringing to light of bits of curious and sometimes terrible belief. Systematic analysis of observed behaviors and of the latent and manifest content of interview material suggests clues as to the stresses and strains of Navaho social organization and the dynamics of social process generally. . . .

But witchcraft is not something which need be viewed with native abhorrence. It has been seen to have its manifest and its latent "functions" both for the individual and for social groups. At the same time, witchcraft has its *cost* for the individual and for the group. Given the conditions of Navaho life and the Navaho socialization process, given the guarantee in the background that the Indian Service will prevent wholesale slaughter of "witches," Navaho witchcraft does constitute an adjustive and an adaptive structure. Its *cost* is projected aggression and some social disruption. Probably, as a natural consequence of the insistence that witchcraft *does* have important adaptive and adjustive effects, the *cost* has been too little stressed. In many cases witchcraft belief undoubtedly does more to promote fear and timidity than to relieve aggressive tendencies. The fears consequent upon witchcraft tend to restrict the life activities of some persons, to curtail their social participation. Perhaps the witchcraft pattern assemblage tends to be mainly adjustive for individuals who tend to be aggressive, mainly disruptive for those who tend to be non-aggressive. Such a view would fit well with the suggestions which have been made of the relationship between witchcraft patterns and war patterns. . . .

Another aspect of the *cost* of witchcraft belief to which attention should be drawn is that probably this is a basis for unwillingness to undertake or to continue the burdens of leadership. For example, a young Navaho who has made a splendid record during the past two years as a judge has told his friends that he was resigning because he felt that his father's serious illness was traceable to witchcraft activities occasioned by resentment at some of the judge's decisions. Likewise, to counterbalance the tendency to economic leveling, there is to be reckoned the power and instrument for domination which accrues to the rich insofar as they are dreaded as witches. . . .

7. An American Sacred Ceremony
W. LLOYD WARNER *

THIS SELECTION HAS A BEARING ON SEVERAL PROBLEMS THAT WE HAVE RAISED.
THE QUESTION OF THE RELATIONSHIP BETWEEN RELIGION AND SOCIAL INTE-
GRATION, THE WAYS IN WHICH A HETEROGENEOUS SOCIETY SECURES A SENSE
OF UNITY, THE FUNCTIONS OF CEREMONY, THE QUESTION OF FUNCTIONAL AL-
TERNATIVES, AND OTHER PROBLEMS ARE EXAMINED HERE.

The integration and smooth functioning of the social life of a modern
community are very difficult because of its complexity. American communities are filled with churches, each claiming great authority and each
with its separate sacred symbol system. Many of them are in conflict,
and all of them in opposition to one another. Many associations, such as
the Masons, the Odd Fellows, and the like, have sacred symbol systems
which partly separate them from the whole community. The traditions of
foreign-born groups contribute to the diversity of symbolic life. The
evidence is clear for the conflict among these systems.

It is the thesis of this chapter that the Memorial Day ceremonies and
subsidiary rites (such as those of Armistice Day) of today, yesterday, and
tomorrow are rituals of a sacred symbol system which functions periodically to unify the whole community, with its conflicting symbols and its
opposing, autonomous churches and associations. It is contended here
that in the Memorial Day ceremonies the anxieties which man has about
death are confronted with a system of sacred beliefs about death which
gives the individuals involved and the collectivity of individuals a feeling
of well-being. Further, the feeling of triumph over death by collective
action in the Memorial Day parade is made possible by re-creating the
feeling of well-being and the sense of group strength and individual
strength in the group power, which is felt so intensely during the wars
when the veterans' associations are created and when the feeling so necessary for the Memorial Day's symbol system is originally experienced.

Memorial Day is a cult of the dead which organizes and integrates the
various faiths and national and class groups into a sacred unity. It is a
cult of the dead organized around the community cemeteries. Its principal themes are those of the sacrifice of the soldier dead for the living
and the obligation of the living to sacrifice their individual purposes for

* Abridged from Chapter 1 of *American Life: Dream and Reality*.

the good of the group, so that they, too, can perform their spiritual obligations.

MEMORIAL DAY CEREMONIES

We shall first examine the Memorial Day ceremony of an American town for evidence. The sacred symbolic behavior of Memorial Day, in which scores of the town's organizations are involved, is ordinarily divided into four periods. During the year separate rituals are held by many of the associations for their dead, and many of these activities are connected with later Memorial Day events. In the second phase, preparations are made during the last three or four weeks for the ceremony itself, and some of the associations perform public rituals. The third phase consists of the scores of rituals held in all the cemeteries, churches, and halls of the associations. These rituals consist of speeches and highly ceremonialized behavior. They last for two days and are climaxed by the fourth and last phase, in which all the separate celebrants gather in the center of the business district on the afternoon of Memorial Day. The separate organizations, with their members in uniform or with fitting insignia, march through the town, visit the shrines and monuments of the hero dead, and, finally, enter the cemetery. Here dozens of ceremonies are held, most of them highly symbolic and formalized. Let us examine the actual ritual behavior in these several phases of the ceremony.

The two or three weeks before the Memorial Day ceremonies are usually filled with elaborate preparations by each participating group. Meetings are held, and patriotic pronouncements are sent to the local paper by the various organizations which announce what part each organization is to play in the ceremony. Some of the associations have Memorial Day processions, memorial services are conducted, the schools have patriotic programs, and the cemeteries are cleaned and repaired. Graves are decorated by families and associations and new gravestones purchased and erected. The merchants put up flags before their establishments, and residents place flags above their houses.

All these events are recorded in the local paper, and most of them are discussed by the town. The preparation of public opinion for an awareness of the importance of Memorial Day and the rehearsal of what is expected from each section of the community are done fully and in great detail. The latent sentiments of each individual, each family, each church, school, and association for its own dead are thereby stimulated and related to the sentiments for the dead of the nation. . . .

Through the early preparatory period of the ceremony, through all its phases and in every rite, the emphasis in all communities is always on sacrifice—the sacrifice of the lives of the soldiers of the city, willingly given for democracy and for their country. The theme is always that the gift of their lives was voluntary; that it was freely given and therefore above selfishness or thoughts of self-preservation; and, finally, that the "sacrifice on the altars of their country" was done for everyone. The red poppy became a separate symbol from McCrae's poem "In Flanders Fields." The poem expressed and symbolized the sentiments experienced by the soldiers and people of the country who went through the first war. The editor makes the poppy refer directly to the "blood of the boys slaughtered." In ritual language he then recites the names of some of the city's "sacrified dead," and "the altars" (battles) where they were killed. "Remember Dexter and Smith killed at Belleau Wood," he says. "Remember O'Flaherty killed near Château-Thierry, Stulavitz killed in the Bois d'Ormont, Kelley killed at Côte de Châtillon, Jones near the Bois de Montrebeaux, Kilnikap in the St.-Mihiel offensive, and the other brave boys who died in camp or on stricken fields. Remember the living boys of the Legion on Saturday."

The names selected by the editor covered most of the ethnic and religious groups of the community. They included Polish, Russian, Irish, French-Canadian, and Yankee names. The use of such names in this context emphasized the fact that the voluntary sacrifice of a citizen's life was equalitarian. They covered the top, middle, and bottom of the several classes. The newspapers throughout the country each year print similar lists, and their editorials stress the equality of sacrifice by all classes and creeds.

The topic for the morning services of the churches on the Sunday before Memorial Day ordinarily is the meaning of Memorial Day to the town and to the people as Christians. All the churches participate. . . .

The Rev. Hugh McKellar chose as his text, "Be thou faithful until death." He said:

Memorial Day is a day of sentiment and when it loses that, it loses all its values. We are all conscious of the danger of losing that sentiment. What we need today is more sacrifice, for there can be no achievement without sacrifice. There are too many out today preaching selfishness. Sacrifice is necessary to a noble living. In the words of our Lord, "Whosoever shall save his life shall lose it and whosoever shall lose his life in My name shall save it." It is only those who sacrifice personal gain and will to power and personal ambition who ever accomplish anything for their nation. Those who expect to save the nation will not get wealth and power for themselves.

Memorial Day is a religious day. It is a day when we get a vision of the unbreakable brotherhood and unity of spirit which exists and still exists, no matter what race or creed or color, in the country where all men have equal rights. . . .

There were many more Memorial Day sermons, most of which had this same theme. Many of them added the point that the Christian God had given his life for all. That afternoon during the same ceremony the cemeteries, memorial squares named for the town's dead, the lodge halls, and the churches had a large number of rituals. Among them was the "vacant chair." A row of chairs decorated with flags and wreaths, each with the name of a veteran who had died in the last year, was the center of this ceremony held in a church. Most of the institutions were represented in the ritual. . . .

In all the other services the same themes were used in the speeches, most of which were in ritualized, oratorical language, or were expressed in the ceremonials themselves. Washington, the father of his country, first in war and peace, had devoted his life not to himself but to his country. Lincoln had given his own life, sacrificed on the altar of his country. Most of the speeches implied or explicitly stated that divine guidance was involved and that these mundane affairs had supernatural implications. They stated that the revered dead had given the last ounce of devotion in following the ideals of Washington and Lincoln and the Unknown Soldier and declared that these same principles must guide us, the living. The beliefs and values of which they spoke referred to a world beyond the natural. Their references were to the supernatural.

On Memorial Day morning the separate rituals, publicly performed, continued. The parade formed in the early afternoon in the business district. Hundreds of people, dressed in their best, gathered to watch the various uniformed groups march in the parade. Crowds collected along the entire route. The cemeteries, carefully prepared for the event, and the graves of kindred covered with flowers and flags and wreaths looked almost gay. . . .

After the several ceremonies in the Elm Hill Cemetery, the parade re-formed and started the march back to town, where it broke up. The firing squad of the American Legion fired three salutes, and a bugler sounded the "Last Post" at the cemetery entrance as they departed. This, they said, was a "general salute for all the dead in the cemetery."

Here we see people who are Protestant, Catholic, Jewish, and Greek Orthodox involved in a common ritual in a graveyard with their common dead. Their sense of separateness was present and expressed in the different ceremonies, but the parade and the unity gained by doing everything at one time emphasized the oneness of the total group. Each ritual also stressed the fact that the war was an experience where everyone sacrificed and some died, not as members of a separate group, but as citizens of a whole community. . . .

HOW SUCH CEREMONIES FUNCTION IN THE COMMUNITY

Memorial Day and similar ceremonies are one of the several forms of collective representations which Durkheim so brilliantly defined and interpreted in *The Elementary Forms of the Religious Life*. He said: "Religious representations are collective representations which express collective realities." Religious collective representations are symbol systems which are composed of beliefs and rites which relate men to sacred beings. Beliefs are "states of opinion and consist in representations"; rites are "determined modes of action" which are expressions of, and refer to, religious belief. They are *visible* signs (symbols) of the invisible belief. The visible rite of baptism, for example, may express invisible beliefs about cleansing the newborn infant of sin and relating him to the Christian community.

Ceremonies, periodically held, serve to impress on men their social nature and make them aware of something beyond themselves which they feel and believe to be sacred. This intense feeling of belonging to something larger and more powerful than themselves and of having part of this within them as part of them is symbolized by the belief in sacred beings, which is given a visual symbol by use of designs which are the emblems of the sacred entities, e.g., the Cross of the Christian churches. . . .

We said earlier that the Memorial Day rites of American towns are sacred collective representations and a modern cult of the dead. They are a cult because they consist of a system of sacred beliefs and dramatic rituals held by a group of people who, when they congregate, represent the whole community. They are sacred because they ritually relate the living to sacred things. They are a cult because the members have not been formally organized into an institutionalized church with a defined theology but depend on informal organization to bring into order their sacred activities. They are called a "cult" here, because this term most accurately places them in a class of social phenomena which can be clearly identified in the sacred behavior of non-European societies.

The cult system of sacred belief puts into the organized form of concepts those sentiments about death which are common to everyone in the community. These sentiments are composed of fears of death, which conflict with the social reassurances that our culture provides us to combat such anxieties. These assurances, usually acquired in childhood and thereby carrying some of the authority of the adults who provided them, are a composite of theology and folk belief. The deep anxieties to which we refer include anticipation of our deaths, of the deaths or possible deaths of loved ones, and, less powerfully, of the deaths or possible deaths of those we know and of men in general.

Each man's church provides him and those of his faith with a set of beliefs and a way of acting to face these problems; but his church and those of other men do not equip him with a common set of social beliefs and rituals which permit him to unite with all his fellows to confront this common and most feared of all his enemies. The Memorial Day rite and other subsidiary rituals connected with it form a cult which partially satisfies this need for common action on a common problem. It dramatically expresses the sentiments of unity of all the living among themselves, of all the living to all the dead, and of all the living and dead as a group to the gods. The gods—Catholic, Protestant, and Jewish—lose their sectarian definitions, limitations, and foreignness among themselves and become objects of worship for the whole group and the protectors of everyone. . . .

The Memorial Day rite is a cult of the dead, but not just of the dead as such, since by symbolically elaborating sacrifice of human life for the country through, or identifying it with, the Christian church's sacred sacrifice of their god, the deaths of such men also become powerful sacred symbols which organize, direct, and constantly revive the collective ideals of the community and the nation.

The Social Psychology of Religion

Having defined the sociology of religion in terms that include social psychological aspects, we can appropriately include readings that are primarily concerned with motivational factors in religious behavior. Analyses that relate individual tendencies to social situations are particularly appropriate. This approach is well illustrated in the papers by Parsons and Fromm. The work of James is more strictly psychological, but his famous description of "the sick soul" is quite readily brought into the framework of contemporary personality studies, with their broader theoretical scope. Eckardt's paper, the last in this section, is an interesting interpretation of current religious trends.

8. Motivation of Religious Belief and Behavior

TALCOTT PARSONS *

PROBABLY NO AMERICAN SOCIOLOGIST HAS CONTRIBUTED MORE TO THE STUDY OF RELIGION THAN PROFESSOR PARSONS. THE SPECIAL SIGNIFICANCE OF HIS WORK HAS BEEN HIS INSISTENCE THAT AN ADEQUATE THEORY, WHETHER IT BE OF RELIGION OR OF ANY OTHER PHASE OF HUMAN BEHAVIOR, MUST BE CONCERNED WITH THE INTERPLAY OF SOCIAL, CULTURAL, AND PERSONALITY FORCES. THE SELECTION HERE IS A BRIEF STATEMENT OF THE MOTIVATIONAL FACTORS IN RELIGION.

. . . we may now turn to some aspects of the "social psychology" of religion, of the characteristics of man as an "actor" in a situation, and of that situation, which helps us to understand his need for and relations to religious institutions. We will develop this theme in two sections; in the present one we will attempt to sketch some of the main sources of the motivation to religious belief and behavior, and in that following to indicate some of the complicated interrelations between religious and secular motivations on this level.

Man is distinguished from the other animals, from the point of view of the social scientist, above all by the fact that he is a creator and bearer of culture. He creates and lives by systems of symbols and of artifacts; he not only modifies his environment but his orientation to it is generalized in terms of systems of symbolic meaning; he communicates with his fellow men through language and other symbols; he perpetuates and develops his knowledge, and he expresses his feelings, not directly and crudely, but in elaborately symbolic form.

A "culture" is not and cannot be just a discrete collection of disconnected artifacts and symbols, but to a greater or lesser degree must constitute a *system*. It must, that is, have coherence as a set of orientations which tie together the many particular aspects of men's experience and needs. Above all it has three types of functions. In the cognitive aspects, as a system of beliefs, it attempts to answer man's questions about himself and the world he lives in, and we all know that we cannot consciously hold contradictory beliefs without strain. Secondly, it provides

* From *Religious Perspectives of College Teaching in Sociology and Social Psychology*, pp. 9–15.

"forms" or expressive symbols for expressing and communicating his feelings, forms which conform to standards of "taste." Finally, and from the sociological point of view perhaps most important, it provides standards for evaluation above all the moral standards which regulate man's conduct, particularly in his relations with his fellows. It can be proved quite definitely that once the step from regulation by "instinct" to the plastic dependence on learned patterns of behavior has been taken by man as organism, a society of men cannot subsist without what sociologists call the institutionalization of a relatively consistent system of patterns of culture, above all of moral values.

The role of culture in human life implies that men must be concerned, in a sense somewhat different from the animals, with the *meaning* of their experience, that is, not merely with whether a given experience gratifies a wish or fills a need or contrariwise involves pain or deprivation, but also with the *fit* between the *expectations* of experience which have been defined for him in his culture, and the *actuality* which he himself experiences.

There is in every system of human action, in every society, a smooth, "normal" pattern of everyday functioning, of ways in which people go "about their business" without particular strain, where the means available to them are adequate to attain the goals they have been taught to strive for, and where the all-important other people fulfill their expectations. But if all human life were like that, religion would certainly not have the significance that it does. We would be much more likely to think of the "problems" of life as mainly of a practical "utilitarian" kind, to be solved by good "horse sense."

There are certain fundamental respects in which this is an inadequate picture of the human life situation. In whatever kind of society *some* human expectations, in the fulfillment of which people have acquired a deep emotional investment, are doomed to frustration. These frustrations are of two main types. One of them consists in the fact that men are "hit" by events which they either cannot foresee and prepare for, or control, or both; to which, however, they must make major adjustments, sometimes practical but always emotional. The type case of this kind of frustration is the occurrence of premature death. Certainly the fact that though we all know we have to die almost no man knows when he will die is one of the cardinal facts of the human situation. But not only for the person facing death himself, if he has time to think about it, but quite clearly for the survivors, there is a major problem of adjustment, for the simple reason that the human individual as an object of emotional attachment is of such fundamental importance. Even the loss of a "beloved enemy" can, we know, be very upsetting. Though religious orientations to death, which are universal and fundamental to religion, contain many shadings of belief about the "life after death," the fundamental feature of this orientation is not "wishful thinking." As one historian of religion has put it, "No major religion has ever claimed to be able to 'beat death.' " [1] The dead are dead, and cannot be brought back to life; but the living must still adjust themselves to that fact. From the point of view of the social scientist, what they believe and do in this situation has significance as a set of "mechanisms" which in some ways facilitate this adjustment. From the secular social point of view to hold funeral ceremonies does not "accomplish anything," the functions of such ceremonies are "latent," but they may none the less be highly important.

In general it is extremely conspicuous that ceremonialism not only concerns the directly bereaved, but directly symbolizes the belongingness of the deceased and of the bereaved in larger social groupings. On the one hand these larger groups which are not so directly affected give their "support" to the bereaved, but on the other they set a "tone" for the occasion which in general says, "the traditional values of the society must be upheld." Death must be only a temporary interruption, the important thing on one level is to "get over it" and to go on living. Though it is by no means obvious, there are many features of funeral ceremonies which are closely similar to those of psychotherapy.

There are other types of uncontrollable events besides death which have what in certain respects is a similar bearing on human interests, natural catastrophes being one of them. Furthermore it should be noted that not only frustration in the usual sense, but unexpected and therefore "unearned" good fortune may also have an upsetting effect and require processes of adjustment. Perhaps our own Thanksgiving fits in that category. The Pilgrim Fathers may well have felt that they were extremely "lucky," or as they said, favored by God, to have survived their first terrible year in the wilderness at all.

A second type of frustrating experience is connected with what has come to be called in a special sense "uncertainty." By this is meant the very common type of situation where there is a strong emotional investment in the success of certain human endeavors, where energy and skill undoubtedly count for much, but where unknown and/or uncontrollable factors may and often do intervene to upset any "reasonable" balance between action and success. The exposure of agriculture the world over, with few exceptions, to the vagaries of uncontrollable and unpredictable weather, is one of the most important examples. No matter how industri-

---

[1] A. D. Nock, in unpublished lectures.

ous and capable a farmer may be, his crops may be ruined by drought or flood. The field of health is another classical example, and there are a variety of others. The unpredictable character of human conduct in many fields, from love to war, is also prominent.

In all these situations rational techniques must of course loom large; no farmer ever grew good crops by magic alone. But these are the classical situations in which what anthropologists call magic flourishes. Whatever the distinction made, magic is always continuous with religion; it always involves some relation to the strains occasioned by uncertainty, and to human emotional adjustment to such situations. Magical beliefs and practices constitute, from the point of view of social psychology, mechanisms of adjustment to these situations of strain. They give an opportunity to "act out" some of the psychological products of that strain, thus to "place the blame" for the frustration—most conspicuous in the cases of belief in witchcraft. They give people the sense of "doing something about it" in areas where their rational techniques are powerless or untrustworthy. Above all they act as a tonic to self-confidence; they are a protection against allowing the risk of failure to lead to a fatalistic discouragement, the attitude that since success cannot be assured, it is no use trying at all. At the same time, magic may act as a stereotyping agency in situations where empirical knowledge and technique are applicable, and thus block technological advance—this in spite of the fact which Malinowski makes so clear, that magic cannot take the place of rational technique. The Trobriand Islander does not believe that he can make up for failing to cultivate his garden properly by more and better magic; it is a supplement, not a substitute.

The frustrations of established expectations of which we have been speaking pose "problems of meaning" in a double sense. On the one hand, man, being a culture-bearing animal, does not merely "take it" when things go as he does not expect. He has to give these things a meaning, in the first instance emotionally, so that his adjustments to such experiences can become integrated in the *system* of experience, which means among other things that his reactions are coordinated and organized with those of his fellows; he can communicate his feelings and receive adequate responses to his expressions of them.

But beyond this, as we have noted at the beginning of this section, the culture in which a social group lives constitutes a more or less integrated system. As such it must have a certain level of consistency; it must "cover" the principal ranges of men's experience in such a way that all of them to some degree "make sense," together as a whole.

Besides the direct problem of emotional adjustment to the frustration of particular experiences, the "generalization" which is involved in the integration of a cultural system brings up two further particularly crucial "problem" areas. The culture links the experience and expectations of any particular individual or sub group with those of others in a society. There is not only the question of why must this happen *to me*, or to those close to me, but why must it happen at all to anyone? Above all, since men universally seek gratification of their wishes and needs there is the generalized problem of suffering, of why men must endure deprivation and pain and so unequally and haphazardly, or, indeed, at all, and, since all societies must live by moral standards, there is equally the problem of "evil," of why men violate the moral standards of their society and why the "economy" of rewards and punishments fails, as it *always* does to some extent, to balance out. Good fortune and suffering must always, to cultural man, be endowed with meaning. They cannot, except in limiting cases, be accepted as something that "just happens." Similarly it is impossible to live by moral standards and yet be wholly indifferent either to the extent of conformity with them or to the fate of conformists and violators respectively. It is necessarily disconcerting that to some degree "the good die young while the wicked flourish as the green bay tree."

The sociologist is in a position to state that some significant degree of discrepancy between expectations in both these respects and the actual state of affairs in a society is inevitable, though it varies greatly in degree and in incidence. Both expectations of gratification and moral standards vary from society to society, but this fundamental fact of discrepancy seems to be a constant, grounded in the nature of human personality, society and culture and their relations to each other.

This complex of circumstances constitutes from a certain sociological point of view [2] the primary focus of the differential significance of religion in human life. It is made up of aspects of the life situation to which, men being what they are, they cannot remain emotionally indifferent, and which at the same time in the long run they cannot evade. But adequate adjustment on either the emotional or the cognitive level to these situations cannot be worked out through the "ordinary" techniques and attitudes of practical utilitarian life. The content and incidence of the problems vary, but their presence is a constant. Almost another way of putting the essential point is to say that tragedy is of the essence of the human situation.

---

[2] More positive aspects of religion, independent of the strains inherent in the human situation, may be equally important, but are more difficult to get at in the context of the intellectual traditions of modern social science.

In one sense all religious ideas involve what may be called a "transcendental reference"; this indeed is what has been meant here by saying that they concern the "supernatural." But this need not imply that the "locus of values" is put primarily in the "other" world. Indeed "naturalism" in the sense of sanctioning the interests of this life in health, wealth, happiness, long life, is more common than not in religious traditions. But the existence of the transcendental reference plus the tension which necessarily to some degree obtains between "ordinary" expectations and the discrepancies of experience with reference to them, may be related to a development by which the primary locus of value is placed in the transcendental sphere itself, in a life after death, or in some other form of "salvation" from the involvements of ordinary human social life. Indeed the problem of balancing the books of the human economy makes this very likely, though the "displacement" may not be into a transcendental world, but may emphasize a future state of human society, as in Western "progressivism" or "revolutionary" utopianism. Furthermore, the degree of radicality of repudiation of the things of "this world" may vary greatly, from a desire to "reform" some secondary unsatisfactory features of it, to the view that ordinary secular human life is intrinsically evil, that man is sunk in utterly hopeless degradation and sin, and that *only* in transcendental terms is any positive value whatever to be found.

Whatever the situation in these respects, the religious problem par excellence in the more generalized sense is the "justification of the ways of God to man," is "making sense" out of the totality of the human situation, both in the cognitive sense of a "theory" in which the discrepancies and the established order can be brought within a single view, and in emotional adequacy so that man can adjust to his own fate and that of the societies with which he is identified. Thus though religious ideas on the sophisticated levels are "philosophical" in content, we will not speak of them being religious so long as the basis of interest is merely intellectual, the solution of baffling cognitive problems. They become religious only so far as a commitment in emotion and action to their implications becomes involved, as, in that sense, to quote Durkheim, they are "taken seriously."

From the psychological point of view, then, religion has its greatest relevance to the points of maximum strain and tension in human life as well as to positive affirmations of faith in life, often in the face of these strains. It is most deeply and intimately involved with the "emotional" problems of men, precisely as these are related to the higher levels of culture, to the problems to which in the widest sense man finds it most difficult to adjust. . . .

9. A Social Psychological Interpretation of Lutheranism and Calvinism

ERICH FROMM *

THIS WELL-KNOWN ANALYSIS BY FROMM MIGHT EQUALLY WELL HAVE BEEN PLACED IN SECTION 2. ALTHOUGH THE TERMINOLOGY OF FUNCTIONAL THEORY IS NOT USED, THE INTERPRETATION IS SUBSTANTIALLY SIMILAR. ONE MIGHT WELL WRITE, PARAPHRASING A SENTENCE FROM FROMM: THE FUNCTION OF THE QUEST FOR CERTAINTY WAS TO CONQUER, OR TO TRY TO CONQUER, THE UN-BEARABLE DOUBT. IN LATER SECTIONS OF THE BOOK FROM WHICH THIS SELECTION IS DRAWN, FROMM APPLIES A SIMILAR ANALYSIS TO NAZISM AND TO THE ANXIETIES OF MEN IN CONTEMPORARY SOCIETY. HIS DISCUSSION SHOWS HOW RELIGIOUS AND NON-RELIGIOUS PHENOMENA MAY GROW FROM THE SAME SOIL. STUDY OF THE CONDITIONS WHICH PROMOTE ONE RATHER THAN ANOTHER OF THE VARIOUS POSSIBLE RESPONSES TO A SITUATION IS AMONG THE PRIMARY TASKS OF THE SOCIOLOGY OF RELIGION.

If we try now to sum up our discussion of the impact of the social and economic changes on the individual in the fifteenth and sixteenth centuries we arrive at the following picture:

We find the same ambiguity of freedom which we have discussed before. The individual is freed *from* the bondage of economic and political ties. He also gains in positive freedom by the active and independent role which he has to play in the new system. But simultaneously he is freed from those ties which used to give him security and a feeling of belonging. Life has ceased to be lived in a closed world the center of which was man; the world has become limitless and at the same time threatening. By losing his fixed place in a closed world man loses the answer to the meaning of his life; the result is that doubt has befallen him concerning himself and the aim of life. He is threatened by powerful suprapersonal forces, capital and the market. His relationship to his fellow men, with everyone a potential competitor, has become hostile and estranged; he is free—that is, he is alone, isolated, threatened from all sides. Not having the wealth or the power which the Renaissance capitalist had, and also having lost the sense of unity with men and the universe, he is overwhelmed with a sense of his individual nothingness and helplessness. Paradise is lost for good, the individual stands alone and faces

* Abridged from *Escape from Freedom*, pp. 62–102.

the world—a stranger thrown into a limitless and threatening world. The new freedom is bound to create a deep feeling of insecurity, powerlessness, doubt, aloneness, and anxiety. These feelings must be alleviated if the individual is to function successfully.

THE PERIOD OF THE REFORMATION

At this point of development, *Lutheranism* and *Calvinism* came into existence. The new religions were not the religions of a wealthy upper class but of the urban middle class, the poor in the cities, and the peasants. They carried an appeal to these groups because they gave expression to a new feeling of freedom and independence as well as to the feeling of powerlessness and anxiety by which their members were pervaded. But the new religious doctrines did more than give articulate expression to the feelings engendered by a changing economic order. By their teachings they increased them and at the same time offered solutions which enabled the individual to cope with an otherwise unbearable insecurity. . . .

Luther's system, in so far as it differed from the Catholic tradition, has two sides, one of which has been stressed more than the other in the picture of his doctrines which is usually given in Protestant countries. This aspect points out that he gave man independence in religious matters; that he deprived the Church of her authority and gave it to the individual; that his concept of faith and salvation is one of subjective individual experience, in which all responsibility is with the individual and none with an authority which could give him what he cannot obtain himself. There are good reasons to praise this side of Luther's and of Calvin's doctrines, since they are one source of the development of political and spiritual freedom in modern society; a development which, especially in Anglo-Saxon countries, is inseparably connected with the ideas of Puritanism.

The other aspect of modern freedom is the isolation and powerlessness it has brought for the individual, and this aspect has its roots in Protestantism as much as that of independence. Since this book is devoted mainly to freedom as a burden and danger, the following analysis, being intentionally onesided, stresses that side in Luther's and Calvin's doctrines in which this negative aspect of freedom is rooted: their emphasis on the fundamental evilness and powerlessness of man.

Luther assumed the existence of an innate evilness in man's nature, which directs his will for evil and makes it impossible for any man to perform any good deed on the basis of his nature. Man has an evil and vicious nature (*"naturaliter et inevitabiliter mala et vitiata natura"*). The depravity of man's nature and its complete lack of freedom to choose the right is one of the fundamental concepts of Luther's whole thinking. In this spirit he begins his comment on Paul's letter to the Romans: "The essence of this letter is: to destroy, to uproot, and to annihilate all wisdom and justice of the flesh, may it appear—in our eyes and in those of others—ever so remarkable and sincere . . . What matters is that our justice and wisdom which unfold before our eyes are being destroyed and uprooted from our heart and from our vain self." [1]

This conviction of man's rottenness and powerlessness to do anything good on his own merits is one essential condition of God's grace. Only if man humiliates himself and demolishes his individual will and pride will God's grace descend upon him. "For God wants to save us not by our own but by extraneous (*fremde*) justice and wisdom, by a justice that does not come from ourselves and does not originate in ourselves but comes to us from somewhere else . . . That is, a justice must be taught that comes exclusively from the outside and is entirely alien to ourselves." [2]

An even more radical expression of man's powerlessness was given by Luther seven years later in his pamphlet "*De servo arbitrio,*" which was an attack against Erasmus' defense of the freedom of the will. ". . . Thus the human will is, as it were, a beast between the two. If God sit thereon, it wills and goes where God will; as the Psalm saith, 'I was as a beast before thee, nevertheless I am continually with thee.' (Ps. 73. 22, 23.) If Satan sit thereon, it wills and goes as Satan will. Nor is it in the power of its own will to choose, to which rider it will run, nor which it will seek; but the riders themselves contend, which shall have and hold it." [3] Luther declares that if one does not like "to leave out this theme (of free will) altogether (which would be most safe and also most religious) we may, nevertheless, with a good conscience teach that it be used so far as to allow man a 'free will,' not in respect of those who are above him, but in respect only of those beings who are below him . . . God-ward man has no 'free will,' but is a captive, slave, and servant either to the will of God or to the will of Satan." [4] The doctrines that man was a powerless tool in God's hands and fundamentally evil, that his only task was to resign to the will of God, that God could save him as the result of an in-

---

[1] Martin Luther, *Vorlesung über den Römerbrief,* Chapter I, i. (My own translation since no English translation exists.)

[2] *Op. cit.,* Chapter I, i.

[3] Martin Luther, *The Bondage of the Will.* Translated by Henry Cole, M.A., B. Erdmans Publishing Co., Grand Rapids, Michigan, 1931, p. 74.

[4] *Op. cit.,* p. 79. This dichotomy—submission to powers above and domination over those below—is, as we shall see later, characteristic of the attitude of the authoritarian character.

comprehensible act of justice—these doctrines were not the definite answer a man was to give who was so much driven by despair, anxiety, and doubt and at the same time by such an ardent wish for certainty as Luther. He eventually found the answer for his doubts. In 1518 a sudden revelation came to him. Man cannot be saved on the basis of his virtues; he should not even meditate whether or not his works were well pleasing to God; but he can have certainty of his salvation if he has faith. Faith is given to man by God; once man has had the indubitable subjective experience of faith he can also be certain of his salvation. The individual is essentially receptive in this relationship to God. Once man receives God's grace in the experience of faith his nature becomes changed, since in the act of faith he unites himself with Christ, and Christ's justice replaces his own which was lost by Adam's fall. However, man can never become entirely virtuous during his life, since his natural evilness can never entirely disappear.[5]

Luther's doctrine of faith as an indubitable subjective experience of one's own salvation may at first glance strike one as an extreme contradiction to the intense feeling of doubt which was characteristic for his personality and his teachings up to 1518. Yet, psychologically, this change from doubt to certainty, far from being contradictory, has a causal relation. We must remember what has been said about the nature of this doubt: it was not the rational doubt which is rooted in the freedom of thinking and which dares to question established views. It was the irrational doubt which springs from the isolation and powerlessness of an individual whose attitude toward the world is one of anxiety and hatred. This irrational doubt can never be cured by rational answers; it can only disappear if the individual becomes an integral part of a meaningful world. If this does not happen, as it did not happen with Luther and the middle class which he represented, the doubt can only be silenced, driven underground, so to speak, and this can be done by some formula which promises absolute certainty. *The compulsive quest for certainty*, as we find with Luther, *is not the expression of genuine faith but is rooted in the need to conquer the unbearable doubt*. Luther's solution is one which we find present in many individuals today, who do not think in theological terms: namely to find certainty by elimination of the isolated individual self, by becoming an instrument in the hands of an overwhelmingly strong power outside of the individual. For Luther this power was God and in unqualified submission he sought certainty. But although he thus succeeded in silencing his doubts to some extent, they never really disap-

---

[5] Cf. *"Sermo de duplici institia"* (*Luthers Werke*, Weimar ed. Vol. II).

peared; up to his last day he had attacks of doubt which he had to conquer by renewed efforts toward submission. Psychologically, faith has
two entirely different meanings. It can be the expression of an inner re-
latedness to mankind and affirmation of life; or it can be a reaction formation against a fundamental feeling of doubt, rooted in the isolation of
the individual and his negative attitude toward life. Luther's faith had
that compensatory quality.

It is particularly important to understand the significance of doubt
and the attempts to silence it, because this is not only a problem concerning Luther's and, as we shall see soon, Calvin's theology, but it has
remained one of the basic problems of modern man. Doubt is the starting
point of modern philosophy; the need to silence it had a most powerful
stimulus on the development of modern philosophy and science. But although many rational doubts have been solved by rational answers, the
irrational doubt has not disappeared and cannot disappear as long as man
has not progressed from negative freedom to positive freedom. The modern
attempts to silence it, whether they consist in a compulsive striving for
success, in the belief that unlimited knowledge of facts can answer the
quest for certainty, or in the submission to a leader who assumes the responsibility for "certainty"—all these solutions can only eliminate the
awareness of doubt. The doubt itself will not disappear as long as man
does not overcome his isolation and as long as his place in the world
has not become a meaningful one in terms of his human needs.

What is the connection of Luther's doctrines with the psychological
situation of all but the rich and powerful toward the end of the Middle
Ages? As we have seen, the old order was breaking down. The individual
had lost the security of certainty and was threatened by new economic
forces, by capitalists and monopolies; the corporative principle was being replaced by competition; the lower classes felt the pressure of growing exploitation. The appeal of Lutheranism to the lower classes differed
from its appeal to the middle class. The poor in the cities, and even more
the peasants, were in a desperate situation. They were ruthlessly exploited and deprived of traditional rights and privileges. They were in a
revolutionary mood which found expression in peasant uprisings and in
revolutionary movements in the cities. The Gospel articulated their hopes
and expectations as it had done for the slaves and laborers of early Christianity, and led the poor to seek for freedom and justice. In so far as
Luther attacked authority and made the word of the Gospel the center
of his teachings, he appealed to these restive masses as other religious
movements of an evangelical character had done before him.

Although Luther accepted their allegiance to him and supported them, he could do so only up to a certain point; he had to break the alliance when the peasants went further than attacking the authority of the Church and merely making minor demands for the betterment of their lot. They proceeded to become a revolutionary class which threatened to overthrow all authority and to destroy the foundations of a social order in whose maintenance the middle class was vitally interested. For, in spite of all the difficulties we earlier described, the middle class, even its lower stratum, had privileges to defend against the demands of the poor; and therefore it was intensely hostile to revolutionary movements which aimed to destroy not only the privileges of the aristocracy, the Church, and the monopolies, but their own privileges as well.

The position of the middle class between the very rich and the very poor made its reaction complex and in many ways contradictory. They wanted to uphold law and order, and yet they were themselves vitally threatened by rising capitalism. Even the more successful members of the middle class were not wealthy and powerful as the small group of big capitalists was. They had to fight hard to survive and make progress. The luxury of the moneyed class increased their feeling of smallness and filled them with envy and indignation. As a whole, the middle class was more endangered by the collapse of the feudal order and by rising capitalism than they were helped.

Luther's picture of man mirrored just this dilemma. Man is free *from* all ties binding him to spiritual authorities, but this very freedom leaves him alone and anxious, overwhelms him with a feeling of his own individual insignificance and powerlessness. This free, isolated individual is crushed by the experience of his individual insignificance. Luther's theology gives expression to this feeling of helplessness and doubt. The picture of man which he draws in religious terms describes the situation of the individual as it was brought about by the current social and economic evolution. The member of the middle class was as helpless in face of the new economic forces as Luther described man to be in his relationship to God.

But Luther did more than bring out the feeling of insignificance which already pervaded the social classes to whom he preached—he offered them a solution. By not only accepting his own insignificance but by humiliating himself to the utmost, by giving up every vestige of individual will, by renouncing and denouncing his individual strength, the individual could hope to be acceptable to God. Luther's relationship to God was one of complete submission. In psychological terms his concept of faith means: if you completely submit, if you accept your individual insignificance, then the all-powerful God may be willing to love you and

save you. If you get rid of your individual self with all its shortcomings
and doubts by utmost self-effacement, you free yourself from the feeling
of your own nothingness and can participate in God's glory. Thus, while
Luther freed people from the authority of the Church, he made them
submit to a much more tyrannical authority, that of a God who insisted
on complete submission of man and annihilation of the individual self as
the essential condition to his salvation. *Luther's "faith" was the conviction of being loved upon the condition of surrender,* a solution which
has much in common with the principle of complete submission of the
individual to the state and the "leader."

Luther's awe of authority and his love for it appears also in his political
convictions. Although he fought against the authority of the Church,
although he was filled with indignation against the new moneyed class—
part of which was the upper strata of the clerical hierarchy—and although
he supported the revolutionary tendencies of the peasants up to a certain
point, yet he postulated submission to worldly authorities, the princes,
in the most drastic fashion. "Even if those in authority are evil or without faith, nevertheless the authority and its power is good and from God.
. . . Therefore, where there is power and where it flourishes, there it
is and there it remains because God has ordained it." [6] Or he says: "God
would prefer to suffer the government to exist no matter how evil, rather
than allow the rabble to riot, no matter how justified they are in doing
so . . . A prince should remain a prince no matter how tyrannical he
may be. He beheads necessarily only a few since he must have subjects
in order to be a ruler."

The other aspect of his attachment to and awe of authority becomes
visible in his hatred and contempt for the powerless masses, the "rabble,"
especially when they went beyond certain limits in their revolutionary
attempts. In one of his diatribes he writes the famous words: "Therefore
let everyone who can, smite, slay, and stab, secretly or openly, remembering that nothing can be more poisonous, hurtful, or devilish than a rebel.
It is just as when one must kill a mad dog; if you do not strike him he
will strike you, and a whole land with you." [7]

Luther's personality as well as his teachings shows ambivalence toward
authority. On the one hand he is overawed by authority—that of a worldly
authority and that of a tyrannical God—and on the other hand he rebels
against authority—that of the Church. He shows the same ambivalence

[6] *Römerbrief,* 13, 1.
[7] "Against the Robbing and Murdering Hordes of Peasants" (1525); *Works of
Martin Luther,* translation: C. M. Jacobs. A. T. Holman Company, Philadelphia,
1931. Vol. X, IV, p. 411. Cf. H. Marcuse's discussion of Luther's attitude toward
freedom in *Autorität und Familie,* F. Alcan, Paris, 1926.

in his attitude toward the masses. As far as they rebel within the limits he has set he is with them. But when they attack the authorities he approves of, an intense hatred and contempt for the masses comes to the fore. In the chapter which deals with the psychological mechanism of escape we shall show that this simultaneous love for authority and the hatred against those who are powerless are typical traits of the "authoritarian character."

At this point it is important to understand that Luther's attitude towards secular authority was closely related to his religious teachings. In making the individual feel worthless and insignificant as far as his own merits are concerned, in making him feel like a powerless tool in the hands of God, he deprived man of the self-confidence and of the feeling of human dignity which is the premise for any firm stand against oppressing secular authorities. In the course of the historical evolution the results of Luther's teachings were still more far-reaching. Once the individual had lost his sense of pride and dignity, he was psychologically prepared to lose the feeling which had been characteristic of the medieval thinking, namely, that man, his spiritual salvation, and his spiritual aims were the purpose of life; he was prepared to accept a role in which his life became a means to purposes outside of himself, those of economic productivity and accumulation of capital. Luther's views on economic problems were typically medieval, still more so than Calvin's. He would have abhorred the idea that man's life should become a means for economic ends. But while his thinking on economic matters was the traditional one, his emphasis on the nothingness of the individual was in contrast and paved the way for a development in which man not only was to obey secular authorities but had to subordinate his life to the ends of economic achievements. In our day this trend has reached a peak in the Fascist emphasis that it is the aim of life to be sacrificed for "higher" powers, for the leader or the racial community.

Calvin's theology, which was to become as important for the Anglo-Saxon countries as Luther's for Germany, exhibits essentially the same spirit as Luther's, both theologically and psychologically. Although he too opposes the authority of the Church and the blind acceptance of its doctrines, religion for him is rooted in the powerlessness of man; self-humiliation and the destruction of human pride are the *Leitmotiv* of his whole thinking. Only he who despises this world can devote himself to the preparation for the future world. . . .

There are a number of subtle differences betweeen Calvin's and Luther's teachings which are not important for the main line of thought of this book. Only two points of difference need to be stressed. One is

Calvin's doctrine of predestination. In contrast to the doctrine of predestination as we find it in Augustine, Aquinas and Luther, with Calvin it becomes one of the cornerstones, perhaps the central doctrine, of his whole system. He gives it a new version by assuming that God not only predestines some for grace, but decides that others are destined for eternal damnation.

Salvation or damnation are not results of anything good or bad a man does in his life, but are predetermined by God before man ever comes to life. Why God chose the one and condemned the other is a secret into which man must not try to delve. He did so because it pleased him to show his unlimited power in that way. Calvin's God, in spite of all attempts to preserve the idea of God's justice and love, has all the features of a tyrant without any quality of love or even justice. In blatant contradiction to the New Testament, Calvin denies the supreme role of love and says: "For what the Schoolmen advance concerning the priority of charity to faith and hope, is a mere reverie of a distempered imagination. . . ." [8]

The psychological significance of the doctrine of predestination is a twofold one. It expresses and enhances the feeling of individual powerlessness and insignificance. No doctrine could express more strongly than this the worthlessness of human will and effort. The decision over man's fate is taken completely out of his own hands and there is nothing man can do to change this decision. He is a powerless tool in God's hands. The other meaning of this doctrine, like that of Luther's, consists in its function to silence the irrational doubt which was the same in Calvin and his followers as in Luther. At first glance the doctrine of predestination seems to enhance the doubt rather than silence it. Must not the individual be torn by even more torturing doubts than before to learn that he was predestined either to eternal damnation or to salvation before he was born? How can he ever be sure what his lot will be? Although Calvin did not teach that there was any concrete proof of such certainty, he and his followers actually had the conviction that they belonged to the chosen ones. They got this conviction by the same mechanism of self-humiliation which we have analyzed with regard to Luther's doctrine. Having such conviction, the doctrine of predestination implied utmost certainty; one could not do anything which would endanger the state of salvation, since one's salvation did not depend on one's own actions but was decided upon before one was ever born. Again, as with Luther, the fundamental doubt resulted in the quest for absolute certainty; but though the doctrine of predestination gave such certainty, the doubt re-

[8] F. Borkenau, *Der Übergang vom Feudalen zum bürgerlichen Weltbild,* Alcan, Paris, 1934, Book III, Chapter 2, 41.

mained in the background and had to be silenced again and again by an ever-growing fanatic belief that the religious community to which one belonged represented that part of mankind which had been chosen by God.

Calvin's theory of predestination has one implication which should be explicitly mentioned here, since it has found its most vigorous revival in Nazi ideology: the principle of the basic inequality of men. For Calvin there are two kinds of people—those who are saved and those who are destined to eternal damnation. Since this fate is determined before they are born and without their being able to change it by anything they do or do not do in their lives, the equality of mankind is denied in principle. Men are created unequal. This principle implies also that there is no solidarity between men, since the one factor which is the strongest basis for human solidarity is denied: the equality of man's fate. The Calvinists quite naïvely thought that they were the chosen ones and that all others were those whom God had condemned to damnation. It is obvious that this belief represented psychologically a deep contempt and hatred for other human beings—as a matter of fact, the same hatred with which they had endowed God. While modern thought has led to an increasing assertion of the equality of men, the Calvinists' principle has never been completely mute. The doctrine that men are basically unequal according to their racial background is confirmation of the same principle with a different rationalization. The psychological implications are the same.

Another and very significant difference from Luther's teachings is the greater emphasis on the importance of moral effort and a virtuous life. Not that the individual can *change his fate* by any of his works, but the very fact that he is able to make the effort is one sign of his belonging to the saved. The virtues man should acquire are: modesty and moderation (*sobrietas*), justice (*iustitia*) in the sense of everybody being given what is his due share, and piousness (*pietas*) which unites man with God. In the further development of Calvinism, the emphasis on a virtuous life and on the significance of an unceasing effort gains in importance, particularly the idea that success in worldly life, as a result of such efforts, is a sign of salvation.

But the particular emphasis on a virtuous life which was characteristic for Calvinism had also a particular psychological significance. Calvinism emphasized the necessity of unceasing human effort. Man must constantly try to live according to God's word and never lapse in his effort to do so. This doctrine appears to be a contradiction of the doctrine that human effort is of no avail with regard to man's salvation. The fatalistic attitude of not making any effort might seem like a much more appropriate response. Some psychological considerations, however, show that this is not so. The state of anxiety, the feeling of powerlessness and insignificance, and especially the doubt concerning one's future after death, represent a state of mind which is practically unbearable for anybody. Almost no one stricken with this fear would be able to relax, enjoy life, and be indifferent as to what happened afterwards. One possible way to escape this unbearable state of uncertainty and the paralyzing feeling of one's own insignificance is the very trait which became so prominent in Calvinism: the development of a frantic activity and a striving to do *something*. Activity in this sense assumes a compulsory quality: *the individual has to be active in order to overcome his feeling of doubt and powerlessness*. This kind of effort and activity is not the result of inner strength and self-confidence; it is a desperate escape from anxiety. . . .

We have so far spoken mainly of the anxiety and of the feeling of powerlessness pervading the personality of the member of the middle class. We must now discuss another trait which we have only touched upon very briefly: his *hostility* and *resentment*. That the middle class developed intense hostility is not surprising. Anybody who is thwarted in emotional and sensual expression and who is also threatened in his very existence will normally react with hostility; as we have seen, the middle class as a whole and especially those of its members who were not yet enjoying the advantages of rising capitalism were thwarted and seriously threatened. Another factor was to increase their hostility: the luxury and power which the small group of capitalists, including the higher dignitaries of the Church, could afford to display. An intense envy against them was the natural result. But while hostility and envy developed, the members of the middle class could not find the direct expression which was possible for the lower classes. These hated the rich who exploited them, they wanted to overthrow their power, and could thus afford to feel and to express their hatred. The upper class also could afford to express aggressiveness directly in the wish for power. The members of the middle class were essentially conservative; they wanted to stabilize society and not uproot it; each of them hoped to become more prosperous and to participate in the general development. Hostility, therefore, was not to be expressed overtly, nor could it even be felt consciously; it had to be repressed. Repression of hostility, however, only removes it from conscious awareness, it does not abolish it. Moreover, the pent-up hostility, not finding any direct expression, increases to a point where it pervades the whole personality, one's relationship to others and to oneself —but in rationalized and disguised forms.

Luther and Calvin portray this all-pervading hostility. Not only in the sense that these two men, personally, belonged to the ranks of the greatest haters among the leading figures of history, certainly among religious leaders; but, which is more important, in the sense that their doctrines were colored by this hostility and could only appeal to a group itself driven by an intense, repressed hostility. The most striking expression of this hostility is found in their concept of God, especially in Calvin's doctrine. Although we are all familiar with this concept, we often do not fully realize what it means to conceive of God as being as arbitrary and merciless as Calvin's God, who destined part of mankind to eternal damnation without any justification or reason except that this act was an expression of God's power. Calvin himself was, of course, concerned with the obvious objections which could be made against this conception of God; but the more or less subtle constructions he made to uphold the picture of a just and loving God do not sound in the least convincing. This picture of a despotic God, who wants unrestricted power over men and their submission and humiliation, was the projection of the middle class's own hostility and envy.

Hostility or resentment also found expression in the character of relationships to others. The main form which it assumed was moral indignation, which has invariably been characteristic for the lower middle class from Luther's time to Hitler's. While this class was actually envious of those who had wealth and power and could enjoy life, they rationalized this resentment and envy of life in terms of moral indignation and in the conviction that these superior people would be punished by eternal suffering.[9] But the hostile tension against others found expression in still other ways. Calvin's regime in Geneva was characterized by suspicion and hostility on the part of everybody against everybody else, and certainly little of the spirit of love and brotherliness could be discovered in his despotic regime. Calvin distrusted wealth and at the same time had little pity for poverty. In the later development of Calvinism warnings against friendliness towards the stranger, a cruel attitude towards the poor, and a general atmosphere of suspiciousness often appeared.

Aside from the projection of hostility and jealousy onto God and their indirect expression in the form of moral indignation, one other way in which hostility found expression was in turning it against oneself. We have seen how ardently both Luther and Calvin emphasized the wickedness

---

[9] Cf. Ranulf's *Moral Indignation and Middle Class Psychology,* a study which is an important contribution to the thesis that moral indignation is a trait typical of the middle class, especially the lower middle class.

of man and taught self-humiliation and self-abasement as the basis of all virtue. What they consciously had in mind was certainly nothing but an extreme degree of humility. But to anybody familiar with the psychological mechanisms of self-accusation and self-humiliation there can be no doubt that this kind of "humility" is rooted in a violent hatred which, for some reason or other, is blocked from being directed toward the world outside and operates against one's own self. In order to understand this phenomenon fully, it is necessary to realize that the attitudes toward others and toward oneself, far from being contradictory, in principle run parallel. But while hostility against others is often conscious and can be expressed overtly, hostility against oneself is usually (except in pathological cases) unconscious, and finds expression in indirect and rationalized forms. . . .

Thereby the new religious doctrines not only gave expression to what the average member of the middle class felt, but, by rationalizing and systematizing this attitude, they also increased and strengthened it. However, they did more than that; they also showed the individual a way to cope with his anxiety. They taught him that by fully accepting his powerlessness and the evilness of his nature, by considering his whole life an atonement for his sins, by the utmost self-humiliation, and also by unceasing effort, he could overcome his doubt and his anxiety; that by complete submission he could be loved by God and could at least hope to belong to those whom God had decided to save. Protestantism was the answer to the human needs of the frightened, uprooted, and isolated individual who had to orient and to relate himself to a new world. The new character structure, resulting from economic and social changes and intensified by religious doctrines, became in its turn an important factor in shaping the further social and economic development. Those very qualities which were rooted in this character structure—compulsion to work, passion for thrift, the readiness to make one's life a tool for the purposes of an extra personal power, asceticism, and a compulsive sense of duty—were character traits which became productive forces in capitalistic society and without which modern economic and social development are unthinkable; they were the specific forms into which human energy was shaped and in which it became one of the productive forces within the social process. To act in accord with the newly formed character traits was advantageous from the standpoint of economic necessities; it was also satisfying psychologically, since such action answered the needs and anxieties of this new kind of personality. To put the same principle in more general terms: the social process, by determining the mode of life of the individual, that is, his relation to others and to work, molds his character structure; new ideologies—religious, philosophical, or political—result from and appeal to this changed character structure and thus intensify, satisfy, and stabilize it; the newly formed character traits in their turn become important factors in further economic development and influence the social process; while originally they have developed as a reaction to the threat of new economic forces, they slowly become productive forces furthering and intensifying the new economic development.

10. The Sick Soul

WILLIAM JAMES *

IT IS DOUBTLESS TRUE THAT NO BOOK HAS CONTRIBUTED MORE TO THE SCIENTIFIC STUDY OF RELIGION THAN THE GIFFORD LECTURES OF WILLIAM JAMES. HIS THEORETICAL SCHEME IS SCARCELY ADEQUATE FOR OUR PURPOSES, BUT HIS GREAT RESPECT FOR EVIDENCE AND HIS KEEN INSIGHT HAVE PROMPTED TWO GENERATIONS OF STUDENTS OF RELIGION TO TRY TO BRING THE ANALYSIS OF RELIGIOUS PHENOMENA FULLY INTO THE STRUCTURE OF THE SCIENCES OF HUMAN BEHAVIOR.

. . . we must address ourselves to the unpleasant task of hearing what the sick souls, as we may call them in contrast to the healthy-minded, have to say of the secrets of their prison-house, their own peculiar form of consciousness. Let us then resolutely turn our backs on the once-born and their sky-blue optimistic gospel; let us not simply cry out, in spite of all appearances, "Hurrah for the Universe!—God's in his Heaven, all's right with the world." Let us see rather whether pity, pain, and fear, and the sentiment of human helplessness may not open a profounder view and put into our hands a more complicated key to the meaning of the situation.

To begin with, how *can* things so insecure as the successful experiences of this world afford a stable anchorage? A chain is no stronger than its weakest link, and life is after all a chain. In the healthiest and most prosperous existence, how many links of illness, danger, and disaster are always interposed? Unsuspectedly from the bottom of every fountain of

* From *The Varieties of Religious Experience*, pp. 135–144, 152–157.

pleasure, as the old poet said, something bitter rises up: a touch of nausea, a falling dead of the delight, a whiff of melancholy, things that sound a knell, for fugitive as they may be, they bring a feeling of coming from a deeper region and often have an appalling convincingness. The buzz of life ceases at their touch as a piano-string stops sounding when the damper falls upon it.

Of course the music can commence again;—and again and again—at intervals. But with this the healthy-minded consciousness is left with an irremediable sense of precariousness. It is a bell with a crack; it draws its breath on sufferance and by an accident.

Even if we suppose a man so packed with healthy-mindedness as never to have experienced in his own person any of these sobering intervals, still, if he is a reflecting being, he must generalize and class his own lot with that of others; and, doing so, he must see that his escape is just a lucky chance and no essential difference. He might just as well have been born to an entirely different fortune. And then indeed the hollow security! What kind of a frame of things is it of which the best you can say is, "Thank God, it has let me off clear this time!" Is not its blessedness a fragile fiction? Is not your joy in it a very vulgar glee, not much unlike the snicker of any rogue at his success? If indeed it were all success, even on such terms as that! But take the happiest man, the one most envied by the world, and in nine cases out of ten his inmost consciousness is one of failure. Either his ideals in the line of his achievements are pitched far higher than the achievements themselves, or else he has secret ideals of which the world knows nothing, and in regard to which he inwardly knows himself to be found wanting.

When such a conquering optimist as Goethe can express himself in this wise, how must it be with less successful men?

"I will say nothing," writes Goethe in 1824, "against the course of my existence. But at bottom it has been nothing but pain and burden, and I can affirm that during the whole of my 75 years, I have not had four weeks of genuine well-being. It is but the perpetual rolling of a rock that must be raised up again forever."

What single-handed man was ever on the whole as successful as Luther? yet when he had grown old, he looked back on his life as if it were an absolute failure.

"I am utterly weary of life. I pray the Lord will come forthwith and carry me hence. Let him come, above all, with his last Judgment: I will stretch out my neck, the thunder will burst forth, and I shall be at rest."—And having a necklace of white agates in his hand at the time he added: "O God, grant that it may come without delay. I would readily eat up this necklace to-day, for the Judgment to come to-morrow."—The Electress Dowager, one day when Luther was dining with her, said to him: "Doctor, I wish you may live forty years to come." "Madam," replied he, "rather than live forty years more, I would give up my chance of Paradise."

Failure, then, failure! so the world stamps us at every turn. We strew it with our blunders, our misdeeds, our lost opportunities, with all the memorials of our inadequacy to our vocation. And with what a damning emphasis does it then blot us out! No easy fine, no mere apology or formal expiation, will satisfy the world's demands, but every pound of flesh exacted is soaked with all its blood. The subtlest forms of suffering known to man are connected with the poisonous humiliations incidental to these results.

And they are pivotal human experiences. A process so ubiquitous and everlasting is evidently an integral part of life. "There is indeed one element in human destiny," Robert Louis Stevenson writes, "that not blindness itself can controvert. Whatever else we are intended to do, we are not intended to succeed; failure is the fate allotted." [1] And our nature being thus rooted in failure, is it any wonder that theologians should have held it to be essential, and thought that only through the personal experience of humiliation which it engenders the deeper sense of life's significance is reached? [2]

But this is only the first stage of the world-sickness. Make the human being's sensitiveness a little greater, carry him a little farther over the misery-threshold, and the good quality of the successful moments themselves when they occur is spoiled and vitiated. All natural goods perish. Riches take wings; fame is a breath; love is a cheat; youth and health and pleasure vanish. Can things whose end is always dust and disappointment be the real goods which our souls require? Back of everything is the great spectre of universal death, the all-encompassing blackness:—

---

[1] He adds with characteristic healthy-mindedness: "Our business is to continue to fail in good spirits."

[2] The God of many men is little more than their court of appeal against the damnatory judgment passed on their failures by the opinion of this world. To our own consciousness there is usually a residuum of worth left over after our sins and errors have been told off—our capacity of acknowledging and regretting them is the germ of a better self *in posse* at least. But the world deals with us *in actu* and not *in posse:* and of this hidden germ, not to be guessed at from without, it never takes account. Then we turn to the All-knower, who knows our bad, but knows this good in us also, and who is just. We cast ourselves with our repentance on his mercy: only by an All-knower can we finally be judged. So the need of a God very definitely emerges from this sort of experience of life.

"What profit hath a man of all his labour which he taketh under the Sun?
I looked on all the works that my hands had wrought, and behold, all was
vanity and vexation of spirit. For that which befalleth the sons of men befalleth beasts; as the one dieth, so dieth the other; all are of the dust, and all
turn to dust again. . . . The dead know not anything, neither have they
any more a reward; for the memory of them is forgotten. Also their love and
their hatred and their envy is now perished; neither have they any more a
portion for ever in anything that is done under the Sun. . . . Truly the light
is sweet, and a pleasant thing it is for the eyes to behold the Sun: but if a man
live many years and rejoice in them all, yet let him remember the days of
darkness; for they shall be many."

In short, life and its negation are beaten up inextricably together. But
if the life be good, the negation of it must be bad. Yet the two are equally
essential facts of existence; and all natural happiness thus seems infected
with a contradiction. The breath of the sepulchre surrounds it.

To a mind attentive to this state of things and rightly subject to the joy-
destroying chill which such a contemplation engenders, the only relief
that healthy-mindedness can give is by saying: "Stuff and nonsense, get
out into the open air!" or "Cheer up, old fellow, you'll be all right erelong,
if you will only drop your morbidness!" But in all seriousness, can such
bald animal talk as that be treated as a rational answer? To ascribe religious value to mere happy-go-lucky contentment with one's brief chance
at natural good is but the very consecration of forgetfulness and superficiality. Our troubles lie indeed too deep for *that* cure. The fact that we
can die, that we *can* be ill at all, is what perplexes us; the fact that we now
for a moment live and are well is irrelevant to that perplexity. We need a
life not correlated with death, a health not liable to illness, a kind of good
that will not perish, a good in fact that flies beyond the Goods of nature.

It all depends on how sensitive the soul may become to discords. "The
trouble with me is that I believe too much in common happiness and goodness," said a friend of mine whose consciousness was of this sort, "and
nothing can console me for their transiency. I am appalled and discon-
certed at its being possible." And so with most of us: a little cooling down
of animal excitability and instinct, a little loss of animal toughness, a little
irritable weakness and descent of the pain-threshold, will bring the worm
at the core of all our usual springs of delight into full view, and turn us
into melancholy metaphysicians. The pride of life and glory of the world
will shrivel. It is after all but the standing quarrel of hot youth and hoary
eld. Old age has the last word: the purely naturalistic look at life, however enthusiastically it may begin, is sure to end in sadness.

This sadness lies at the heart of every merely positivistic, agnostic, or naturalistic scheme of philosophy. Let sanguine healthy-mindedness do its best with its strange power of living in the moment and ignoring and forgetting, still the evil background is really there to be thought of, and the skull will grin in at the banquet. In the practical life of the individual, we know how his whole gloom or glee about any present fact depends on the remoter schemes and hopes with which it stands related. Its significance and framing give it the chief part of its value. Let it be known to lead nowhere, and however agreeable it may be in its immediacy, its glow and gilding vanish. The old man, sick with an insidious internal disease, may laugh and quaff his wine at first as well as ever, but he knows his fate now, for the doctors have revealed it; and the knowledge knocks the satisfaction out of all these functions. They are partners of death and the worm is their brother, and they turn to a mere flatness.

The lustre of the present hour is always borrowed from the background of possibilities it goes with. Let our common experiences be enveloped in an eternal moral order; let our suffering have an immortal significance; let Heaven smile upon the earth, and deities pay their visits; let faith and hope be the atmosphere which man breathes in;—and his days pass by with zest; they stir with prospects, they thrill with remoter values. Place round them on the contrary the curdling cold and gloom and absence of all permanent meaning which for pure naturalism and the popular science evolutionism of our time are all that is visible ultimately, and the thrill stops short, or turns rather to an anxious trembling.

For naturalism, fed on recent cosmological speculations, mankind is in a position similar to that of a set of people living on a frozen lake, surrounded by cliffs over which there is no escape, yet knowing that little by little the ice is melting, and the inevitable day drawing near when the last film of it will disappear, and to be drowned ignominiously will be the human creature's portion. The merrier the skating, the warmer and more sparkling the sun by day, and the ruddier the bonfires at night, the more poignant the sadness with which one must take in the meaning of the total situation.

The early Greeks are continually held up to us in literary works as models of the healthy-minded joyousness which the religion of nature may engender. There was indeed much joyousness among the Greeks— Homer's flow of enthusiasm for most things that the sun shines upon is steady. But even in Homer the reflective passages are cheerless,[3] and the

---

[3] E.g., Iliad XVII. 446: "Nothing then is more wretched anywhere than man of all that breathes and creeps upon this earth."

moment the Greeks grew systematically pensive and thought of ultimates, they became unmitigated pessimists.[4] The jealousy of the gods, the nemesis that follows too much happiness, the all-encompassing death, fate's dark opacity, the ultimate and unintelligible cruelty, were the fixed background of their imagination. The beautiful joyousness of their polytheism is only a poetic modern fiction. They knew no joys comparable in quality of preciousness to those which we shall erelong see that Brahmans, Buddhists, Christians, Mohammedans, twice-born people whose religion is non-naturalistic, get from their several creeds of mysticism and renunciation.

Stoic insensibility and Epicurean resignation were the farthest advance which the Greek mind made in that direction. The Epicurean said: "Seek not to be happy, but rather to escape unhappiness; strong happiness is always linked with pain; therefore hug the safe shore, and do not tempt the deeper raptures. Avoid disappointment by expecting little, and by aiming low; and above all do not fret." The Stoic said: "The only genuine good that life can yield a man is the free possession of his own soul; all other goods are lies." Each of these philosophies is in its degree a philosophy of despair in nature's boons. Trustful self-abandonment to the joys that freely offer has entirely departed from both Epicurean and Stoic; and what each proposes is a way of rescue from the resultant dust-and-ashes state of mind. The Epicurean still awaits results from economy of indulgence and damping of desire. The Stoic hopes for no results, and gives up natural good altogether. There is dignity in both these forms of resignation. They represent distinct stages in the sobering process which man's primitive intoxication with sense-happiness is sure to undergo. In

---

[4] E.g., Theognis, 425–428: "Best of all for all things upon earth is it not to be born nor to behold the splendors of the Sun; next best to traverse as soon as possible the gates of Hades." See also the almost identical passage in Œdipus in Colonus, 1225.—The Anthology is full of pessimistic utterances: "Naked came I upon the earth, naked I go below the ground—why then do I vainly toil when I see the end naked before me?"—"How did I come to be? Whence am I? Wherefore did I come? To pass away. How can I learn aught when naught I know? Being naught I came to life: once more shall I be what I was. Nothing and nothingness is the whole race of mortals."—"For death we are all cherished and fattened like a herd of hogs that is wantonly butchered."

The difference between Greek pessimism and the oriental and modern variety is that the Greeks had not made the discovery that the pathetic mood may be idealized, and figure as a higher form of sensibility. Their spirit was still too essentially masculine for pessimism to be elaborated or lengthily dwelt on in their classic literature. They would have despised a life set wholly in a minor key, and summoned it to keep within the proper bounds of lachrymosity. The discovery that the enduring emphasis, so far as this world goes, may be laid on its pain and failure, was reserved for races more complex, and (so to speak) more feminine than the Hellenes had attained to being in the classic period. But all the same was the outlook of those Hellenes blackly pessimistic.

the one the hot blood has grown cool, in the other it has become quite cold; and although I have spoken of them in the past tense, as if they were merely historic, yet Stoicism and Epicureanism will probably be to all time typical attitudes, marking a certain definite stage accomplished in the evolution of the world-sick soul. They mark the conclusion of what we call the once-born period, and represent the highest flights of what twice-born religion would call the purely natural man—Epicureanism, which can only by great courtesy be called a religion, showing his refinement, and Stoicism exhibiting his moral will. They leave the world in the shape of an unreconciled contradiction, and seek no higher unity. Compared with the complex ecstasies which the supernaturally regenerated Christian may enjoy, or the oriental pantheist indulge in, their receipts for equanimity are expedients which seem almost crude in their simplicity. . . .

At about the age of fifty, Tolstoy relates that he began to have moments of perplexity, of what he calls arrest, as if he knew not "how to live," or what to do. It is obvious that these were moments in which the excitement and interest which our functions naturally bring had ceased. Life had been enchanting, it was now flat sober, more than sober, dead. Things were meaningless whose meaning had always been self-evident. The questions "Why?" and "What next?" began to beset him more and more frequently. At first it seemed as if such questions must be answerable, and as if he could easily find the answers if he would take the time; but as they ever became more urgent, he perceived that it was like those first discomforts of a sick man, to which he pays but little attention till they run into one continuous suffering, and then he realizes that what he took for a passing disorder means the most momentous thing in the world for him, means his death.

These questions "Why?" "Wherefore?" "What for?" found no response.

"I felt," says Tolstoy, "that something had broken within me on which my life had always rested, that I had nothing left to hold on to, and that morally my life had stopped. An invincible force impelled me to get rid of my existence, in one way or another. It cannot be said exactly that I *wished* to kill myself, for the force which drew me away from life was fuller, more powerful, more general than any mere desire. It was a force like my old aspiration to life, only it impelled me in the opposite direction. It was an aspiration of my whole being to get out of life.

"Behold me then, a man happy and in good health, hiding the rope in order not to hang myself to the rafters of the room where every night I went to sleep alone; behold me no longer going shooting, lest I should yield to the too easy temptation of putting an end to myself with my gun.

"I did not know what I wanted. I was afraid of life; I was driven to leave it; and in spite of that I still hoped something from it.

"All this took place at a time when so far as all my outer circumstances went, I ought to have been completely happy. I had a good wife who loved me and whom I loved; good children and a large property which was increasing with no pains taken on my part. I was more respected by my kinsfolk and acquaintance than I had ever been; I was loaded with praise by strangers; and without exaggeration I could believe my name already famous. Moreover I was neither insane nor ill. On the contrary, I possessed a physical and mental strength which I have rarely met in persons of my age. I could mow as well as the peasants, I could work with my brain eight hours uninterruptedly and feel no bad effects.

"And yet I could give no reasonable meaning to any actions of my life. And I was surprised that I had not understood this from the very beginning. My state of mind was as if some wicked and stupid jest was being played upon me by some one. One can live only so long as one is intoxicated, drunk with life; but when one grows sober one cannot fail to see that it is all a stupid cheat. What is truest about it is that there is nothing even funny or silly in it; it is cruel and stupid, purely and simply.

"The oriental fable of the traveler surprised in the desert by a wild beast is very old.

"Seeking to save himself from the fierce animal, the traveler jumps into a well with no water in it; but at the bottom of this well he sees a dragon waiting with open mouth to devour him. And the unhappy man, not daring to go out lest he should be the prey of the beast, not daring to jump to the bottom lest he should be devoured by the dragon, clings to the branches of a wild bush which grows out of one of the cracks of the well. His hands weaken, and he feels that he must soon give way to certain fate; but still he clings, and sees two mice, one white, the other black, evenly moving round the bush to which he hangs, and gnawing off its roots.

"The traveler sees this and knows that he must inevitably perish; but while thus hanging he looks about him and finds on the leaves of the bush some drops of honey. These he reaches with his tongue and licks them off with rapture.

"Thus I hang upon the boughs of life, knowing that the inevitable dragon of death is waiting ready to tear me, and I cannot comprehend why I am thus made a martyr. I try to suck the honey which formerly consoled me; but the honey pleases me no longer, and day and night the white mouse and the black mouse gnaw the branch to which I cling. I can see but one thing: the inevitable dragon and the mice—I cannot turn my gaze away from them.

"This is no fable, but the literal incontestable truth which every one may understand. What will be the outcome of what I do to-day? Of what I shall do to-morrow? What will be the outcome of all my life? Why should I live? Why should I do anything? Is there in life any purpose which the inevitable death which awaits me does not undo and destroy?

"These questions are the simplest in the world. From the stupid child to the wisest old man, they are in the soul of every human being. Without an answer to them, it is impossible, as I experienced, for life to go on.

" 'But perhaps,' I often said to myself, 'there may be something I have failed to notice or to comprehend. It is not possible that this condition of despair should be natural to mankind.' And I sought for an explanation in all the branches of knowledge acquired by men. I questioned painfully and protractedly and with no idle curiosity. I sought, not with indolence, but laboriously and obstinately for days and nights together. I sought like a man who is lost and seeks to save himself—and I found nothing. I became convinced, moreover, that all those who before me had sought for an answer in the sciences have also found nothing. And not only this, but that they have recognized that the very thing which was leading me to despair—the meaningless absurdity of life—is the only incontestable knowledge accessible to man."

To prove this point, Tolstoy quotes the Buddha, Solomon, and Schopenhauer. And he finds only four ways in which men of his own class and society are accustomed to meet the situation. Either mere animal blindness, sucking the honey without seeing the dragon or the mice—"and from such a way," he says, "I can learn nothing, after what I now know;" or reflective epicureanism, snatching what it can while the day lasts—which is only a more deliberate sort of stupefaction than the first; or manly suicide; or seeing the mice and dragon and yet weakly and plaintively clinging to the bush of life.

Suicide was naturally the consistent course dictated by the logical intellect.

"Yet," says Tolstoy, "whilst my intellect was working, something else in me was working too, and kept me from the deed—a consciousness of life, as I may call it, which was like a force that obliged my mind to fix itself in another direction and draw me out of my situation of despair. . . . During the whole course of this year, when I almost unceasingly kept asking myself how to end the business, whether by the rope or by the bullet, during all that time, alongside of all those movements of my ideas and observations, my heart kept languishing with another pining emotion. I can call this by no other name than that of a thirst for God. This craving for God had nothing to do with the movement of my ideas—in fact, it was the direct contrary of that movement—but it came from my heart. It was like a feeling of dread that made me seem like an orphan and isolated in the midst of all these things that were so foreign. And this feeling of dread was mitigated by the hope of finding the assistance of some one." [5]

Of the process, intellectual as well as emotional, which, starting from this idea of God, led to Tolstoy's recovery, I will say nothing in this lecture, reserving it for a later hour. The only thing that need interest us

---

[5] My extracts are from the French translation by "ZONIA." In abridging I have taken the liberty of transposing one passage.

now is the phenomenon of his absolute disenchantment with ordinary life, and the fact that the whole range of habitual values may, to a man as powerful and full of faculty as he was, come to appear so ghastly a mockery.

When disillusionment has gone as far as this, there is seldom a *restitutio ad integrum*. One has tasted of the fruit of the tree, and the happiness of Eden never comes again. The happiness that comes, when any does come —and often enough it fails to return in an acute form, though its form is sometimes very acute—is not the simple ignorance of ill, but something vastly more complex, including natural evil as one of its elements, but finding natural evil no such stumbling-block and terror because it now sees it swallowed up in supernatural good. The process is one of redemption, not of mere reversion to natural health, and the sufferer, when saved, is saved by what seems to him a second birth, a deeper kind of conscious being than he could enjoy before.

11. The New Look in American Piety
ROY A. ECKARDT *

This paper by Eckardt can scarcely be called an essay in the sociology of religion, even were the field defined in very broad terms. Yet the student of the social psychological aspects of contemporary religious movements—some of which we have discussed in Chapter 5— can profit from its description and its sharp criticism of several of these movements. Its interpretations are an effective defense against an overly-easy functionalism. It is interesting that attention to dysfunctional aspects of religion are as likely—it sometimes appears more likely—to be found in the writings of contemporary theologians as in the analyses of social scientists.

When the Apostle Paul visited the Athenians he perceived that in every way they were very religious. Paul would probably make a similar observation about this country at mid-20th century. "Religion," Ralph Sockman recently pointed out, "seems to have become the vogue in America."

Piety is more and more diffusing itself among our people, particularly in ways that supplement the regular ministry of the churches. A nationally circulated "slick" magazine carries a page on which a well known

* From *Christian Century*, November 17, 1954, pp. 1395–1397.

clergyman dispenses "peace-of-mind" religion to people writing in with spiritual problems. Religious books continue to lead best-seller lists. Popular song writers profitably emphasize religious themes. Radio stations pause not simply for the usual station breaks but for recommended moments of meditation. The movie makers know that few productions can out-box-office religious extravaganzas. The new piety has successfully invaded the halls of government. Attendance at prayer breakfasts is quite the thing for politicians these days. Ostensibly, even cabinet meetings can function better after a "word of prayer." And the pledge of allegiance is given the new religious look by the addition of the words "under God."

ELEMENTS OF AMERICAN "CULTURE RELIGION"

John C. Bennett has pointed out that today's religious revival is largely a matter of American "culture religion," involving the following elements:

1. The tendency to reduce Christianity to a gospel of happiness and success with no place for . . . the biblical warning against idolatry, judgment, repentance on the cross.
2. The loss of any basis of criticism of our culture as a whole and the close alliance of religion with the forces of nationalism.
3. The capitalizing on the fact that communism is atheistic and the strong suggestion that because we are against communism, God must be on our side.
4. The close cooperation between many of the leaders of this religious movement and the forces of social reaction. ["Billy Graham at Union," *Union Seminary Quarterly Review*, May 1954.]

The divergent voices of American culture religion are one in the faith that God is an exceedingly handy fellow to have around.

It is hardly fair to condemn out of hand revivals of religion. There is doubtless sincerity of motive in much of the new piety. Besides, God is able to use not alone the wrath but also the foibles of men to praise him. For St. Paul the thing that counted was that Christ was preached, whether in pretense or in truth. The extent to which a reawakening religion may be born of the Spirit and may indicate genuine religious devotion is immeasurable.

It hardly follows that the new piety is to be accepted uncritically. There is nothing in the Bible to support the view that religion is necessarily a good thing. Scripture has no ax to grind for religion; on the contrary, it is highly suspicious of much that passes for religion. The lamentable thing about the current revival is the failure of many people to make discriminating judgments of differing religious outlooks. The truth is that a given brand of piety may represent nothing more than nice, virile idol worship.

"PEACE OF MIND"

Consider three aspects of the new piety which should cause Christians concern.

1. The cult of "peace of mind." The Christian church speaks in the name of the Great Physician who makes whole minds, souls and bodies. Were we to turn away those who hunger and thirst for spiritual peace, we would betray part of our pastoral function. That this cult has spread so phenomenally may well represent a divine judgment upon our ministry.

The fact remains that the peace-of-mind cult readily turns into religious narcissism. The individual and his psycho-spiritual state occupy the center of the religious stage. Here is piety concentrating on its own navel. The Christian gospel, we must object, is in its redemptive wholeness a challenge to men to surrender themselves for the sake of Christ with the result that their hearts will go out to their brethren. The New Testament forcibly reminds them that in this world they have tribulation. They are to be of good cheer, but only because *Christ* has overcome the world. The shadow of his cross may indeed fall across their own lives.

The peace-of-mind movement is deficient morally and empirically. It has no grasp of the deep paradox that "whoever would save his life will lose it, and whoever loses his life for [Christ's] sake will find it." Lasting peace of mind is impossible apart from peace with God; yet enduring peace with God comes only when a man is ready to surrender his own peace of mind.

"PERSONAL ADJUSTMENT"

This new cult counsels "personal adjustment." But adjustment to what? New Testament Christianity is hardly adjusted to its environment. It makes us seriously wonder, in fact, how much the social order is *worth* adjusting to. The gospel urges us to nonconformity: "Do not be conformed to this world but be transformed."

An evil aspect of peace-of-mind religion is its acceptance, by default, of the social status quo. An unannounced assumption is that the present condition of the social order is irrelevant to one's true needs and outside the scope of one's obligations. In truth, to limit religion to "spiritual" concerns is to abdicate responsibility in the struggle against man's inhumanity to man. The tragedy is that the peace-of-mind cult unwittingly furthers the rise of radical politico-economic movements which step in to fill the void left by the absence of a social gospel.

A final irony is that peace-of-mind religion fails to address itself to the very cultural crisis which helps produce more distraught souls than the practitioners could ever handle. But its greatest sin lies in using God as a means for human ends. This is blasphemous. The Bible tells us that God uses *us* for *his* ends. "Woe to those who are at ease in Zion, and to those who feel secure on the mountain of Samaria."

"THE MAN UPSTAIRS"

2. The cult of the "Man Upstairs." A rhapsodic inquiry greets us from the TV screen and the radio: "Have you talked to the Man Upstairs?" God is a friendly neighbor who dwells in the apartment just above. Call on him anytime, especially if you are feeling a little blue. He does not get upset over your little faults. He understands. We have been assured by no less a theologian than Jane Russell that the Lord is a "livin' Doll," a right nice guy. Thus is the citizenry guided to divine-human chumminess.

This view of religion is not wholly unlike the one just considered. However—to borrow William James' terminology—the peace-of-mind cult makes more of an appeal to the "sick soul" religionist, while the cult of the Man Upstairs attracts more the "healthy-minded" type. The latter individual is not so much weighed down by fears and complexes. On the surface at least he is well adjusted. The appeal of religion is that it can make him get even more pleasure out of life. Fellowship with the Lord is, so to say, an extra emotional jag that keeps him happy. The "gospel" makes him "feel real good."

In this cult religion verges on entertainment, perhaps merges with it. Thus "gospel boogie," replete with masters of ceremonies, gospel quartets, popcorn and soda pop, is able to play to jam-packed audiences in many cities. The financial take from the paid admissions is considerable.

Those whose God is the Friendly Neighbor would not dream of hearing him say,

> For three transgressions of America, yea for four,
> I will not turn my wrath away.

Our new culture religion is helping to mold us into a people possessed of the certainty that the Lord is squarely on our side. Whatever we think and do can be carried on in good conscience.

BURIED IN TRIVIALITY

The stern fact remains that to behave as if man *as man* were not anxious with himself in the presence of his fellows and, especially, of God, is to dull the moral sense. It is to destroy man's dignity as a free being. He is dehumanized. His life is reduced, as Will Herberg says, "to the level of subhuman creation which knows neither sin nor guilt." The moral and spiritual life is buried in triviality.

The Christian whose norm is Scripture must always have a particularly uneasy conscience. He recognizes the gulf between the quality of his life and the sacrifice of God's only Son on the cross. He knows the love that came down on Calvary. He knows the judgment too. And he knows that the love cannot be separated from the judgment.

The Man Upstairs is a foolish idol fabricated from out of the proud imaginations of the human spirit, a childish projection of granddaddy. The real God is the relentless One who pursues us and gives us no peace until our religiosity is transformed by repentance. In the very hour that the gospel quartet soothes with the universalist-hedonist refrain, "Everybody's gonna have a wonderful time up there," the sheep and the goats are being sorted out. "It is a fearful thing to fall into the hands of the *living* God." Old Testament scary stuff? No, the Epistle to the Hebrews. The adjective in the phrase "livin' Doll" is precisely what causes us so much trouble. The real God is the Hound of Heaven. We wish he would go and live somewhere else. But the Lord refuses to move, no matter how we try to take the threat out of him by reducing him to a friendly neighbor. The cult of the Man Upstairs meets its nemesis before the Holy Presence.

"CHOSEN PEOPLE"

3. The cult of "we" versus "they." This cult is more tangibly sinister than the other two. It is just a short step from a god who is the Great Adjuster and/or the Friendly Neighbor to the god who fights on the side of his chosen people, supporting their racial, economic or national interests. The crucial point is that the first two cults have already stimulated and endorsed powerful human emotions. The obvious outcome is that it is un-American to be unreligious. We are the good spiritual people. The God of judgment has died.

In a searching analysis Joseph E. Cunneen describes our third cult as follows:

At present there seems to be a wave of enthusiasm for a rather undefined "religion" in America. What is its origin? There is fear in the atmosphere: fear of the unknown forces in man, fear of the natural forces he has learned to release without yet knowing how to control. But the fear emphasized by the new religionists is chiefly fear of "the others" as "we" feel it. Well publicized and shrewdly aware of our general uncertainty, the movement appears to give calculated encouragement to an attitude which at its mildest is the vague, almost unconscious resentment against the neighbor who always crosses our lawn to get to his back door; at its worst, it is that of a lynching mob. [*Cross Currents*, Fall 1954.]

Only the ethically blind will, for example, equate the moral health of world communism and the United States when it comes down to how "they" should be treated. Yet it is perverse to conclude that our cause is God's cause. To equate the two is to be in for a shock before the transcendent justice of God.

The dangers in the "we" versus "they" cult are especially evident today in relations between this country and the rest of the world. The nation that best fulfills its God-given responsibilities is not necessarily the nation that displays the most religiosity. A country possessed of the might of the United States might do better to go into its closet and pray to its Father in secret rather than standing on the street corners parading its piety before men. The piety of individuals stands a relatively better chance of inducing repentance than does the public piety of nations. The temptation is just about irresistible for a powerful nation to rely on its religiosity as proof of its own virtue. Thus is threatened the possibility of sober and responsible political action.

Against all human idolatries we may set the peace of Christ which passes all understanding. We have not earned his peace. It is a gift we have received. It does not center in the self or the group. It centers in the cross and the empty tomb. It provides an ultimate vantage point from which the whole drama of life may be viewed. It is the peace of a disturbing forgiveness. God ceases to be fashioned in our image; we are made over into his. We are granted not a short-cut or trivial solution to our anxieties but the grace to laugh and to know that our anxieties are of no ultimate consequence. The peace of Christ comes, mysteriously, when we forget all about our peace, when we prostrate ourselves before the holiness of God, and when we discern the source of evil not in "them" but in our own hearts. What is more humiliating than to be forgiven by the Lord of heaven and earth, to be accepted just as we are—petty and full of pride?

The peace of Christ issues in the nonchalance of faith and service. The gospel meets the desperate human need of which the cults are an ominous symptom. It does so in the very act of defeating idolatry.

The Socio-Cultural Setting of Religion

The readings in this section document, in various ways, the thesis that religion is part of a socio-cultural system, that it cannot be understood in isolation from its cultural and social context. One of the clearest manifestations of this fact is that religious differentiation appears in socially differentiated societies. It is from this point of view that typologies of religious groups and of religious-group participants become important. Readings 12, 13, and 14 relate to that question. The two that follow describe various ways in which the social context of religion affects patterns of belief, church structure, and the interaction of religious groups with each other.

12. Church and Sect

ERNST TROELTSCH *

HERE IS THE STARTING POINT FOR MOST CURRENT TYPOLOGIES OF RELIGIOUS
GROUPS. ALTHOUGH THE CATEGORIES HAVE PROVED TO BE TOO BROAD FOR PRE-
CISE ANALYSIS, TROELTSCH'S FORMULATION HAS BEEN OF ENORMOUS SIGNIFICANCE
IN THE DEVELOPMENT OF THE SOCIOLOGY OF RELIGION. THERE HAS BEEN SOME
TENDENCY TO REIFY THE CONCEPTS OF CHURCH AND SECT RATHER THAN TO
USE THEM AS TOOLS, BUT IF THIS ERROR IS AVOIDED AND IF FULL ATTENTION
IS GIVEN TO VARIATION IN TIME AND PLACE—THE MORE WIDELY APPLICABLE
A TYPE IS, THE MORE ABSTRACTLY IT MUST BE DRAWN—TYPOLOGICAL DESCRIP-
TION CAN MAKE AN IMPORTANT CONTRIBUTION TO SCIENTIFIC ANALYSIS.

SECT-TYPE AND CHURCH-TYPE CONTRASTED

At the outset the actual differences are quite clear. The Church is that
type of organization which is overwhelmingly conservative, which to a
certain extent accepts the secular order, and dominates the masses; in
principle, therefore, it is universal, i.e. it desires to cover the whole life
of humanity. The sects, on the other hand, are comparatively small
groups; they aspire after personal inward perfection, and they aim at a
direct personal fellowship between the members of each group. From the
very beginning, therefore, they are forced to organize themselves in small
groups, and to renounce the idea of dominating the world. Their attitude
towards the world, the State, and Society may be indifferent, tolerant, or
hostile, since they have no desire to control and incorporate these forms
of social life; on the contrary, they tend to avoid them; their aim is usually
either to tolerate their presence alongside of their own body, or even to
replace these social institutions by their own society.

Further, both types are in close connection with the actual situation
and with the development of Society. The fully developed Church, however, utilizes the State and the ruling classes, and weaves these elements
into her own life; she then becomes an integral part of the existing social
order; from this standpoint, then, the Church both stabilizes and determines the social order; in so doing, however, she becomes dependent upon
the upper classes, and upon their development. The sects, on the other

* From *The Social Teaching of the Christian Churches*, pp. 331–333, 338–341.

hand, are connected with the lower classes, or at least with those elements in Society which are opposed to the State and to Society; they work upwards from below, and not downwards from above.

Finally, too, both types vary a good deal in their attitude towards the supernatural and transcendent element in Christianity, and also in their view of its system of asceticism. The Church relates the whole of the secular order as a means and a preparation to the supernatural aim of life, and it incorporates genuine ascetism into its structure as one element in this preparation, all under the very definite direction of the Church. The sects refer their members directly to the supernatural aim of life, and in them the individualistic, directly religious character of asceticism, as a means of union with God, is developed more strongly and fully; the attitude of opposition to the world and its powers, to which the secularized Church now also belongs, tends to develop a theoretical and general asceticism. It must, however, be admitted that asceticism in the Church, and in ecclesiastical monasticism, has a different meaning from that of the renunciation of or hostility to the world which characterizes the asceticism of the sects.

The asceticism of the Church is a method of acquiring virtue, and a special high watermark of religious achievement, connected chiefly with the repression of the senses, or expressing itself in special achievements of a peculiar character; otherwise, however, it presupposes the life of the world as the general background, and the contrast of an average morality which is on relatively good terms with the world. Along these lines, therefore, ecclesiastical asceticism is connected with the asceticism of the redemption cults of late antiquity, and with the detachment required for the contemplative life; in any case, it is connected with a moral dualism.

The asceticism of the sects, on the other hand, is merely the simple principle of detachment from the world, and is expressed in the refusal to use the law, to swear in a court of justice, to own property, to exercise dominion over others, or to take part in war. The sects take the Sermon on the Mount as their ideal; they lay stress on the simple but radical opposition of the Kingdom of God to all secular interests and institutions. They practise renunciation only as a means of charity, as the basis of a thoroughgoing communism of love, and, since their rules are equally binding upon all, they do not encourage extravagant and heroic deeds, nor the vicarious heroism of some to make up for the worldliness and average morality of others. The ascetic ideal of the sects consists simply in opposition to the world and to its social institutions, but it is not opposition to the sense-life, nor to the average life of humanity. It is therefore only related with the asceticism of monasticism in so far as the latter also creates special conditions, within which it is possible to lead a life according to the Sermon on the Mount, and in harmony with the ideal of the communism of love. In the main, however, the ascetic ideal of the sects is fundamentally different from that of monasticism, in so far as the latter implies emphasis upon the mortification of the senses, and upon works of supererogation in poverty and obedience for their own sake. In all things the ideal of the sects is essentially not one which aims at the destruction of the sense life and of natural self-feeling, but a union in love which is not affected by the social inequalities and struggles of the world. . . .

The essence of the Church is its objective institutional character. The individual is born into it, and through infant baptism he comes under its miraculous influence. The priesthood and the hierarchy, which hold the keys to the tradition of the Church, to sacramental grace and ecclesiastical jurisdiction, represent the objective treasury of grace, even when the individual priest may happen to be unworthy; this Divine treasure only needs to be set always upon the lampstand and made effective through the sacraments, and it will inevitably do its work by virtue of the miraculous power which the Church contains. The Church means the eternal existence of the God-Man; it is the extension of the Incarnation, the objective organization of miraculous power, from which, by means of the Divine Providential government of the world, subjective results will appear quite naturally. From this point of view compromise with the world, and the connection with the preparatory stages and dispositions which it contained, was possible; for in spite of all individual inadequacy the institution remains holy and Divine, and it contains the promise of its capacity to overcome the world by means of the miraculous power which dwells within it. Universalism, however, also only becomes possible on the basis of this compromise; it means an actual domination of the institution as such, and a believing confidence in its invincible power of inward influence. Personal effort and service, however fully they may be emphasized, even when they go to the limits of extreme legalism, are still only secondary; the main thing is the objective possession of grace and its universally recognized dominion; to everything else these words apply: *et cetera adjicientur vobis.* The one vitally important thing is that every individual should come within the range of the influence of these saving energies of grace; hence the Church is forced to dominate Society, compelling all the members of Society to come under its sphere and influence;

but, on the other hand, her stability is entirely unaffected by the fact of the extent to which her influence over all individuals is actually attained. The Church is the great educator of the nations, and like all educators she knows how to allow for various degrees of capacity and maturity, and how to attain her end only by a process of adaptation and compromise.

Compared with this institutional principle of an objective organism, however, the sect is a voluntary community whose members join it of their own free will. The very life of the sect, therefore, depends on actual personal service and co-operation; as an independent member each individual has his part within the fellowship; the bond of union has not been indirectly imparted through the common possession of Divine grace, but it is directly realized in the personal relationships of life. An individual is not born into a sect; he enters it on the basis of conscious conversion; infant baptism, which, indeed, was only introduced at a later date, is almost always a stumbling-block. In the sect spiritual progress does not depend upon the objective impartation of Grace through the Sacrament, but upon individual personal effort; sooner or later, therefore, the sect always criticizes the sacramental idea. This does not mean that the spirit of fellowship is weakened by individualism; indeed, it is strengthened, since each individual proves that he is entitled to membership by the very fact of his services to the fellowship. It is, however, naturally a somewhat limited form of fellowship, and the expenditure of so much effort in the maintenance and exercise of this particular kind of fellowship produces a certain indifference towards other forms of fellowship which are based upon secular interests; on the other hand, all secular interests are drawn into the narrow framework of the sect and tested by its standards, in so far as the sect is able to assimilate these interests at all. Whatever cannot be related to the group of interests controlled by the sect, and by the Scriptural ideal, is rejected and avoided. The sect, therefore, does not educate nations in the mass, but it gathers a select group of the elect, and places it in sharp opposition to the world. In so far as the sect-type maintains Christian universalism at all, like the Gospel, the only form it knows is that of eschatology; this is the reason why it always finally revives the eschatology of the Bible. That also naturally explains the greater tendency of the sect towards "ascetic" life and thought, even though the original ideal of the New Testament had not pointed in that direction. The final activity of the group and of the individual consists precisely in the practical austerity of a purely religious attitude towards life which is not affected by cultural influences. That is, however, a different kind of asceticism, and this is the reason for that difference between it and

the asceticism of the Church-type which has already been stated. It is
not the heroic special achievement of a special class, restricted by its very
nature to particular instances, nor the mortification of the senses in order
to further the higher religious life; it is simply detachment from the world,
the reduction of worldly pleasure to a minimum, and the highest possible
development of fellowship in love; all this is interpreted in the old
Scriptural sense. Since the sect-type is rooted in the teaching of Jesus,
its asceticism also is that of primitive Christianity and of the Sermon on
the Mount, not that of the Church and of the contemplative life; it is
narrower and more scrupulous than that of Jesus, but, literally understood,
it is still the continuation of the attitude of Jesus towards the world. The
concentration on personal effort, and the sociological connection with a
practical ideal, makes an extremely exacting claim on individual effort,
and avoidance of all other forms of human association. The asceticism of
the sect is not an attempt to popularize and universalize an ideal which
the Church had prescribed only for special classes and in special circumstances. The Church ideal of asceticism can never be conceived as a
universal ethic; it is essentially unique and heroic. The ascetic ideal of
the sect, on the contrary, is, as a matter of course, an ideal which is
possible to all, and appointed for all, which, according to its conception,
united the fellowship instead of dividing it, and according to its content
is also capable of a general realization in so far as the circle of the elect
is concerned.

Thus, in reality we are faced with two different sociological types.
This is true in spite of the fact (which is quite immaterial) that incidentally in actual practice they may often impinge upon one another. If
objections are raised to the terms "Church" and "Sect," and if all sociological groups which are based on and inspired by monotheistic, univer-
salized, religious motives are described (in a terminology which is in itself
quite appropriate) as "Churches," we would then have to make the
distinction between institutional churches and voluntary churches. It does
not really matter which expression is used. The all-important point is
this: that both types are a logical result of the Gospel, and only conjointly
do they exhaust the whole range of its sociological influence, and thus
also indirectly of its social results, which are always connected with the
religious organization.

13. Types of Sects in the United States

E. T. CLARK *

TYPOLOGIES THAT FOLLOW THE LEAD OF TROELTSCH ARE PRIMARILY FUNCTIONAL: TO DEFINE A "CHURCH" IS TO EXPLAIN THE WAYS IN WHICH IT IS RELATED TO THE SECULAR ASPECTS OF SOCIETY AND TO THE NEEDS AND TENDENCIES OF ITS ADHERENTS. CLARK'S CLASSIFICATION OF SECTS IS BASED PREDOMINANTLY ON CULTURAL DIFFERENCES: VARIATIONS IN BELIEF, IN RITUAL, IN GROUP STRUCTURE ARE THE CRITERIA BY WHICH ONE TYPE IS DISTINGUISHED FROM ANOTHER. NO ONE CLASSIFICATION, OF COURSE, IS SUITABLE FOR ALL PURPOSES.

A study of the small American sects, however, reveals that they may be grouped roughly into seven main categories, according to the types of mind to which their leading principles appeal. The lines of demarcation cannot be strictly drawn, however, for here, as elsewhere, training and social pressure have operated, and since any given sect embraces several different principles there will be considerable overlapping. The categories are as follows:

1. *The Pessimistic or Adventist Sects.* These are typical groups of the disinherited, in final despair of obtaining through social processes the benefits they seek. They see no good in the world and no hope of improvement; it is rushing speedily to hell, according to the will and plan of God. The adherents of such sects magnify millenarianism and see the imminent end of the present world-order by means of a cosmic catastrophe. They have turned on the world, and they seek escape through a cataclysm which will cast down those who have been elevated, and secure to the faithful important places in a new temporal kingdom as well as eternal bliss in heaven. Adventists are the best representatives of this class, although this philosophy is the leading principle of the so-called Fundamentalist movement and is found in nearly all of the denominations and in many small sects.

2. *The Perfectionist Subjectivist Sects.* These seek holiness, personal perfection of life, or freedom from the temptations and "desires of the flesh." They are of the experiential type, realizing their hopes through strong emotional reactions. The early Methodists were fine examples of

* From *The Small Sects in America*, pp. 22–24.

this type of mind, and the present-day perfectionists are nearly all off-shoots of Methodism. Among these sects are the Nazarene, Holiness, and similar bodies.

3. *The Charismatic or Pentecostal Sects.* These are the left-wing of the subjectivist groups. They seek "gifts," the "spirit of prophecy," the "blessing," and spiritual enduements of various kinds. "Speaking with tongues," trances, visions, and various motor reactions characterize their worship. Examples are found in the pentecostal sects, some of the Church of God groups, and many Negro bodies.

4. *The Communistic Sects.* These groups withdraw from "the world" into colonies where they secure the social approval which is denied them elsewhere and where they engage in economic experiments. Community of goods is the common characteristic. Some of these groups have espoused free love or community of women and their rites have run into antinomian excesses. None of these sects have been able to preserve their pure communistic character over a long period; many have appeared and died, some have gradually merged with the society about them, and a few are maintaining a struggling existence. Among these religious colonies may be mentioned the Shakers, the Amana Church Society, the House of David, the Church of God and Saints of Christ, at Belleville, Virginia, and the now-defunct Llano Colony.

5. *The Legalistic or Objectivist Sects.* For want of a better name the term "legalistic" is used to designate a group of sects which stress certain rules, objective forms, observances, or "things" which can be definitely performed as essential to true religion. Frequently the distinguishing mark is the *rejection* or *denial* of some practice. The sects derive their rites or taboos from some portion of the Bible and sometimes look upon themselves as the "true church" or restorers of primitive Christianity. In this group are the foot-washing sects, those which insist upon some peculiarity of dress, as the "hook-and-eye" Mennonites, and those that cover the heads of the women, the Presbyterians who sing only the Psalms and reject the hymns, the Churches of Christ, with their antipathy to musical instruments and missionary societies, and the Primitive Baptists, who oppose Sunday schools. Included also are the sacramentarian or sacerdotal sects, which set great store by their sacraments and the "apostolic succession" of their higher clergy. Examples are the Old Catholic Churches, of which there are three in America, and the African Orthodox Church, a Negro body.

6. *The Egocentric or New Thought Sects.* These have physical comfort, personal exhilaration, and freedom from pain, disease, and ennui as their

objectives. The Christian Scientists, Divine Scientists, Unity School of Christianity, and New Thought groups are examples of this type.

7. *The Esoteric or Mystic Sects.* These are devotees of the mystic. They espouse doctrines into which one needs to be initiated. They are nearly all offshoots of Hinduism and can hardly be called Christian sects. They specialize on mysteries and the occult, and their literature is scarcely understandable to the ordinary man. The best examples are the Theosophists and the Spiritualists.

14. The Marginal Catholic: An Institutional Approach

JOSEPH H. FICHTER *

TYPOLOGIES OF RELIGIOUS PARTICIPANTS ARE POTENTIALLY AS USEFUL TO A SCIENCE OF RELIGION AS TYPOLOGIES OF GROUP STRUCTURE. RELATIVELY FEW, HOWEVER, HAVE BEEN DEVELOPED. WEBER GAVE GREAT ATTENTION TO DIFFERENCES IN RELIGIOUS INTEREST, BUT HIS TYPOLOGICAL WORK AT THIS POINT, AS WE HAVE SEEN IN CHAPTER 11, WAS PRIMARILY CONCERNED WITH RELIGIOUS LEADERS. FICHTER'S PAPER IS ESSENTIALLY DESCRIPTIVE AND THE APPLICABILITY OF HIS CLASSIFICATION TO OTHER SETTINGS IS UNTESTED; BUT WE HAVE HERE A USEFUL BEGINNING.

Any attempt to arrange a typology of the persons participating in a religious structure involves a number of complicated abstractions. The dividing line between any two categories is admittedly "fuzzy" in that some people do not fall unambiguously into either of them. The criteria employed are relatively arbitrary, and the psycho-social analysis of the persons within each category is not satisfactorily conclusive.

In spite of these difficulties we have made certain generalizations from our research in urban Catholic parishes.[1] We have tentatively classified the urban white Catholics of this study into four general groupings: (a) *nuclear*, who are the most active participants and the most faithful be-

* From *Social Forces*, December, 1953, pp. 167–173.
[1] The basic data of this article are an extension of the *Southern Parish* research project, financed from funds made available jointly by the Carnegie Foundation and Loyola University of the South. The first of the four-volume series reporting this project was *Dynamics of a City Church* (Chicago: University of Chicago Press, 1951).

lievers; (b) *modal*, who are the normal "practicing" Catholics easily identifiable as parishioners; (c) *marginal*, who are conforming to a bare, arbitrary minimum of the patterns expected in the religious institution; (d) *dormant*, who have "given up" Catholicism, but have not joined another denomination.

This paper is concerned only with the marginal, or "fringe" Catholic, and it takes into consideration the several facets of cultural marginality which have beguiled sociological thinking ever since Robert Park first introduced it and Everett Stonequist elaborated upon it.[2] We have employed the marginal concept in analyzing our data on 14,838 white Catholics living in three ecclesiastical parishes of a southern city. The basic information was gathered through census schedules and personal interviews and is chronologically valid as of April 1951.

The several important aspects of marginality have been combined in the present analysis: (a) the individual's internal psychological conflict, symbolized in the general term *value conflict*, which seems to have been paramount in the original discussions of the marginal man; [3] (b) the *imperfectly institutionalized role*, which implies a kind of ambiguity and inconsistency in both the behavior of the marginal man and the sanctions attending his behavior; [4] (c) *socio-religious distance*, because a classification of religious participants requires a social stratification of the religious structure according to the behavioral and value norms employed.

It appears that all three of these aspects of marginality may be fruitfully combined in a basic "institutional approach" to the problem of the marginal Catholic parishioner. If the urban cultural system is conceived as a series of interlocking circles, each of which represents a major institution, the human being may be said to occupy a position somewhere inside each circle. Conformity to the behavioral norms and acceptance of the goals and values of any particular institution may be measured along the

[2] The original contributions on marginality have become almost classic. See Robert E. Park, "Human Migration and the Marginal Man," *American Journal of Sociology*, 33 (May 1928), pp. 881–893; also Everett V. Stonequist, "The Problem of the Marginal Man," *American Journal of Sociology*, 41 (July 1935), pp. 1–12, and *The Marginal Man: A Study in Personality and Culture Conflict* (New York: Scribner's, 1937).

[3] The over-simplified version of this cultural and personality conflict has been discussed in the following articles: Milton M. Goldberg, "A Qualification of the Marginal Man Theory," *American Sociological Review*, 6 (February 1941), pp. 52–58; Arnold W. Green, "A Re-examination of the Marginal Man Concept," *Social Forces*, 26 (December 1947), pp. 167–171; and David I. Golovensky, "The Marginal Man Concept: An Analysis and Critique," *Social Forces*, 30 (March 1952), pp. 333–339.

[4] This aspect is competently analyzed by Walter I. Wardwell, "A Marginal Professional Role: The Chiropractor," *Social Forces*, 30 (March 1952), pp. 339–348.

radius of the circle. The more distant from the center, the less conforming and the less accepting would one be.

Two sociological generalizations concerning the major institutions underlie the present analysis. The first is that the major institutions are universal in the American culture in the sense that every individual is somehow affected by all of them. This seems true of the religious institution even in regard to those who disclaim any affiliation with organized religion. Cuber put this fact accurately when he said that there no longer exists the "either-or" proposition of Church membership and affiliation, and that the measure must be in degrees of participation rather than on clear-cut lines. "To the degree that a given person is observably controlled in his behavior by the institution in however slight a degree, he cannot be said to be wholly outside its 'culture.' He is a marginal participant, perhaps even with non-Church culture ascendant over Church culture—but marginal to the Church culture, nevertheless." [5]

The second generalization is the fact that the several major institutions in our culture are, at various points of comparison, inconsistent with one another. This is indicated when Golovensky remarks that American culture "is not a monolithic organism but rather a pluralistic mosaic, a congeries of conflicting and contradictory values." [6] As Williams points out, we do not find a neatly unified "ethos" or an irresistible "strain toward consistency" in our society. And in reference to religion he italicizes the statement that "American religious organizations are extraordinarily segregated from other institutionalized structures." [7]

While the culmination of institutional inconsistency which Lynd analyzed would be complete social chaos, and would probably be accompanied by an almost culture-wide phenomenon of neurotic personalities which Horney described, the present concept of a "pluralistic mosaic" of overlapping institutional circles seems to be a necessary and useful instrument of analysis for marginality. Without suggesting a complete fragmentation of the culture, we may say analogously that the division of labor, which Durkheim analyzed so brilliantly, has extended to a sort of "division of institutions." The functions of institutions have become compartmentalized as well as ritualized. Social values and goals have be-

[5] John F. Cuber, "Marginal Church Participants," *Sociology and Social Research*, 25 (September–October 1940), pp. 57–62. Cuber's concept of religious marginality would embrace also those whom we have termed "dormant Catholics."
[6] David I. Golovensky, "The Marginal Man Concept: An Analysis and Critique," *loc. cit.*, p. 335.
[7] Robin M. Williams, *American Society: A Sociological Interpretation* (New York: Alfred A. Knopf, 1951), p. 339.

come functionally specific in each institution. Behavioral patterns, both expected and actual, differ according to the institution in which they operate. Again it must be said that as these institutional divergences increase, the individual who attempts to perform his roles in the several major institutions tends to be pulled in different directions.

The marginal Catholic, the "individual" in question here, is not "all of a piece." He must be conceptualized as both dynamic and pluralistic. In other words, the persons measured by socio-religious distance are not held in permanently static positions. If they are Catholics who are "going away" from the central values of the religious institution and from the nuclear parishioners in the social structure, they probably are not, nor do they consider themselves, "institutional hybrids" or "split personalities." If, on the other hand, they are returning to the modal or nuclear status, they are probably experiencing the soul-searching and the psychological turmoil which seem to accompany the preliminary steps toward spiritual conversion.

The Catholic parishioner, like other church-participants, is faced, in varying degrees of intensity, with the conflict of institutions which exists in the American culture. He, too, like other Americans, is subject to the "patterned evasions" which are found particularly in urban society. For example, certain values current in our capitalistic business system are incompatible with those of the Catholic Church. The Catholic's proximate conformity to the role-demands and vocational values of the business institution may imply his growing distance from the ideals of the religious institution. His economic role may have little integration with his familial role, and even less with his religious role.

The marginal Catholic is still under some influence and control of the religious institution, yet he may be very near its circumference because he is being pulled toward the center of one or more other institutions.[8] He may be said to be partially accepting the values of the religious institution, yet partially rejecting them because of their disagreement with other institutionalized values. His religious role in the Church structure is ambiguous because in the clear-cut formal institutionalism of the Catholic Church there seems to be no patterned status for the person who is "neither hot nor cold."

The concept of socio-religious distance among the members of a Church implies that certain subjective and objective criteria can be employed to identify the marginal participant (as well as the nuclear, modal,

---

[8] Yet he often interprets this influence obversely as a "push" from the religious institution because the Church in its doctrines and practices refuses to "change with the times" or to "keep up with modern progress."

and dormant Catholics). The generalized criteria of religious belief and behavior must be specified and graded in order to discover the number of persons to be included in each category. From the formal teaching of the Church we know that certain elements of religion are more important than others. From the observation of the persons in action relative to the religious structure we can learn the frequency with which they perform the more important functions. From personal interviews we can gain an approximate estimate of the attitudes toward religious doctrines, values and practices.[9]

For example, *nuclear* parishioners cooperate with other lay persons and with the priests in parochial activities, exemplify Christian behavior in their personal lives, hold high religious values and follow the formal sacramental expectations of the Church. This combination of standards obviously cannot be employed to measure the number of marginal Catholics. On the other hand, certain criteria mark the *dormant* Catholic—a sort of outside limit, such as his baptism in infancy, probably his reception of the sacrament of matrimony, occasional attendance at a church service, refusal to join any other Church. He is quite likely also to follow the accepted custom of infant "Christening" for his children. A person who is measured by this combination of norms is already beyond our definition of marginality.

Objectively we employed three criteria in order to determine the extent and percentage of marginals among the 9,052 Catholics in this study. These were Mass attendance, the pascal reception of the sacraments of Communion and Penance, and the religious education of children. The statistics given here are combined from Church records, a house-to-house canvass, census questionnaires, and interviews. The territory in which these data were gathered comprised three urban southern parishes. In this area there lived 14,838 white baptized Catholics seven years of age and older. Since the large number of 5,786 dormant Catholics are really "outside" the Church we exclude them also from our percentages in this analysis. We estimate that approximately one-fifth of the remaining 9,052 persons are marginals.

Mass Attendance. Unless they have a valid excuse, all Catholics above the "age of reason" are morally obliged to attend Mass on Sundays and on the designated feast days of the liturgical year. We found that 1,792 persons (or 19.8 percent) out of the 9,052 Catholics did not even approach this standard of religious observance. As a matter of fact, less

[9] For a rough example of an attempt to measure religious ideology, see the chapter on "The Catholic Mind of the Parish" in the writer's *Dynamics of a City Church*, pp. 259–271.

than half of these individuals attended Mass only once during the year, mainly at Christmas or Easter, at a wedding or funeral. The remainder admitted that they did not go to Mass at all during the preceding year.

Sacraments of Communion and Penance. Every Catholic knows that he has the strict obligation to confess his sins and to receive the Eucharist at least once a year during the pascal time. This is common called "making one's Easter Duties," and its symbolism is very strong in Catholic culture. We found that 1,946 persons (or 21.5 percent) admitted their failure in this obligation during the preceding year. This percentage is somewhat higher than that given for Mass attendance, but the difference indicates that there are some Catholics who go to Mass occasionally during the year but do not receive the sacraments.

Catholic Education of Children. All of these 9,052 Catholics lived in an urban area within easy reach of parochial and other Catholic elementary schools. We suspected that the marginal Catholic parent is most likely to neglect the formal religious education of his children and permit them to attend the public schools of the community. Among the Catholics of this study there were 1,223 families with children of elementary school age. 283 of these families (or 23.1 percent) sent one or more of their children to the public school. While this criterion does not give us the total number of marginal Catholics, it indicates that the percentages of those who seldom attend Mass or receive the sacraments are roughly the same as the percentage of parents who neglect the Catholic elementary education of their children.

While there are some exceptions [10] in each of the three categories of religious duties, we have found that for the most part the *same people* are negligent in all three religious obligations. This rough congruence makes it possible to assert that the marginal parishioner is marked by the same general negative characteristics. When we compare this grouping with others, our study reveals, as a tentative estimate, that approximately 21 percent of these Catholics are marginal; 68 percent are modal, and 11 percent are nuclear (out of 9,052 persons seven years of age and older).

It was relatively easy to arrive at these statistical conclusions, drawn from measurable norms of Catholic behavior. It was much more difficult to determine *the reasons why* a little more than one-fifth of these Catholics seem to hover near the fringe of the religious institution, neither completely inside nor completely outside it. We felt that the subjective attitudes of these persons would provide an important clue to at least a partial and tentative explanation of marginality among Catholics. We wanted

---

[10] As we have seen, some persons attend Mass but do not make their Easter Duties; also, some parents who are otherwise model Catholics send their children to the public school.

to find out more about these marginals, e.g., whether they consider themselves "not-so-good" Catholics, whether they showed symptoms of religious ambivalence, whether their religious roles were more or less ambiguous.

We tried to relate the results of random interviews with marginals, their relatives and with priests, to the general theory of institutional inconsistency in urban culture. As noted above, this hypothesis states that the various major institutions tend to come in conflict with one another and tend to pull the participants in different directions. The results of our interviews partially confirm this institutional approach to religious marginality.

It is an axiom of social science that the value attitudes and the expectations of the social roles of the individual are patterned within the institutional framework of the community in which he lives. It seems quite clear also that the folkways and mores which have gradually accumulated in the recreational, economic, familial, and even political and educational institutions, and which form the content of the social behavior and thinking of the urban Catholic, have an ascendancy over the folkways and mores of the religious institution. The lack of consistency and integration among these basic institutions seems to be clearly reflected in the marginal Catholic.

The following are the four most frequently obvious generalizations which apply to the analysis of marginal Catholics. They appear to be the most influential factors in the formation of this type of religious participant. It must be noted, of course, that these factors are at work on all Catholics, to a lesser extent on nuclear and modal parishioners, to a much greater extent among dormant Catholics.

a) *Contrasting Assumptions.* Among the marginal Catholics in this southern city there is a noticeable attempt to reconcile values and patterns of conduct which are contradictory. The most blatant example of this is the assumption that democracy is a practical ideal worthy of pursuit, coupled at the same time with another assumption to the effect that Negro Catholics are not fit persons to belong to the same parish or to attend the same school with whites. The norms of brotherhood and love which are deeply imbedded in religious ideology are not sufficiently strong to draw the marginal parishioner closer to the center of Catholic life. The traditional cultural patterns of "white" thought and behavior tend to weaken his adherence to religious teachings.[11]

Another example is current in the contrast between professed honesty

---

[11] In some instances we found dormant Catholics who professed racial equality and used, as an argument against religion, the segregation policies and practices of church-goers.

and the demands of occupational roles. The religious ideal firmly asserts the doctrine that a lie is always a lie and that the virtue of justice must be operative at all times. The religious institution is here in conflict with the known practices of the economic institution. The marginal Catholic tends to think that "you can cut corners" with little white lies and little dishonesties in the business world. After all, he says, "Everybody does it, and you don't want to be over-scrupulous about these things."

It must not be implied that the marginal Catholic is morally more sensitive than other Catholics, or that he is *always* conscious of the contrast between the assumptions according to which he behaves. While he is aware of the Church's teaching—at least in a general way—he may also feel that one has to be practical in everyday life. There are, of course, many modal parishioners who accept and fulfill all the rituals and formalities of religion, and at the same time conform largely to the secular patterns and values of the culture. In this respect the difference between the modal and the marginal Catholic seems to be one of general awareness of inconsistency.

b) Relative Morality. This moral phenomenon represents an attitude closely allied to the concept of contrasting assumptions. In the latter case the individual is attempting to accept both of the contrasting beliefs, and finds himself pulled in both directions. Relative morality here means that the goodness and badness of social behavior depends upon the social situation in which a person is involved. It is reflected in the statement of one interviewee: "Every man's ethics are his own and change with his circumstances."

Perhaps this concept of the relativity of morals is met most frequently in the difficult problems of sex, love, and marriage. Personal interviews with marginal Catholics show that birth prevention is often given as a reason for "losing interest" in the Church. The individual "wants to do the right thing" according to the teachings of religion, but circumstances *make it impossible.* "God understands my position. He will not hold me responsible because he knows that *in my case* the Church's stand on birth control is unreasonable."

The marginal Catholic usually does not go so far as to deny the validity of the Church's doctrines on sex sins, birth prevention, divorce, and so forth. In fact, he is likely to praise and defend the "high morality" of Catholicism in a society which seems to be losing its moral standards. He indicates that the Church is correct in its general principles, and that every Catholic should try to conform his life to these principles. But even though sacramental absolution is refused to him because he is himself "unable" to follow the principles, he is sure that God understands his position better than any priest in the confessional. It is manifest that an attitude of this kind will tend also to belittle the other behavioral aspects of Catholicism.

c) *Anti-Authoritarianism.* A third important factor is, according to Catholic doctrine, a misapplication to the religious institution of the traditional American ideal of personal independence. The hierarchical structure of Catholicism shows the hand of Christ ruling through a formally stratified religious monarchy. The principal functionaries of the Catholic Church are arranged in a relatively clear-cut pattern of rank, based on appointment from above. To the marginal Catholic this often seems to be an arbitrary and authoritarian arrangement which conflicts with the American ideal of equal representation for all.

The apparent emphasis on rights and privileges (with a corresponding neglect of the concepts of duties and responsibilities) which is characteristic of the American culture, has helped to crystallize this spirit of religious anti-authoritarianism. Many of these marginal Catholics apparently fail to realize that they are already living under different forms of social control in the various social structures in which they participate. The *laissez-faire* philosophy is expressed in a strange way in this southern urban culture when the same person on the one hand heartily endorses the authoritarian southern political demagogue and on the other hand resists the authority of Bishops and pastors within the ecclesiastical structure.

The way in which priests and parishioners carry out their reciprocal social roles is also relevant in this particular attitude of marginal Catholics. The charge is often made by marginal Catholics that the priests tend to be "dictatorial" in those functions of the Church which are not primarily religious and which do not require "dictation." The marginal parishioner, like the dormant Catholic, is insistent that the priest should confine himself strictly to Mass, sacraments, and rituals. When the priest does otherwise—for example, speaks out on social questions—the marginal Catholic accuses him of interfering with the freedom of the parishioners.

d) *The Dysfunctional Parish.* This fourth factor influencing the behavior of the marginal Catholic is more complex than any of the three others. The general hypothesis is that both the social structure and the cultural values of the urban secular society have interfered with the functioning of the Catholic parish *as a community of persons*.[12] This is a func-

---

[12] This is a variation of the basic sociological theme running through the writings of Suhard, Michonneau, Loew, Le Bras, Lebret, and Godding. The last-named thinks that the "fundamental cause of de-Christianization" has been the "extinction of all

tional as well as structural problem, and it seems to influence both the attitudes and behavioral patterns of religious participants.

The multiple functions of the old-fashioned, solidaristic, community parish have been attenuated. Like the functions of the family, those of the parish have been largely absorbed by other institutions, and they have been partially replaced by the "escape mechanisms" of urban society. This seems especially true in the so-called leisure-time activities of urban Catholics. Radio and television, the picture magazines, commercial movies, sports and dances, are now enjoyed outside the context of the parish. They are also generally outside (or at least indifferent to) the system of typical religious values.

From an abstract point of view, one may suggest that the higher values of the religious institution could offer psychological compensation for the person who is regimented and thwarted in the daily pursuit of economic goals. The materialistic and sensate functions of the working day could be balanced by the more humane and social functions of a highly integrated and active parish. Ideally, the religious institution might be placed in "balance" with the economic institution, or at least provide an escape or outlet for social needs.

It seems, however, that the modern urban Catholic parish has been unable to cope with these institutional changes in American culture. Instead of a "balance of institutions" there has been a substitution of secular institutions. The marginal Catholic leans toward secularized activities and the use of secular escape mechanisms. He claims that he "sees nothing sinful in this" but because of it he logically becomes more worldly in his thinking, and thus marginal to the religious center. Whether the priests and the parishioners have failed by allowing the socially-orientated functions of the parish to lapse, or whether the marginal Catholic has failed in a too-ready acceptance of secular substitutes, is a question beyond our inquiry at this point.

In broadest summary of the factors described above, it may be suggested that the marginal Catholic is largely a product of institutional inconsistency. Hertzler, in writing about organized religion, says that "its power to standardize behavior and exercise social control, either for groups or for individuals, *has diminished as that of various other institutions has been augmented;* its influence has evaporated from one department of life after another." [13] This does not mean that the moral responsi-

---

those basic communities which help men to develop." See Mazie Ward, *France Pagan?* (New York: Sheed and Ward, 1949), pp. 178 ff.

[13] See J. O. Hertzler, "Religious Institutions," *The Annals of the American Academy of Political and Social Sciences,* 256 (March 1948), p. 13.

bility of the individual to make choices among institutional values can be omitted as a factor of marginality.

Presumably, any marginal Catholic can at any time stop to meditate his religious status, and with the help of divine grace make the decision to return to the Church as a fully participating nuclear Catholic. The enthusiastic apologist of religion may say that "the grace of God is sufficient for him. The sacraments and Church services are available. He need but make up his mind." This presumption can never be denied by a religious believer, but it views the ordinary human being as though he were isolated from other persons and uninfluenced by institutional and cultural contacts. It by-passes the fundamental sociological fact of the cultural environment.

15. Characteristics of American Organized Religion
WINFRED E. GARRISON *

THIS PAPER AND THE NEXT DESCRIBE, FROM DIFFERENT PERSPECTIVES, THE WAYS IN WHICH RELIGION IN AMERICA HAS BEEN AFFECTED BY THE TOTAL SOCIO-CULTURAL ENVIRONMENT. THEY MAKE CLEAR THAT THE SOCIETY IN WHICH A RELIGION IS FOUND HAS A VITAL INFLUENCE ON THE COURSE OF ITS DEVELOPMENT.

When organized religion in America is viewed in one continuous panorama, from the beginning of the Federal period to the present time, its most conspicuous and distinctive features seem to be these: the full flowering of the denominational system; revivalism, or evangelism; the "social gospel"; and the trend toward co-operation and union among denominations.

Back of these characteristics of organized religion lie certain environmental factors which are primarily political, geographic, social, and economic. The chief of these are: the complete equality of all churches and of all citizens before the law, regardless of their religion or lack of it, and the absence of governmental control or support for the churches; the newness of the country at the beginning of the Federal period, with a small population in a vast area; the small proportion of church members in the

* Abridged from Annals of the American Academy of Political and Social Science, March, 1948, pp. 14–24.

total population at that time; the volume and variety of immigration; an
expanding economy, with rapid increase of population, wealth, occupied
area, and social and cultural institutions; urbanization and the shift from
an agricultural to an industrial economy.

Putting these causes and consequences together, we may arrive at some
such list of topics as the following which will guide our exploration of the
phenomena of institutional religion in America: (1) free churches in a
free society—a new idea; (2) the denominational system; (3) a new
country and an advancing frontier; (4) revivalism; (5) immigration and
its consequences; (6) the recovered sense of social responsibility; (7)
trends toward unity. . . .

FREE CHURCHES IN A FREE SOCIETY

The religious situation in America was radically altered by a series of
changes which preceded and accompanied the American Revolution and
were clinched by its success. The establishments of religion in the separate
colonies faded out. One or two lingered on, vestigially, into the next century, but they were obviously outworn. The Virginia "Declaration of
Rights," adopted June 12, 1776, expresed an idea which was widely current in all the colonies and was to become the keystone of the national
policy with respect to religion. It declared:

XVI. That Religion, or the Duty which we owe to our Creator, and the
Manner of discharging it, can be directed only by Reason and Conviction, not
by Force or Violence; and therefore, all Men are equally entitled to the free
Exercise of Religion, according to the Dictates of Conscience; and that it
is the mutual Duty of all to practice Christian Forbearance, Love and Charity,
towards each other.

Ten years later, the Virginia "Act for Establishing Religious Freedom,"
written by Thomas Jefferson and adopted January 16, 1786, went still
farther. The 1776 declaration had freed the consciences but not the purses
of citizens from compulsion by the state on behalf of the church. The 1786
act laid down these principles: (1) that the state has no right to compel
the citizen to support with money the propagation even of those religious
opinions which he believes, much less those which he disbelieves; (2)
that "civil rights have no dependence on our religious opinions"; (3) that
eligibility to public office ought not to be conditioned upon the profession
or renunciation of any religious opinion; (4) that all men are free to worship as they will, or not to worship at all, without restraint or penalty; and
(5) that all are equally "free to profess, and by argument to maintain,

their opinion in matters of religion"—which would even include anti-religious opinions.

The effect of this act was not only to disestablish the Episcopal Church but to reject decisively the proposal, strongly urged by some, that Christianity should be declared "the religion of the state" and that ministers of all denominations should be supported by taxation. There was a real battle on this point. The sweeping action which brought about genuine separation of church and state was not taken by inadvertence.

Nor was the Congress of the United States unaware of this issue and the implications of Virginia's decision when, only three years later, it voted to submit for ratification the First Amendment to the Constitution. This declared that "Congress shall make no law respecting an establishment of religion." In the light of the Virginia debates and decision, which were a matter of common knowledge, the First Amendment clearly meant: no Federal establishment of any one church (which would have been patently impossible anyway); no establishment of several or all churches by levying a tax to be divided among them; in short, no law whatsoever looking toward the establishment or support of religion by the Government. The phrase "separation of church and state," coined later, describes the situation produced and guaranteed by this amendment.

A NEW IDEA

The separation of church and state was a thing unheard of in Christendom since the fourth century. It is the one thing to which, more than to anything else, the distinguishing characteristics of organized religion in America are due. The fact that the American churches were in an unprecedented position in relation to the political and social order must be emphasized by contrasting the new arrangement with the one which it supplanted.

For more than fourteen hundred years—that is, from a little after the time of Constantine—it was a universal assumption that the stability of the social order and the safety of the state demanded the religious solidarity of all the people in one church. Every responsible thinker, every ecclesiastic, every ruler and statesman who gave the matter any attention, held to this as an axiom. There was no political or social philosophy which did not build upon this assumption. . . .

. . . . On the administrative side, the two most profound revolutions which have occurred in the entire history of the church have been these: first, the change of the church, in the fourth century, from a voluntary society having in its membership only those who were members by their own choice, to a society conceived as necessarily coextensive with the civil community and endowed with the power to enforce the adherence of all members of the civil community; second, the reversal of this change. That reversal was completed in America.

This was not an issue between Catholics and Protestants. The theory of compulsory solidarity was, indeed, of Roman Catholic origin, was practiced consistently by the medieval church, and has continued to be practiced with some necessary modifications in Catholic countries; but it was also taken over by the major divisions of Protestantism in so far as these secured establishment as state churches. England concerns us most. Tudor, Stuart, and Commonwealth Protestantism saw an established church, of whatever complexion, struggling to maintain its monopoly and to convince the government that dissent from its norms would be dangerous to the state. This attitude was carried into Puritan New England and into other colonies.

In mother country and colonies alike, the growing sense of man's natural rights made this theory difficult to maintain, and experience proved it false. The pressure of increasing numbers of dissenters was irresistible, and their complete suppression or assimilation was impracticable. It was found that, in actual fact, dissenters were not necessarily disloyal to the state, and that compulsory religious conformity was not the cement of the social order. England learned this slowly and relaxed the pressure on her nonconformists while keeping her established church. The colonies learned it more rapidly and more completely. The founders of Rhode Island and Pennsylvania had known it from the start. Virginia made splendid and memorable record of its discovery.

THE DENOMINATIONAL SYSTEM

By the time the Federal Government was launched, this second revolution in church history—the one in the interest of religious liberty—had been sufficiently achieved in America to ensure the complete detachment of all the churches from the Central Government and the equal treatment of them all by the Government in so far as it had any relations with them. This was the first great distinguishing fact about organized religion in Federal America.

Visitors from Europe frequently mention the multiplicity of sects as the first feature of the religious scene that strikes their attention. The explanation is simple and not too discreditable. America has more sects than any European country because she has received immigrants from all of them—often as refugees. And America has more sects because nowhere else, in the formative period, did all sects enjoy complete freedom, including freedom from the overshadowing prestige of a long-established state church. . . .

A NEW COUNTRY AND AN ADVANCING FRONTIER

Frederick J. Turner discovered and publicized the significance of the frontier in American history. Mode, Sweet, and others have explored the influence of the frontier on the American churches. The point is valid. America is still young. A British visitor remarks that, by contrast with his own land, America "has no medieval churches." Except for rare colonial landmarks, America has not even any seventeenth-century and very few eighteenth-century churches. As seen through European eyes, this gives a sense of shallow rootage.

But the churches are no newer than the country. In 1800 the United States was a ribbon of settlements along one coast, with a vast and almost empty and unknown hinterland. Ninety per cent of its 5,300,000 people lived east of the Alleghenies, and more than half of the other 10 per cent were in Kentucky and Tennessee. . . .

The notable fact is that here was a great new country to be occupied by settlers and by the churches at the same time. Or, to put it in another way, the new communities which were coming into existence had to create simultaneously their social, political, and religious institutions. The separation of church and state meant that the religious effort had to be supported on an entirely voluntary basis. The churches had neither subsidies nor endowments; they were strictly on their own.

Though the institutions of the frontier had to be created on the ground, the basic patterns were imported from the east and from overseas. The churches which grew up in the Middle West were new congregations of old types, their coloration but not their fundamental structure determined by environment. . . .

REVIVALISM

Revivalism was for many years a conspicuous characteristic of religion in America. Its first large-scale manifestation was in colonial days, about 1740, with the "Great Awakening." The names of Jonathan Edwards and George Whitefield stand forth here, but the drive for converts was continued by the "New Light" Presbyterians, who, through the remainder of that century, stressed evangelism more than creed. Methodism was vigorously evangelistic from its first days in America, about 1770. The next notable event was the Great Western Revival, about 1800, in which

Methodists, Presbyterians, and Baptists were involved, all using Methodistic methods. Out of this grew the camp meeting, which became a famous frontier institution and (after the manner of institutions generally) lingered on after the passing of the conditions that gave rise to it.

Later waves of revivalism swept the country periodically. The three decades before the Civil War were especially marked by this phenomenon. Neither the more sober denominations, such as Presbyterians and Congregationalists, nor the large eastern centers of population were immune to this contagion of religious enthusiasm, as witness the spectacular successes of Charles G. Finney in New York, Boston, and Rochester. Conservative Calvinists on the one hand and such relatively liberal theologians as Lyman Beecher and Horace Bushnell on the other tried, but in vain, to stem the torrent. It ran its course and, to a great extent, was swallowed up in the greater and more mundane excitement induced by the issues of slavery and secession.

When the revival returned in the Moody and Sankey era, it was to sound a less strident note with a less furious tempo. Subsequent types of evangelistic campaigning—from the sanctified wit of "Sam" Jones (a Methodist) to the morally earnest billingsgate and acrobatics of "Billy" Sunday (a Presbyterian) and the mellifluous pleading of "Gypsy" Smith —appealed to a diversity of tastes and interests in what had become a highly heterogeneous society. These campaigns were prominent in the news but were marginal in the life of the churches and spasmodic in any given community. No attempt is made here to evaluate their good and bad results. They had both. All these great revival movements tended to ignore sectarian walls, to play down denominational distinctions, and to present the elements of Christianity common to all.

CONVERSION FOR 90 PER CENT

The rise and progress of revivalism presupposed a large nonchurch public to which the appeal was directed. This state of affairs existed, and was another distinctive characteristic of the American scene. In 1800, less than 10 per cent of the people in the United States were members of any church. There was probably not another country in Christendom with so small a percentage of professed Christians. There is no way of knowing what proportion of the people in Great Britain or on the Continent were more than nominal Christians, but most of them were members of churches. The state church system had produced that result even in those Protestant countries which permitted nonconforming bodies to exist. In Roman Catholic countries, of course, everything possible was done to prevent them from existing. But everywhere outside of the United States, persons who took no interest in religion one way or the other were church members by default. In America the opposite was true.

With 90 per cent of the population outside the churches, the task of organized religion could not be limited to encouraging "Christian nurture" (the title of Bushnell's great antirevival book) in Christian families, or to ministering to old members as they moved to new places farther west. It had to be directed toward that 90 per cent. What they needed first was not nurture or edification, but radical conversion. Nowhere since Christianity was carried into northern Europe to drive out the old Germanic and Scandinavian gods had there been such a field for a campaign of evangelism; and here the pagans (of Christian heritage, to be sure, but non-Christians just the same) could not be swept into the church by a mass movement or by winning over their chiefs. The American pagans followed no chiefs, and they had to be brought in one by one. It is small wonder that the revivalists put on all the heat they could and, with some notable exceptions, appealed to the emotions more than to the intelligence. . . .

IMMIGRATION AND ITS CONSEQUENCES

Immigration augmented the general percentage of church members and, more specifically, brought an enormous increase in both the number and the percentage of Roman Catholics. Until 1830, immigration was light enough to leave relatively unchanged the racial, cultural, and religious characteristics of the later colonial and early Federal days. The racial strain and the cultural tradition were chiefly British, and the background was Protestant even though the backsliders and the unregenerate far outnumbered the communicants. There were also German, Dutch, Swedish, and French elements, the last including colonies of Huguenot refugees in the east and Roman Catholic early settlers in the Mississippi Valley. The Irish were Scotch-Irish, Ulster Presbyterians of Scottish ancestry.

At the time of the first Federal census, in 1790, less than 1 per cent of the population was Roman Catholic—30,000 out of 3,900,000. There had been restrictive legislation against Roman Catholics in some of the colonies, though nothing to compare with the proscription of Protestants at the same period and later in Catholic countries. But from the beginning of the Federal period, Catholics had full liberty of worship and civil equality. . . .

Immigration increased greatly after 1830, and enormously after 1840. The chief influx was from Ireland, and all the Irish were Roman Catholics.

Most of them stayed in the eastern cities. There was also heavy Catholic immigration from Germany. By 1860 the initial 30,000 Catholics had become 3,000,000, and their proportion of the total population had increased from .78 to 9.65 per cent. Roughly, the population of the country had been multiplied by 10, the Catholic population by 100. Immigration was the chief source of this increase, aided by the high birth rate in immigrant families.

NATIVISM

The tensions that arose were the resultant of several causes, of which religion was the least. Antialien, specifically anti-Irish, and anti-cheap-labor feeling and the fear of antirepublican influences were more basic than anti-Catholic "prejudice." The belief that Catholicism was hostile to what were deemed fundamental American principles seemed plausible because the Vatican was in active alliance with every reactionary and antidemocratic force in Europe during the forty years after Napoleon, and the Popes were constantly denouncing every form of liberalism and declaring that the demand for religious liberty was nothing else than the essentially irreligious attitude of "indifferentism."

Nativist feeling found expression in a series of "American" political parties, under various names, which demanded a period of twenty-one years' residence in the United States prior to naturalization and opposed any candidate for public office who "owes allegiance to any foreign prince or potentate"—meaning, of course, the Pope. The slogan, "No Irish need apply"—often humorously used but meant to be taken as a true word spoken in jest—signified that the Irish were regarded as a lower order of humanity, ignorant, vicious, and unclean, who, if they no longer "kept the pig in the parlor" as they were reputed to do in the old country, would naturally do so if they were not too miserably poor to have either parlors or pigs. That they were Catholics was significant only because of the presumption that such ignorant and superstitious people would vote as their priests told them, and most of the priests were also recent immigrants. Gone were the days when a "Charles Carroll of Carrollton," signer of the Declaration of Independence, could be considered as the typical American Catholic. In the Massachusetts mill towns, the Irish lived in hovels on the other side of the track. In the cities, they crowded the ranks of unskilled labor and competed with "real Americans" for jobs. Labor was unorganized, its condition was bad, and the heavy immigration made it worse.

The anti-Catholic angle, which became very real, had nothing to do with Catholicism as a form of faith and worship. Aside from the fact that these odious immigrants happened to be Catholics, the feeling against the Roman Catholic Church rested on these alleged grounds: (1) that the Pope is a foreign ruler to whom all Catholics give prior loyalty and from whom they, and especially their priests, receive instructions which govern their political action as citizens; (2) that the Catholic hierarchy, from the Pope down, is hostile to democracy and to the civil rights guaranteed by the Constitution, and plans to gain control of the United States so as to transform it into a typical "Catholic country" in which civil and religious liberty would be suppressed, as in Spain and the Papal State itself; (3) that this control is sought by directing the masses of Catholic voters at the polls, and perhaps by armed insurrection when the time is ripe; (4) that the personal morals of the clergy are low and the internal administration of monasteries and convents amounts to a tyranny and a scandal.

Some of the Protestant clergy lent their support to one or all of these charges, but the main force of the organized attack upon what was commonly called "political Romanism" did not come from Protestants as such. Its impulse, its leadership, and its personnel were akin to those of the anticlerical movements which have occurred, with even more vigor and effectiveness, in some Catholic countries where there were practically no Protestants at all. No important leader of any of the nativist and anti-Catholic parties, from the Native Americans of 1836 to the Know-Nothings of 1855, was a figure of any consequence in any Protestant church. This is true also of such later organizations as the A.P.A. (American Protective Association—not American Protestant Association as sometimes supposed) and the Ku Klux Klan.

Nevertheless, the great growth of the Roman Catholic Church in numbers, wealth, and power in a country which began its national life on a set of principles radically at variance with the political and social philosophy of that church as exhibited everywhere else throughout history, has produced a situation which is not only distinctive of organized religion in America but is unique in the history of Christendom.

THE RECOVERED SENSE OF SOCIAL RESPONSIBILITY

"Activism" is a quality which has often been ascribed to American religion, with an unfavorable connotation, implying a culpable indifference to doctrine, sacraments, and the things of the spiritual life, and an equally culpable absorption in the operation of the church's machinery and in efforts to "do good" by improving the conditions of the community and the social order. It is charged with being too optimistic, too confident of man's power to do what needs to be done, too little inclined to "wait on God."

Passing over the implied judgment, one may say that there is much truth in the statement that American churches have been active. The preceding pages have suggested some reasons why they had to be. They inherited the Christian gospel which it is their business to disseminate and apply, but they were completely on their own when they created the necessary institutions; they worked up from the grass roots when they built themselves into communities which were as new as they were. They had to win the necessary financial support as they went along—an experience unknown to the European established churches from which the charge of "activism" emanates. Further, they had to win and hold their members in a society in which church membership is not taken for granted as something almost as automatic as allegiance to the flag under which one is born. They had to be active or die.

Looking at the American churches from the inside, one can only regret that they have not been more active in the promotion of social welfare, and more wisely active in some of the matters that have enlisted their effort. The "social gospel" became a slogan in the 1890's, but this was an awakening rather than a new birth. During most of its long history, the church has been concerned about the structure and the functioning of society. A reaction against what seemed a dangerous usurpation of control by the church over secular affairs led to a withdrawal by some churches, including most Protestant churches, to a more restricted field. The American churches emerged from this seclusion to take sides in the War of Independence, in the early campaigns for temperance, both for and against the slavery question, and on prohibition. But it was only when questions of social justice became acute, toward the end of the nineteenth century, that Christian leaders became morally sensitive and intelligently articulate on fundamental issues involving human rights and welfare, and the "social gospel" emerged under that name. The term has lost the charm of novelty and has passed out of common use, but that for which it stands continues, with wider and deeper extensions suggested by conditions arising out of two world wars.

TRENDS TOWARD UNITY

The most conspicuous present trend of organized religion is toward unity. Re-examination of the intellectual foundations of religion has raised new issues unrelated to the old divisions, with consequent planes of cleavage and areas of agreement running across denominational lines. The growing sense of social responsibility shared by all the churches has brought co-operation in fields where sectarian distinctions are obviously irrelevant. The habit of co-operation has bred friendship; friendship has led to better mutual understanding; understanding is an approach to union. The most significant agencies of Protestant co-operation since the beginning of the twentieth century have been the Federal Council of the Churches of Christ in America and the International Council of Religious Education, but there are many others. Several mergers of related or congenial denominations have been consummated, and several more are in various stages of preparation. . . .

The urge toward unity reaches beyond national boundaries. It does not exhaust itself in promoting co-operations and mergers among American denominations. In harmony with a similar impulse which exists in all countries, it envisages the integration of all churches into The Church embracing a world-wide Christianity. This is the "ecumenical movement" which has been taking form through a series of great international and interdenominational conferences, beginning in Edinburgh in 1910. It reaches a landmark in the meeting of the assembly which is to complete the organization of the World Council of Churches in Amsterdam in August 1948. Deep interest and hearty participation in this "ecumenical movement" do not define a distinctively American trait, for, by definition, such a movement is nothing if it does not approximate universality. However, this trait is a characteristic in which American organized religion shares. Its goal is a distant one, and there are apparently insuperable obstacles in the way of its complete attainment. But the movement is in the direction of universality.

16. Some Consequences of Religious Heterogeneity in America
ROBIN M. WILLIAMS *

LACK OF AN ESTABLISHED CHURCH

The first clause of the Bill of Rights, prohibiting the establishment of a state church, simply legalized the social condition already existing in America. From the colonial beginnings, the immigrating population had

* From *American Society*, pp. 318–321.

a variegated religious composition—a sizeable Catholic minority, a few Jewish people, and an enormously varied aggregate of dissenting Protestant sects. Perhaps much more significant, no single one, nor any practicable combination of these groups, was powerful enough to dominate the national government or to wield completely authoritative power in any one of the newly formed states. It was accordingly impossible to secure political consensus as to which *one* church should enjoy state establishment, and the strongly sectarian groups were certainly unwilling to see any rival receive such privileges.

Out of this heterogeneity, therefore, emerged the separation of church and state, which tended to produce further religious diversity. The taxgatherer was separated from the tithecollector, and the religious aspects of the total social structure barred both unitary church organization and any major state support of a particular religious body. The culture remained dominantly Protestant and overwhelmingly Christian, but politically supported religious monopoly was gone—a decisive departure from the European tradition. The single fact of the absence of an established church was therefore centrally important for the total character of religious institutions in this country.[1] It was both the product and cause of denominationalism, with its attendant evangelism, and imposed on the churches the necessity of competitive financing through voluntary contributions. It also encouraged lay representation and control in church organization, as opposed to control by an ecclesiastical hierarchy, and facilitated local independence and secession tendencies in the individual denominations. It tended to reduce the symbolic reinforcement of mutually supportive political and religious authority by largely insulating religious from political organization. This eventually strongly encouraged jealous defensiveness among Protestant sects against the state. Although the Catholic churches (and to a lesser degree, the Lutheran denominations) have not held this attitude strongly, they also have been profoundly affected by lack of establishment.

No one church in American communities can speak for the entire people; as private associations all religious bodies are legally equal to each other. Although religious groupings throughout this society are stamped by recognizably "American" qualities, they are diverse, pluralistic, and incessantly changing; the principle of nonestablishment in religion operates somewhat like *laissez faire* in the economy.

---

[1] Cf. Henry K. Rowe: *The History of Religion in the United States* (New York: 1924), pp. 52 ff.; Thomas C. Hall: *The Religious Background of American Culture* (Boston: 1930); William W. Sweet: *The Story of Religions in America* (New York: 1930); Sperry: *Religion in America.*

As Sperry indicates, the United States as a total culture does not understand the idea of a universal church; it comprehends only the environing facts of numerous types of churches, cults, sects, denominations. Whatever unity there is in American religion is cultural rather than organizational, diffuse convergence rather than an authoritative and centrally controlled system of beliefs and symbols.

RELIGIOUS FREEDOM AND TOLERATION [2]

Each dissenting group that came to colonial America wanted religious freedom for itself, but was by no means prepared to grant religious liberty, or even toleration (a different thing), to all other sectarian movements. Freedom and toleration were only very gradually established in the face of the rival imperialism of sectarian groups, each holding staunchly to its own cherished version of the true faith, and in most cases utterly impatient of dissent. Intolerance pervaded the early period of intense religious interest [3] and internecine religious competition. Orthodoxy was intense, group contrasts great. Aside from the early efforts of Roger Williams and the Calverts to establish toleration, there was no initial commitment to a religious freedom.

Major factors in the rise of religious freedom and toleration include the following: (1) there was no cleavage between two or only a few opposing religious groupings, but rather a fragmented diversity of numerous small sects; ingroup solidarity was diffused, and conflict could not be massive or unitary; (2) no one religious groupings had the opportunity to seize a dominant political position; (3) due to the circumstances of settlement, there was no prior established church common to all the colonies [4] and therefore no vested ecclesiastical interests in property, office, and institutional prestige; (4) outside the solid centers of intense religious orthodoxy there was much public indifference to organized religion in the late eighteenth century; expanding economic and social opportunities tended to distract men from religion; many important political and intellectual leaders were thoroughly secular; (5) the dissenting varie-

---

[2] Convenient background sources: Hall: *The Religious Background of American Culture*, pp. 127–46; Laski: *The American Democracy* (New York: 1948), pp. 264–6; Sperry: *Religion in America*, pp. 6 ff.; M. Searle Bates: *Religious Liberty: An Inquiry* (New York: 1945).

[3] Men are always likely to be intolerant of opposition to their central ultimate values. In the formative period of the American political community, differences in formal religious beliefs and practices were widely interpreted as *ultimate* value-differences.

[4] Although most of the colonies did have some form of establishment, and some states persisted in it until the 1830's.

ties of Protestantism had the incipient principle of toleration: since the individual believer had direct access to Divine truth through the Bible, valid religious experience could be approached by divergent paths; (7) settlers were needed to provide labor, to aid in military security, and to increase capital gains, and the colonies accepting immigrants of various faiths could foresee tangible economic advantages. The factors named [5] are enough to indicate how power considerations, economic interest, religious organization, and creeds converged to produce religious freedom— even though in a broad sense, "nobody intended it." [6]

Religious liberty, once established as an official national doctrine, reinforced the continuing forces of a pluralistic society until the broad principle had worked deeply into the whole cultural fabric. Intolerance and conflict still occur in very substantial proportions, but they are opposed to, and not supported by, the dominant institutions.

[5] Other factors were the loose contacts with the parent organizations in Britain and on the Continent; the pressure of British proprietors to increase settlements; the fact that at the time of the Revolution there were only a few thousand Catholics and a negligible number of Jews in the whole country.

[6] A specific example of the fact that unforeseen and even unwanted consequences are common in collective social processes.

Religion and Social Stratification

The relationship between religion and social stratification has been as fully explored as any part of the sociology of religion. The basic work of Weber and Troeltsch has been followed by a large number of studies which document the ways in which religious patterns vary among the strata of a society. A functional interpretation has been made in most cases: since the needs and tendencies of persons in the different strata vary and since the strata differ in their relationship to the whole social structure, there will be differences in religious inclinations.

17. Occupation and Religion

MAX WEBER *

OCCUPATION IS NOT PRECISELY THE WORD TO USE IN CONNECTION WITH THIS
EXCERPT FROM WEBER, YET IT IS CLOSER THAN THE TERMS CLASS OR STRATUM.
IN ANY EVENT, HIS THESIS IS THAT THE ROAD TO SALVATION THAT WILL SEEM
APPEALING VARIES AMONG GROUPS WHO HAVE HAD DIFFERENT TRAINING, WHO
HAVE DIFFERENT KINDS OF WORK, WHO HAVE A DIFFERENT PLACE IN THE TOTAL
SOCIAL SYSTEM.

The kind of empirical state of bliss or experience of rebirth that is sought after as the supreme value by a religion has obviously and necessarily varied according to the character of the stratum which was foremost in adopting it. The chivalrous warrior class, peasants, business classes, and intellectuals with literary education have naturally pursued different religious tendencies. As will become evident, these tendencies have not by themselves determined the psychological character of religion; they have, however, exerted a very lasting influence upon it. The contrast between warrior and peasant classes, and intellectual and business classes, is of special importance. Of these groups, the intellectuals have always been the exponents of a rationalism which in their case has been relatively theoretical. The business classes (merchants and artisans) have been at least possible exponents of rationalism of a more practical sort. Rationalism of either kind has borne very different stamps, but has always exerted a great influence upon the religious attitude.

Above all, the peculiarity of the intellectual strata in this matter has been in the past of the greatest importance for religion. At the present time, it matters little in the development of a religion whether or not modern intellectuals feel the need of enjoying a "religious" state as an "experience," in addition to all sorts of other sensations, in order to decorate their internal and stylish furnishings with paraphernalia guaranteed to be genuine and old. A religious revival has never sprung from such a source. In the past, it was the work of the intellectuals to sublimate the possession of sacred values into a belief in "redemption." The conception of the idea of redemption, as such, is very old, if one understands by it a liberation from distress, hunger, drought, sickness, and ultimately from

* From *From Max Weber*, pp. 279–285.

suffering and death. Yet redemption attained a specific significance only where it expressed a systematic and rationalized "image of the world" and represented a stand in the face of the world. For the meaning as well as the intended and actual psychological quality of redemption has depended upon such a world image and such a stand. Not ideas, but material and ideal interests, directly govern men's conduct. Yet very frequently the "world images" that have been created by "ideas" have, like switchmen, determined the tracks along which action has been pushed by the dynamic of interest. "From what" and "for what" one wished to be redeemed and, let us not forget, "could be" redeemed, depended upon one's image of the world.

There have been very different possibilities in this connection: One could wish to be saved from political and social servitude and lifted into a Messianic realm in the future of this world; or one could wish to be saved from being defiled by ritual impurity and hope for the pure beauty of psychic and bodily existence. One could wish to escape being incarcerated in an impure body and hope for a purely spiritual existence. One could wish to be saved from the eternal and senseless play of human passions and desires and hope for the quietude of the pure beholding of the divine. One could wish to be saved from radical evil and the servitude of sin and hope for the eternal and free benevolence in the lap of a fatherly god. One could wish to be saved from peonage under the astrologically conceived determination of stellar constellations and long for the dignity of freedom and partaking of the substance of the hidden deity. One could wish to be redeemed from the barriers to the finite, which express themselves in suffering, misery and death, and the threatening punishment of hell, and hope for an eternal bliss in an earthly or paradisical future existence. One could wish to be saved from the cycle of rebirths with their inexorable compensations for the deeds of the times past and hope for eternal rest. One could wish to be saved from senseless brooding and events and long for the dreamless sleep. Many more varieties of belief have, of course, existed. Behind them always lies a stand towards something in the actual world which is experienced as specifically "senseless." Thus, the demand has been implied: that the world order in its totality is, could, and should somehow be a meaningful "cosmos." This quest, the core of genuine religious rationalism, has been borne precisely by strata of intellectuals. The avenues, the results, and the efficacy of this metaphysical need for a meaningful cosmos have varied widely. Nevertheless, some general comments may be made.

The general result of the modern form of thoroughly rationalizing the conception of the world and of the way of life, theoretically and practically, in a purposive manner, has been that religion has been shifted into the realm of the irrational. This has been the more the case the further the purposive type of rationalization has progressed, if one takes the standpoint of an intellectual articulation of an image of the world. This shift of religion into the irrational realm has occurred for several reasons. On the one hand, the calculation of consistent rationalism has not easily come out even with nothing left over. In music, the Pythagorean "comma" resisted complete rationalization oriented to tonal physics. The various great systems of music of all peoples and ages have differed in the manner in which they have either covered up or bypassed this inescapable irrationality or, on the other hand, put irrationality into the service of the richness of tonalities. The same has seemed to happen to the theoretical conception of the world, only far more so; and above all, it has seemed to happen to the rationalization of practical life. The various great ways of leading a rational and methodical life have been characterized by irrational presuppositions, which have been accepted simply as "given" and which have been incorporated into such ways of life. What these presuppositions have been is historically and socially determined, at least to a very large extent, through the peculiarity of those strata that have been the carriers of the ways of life during its formative and decisive period. The *interest* situation of these strata, as determined socially and psychologically, has made for their peculiarity, as we here understand it.

Furthermore, the irrational elements in the rationalization of reality have been the *loci* to which the irrepressible quest of intellectualism for the possession of supernatural values has been compelled to retreat. That is the more so the more denuded of irrationality the world appears to be. The unity of the primitive image of the world, in which everything was concrete magic, has tended to split into rational cognition and mastery of nature, on the one hand, and into "mystic" experiences, on the other. The inexpressible contents of such experiences remain the only possible "beyond," added to the mechanism of a world robbed of gods. In fact, the beyond remains an incorporeal and metaphysical realm in which individuals intimately possess the holy. Where this conclusion has been drawn without any residue, the individual can pursue his quest for salvation only as an individual. This phenomenon appears in some form, with progressive intellectualist rationalism, wherever men have ventured to rationalize the image of the world as being a cosmos governed by impersonal rules. Naturally it has occurred most strongly among religions and religious ethics which have been quite strongly determined by genteel strata of intellectuals devoted to the purely cognitive comprehension of the world and of its "meaning." This was the case with Asiatic and, above all, Indian world religions. For all of them, contemplation became the supreme and ultimate religious value accessible to man. Contemplation offered them entrance into the profound and blissful tranquillity and immobility of the All-one. All other forms of religious states, however, have been at best considered a relatively valuable *Ersatz* for contemplation. This has had far-reaching consequences for the relation of religion to life, including economic life, as we shall repeatedly see. Such consequences flow from the general character of "mystic" experiences, in the contemplative sense, and from the psychological preconditions of the search for them.

The situation in which strata decisive for the development of a religion were active in practical life has been entirely different. Where they were chivalrous warrior heroes, political officials, economically acquisitive classes, or, finally, where an organized hierocracy dominated religion, the results were different than where genteel intellectuals were decisive.

The rationalism of hierocracy grew out of the professional preoccupation with cult and myth or—to a far higher degree—out of the cure of souls, that is, the confession of sin and counsel to sinners. Everywhere hierocracy has sought to monopolize the administration of religious values. They have also sought to bring and to temper the bestowal of religious goods into the form of "sacramental" or "corporate grace," which could be ritually bestowed only by the priesthood and could not be attained by the individual. The individual's quest for salvation or the quest of free communities by means of contemplation, orgies, or asceticism, has been considered highly suspect and has had to be regulated ritually and, above all, controlled hierocratically. From the standpoint of the interests of the priesthood in power, this is only natural.

Every body of *political* officials, on the other hand, has been suspicious of all sorts of individual pursuits of salvation and of the free formation of communities as sources of emancipation from domestication at the hands of the institution of the state. Political officials have distrusted the competing priestly corporation of grace and, above all, at bottom they have despised the very quest for these impractical values lying beyond utilitarian and worldly ends. For all political bureaucracies, religious duties have ultimately been simply official or social obligations of the citizenry and of status groups. Ritual has corresponded to rules and regulations, and, therefore, wherever a bureaucracy has determined its nature, religion has assumed a ritualist character.

It is also usual for a stratum of *chivalrous* warriors to pursue absolutely worldly interests and to be remote from all "mysticism." Such strata, however, have lacked—and this is characteristic of heroism in general—the desire as well as the capacity for a rational mastery of reality. The irrationality of "fate" and, under certain conditions, the idea of a vague and deterministically conceived "destiny" (the Homeric *Moira*) has stood above and behind the divinities and demons who were conceived of as passionate and strong heroes, measuring out assistance and hostility, glory and booty, or death to the human heroes.

Peasants have been inclined towards magic. Their whole economic existence has been specifically bound to nature and has made them dependent upon elemental forces. They readily believe in a compelling sorcery directed against spirits who rule over or through natural forces, or they believe in simply buying divine benevolence. Only tremendous transformations of life-orientation have succeeded in tearing them away from this universal and primeval form of religiosity. Such transformations have been derived either from other strata or from mighty prophets, who, through the power of miracles, legitimize themselves as sorcerers. Orgiastic and ecstatic states of "possession," produced by means of toxics or by the dance, are strange to the status honor of knights because they are considered undignified. Among the peasants, however, such states have taken the place that "mysticism" holds among the intellectuals.

Finally, we may consider the strata that in the western European sense are called "civic," as well as those which elsewhere correspond to them: artisans, traders, enterprisers engaged in cottage industry, and their derivatives existing only in the modern Occident. Apparently these strata have been the most ambiguous with regard to the religious stands open to them. And this is especially important to us.

Among these "civic" strata the following religious phenomena have had especially strong roots: the institutional and sacramental grace of the Roman church in the medieval cities—the pillars of the popes; the mystagogic and sacramental grace in the ancient cities and in India; the orgiastic and contemplative Sufi, and Dervish religion of the Middle Eastern Orient; the Taoist magic; the Buddhist contemplation; the ritualist appropriation of grace under the direction of souls by mystagogues in Asia; all the forms of love for a savior; the beliefs in redemption the world over, from the cult of Krishna to the cult of Christ; the rational ritualism of the law and the sermon of the synagogue denuded of all magic among Jewry; the pneumatic and ancient as well as the asceticist medieval sects; the grace of predestination and the ethical regeneration of the Puritan and the Methodist; as well as all sorts of individual pursuits of salvation. All of these have been more firmly rooted among "civic" strata than among any other.

Of course, the religions of all strata are certainly far from being unambiguously dependent upon the character of the strata we have presented as having special affinities with them. Yet, at first sight, civic strata appear, in this respect and on the whole, to lend themselves to a more varied determination. Yet it is precisely among these strata that elective affinities for special types of religion stand out. The tendency towards a *practical* rationalism in conduct is common to all civic strata; it is conditioned by the nature of their way of life, which is greatly detached from economic bonds to nature. Their whole existence has been based upon technological or economic calculations and upon the mastery of nature and of man, however primitive the means at their disposal. The technique of living handed down among them may, of course, be frozen in traditionalism, as has occurred repeatedly and everywhere. But precisely for these, there has always existed the possibility—even though in greatly varying measure—of letting an *ethical* and rational regulation of life arise. This may occur by the linkage of such an ethic to the tendency of technological and economic rationalism. Such regulation has not always been able to make headway against traditions which, in the main, were magically stereotyped. But where prophecy has provided a religious basis, this basis could be one of two fundamental types of prophecy . . . : "exemplary" prophecy, and "emissary" prophecy.

18. The Churches of the Middle Class
H. RICHARD NIEBUHR *

The religious needs of the middle class are not as well defined as are those of the poor, for the bourgeoisie present a more complex pattern both of sociological structure and of social interests than do the proletarians. Political and cultural interests combine with economic desires in various ways, while the relationship of the governing class—the bureaucracy— and of the professional class with the group engaged in trade is often very close and subjects the latter to many modifying influences. Furthermore, the development of individual self-consciousness, with the resultant love of personal liberties and rights, is responsible for considerable variation in the religion as well as in the politics of the bourgeoisie. Yet the psychology of the middle class contains certain constant features which are reflected in its religious organizations and doctrines. Among these the

* From *The Social Sources of Denominationalism*, pp. 80–89.

most important are the high development of individual self-consciousness
and the prevalence of an activist attitude toward life. To these primary
factors others of secondary importance may be added: the general level
of education and culture in the group, the financial security and physical
comfort which it enjoys, the sense of class which it fosters, and the direct
effect of business and trade upon its code of ethics.

The individuals of no other group, save those of the professional class,
are so highly self-conscious as are the members of the bourgeoisie. Various elements in their situation are responsible for this fact. The character
of their employment which places responsibility for success or failure
almost entirely upon their own shoulders is fundamental. In contrast to
the worker, who, in ancient as in modern times, is accustomed by his cooperative labor to share or to resign responsibility and to cultivate a sense
of dependence for success upon impersonal factors, the business man is
employed in relatively independent activity, in which he must rely upon
his own energy and acumen. His dealings, while not so purely personal
in character as are those of professional men, still remain dealings with
men as buyers and sellers even more than dealings with goods to be
bought and sold. Moreover, the level of education is relatively high in
the middle class and contributes a share to the development of a sense of
self. Finally, the rise of the bourgeoisie in the face of the feudal powers
was conditioned by the development of the doctrines of natural rights
and individual liberty and the ideals forged in that conflict have been
conserved in the literature and tradition of the commercial groups. In
consequence the men of the middle class think in terms of persons more
than of forces, and in terms of personal merit and demerit more than of
fortune and fate.

Hence the religion of these groups is likely to be rather intensely personal in character. The problem of personal salvation is far more urgent
for them than is the problem of social redemption. In middle-class symbolism conceptions of heaven in which individual felicity is guaranteed
are much more important than the millennial hope of the poor man's
faith—a difference, which, of course, is also partly due to the greater
satisfaction of the middle class with the temporal order in which it enjoys
a considerable number of pleasant advantages. The dominance of self-
consciousness is further responsible for the preoccupation of much bourgeois religion with the problem of evil and with the task of justifying
the ways of God to man. Where self-consciousness is highly developed
the sensitiveness of the individual is correspondingly great, the need for
solace in a world "so careless of the single life" is pronounced, and religion is required to exercise the office of the comforter with exceptional

attention and skill. Where the sense of solidarity is greater, as on the whole it is among the poor, a far greater readiness prevails to accept without explanation and without rebellion the common fate of pain and loss and death. The attitude of resignation which the disinherited have imbibed with mother's milk is the difficult achievement of the middle-class man. In harmony with this whole emphasis upon the fate, the salvation, the happiness, the worth of the individual in bourgeois faith, there is a corresponding emphasis upon the personal character of God. The impersonal conceptions of mysticism are quite foreign and unintelligible to this group.

The corollary of the emphasis on self-hood is the activist attitude toward life which prevails in the middle class. The very existence of the class depends on the technical manipulation of things and the management of persons. Life is not regarded as a time of enjoyment and contemplation but as the sphere of labor. Business is the very essence of existence and industry the method of all attainment. This "practical rationalism" characterizes not only the middle-class conduct of economic enterprise but also its conceptions of ethics, politics, and religion. The values of religion are regarded less as a divine, free gift than as the end of striving; the method of religion is held to be the method of constant activity; the conception of God is the conception of dynamic will; the content of the faith is a task rather than a promise. "Active asceticism— not the possession of God or contemplative surrender to the Divine which are regarded as the highest good in the religions influenced by aristocratic and intellectual classes—but activity willed by God and carried on with the sense of being God's tool, could become the preferred religious attitude among the bourgeoisie," says Weber, who finds in this dynamic view of religion and in this practical rationalism in the conduct of life the distinguishing mark of bourgeois faith. This attitude in religion is reflected not only in the conceptions of God and of the content of his will but also in the doctrines of personal responsibility, of the priesthood of all believers and in the ideas of sin and of salvation. The conception of God which prevails in bourgeois faith is that of dynamic will. God is neither the Absolute of the mystic nor the Father of the child-like meek; He is rather the Old Testament Jehovah of energetic activity and of stern legislation, the Creator and the Judge more than the Redeemer and the Savior. The attempt has often been made to correlate the doctrine of predestination, which prevailed in the Calvinist middle-class churches, with the character of the Puritan, but it is difficult to conceive either that the doctrine was the outcome of bourgeois psychology, with all its emphasis on individual responsibility, or that, conversely, the Puritan character of dynamic

activity was the result of the doctrine of predestination. There is truth in
the statement that Calvin, in the doctrine of predestination, "did for the
bourgeoisie of the sixteenth century what Marx did for the proletariat of
the nineteenth" by giving "assurance that the forces of the universe are
on the side of the elect"; [1] but, on the whole, this element derived by
Calvin from purely religious sources was hard to reconcile with the native
interests of the bourgeois mind and suffered an early eclipse wherever
the trading class was dominant. Only in so far as the idea of God as
dynamic force and sovereign will came to expression in the doctrine of
predestination was the latter thoroughly germane to the temper of the
middle classes.

The ideas of sin, righteousness, and salvation which flourish in the
middle-class milieu are profoundly influenced both by this dynamic conception of life and by the sense of individual worth and responsibility. Sin
is not so much a state of soul as a deed or a characteristic; it is not so
much the evil with which the whole social life and structure is infected
as it is the personal failure of the individual. That interpretation of moral
evil which mystic and ascetic achieve and which finds sin the very essence
of mundane and human existence is foreign to the middle-class point of
view. The pluralistic rather than the monistic conception of sin prevails;
sin is not so much status as act. Similarly, righteousness is a matter of
right actions carried out in obedience to a series of divine commandments.
It is very necessary, therefore, that religion establish a code of right conduct; a general spirit of well-doing is insufficient or irrelevant. Such
righteousness, moreover, is an individual matter. Though the righteousness of society be the aim, yet it is the righteousness of a society of discreet selves, who one by one obey the divine precepts under divine and
human compulsion; it is, in short, the righteousness that is by law, not by
faith. The doctrine of salvation falls into line with these conceptions of
sin and of the good life. Salvation is conceived as a process within the
individual, not the construction of a divine kingdom; its results are believed to be given to the individual in conversion or in a process of education which establish him as a holy character, distinguished not so much
by heroic as by conforming virtue. He is delivered not from sin and guilt,
from remoteness from God, from the sense of the utter worthlessness of
all human effort, but from bad habits and evil desires which war against
the divine command.

The religious ethics of the middle class is a product of the same interests
modifying the tradition or the moral deliverances of the religious leader.
As in the case of the poor, the sanction of religion is invoked upon the

[1] R. H. Tawney, *Religion and the Rise of Capitalism,* p. 112.

peculiar virtues of the group itself; honesty, industry, sobriety, thrift, and prudence, on which the economic structure of business as well as the economic and social status of the individual depend, receive high veneration while the virtues of solidarity, sympathy, and fraternity are correspondingly ignored. A very high regard attaches to the ethics of family life; this emphasis is partly due to the special appreciation of the family that prevails in a class which finds its social satisfactions almost limited to this group and which, moreover, can nurture a high type of family life under the prevailing conditions of individual freedom and responsibility. On the other hand this interest in family morals may also be due to the threat to stable family relations which arises out of this same individualism. It may be, too, that the emphasis on family is a natural concession which an individualistic tradition makes to the suppressed social character of religion; interest in this institution is made to do service for the neglected social factors in faith.

The religious ethics of the middle class is marked throughout by this characteristic of individualism. The good which is to be sought in ethical life as in religion is the moral welfare of the individual. Because his economic life has taught him always to weigh cost and price against each other and because it has demonstrated the relationship of personal ability and energy to success, the man of business is inclined to construct his whole view of the providential order on the Deuteronomic pattern. Success in the world is to him a clear evidence of the presence of virtue and failure an almost certain symptom of vice. "Convinced that character is all and circumstances nothing, he sees in the poverty of those who fall by the way, not a misfortune to be pitied and relieved, but a moral failing to be condemned, and in riches, not an object of suspicion—though like other gifts they may be abused—but the blessing which rewards the triumph of energy and will." [2] Such an ethics is capable of producing a real heroism of self-discipline and, in its insistence on personal responsibility, the courage of resistance to the authority of state and church when these conflict with the imperatives of individual conscience. But this morality is incapable of developing a hopeful passion for social justice. Its martyrs die for liberty not for fraternity and equality; its saints are patrons of individual enterprise in religion, politics, and economics, not the great benefactors of mankind or the heralds of brotherhood.

Finally, the organization of the churches of the middle class, like their doctrine and ethics, reflects the individualism and the activism which rise out of the economic life. These churches are typically democratic in constitution, designed to give free scope to the individual, yet to pre-

[2] *Ibid.*, p. 230.

serve morality, to train character, and to fulfil in their very structure the demands of the divine will. Hence the churches of the bourgeoisie tend to accept some type of representative government which will insure liberty and individual responsibility but which will also raise barriers against the license of complete democracy. Their constitutions contain not only a doctrine but also a discipline and their leaders are not only teachers but also guardians. The leader is democratically chosen; he has none of the special unction of the priest, and yet he may assume high authority as the interpreter and executive officer of the divine will. It is significant, however, that in the churches of the middle class this type of organization is justified not by its fitness for the end which it serves but by its conformity to the will of God as expressed in the Scriptures. Others may appeal to expediency, the bourgeois seeks here as elsewhere to observe the letter of the law that he may in no manner violate the sacred principle of contract.

Middle-class religion, so defined, is not only distinguished from the faith of the poor but also from the Christianity of the landed gentry and their allies or dependents. For the latter type is agricultural or military, while bourgeois religion is commercial and industrial in symbolism and attitude. The one kind of organization is paternal and institutional, the other democratic; the best ethics of the one class is the ethics of *noblesse oblige*, that of the other the morality of strict self-discipline without much regard for the neighbor; the doctrine of the one centers in a magic conception of salvation and of the means of grace, that of the other in the teaching of salvation in and by character. Hence the religion of the bourgeoisie seeks separate organization not only on account of the economic conflicts of the class with aristocracy above and the proletariat below but also because of the divergent religious attitudes and desires which arise out of these class differences.

19. The Function of Ethnic Churches: Judaism in the United States

MARSHALL SKLARE *

It was once thought that each ethnic group would—in the space of a few decades—leave their "ghetto" and fuse into the melting pot. Sociologists conceded that groups which came here fairly late, against whom

* Abridged from *Conservative Judaism: An American Religious Movement*, pp. 32–40.

discrimination was practiced, or whose original culture was strikingly different from the dominant one, might be more cohesive than others. But assimilation was considered inevitable. At present it is becoming increasingly evident that ethnicity still remains a significant basis of social stratification. For example, an investigation in New Haven, Connecticut, discloses that Swedes and Danes—who came here earlier than many other groups and whose culture was not strikingly deviant—still constitute recognizable entities in that city. Does this result from prejudice, from rejection by the dominant group? Is it traceable to the influence of ethnic survivalists who are strongly attached to the old culture and who preserve the subcommunity by influencing marginal individuals to remain loyal? Is it that the content of the original culture, once it is adapted to American conditions, retains a degree of attractiveness? Or is it because ethnic solidarity now serves a new purpose: protection from *anomie* —the atomization and disorganization characteristic of present-day society which results in a loss of the feeling of social solidarity?

This last suggestion is a particularly intriguing one since the problem of *anomie* exists for all peoples who live in a society characterized by mobility, by the segregation of kinship, occupation, and leisure-time roles, by shifting norms, and by clashing social systems. One of the structures which compensates for this characteristic feature of modern life is the voluntary association. These groups help to create for the individual additional primary and secondary relationships. Viewing such bonds as a "defense" against *anomie*, it is apparent that they can be elaborated on various levels: class ends, shared life experiences, similar play interests, or *common descent*. While the presentday ethnic is no longer in need of a therapeutic instrument to reduce the trauma resulting from encountering radically new norms and values (as was the case with his father or grandfather), he *is* in need of meaningful social relationships. Participation in the affairs of his ethnic group may be a convenient way of meeting this requirement. The "defense against *anomie*" theory may well help to explain why some of the sub-communities preserve a degree of integration in spite of the participants having shed many old-world culture patterns.

Rejection, the influence of the survivalists, the adapted culture, and the *anomie* problem are undoubtedly all factors which operate to retard —although perhaps only temporarily—the assimilation of ethnics. With the amount of knowledge which we have at our disposal, it is difficult to decide just how much weight should be assigned to each of these forces, as well as to others detailed below. Whatever the situation in other groups, it will be conceded that Jews have shown themselves *particularly* desirous of retaining some form of group identity. . . .

A full explanation of this almost unique desire for survival will not
be attempted here. Some of the causes have already been cited. In addition there is the fact that Jews still possess a feeling of superiority, although more in the moral and intellectual realms now than in the area
of spiritual affairs. While the feeling of superiority is a factor which has
received comparatively little attention from students of the problem, it
is of crucial importance because it operates to retard assimilation. Leaving
the group becomes a psychological threat: such a move is viewed not as
an advancement but as cutting oneself off from a claim to superiority.
However explained, the "will to live" serves to encourage the making of
experiments, like Conservatism, which aim to discover a *modus vivendi*
for the Jewish community. . . .

Judaism constitutes an *ethnic church:* a fellowship whose members are
differentiated from those belonging to other denominations by virtue of
their special *descent* as well as by their doctrines or practices. In America
the uniqueness of this type of church is its articulation of ethnicity and
religiosity in a multi-ethnic society where ethnic groups are essentially
minority groups, i.e., subordinate to a majority group presumed to be
non-ethnic. In addition to Jews and others, this type of body is found
in the three divisions of Christianity: the Protestant, Roman Catholic,
and Eastern Orthodox Churches. To illustrate for the Protestant group,
special Lutheran bodies and synods exist for the Danes, Finns, Germans,
Hungarians, Icelanders, Norwegians, Slovaks, Swedes, and others. Special nationality parishes have been established in the United States for
Roman Catholics who come from Armenia, Croatia, Italy, Poland, Portugal, the Ukraine, and many other places.

These groups are first of all *churches,* for like all religious organizations
they seek to provide ". . . a way of facing the problems of ultimate and
unavoidable frustration, of 'evil,' and the generalized problem of meaning
in some non-empirical sense, of finding some ultimate why." [1] But concur-
rently they have an additional task: the preservation of a particular sub-
culture or ethnic group. Note that the language used in sermons, liturgy,
or hymns may be the one spoken in the homeland; that certain rites and
holidays are observed which are celebrated only by members of the special ethnic group; and that celebrations commemorate events unique to
the history of the group. The ethnic church commonly makes special
educational arrangements designed to teach its youth those special loyalties necessary for group survival. This frequently includes some training
in the language of the homeland. . . .

[1] Robin M. Williams, Jr., *American Society,* p. 307.

. . . these churches have become an important mechanism for the preservation of ethnicity. Religion easily recommended itself for this role. The church was one of the few institutions of the original culture capable of re-establishment in the new land. Also, since the ethnic church is the counterpart of non-ethnic institutions of the same order, it would automatically receive identical formal recognition, although of course its status position may not be on the same level. Furthermore, while ethnic separatism is not very highly valued in our culture, religious distinctiveness is allowable—even esteemed in a way because it is "American." Given the attraction of national culture patterns which have slowly but surely impressed themselves upon the ethnic, group distinctiveness could be preserved—even if emptied of much of its content—under the banner of religion. Thus, because of the challenge to group survival, ethnicity has tended to retreat and to reappear in a very different form.

In summary, the forces working toward the continuation of the special function of the ethnic church converge from the following two directions: (1) From the dynamic of the institution itself. Since the future of the church generally hinges on the persistence of the ethnic group, it must promote ethnic group solidarity in order to survive. (2) From ethnics who—whether consciously or not—realize that religion is an acceptable method of group differentiation, that church functions may include much more than the dissemination of the word of God. Such individuals see suprasocial differences as legitimating the perpetuation of divisions in the social structure. While it is true that in some cases group persistence has been in outright ethnic form, in other instances the main index to continuing ethnicity is to be found in the survival of churches whose membership is relatively homogeneous. Most of the group are still descended from individuals who come from the same homeland. American ethnic groups are tending to change their outward appearances. They can preserve themselves as religious groups.

On the whole, Jews in the United States choose to be regarded as members of a religious denomination. However, the various groups in the community who have arrived at this consensus are differently motivated. There are, of course, those who feel (as well as act) that religion *is* the prime expression of Judaism. The religious designation is, therefore, expressive of their true ideological preferences. Another segment of the community has wider Jewish interests than simply religion (or even possess other Jewish interests which serve to replace religion), but they feel nonetheless that—given American traditions—*religion must become the main expression of Jewish identification as well as the guarantor of Jewish ethnic survival.* At the very least, they would contend that the designation of the Jewish group as constituting a denomination is a highly convenient fiction which it is wise to cultivate. Lastly, there are those whose feelings of Jewish identification are weak or conflicting, and whose survivalistic urges are consequently questionable. Nevertheless, because of public relations considerations, they feel that it is essential that Jews stress the religious designation. The middle group seems to be the predominant one at present. While few Jews—particularly those in the middle group—could succeed in verbalizing their feelings as we have set them down, there is ample evidence available pointing to the existence of these trends.

It is significant that although overall Jewish identification has remained at a high level (and while synagogue affiliation appears to be greater than previously), Jews today hardly seem very observant of religious practices. Their day-to-day religious behavior is readily apparent from data gathered in a poll conducted by the National Opinion Research Center during 1945. This survey revals that only 6% of those who identify themselves as Catholic state that they sedom or never attend religious services, 19% of the Protestants make this statement, but no less than 32% of the Jews are found in this category. Of the Catholics, 69% attend religious services once a week or more, 36% of the Protestants do likewise, but a mere 9% of the Jews attend. Worshipping at least once a month are 81% of the Catholics, 62% of the Protestants, and only 24% of the Jews.[2] It would seem then that many wish to identify themselves as being members of a religious group while at the same time they lack much religious interest. Because of such a trend, one student of Jewish problems speaks of the ". . . paradox of the concentration of Diaspora survivalism on religious channels in the face of increasing weakening of religion."[3] Although the fundamental tie in the Jewish community continues to be on the level of common ethnicity, many apparently share Mordecai M. Kaplan's viewpoint that ". . . [the synagogue] is the only institution that can define our aims to a world that will otherwise be at a loss to understand why we persist in retaining our corporate individuality."[4]

All of this results in the strengthening of the religious structure in spite of increasing secularization. As we noted, reinforcement comes from different directions. The ethnic survivalists concentrate upon religion as the most satisfactory means of Jewish identification, and the more marginal

[2] *Opinion News*, V, 13 (Dec. 25, 1945).

[3] Abraham G. Duker, *Outline of Comprehensive Introductory Course for Adult Jewish Studies* (New York: American Jewish Congress, 1951), p. 25.

[4] In *Jewish Communal Register*, 1917–1918 (New York: Kehillah of New York City, 1918), p. 122.

group seizes upon it as a protective device which will help to raise status, draw allies to the Jewish cause, and in the long run serve to decrease the virulence of anti-Semitism. Both are forced into "making good" on the stereotype by according some support to religious causes. Whatever their real feelings, their very desire to project the stereotype means that they have to concede a responsibility for supporting religious institutions. Additionally, the stereotype—once it is successfully established—reacts back on the Jew himself. Whether because of impressions conveyed by Jews, or because of factors which operate independently of minority-generated pressures, Gentiles may begin to convey that they consider the Jewish group as just another religious denomination. At this juncture, the Jew may find himself propelled into fulfilling the image projected by the Gentile. Although he himself may not actually believe the stereotype to be wholly valid, he feels that he must act like the type of "good Jew" which the Gentile imagines—the Jew who is loyal to his rabbi, interested in his synagogue.

Such developments do not prepare the ground for any kind of true religious revival. Attendance at services may not even grow very substantially. However, religious institutions will receive increasing financial support and community esteem, particularly if they offer a program which includes non-religious activities and is strongly oriented toward ethnic values. We can assume that Conservatism resulted in part from the feeling that the Orthodox synagogue was inadequate to meet the demands of the environment—that ethnic solidarity would have to be perpetuated chiefly under religious auspices and that consequently a new type of institution was required.

20. Holiness Religion: Cultural Shock and Social Reorganization

JOHN B. HOLT *

When, through migration or social change, the occupation, the community structure, the status aspirations, and other aspects of their social situation change dramatically for a group of people, their religious life also changes. This selection might well be included in section 7, but it is placed here because it indicates so clearly how position in the pattern of social stratification influences the religious life.

* Abridged from *American Sociological Review*, October, 1940, pp. 740–747.

The purpose of this paper is to suggest further research in the field of social organization and culture conflict. Within both these fields lies the problem of describing the social reorganization of migrants from rural to urban areas and, in some cases, to other rural areas. For reasons which will become obvious as we proceed, this discussion is limited in its application to the South and more particularly to the southeastern states. It is thus quite regional in scope.

The writer's attention was drawn to the subject less by an abstract interest in the social factors of population migration than by his curiosity concerning the phenomenal growth of the Holiness and Pentecostal denominations or sects in the southeastern states. The largest of these groups, the Assemblies of God, increased from 11,000 members in 1916 to 148,043 in 1936, and to around 200,000 in 1939. The second largest, the Nazarene, increased from 6657 in 1906 to 136,227 in 1936, and seems to have continued to grow rapidly since then. The three branches of the third largest group have today an aggregate membership of about 90,000, as compared with 23,000 in 1926.

Included in the following discussion are white churches only, exclusive of the Lutheran. The data cover the seven strongest bodies, which seem to be representative of the movement in its more organized phases.[1] These seven are: (1) The Assemblies of God; (2) The Church of the Nazarene; (3) The Church of God, with headquarters at Cleveland, Tennessee; (4) The Church of God, with headquarters at Anderson, Indiana; (5) The Pentecostal Assemblies of the World; (6) The Pentecostal Holiness Church; (7) The Pilgrim Holiness Church. An eighth, on which no figures have yet been obtained, is the Pentecostal Assemblies of Jesus Christ, founded since 1930.

These groups are frequently classed indiscriminately as "holy rollers." This epithet is inspired by their highly emotional and physically energetic behavior at religious services. This behavior is characterized by themselves as the outward expression of their beatific or ecstatic feeling of "sanctification," when God bestows upon their souls His so-called "second blessing" in evidence of His forgiveness of sin. The Pentecostal groups, as distinguished from the Holiness groups, believe further in the gift of tongues as an additional evidence of God's grace, awakened in the more select of these who have been sanctified by the "second blessing." The

---

[1] It should be recognized that not all Holiness and Pentecostal religion is organized. Of all formalized types of denominational religion, it is closest to the unorganized waves of summer revivals which sweep the South when the crops are "laid by," leaving no permanent traces, because the poor are too poor or too mobile to build a church or meeting house. Research concerning unorganized Pentecostal and Holiness religion should be done as soon as possible.

involuntary jerking, twitching, running, writhing, rolling on or beating the floor, shouting, shrieking, or clapping of hands, while in the emotionally exalted state is merely evidence of the "spirit" working within. Leading up to this emancipated state of religious ecstasy and seemingly a prerequisite to it, is the subjectively distressing state of being under "conviction," that is, being convinced of one's sins to the point of intolerable misery. From this state, one can be "saved" only by full confession, desire for forgiveness, and intercession on the part of Jesus Christ.

This pattern of religious behavior and belief has been, at least in part, common to most of the denominations which have grown to maturity in the South and Southwest of the United States. However, liberalization of these churches has eliminated, for the most part, the highly emotional and experiential character of their religion.

The following hypotheses are presented regarding the factors in and the significance of the growth of these sects.

1. This religious movement is largely the natural product of the social disorganization and cultural conflict which have attended the over-rapid urbanward migration and concomitant urbanization of an intensely rural, and among other things, religiously fundamentalist population.

2. The movement is typically a social movement in that it is an attempt on the part of certain groups experiencing acute social maladjustment to recapture their sense of security through religious revival and reform.

3. This present attempt at social readjustment and reintegration tends to be reactionary and reformist rather than revolutionary or constructive in character, and does not promise to help eradicate the maladjustment which brought it forth. Its beliefs and ethics are drawn from a disintegrating rural agricultural tradition. However, they are successful in inspiring hope and a type of behavior in individuals which may raise their individual or group status above that of their class.

4. The growth of these sects comprises a religious movement which is definitely regional and primarily southern in character.

So much for the theses. Their elaboration and the supporting data follow. They must be explored much more deeply than has been possible in the preparation of this paper. It will aid the clarity of exposition if the order of discussing these hypotheses is altered, so that we may first discuss the geographical distribution of the movement with respect to the statement that the religious movement is southern and regional in character. Membership in the seven largest Holiness and Pentecostal groups in 1926 was ten times stronger in the Southeast and Southwest, compared to the membership in all denominations, than it was in the New England

and the Middle Atlantic states. Next to the South, the movement was strongest in the southern portions of the North Central states. In the Pacific states, it was nearly as weak as in the Northeast. . . .

The growth of the new Pentecostal and Holiness churches tends geographically to be associated with industry, manufacturing, mining, developing agriculture, and low-cost recreational areas. The concentrations of these churches coincide rather well throughout with the concentration of white population. Furthermore, a map showing the net change in the total population, 1890 to 1930, suggests that these are the areas of greatest population increase. Areas of net decrease do not contain many congregations of the Church of God.

It is perhaps worth noting that few or no churches have become organized in the older commercial farming areas of these states, most of which have suffered a net decline in population since 1890. These areas have been largely the plantation areas which possessed in general the highest rates of tenant and cropper-operated farms and the highest proportion of Negro to white population.

But more important for the understanding of the growth of Pentecostal and Holiness sects than the simple facts of geographic location and the numerical increase of population, seem to be the facts about who the people are, where they come from, facts about their religious and social heritage, and about the situation to which they have attempted to adjust themselves.

Immediately we are confronted in the Southeast with the fact of a heavy migration of rural farm population to the cities. Woofter points out that between one third and one half of the urban population of the Southeast in 1930 had been born in rural areas. . . .

Moreover, a basic shift in occupational distribution has occurred. Opportunities in other than extractive industries have been increasing in the southern states more rapidly than in any other part of the country. Although the South is still more agricultural than any other part of the country, it has had a more rapid growth in the proportion of its workers in nonagricultural occupations than has any other section.

Attention has been drawn to the heavy incidence of migration since 1890. Now consider Odum's observation concerning the evidences of tension or maladjustments which arise among migrants to urban areas:

There has been very little research on the effects of the inflow of young people and adults nurtured in rural areas on the characteristics and institutions of the city populations. It would be interesting to know how this movement affects religious associations, labor activities, political alinements, et cetera. It would also be interesting to know the effects of this change in environment on individual and family adjustment. . . . It is a subject that merits the critical attention of social scientists. In this connection, one very interesting analysis that . . . may have an important bearing on this problem, has been reported by Malzberg. He reports that the admission rate to hospitals for mental disease in New York State is significantly higher for the native population born in other states than for the population born in that state. In fact, he finds that among native whites the crude rates are about $3\frac{1}{2}$ times as high for those born without as for those born within the state, both for all psychoses and for each of the five major classes treated separately.[2]

Faris and Dunham have made a valuable contribution to the exploration of this field of research in the work, *Mental Disorder in Urban Areas.*

Regarding the possible connection between the rapid rate of urbanization and social maladjustment in the Southeast, Odum observes, "The South, more than the other regions, fitted by habit and tradition to a life closely attuned to natural processes, finds rapid shift to artificial industrialism beyond its power for quick absorption and effective adaptation." The administrator of a farm program in Kentucky is reported to have said, "The physical 'bends' of deep-sea divers exposed too rapidly to lighter atmospheric pressure is nothing compared to the psychological or spiritual bends produced in our mountain communities when subjected too rapidly to urban standards and ways of doing things."

All these citations suggest the "culture shock" arising from the precipitation of a rural person or group into an urban situation characterized by a loosening of mores from a strict social control, a liberation of the individual from his group, an increasing impersonalism as against the personal character of the rural environment, an increasing mobility as contrasted with the old stability and isolation, and on top of these changes, a blasting disruption of personal and occupational habits and status.

This process of urbanization fits the concept of social disorganization as defined by Thomas and Znaniecki in their book, *The Polish Peasant in Europe and America.* They define a state of disorganization as existing when a conflict of standards arises and the new standards begin to take root one by one, disrupting the fairly well integrated pattern of old standards. "The decay of traditional social organization is, as we have seen, due to the appearance and development of new attitudes leading

<hr/>

[2] Quoted from the National Resources Committee *Report on the Problems of a Changing Population,* III, May 1938, citing Benjamin Malzberg's "Rates of Mental Disease Among Certain Population Groups in New York State," in the *J. Amer. Statist. Assn.,* XXX: 1, September 1936, 545–548.

to activities which do not comply with the socially recognized and sanctioned schemes of behavior." [3]

Here it may be profitable to distinguish between two phases of this process which is called urbanization. The first phase is the destruction of the old rural values, social controls, and ways of living by the invasion of urban values, standards, and ways of doing things. This process envelops the migrant to towns and cities, but it is also common to every rural area in the United States touched by paved highways and moving picture houses. It takes place through the extension of good roads, consolidated school systems, movies and other techniques for expanding the mental horizon and accelerating the pace of experience of the rural dweller.

The second and perhaps equally important part of the process of urbanization in the Southeast has been that of the disruption of social ties, the social disorganization in terms of individual isolation from previously stable and durable personal ties which attends heavy migration of persons from their home communities to new areas. . . .

Moreover, mass migration generally takes place at low economic and social levels. This fact has a twofold significance. In the first place, the migrants enter their new social milieu at its most poorly organized level. Their own poverty and that of their low-income neighbors, also the very fact that they are newcomers, without having had the necessary time to develop new ties and to build or find their place in local institutions, account in part for the social disorganization characteristic of these areas. In the second place, the low economic level of entry is significant because to the better established families and groups in the new areas, the migrants appear as an inferior social group of wage hands, miners, or tenants, in most cases as just "poor whites." Segregated occupationally, economically, and by the social discrimination of the longer or better established families and groups in the new areas, the migrants would tend to become acutely aware of their lack of status. Disturbed emotionally by the necessity to adjust to a changed situation and subjected perhaps also to economic insecurity and want, this group of in-migrants would find the situation psychologically distressing.

But why should the culture shock result in religious revivalism? Boisen has already advanced the proposition that there is or can be a close relationship between economic distress and religious experience. [4] Boisen maintains, probably with considerable insight, that these sects are "mani-

---

[3] W. I. Thomas and Florian Znaniecki, *The Polish Peasant in Europe and America,* Vol. II, 1303 (Knopf ed.).

[4] "Economic Distress and Religious Experience," in *Psychiatry,* II: 2, May 1939.

festations of nature's power to heal." He says, "They are the spontaneous attempts of the common people to deal constructively with the stresses and trials which fall with peculiar severity upon them." [5] As a trained psychiatrist, he supports his conclusions with findings from case history investigations, which, after all, would be the only technique for dealing with this whole problem on a sound basis. While Boisen emphasizes the religious experience which may under certain conditions come out of economic distress, it seems to the writer that such religious experience would tend to develop also under the conditions of personal isolation and insecurity incidental to migration and social discrimination. The urgent demand of the migrant's personality for stable and secure social status in the midst of a feeling of isolation, social and economic insecurity, and lack of social adequacy would probably tend to cause the migrant to exploit emotionally any escape-activity or reorganization which presented itself, particularly one in his cultural tradition.

Of the possible types of reorganization or adjustment which the group may attempt to effect as outlined by Thomas and Znaniecki, the adjustment of the Holiness and Pentecostal groups represents the defense of the old standards and modes of behavior rather than a reconstruction of attitudes and behavior to fit the altered situation or a revolution against both the old and the new, which would merely postpone the necessary reconstruction. The rise of the Holiness and Pentecostal groups represents a definite desire to secede from the established denominations. These new denominations are definitely sectarian in nature, thoroughly reformist, voicing decided disapproval of the liberal trends in the older churches. They are orthodox-minded to the point of emotional fanaticism, exclusive to the point of admitting members only upon convincing evidence of proper religious experience and close observance of the old strict codes of behavior. These are the elements and outline of the culture conflict which the writer proposes is involved in the urbanization of the rural migrants in the southeastern states.

The reference to the role of the cultural heritage or tradition of the migrant in determining his adjustment to the social disorganization incidental to migration and urbanization probably explains the regional character of this religious movement of Holiness and Pentecostal churches. The movement seems most prevalent in areas in which have tended to concentrate the migrant groups whose most recent heritage is that of the fundamentalist, revivalistic tradition of the southern rural areas.

Why the religious revolt took place outside of, in the form of a secession, rather than within the established denominations is best explained

[5] *Ibid.*, 193.

by the failure of the established churches to provide the type of religion which proved satisfying to the migrant newcomers or even to cater to them at all. The established churches became a symbol of the migrant's isolation and of the strange and unfriendly society with which he was confronted.

The supporting data reviewed in this paper appear quite inadequate as full proof of any of its hypotheses. This fact indicates the amount of research which must be done to clarify our knowledge of the factors operating in and the social implications of the rise in Holiness and Pentecostal religious movements. Boisen has done excellent work in analysing the significance of the concepts of guilt and sin in this religion of personal salvation and their relationship to economic distress. Many case studies of the migrant devotee of Pentecostal or Holiness religion might throw some light on the problem of social disorganization and cultural conflict incidental to urbanization and isolation of rural migrants. Certainly we should know more about the social and psychological characteristics of migrants under different conditions and at different stages of their migratory process. Would it be true, for instance, that in the clash of cultures, the resultant type of adjustment would be a function of the relative strength or numbers of migrants compared with the population in the new situation into which they moved? In a large manufacturing city, their attempted defense might prove utterly useless, whereas in a small mill town, where the majority of the population possess the same religious heritage, their attempted defense of traditional ways and attitudes might be relatively successful for a considerable period. There would tend to be something in this latter situation comparable to the retention of the paternalistic social structure in southern mill towns as a holdover from large scale ownership social patterns among the farm population, a situation to which Raper and Reid are calling attention in a forthcoming book. Finally, it would be interesting to determine whether the distribution of this growth of Pentecostal and Holiness religion is functionally related to the distribution and strength of the labor union movement, since the latter might be another type of adjustment to the urban situation by workers in the lower income brackets, an adjustment which Thomas and Znaniecki would probably term reconstructive rather than a defense of the traditional.

21. Church-Sect Typology and Socio-Economic Status

RUSSELL R. DYNES [*]

THIS PAPER AND THE TWO THAT FOLLOW ARE VERY CLOSELY RELATED TO THE TOPIC OF SECTION 4; BUT TO THE INTEREST IN TYPOLOGY THEY ADD AN EX-PLICIT APPLICATION TO THE QUESTION OF THE INFLUENCE OF SOCIAL STRAT-IFICATION. THIS STUDY BY DYNES IS VALUABLE FOR ITS CAREFULLY WORKED-OUT SCALE AND AN EMPIRICAL EMPHASIS OFTEN LACKING IN THE SOCIOLOGY OF RELIGION.

Although the polar types of Church and Sect were introduced by Max Weber,[1] they are most often identified with one of his students, Ernst Troeltsch.[2] Others, in both theology and sociology, have used variations of these types primarily to categorize historical data.[3] While these con-structs have had their roots in the sociology of religion, their theoretical implications extend into other areas of specialization, notably, power, stratification and the sociology of knowledge.

The construct of the Church has generally signified a type of religious organization which accepts the social order and integrates existing cul-tural definitions into its religious ideology. The Sect, as a contrasting type, rejects integration with the social order and develops a separate sub-culture, stressing rather rigid behavioral requirements for its members. While these types have been useful in historical and theoretical analysis, there have been few efforts to apply them empirically to contemporary religious phenomena. This paper reports one attempt to quantify them and to ascertain their relationship to socio-economic status.

[*] From *American Sociological Review*, October, 1955, pp. 555–560.

[1] See Max Weber, *The Protestant Ethic and the Spirit of Capitalism* [Translated by Talcott Parsons], London: Allen and Unwin, 1930; and the "The Protestant Sects and the Spirit of Capitalism" in *From Max Weber, Essays in Sociology* [Translated by Hans Gerth and C. Wright Mills], New York: Oxford University Press, 1946.

[2] See Ernst Troeltsch, *The Social Teachings of the Christian Churches* [Translated by Olive Wyon], New York: The Macmillan Company, 1932.

[3] See, for example, H. Richard Niebuhr, *The Social Sources of Denominationalism*, New York: Henry Holt and Company, 1929; Leopold von Weise and Howard Becker, *Systematic Sociology*, New York: John Wiley and Sons, Inc., 1932; J. Milton Yinger, *Religion in the Struggle for Power*, Durham: Duke University Press, 1946; S. D. Clark, *Church and Sect in Canada*, Toronto: University of Toronto Press, 1948; and Joachim Wach, "Church, Denomination and Sect" in *Types of Religious Experience*, Chicago: The University of Chicago Press, 1951.

THEORETICAL BASIS

Restricting the study to Protestantism, the types are posed in terms of a number of specific distinctions drawn primarily from the work of Liston Pope: [4]

1. The Sect renounces or is indifferent to the secular value systems, while the Church accepts and reinforces them.
2. The Sect emphasizes a literal Biblical interpretation of life and rejects worldly success, while the Church incorporates some degree of scientific and humanistic thinking in its interpretation of life and accepts success in *this* world as a not unworthy goal.
3. The Sect maintains a moral community, excluding unworthy members, and depreciates membership in other religious institutions, while the Church embraces all who are socially compatible with it and accepts other established religious institutions.
4. The Sect emphasizes congregational participation and an unprofessionalized ministry, while the Church delegates religious responsibility to a professionalized group of officials.
5. The Sect stresses a voluntary confessional basis for membership and its primary concern is for adults, while the Church stresses social and ritual requisites for all.
6. The Sect values fervor in religious observance through its use of folk hymns and its emphasis on evangelism, while the Church values passivity through its use of liturgical forms of worship and its emphasis on education.

SCALE CONSTRUCTION

Although the distinctions above are phrased in terms of religious behavior and concepts, this study translated them into statements of personal preference and used them in the construction of an initial thirty-five item Likert-type scale. The scale was pretested on a sample drawn from a large Protestant church in Columbus. The initial scale was analyzed by the method of internal consistency [5] and was revised eliminating eleven items. The twenty-four items retained had the largest scale value differences and gave the best coverage to the theoretical types. The items utilized five responses—Strongly Agree to Strongly Disagree—and were

[4] Liston Pope, *Millhands and Preachers*, New Haven: Yale University Press, 1942.
[5] The method is briefly as follows: First, after the scale had been scored, the items were ranked in terms of their total score. Second, the extremes of the distribution were segregated. In this instance, quartiles were used. Third, the differences between these quartiles were computed. In this scale, since there were different weighted responses from one to five, the mean was computed for each item in both quartiles. Fourth, the statistical significance was determined for each difference. For further details, see, R. F. Sletto, *The Construction of Personality Scales by the Criterion of Internal Consistency*, Hanover, N. H.: The Sociological Press, 1937.

scored from one, indicating a Sect response, to five, indicating a Church response.[6] A total score was computed—low scores indicating the acceptance of the Sect type of religious organization and high scores indicating the acceptance of the Church type.

The scale was analyzed for reliability in two different samples using the split-half method. On the pretest sample (N=55), using a Pearsonian product-moment correlation, the uncorrected split-half correlation was +.86 with a standard error of ±.04. Taking account of attenuation, the estimated correlation by the Spearman-Brown formula was +.92. From the final sample, one hundred cases were selected at random for analysis.

[6] In the scale, when an item stated a Sectarian trait, Strongly Agree was scored as one. When the item stated a Church trait, the scoring was reversed and Strongly Agree was scored as five. The items are listed below by their means scores and the items representing a Church trait are indicated by an asterisk.

1. I think a minister should preach without expecting to get paid for it. ($\bar{X}$—3.98)

2. I think it is more important to live a good life now than to bother about life after death.* ($\bar{X}$—3.74)

3. I think a person who is not willing to follow *all* the rules of the church should not be allowed to belong. ($\bar{X}$—3.58)

4. Testifying about one's religious experience should be a part of regular church services. ($\bar{X}$—3.52)

5. I feel that a congregation should encourage the minister during his sermon by saying *amen*. ($\bar{X}$—3.51)

6. I think that we should emphasize education in religion and not conversion.* ($\bar{X}$—3.50)

7. I think that there is practically no difference between what the different Protestant churches believe.* ($\bar{X}$—3.25)

8. I think a person should make a testimony about his religion before he joins a church. ($\bar{X}$—3.20)

9. In church, I would rather sing the hymns myself than hear the choir sing. ($\bar{X}$—3.19)

10. I think being a success in one's job is one mark of a good Christian.* ($\bar{X}$—3.01)

11. A minister who is "called" is better than one who is "trained." ($\bar{X}$—3.00)

12. I like the "old-time" religion. ($\bar{X}$—2.98)

13. I think churches should have more revivals. ($\bar{X}$—2.94)

14. I think it would be wrong for a church member to have a job as a bartender. ($\bar{X}$—2.77)

15. I think a person should feel his religion before he joins a church. ($\bar{X}$—2.71)

16. I like to sing the old gospel songs rather than the new hymns. ($\bar{X}$—2.64)

17. I don't believe churches do enough about saving souls. ($\bar{X}$—2.63)

18. Heaven and Hell are very real to me. ($\bar{X}$—2.53)

19. All the miracles in the Bible are true. ($\bar{X}$—2.45)

20. Children should not become members of the church until they are old enough to understand about it. ($\bar{X}$—2.39)

21. I think it is more important to go to church than to be active in politics. ($\bar{X}$—2.18)

22. I wish ministers would preach more on the Bible and less on politics. ($\bar{X}$—2.07)

23. I think it is more serious to break God's law than to break man's law. ($\bar{X}$—2.00)

24. I think every family should have family prayers or say grace before meals ($\bar{X}$—1.92)

* For further details on scale construction, see the writer's unpublished doctoral dissertation, *Church-Sect Typology: An Empirical Study*, The Ohio State University, 1954.

The split-half correlation was +.70 with a standard error of ±.05. Taking account of attenuation, the estimated correlation was +.82.

The validity of the scale was inferred from two different sources. The first aspect involved judgment of the scale's conformity to the types to be measured. Ten judges were asked to identify both the general type and the specific polarity to which each item was related. All of the judges were sociologists, either by present occupation or by choice of advanced graduate study. They represented a variety of religious backgrounds (i.e. Methodist, Congregational, Brethren, Orthodox Jewish, Lutheran, Baptist, Disciples of Christ) and a variety of degrees of present interest. Of five judges who had had some theological training, four had received B.D. degrees from seminaries representing this number of different Protestant denominations. There was a mean agreement of 98 per cent among the judges on each item's relation to the general type, either Church or Sect, and a mean agreement of 84 per cent on each item's relation to one of sixteen specific polarities.[7] The second aspect of validity was based on the conception that individuals, belonging to religious organizations which manifest either Church or Sect traits, would presumably hold favorable attitudes toward these traits, and this would be reflected by a valid scale. Sampling procedure necessitated combining Episcopalian and Presbyterian members to represent the Church type and the Holiness Pentecostal, Church of God, Church of the Nazarene and Baptist members to represent the Sect type. Table 1 shows the mean scale score differences between the members of these criterion groups. The scale, then, not only had tested reliability but also both logical and empirical validity.

TABLE 1. MEAN CHURCH-SECT SCORES OF CRITERION GROUPS

Criterion Group	N	Mean	Standard Deviation	Critical Ratio *	P
"Church" members	62	76.1	10.7		
"Sect" members	53	51.8	13.4	10.6	.001

* The difference between mean scores has a Critical Ratio of 10.6, a probability of <.001 that it is due to chance.

The scale, in questionnaire form, was sent to a random sample of the adult population listed in the City Directory of the Columbus metropolitan area. The questionnaire contained other attitude items and elicited information on social participation, denominational affiliation and other social background characteristics, including the three different measures

[7] The six distinctions mentioned above between Church and Sect are a summary of these sixteen specific polarities.

of socio-economic status used here. Random sampling was chosen in preference to using the usually inaccurate church records, since it would approximate actual denominational proportions and would include "marginal" church members, i.e., those with a denominational preference but no active affiliation. As the scale was designed to measure Church-Sect tendencies within Protestantism, an initial loss of 25 per cent was anticipated from the presence of non-Protestants in the sample. Actually 22 per cent of the final returns were from non-Protestants. Returns of the questionnaire were elicited by the initial mailing, two follow-up postcards and a second questionnaire mailed to every fifth non-respondent. This study was based on 360 returns or 53 per cent of the estimated Protestant sample.[8]

CHURCH-SECT SCORES AND SOCIO-ECONOMIC STATUS

Although there were other aspects to this research, this paper is confined to the relation between socio-economic status and the attitudes measured by the Church-Sect Scale. It was hypothesized that the higher the socio-economic status, the greater would be the acceptance of the Church type of religious organization. Operationally, this would be indicated on the scale by higher scores. Socio-economic status was estimated by three different measures: first, by differences in education; second, by the Census Occupational classification; third, by ratings of occupational prestige on the North-Hatt Scale.[9]

Using education as the first-measure of socio-economic status, Table 2 indicates that consistent differences in mean scale scores occur among all of the different educational levels. Although only two of the differences between adjacent categories were significant at the .05 level, this was, in part, a product of small categories, since both high school and college were sub-divided into graduates and non-graduates. It is evident that the degree of acceptance of the Church type of organization increases with an increase in the amount of education.

[8] Use of the City Directory as a sampling source obviously excludes recent migrants to the city from the sample. The final returns, also, came more frequently from the higher socio-economic groups. Assuming 25 per cent of the non-returns would be from non-Protestants, the highest occupational prestige category (80 and above on the North-Hatt scale, see footnote 9) had a 73 per cent return, and the lowest prestige category (under 60) had a 33 per cent return. It is probable that the non-Protestant population would be more heavily concentrated in the lower prestige categories, so perhaps the differential return is not quite so great. The interest of this paper, however, is to investigate the relationship between Church-Sect attitudes and socio-economic status and not the distribution of these attitudes in the general population.

[9] Cecil C. North and Paul K. Hatt, "Jobs and Occupations: A Popular Evaluation," *Opinion News,* 9 (1947) pp. 3–13.

TABLE 2. MEAN CHURCH-SECT SCORES BY AMOUNT OF
EDUCATIONAL TRAINING

Amount of Educational Training	N	Mean	Standard Deviation	Critical Ratio *	P
Post-graduate and professional	40	79.8	12.1		
				.9	.40
College graduate	39	77.7	11.2		
				2.1	.05
One to three years of college	55	72.9	12.2		
				1.7	.10
High school graduate	93	69.2	13.4		
				1.4	.20
One to three years of high school	48	66.3	10.6		
				2.8	.01
Elementary school	54	59.9	12.4		

* Critical Ratios are for differences between mean scores of adjacent categories.

The Census Occupational Classification was used as the second indicator of socio-economic status since this classification reflects, in part, a prestige hierarchy. Table 3 indicates that mean differences in Church-Sect scores occurred among all of the major categories. (Service workers and laborers were combined.) The only discrepancy, if it is one, is the higher mean score of the managers, since the professional category is usually assumed to be highest in prestige. One possible explanation for this "discrepancy" was the relative grossness of the Census category of "Professional, technical and kindred workers." Some who were so classified, e.g., draftsmen, technical clerks, etc., were professionals more by classification than by public acceptance, and these "quasi-professionals" produced greater prestige and attitude heterogeneity. Dividing them into more homogeneous prestige groupings, both the managers and the "traditional" professionals had somewhat similar Church-Sect scores.[10] Additional data on the managerial and professional categories are presented below, but this "discrepancy" should not obscure the close association between the occupational classification, indicating prestige differences, and variations in Church-Sect scores.

[10] The greater heterogeneity of the professional category is shown in Table 3 by its larger standard deviation. Both the managerial and professional categories were sub-divided into more homogeneous prestige groupings using the North-Hatt scale. The managers with higher prestige (72 and over on the North-Hatt scale) had a mean Church-Sect score of 79.9 (N=21) and the managers with lower prestige (under 72) had a mean score of 79.1 (N=20). The professionals were divided into three groups. Professionals with the highest prestige (80 and above on the North-Hatt scale) had a Church-Sect score of 78.8 (N=33), the middle group (78–79) had a mean score of 77.3 (N=23) and the lowest (77 and below) had a mean score of 74.7 (N=25).

TABLE 3. MEAN CHURCH-SECT SCORES FOR MAJOR
OCCUPATIONAL CATEGORIES

Occupational Categories *	N	Mean	Standard Deviation	Critical Ratio †	P
Managers, officials and proprietors	41	79.5	7.8		
				1.8	.10
Professional, technical and kindred workers	81	76.3	11.2		
				1.6	.20
Sales workers	32	71.7	14.6		
				.9	.40
Craftsmen, foremen and kindred workers	54	69.0	11.8		
				1.2	.30
Clerical and kindred workers	53	66.2	11.6		
				1.1	.30
Operatives and kindred workers	40	63.6	12.1		
				3.1	.01
Service workers and laborers	27	53.9	12.6		

* Source of occupational categories is U. S. Bureau of the Census, *Alphabetical Index of Occupations and Industries: 1950,* Washington, D. C., 1950.
† Critical Ratios are for differences between mean scores of adjacent categories.

The third measure of socio-economic status used was the North-Hatt scale which expresses occupational prestige by a numerical score between twenty and one hundred.[11] Using this more precise measure of prestige, systematic differences in Church-Sect scores again occurred among North-Hatt categories. (See Table 4.) One reversal in the differences in the attitude scores occurs in the 70–74 range of the North-Hatt scale. Since the highest mean Church-Sect score of the occupational categories was for managers, it seemed plausible that many of this category might be concentrated within this prestige range of the North-Hatt scale. Analysis proved this to be correct, and this concentration increased the mean Church-Sect scores.[12] Again, this aberration should not con-

[11] *Op. cit.,* The original prestige evaluations in the North-Hatt study included only 90 different occupations. Since ratings for other occupations were needed to make it a useful research tool, several different studies at Ohio State have expanded the initial list. All have used a standard method of interpolation, using five judges to evaluate an occupation in terms of the original scale. This expanded list is available in mimeographed form from the writer.

[12] The managerial category was analyzed for its composition of occupational prestige. A mean North-Hatt score of 73 was found for this category, and this mean lies within the range where the "discrepancy" occurred in the North-Hatt scale shown in Table 4. One might expect, however, this similarity in Church-Sect scores between the managers and the more "traditional" professions, represented by the top categories of the North-Hatt scores. Income may be one intrusive factor. While the managers

TABLE 4. MEAN CHURCH-SECT SCORES BY CATEGORIES
ON THE NORTH-HATT SCALE

North-Hatt Score	N	Mean	Standard Deviation	Critical Ratio [*]	P
80 and above	39	80.5	9.7	1.6	.20
75–79	48	77.0	10.6		
70–74	49	78.2	9.7	4.6	.001
65–69	93	69.9	10.9	4.0	.001
60–64	54	62.2	11.4	2.1	.05
Under 60	47	56.8	14.1		

[*] Critical Ratios are for differences between mean scores of adjacent categories.

ceal the general association between the Church-Sect scores and occupational prestige.

The relationships between Church-Sect scores and these three indices of socio-economic status indicate, as hypothesized, that *Churchness is associated with high socio-economic status and, conversely, that Sectness is associated with low socio-economic status.* In other words, as education increases, emotionalism, evangelism and other Sectarian characteristics are increasingly rejected. An increase in occupational prestige, whether measured by the Census Occupational Classification or by the North-Hatt scale, is associated with a greater acceptance of the more institutional and liturgical Church.

CHURCH-SECT SCORES AND DENOMINATIONAL MEMBERSHIP

It might be argued that the Church-Sect Scale measures only differences in denominational affiliation, since certain denominations manifest behaviorally the traits which the scale attempted to measure. (For example, denominational groups were used as criterion groups in a test of validity. See Table 1.) It is hypothesized here, however, that these differences are the result of socio-economic factors correlated with membership in certain denominations and are not just the simple consequence of doctrinal position. In other words, when a denomination, or a specific church, has a

have slightly less occupational prestige than the professionals, as a group, managers have a higher income. (For evidence on this point, see, Otis Dudley Duncan and Beverly Duncan, "Residential Distribution and Occupational Stratification," *American Journal of Sociology,* 60 (March, 1955), pp. 493–503). The Church-Sect scores may bear a closer relationship to income than to education and occupation; however, in this study, no income data were collected. In addition, if part of the constellation of the Church type of organization is the acceptance and reinforcement of secular value systems, then, a high score of the managerial category would be expected.

membership drawn from a certain socio-economic level, these members will manifest certain attitudes and other characteristic traits of that level, regardless of the specific doctrinal emphasis. Thus, individuals of different denominations but equivalent in socio-economic status may be more similar in certain religious attitudes than individuals of the same denomination who differ in socio-economic status.

If these attitudes, measured by the scale, actually vary with socio-economic status, members of the same denomination differing in occupational prestige, for example, should show corresponding differences in scale scores. To determine whether this is valid, an analysis was made of two denominational groups, Methodists and Presbyterians, which were frequent enough in the sample to permit subdivision into prestige categories. The results are shown in Table 5. Both of these groups were dichotomized on the North-Hatt Scale using seventy as the dividing line. The Methodists categorized this way showed a mean difference of almost eleven scale points, significant at the .001 level. The Presbyterians, a more homogeneous group in prestige, showed a scale difference of almost seven points, significant at the .05 level. *Holding denominational affiliation constant, then, the difference in the degree of Churchness and Sectness is still associated with socio-economic status.*

TABLE 5. MEAN CHURCH-SECT SCORES OF METHODISTS AND PRESBYTERIANS BY CATEGORIES ON THE NORTH-HATT SCALE

Denominational Affiliation	North-Hatt Score	N	Mean	Standard Deviation	Critical Ratio *	P
Methodists	70 and over	43	78.0	9.9	5.1	.001
	Under 70	54	67.1	11.2		
Presbyterians	70 and over	24	78.4	8.5	2.4 †	.05
	Under 70	24	71.7	10.5		

* Critical Ratios are for differences between mean scores.
† "t" test was used.

SUMMARY

The Church-Sect typology, introduced by Weber and Troeltsch and used in various forms by others, served as the theoretical basis for this study. An attitude scale was constructed to measure these types and it was administered in questionnaire form to a random sample of the Columbus, Ohio, Protestant population. The scale scores were related to socio-economic status, measured three different ways. Significant relationships were found between the acceptance of the Sect type of organization and lower socio-economic status and between the acceptance of the Church type of organization and higher socio-economic status. In two instances, holding denominational affiliation constant, differences in the degree of acceptance of Church or Sect characteristics were still found to be associated with socio-economic status.

If vertical social mobility in America is as prevalent as alleged, these relationships would have implications for shifts in religious ideology and organizational structure. The research reported here, however, does not imply that economic determinism is a sufficient explanation of religious ideology. The insufficiency of one factor theories is well recognized, but in attempting to develop an adequate theory of the function of religion, points of origin have to be selected in tracing functional interrelationships. This research should indicate that knowledge of socio-economic factors is important in understanding religious behavior.

22. From Sect to Church

WALTER MUELDER *

IF RELIGION IS FUNCTIONALLY INTERRELATED WITH ONE'S POSITION IN THE PATTERN OF SOCIAL STRATIFICATION, IT SEEMS LIKELY THAT CHANGE IN ONE WOULD INFLUENCE THE OTHER. IMPROVEMENT IN CLASS STATUS, FOR EXAMPLE, IS OFTEN ACCOMPANIED BY A SHIFT FROM SECT TO CHURCH. THIS PROCESS, HOWEVER, IS NOT WHOLLY TO BE ACCOUNTED FOR BY WHAT HAPPENS TO INDIVIDUAL MEMBERS OF A RELIGIOUS GROUP. THERE ARE IMPORTANT DEVELOPMENTS IN THE SOCIOLOGICAL STRUCTURE OF THE GROUP THAT PROMOTE A DEVELOPMENT FROM SECT TO CHURCH, AS THIS PAPER SHOWS.

Sociology of religion is a very complex discipline. One of the difficulties in the field is the stereotype of holiness sects which one finds on every hand. In this paper a brief survey is made of recent studies on the West Coast as they bear on the problem of institutional development from sect-type groups into church-type denominations.[1] The two groups particularly

* Abridged from *Christendom*, Autumn, 1945, pp. 450–462.
[1] The writers of two doctoral dissertations at the University of Southern California have consented to a liberal use of their researches in this article. Harold W. Reed studied *The Growth of a Contemporary Sect-Type Institution as Reflected in the Development of the Church of the Nazarene*, 1943. James B. Wilson investigated *Religious Leaders, Institutions and Organizations Among Certain Agricultural Workers in the Central Valley of California*, 1944.

under examination are Nazarenes and Pentecostals. They are frequently confused with each other as are other rural and urban phenomena. We shall devote the first part of the discussion to some findings concerning the institutional evolution of rural Pentecostal sects and the second part to the recapitulation of the institutional development of the Church of the Nazarene which is mostly an urban denomination. Rural California is becoming industrialized so rapidly, however, that the social conflict attendant upon "factories in the field" reflects itself quite as much there as in the city. Religious institutions reflect these conflicts as they also reflect the great social accommodations which the established people have made to the social values of the community they have helped to generate. Dissent is characteristic of the sects. Accommodation is characteristic of the churches. Institutional development moves from dissent to accommodation.

I

There is bound to be a significant and fundamental difference between the growth, development, stability, stratification, and the degrees and types of co-operation among marginal churches and sects in the rural areas and the expression of the same factors in the cities. In the cities there is obviously a more stable resident population. In rural California industrialization has become so widespread that migratory workers, the constituency of holiness churches, are the dominant type of labor. No great institutional development either of labor unions or of churches is possible without a relative residential stability. Hence the comparatively greater primitiveness of holiness sects in the rural districts as compared with the city. Churches in rural California inevitably depend for membership and support on the permanent residents, and these are for the most part ranchers, professional and business people. The churches tend to be ranchers' societies.

In one rural village the Methodist Church consists chiefly of ranchers, although the church is completely surrounded by agricultural workers. Many of the latter had belonged to regular churches "back east" and had been active; but their new class status in California changed all that. The farmers did "not want their little church molested by them." Rancher Methodists regarded migrant Methodists as "dirt under their feet." The migrants felt that the landowners' church was a good place to avoid. These people therefore were open to cultivation by the transient sect preacher and the migratory evangelist. The migrant camps are generally avoided by old-line churches. . . .

Walter R. Goldschmidt's study of the social structure of a California rural community deserves widespread attention.[2] His thorough anthropological analysis of Wasco in the Central Valley confirms, in its examination of religious groups, the general theories of men like Richard Niebuhr and the specialized studies of Pope, Reed, and Wilson. The religious situation in Wasco throws light on the function of Pentecostalism in the social life of the area and on the evolution of institutional structures through the interplay of dissent and accommodation among groups. There are two distinct classes in Wasco, the upper (called the nuclear group) and the lower (called the outsider group). The former comprises that group of persons which grew up with the town and inherited the institutions of the community. The latter is composed of those who arrived somewhat later to serve as agricultural laborers. Both groups have the same basic values but differ in social experience and in economic interests. In the nuclear group there is a threefold division, the elite, the middle group, and the marginal group. In the outsider group are whites, Negroes, and Mexican workers. They are subgroups in the same social class. It is the ambition of the outsiders to become accepted members in the community, a desire which is frustrated by the social situation, but which at the same time determines the institutional development from sects (dissent) to churches (accommodation).

The elite group of churches comprises two old-line churches and a third, the Seventh Day Adventist, which in some areas of the U.S.A. would be classified among the sects. In Wasco, however, its social function is exactly the same as that of the other older denominations. Differences in theology fade into insignificance in comparison with the social distance which exists between the membership of this church and the agricultural laborer's religious societies. Seventh Day Adventists have a theology very much like that of Pentecostals in important respects; but similarity in doctrine and ecclesiastical goal is not sufficient to provide solidarity between the rancher and professional groups, on the one hand, and the migrant or other agricultural worker, on the other hand. This same relationship is demonstrable for all the other nuclear-type churches. Though the workers "back home" belonged to nuclear-type churches, in Wasco they are welcome only in outsider organizations. In the total church population, eighteen per cent are from the professional, managerial, or proprietary groups, but there are none of these in the Pentecostal sect. In the total church population, nineteen per cent are unskilled

    [2] Walter R. Goldschmidt, *Social Structure of a California Rural Community* (unpublished doctoral dissertation in anthropology, The University of California, Berkeley, California, August, 1942).

laborers, but in the Pentecostal sect they represent eighty-two per cent of the membership.

The internal development of denominational patterns and the co-operation of sects and churches are definitely limited by the class structure of both older denominations and the outsider sects. Schisms among the Pentecostal churches are frequent, being an outward manifestation of internal strife. But as the social status of the membership changes the factors making for their type of social group will disappear, and we may look forward to a new relationship both within the sect and between the churches and the sects. Pentecostal sects in California as elsewhere are related to such social vectors as: (1) appeal to the economically disinherited, (2) mobility, in part, (3) cultural alienation, (4) leadership of and by their own group, (5) emotional starvation, (6) inexpensive religious release and status, (7) simplicity and comprehensibility of religious ideas, (8) a putative society, and (9) revivalism. In these respects the general pattern is like that noted already by Clark, Pope, Boisen and others. Just to the degree that these factors in group life are modified by a dynamic and developing socio-economic pattern in rural California, to that same degree the internal and external social relationships will show accommodation. In the rural sects conflict is paramount; in the churches social accommodation is paramount. The gradual shift from social ostracism to social acceptability, all other things being equal, will determine the transition from sects to churches. This shift is made very difficult because of the present unconcern, ineptness, and caste feelings of the churches and many of their ministers as they are confronted by the "outsiders."

Not all Pentecostal churches, of course, are at the same stage of social evolution as religious institutions. Conflict and accommodation are always in operation. What Clark and Pope have clearly demonstrated in other areas of the United States repeats itself here again. The evidence here used comes from Pentecostal leaders in the great Central Valley, from leaders who recognize clearly that certain Pentecostal churches are losing their sect characteristics. One of them, the minister of Bethel Assembly of God, in M., observed this trend in his national organization:

We are going through the same process as the Methodists did. We are in the cycle. We are gradually giving more attention to the form of government, control by the bishops, and following formal services. If divisions come it will be over these matters. The younger churches will say, "Let us go out into the highways and bring them in," whereas the formal churches will say, "They know where we are; let them come to us." That is a picture of what is taking place within my own denomination.

The Assemblies of God Churches in cities like F., S., and B. "get a fine type of people." In B. the membership consists mainly of a "very good middle class," most of the constituency being home owners and only a few being migrants.

In the town of M. the Pentecostal Assembly of God Tabernacle is a "split-off" from the Bethel Assembly of God mentioned above. The ministers of both congregations recognize that the division was not over questions of doctrine but was determined by the relative social and economic status of the two elements in the church. The comment of the minister of the "split-off" group is instructive:

The common people felt they were squeezed out. They were given to an emotional type of service and the better class resented it. My members are mostly just plain working folks, but [X] has a lot of white collar professional people. . . . Some of our churches are becoming formal. I've been in some of them and the manner of their services is such that you could never tell they were Pentecostal. They had just as much ritual as any other church. They had a set program of slow songs, no general participation by the congregation, not even saying "Amen." Just nice and quiet all the way round. The preacher did it all. The big tabernacle in F. is like that. . . .

In one of the towns it was possible to trace the evolution of a holiness congregation through ten years. It began in a cottage, grew to a store front, then expanded to a tabernacle structure, and finally built a modest modern-appearing church building. The corresponding changes in the group life and religious expression of the congregation can be measured by the fact that while the nucleus of this congregation was migrant, migrants who came ten years later found it too "cold" and "formal." Consequently they rallied to a new holiness group which was started by some elements in the society who no longer felt "at home" and who therefore "split off."

II

A more advanced stage of accommodation and assimilation to the patterns of established Protestantism is observable in the development of the Church of the Nazarene. In the common scholarly conception of sect the factor of conflict and dissent is made a point of focus. While this emphasis is essential in the definition of the sect, the principle of unity may be equally significant and may even at times overshadow the element of conflict. Thus a religious sect is a dissenting group of individuals differing in birth, in education, in profession, and in social status, but united and, indeed, voluntarily cemented together by an extremely strong bond, a common religious faith and ideal. As one studies the development of the Church of the Nazarene one is impressed with the spirit of unity not only within the "in-group" but also in its inception as simply a movement within the regular denominations, and even more as exhibiting a kind of ecumenical institutional growth among the myriad of holiness sects and quasi-sects within the perfectionist movement as a whole. The Church of the Nazarene must thus be viewed partly as the crystallization of institutional tendencies of a movement and partly as a split-off or organized revolt against "major" denominations.

There prevails among the "major" denominations an assumption, stimulated by certain sociologists and historians of religion, that Pentecostal and Holiness sects are simply expressions of the "religion of the disinherited." Although through the preaching of holiness "many plow-boys and mechanics were called to preach," it must be emphasized that the disinheritance was sometimes more ecclesiastical than it was strictly socioeconomic. This is especially true of the Church of the Nazarene. It emerged as a denomination out of the convergence of numerous factors, among them the fact that many persons, who at the turn of the century were active in holiness camp meetings, "were expelled from their communions" or "were made to feel uncomfortable in their churches." Anyone acquainted with the development of the Church of the Nazarene as an institution can hardly avoid the conclusion that personality factors, religious incentives, and doctrinal issues are equally important with the social situation more widely conceived. At the same time it must be recognized that at its inception the sect gathered most of its constituency from the poor and flourished among the depressed income groups of wage earners.

The evolution of this particular Nazarene group must be read against the general background of American church history. American perfectionism since the Civil War has contributed over twenty perfectionist sects to what may be called the sect-type denominational pattern. In the latter half of the nineteenth century this perfectionism first took the form of a holiness movement, which rapidly developed national, state, and county organizations. As the movement grew it also crystallized into many independent churches and loosely organized bands which may be designated as quasi-sects. Some of these groups constituted what has been called a right-wing and some a more "radical" or left-wing division. The former followed Wesleyanism quite closely, although their emphasis upon the "secondness" of experience was probably more specialized than had been early Methodism. The latter emphasized speaking in tongues, the second coming of Christ, and divine healing. There was conflict between these groups especially over the idea of speaking in tongues. About 1894 the independent churches of the right wing began to organize into small groups and form small sects or semi-sects. By 1908 three of these quasi-sects united and formed a new sect-type institution known as the Pentecostal Church of the Nazarene. In the next ten years five other independent groups were brought into the organization. The use of the term Pentecostal was a concession made in 1907 to the Pentecostal Association. But in 1919 in response to memorials from thirty-five districts the General Assembly changed the name to "Church of the Nazarene." This change was deliberately made in order that the Church of the Nazarene might not be confused with the "tongues" movement.

In religious expressive movements, as Professor Robert E. Park has pointed out, the individuals involved do not seek to change the prevailing institutions of the social order. Their tension and unrest do not ordinarily carry over into purposive action. The individuals are rather content to release the tension of their inner disturbed feelings by some type of expressive behavior. The expressive behavior is such as to arouse feelings of intense intimacy, constituting the participating members as "in-group." Their tendency is to be conscious of a heightened feeling of exaltation and ecstasy, which leads them to experience personal expansion and a sense of being possessed by some transcendental spirit. In addition the collective feelings are projected on outside objects, persons, and behavior. Songs, phrases, words, and material objects acquire a more or less sacred character. Eventually heightened feelings of dissent yield to the less emotionalized feeling-tone of accommodation. Conflict gives way to cooperation.

Indeed from the beginning the Holiness Associations from which the Church of the Nazarene emerged were opposed to the extreme degree of dissent which expressed itself in the "Comeouter Movement." Being neither denominations, nor designed to take the place of the church, the Holiness Associations were interdenominational interest groups whose members could be and were members of the evangelical churches. They had no more organization than many missionary, Bible, or temperance societies. From the standpoint of their leadership the Associations claimed to have a two-fold objective, namely, that of the conversion of the lost and the spreading of "scriptural holiness" among believers of whatever name they might be called. . . .

As an earnest of faith in the essential unity of the faith and as a demonstration of peace and united aggressive action in the promulgation of truth, the National Holiness Association taught the principle of unsectarian affiliation.

The group instruments of the camp meetings, doctrinal literature, and committees of correspondence were destined, however, to lead to greater organizational self-consciousness. Some of the functions performed by the Holiness Associations overlapped those of regularly organized denominations. They held property. They received members with certain rights and financial obligations. They had well-developed rules and regulations to govern county, state, and national associations. They developed a considerable self-conscious literature, both periodicals and tracts. They established Bible Schools and colleges. They carried on regular meetings, including camp meetings. As time passed the loosely institutional pattern became more firmly set. . . .

By 1896 the National Holiness Association was definitely more than a loose confederation of holiness associations and independent congregations: it was virtually a denomination. . . .

As the denominational life of the church has progressed there has been the inevitable accommodation which is associated with the church-type pattern. The laws of institutional growth from sect to church are clearly evident. Less and less do the extreme sect-type conflict-patterns present themselves. More and more the techniques of accommodation are employed. Membership for example, is stressed in the reports of ministers. And members are recruited increasingly from the church school and less from adult evangelistic campaigns. Moreover, less attention is given to worldliness, as is easily demonstrated by the most casual perusal and comparison of early and present literature of the denomination. Church finances have bettered and the ministers, like the laity, are implicated in the usual accommodations associated with security and higher salaries.

The second and third generation church members have not battled over religious doctrine, and hence lack the conflict consciousness of their elders. They more readily make concessions, at least on detail of doctrine. The young people come increasingly from urban homes (the Nazarene Church is not a rural institution, as many suppose) which reflect a growing economic security. Companions and associates are found among those who are quite secularized. Indeed, Nazarene youth are not conspicuously different in their basic values from those with whom they fraternize in high school and college. The colleges themselves are making every effort to be accepted by the accrediting and standardizing agencies of the general college associations. More and more the leadership of the Church of the Nazarene is achieving the scholarship level of the doctorate in America's leading universities. . . .

Given a generation or two for their members to adjust to urban economic and social opportunity and they will present the church historian with a pattern of the same internal institutional growth and accommodation which the major denominations have undergone. On the West Coast, where the ruts of traditional denominationalism are not so deep as in the East, there are numerous hints even of co-operation and unity across previous barriers. With most of the major denominations the Church of the Nazarene has long been a member of the International Council of Religious Education. The First Church of the Nazarene, the mother church, founded by Phineas Bresee, and the largest congregation of the denomination in Los Angeles, now co-operates with the Church Federation of Los Angeles in the program of week-day or released time religious education. In line with its conservative theology it also co-operates with the National Association of Evangelicals. Some Nazarene women now participate in the Los Angeles Council of Church Women, which is integrally related to the Church Federation of that city. This trend is also apparent in some of the Assemblies of God, representatives of which are in the Women's Council. In Pasadena, the Nazarene churches co-operate with the Pastors' Union, as well as with the more conservative interchurch agencies. If the present trend continues we may soon find the Nazarene Church quite fully participating in ecumenical organizations. This would mark a decisive step in accommodation to the church-type.

23. Aspects of the Movement from Sect to Church

LISTON POPE *

THIS BRIEF EXCERPT FROM DEAN POPE'S WELL-KNOWN STUDY FORMULATES IN GENERAL TERMS WHAT HAS BEEN ILLUSTRATED IN THE PRECEDING SELECTION. THE BOOK FROM WHICH THIS QUOTATION IS DRAWN HAS BEEN VERY INFLUENCIAL IN THE SOCIOLOGY OF RELIGION, BECAUSE IT COMBINES, IN A HIGHLY EFFECTIVE WAY, EMPIRICAL RESEARCH WITH THEORETICAL INTEREST.

After close observation of religious institutions of all types, the following scale has been worked out to indicate the various facets of this transition:

1. *From* membership composed chiefly of the propertyless *to* membership composed of property owners.

* From *Millhands and Preachers,* pp. 122–124.

2. *From* economic poverty *to* economic wealth, as disclosed especially in the value of church property and the salary paid to ministers.

3. *From* the cultural periphery *toward* the cultural center of the community.

4. *From* renunciation of prevailing culture and social organization, or indifference to it, *to* affirmation of prevailing culture and social organization.

5. *From* self-centered (or personal) religion *to* culture-centered religion, from "experience" to a social institution.

6. *From* noncooperation, or positive ridicule, toward established religious institutions *to* cooperation with the established churches of the community.

7. *From* suspicion of rival sects *to* disdain or pity for all sects.

8. *From* a moral community excluding unworthy members *to* a social institution embracing all who are socially compatible with it.

9. *From* an unspecialized, unprofessionalized, part-time ministry *to* a specialized, professional, full-time ministry.

10. *From* a psychology of persecution *to* a psychology of success and dominance.

11. *From* voluntary, confessional bases of membership *to* ritual or social prerequisites only (such as a certificate of previous membership in another respected denomination, or training in an educational process established by the denomination itself).

12. *From* principal concern with adult membership *to* equal concern for children of members.

13. *From* emphasis on evangelism and conversion *to* emphasis on religious education.

14. *From* stress on a future in the next world *to* primary interest in a future in this world—a future for the institution, for its members, and for their children; *from* emphasis on death *to* emphasis on successful earthly life.

15. *From* adherence to strict Biblical standards, such as tithing or nonresistance, *to* acceptance of general cultural standards as a practical definition of religious obligations.

16. *From* a high degree of congregational participation in the services and administration of the religious group *to* delegation of responsibility to a comparatively small percentage of the membership.

17. *From* fervor in worship services *to* restraint; *from* positive action *to* passive listening.

18. *From* a comparatively large number of special religious services *to* a program of regular services at stated intervals.

19. *From* reliance on spontaneous "leadings of the Spirit" in religious services and administration *to* a fixed order of worship and of administrative procedure.

20. *From* the use of hymns resembling contemporary folk music *to* the use of slower, more stately hymns coming out of more remote liturgical tradition.

21. *From* emphasis on religion in the home *to* delegation of responsibility for religion to church officials and organizations.

24. Cultural Significance of the Ghost Dance

ALEXANDER LESSER *

THE FOUR PAPERS THAT MAKE UP THE REMAINDER OF THIS SECTION DEAL WITH RELIGIOUS MOVEMENTS AMONG MINORITY GROUPS—THE DISPRIVILEGED AND DISINHERITED. THEY DIFFER IN THE DEGREE TO WHICH A FUNCTIONAL THEORETICAL INTERPRETATION IS MADE EXPLICIT, BUT EACH ONE FITS READILY INTO THIS PATTERN.

Few religious movements have been so fortunate in their contemporary chroniclers as the Ghost Dance of 1890 in the sympathetic record of James Mooney. In his long historical account and commentary, Mooney enlarged upon earlier movements of a similar nature, ghost dance origins and sources, the doctrine, the forms of the dance, its psychological aspects in the trances, the spread of the religion in detail, the local forms of the religion among a number of the tribes, and the actual historical events which brought some tribes into conflict with the government over the doctrine. But Mooney's report was at once so voluminous and full a record, that since its publication there has been a tendency to regard the Ghost Dance as a closed book, finished and forever settled in this definitive treatment.

James Mooney investigated the Ghost Dance at intervals in the years from 1890 to 1893. Of his own work he states that his investigations brought "personal observation and study of the Ghost Dance down to the beginning of 1894." In his introductory remarks, Mooney comments that "the investigation . . . might be continued indefinitely, as the dance still exists [in 1896] and is developing new features at every performance."

* From *American Anthropologist,* January–March, 1933, pp. 108–115.

Thus Mooney himself recognized that he had not written the final chapter.

And in truth the Ghost Dance, like all vital cultural manifestations, was not, and could not be, an episode that had an arbitrary beginning and an arbitrary close. In human culture, as in human experience, what has come to attention and prominence never disappears. Either it is retained in some form as a part of culture thereafter, or it leaves its impress and influence upon other aspects of culture.

To measure the pulse of the Ghost Dance movement, Mooney found it necessary to consider the religious revivals of earlier American Indian prophets, demonstrating that no mere arbitrary point could be selected as the beginning of the Ghost Dance. In a passage of his concluding remarks, Mooney called attention to the fact that among some of the tribes which participated in the Ghost Dance, "the Ghost Dance has become a part of the tribal life and is performed at regular intervals," indicating that no arbitrary date could be set upon its close. If the Ghost Dance did not suddenly arise, flourish, and disappear, but rather had a natural growth upon the basis of earlier culture in response to cultural needs, and after the excitement of its period of storm and stress settled down to become a more or less integrated part of a newer, changed culture, then Ghost Dance effects are a significant ethnological problem. For if the field ethnologist today is to penetrate to older levels of aboriginal culture, he must attend to the local Ghost Dance and mark off the changes it has caused.

According to James Mooney's concept of the Ghost Dance it was a movement of revolt, religiously directed, an attempt to throw off an alien yoke, and recover aboriginal freedom. In the course of that movement, the activities which composed it could not fail to influence directly the rest of culture. I should like to call attention to certain phases of this influence, of how changes which came about were related to the doctrine and to the activities of the dance. While I shall use facts from the Pawnee to illustrate my meaning, I believe that the general bearing of the point of view will be found relevant to the situation among other tribes.

The Ghost Dance spread among American Indian tribes at a time when the final destruction of native culture was well advanced. Perhaps the greatest destructive influence was not so much the influx of white settlers or the consequent appropriation of tribal lands, as the annihilation of the great herds of buffalo. With the disappearance of the buffalo, the economic stability and security of the Indian tribes vanished. In its place came want and hunger. A feeling of desolation which spread among these tribes made them ripe for any message of hope.

The Ghost Dance doctrine brought hope. It promised a destruction of the invading white man, a return of the buffalo and old Indian ways, and a reunion of the Indians and their deceased forebears. The last may well have been a Christian element, as well as the moral precept accompanying it that Indians were not to fight any more, but live together in one great brotherhood. But the sanction for this hope was native to the Indian mind. It was based on the vision, on the direct supernatural experience. In the vision a message came from the deceased, telling the living what to do, telling the living what would happen.

With the destruction of the buffalo and the influx of the white man, Indian ways of life were vanishing. This was clearly the case if we read the Pawnee story aright. The old Pawnee societies had long since ceased to function. Practically all these societies were concerned with war and hunting. Intertribal warfare had been legally eliminated, although of course occasional skirmishes occurred. But the Pawnee steadfastly maintained their treaty obligations and avoided warfare with their ancient enemies, appealing, as in the case of the Sioux massacre of the Pawnee in 1873, to the federal government for redress. In the same way, tribal hunting became a memory. With the disappearance of warfare and hunting, the societies no longer had a function.

The great esoteric bundle ceremonies of the Pawnee had also ceased. The reason given by old men today is not a failure of belief, but the same failure of the supply of buffalo which destroyed many of the societies. A cardinal tenet of Pawnee ideology was the sacred character of buffalo meat. None but buffalo meat could be used in the great ceremonies; in fact, not only was buffalo meat essential, but in many of the bundle ceremonies buffalo concepts and orientations of powers concerned primarily with the buffalo were part and parcel of the ritual and ceremony itself. Without these aspects of the ritual and ceremony, the performance became meaningless.

The medicine-men's phase of Pawnee religion had not entirely died out. Many leading doctors who controlled the right to demonstrate dances had died, taking their esoteric teachings with them to the grave; but one or two Doctor Dances were still held almost every year. For these a sufficient supply of buffalo meat could be obtained, or the medicine-men themselves found justification for substituting ordinary beef for buffalo meat. The great Doctor Performances involving feats of magic and sleight of hand had ceased. The last one occurred among the Pawnee in 1878 or 1879.

The ordinary social activities of daily life had also broken down to a great extent. Most of the games were no longer played, or were revived here and there intermittently. Thus while in former times the spring was not only a time of great religious and ceremonial activity, of great economic and industrial activity, but also a time for the revival of games for the young and old, in the years before the Ghost Dance there was no general spring revival of social activity.

This decline of Pawnee culture was not altogether a direct result of the changing conditions, but in considerable part was connected with the Pawnee pattern for handing on traditional knowledge.

According to the Pawnee conception, the knowledge and learning of an individual had to be handed down by actual instruction of the young. This was somewhat different for the two basic types of bundles: the sacred bundles (with which can be associated the society bundles, probably derivative), and the doctor bundles. A sacred bundle was physically owned by a man who did not necessarily know its significance and ritual, although he did carry out his obligations toward it according to the instruction of a priest; it was physically cared for by the owner's wife; and its ritual learning was controlled or owned by a priest. The bundle itself was inherited in the male line (ordinarily). The ritual learning was taught by the priest to his successor, usually a close relative (though not necessarily in the male line alone), but lacking close kin of the right temperament and character, the priest taught whom he wished. On the other hand, a medicine man owned his bundle *and* its correlative teachings, performances, rites. He turned these over to his successor, who was usually a close relative (son or nephew, etc.), but again, if the medicine man found his own kin unwilling to take over his bundle, he would teach someone else who came to him desiring to learn.

Ordinarily, a man taught his successor largely by demonstration. That is, the apprentice took part in the actual demonstrations of the ritual, watching what went on. In the course of the procedure, his master explained details. As the teacher found his pupil mastering phases of the activity, he turned over to the pupil such parts of the ritual, performance, etc., as he found were understood. In this way, as a rule, a man learned *all* of another's teachings only if the teacher lived to be an old man. In fact, the Pawnee conception was that as a man taught what he knew he gave up part of his life, and that when he had given over all his teachings, he would die. Hence the old and learned always held back something until they were ready to die. If a priest or medicine man died, what he had not taught to his successor was lost. Usually, when an old man knew he was on his deathbed, and valued his learning and his apprentice, he called the apprentice in, and in dying whispers told him the essentials of what he had not before that time communicated. Now since among the

Pawnee a man has no right to handle in a ceremonial manner what he does not understand, what he has not learned to carry out, it happened in most cases that doctor bundles were broken up upon the death of the owner. Some part of the bundle had already been transferred to the medicine man's apprentice; some further part which the apprentice understood but had not already been given, was now handed over to him; and the rest was buried with the deceased medicine man. As the ownership of the sacred bundles was divorced from the knowledge of their rituals, the same did not happen to them. The physical bundle survived, but gradually less and less of its contents were understood by living men.

The important point to remember in this is that in old Pawnee ideology what of traditional learning was lost through death was lost beyond recovery. There was no sanction for carrying out any ritual, other than that the one who attempted to carry it out had learned about it from the man who formerly had controlled it and demonstrated it.

As conditions became unfavorable for carrying out the activities and demonstrating the rituals of the ceremonies and societies, there was neither the stimulus for the old to teach and for the young to learn, nor the customary mechanism in operation for the transfer of learning. Hence the normal rate of cultural forgetting was accelerated, and in the course of only a few years, relatively, most of the old traditional ways were buried in the grave.

Into this situation of cultural decay and gradual darkness, the Ghost Dance doctrine shone like a bright light. Indian ways were not gone, never to be recovered. Indian ways were coming back. Those who had lived before in the "golden age" were still carrying on old ceremonies, old dances, old performances, and old games in the beyond. They were coming back; they were bringing the old ways and the buffalo. Dance, dance, dance. The white man would be destroyed by a great wind. The Indian would be left with the buffalo, with his ancestors, with his old friends and his old enemies. Cast aside the white man's ways like an old garment; put on the clothes of the Indian again. Get ready for the new day and the old times.

The dancers shook and fell in hypnotic trances. They saw the people in the beyond dancing too. They saw them playing games, ring and pole games, hand-games; they saw them gathering for war dances and the hunt; they saw them gathered in their old society brotherhoods.

The visionaries awoke and told what they saw. *They* are doing all these things; we must too. So the people began games and dances. They revived war dances and societies; they revived the Horn Dance, the Young Dog Dance, the Iruska, the Big Horse Society, the Roached Heads, the

Crazy Dogs. Again they carried out the Pipe Dance; they renewed interest in the Doctor Dances. They played handgames.

In short, the activity of the Ghost Dance times was not a mere revival of old ways, it became a renaissance of Pawnee culture.

This effect occurred in the following way: In a vision the subject would "see" some old way of life which had come to be disregarded. He would "remember" it. His vision then became a command upon those alive who knew how it must be carried out, to do so. Sometimes there were men alive who knew the thing thoroughly and were persuaded by the demand of such a supernatural message to begin it again. But often a ritual or dance was only partially remembered. Then many men would get together and pool their memories to revive the affair. If the "seen" phase of old life was social and non-esoteric, the visionary himself would revive the old way. Hence games, and handgames.

Most important of all were revivals of those old ways which had been utterly lost. In older Pawnee theory, as we saw, only direct learning from the owner sanctioned use and demonstration. But in a vision in the Ghost Dance one saw the deceased (the "ghost," in other words); one saw those who had known how to do these things and had died without handing them on. The deceased in the vision told the visionary what to do just as he would have done in life. He appealed to the visionary to revive his ways because the old life was soon to reappear in its entirety. Thus an entirely new form of sanction came into Pawnee thought. Where it would have been sacrilege formerly to have carried out a dance or ceremony to which one had no right, where before such behavior would have invited supernatural punishment, the trance vision now constituted a supernatural command that the performance *be* revived.

This renaissance meant not only the revival of activities. It meant also that a good deal of ceremonial paraphernalia which had been lost or buried in times past, was duplicated from memory and vision. Many of the society regalia and ritual objects which were purchased by the museums around 1900 from the Pawnee were not the old sacred objects. Those had long before disappeared, many of them prior to the movement of the Pawnee to Oklahoma in 1874–76. They were the Ghost Dance revival objects, the Ghost Dance reincarnations of the old lances, drums, regalia and pipes.

Following this revival of old ways, there was a new reintegration of Ghost Dance suggestions, old ways, and current thought. In terms of this the Ghost Dance handgames arose, and passed through many transformations. In some of these, special revivals of old societies were incorporated. New forms of intertribal visiting were founded on revivals of old customs and Ghost Dance ideas. Society and dance revivals were integrated with Ghost Dance thought. Thus vital phases of Pawnee life which survived until recent years were not exactly what Pawnee life had been in the 19th century; they were based on old forms and traditions, but they were changed permanently into new forms by the cultural stimulant of the Ghost Dance years.

The Ghost Dance was not merely a religious revival movement. Its roots lie deep in the gradual cultural destruction which preceded it. Its doctrine and the activities it demanded infused new life into the culture, and constituted instrumentalities for an actual renaissance of the forms of old culture. Along with this renaissance there came into being also new cultural forms, unknown before.

25. A Socio-Cultural Interpretation of the Peyote Cult

BERNARD BARBER *

Nativistic movements among the North American Indians have emerged from the cultural disorganization which the aboriginal groups experienced under the impact of the white culture. They were attempts, in the face of pervasive cultural disorganization, to restore to their adherents a stable orientation, a sense of satisfaction and meaningfulness in life. The Ghost Dance Movements of 1870 and 1890, for example, sought to do so by messianic prophecy of a millennium where the aboriginal way of life would again prevail. They furnished an escape from the cultural impasse that the tribes faced. In 1870, the Ghost Dance diffused from the North Paiute of Nevada to California, where disorganization prevailed; it did not spread among the Plains Indians. In 1890, when the Plains Indian culture was crumbling, the Ghost Dance spread again, and again from the Paiute, but this time it was taken up only on the Plains. Among the Klamath, Nash has shown, the Ghost Dance of 1870 was adopted in different degrees, its acceptance being directly correlated with what he calls the degree of "deprivation," i.e., the amount of cultural disorganization. It is my present aim to point out the significance of this variable for comprehension of the diffusion of the Peyote cult and to show the connection between the Peyote cult and the collapse of the Ghost Dance.

* From *American Anthropologist*, October–December, 1941, pp. 673–675.

Use of peyote among the natives of Mexico was reported as early as 1569. Among the Mexicans, peyotism centered around the tribal shaman: it was considered a potent ally in his pursuit of the tribal welfare. Not until the nineteenth century, however, did peyote diffuse northward. About 1870, the Mescalero were using it, in a manner which was "truly transitional" between the Mexican and the Plains Indian. In the eighties, the Kiowa and Comanche initiated the tribal and ceremonial use of peyote; and they were the chief sources for its dissemination in the Plains area. After 1890, its spread was extensive and rapid: whereas previously it had been limited to five or six tribes north of the Rio Grande, in the following thirty-four years it was carried to some thirty additional tribes.

Thus, the Peyote cult as a significant nativistic movement came in approximate temporal succession to the Ghost Dance of 1890. The Ghost Dance movement collapsed because its prophecies had not been fulfilled and because, its doctrine being passively anti-white, it was construed as a threat to white supremacy. Indeed, it had even become adventitiously connected with the "Sioux outbreak" of 1890, and the government agents on the reservations were ordered to exterminate it. The cultural disorganization of the Plains groups still existed, however, and it was this which facilitated the acceptance of the Peyote cult. The doctrine of the Peyote cult was peaceful, in no way did it threaten the white culture. The essential orientation crystallized around passive acceptance, resignation, around conciliation and compromise with the existing world. It called for renunciation of mundane aspirations and for maintenance of "a loftier spiritual realm which it is beyond the reach of the whites to destroy." Peyote, like the Ghost Dance, transcended tribal boundaries. It took advantage of the new sympathetic attitudes among the tribal units, attitudes stemming from the destruction of the old tribal animosities by the reservation system. Peyote is spoken of as "the Indian Religion." The Ghost Dance had also stimulated friendly inter-tribal contacts; it had created channels along which the Peyote cult could flow all over the Plains.

Connections between the Ghost Dance and the Peyote cult, mediated through particular individuals, in some cases were quite direct. Frank White, the Pawnee Ghost Dance prophet, became an ardent devotee of the new cult. John Wilson, perhaps the most important figure in the Peyote cult, was a leader of the Ghost Dance among the Caddo. A Kiowa named Baigya had a revelation in 1888 on the authority of which he predicted that a great whirlwind would come in the Spring, followed by a four-day prairie fire that would destroy all the whites and restore the buffalo and the old Indian life. When the catastrophe was not realized, his adherents lost faith and turned to Peyote. He and his disciples, of course, strongly opposed the innovation.

The Ghost Dance and the Peyote cult, then, may in part be understood as alternative responses to a similar socio-cultural constellation. As such a response, the Peyote cult performs certain important adaptive functions. On those whom it honors with leadership, it bestows prestige and status, serving as a path to social advancement. Public confession of sins in Peyote ceremonies is at once a mechanism for the dissolution of individual anxieties and a mode of social control. Like the old buffalo societies of the Teton Sioux, the cult can become a focus of tribal ceremonial and social activity. This interpretation, however, does not pretend to exhaust the possible understanding of these phenomena. It does not preclude the necessity for understanding the particular cultural patterns to which peyotism diffused and tracing their influence in the process of its assimilation. It does indicate the socio-cultural situation from which the Peyote cult was precipitated.

An opportunity for the further testing of this hypothesis exists among the Navaho. Although they have known about it for at least two generations, the Navaho have had recourse to Peyote only recently, under the impulsion of the incipient cultural disorganization that is now affecting them. Further research should seek to answer the following questions, among others: Do the leaders of the new cult come from among the old elite? What satisfactions accrue to its adherents? In what ways does the cult help the group adjust, contribute to its stability?

26. Moorish Science Temple of America
ARTHUR H. FAUSET *

This cult was founded about 1913 by Timothy Drew, who came from North Carolina where he was born in 1886. Somewhere in his life he came upon two facts which radically influenced his thinking:

He encountered some forms of oriental philosophy and was impressed with its racial catholicity. The fruits of his research have been compressed into the *Holy Koran* of the Moorish Holy Temple of Science, which is not to be confused with the orthodox Mohammedan Koran.

He became obsessed with the idea that salvation for the Negro people lay in the discovery by them of their national origin, i.e., they must know

* From *Black Gods of the Metropolis,* pp. 41–51.

whence they came, and refuse longer to be called Negroes, black folk, colored people, or Ethiopians. They must henceforth call themselves Asiatics, to use the generic term, or, more specifically, Moors or Moorish Americans.

Drew would harangue small groups of Negroes on street corners, in basements, or empty lots. Although he had little formal education, a certain magnetic charm, a sincerity of purpose, and a real determination to lead his people out of the difficulties of racial prejudice and discrimination brought him followers.

He established his first temple in Newark, New Jersey. Gradually, as his following increased, temples were established in Pittsburgh, Detroit, and in numerous cities in the South. His greatest achievement was the founding of a temple in Chicago. But this was to prove his personal undoing.

Many Negroes on the South Side of Chicago flocked to the new teacher. Complete emancipation through a change of status from "Negro" to "Asiatic" promised an easy way to salvation.

When the initiate became a full member of the cult, he was given a card, slightly larger than a calling card, which bore the following inscription:

UNITY

(Replica of star and crescent)	(Replica of clasped hands)	(Replica of circle "7")
ISLAM		ALLAH

This is your Nationality and Identification Card for the Moorish Science Temple of America, and Birthrights for the Moorish Americans, etc., we honor all the Divine Prophets, Jesus, Mohammed, Buddha and Confucius. May the blessings of the God of our Father Allah, be upon you that carry this card. I do hereby declare that you are a Moselm under the Divine Laws of the Holy Koran of Mecca, Love, Truth Peace Freedom and Justice. "I AM A CITIZEN OF THE U. S. A."

NOBLE DREW ALI, THE PROPHET, 3603 INDIANA AVE.,
CHICAGO, ILL.

The hundreds of Chicago Negroes who carried these cards believed that the mere sight of the card would be sufficient to restrain a white man who was bent on disturbing or harming its holder.

The members were also taught to believe that a sign, a star within a crescent moon, had been seen in the heavens, and that this betokened the arrival of the day of the Asiatics, and the destruction of the Europeans (whites).

A number of disturbances developed. The Moors, made conspicuous by their fezzes, walked the streets, treating white folk with open contempt. In various parts of the Middle West they became anathema to the police.

In Chicago, affairs reached the point where members of the cult would accost white people on the streets and, showing their membership cards or the button they wore in their coat lapels, would sing the praises of their prophet, now known as Noble Drew Ali, because he had freed them from the curse of European (white) domination. The prophet was compelled to call a halt to their zeal with the following admonition:

I hereby warn all Moors that they must cease from all radical or agitating speeches while on their jobs, or in their homes, or on the streets. Stop flashing your cards before Europeans as this only causes confusion. We did not come to cause confusion; our work is to uplift the nation.

Climaxing these public difficulties, came troubles within the cult itself. Recognizing the need of assistance to extend his work, Noble Drew Ali took into his confidence some Negroes whose prior education fitted them to lead. Unfortunately they proved to have questionable motives, and before long had introduced practices which the prophet had not anticipated. Various methods were employed to exploit the members of the cult, including the sale of herbs, magical charms and potions, and literature pertaining to the cult. Some of the leaders of the cult grew rich.

When it became apparent that Noble Drew Ali stood in the way of further expansion along these lines, attempts were made to displace him. The internal strife reached menacing proportions, and eventually one of the leaders was killed. Noble Drew Ali who was not in Chicago at the time of the slaying, nevertheless, was arrested on his return to the city. He was remanded to prison to await trial for the death of the victim.

The trial never took place, for Noble Drew Ali, who had been released on bond, died a few weeks later, under mysterious circumstances. Some say he died from the effects of a third degree; others declare that his death was the result of a severe beating at the hands of dissident members.

Nevertheless he had lived long enough to imprint his life and reflections on the minds of his followers. Since his death they have split into numerous sects. Some claim to follow the spirit of the dead Noble Drew Ali, while others go so far as to believe that they now follow the reincarnation of Noble Drew Ali, that is, that their present leader rightfully claims to be the former prophet returned to the earth in another body. The Philadelphia temple which furnishes the chief data for this study holds to this belief.

ORGANIZATION

Because of the secret character of this cult, full details of its present organization are lacking. This much has been divulged to the author: The prophet (reincarnated) is the final authority. Nothing whatever can be done in any of the branches without his prior knowledge and assent; any command or instruction from him must be obeyed summarily. The leader of each branch temple is known as Grand Sheik or Governor. There are elders and stewards. Ordinary members are known as brothers and sisters (as for that matter the grand sheik is also). Every member is required to attach the term "el" (pronounced "eel") or "bey" to his name. The term "bey" appears to have a somewhat more distinguished connotation than "el." The insistence upon the addition of these titles has involved members of the cult in numerous legal disputes.

MEMBERSHIP

Membership is open to all "Asiatics." By Asiatic is meant any person not of "pale" hue (i.e., non-Caucasian). However, the author has not seen any Moors who were not Negroes.

Affirmation of a desire to be included on the rolls of the cult is the only prerequisite to admission. There is an initiation fee of $1.00, with certain stipulated dues thereafter.

FINANCE

Financial support is derived from two main sources: collections during the services of the temple, and dues. Members frequently pay dues while they are attending the regular services of the temple.

SACRED TEXT

The various sects of the Moorish Science Temple of America live in accordance with the teachings divulged to and by Noble Drew Ali, as contained in the *Holy Koran* of the Moorish Holy Temple of Science. This book is secret. There is also a catechism or questionary derived from the *Holy Koran,* which I was permitted to see.

The *Holy Koran* consists of 64 pages, rather compactly printed. The cover page reads as follows:

THE HOLY KORAN
of the
MOORISH HOLY TEMPLE
OF SCIENCE
Divinely Prepared by the Noble Prophet
DREW ALI

BY the guiding of his father God, Allah; the great God of
the universe. To redeem man from his sinful and
fallen stage of humanity back to the highest plane
of life with his father, God, Allah.

On the inside cover are the words:

KNOW THYSELF AND ALLAH
THE GENEOLOGY
OF 'JESUS'

Life and Works of Jesus in India
Europe and Africa, in the
land of Egypt.

The first page of the *Holy Koran* contains a picture of Noble Drew Ali.
We see a tall, slender, dark Negro, with rather pronounced qualities of
the dreamer suggested in his physiognomy. He is clad in dark trousers,
dark shoes, a white robe and sash, collar and necktie, and fez. His right
hand, which is distinguished by long, slender, sentient fingers, is stretched
across his breast. Under the picture is the sub-title:

THE PROPHET AND FOUNDER OF THE MOORISH SCIENCE
TEMPLE OF AMERICA, TO REDEEM THE PEOPLE
FROM THEIR SINFUL WAYS.

On the second page is a portrait of a Mohammedan priest or sheik,
with title:

SULTAN ABDUL AZIZ IBU SUAD
THE DESCENDANT OF HAGAR, NOW THE HEAD OF THE
HOLY CITY OF MECCA

Then follows an introductory page of instructions.
The introductory page of instructions indicates clearly certain outlines
in the beliefs of the Moors:

1. Although they are a Moslem sect, Jesus figures prominently.
2. The cult is secret.

3. Noble Drew Ali is a prophet ordained by Allah.

4. Allah is God, and He has ordained His prophet, Noble Drew Ali, to divulge His secrets to the dark folk of America.

5. Moslems (i.e., people of dark hue) belong to certain areas of the world including the American continent.

6. The guiding spirit of the universe is love.

After the introductory page, there follow many pages containing apocryphal chapters from the life of Jesus, and further pages of instruction, admonition, caution, warning, and reference to the rôle of the dark races in the world's development.

The concluding chapters, which are numbered 45–48, treat of the divine origin of Asiatic nations, the beginning of Christianity, Egypt as the capital empire of the dominion of Africa, and the End of Time and the fulfilling of the prophesies. In these chapters many of the racial principles of the cult are expounded.

On the inside of the back cover are these words:

The fallen sons and daughters of the Asiatic Nation of North America need to learn to love instead of hate; and to know of their higher self and lower self. This is the uniting of the Holy Koran of Mecca, for the teaching and instructing of all Moorish Americans, etc.

On the back cover occur the following words:

THE HOLY KORAN
of the
MOORISH SCIENCE TEMPLE
OF AMERICA
KNOW YOURSELF AND YOUR FATHER
GOD ALLAH
THAT YOU MAY LEARN TO LOVE INSTEAD OF HATE
EVERYMAN NEED TO WORSHIP UNDER HIS OWN
VINE AND FIG TREE
THE UNITY OF ASIA

BELIEFS

The charter of the Moorish Science Temple came from the great capital empire of Egypt.

Before you can have a God, you must have a nationality.

Noble Drew Ali gave his people a nation (Morocco).

There is no Negro, black, colored, or Ethiopian—only "Asiatic" or Moorish-American.

Ethiopian signifies a division.

Negro (black) signifies death.

"Colored" signifies something that is painted.

For the above reasons, the term Moorish-American must be used, and not other, opprobrious terms.

The name means everything; by taking the Asiatic's name from him, and calling him Negro, black, colored, or Ethiopian, the European stripped the Moor of his power, his authority, his God, and every other worth-while possession.

Christianity is for the European (paleface); Moslemism is for the Asiatic (olive-skinned). When each group has its own peculiar religion, there will be peace on earth.

Noble Drew Ali is a kindred personage and spirit to Confucius, Jesus, Buddha, and Zoroaster.

Marcus Garvey was to Noble Drew Ali as John the Baptist was to Christ.

RITUAL

TYPICAL SERVICE

At 8 p.m. promptly, the leader, who sits at the front of the temple facing the congregation, begins to chant a hymn softly, and this is taken up by the members of the congregation. Unlike the singing in many Negro services, the chants of the Moors are very soft. Next the leader reads from the *Holy Koran* of Noble Drew Ali, and his voice is very low, scarcely above a whisper. When he has finished his reading, he makes a brief discourse to the members. He reminds them that they are the descendants of the Moabites and Canaanites, that they have a charter and that this charter was procured in the great capital in Egypt, and that it entitles the Moors to possession of northwest and southwest Africa. He emphasizes that Egypt is a greater capital than Washington. He reminds his followers that there is no Negro, black, colored, or Ethiopian, and that before they can have a God they must have a nationality. He proclaims the reincarnation of their Prophet, Noble Drew Ali, and states that he is in reality Mohammed III, who gave them a nation which he called Morocco. Christianity, he tells them, is the religion for the Europeans, but Islam is the religion for the Asiatics. When Europe and Asia each has its own religion, then there will be peace.

Christianity, he continues, is a European religion which was founded in Rome. The Romans killed Jesus, who was a Canaanite, and following the death of Jesus there was peace for a time. But Mohammed II came, and then there was no longer any peace. The name means everything, and by taking away the name of the Moors the palefaces stripped the power, authority, God, and everything from the darker peoples. Thus the Europeans have taken away their flag, their land, their God, their name—everything. The Moors must struggle on, establishing a world in which love, truth, peace, freedom, and justice will flourish. Always there must be peace, and although the Moors are hostile to the palefaces there must be no question of obedience to the American flag and loyalty to the United States.

After the leader has spoken, an elder reads the special laws of the temple which are in the questionary, and which also hang in a frame on the wall. This copy he takes down from the wall and reads. The elder makes comments as he goes along, similar to the remarks already made by the grand sheik. After he has concluded his reading, the leader again rises and picks up the *Holy Koran,* and invites members to come forward and speak. One after the other they approach the front, take the *Holy Koran* to testify. Each begins by saying, "I rise to give (do) honor to Allah, and to his Holy Prophet, Noble Drew Ali, Reincarnated, who gave to us this Holy Koran." Then follows reading from the *Koran* and a talk in the same vein as the one given by the leader. The individual talks will bear testimony to the efficacy of the spirit of Noble Drew Ali, Reincarnated, and how that spirit, or perhaps an actual word from the living prophet, has illuminated the life of the follower. Frequent reference is made to the fact that the prophet has removed the stigma of color and of race.

At 9:30 promptly, several members move forward with collection plates; the leader begins a chant, which is taken up quietly by the followers. Usually the chants are ordinary hymn tunes set to words which conform to Moslem teaching. For example:

> Give me that old time religion . . .

becomes:

> Moslem's that old time religion . . .

The collection takes about fifteen minutes, after which the followers continue to come forward, read from the *Koran* and testify until, exactly at 10 p.m., the leader gives a signal, everyone stands, faces east, raises the arms horizontally, with first and second fingers of the right hand uplifted, and says, "Allah, the Father of the Universe, the Father of Love, Truth, Peace, Freedom and Justice. Allah is my Protector, my Guide, and my

Salvation by night and by day, through His Holy Prophet, Drew Ali. Amen." . . .

PRACTICES

In connection with the services in the temple the following practices are especially to be noted, for they are quite distinct from practices to be observed at most Negro religious services.

When sitting in the temple, men and women are segregated. In Philadelphia it is customary to have the women seated in front, the men to the rear.

All members are particular about having everyone pay strict attention to the service. Older members frequently are prodded because they nod during the service. But the pranks of the young children are regarded with an amazing patience and with an unusual degree of sympathy for the restlessness of children.

All services are extraordinarily quiet, belying the generally accepted beliefs regarding the Negro and his religious worship. Thus it often is extremely difficult to make out the words of a speaker addressing the congregation from the front of the temple despite the tomb-like stillness. Although there is some bustle as the women take care of the needs of their children, this is accomplished with a minimum of commotion or noise. Exclamations from the congregation are few and almost inaudible; there is a complete absence of that emotionalism which is considered characteristic of Negro services, and this is the more surprising because the basic principles of the cult involve those very elements which would be expected to arouse the emotions to an extreme degree. Finally, the meetings begin punctually and end punctually, a most unusual condition in Negro churches.

The place of worship is not called a church; it is the temple.

Friday is the Sabbath of the cult.

"Christmas" is observed on January 5, the anniversary of the day when the prophet, Noble Drew Ali, was reincarnated.

Meetings of the cult are held Friday, Sunday, and Wednesday evenings. They begin at 8 p.m. and end at 10. There also is Sunday School from 5 p.m. to 7 on Sunday.

There is no baptism or communion and little singing. There are few hymns, and these are mostly chants.

Members must pray three times daily, at sunrise, noon, and at sunset. When praying, members stand facing the east (Mecca), and raise their hands but do not prostrate themselves.

There are two words of greeting: "Peace!" and "Islam!" These are usually spoken with the right hand upraised, palm out.

All Moorish Americans must obey the laws of their (American) government. "Radicalism" is forbidden.

Marriages are monogamous. The grand sheik gives in marriage, and he may approve a union which would be forbidden under Christian auspices.

Divorce rarely is permitted.

Husbands must support their families. Wives must obey their husbands and care for their homes. Children must obey their parents.

Masters must be just to servants, and servants are to be patient under reproof.

Bodies must be kept clean by bathing.

The red fez should be worn by the men at all times, inside the house and temple as well as on the street.

Use of meat of any kind and eggs is forbidden. But fish and vegetables may be eaten.

Indulgence in European games, attendance at motion picture shows, and secular dancing are forbidden.

Shaving, cosmetics, straightening the hair, use of intoxicants, and smoking are forbidden.

27. The Ras Tafari Movement in Jamaica: A Study of Race and Class Conflict

GEORGE EATON SIMPSON * †

THE RAS TAFARI MOVEMENT IS NOT EXPLICITLY RELIGIOUS. ITS ORIENTATION IS POLITICAL AND ITS TERMINOLOGY SECULAR. THE SIMILARITY IN FUNCTION TO MANY RELIGIOUS SECTS AND CULTS, HOWEVER, IS READILY APPARENT. THUS THE STUDY RAISES CLEARLY THE QUESTION OF FUNCTIONAL ALTERNATIVES.

The contra-acculturative aspects of Messianic cults and nativistic movements have long been of interest to anthropologists and sociologists.[1] Ras

* From *Social Forces*, December, 1955, pp. 167–170.

† With the support of a grant from the American Philosophical Society. I am indebted to Mr. Arthur Bethune, of Kingston, Jamaica, for assistance in the collection of data on the Ras Tafari movement. Paper read at the annual meeting of the American Sociological Society, September, 1954.

[1] See James Mooney, "The Ghost Dance Religion and Sioux Outbreak of 1890," *Bureau of American Ethnological Reports*, 14, part 2 (1892); A. H. Gayton, "The

Tafari, a Jamaican cult which originated in 1930, is violently anti-white on the verbal level. Its members regard Haile Selassie (Ras Tafari), Emperor of Abyssinia, as the living God, see no hope for black men in the British West Indies, and look forward to an early return to Ethiopia.

The "Rasta" people consider Marcus Garvey, revered founder of the Universal Negro Improvement Association, as the forerunner of their movement. They claim that Garvey, "the world's greatest statesman," was sent by Ras Tafari "to cut and clear." [2] Garvey advocated a mass migration to Africa, and his slogans "Africa for the Africans—At Home and Abroad" and "One God! One Aim! One Destiny!" are proclaimed at every Ras Tafari meeting.

In the early days of the movement, opposition came from both the ordinary Jamaicans and the police. Lower class Jamaicans stoned speakers, slashed banners, and smashed lamps at street meetings. An active early leader of the cult was arrested, jailed, and tried seven times, but never convicted, on charges of disorderly conduct, ganja (marihuana) smoking, and lunacy. Open hostility to the movement has declined to some extent in recent years due, in part, to the well-disciplined control of members during meetings. Middle and upper class Jamaicans, as well as foreigners, still fear the Ras Tafarians, but available evidence does not support the widespread belief that they are bearded hoodlums.

Western Kingston and Eastern St. Andrew constitute the center of the Ras Tafari movement, but groups have been formed in other parts of the island. Participants are lower class Jamaicans, many of them unemployed or underemployed, who reside in crowded, blighted areas.

At present, twelve or fifteen Ras Tafari groups operate in Kingston and St. Andrew, with memberships ranging from twenty-five to one hundred and fifty or more. Groups form, split, and dissolve, and some individuals accept cult beliefs without attaching themselves to an organization. In contrast to a Revivalist group, which is dominated by a leader, a Ras Tafari band is extremely democratic. Everyone who wishes to speak must be heard, often at some length, and no action is taken without a vote of the membership, or, at the least, the executive committee. Names of these groups include: Ethiopian Coptic League, United Ethiopian Body, Ethio-

---

Ghost Dance of 1870 in South-Central California," *University of California Publication in Archaelogy and Ethnology,* 28 (1930); Bernard Barber, "Acculturation and Messianic Movements," *American Sociological Review,* 6 (1941), pp. 663–669; Ralph Linton, "Nativistic Movements," *American Anthropologist,* 45 (1943), pp. 230–240; M. J. Herskovits, *Man and His Works* (New York: Knopf, 1948), pp. 531–532.

[2] This expression is used in the Jamaican Revivalist cults (Pocomania and Revival Zion) to refer to the process of removing evil spirits by ritualistic means.

pian Youth Cosmic Faith, United Afro-West Indian Federation, and African Cultural League.

BASIC DOCTRINES OF THE RAS TAFARI MOVEMENT

1. Ras Tafari (Haile Selassie) means "Lord Jehovah" or "Power of the Trinity." Haile Selassie is the only living King who is sitting on a throne, and he is on the throne of David. He is the King of Kings, the Lion of Judah, and the heads of other countries bow down before him. Proof of this assertion is found in such Biblical passages as Revelation 5:2,5— "And I saw a strong angel proclaiming with a loud voice, Who is worthy to open the book, and to loose the seals thereof? . . . And one of the elders saith unto me, Weep not; behold, the Lion of Judah, the Root of David, hath prevailed to open the book, and to loose the seven spirits of God sent forth into all the earth."

2. Haile Selassie, with whom the Ras Tafarians have had no direct contact nor any correspondence, is believed to be invincible, even to the point of being the only one who can control the atomic bomb. The proof offered for this claim is a picture of the Emperor of Abyssinia standing with one foot on a large unexploded bomb at the time his country was invaded by Italian forces.[3]

3. Black men are Ethiopians. They are the true Israelites, once the greatest people in the world. God is black, Christ was black, Solomon was black, and black Jamaicans are reincarnations of the ancient Hebrews. Residence in the West Indies is punishment for past stubbornness and transgression. However, black men have now suffered enough and it is time for them to go home.[4]

4. The Romans made idols of wood and stone, stood them up and worshipped them. The English thought that was too simple, so they invented the idea that God is a spirit in Heaven that men cannot see. Since

[3] Interesting in this connection is the claim that Haile Selassie started Mau Mau, that Mau Mau fighters use bows and arrows instead of guns, and that the bombs of white men cannot hurt the Mau Mau. Lowie has pointed out that one of the recurrent themes in Messianic cults is the belief that the superior weapons of the enemy can be nullified by supernatural power. Robert Lowie, "American Culture History," *American Anthropologist*, 42 (1940), p. 424. At least two leaders in Haiti's revolution against the French, Hyacinthe Ducoudray and Halaou, carried ox-tails into battle and claimed that these could turn aside all bullets. See G. E. Simpson, "The Belief System of Haitian Vodun," *American Anthropologist*, 47 (1945), p. 37.

[4] Frequently cited Biblical passages to support this viewpoint include Psalms 68:31 —"Princes shall come out of Egypt; Ethiopia shall soon stretch out her hands unto God"; and Ezekiel 36:28—"And ye shall dwell in the land that I gave to your fathers; and ye shall be my people, and I will be your God."

white men have given no proof to support this belief, it can only be regarded as a racket. Ras Tafari is the living God.

5. Heaven is an invention of the white man which is used to deceive black men by promising them everything after death. Since dead men tell no tales, there is no proof of the existence of the Englishman's Heaven. Ethiopia is the only real heaven.

RAS TAFARI MEETINGS

Most Ras Tafari bands hold one meeting at their headquarters and two street meetings weekly. A typical Sunday night meeting in the leader's yard consists mainly of speeches expounding the doctrines of the movement interspersed with the singing of original songs and modified Sankey and Methodist hymns. Examples of the latter include "Let the Song Go Round the Earth," "Beulah Land," and "From Greenland's Icy Mountains." The words of one of the favorite original compositions are:

HERE WE ARE IN THIS LAND

Here we are in this land.
No one think how we stand
The hands that are on us all day.
So we cry and we sigh
For we know not our God.
So we always be crying in vain.

Our forefathers cried;
Feel the pangs of the chain
See the blood running out of his vein.
And our slave masters did pierce
Our forefathers' hearts
So they die like a brute in the chain.

These meetings end with the singing of the Ethiopian national anthem and the recitation of the Ethiopian prayer, both composed in Western Kingston. The prayer ends with the words: "Deliver us from the hands of our enemies that we might prove fruitful for the last days. When our enemies are passed and decayed in the depths of the sea, in the depths of the earth, or in the belly of a beast, Oh give us all a place in Thy Kingdom for ever and ever. Selah."

Special meetings are occasionally held, especially in November on the anniversary of Haile Selassie's coronation. On such occasions, the special decorations, music, and refreshments, and the dedication of babies to Ras Tafari, attract a large assembly.

SIX RAS TAFARI THEMES

In private conversations, small group discussions, regular meetings and street meetings, six constantly recurring themes appear, namely: The Wickedness of the White Man; The Superiority of the Black Man; Jamaica's False Prophets; The Hopelessness of the Jamaican Situation for Black Men; Revenge; and Africa, the Homeland, Is Heaven and the Only Hope for the Black Man.

The Wickedness of the White Man. According to this theme, white slave masters were murderers and criminals. A favorite saying is that during slavery, the white man killed the baby of a black woman and said: "Mary Jane, go back to work." Today the white man accuses the black man of being a thief, but the white man has stolen continents and men. White men of today are hypocrites, murderers, and criminal thieves, and they cannot escape responsibility for what happened in the past because the tree bears fruit and the seeds of the fruit become trees (the doctrine of reincarnation).

The Superiority of the Black Man. Black men were civilized when the white man was living in the caves of northern Europe. The throne of Ethiopia is older than the throne of St. George. The white man says that black men are no good, but David, Solomon, and the Queen of Sheba were black. The knowledge black men have cannot be obtained in college. They are born with the knowledge they possess because they have been with God from the beginning of Creation, and they have been with God everywhere. They have been through these things before. The white man cannot beat them on history. The white man lies, but black men can contradict everything he says. The white man tells black men they are inferior, but they are not inferior. They are superior and the white man is inferior.

Jamaica's False Prophets. The two wickedest kinds of men are the preachers and the police. The fraud of religion and politics have kept black men in ignorance and have kept them back. The church robs men, not of their pockets, but of their mentality. Because of the church, the black man in Jamaica is concerned more with death than with life. School teachers never teach black men anything but foolishness, and black men want no more of the white man's indoctrination. Everything about the white man is false.

The Hopelessness of the Jamaican Situation for Black Men. The Jamaican Government, the worst government in the world, is corrupt and nothing can be expected from it. The politicians are out only for themselves;

they want your vote and nothing else. Bustamante and Manley (leaders of the two principal political parties in Jamaica) are as bad as the other (English) politicians. Black men are slaves today, and their slavery is worse than that during the days of slavery because they are mentally enslaved. The white man keeps black men in poverty. "It is like being in prison, and there will be no freedom until we go back home."

Revenge. "We understand what the white man has done to us and we are going to do unto them as they have done unto us. In Ethiopia, the white man will have to serve us." Isaiah 14 says: ". . . and the house of Israel shall possess them [the strangers] in the land of the Lord for servants and handmaids; and they shall take them captives, whose captives they were; and they shall rule over their oppressors." Mau Mau is a war between black men and white men, and the Mau Mau are angels of deliverance sent by Haile Selassie to drive white men out of Africa. Ras Tafari says: "Death to the white man and to the black traitors." Today it is nation against nation, and the time is short. The King of Israel shall rule over all, and anyone who stands in the way, including the big, fat Negroes (middle class Jamaicans), will be removed; there will be a remission of blood.

Africa, the Homeland, Is Heaven and the Only Hope for the Black Man. The Chinese have a native land—China, and the Indian has his native land—India. The black man has his native land too—Ethiopia. "The white man tells us to wait until Jesus comes, but we're not going to wait. In the near future, we are going back to our Homeland. The only future for the black man is with Ras Tafari. Our God and Our King is here to deliver us, and when we go back to that land no one will ever get us again."

DIFFERENCES BETWEEN THE RAS TAFARI CULT AND THE REVIVALIST CULTS

A detailed examination of the differences between the Ras Tafari cult and the Revivalist cults known as Pocomania and Revival Zion cannot be given here. All of these cults draw their members from the economically depressed, uneducated lower class of Jamaica. Revivalists and Ras Tafarians are bitter enemies and have nothing but contempt for one another. We have referred earlier to the authoritarianism of Revivalist cults and the democracy of the Ras Tafari movement. Spirit possession, a prominent feature of Revivalist meetings, never occurs in a Ras Tafari gathering. Witchcraft and healing, exceedingly important activities in most Revivalist bands, are not practiced by the Rasta people. In the four Ras

Tafari groups I observed, the ubiquitous drums of the Revivalists were replaced by rhumba boxes. Otherwise, the musical instruments were much the same, consisting mainly of rattles and tambourines.

FUNCTIONS AND DYSFUNCTIONS OF THE RAS TAFARI MOVEMENT

The social psychological functions of the Ras Tafari movement, like those of esoteric cults in general, include: compensation for the humiliations and deprivations of a lowly social station; emotional warmth and friendship of the leader and like-minded believers; hope for a better life in the other-world; recreation; opportunities for self-expression through singing, speech-making, procession-leading, and costume-wearing; recognition through office-holding or as a speaker, musician, organizer or fund-raiser; and economic assistance at such critical times as serious illness, death in the family, and court trials.

Unquestionably there are dysfunctional aspects of the Ras Tafari movement. It is conceivable that the verbal violence which characterizes the cult at present might lead to other kinds of violence. The constant stress upon the hopelessness of the Jamaican situation and the desirability of returning to Africa tends to undermine any desire an individual might have to try to achieve a more satisfactory adjustment for himself. While Ras Tafari activities relieve the tensions of some, it seems likely that they contribute to the deepening of the anxieties and to the paranoid and schizoid tendencies of others.

TYPES OF ADJUSTMENT TO DISPRIVILEGED SOCIAL POSITIONS

Studies of race and class conflict suggest several types of adjustment to disprivileged social positions in terms of avoidance, acceptance, and aggression. A tentative formulation of this thesis is:

Type 1. Acceptance. Members of subordinate groups embrace their disprivileged position and accept the dominant group's definition of their status and role. These isolated individuals have no religious or political affiliations. This might be called the simplest type of acculturation.

Type 2. Withdrawal through the invention of a symbolic Utopia. The Revivalist groups in Jamaica and elsewhere illustrate this type of adjustment, a "live right" or fundamentalist religious orientation which stresses preparation for the next world.

Type 3. Political withdrawal combined with verbal aggression. Members of a subordinate group are sufficiently acculturated to embrace the values of the dominant group but believe they cannot succeed under existing institutions and conditions. Ras Tafari, a semi-religious, semi-political movement, would fall at this point. Ras Tafarians withdraw from such activities as attending political rallies, voting, etc., and they expect no real achievements from labor unions. Members talk of returning to Africa, meanwhile keeping up a violent verbal attack on "the white man." This type of adjustment indicates more acculturation than is the case with those who are involved only in supernatural withdrawal (Heaven).

Type 4. A type of adjustment between Ras Tafarianism and active participation in protest organizations in the United States. This outlook would be a less hopeless one than that of the Ras Tafarians, but not as advanced as that of members of politically active organizations such as the N.A.A.C.P. This type of adjustment is seen in the less aggressive members of a racial or cultural minority in the United States. Such persons are partially assimilated, but they fall back on religion as a second line of defense. Perhaps the average small town northern Negro, if not the average northern Negro, illustrates this kind of adjustment.

Type 5. Full acculturation to the values of the dominant society. This type of adjustment includes those who drop the withdrawal (supernatural, political, or geographical) theme completely and work for full assimilation. Active participants in the N.A.A.C.P. program illustrate this kind of adjustment.

Type 6. Political withdrawal combined with physical aggression. Members of a subordinated group renounce the values of the dominant group and attempt to free themselves from its control. The Mau Mau movement in Kenya illustrates this reaction.

These types of adjustment are thought of as constituting a continuum [5] rather than as a set of absolute categories. Such a continuum might be useful in making comparisons of the degrees of acculturation and assimilation of subordinated groups in a variety of situations.

---

[5] I am indebted to a colleague, J. Milton Yinger, for suggesting this continuum of adjustment. Ralph Linton, *op. cit.*, p. 233, suggested a fourfold typology of nativistic movements: Revivalistic-magical; Revivalistic-rational; Perpetuative-magical; and Perpetuative-rational.

Religion, Economics, and Politics

As we have seen in Chapters 8 and 9, the way in which a religion is embedded in a total social system is nowhere more clearly indicated than in its relationship to economics and politics. The first four selections in this section are concerned with Weber's thesis that the Protestant ethic was of great importance in determining the spirit of western capitalism. The two that follow describe the ways in which religion is related to political processes in different societies.

28. The Protestant Ethic and the Spirit of Capitalism

MAX WEBER *

WITHOUT DOUBT THIS FAMOUS ESSAY HAS PROMPTED MORE DISCUSSION, AND
MORE CONTROVERSY, THAN ANY OTHER STUDY IN THE SOCIOLOGY OF RELIGION.
AS ONE OF WEBER'S EARLIEST PAPERS IN THE FIELD, IT DID NOT BENEFIT FROM
THE FULL DEVELOPMENT OF HIS THEORETICAL SYSTEM, BUT MANY OF ITS CENTRAL
CONCEPTS ARE CONTAINED HERE IN GERM.

A glance at the occupational statistics of any country of mixed religious
composition brings to light with remarkable frequency a situation which
has several times provoked discussion in the Catholic press and literature,
and in Catholic congresses in Germany, namely, the fact that business
leaders and owners of capital, as well as the higher grades of skilled
labour, and even more the higher technically and commercially trained
personnel of modern enterprises, are overwhelmingly Protestant. This is
true not only in cases where the difference in religion coincides with one
of nationality, and thus of cultural development, as in Eastern Germany
between Germans and Poles. The same thing is shown in the figures of
religious affiliation almost wherever capitalism, at the time of its great
expansion, has had a free hand to alter the social distribution of the
population in accordance with its needs, and to determine its occupational structure. The more freedom it has had, the more clearly is the
effect shown. It is true that the greater relative participation of Protestants
in the ownership of capital, in management, and the upper ranks of labour
in great modern industrial and commercial enterprises, may in part be
explained in terms of historical circumstances which extend far back into
the past, and in which religious affiliation is not a cause of the economic
conditions, but to a certain extent appears to be a result of them. Participation in the above economic functions usually involves some previous
ownership of capital and generally an expensive education; often both.
These are to-day largely dependent on the possession of inherited wealth,
or at least on a certain degree of material well-being. A number of those
sections of the old Empire which were most highly developed economi-

* Excerpts from *The Protestant Ethic and the Spirit of Capitalism*, pp. 35–37, 113–
117, 153 ff.

cally and most favoured by natural resources and situation, in particular a majority of the wealthy towns, went over to Protestantism in the sixteenth century. The results of that circumstance favour the Protestants even to-day in their struggle for economic existence. There arises thus the historical question: why were the districts of highest economic development at the same time particularly favourable to a revolution in the Church? The answer is by no means so simple as one might think.

The emancipation from economic traditionalism appears, no doubt, to be a factor which would greatly strengthen the tendency to doubt the sanctity of the religious tradition, as of all traditional authorities. But it is necessary to note, what has often been forgotten, that the Reformation meant not the elimination of the Church's control over everyday life, but rather the substitution of a new form of control for the previous one. It meant the repudiation of a control which was very lax, at that time scarcely perceptible in practice, and hardly more than formal, in favour of a regulation of the whole of conduct which, penetrating to all departments of private and public life, was infinitely burdensome and earnestly enforced. The rule of the Catholic Church, "punishing the heretic, but indulgent to the sinner," as it was in the past even more than to-day, is now tolerated by peoples of thoroughly modern economic character, and was borne by the richest and economically most advanced peoples on earth at about the turn of the fifteenth century. The rule of Calvinism, on the other hand, as it was enforced in the sixteenth century in Geneva and in Scotland, at the turn of the sixteenth and seventeenth centuries in large parts of the Netherlands, in the seventeenth in New England, and for a time in England itself, would be for us the most absolutely unbearable form of ecclesiastical control of the individual which could possibly exist. That was exactly what large numbers of the old commercial aristocracy of those times, in Geneva as well as in Holland and England, felt about it. And what the reformers complained of in those areas of high economic development was not too much supervision of life on the part of the Church, but too little. Now how does it happen that at that time those countries which were most advanced economically, and within them the rising bourgeois middle classes, not only failed to resist this unexampled tyranny of Puritanism, but even developed a heroism in its defence? For bourgeois classes as such have seldom before and never since displayed heroism. It was "the last of our heroisms," as Carlyle, not without reason, has said. . . .

[There follows a description of "the spirit of capitalism," as Weber conceives it, and then an analysis of the Lutheran and Calvinistic sources of "worldly asceticism." The problem of the essay is to determine whether the latter contributed notably to the development of the former. Weber, of course, answered yes.]

The religious believer can make himself sure of his state of grace either in that he feels himself to be the vessel of the Holy Spirit or the tool of the divine will. In the former case his religious life tends to mysticism and emotionalism, in the latter to ascetic action; Luther stood close to the former type, Calvinism belonged definitely to the latter. The Calvinist also wanted to be saved *sola fide*. But since Calvin viewed all pure feelings and emotions, no matter how exalted they might seem to be, with suspicion, faith had to be proved by its objective results in order to provide a firm foundation for the *certitudo salutis*. It must be a *fides efficax*, the call to salvation an effectual calling (expression used in Savoy Declaration).

If we now ask further, by what fruits the Calvinist thought himself able to identify true faith? the answer is: by a type of Christian conduct which served to increase the glory of God. Just what does so serve is to be seen in his own will as revealed either directly through the Bible or indirectly through the purposeful order of the world which he has created. . . .

. . . however useless good works might be as a means of attaining salvation, for even the elect remain beings of the flesh, and everything they do falls infinitely short of divine standards, nevertheless, they are indispensable as a sign of election. They are the technical means, not of purchasing salvation, but of getting rid of the fear of damnation. In this sense they are occasionally referred to as directly necessary for salvation or the *possessio salutis* is made conditional on them.

In practice this means that God helps those who help themselves. Thus the Calvinist, as it is sometimes put, himself creates his own salvation, or, as would be more correct, the conviction of it. But this creation cannot, as in Catholicism, consist in a gradual accumulation of individual good works to one's credit, but rather in a systematic self-control which at every moment stands before the inexorable alternative, chosen or damned. . . .

The rationalization of the world, the elimination of magic as a means to salvation, the Catholics had not carried nearly so far as the Puritans (and before them the Jews) had done. To the Catholic the absolution of his Church was a compensation for his own imperfection. The priest was a magician who performed the miracle of transubstantiation, and who held the key to eternal life in his hand. One could turn to him in grief and penitence. He dispensed atonement, hope of grace, certainty of for-

giveness, and thereby granted release from that tremendous tension to
which the Calvinist was doomed by an inexorable fate, admitting of no
mitigation. For him such friendly and human comforts did not exist. He
could not hope to atone for hours of weakness or of thoughtlessness by
increased good will at other times, as the Catholic or even the Lutheran
could. The God of Calvinism demanded of his believers not single good
works, but a life of good works combined into a unified system. There was
no place for the very human Catholic cycle of sin, repentance, atonement,
release, followed by renewed sin. Nor was there any balance of merit for
a life as a whole which could be adjusted by temporal punishments or the
Churches' means of grace.

The moral conduct of the average man was thus deprived of its plan-
less and unsystematic character and subjected to a consistent method
for conduct as a whole. It is no accident that the name of Methodists
stuck to the participants in the last great revival of Puritan ideas in the
eighteenth century just as the term Precisians, which has the same meaning, was applied to their spiritual ancestors in the seventeenth century. . . .

It is our next task to follow out the results of the Puritan idea of the
calling in the business world, now that the above sketch has attempted
to show its religious foundations. With all the differences of detail and
emphasis which these different ascetic movements show in the aspects
with which we have been concerned, much the same characteristics are
present and important in all of them. But for our purposes the decisive
point was, to recapitulate, the conception of the state of religious grace,
common to all the denominations, as a status which marks off its possessor
from the degradation of the flesh, from the world.

On the other hand, though the means by which it was attained differed
for different doctrines, it could not be guaranteed by any magical sacraments, by relief in the confession, nor by individual good works. That
was only possible by proof in a specific type of conduct unmistakably
different from the way of life of the natural man. From that followed for
the individual an incentive methodically to supervise his own state of
grace in his own conduct, and thus to penetrate it with asceticism. But,
as we have seen, this ascetic conduct meant a rational planning of the
whole of one's life in accordance with God's will. And this asceticism
was no longer an *opus supererogationis,* but something which could be
required of everyone who would be certain of salvation. The religious life
of the saints, as distinguished from the natural life, was—the most important point—no longer lived outside the world in monastic communities, but within the world and its institutions. This rationalization of con-

duct within this world, but for the sake of the world beyond, was the consequence of the concept of calling of ascetic Protestantism.

Christian asceticism, at first fleeing from the world into solitude, had already ruled the world which it had renounced from the monastery and through the Church. But it had, on the whole, left the naturally spontaneous character of daily life in the world untouched. Now it strode into the market-place of life, slammed the door of the monastery behind it, and undertook to penetrate just that daily routine of life with its methodicalness, to fashion it into a life in the world, but neither of nor for this world. . . .

Let us now try to clarify the points in which the Puritan idea of the calling and the premium it placed upon ascetic conduct was bound directly to influence the development of a capitalistic way of life. As we have seen, this asceticism turned with all its force against one thing: the spontaneous enjoyment of life and all it had to offer. . . .

This worldly Protestant asceticism, as we may recapitulate up to this point, acted powerfully against the spontaneous enjoyment of possessions; it restricted consumption, especially of luxuries. On the other hand, it had the psychological effect of freeing the acquisition of goods from the inhibitions of traditionalistic ethics. It broke the bonds of the impulse of acquisition in that it not only legalized it, but (in the sense discussed) looked upon it as directly willed by God. The campaign against the temptations of the flesh, and the dependence on external things, was, as besides the Puritans the great Quaker apologist Barclay expressly says, not a struggle against the rational acquisition, but against the irrational use of wealth. . . .

. . . the full economic effect of those great religious movements, whose significance for economic development lay above all in their ascetic educative influence, generally came only after the peak of the purely religious enthusiasm was past. Then the intensity of the search for the Kingdom of God commenced gradually to pass over into sober economic virtue; the religious roots died out slowly, giving way to utilitarian worldliness. Then, as Dowden puts it, as in *Robinson Crusoe*, the isolated economic man who carries on missionary activities on the side takes the place of the lonely spiritual search for the Kingdom of Heaven of Bunyan's pilgrim, hurrying through the market-place of Vanity.

When later the principle "to make the most of both worlds" became dominant in the end, as Dowden has remarked, a good conscience simply became one of the means of enjoying a comfortable bourgeois life, as is well expressed in the German proverb about the soft pillow. What the great religious epoch of the seventeenth century bequeathed to its utilitarian successor was, however, above all an amazingly good, we may even say a pharisaically good, conscience in the acquisition of money, so long as it took place legally. Every trace of the *deplacere vix potest* has disappeared.

A specifically bourgeois economic ethic had grown up. With the consciousness of standing in the fullness of God's grace and being visibly blessed by Him, the bourgeois business man, as long as he remained within the bounds of formal correctness, as long as his moral conduct was spotless and the use to which he put his wealth was not objectionable, could follow his pecuniary interests as he would and feel that he was fulfilling a duty in doing so. The power of religious asceticism provided him in addition with sober, conscientious, and unusually industrious workmen, who clung to their work as to a life purpose willed by God.

Finally, it gave him the comforting assurance that the unequal distribution of the goods of this world was a special dispensation of Divine Providence, which in these differences, as in particular grace, pursued secret ends unknown to men. Calvin himself had made the much-quoted statement that only when the people, i.e. the mass of labourers and craftsmen, were poor did they remain obedient to God. In the Netherlands (Pieter de la Court and others), that had been secularized to the effect that the mass of men only labour when necessity forces them to do so. This formulation of a leading idea of capitalistic economy later entered into the current theories of the productivity of low wages. Here also, with the dying out of the religious root, the utilitarian interpretation crept in unnoticed, in the line of development which we have again and again observed. . . .

. . . when asceticism was carried out of monastic cells into everyday life, and began to dominate worldly morality, it did its part in building the tremendous cosmos of the modern economic order. This order is now bound to the technical and economic conditions of machine production which to-day determine the lives of all the individuals who are born into this mechanism, not only those directly concerned with economic acquisition, with irresistible force. Perhaps it will so determine them until the last ton of fossilized coal is burnt. In Baxter's view the care for external goods should only lie on the shoulders of the "saint like a light cloak, which can be thrown aside at any moment." But fate decreed that the cloak should become an iron cage. . . .

The modern man is in general, even with the best will, unable to give religious ideas a significance for culture and national character which they deserve. But it is, of course, not my aim to substitute for a one-sided materialistic an equally one-sided spiritualistic causal interpretation of culture and of history. Each is equally possible, but each, if it does not serve as the preparation, but as the conclusion of an investigation, accomplishes equally little in the interest of historical truth.

29. The Social Setting of Calvinist Development

R. H. TAWNEY *

THIS SELECTION IS PART OF THE FOREWARD TO WEBER'S BOOK FROM WHICH THE PRECEDING EXCERPTS WERE TAKEN. IT GIVES IN BRIEF FORM THE SUBSTANCE OF THE INTERPRETATION OF WEBER'S THESIS THAT TAWNEY HAS DEVELOPED IN FULL AND WITH GREAT BRILLIANCE IN RELIGION AND THE RISE OF CAPITALISM.

It is the temptation of one who expounds a new and fruitful idea to use it as a key to unlock all doors, and to explain by reference to a single principle phenomena which are, in reality, the result of several converging causes. Weber's essay is not altogether free, perhaps, from the defects of its qualities. It appears occasionally to be somewhat over-subtle in ascribing to intellectual and moral influences developments which were the result of more prosaic and mundane forces, and which appeared, irrespective of the character of religious creeds, wherever external conditions offered them a congenial environment. "Capitalism" itself is an ambiguous, if indispensable, word, and Weber's interpretation of it seems sometimes to be open to the criticism of Professor Sée, that he simplifies and limits its meaning to suit the exigencies of his argument. There was no lack of the "capitalist spirit" in the Venice and Florence of the fourteenth century, or in the Antwerp of the fifteenth. Its development in Holland and England, it might not unreasonably be argued, had less to do with the fact that they, or certain social strata in them, accepted the Calvinist version of the Reformation, than with large economic movements and the social changes produced by them. "Ce que MM. Weber et Troeltsch," writes Professor Pirenne,[1] "prennent pour l'esprit Calviniste, c'est précisément l'esprit des hommes nouveaux que la révolution économique du temps introduit dans la vie des affaires, et qui s'y oppo-

---

* From *The Protestant Ethic and the Spirit of Capitalism*, pp. 7–11.
[1] H. Pirenne, *Les Périodes de l'Histoire Sociale du Capitalisme* (1914).

sent aux traditionalistes auxquels ils se substituent." Why insist that
causation can work in only one direction? Is it not a little artificial to
suggest that capitalist enterprise had to wait, as Weber appears to imply,
till religious changes had produced a capitalist spirit? Would it not be
equally plausible, and equally one-sided, to argue that the religious
changes were themselves merely the result of economic movements?

If Weber, as was natural in view of his approach to the problem, seems
to lay in the present essay somewhat too exclusive an emphasis upon
intellectual and ethical forces, his analysis of those forces themselves
requires, perhaps, to be supplemented. Brentano's criticism, that the political thought of the Renaissance was as powerful a solvent of conventional restraints as the teaching of Calvin, is not without weight. In
England, at any rate, the speculations of business men and economists as to
money, prices, and the foreign exchanges, which were occasioned by the
recurrent financial crises of the sixteenth century and by the change in
the price level, were equally effective in undermining the attitude which
Weber called traditionalism. Recent studies of the development of economic thought suggest that the change of opinion on economic ethics
ascribed to Calvinism was by no means confined to it, but was part of
a general intellectual movement, which was reflected in the outlook of
Catholic, as well as of Protestant, writers. Nor was the influence of
Calvinist teaching itself so uniform in character, or so undeviating in
tendency, as might be inferred by the reader of Weber's essay. On the
contrary, it varied widely from period to period and country to country,
with differences of economic conditions, social tradition, and political
environment. It looked to the past as well as to the future. If in some of
its phases it was on the side of change, in others it was conservative.

Most of Weber's illustrations of his thesis are drawn from the writings
of English Puritans of the latter part of the seventeenth century. It is
their teaching which supplies him with the materials for his picture of
the pious *bourgeois* conducting his business as a calling to which Providence has summoned the elect. Whether the idea conveyed by the word
"calling" is so peculiar to Calvinism as Weber implies is a question for
theologians; but the problem, it may be suggested, is considerably more
complex than his treatment of it suggests. For three generations of economic development and political agitation lay between these writers and
the author of the *Institutes*. The Calvinism which fought the English Civil
War, still more the Calvinism which won an uneasy toleration at the
Revolution, was not that of its founder.

Calvin's own ideal of social organization is revealed by the system
which he erected at Geneva. It had been a theocracy administered by a

dictatorship of ministers. In "The most perfect school of Christ ever seen on earth since the day of the Apostles," the rule of life had been an iron collectivism. A godly discipline had been the aim of Knox, of the Reformed Churches in France, and of the fathers of the English Presbyterian Movement; while a strict control of economic enterprise had been the policy first pursued by the saints in New England. The Calvinism, both of England and Holland, in the seventeenth century, had found its way to a different position. It had discovered a compromise in which a juster balance was struck between prosperity and salvation, and, while retaining the theology of the master, it repudiated his scheme of social ethics. Persuaded that "godliness hath the promise of this life, as well as of the life to come," it resisted, with sober intransigeance, the interference in matters of business both of the state and of divines. It is this second, individualistic phase of Calvinism, rather than the remorseless rigours of Calvin himself, which may plausibly be held to have affinities with the temper called by Weber "the spirit of Capitalism." The question which needs investigation is that of the causes which produced a change of attitude so convenient to its votaries and so embarrassing to their pastors.

It is a question which raises issues that are not discussed at length in Weber's essay, though, doubtless, he was aware of them. Taking as his theme, not the conduct of Puritan capitalists, but the doctrines of Puritan divines, he pursues a single line of inquiry with masterly ingenuity. His conclusions are illuminating; but they are susceptible, it may perhaps be held, of more than one interpretation. There was action and reaction, and, while Puritanism helped to mould the social order, it was, in its turn, moulded by it. It is instructive to trace, with Weber, the influence of religious ideas on economic development. It is not less important to grasp the effect of the economic arrangements accepted by an age on the opinion which it holds of the province of religion.

30. Modifications of Calvinism
H. RICHARD NIEBUHR *

Yet the agreement between the interests of the middle classes and the religious temper of the Reformation movement was not so complete but that the former should not find in the doctrine of the God-intoxicated

* From *The Social Sources of Denominationalism*, pp. 98–104.

French reformer inconvenient elements which they felt impelled to modify. However close the relationships between economics and theology may have been in the sixteenth century and however practical may have been the genius of Calvin, he was after all, like Augustine and Luther and Wesley, a prophetic personality in whom the religious interest was quite supreme; to it he ruthlessly subordinated all other values which less radically Christian men continued to hold dear. The Genevan discipline illustrates the point. The complete dominance of the church over the political and economic life of the city was the fundamental assumption of Calvin's theocratic régime as it was in the repristinated Calvinism of New England a century later. The preachers of Geneva continued to fear money as the root of all evil and surrounded its acquisition with many prohibitions supported by threats of everlasting punishment. Despite their insistence on individual responsibility, their distrust of human nature was so profound and their theocratic ideal so compelling that they sacrificed liberty to authority without a qualm. "Calvinism had little pity for poverty," says Tawney, "but it distrusted wealth, as it distrusted all influences that distract the aim or relax the fibers of the soul, and, in the first flush of its youthful austerity, it did its best to make life unbearable for the rich." [1] But this position was not long tenable before the assaults of the class which had found the doctrine otherwise so attractive and to which the church needed to look for its chief support.

It may well be that the failure of the restrictive ethics was due to an antinomy within the soul of Calvinism itself—to the clash of the dynamic individualism fostered by its religious teaching with the repressive character of its morality. Individualism truimphed, however, only after the commercially and politically interested groups within the church threw their influence into the scale—quite unconsciously—and conveniently forgot the discipline while they remembered the liberty their faith inculcated. The modification of primitive Calvinism under this influence is marked in four particular areas: in the democratization of the originally autocratic and authoritative plan of government, in the abandonment of the essentially medieval social ethics, in the substitution of independency and tolerance for the conception of the church-state, and in the acceptance of doctrinal modifications under the influence of the humanism and rationalism which were prevalent in the middle classes.

Calvin's distrust of the common man and his aristocratic temper, as well as his doctrine of the divine sovereignty, inclined him toward an essentially autocratic plan of church government. Both in Geneva and in

[1] R. H. Tawney, *Religion and the Rise of Capitalism*, p. 132.

early New England the theocratic ideal was associated with oligarchical rather than with democratic polity. Yet Calvinism has everywhere entered into close alliance with democratic movements in both church and state. While the origin of such tendencies was usually humanist or radical rather than religious, yet the Reformed faith was predisposed to their acceptance partly by its insistence on individual responsibility and the priesthood of believers, partly by the influence of republican Geneva on the ideas and habits of its youth, and partly by the convenience of the liberal doctrine in the conflicts of Protestants with Catholic monarchs in France, the Netherlands, Scotland, and England. Under the further influence of the commercial classes who became the leaders of the democratic revolts of the sixteenth and seventeenth century in order that they might be delivered from royal monopolies and restrictions on commerce Calvinism took on an increasingly republican character. Yet the same middle class which sought in religion the sanction of its efforts to achieve liberty from royal control found in that very faith a convenient reason for denying the same liberty to the poor and the ungodly. The doctrine of predestination and the practice of government by the righteous and respectable few were corollaries in Switzerland, Holland, and New England. Not until the genuinely democratic ideals issuing out of humanism and the revolts of the poor had come into decided conflict with the oligarchical principles of Calvinism did these countries achieve really democratic constitutions. Nevertheless, the individualism of the commercial class broadened the popular basis of the Calvinist church and state, far removed as they were from any desire to recognize the principle of universal equality.

The second modification of primitive Calvinism which resulted from its alliance with the middle class was the relaxation of its restrictive social ethics. Calvin was little inclined to abandon the medieval principle of the supremacy of the church over all other institutions and of religion over all other interests of life. Indeed the ecclesiastical regulation of economic life was far more rigorously enforced at Geneva by the new than it had been by the old church. But under the subtle influence of the business interests which the church had welcomed into its fold the restrictive regulation soon lost its force, while the commendation of the commercial life as a sphere of divine vocation and the religious invigoration of individual activity remained effective. So, in discipline more than in doctrine, there was substituted for the collective authority of the church the equally orthodox authority of individual conscience. While the church continued to be regarded as the rightful arbiter of family morals and even of political conduct, its official representatives were persuaded of the self-sufficiency of economic ethics. So the Calvinism which "had begun by being the very soul of authoritarian regimentation," "ended by being the vehicle of an almost Utilitarian individualism." [2]

Finally, Calvinism was modified so as to assume a more definitely middle-class character through the influence of humanism and rationalism, and nineteenth-century science. The middle classes developed their interest in the liberal movements of thought because of the education which their economic circumstances enabled them to afford, because of the close relationship existing between rationalism and the social philosophy of modern business enterprise and, in later times, because of the technical interest which industry and commerce were required to take in the development of modern science. It has been pointed out by critics of Weber's thesis of the Calvinist parentage of capitalism that such typical representatives of the bourgeois spirit as Franklin and Carnegie derived their social ethics from the Illumination rather than from the Reformation. Yet the middle classes in general received this new influence quite unconsciously, unaware of any antagonism between the rationalism they absorbed in education and business and the teachings of their churches. Moreover their increasing affluence inspired them with ever greater self-respect—the reflection of the esteem, it may be, in which they were held by other groups. The desire to achieve a demonstrable success, regarded as a token of election, the ethics of merit and reward in the mundane life, the activism and individualism of Calvinist religious attitudes combined with rationalist appreciations of progress in the conquest of nature and of the value of the human reason to liberalize the strict teachings of early Calvinism. The supreme doctrine of the sole sovereignty of God lost its significance as the rather considerable sovereignty of man over nature came to light and as his imperial instincts were aroused in the competition of economic life. Under such influences Grotius and Locke were eventually alienated from the Calvinist system of thought and such movements as Arminianism and Unitarianism broke away from the parent stem. In them the related doctrines of human ability and of limited divine sovereignty were combined with the teaching of self-help and with faith in human progress. But even where the modification of the original doctrine did not go to such lengths as in these instances, the slow deterioration of the early Calvinist doctrines was nevertheless noticeable, though its explicit expression was held in

[2] *Ibid.*, p. 227.

check by the confessionalism fastened on the church in the sixteenth century. In the one case the victory of middle-class psychology over the religious spirit of Calvin came patently to light, in the other cases it was no less present though it was obscured. In New England Congregationalism, in Dutch Calvinism, and in English and Scotch Presbyterianism, as well as in Unitarianism and Arminianism, the accommodation of the doctrine and attitude of the erstwhile strictly theocentric faith to the spirit of the middle class resulted in the blunting of the sharp edges of the doctrine of divine sovereignty and in a practical emphasis on salvation by character. The ultimate result of this victory of middle-class attitudes over Calvinism was the substitution for the spiritual exaltation of the early devotees of a decent morality which believed with Defoe that "with energy, ingenuity and resolution it is possible under the most unfavorable conditions to make this life more than tolerable and even to arrange one's future affairs on a satisfactory footing with an offended Deity." [3] What a far cry this is from the pilgrim's heroic progress toward the celestial city! No better description of this decline of Calvinism is possible than Dowden's much quoted paragraph: "After the jagged precipices and forlorn valleys—scenes of spiritual exaltation and despair—a tableland was reached—safe, if unheroic—where men might plow and build. To make the best of both worlds was the part of prudence, and of the two worlds that on which our feet are planted is, at least, the nearer and the more submissive to our control. Divine providence is doubtless to be acknowledged, but it is highly desirable to supplement Divine providence by self-help." [4]

The victory of the bourgeoisie over Calvinism, however, was to be made even more complete than appeared in later English Puritanism. It remained for America to carry the accommodation of the faith to bourgeois psychology to its extremes. A single line of development leads from Jonathan Edwards and his great system of God-centered faith through the Arminianism of the Evangelical revival, the Unitarianism of Channing and Parker, and the humanism of transcendental philosophy, to the man-centered, this-worldly, lift-yourself-by-your-own-bootstraps doctrine of New Thought and Christian Science. The common strand that runs through these various movements is the adaptation of the early faith to the changing attitudes of the bourgeoisie.

[3] Edward Dowden, *Puritan and Anglican,* p. 276.
[4] *Ibid.,* p. 275.

31. A Critique of Weber's Thesis

J. MILTON YINGER *

Church and sect make opposite interpretations of the inherent dualism of Christian teachings. If a religious movement spreads to a larger and larger group and moves away from the religious preoccupation and fervor of its founders, to become involved as one factor among others in the daily lives of its members, it becomes adjusted to suit the needs of the people who come in contact with it. The nature of the adjustment is of great importance in determining the influence and further spread of the movement.

These two choices—the paths of church and sect—were open to religious groups in the sixteenth century, a time of significant social change. A study of the nature of the choice made by Calvinism and of the process by which it was made—for it was a process and not an instantaneous decision—reveals a great deal of the essential relationship between religious groups and social organization. The church-sect dilemma is not at first apparent, and the leader of a movement may not recognize it. But it is revealed in the process of interaction with the social situation of the time. It is essential in connection with our problem, therefore, to study not only what Calvin taught, but what happened to Calvinism. Only in that way can we understand its relation to the development of capitalism. What was Calvinism in the sixteenth century was not Calvinism in the eighteenth, and we must know the reasons for the difference. Moreover, we cannot wholly accept the Weber-Troeltsch assumption that at the start Calvinism was largely independently determined out of an inner dialectic of religious phenomena. We must inquire into the socio-economic setting out of which came some of the very assumptions with which Calvin *starts*. It is not likely that he would reason from premises contradictory to his time and place and still be successful. Capitalism was already fairly well under way in Geneva; or, at the least, many of the forces which were to produce capitalism were operating. It is not surprising therefore that his thought was somewhat less medieval than his predecessors.

When Troeltsch writes: "I would rate still higher the difference which *Weber* emphasizes between Calvin and Calvinism . . . ,"[1] he is putting

* Abridged from *Religion in the Struggle for Power*, pp. 85–118.
[1] *The Social Teaching of the Christian Churches*, p. 894 n.

the case mildly, for Weber gives it too little attention. As Troeltsch rightly points out, there are contradictory currents in every mass movement. This is scarcely less true of Calvinism than of the primitive church. The Geneva movement was at the same time traditional and radical, collectivistic and individualistic; it contained a sober prudence and a divine recklessness. "Primitive Calvinism is the daughter of Lutheranism." It emphasized obedience to the word of God revealed in the Bible, and stressed its connection with the primitive church. Like Lutheranism, it accepted secular culture and the idea of a calling which was the fulfilling of one's place in the divine scheme. It identified the Decalogue and law of nature. In other regards, however, primitive Calvinism had distinctive features. It had a strong element of individualism. For Luther, happiness because of the assurance of the forgiveness of sin was the important thing; but expression of the glory of God was central with Calvin; therefore, let there be activity. As we have seen, Calvinism also emphasized predestination: pure, unmerited grace as an expression of God's absolute will. And this grace fell only to the few. Luther, who had held to this doctrine in the early days, never wholly abandoned it; but under the pressure of conditions he was forced to adopt a creed that taught that grace was revocable, and able to be won and rewon by humility and faith.

Now it is of the utmost importance to discover what influences selected the teachings of Calvin that were to survive, what teachings were reinterpreted, what new doctrines added, as well as to understand the original setting which may have influenced the nature of this religious development. By means of the concept of the "church" as a type and a comprehension of the sect-to-church process, one can begin to understand the development of Calvinist teachings.

The doctrine of predestination, for instance, underwent a rather important change and development. With Calvin himself, the elect were God's invisible church. For ordinary men, however, the *recognizability* of the state of grace was of supreme importance; all men did not have Calvin's self-assurance—they wanted a visible sign of salvation. There were also institutional reasons for wanting to know who the elect were. Who were to take and administer the sacraments? For the laymen it came about, therefore, that self-assurance was the chief proof of divine grace. How could God's favor better be demonstrated to businessmen than by success in this world's activities? Worldly achievement and good works came to be, not the technical means of winning salvation, as in Catholicism, but the best way to get rid of the fear of damnation. We get, therefore, in place of the humble sinners to whom Luther promises grace, a group of self-confident saints. It is not difficult to see how, as

Weber shows, this kind of doctrine leads to enterprise. In practice it becomes: God helps those who help themselves.

It is of great importance to ask at this point, however: Why did this particular solution to the problem of salvation—a solution which is not necessarily the logical development of original Calvinism—appear, in contrast to the Lutheran and Catholic solutions of the same problem? Why is it that among the various tendencies within Calvinism, those which were favorable to the rising economic system were "sorted out" so to speak and emphasized to the minimization of other tendencies which were just as important in early Calvinism? Why did not the quietistic tendencies, to which predestination can as logically lead, prevail instead of its stimulating effects? This may be explained in terms of the origin of Calvinism and its setting. What could be more convincing to a businessman, who also was seriously interested in his eternal salvation, than that worldly success was a sign of God's favor? (Just as vast numbers of the poor had been taught for centuries, and continued to be taught by Calvin, Baxter, and other churchmen, that their salvation was the better because of their worldly "failure.") It was not inevitable in the logic of the idea nor in Calvin's use of it that the doctrine of predestination should become a stimulus to worldly success. The earlier teachings in Geneva had put severe restriction on the businessman. Calvin and the church in general preached unceasingly against unjust moneylenders and avarice. The Council of Geneva, who were businessmen, heard the ministers on thrift and simplicity, sent their children to catechism, and supported the church. On business matters, however, they were obdurate. They were glad to invoke the sanction of religion on traits which their secular activity found valuable—honesty, industry, sobriety, as well as the dynamic interpretation of predestination. But, as H. R. Niebuhr points out, the less useful virtues of solidarity, sympathy, and fraternity were ignored. The ministers did not capitulate to the businessmen; but those who emphasized the elements in the all-embracive Calvinist doctrine which were in tune with the times secured an audience and prospered. Calvin himself, unlike Luther, was a man of affairs. His movement was an urban movement. Although he preached against the dangers of riches and commerce, he started with the assumption that they were an acceptable part of the Christian order. ". . . the Geneva situation helped determine Calvin's political, social, and economic ideal. . . ." [2]

As was to be expected in the exponents of a faith which had its headquarters at Geneva, and later its most influential adherents in great business centers,

[2] *Ibid.*, p. 625.

like Antwerp, with its industrial hinterland, London and Amsterdam, its leaders addressed their teaching, not of course exclusively, but none the less primarily, to the classes engaged in trade and industry, who formed the most modern and progressive elements in the life of the age.

In doing so they naturally started from a frank recognition of the necessity of capital, credit and banking, large-scale commerce and finance, and the other practical facts of business life. . . . It is not that they abandon the claim of religion to moralize economic life, but that the life which they are concerned to moralize is one in which the main features of commercial civilization are taken for granted, and that it is for application to such conditions that their teaching is designed.[3]

Misuse, not the accumulation of riches, was declared to be the enemy of religion. Only by such a stand could Calvinism hope to have a practical influence in Geneva. . . .

Calvin himself shared the Lutheran view of the value of work, emphasizing its moral qualities, the need for moderation in wealth, and even the value of poverty in fostering Christian virtues. By preaching rigorous self-denial and condemning greed and profit, Calvin, especially in his early years, restricted trade and sponsored disdain of this world scarcely less than did Luther. In the *Institutes* he writes:

With whatever kind of tribulation we may be afflicted, we should always keep this end in view, to habituate ourselves to a contempt of the present life that we may thereby be excited to meditation on that which is to come. . . . There is no medium between these two extremes, either the earth must become vile in our estimation, or it must retain our immoderate love. Wherefore if we have any concern about eternity, we must use our most diligent efforts to extricate ourselves from these fetters. . . . But believers should accustom themselves to such a contempt of the present life, as may not generate either hatred of life, or ingratitude towards God. For this life, though it is replete with innumerable miseries, is yet deservedly reckoned among the Divine blessings which must not be despised. . . . It should be the object of believers, therefore, in judging of this mortal life that, understanding it to be of itself nothing but misery, they may apply themselves wholly with increasing cheerfulness and readiness to meditate on the future and eternal life. When we come to this comparison, then indeed the former will be not only securely neglected, but in competition with the latter altogether despised and abhorred. For if heaven is our country, what is the earth but a place of exile? If the departure out of the world is an entrance into life, what is the world but a sepulchre? What is a continuance in it but an absorption in death? If deliverance from the body is an introduction into genuine liberty, what is the body but a prison? If to enjoy the presence of God is the summit of felicity, is it not misery to be destitute of it? But till we escape out of the world "we

---

[3] R. H. Tawney, *Religion and the Rise of Capitalism*, pp. 104–105.

are absent from the Lord." Therefore, if the terrestrial life be compared with the celestial, it should undoubtedly be despised and accounted of no value.[4]

How far this is from a call to vigorous worldly activity to prove one's divine election! And surely if it is claimed, as Weber does, that it was not the intention of the reformers, but the unconscious and quite unexpected effects of their teachings which were crucial in producing the capitalistic spirit, then it is quite meaningless to say that the religious ethic "caused" the spirit, for in truth it was the interpretation given to the ethic that is associated with the spirit. The important question becomes, therefore: Why was the original meaning of Calvinism interpreted in the way it was, rather than in other possible and equally "logical" ways?

The process of adjustment to external circumstances is well illustrated by the English churches, which were so largely under the influence of Calvin. The doctrine that Calvin himself taught differs from the doctrine of seventeenth-century England. . . . The Puritan before the Civil War in Great Britain would have been as astounded as his opponents to learn that he has been labeled a friend of unbridled economic activity. The contrast between Calvin's rigorous teachings on the one hand and the impatient rejection of traditional economics on the other was at first, as we have seen, extreme. There were tendencies in Calvinism, however, which favored capitalism, and these were encouraged by the economic and political situation. ". . . the Puritan conscience lost its delicacy where matters of business were concerned."[5] Calvin himself had fused two elements: ascetic discipline and activity. In Geneva, a small, homogeneous city, the restraining hand of discipline had dominated, although even there there was conflict. In Britain, however, a civil war gave evidence of the irreconcilability of these two aspects of Calvinism. What had been held together in the work of Calvin, because of the domination of religious motives, proved to be an unstable union in the lives of the less intensely religious. . . .

Richard Baxter, whom Weber cites frequently, stands midway in the process of transition from early to late Calvinism, and consequently refutes Weber's claim as often as he validates it. ". . . he was constantly wavering between the two opposing camps of Puritanism on the one hand and its deadly enemy at that time, 'Independency,' on the other. His very influence was to some degree based upon his blowing neither too hot nor too cold to displease any, and even in Anglo-Catholic circles he was read and enjoyed."[6] Baxter, who was a man of great practical experience, is

[4] *Institutes* (translated by John Allen), I, pp. 639–642.
[5] Tawney, *op. cit.*, p. 232.
[6] T. C. Hall, *The Religious Background of American Culture*, p. 217.

an excellent example of the way churchmen attempt to moralize from within a social order. He did not want to alienate an important group who had taken to a life of trade, with or without the church's permission, for England had already gone far toward capitalism, but neither did he give up the task of trying to control their behavior. He stressed the dangers of trade and wealth, but did not condemn them. Baxter allowed lending upon pledges, pawns, and mortgages for security, provided that they were not against something necessary to a poor man's livelihood. And the mortgage might be taken if the pledge is "among merchants and rich men." Taking of interest is also lawful when the borrower has profited by the use of the money; it is unlawful when it violates justice and charity. The two great principles of justice in trade he held to be love of neighbor and self-denial. "When the tempter draweth you to think only of your own commodity and gain, remember how much more you will lose by sin, than your gain can any way amount to." [7] One gets the impression in reading his "directions for the rich" that Baxter is preaching to a group who are already, willy-nilly, involved in a life of business and wealth: he seeks only to enfold that group within the Christian doctrine.

To the poor he counsels patience, eyes on the next world, content with one's status, lack of covetousness. There the traditional element in his preaching looms large, and is a long way from giving the dynamic impetus to the capitalistic spirit that Weber held was in *the* Protestant ethic.

We are like runners in a race, and heaven or hell will be our end; and therefore woe to us, if by looking aside, or turning back, or stopping, or trifling about these matters, or burdening ourselves with worldly trash, we should lose the race, and lose our souls. O sirs, what greater matters than poverty or riches have we to mind! Can these souls that must shortly be in heaven or hell, have time to bestow any serious thought upon these impertinencies?

. . . "Stedfastly believe that, ordinarily, riches are far more dangerous to the soul than poverty, and a greater hindrance to men's salvation." Believe experience; how few of the rich and rulers of the earth are holy, heavenly, self-denying, mortified men? Believe your Saviour, "How hardly shall they that have riches enter into the kingdom of God! For it is easier for a camel to go through a needle's eye than for a rich man to enter into the kingdom of God. And they that heard it said, who then can be saved? And he said, The things which are impossible with men, are possible with God." So that you see the difficulty is so great of saving such as are rich that to men it is a thing impossible, but to God's omnipotency only it is possible.

. . . Also you will be tempted to be coveting after more; satan maketh poverty a snare to draw many needy creatures, to greater covetousness than many of the rich are guilty of; none thirst more eagerly after more; and yet

[7] Richard Baxter, *A Christian Directory*, Vol. VI, p. 287.

their poverty blindeth them, so that they cannot see that they are covetous, or else excuse it as a justifiable thing. They think that they desire no more but necessaries, and that it is not covetousness; if they desire not superfluities. But do you not covet more than God allotteth you? And are you not discontent with his allowance? And doth not he know best what is necessary for you, and what superfluous? What then is covetousness, if this be not? [8]

How far all this is removed from ascetic rational pursuit of gain! Baxter is a direct descendant of medieval doctrine. "The Christian avoids sin rather than loss." He modifies his teachings only enough—and that rather reluctantly—to bring the businessmen within the fold of the church, for only then may it have a claim upon their conduct. Baxter's work may be somewhat contradictory and ambiguous, although of the utmost sincerity; but what effective "political" action is not?

Other clergymen of the time, less subtle or sincere, or less alive to the movements of history, preached a far sterner traditionalism, calling down fire from heaven on those who called attention to abuses of landownership, declaring that they were stirring up class hatred. That kind of traditionalism was disregarded for the most part, however, and those elements in Calvinism which supported the rising tide of industry received more and more attention. "Tillotson was eloquent in a sermon on the *Advantages of Religion,* proving that God increased the wealth of the godly, both by special Providence, and by making religious graces conducive to worldly success." [9] The church-type mind, having accepted the legitimacy (inevitability) of trade, was devoted to the task of controlling the new activities. Baxter's work was soon followed by a series of books attempting to encompass the economic life of the time: *The Religious Weaver, Navigation Spiritualized,* Defoe's *The Complete English Tradesman,* and Steele's *The Tradesman's Calling.* It is apparent that these men were by no means entirely successful in their aim. As Bates observes, they sought to idealize commerce, not to materialize religion, but that was not always the result: "Calvin's legalization of interest 'took with the brethren . . . like polygamy with the Turks,' and the injunction to exact interest for the sake of widows and orphans appealed to 'divers zealous ministers who themselves desired to pass for orphans of the first rank.'" [10] . . .

This discussion of the gradual modification of Calvinism through two centuries requires at the least a restatement of Weber's thesis. It is not that the relationship which he observes between Calvinism and the spirit of capitalism is nonexistent (although he probably states the case

[8] *Ibid.,* Vol. IV, pp. 379–384.
[9] R. B. Schlatter, *The Social Ideas of Religious Leaders, 1660–1688,* p. 199.
[10] E. S. Bates, *American Faith,* p. 70.

too strongly). The important thing is that when one interprets the meaning of this relationship in connection with the development of Calvinism, he finds nothing surprising about the harmony between the spirit of capitalism and Calvinist ethics. Moreover, there are limitations to the assumption of Weber and Troeltsch—and it is scarcely more than an assumption in the essay under discussion—that original Calvinism was a product of an inner religious dialectic, and that it became conjoined with capitalism only by a historical accident (the crossing of two theretofore independent causal systems). This assumption is absolutely crucial to their argument, and yet by the nature of the case it is very difficult to validate. In fact, there is more than a little tendency to get this assumption in, in the early stages of the debate, as a kind of first premise, and thus to beg the whole question under dispute. That is perhaps to put the case a little too strongly, for Weber's concept of the inner development of religious ideas is part of a carefully worked-out religious typology. According to his conception, the immanent development of a religion is largely the result of "prophecy," which is the religious aspect of the destruction of traditionalism, carried on under the claim of charismatic authority. This break with traditionalism is the result of a religious "interest" in interpreting the meaning of the world. The genuine prophet, according to Weber, establishes *new* obligations; he repudiates the past. His claims cannot be reduced to various secular interests; they are a primary revolutionary force.

Clearly it is very difficult to prove the immanent quality of the development of religion by prophecy. At least two questions are involved: What might be some of the social factors conditioning the appearance and the nature of prophecy? And how is the purely religious development transferred into a realm of secular influence? Weber, of course, was not unaware of these problems. He noted that the appearance of prophecy was itself dependent upon social conditions. Social crises, in which traditionalism was already being challenged, encouraged the development of prophecy. Moreover, in a differentiated society, the interpretations of the meaning of the world will vary with the interests and problems of the various classes. And the likelihood of prophecy having a dominant influence depends upon the power of the group who become its principle adherents. On the other hand, says Weber, the prophecy would not enter the field of interaction at all were it not for a religious "interest." It cannot, therefore, be reduced to conditions which influenced it. . . .

The argument of a "historical accident" might be more convincing were it not necessary to explain the fact that at the time Calvinism was emerging there also appeared a new legal situation, a political revolutionary tendency, a new theory of poverty and its treatment, individualistic theories in philosophy, all of which also harmonized with the capitalistic spirit. Are we to assume that these connections are the result of an amazing series of historical accidents? Or are these human products to be seen as on a different level from religious phenomena? Until these problems are more fully solved, no argument can rest solidly on this premise. It is easily conceivable that the appeal to moral action on the basis of individual character, which is characteristic of Calvinism, is the expression of the same forces that created other kinds of individualism.

We must not, however, exaggerate the extent of our criticism of Weber. It may be that he would accept most of the above discussion of the evolution of Calvinism. It is not entirely clear how large a part of the total explanation of capitalism he intended the Protestant ethic to fill. When he says only: To all other sources of capitalism Calvinism added a peculiarly rigorous and ascetic discipline and furnished ready at hand a religious dynamic that *could be made into* a stimulus of enterprise: if that in his thesis, the idea of a "historical accident" is more readily established. There is perhaps very little in the pre-Calvinistic development of capitalism that would have enabled one to predict the emergence of this peculiarly ascetic rationalism, although indeed there are some instances of it in earlier times. Such a limited interpretation of the essay, however, scarcely fulfills the herculean task of disproving the economic interpretation of the rise of capitalism, as some of its supporters claimed. Nor does it establish the basic role of Calvinism in the development of the spirit of capitalism, for it must be seen in relation to the many other factors which stimulated that spirit. Above all, one must not forget the important ways in which Calvinism was molded to fit the needs of the class who had found in it the possibilities of the kind of religious sponsorship that they required in their struggle for advancement. They would have advanced in any event; they probably would have found a religious sponsor in any event. Nevertheless, it is not unimportant that Calvin's formulations appeared when and where they did. Without them capitalism would have evolved along somewhat different lines.

THE QUESTION OF USURY

In addition to the matter of the origin and evolution of Calvinism there are other related questions which can throw light on the nature of the relationship between religious teachings and secular interests. While Weber gives scant attention to the question of usury, it is not unimportant for our problem, for the development of religious doctrine on interest-taking demonstrates the adjustment of churches to new secular situations. In a local economy where self-sufficient production is the rule, persons borrow only in unusual circumstances—when they have suffered some loss by fire, theft, crop failure, and the like. Lending for gain under such circumstances was almost synonymous with extortion and oppression. The Aristotelian theory that money was barren was not only accepted but largely true. It is not surprising that the church condemned all interest as sinful, although it overlooked, and thereby accepted, the transactions of merchants and governments and even of church officials, whose borrowings were obviously not expressions of immediate need.

With the growth of trade and large-scale enterprise, however, credit came to be, not an exception to the usual practice, but a normal part of business, and the old restrictions seemed more and more unreasonable. ". . . it was clear that a man who borrowed in order to speculate or take advantage of some opportunity for profit was not being oppressed." [11] How did the church deal with the new developments? The first reaction was to make the original prohibition more emphatic and universal. The Lateran Council of 1179 issued the first of a series of stringent prohibitions of usury. Gradually, however, modifications appeared in the pronouncements of the church; they came as the granting of exceptions rather than the abandonment of the principle. In the early stages the taking of interest was allowed by the overlooking, if not the actual permission, of rent charges and triple contracts. This did not mean, of course, the complete abandonment of the rulings against interest, but it allowed interest payments to be made where there seemed to be moral justification. This permitted the church to maintain unity of principle at the same time that it allowed flexibility of practice. It was an adjustment to the development of trade while still preserving the basic condemnation of interest-taking as it applied to the traditional economy. This is the kind of reconciliation that one would expect from the church of St. Thomas, because it had as many moral problems to solve as there were classes of people to whom it wished to appeal. If it did not capitulate quickly and easily to the demand for justifying interest-taking, the reason was that the church had among its members the vast number who still borrowed only for consumption purposes, to whom interest was a genuine injury. Medieval teachings were repeated, in spite of new economic developments, because economic conditions continued, over a wide range, to be what they had been when the teachings were first formulated. Like an effective political party, the Catholic Church tried to balance the demands and needs of its various contradictory groups, so

[11] Schlatter, *op. cit.*, p. 216.

that justice would be at a maximum and so that none would be tempted to desert the fold. This is the inevitable program of any group that tries to appeal to all people.

Further modification of the doctrine of the church was made as the external situation changed, although the process of transition was very slow. Calvin appeared in the midst of this process of modification of the principle of usury. It is not surprising that as a citizen of the commercial center of Geneva, as a man of affairs and associate of businessmen and traders, Calvin did not oppose the modification of principle. He wrote: ". . . by no testimony of scripture am I resolved that usuries are altogether condemned . . . we do not see usuries simply forbidden to us, unless so far as they are repugnant both to justice and charity." Calvin examined the idea that money does not breed money, and decided that money lent created more, just as did money invested in a farm. To the taking of interest, however, he laid down these seven restrictions: it is wrong to exact usury from the needy, to exact from the poor more security than they can afford, to violate natural justice, to take payment for a loan that does not equally benefit the borrower; contracts must be for the benefit of the state, with no higher interest than civil authorities allow; and the fact of common usage is not justification of usury.

Even this moderate justification of interest was not quickly and easily accepted by the followers of Calvin. Interest was legally prohibited in England until 1571, although there were exceptions for borrowings of the crown. Of the writers against usury listed in Blaxton's *English Usurer* (1634), most were Puritans. It was the second decade of the seventeenth century before any important Protestant writer dealt with the problem of usury in a way at all comparable with Calvin's letter of 1545. Then Johann Gerhard, a Lutheran, published his *Loci Theologici,* in which he discussed the subject at length, coming to the conclusion that only an immoderate rate of interest was usury. Not until 1631 did a Calvinist pastor (Ames) make a thorough review of the subject of usury and decide in the liberal favor.

Baxter, a century and a quarter after Calvin, stands on about the same ground. Usury is a sin in most cases when it violates principles of charity, when it takes advantage of another's need. When borrowed money is put to productive use, Baxter holds that interest is justifiably taken. In the main, he holds that moral issues cannot be judged in the abstract but only with reference to practical experience:

As all oppression and unmercifulness must be avoided and all men must do as they would (judiciously) be done by; so it is a bad thing to corrupt religion, and fill the world with causeless scruples, by making that a sin which is no sin. Divines that live in great cities and among merchandize, are usually fitter judges in this case, than those that live more obscurely (without experience) in the country.[12]

While Catholic teachings are seldom so forthright as this regarding the necessary flexibility in moral judgments, in practice, as we have seen, they too adjusted to the new situation regarding interest. Although Calvinist churches adjusted more quickly and easily perhaps, it should be remembered that they had a far higher percentage of businessmen in their congregations. Any religious group which hoped to influence the increasingly powerful business class was forced to accept the legitimacy of interest-taking as a moral principle, for business enterprise depended more and more on credit. . . .

The whole history of the spread of Calvinism teaches us to beware of facile generalizations regarding its influence, for it could evolve in many directions. Its rigorous asceticism could be a tonic to those who stood to gain by vigorous activity. But the doctrine of the depravity of the flesh, taken emotionally, could lead to a deadening of earthly activity. This was manifest in some aspects of Pietism, which emphasized that aspect of asceticism which meant withdrawal from the world, in contrast to the activist tendencies in Calvinism in general. As we have shown above, it is of great importance to know why these tendencies toward withdrawal were not dominant. Weber himself noted that "the doctrine of predestination could lead to fatalism if, contrary to the predominant tendencies of rational Calvinism, it were made the object of emotional contemplation." [13]

One may note too, alongside the main emphases of Calvinism, a kind of Christian socialism, which taught that goods ought to be inexpensive, interest rates low (Calvin held that 2.5 per cent was high enough), and regard for others the dominant ethic. Weber wrote: ". . . the desire to separate the elect from the world could, with a strong emotional intensity, lead to a sort of monastic community life of half-communistic character, as the history of Pietism, even within the Reformed Church, has shown again and again." [14] This is one of the sources of Christian socialism today; but it did not (and one may perhaps say does not) receive much attention because it was moving against contemporary developments. When one understands "the social sources of denominationalism," he is surprised neither at the infrequency of this interpretation of Calvinism, nor at its occasional appearance.

[12] Baxter, *op. cit.*, Vol. VI, p. 328.
[13] *The Protestant Ethic*, p. 131.
[14] *Ibid.*

These inner contradictions in Calvinism, these "radical" elements, were not able to swim upstream and hence remained obscured. The most powerful opponent of prevailing Calvinism, however, was that very capitalism which it helped to support. Calvinism recognized secular activities—political participation and economic enterprise—but only as means to a spiritual end—the glory of God and the demonstration of salvation. Material motives were kept under control by rigorous discipline and limitation of the sense life. Such asceticism, however, was not for most men. Anyone who could endure a sermon became a Calvinist. The new doctrine helped to free men from traditionalism but was unable to establish its own tradition of ascetic self-denial, until, as Weber says: "The people filled with the spirit of capitalism today tend to be indifferent, if not hostile, to the Church." "In Baxter's view the care for external goods should only lie on the shoulders of the 'saint like a light cloak, which can be thrown aside at any moment.' But fate decreed that the cloak should become an iron cage." [15] The Puritans were well aware that their ideals tended to give way under the influence of wealth, once it was achieved. The genuine adherents to the doctrine always were found in the classes rising from a lowly status, while those who had gained wealth continually repudiated the ethic. Monasticism underwent the same fate throughout the Middle Ages: penniless monks were outspoken and sincere; but wealthy monasteries, with large financial interests, lost some of their ardor. The Christian ethic needed constant regeneration from the bottom. Methodism, says Weber, may be regarded as a kind of monastic reform of Puritanism. It furnished a religious basis for ascetic conduct after the doctrine of predestination had been given up. Wesley was well aware of this contradiction into which the Puritan church fell: "I fear, wherever riches have increased, the essence of religion has decreased in the same proportion. Therefore I do not see how it is possible, in the nature of things, for any revival of true religion to continue long. For religion must necessarily produce both industry and frugality, and these cannot but produce riches. But as riches increase, so will pride, anger, and love of the world in all its branches." [16] The form of religion remains, but its spirit swiftly vanishes.

Thus we see that Protestant asceticism was molded by "the totality of social conditions, especially economic" (Weber). While recognizing that a fully developed Calvinism became a powerful ideological weapon for the business classes, we must avoid misinterpreting the significance of this fact for the sociology of religion. We do not have a complete un-

[15] *Ibid.*, p. 70 and p. 181.
[16] *Ibid.*, p. 175.

derstanding of the importance of a religious ethic until we study the
process by which it developed.

32. Religious Opposition to Nationalism in the Middle East

EMILE MARMORSTEIN *

THE INTRICATE CONNECTIONS BETWEEN NATIONALISM AND RELIGION RAISE SOME
OF THE MOST DIFFICULT AND IMPORTANT QUESTIONS FOR A SCIENCE OF RELIGION.
THAT RELIGION COMMONLY SUPPORTS NATIONALISM IN THE CONTEMPORARY
SCENE HAS FREQUENTLY BEEN OBSERVED. THIS PAPER DESCRIBES TWO RELIGIOUS
MOVEMENTS THAT OPPOSE NATIONALISM. ALTHOUGH IT IS PRIMARILY DESCRIP-
TIVE, IT SUGGESTS SOME OF THE CONDITIONS UNDER WHICH SUCH A RELATION-
SHIP APPEARS. THERE ARE VALUABLE LEADS HERE THAT DESERVE CAREFUL
ATTENTION AND FURTHER RESEARCH.

Turkey and Israel are popularly considered to be the two most stable
States in the Middle East. Their parliamentary institutions work comparatively well, their armies seem prepared to fight in defence of their
countries, and their governments have indicated their intention to side
with the Western bloc in the event of an international conflict. There is
also another point of resemblance. While in all other Middle Eastern
countries religious-political organizations are devoted to the support of
nationalist aspirations, in Turkey and Israel religious groups with an
aversion to nationalist thought and conduct have emerged. This statement must be qualified by two admissions. First, there are in both these
countries individuals and groups who combine nationalist loyalties with
devotion to their faith. Secondly, in the other Middle Eastern countries,
a small number of conservative religious people still harbour in their
hearts suspicion of the all-embracing claims of nationalist doctrine and
fear of the results of the atmosphere which it fosters. Moreover, there is
an obvious reason for the development of religious opposition to nationalism in Turkey and Israel and not elsewhere in the Middle East.
Only in Turkey and Israel has anti-religious nationalism become powerful
enough to arouse and justify the formation of anti-nationalist religious
groups.

Throughout much of the latter half of the history of Islam, the func-

* Abridged from *International Affairs*, July, 1952, pp. 344–359.

tions relating to the spiritual guidance of the community have been shared by two distinct groups of religious functionaries. The doctrinal, ritual, and legal traditions of the faith are safeguarded by men of learning, who give authoritative decisions on religious problems, administer justice in the religious courts, preach sermons and compile works of devotion for the instruction and entertainment of those Muslims who have enjoyed the benefits of a sound religious education. The enthusiasm of the masses, however, has been largely sustained not by the erudition of the official leaders of the faithful but by the heirs to the traditions of Islamic mysticism, the orders of dervishes. In the last century of the Ottoman Empire, both the official and unofficial groups occupied positions of dignity and respect. Not only had the sense of conflict between them lessened but they were even in some cases closely linked together by personal ties and by a feeling of solidarity and alliance. The official groups were supported by the State and headed by the Sheikh-ül-Islam, to whom all proposed measures were submitted for his decision as to their compatibility with Islamic teaching, while the unofficial groups had gained power and wealth as a result of the affection which the masses felt towards them.

With the disintegration of the Ottoman Empire and the abolition of the Caliphate, religious functionaries were reduced to the level of ordinary citizens. Secularism, one of the six guiding principles on which the new Turkey was based, meant that Islam was no longer to be the official faith but merely one of the religions of Turkey and, in fact, subject to more strict government supervision than the others. A host of restrictions such as the prohibition of religious instruction in government schools and, in practice, of the establishment of private institutions for religious activities of almost any kind were introduced. In 1925, the orders were dissolved on the grounds that they had actively participated in reactionary conspiracies. The prohibition of the Arabic call to prayer, the substitution of Latin for Arabic characters, the introduction of European clothing and headgear, the limitation of the right to wear traditional clothing to the heads of recognized religious communities, and the general attitude of Kemal Atatürk made it clear to all that religious practices were unfashionable and unlikely to advance the careers of government officials.

On 14 May 1950, as a result of the general election, the Republican People's Party was defeated by the Democratic Party and two of the fundamentals of Atatürk's system, statism and secularism, were threatened. This victory had been due largely to the support of rich peasants, merchants, and shopkeepers who had made considerable fortunes during the war. As in Britain during the nineteenth century, the growth of the prosperity of the mercantile middle classes coincided with an increase in their political influence, a prejudice in favour of *laissez-faire* in economic matters and a tendency to favour the maintenance of the religious traditions in which they were reared. In fact, some of these self-made Turks regard the improvement of their material circumstances as a reward for their attachment to Islam throughout the period of anticlerical predominance. The new government in their hour of triumph decided to lift a number of restrictions on religious freedom. The Arabic call to prayer was allowed. Training colleges for Imams were opened and religious instruction encouraged in the schools. Festivals of a religious character were accorded a fair amount of official recognition. These activities are, however, strictly controlled by the State. Religious teaching at all levels comes under the Ministry of Education and not under the Director General of Religious Affairs. The aim of the government was to restore Islam to respectability but not to power.

These plans for a loyal and docile Islam, domesticated within the framework of a slightly modified Kemalist regime, reckoned without the orders which had gone underground after their dissolution and persisted in their efforts to prolong the attachment of the people to their faith. They now emerged with their prestige almost intact and with a new self-confidence born in the underground struggle and stimulated by unexpected victory. Within the course of a few months, they showed very clearly that they were not content that Islam should become a semi-official appendage of the new Turkey. In their visions, Islam was to become once again the guiding influence of Turkey and, eventually, of the whole Islamic world. Early in 1951 their aspirations were translated into actions which could not be ignored. Reports of the mutilation or decapitation of busts of Atatürk began to appear in Turkish newspapers, followed by accounts of rehabilitation ceremonies to the accompaniment of speeches expressing the devotion of the nation to the memory and ideals of Atatürk. No information was given as to the identity of the culprits. They were generally described as "dark forces" or "vandals" and only occasionally as "reactionaries." New "outrages" continued to be reported from April to June. In May, the government introduced a bill inflicting exemplary penalties on all who should venture to insult the memory of Atatürk but this had little immediate effect. On the night of 17 June 1951 the head of the marble statue of Atatürk in the Park of the Republic at Turgutlu was severed and, on 26 June, another standing in front of the officers' club in Ankara was the victim of a similar "outrage."

Towards the end of June the veil of anonymity was lifted and the culprits were exposed as members of the Tijani order. A sheikh of the order—Kemal Pilâvoğlu—was arrested together with over a hundred other Tijanis. A statement, issued by the Director General of Religious Affairs, gave a brief account of the history of the order, in which the founder's pretensions to the privilege of prophetic revelation were ridiculed. The newspaper campaign, which followed, went much further. "The problem has become serious," wrote *Hurriyet* on 18 July. "The existence of the bearded Tijanis must be ended immediately if Turkey is to live in freedom and independence." Other writers cast doubt on their financial aims, their sanity, and their patriotism. . . .

Now, in view of the rebellious attitude of the Tijanis in modern Turkey, it might seem strange that they should have assisted foreign conquerors against their own countrymen and co-religionists. Yet, time after time in the history of groups of religious rebels such as the Anabaptists of Münster or the Prophets of Zwickau and others—and it is a characteristic of the Guardians of the City in modern Israel—one notices the contrast between loyal submission to a tolerant pagan or avowedly infidel government and open revolt against the rule of co-religionists, who fall short of very exacting standards of faith and conduct.

The allegations levelled against the Tijanis by their opponents are largely justified. Islam, like Judaism, is a nomocracy. In theory, a Muslim State must be administered in accordance with the principles of the Sacred Law. It is not sufficient for the Tijanis that modern Turkey tolerates Islam as a respectable form of religious activity. Nor would it satisfy them if government controls were entirely removed and Islam granted unlimited internal autonomy in the administration of Islamic institutions in Turkey. They would argue that the whole purpose of the State in Islam is to organize the community of the faithful in such a way as to enable them to follow the precepts of Islam under the most favourable conditions. The State should be an Islamic institution rather than Islam a State institution. The form of posthumous revenge taken by the Tijanis on Atatürk is due not only to memories of the persecution to which they had been subjected by him. It can also be attributed to their detestation of him as the embodiment of Turkish nationalism, of the doctrine which under his leadership dethroned Islam so successfully and so ruthlessly, which substituted the ties of language and race for the bonds of a common faith and law and which replaced the gulf dividing Muslims and non-Muslims with another separating Turks from everyone else. When their opponents accuse the Tijanis of "hating everything that is Turkish," that is what they mean. When they charge them with opposition to "modern life," they mean that the Tijanis attach more importance to obedience to the precepts of Islam than to material progress, to the day of judgment than to an improvement of the standard of living, to the efficacy of prayer than to the laws of hygiene. However, while all these accusations are justified, there is no concrete evidence to confirm allegations of Communist views and affiliations. In fact, all the available evidence suggests that they regard faith as a more than adequate substitute for economic planning and that they have no links with anyone outside their country at all.

Reports of arrests suggest that they are distributed all over Turkey but they seem to be concentrated in the Turkish-Syrian frontier regions, as well as in the neighborhood of Smyrna and the shores of the Aegean. Estimates of their numbers vary between 8,000 and 100,000. If loyal members of the order are intended, the former would seem the more reliable; if the estimate is meant to cover sympathizers the latter may be correct. But it would appear as if the Tijanis were merely the "shock troops" of a larger movement. Some of the other orders are larger and more influential. There are also many sympathizers, unconnected with the orders, men active in the business and political life of the country, whose consciences occasionally tell them that if only their hearts were granted more scope than their heads, their place should be among those who protest rather than among those who acquiesce. Their feelings have been cautiously expressed even at provincial conferences of the Democratic Party, and government spokesmen have felt it necessary to provide an authoritative reply. Fevzi Lutfi Karaosmanoğlu, a recent Minister of the Interior, made an impassioned protest at Bursa on 13 May 1951 against demands for "canonical legislation" and attempts "to mingle religious and worldly affairs. . . . While not forgetting our faith as Muslims, we shall uphold our Turkish character above all else." The question of priority appears to be troubling many Turkish Muslims at the present time. The majority would be content with moderate concessions. They have been shocked by the decapitations. They think that the Tijanis have gone too far. Yet in their hearts they feel thrilled at the daring of these red-beards. The Tijanis themselves are under a cloud. They are trying to survive "elimination." One cannot prophesy the role which they will play in the future but one can say with a certain amount of confidence that they have struck the first blow in a campaign which— whether it succeeds or not in achieving their maximum aspirations—has strengthened Islam in Turkey.

There are a number of points of genuine resemblance between Judaism and Islam. They are both loosely organized but tightly bound by the conception of a divinely revealed law. Their methods of interpretation, argument, and acceptance of tradition are very similar. They both depend on the existence of a small but influential minority of learned and devout men upon whose consent the theory and practice of the faith depend. One may also point out the likeness between the relationship of the *ulema* to the orders in Islam and that of the recognized rabbinical authorities to the Hasidic dynasties in Judaism. It is, therefore, quite natural that the Tijanis and the Guardians of the City, two groups engaged in fighting against the same kind of adversary, should have a number of things apart from their beards in common. Neither of them are sects. Neither offer new religious or social doctrines. Both cling stubbornly to tradition. But however similar the broader outlines of the struggle, political variations are responsible for a number of differences in detail, which must be traced back to their origins. . . .

The reasons for the rise of a group of this nature [Guardians of the City] must be sought in the general pattern of the development of Judaism, the struggle between orthodoxy and secularism and the history of Jewish settlement in the Holy Land over the last 150 years. From Talmudical times, the differences between Jews who maintained the yoke of the Sacred Law firmly on their shoulders and those who had more or less shaken it off, were stressed by the rabbis. Restrictions were introduced into the religious-social life of the Jew, which, in some cases, created an even more formidable barrier between the observant and unobservant Jew than between Jew and gentile. In times of laxity, sectarianism, and heresy, the importance of these restrictions was emphasized. Thus, in the middle and latter half of the nineteenth century, the inclination of many Jews to neglect traditional practices and the growth of reform movements resulted in the determination of considerable sections of the devout to separate themselves from those who did not lead uncompromisingly traditional lives and to form distinct communities. Their leaders went so far as to proclaim the view that it was forbidden by the Sacred Law to join in prayer, intermarry, or be buried with those belonging to reforming communities. This tendency towards withdrawal within a camp of one's own, accompanied by a purge of the community of the faithful from all sources of heretical infection, is of very great importance for our purpose because the parents and grandparents of the Guardians of the City largely consisted of men and women who were nurtured in this atmosphere. They came to the Holy Land in the latter half of the nineteenth century in order to await the final redemption—like the German Templars and the American Colony—and to spend their lives in the traditional manner in prayer and study. Their disgust at the pollution of Jewish life in Europe led them to seek refuge in the unspoiled sanctity of the Holy Land.

Their descendants speak of Ottoman Jerusalem with undisguised nostalgia. Some of their families had brought substantial sums of money with them and acquired houses in the Old City or built new quarters outside the walls. Life was cheap, and for citizens of the Austro-Hungarian Empire protected by the Capitulations, delightfully free. Many, it is true, were subjects of the Sultan, but Ottoman officials were, on the whole, easy-going and it was always possible to intervene on behalf of victims of oppression. Money came in from all over Europe. Children grew up, married, and multiplied on the bounty of the devout. They spent their days in study, they prayed at the shrine of the Patriarchs in Hebron, at Rachel's tomb in Bethlehem, at the Western Wall, at the graves of the sages, and, finally, even in their dying moments, they were sustained by the thought that they would be buried on the Mount of Olives overlooking the site of the Holy of Holies.

This idyll was only slightly disturbed in 1908 when the Young Turks seized power and proclaimed the equality of all Ottoman citizens. The abolition of the poll tax and the extension of conscription to the minorities were put into effect. There was an end to the almost absolute power which the heads of religious communities had to punish sinners, but they retained a large measure of autonomy, especially in matters of personal law. A more pronounced disturbance arose from the growth of Zionism and the arrival of a new type of settler, who appeared to the devout to be the very same kind of individual from whom they and their fathers had fled from Europe. The Balfour Declaration and the Mandate proved an even severer blow. Foreign citizens were deprived of the protection of the Capitulations. Under the new dispensation, the Zionist authorities were recognized as the spokesmen of the Jewish population of Palestine. The administration with the help of Zionist advisers drew up new regulations for the election of rabbis and the establishment of community councils, and Zionists were naturally given a certain share in the control of these organizations. A section of the Jews of Jerusalem, Safad, and Tiberias revolted against this decision and appealed to the League of Nations in 1924 for permission to set up separate communities. This right was conceded by the Mandatory Power on the instructions of the Mandates Commission of the League and a separate community was formed in Jerusalem under the title of The Ashkenazi Council of the City, which elected its own Chief Rabbi, organized its own institutions and refused to recognize or to co-operate with the official community. Politically, it was allied with the Agudath Yisrael under the leadership of the late Rabbi Moshe Blau, an astute politician and an impressive orator. Under his guidance the party and the community preserved their independence but the demands of their members for immigration certificates for their relations—particularly after the rise of Hitler—forced him into a certain amount of clandestine collaboration with the Labour Party, the controlling force in the Jewish Agency, which had been entrusted by the administration with the distribution of immigration certificates. Consequently, the Agudath Yisrael made an electoral pact with the Labour Party in the Municipal Elections in Jerusalem and Tiberias in 1935 and in the same year Rabbi Blau accompanied Zionist leaders to Government House to protest against the proposal to set up a Legislative Council.

It was in this atmosphere that the Guardians of the City began to emerge. The Agudath Yisrael was being torn by internal dissension. The compromisers included most of the members of the Agudath Yisrael Workers' Party, a youthful and energetic group. The other wing consisted of the most uncompromising elements among the old settlers reinforced by recent immigrants of a similar outlook. As long as Rabbi Blau was alive, his political skill and knowledge of local personalities and conditions sufficed to maintain a façade of unity, but with his untimely death a large proportion of the uncompromising wing openly left the party and combined with those elements of the old settlement, which had always suspected the members of Agudath Yisrael of being "Zionists in disguise," under the banner of the Guardians of the City. They adopted the old methods of campaign so familiar to Jerusalem life, i.e., sticking leaflets on the outer walls of synagogues, and soon managed to collect a number of adherents. In 1945, on the same day as the General Election in Great Britain, they succeeded in gaining control of the Ashkenazi Council of the City by a large majority. Their power and influence increased. Chief Rabbi Duschinsky, the head of their community, and his rabbinical court openly favoured their cause. So did a number of other rabbis including the Hazon Ish, who is regarded as the outstanding rabbinical authority in the world today, and Rabbi Soloveitchik of Brest-Litovsk, who allowed himself to be appointed their spiritual leader for the whole country. They began to publish a periodical and a host of pamphlets.

Then came the British decision to leave Palestine and the war with the Arabs. It was a decision which the Guardians of the City profoundly deplored. . . .

The only hope of the Guardians of the City remained the possibility of the internationalization of Jerusalem. They petitioned the late Count Bernadotte on the subject and followed the debates in the United Nations Assembly with eager expectation. But with the waning of their hopes, their attitude towards the new situation became clearer. The State was to be refused recognition *de facto* as well as *de jure*. The State was not to be referred to as the State of Israel but as "the realm of the Sadducees"—a reference to the period of Sadducean predominance during the Second Commonwealth. Israel was a holy name which had been usurped by "transgressors" who were defiling it. Nationalism was "idolatry" and would lead to divine punishment. It was absurd to refer to the rise of this State as "the beginning of the Redemption"—a rabbinic phrase applied by many religious Zionists. The community of Israel had been exiled from the land for three sins: bloodshed, sexual immorality, and idolatry. It was hardly possible to believe that the practice of those very sins could bring about the redemption. On the contrary, "nationalist idolatry" by its aggressive tactics was leading to a dreadful calamity. Israel was alone and unprotected among the nations, "a sheep among seventy wolves." The only guarantee of divine protection was obedience to the Sacred Law. Disobedience could only lead to destruction. Had the Zionists learned nothing from the slaughter of 6 million Jews in Europe, the direct result of a wave of apostasy without parallel in Jewish history? No, the creation of this State was not a miracle but a test.

Fortunately, they argued, the State suffered from lack of money and was dependent on the good will of Jews outside its frontiers. Had it not been for this, the Zionist leaders would have sought to uproot Judaism with all the means at their disposal. As it is, they have to confine themselves to corrupting the youth and undermining their faith, to kidnapping the children of pious parents and cutting off their ear-locks and indoctrinating them in their pernicious doctrines in the haunts of vice, which they call collective settlements; and in this they were being supported by religious men of the Mizrahi and the Agudath Yisrael, who join with them in their government and attend their idolatrous ceremonies such as that accompanying the transfer of the bones of "the false prophet" (Herzl) from Vienna to the holy soil of Jerusalem for its pollution. They were being used by the "wicked" for the purpose of ensnaring innocent minds and leading them away from "the straight path." Pious Jews must stand firm and refuse to acknowledge the State in any form. They must not pay taxes, vote in elections, accept ration books, register for military service, recognize the courts or any branch of the administration and, if they are sent to prison for disobedience, they must gladly accept any sufferings which they may be called upon to endure. They must raise their voice in protest against any defilement of the Holy City even if it means personal ill-treatment. Then, if they withstand the temptation to compromise, the Almighty may relent and bring about the real redemption of Israel.

This theory of the duty to protest unceasingly is based on a talmudic doctrine that a failure to protest is equal to acquiescence in, or even connivance at, a wrong. It has certainly been put into effect. Meetings of protest are held very frequently at which violent harangues are delivered. The anniversary of the foundation of the State, which is celebrated as a day of rejoicing by the Zionists, is observed as a day of fasting and mourning by the Guardians of the City, who take the opportunity to denounce the alleged iniquities of the regime. A few hundred suffer considerable privations as a result of their refusal to acknowledge the existence of rations. Their general poverty reduces their opportunities of buying in the black market. Some have suffered imprisonment. . . .

There are a few indications as to the numbers of the Guardians of the City. In 1945, when they won the elections to the Ashkenazi Council of the City, they polled just over 6,000 votes. As the vote is confined to married males, and families are very large in their circles, this would amount to a total of 24,000 souls for Jerusalem alone, given an average of four members for each family. According to eyewitnesses, their demonstrations attract between two and three thousand men. Their educational institutions are attended by nearly two thousand pupils. In addition, a small proportion of the newcomers from the Yaman and Iraq have joined their ranks. An estimate of 30,000 supporters within the State and of a few thousand contributors to their funds in Europe and America might err on the side of caution. But, as with the Tijanis, their strength is not confined to open sympathizers. There are many religious Jews, who support Zionist parties in elections and yet have a sneaking feeling of sympathy for the Guardians of the City. There is a growing tendency among religious Jews in Israel to feel themselves "a nation within a nation," subject to discrimination in State appointments on account of Sabbath observance and in the distribution of food as a result of their observance of the dietary laws. They have already put forward demands, which have been refused, for distinct religious units in the armed forces. Their schools are under their own control and they strongly oppose attempts to create a unified school system. They marry among themselves and both in work and social intercourse are largely self-contained. This feeling of solidarity must eventually strengthen the hands of the Guardians of the City. . . .

This comparison may serve to stress the fundamental difference between religious nationalists of the Ikhwan al-Muslimun type, and religious anti-nationalists of the Tijani type. The former, in common with other nationalists, regard the prestige of their own particular nation as an end in itself. They are attached to their own religious traditions and would like their national State to be influenced by them. They also feel that the majority of their countrymen, especially in the villages, have a senti-mental prejudice in favour of religious forms and can easily be induced to support politicians who appeal to such feelings. The latter, on the other hand, regard their religion as the main, if not the only, purpose of life. Any attempt to grant the nation a status approaching equality with that of the creed appears to them both blasphemous and idolatrous. They maintain the old view of Oriental pietists that government is a necessary evil, sinful, and imperfect at the best of times, to be avoided when pos-sible and rebuked when necessary. Their hopes are centered on the King-dom of Heaven rather than on the regime under which they are forced to live. In the Middle East where nationalism and Anglophobia are almost inseparable, the difference between these two movements is perhaps best illustrated by their respective positions with regard to Britain. Religious nationalists like other nationalists regard the British with suspicion as greedy imperialists, striving unceasingly to satisfy their appetites for greater power. When help is expected of Britain, flattering references to her sense of justice and fairness appear in the press and political speeches, but the underlying sense of fear and hostility persists, reinforced by re-ligious prejudice. Religious opponents of nationalism, however, have sub-ordinated their suspicions of the infidel without to their struggle against the infidel within. The British appear to them, by way of contrast, to be liberal people with a respect for the beliefs and practices of others and a reluctance to interfere in their religious affairs.

All this is really a much bigger story than that of the Tijaniya or of the Guardians of the City or even of the attempts of traditional Judaism and Islam to recover their lost positions within their own communities. The peoples of the Middle East are troubled by new problems resulting from a combination of interdependent developments, the rise of nationalist movements, the introduction of new technique, means of communication and methods of administration, the spread of monopoly capitalism and the decay of traditional ways of life. They are looking for solutions which provide all the answers to all their questions as to why these things are happening to them and what they must do about them. Those who wish to adopt a positive attitude towards their world are forced to decide be-tween the philosophy of national regeneration, the path of revolutionary Communism, and devotion to the beliefs and practices of their ancestors. This paper has described the struggle of those who have chosen to come to terms with their Creator and, with His help, to attempt the conversion of their fellow-men. A remarkable contrast has emerged from their struggle. On the one hand, Zionists and Arab Nationalists, inspired by roughly the same ideals, are fighting for the same piece of territory but on opposite sides. On the other, Jews and Muslims are waging another war on different sectors of the front against one and the same enemy, the eternal Amalek which they believe to be within us all.

33. The Protestant Churches and Totalitarianism (Germany, 1933-1945)

FRANKLIN H. LITTELL *

IT IS OFTEN ARGUED THAT NATIONALISM IS THE WORKING RELIGION OF MANY CONTEMPORARY PEOPLE, THAT TRADITIONAL RELIGIONS CANNOT RESIST THE INTRUSIONS OF STATES—PARTICULARLY THE TOTALITARIAN STATES—INTO THEIR SPHERES. IN ADDITION TO THE IMPORTANT VALUE QUESTIONS INVOLVED IN THIS PROBLEM, IT IS AN ISSUE OF GREAT SIGNIFICANCE FOR THE SOCIOLOGY OF RELIGION. THE FOLLOWING SELECTION SUGGESTS SOME OF THE VARIABLES INVOLVED IN AFFECTING THE RESPONSE OF A CHURCH TO TOTALITARIANISM AND THEN PROPOSES THE HYPOTHESIS THAT CHURCHES WHICH WERE MOST CONSERVATIVE THEOLOGICALLY WERE THE MOST STAUNCHLY OPPOSED TO HITLER. THE EVIDENCE FAVORS THIS HYPOTHESIS. THERE IS FURTHER NEED, HOWEVER, TO EXPLORE THE CAUSES OF THEIR OPPOSITION AND TO ANALYZE THE TOTAL, LONG-RUN CONSEQUENCES OF CONSERVATIVE THEOLOGY FOR POLITICS. TO DEMONSTRATE THE VIGOR OF A CHURCH'S OPPOSITION TO A TOTALITARIAN GOVERNMENT IS NOT TO PROVE THAT THE CHURCH WAS UNINVOLVED IN THE SOCIAL PROCESSES THAT LED TO THAT GOVERNMENT.

It would be well if, before correspondence and records are scattered and the principals departed from the scene, a team of social and political scientists could make a study of certain basic issues (parallel to the concerns of the Strategic Bombing Survey and the Psychological Warfare units): (1) How did internal structure affect the ability to resist; i.e., did a church with a more democratic pattern (lay officers, decentralization of power toward the local parish) prove better or less able to resist than one highly centralized? (2) At what points did the confessing churches stand for humane and democratic traditions, and where was their resist-

---

* From *Totalitarianism,* Carl J. Friedrich, editor, abridged from pp. 109–116.

ance primarily ecclesiastical? (3) What factors (i.e., traditional relation between altar and throne) weakened and what strengthened the churches' influence as centers of resistance? (4) At what points was the traditional Land Church pattern abandoned (that is, did the Confessing Church become temporarily a "free church") to effect resistance? (5) What part did dogmatic formulation play in capitulation (for instance, the traditional Lutheran position on Romans 13) or resistance (e.g., in the power of the dialectic theology of Karl Barth)? Was this an historical accident, or is there a more general lesson to be learned? (6) To what extent did the witness of the BK martyrs provide a control element and disciplinary function in strengthening general antipathy to the policy of *Reichsbischof* Müller and the *Deutsche Christen?* (Are martyrs "useful"? If so, how and at what point early or late?) (7) What is the significance of the fact that major resistance centered in the old Prussian Union? Is it to be attributed to strong leadership, light ecclesiastical machinery, theological orientation (e.g., Calvinist influence), or is there another factor related to the general "legitimist" resentment against Hitler and his parents? (What is the connection of the resisting Churches with the conservative opposition in the Prussian Army officer caste, etc.?) . . .

The burden of this paper will be to review a matter too little considered outside the theological faculties, yet of basic significance to an understanding of the capacity of religious bodies to resist totalitarianism: *the role of dogmatic formulas in laying the grounds for and developing a disciplined community of opposition.* This field, a happy hunting ground for professional theologians for some years, deserves more serious attention from social and political scientists than it has yet received. The problem may be bluntly introduced by quoting from one of Hitler's most gallant and persistent opponents on the Continent:

"The liberal theology in Germany and in her orbit utterly failed. It was willing to compromise on the essential points of divine law and of 'the law of nature'; to dispose of the Old Testament and to accept the law of the Nordic race instead; and to replace the 'Jewish' law of the Old Testament by the autonomous law of each race and nation respectively. It had made all the necessary preparation for the 'Germanization of Christianity' and for a racial Church." [Quoting Joseph L. Hromodka] . . .

In what respect did the nineteenth-century liberal theology of Schleiermacher, Ritschl, and Harnack fail the church in the middle twentieth century? How were even the exaggerations of the Crisis Theology a source of strength to the centers of resistance? . . . At one time it was hotly debated whether there could be traced through the underbrush a road leading from Luther to Hitler. However this may be, there is a rather plain path through the maze from Schleiermacher to the *Deutsche Christen,* via Ritschl and Harnack. . . .

The resisting church, with the exception of defense of the Jews and protection of defectives (for example, in the epilepsy center at Bethel bei Bielefeld), seems to have taken its stand on ground which was narrowly churchly and theological rather than general and humane. This seems to be true, although very early in 1933 Church leaders issued warnings against idolatry of the state, against the new political *Schwärmerei,* and proclaimed that a just state needs and requires the corrective critique of the true church. The first open resistance, led by Professor Karl Barth at the University of Bonn and Pastor Martin Niemöller at Barmen Synod (May 28, 1934), was at any level far in advance of the educated conscience in England and America. With firm grounding in the Bible and the theology of the Reformers, a stand was taken at Barmen, Dahlem, Steglitz, Augsburg, and succeeding synods, against anti-Semitism, against forced introduction of the Führerprinzip into the Church, against illegal imprisonments and the subversion of an objective justice, against abuse of minority peoples, against the "new revelation" claimed to be embodied in the Third Reich; later actions dealt with sterilization and murder of defectives, refusal to pray for a Hitler victory, and so forth. Within the ramparts of this theological fortress young men were educated for the ministry in bootleg seminaries, pastors expelled by the Nazis were supported by free collections, and a leadership of integrity maintained to take control of the church organizations after the collapse by a group which could only testify by the boldness of hope in 1935: *"We will not abandon this our Church and become a 'free church'; we are the church."*

Religion and Social Change

Several of the questions which we have discussed in Chapters 10 and 11 are explored in the readings found in this section. The papers by Parsons and by Vogt and O'Dea are concerned with the degree to which religious values influence social action. In his study of "Messiahs," Wallis examines not only the socio-cultural settings in which the messianic idea develops, but also the influences on the prophets who proclaimed this idea. His book in part, therefore, is a study of religious leadership. The dilemma of religious leaders is sharply revealed in Burchard's study of military chaplains. By their explicit connection with both the armed forces and the church, they experience in heightened form the pull of diverse forces which affect—whether or not they are consiously recognized—the lives of most religious leaders. The two final papers discuss some of the value questions that were examined briefly at the end of Chapter 11: What are the consequences of the sociological study of religion? What kind of religion best expresses the needs of contemporary men? The present writer does not agree with all the values expressed in these selections, but he believes that the questions which they raise are of great importance and is eager to support their further exploration.

34. Religion as a Source of Creative Innovation

TALCOTT PARSONS *

PARSONS DESCRIBES THE WAY IN WHICH A MAJOR RELIGION SETS THE TONE
OF A CIVILIZATION IN IMPORTANT WAYS. THIS POINT IS LEAST LIKELY TO BE
MISUNDERSTOOD, AS HE RECOGNIZES, IF ONE ALSO STUDIES THE CONDITIONS WHICH
ENCOURAGED THE APPEARANCE OF A RELIGION WITH A PARTICULAR EMPHASIS
AND THE CONDITIONS WHICH SELECT A GIVEN THEME FROM THE SEVERAL THAT
ARE FOUND IN A COMPLEX RELIGION.

In most "primitive" societies, and in highly stabilized and traditionalized
higher cultures, religion tends to be mainly a conservative force; it is as
it were the balance wheel of the society which prevents it from departing
from the established ways. So much is this the case that it is highly probable, for instance, that as Max Weber put forward cogently, the fact that
a traditional priestly class did not have great social power in classical
Greece was an essential condition of the great cultural creativity of the
Greeks. Conversely the social ascendancy of the Brahman priestly caste
in India is inseparable from the fact that Indian caste society is perhaps
the most conservative large scale society the world has even seen.

But this relationship by no means holds without exception. The very
fact of the association of religion with the areas of strain and tension in
human life on the deepest emotional levels means that it is likely to be one
of the main areas in which responses to such situations are creative rather
than traditional. But for the same reasons this creativeness is very likely
to be inextricably intermingled with turmoil and many of the types of
"irrational" reaction of which we have spoken above. Furthermore the
most creative periods of religious development tend also to be times of
social turmoil rather than settled peace.

It is a remarkable fact that roughly the same period saw the development of Confucianism in China, of philosophical Brahmanism and the beginnings of Buddhism in India, and the prophetic movement in Judea, to
say nothing of the beginnings of the great development of the classical
culture in Greece of the seventh and sixth centuries B.C. which certainly

* From *Religious Perspectives of College Teaching in Sociology and Social Psychology*, pp. 29–34.

had a most important religious component as well as later religious consequences. In each of these countries, furthermore, it was a period of rapid social change and considerable unsettlement. The warring feudal principalities of China were beginning the process by which eventually a great unified empire arose. India likewise was involved in many internal conflicts, in the difficult relations between the Aryans and the indigenous populations, in feudal wars, and in rivalry for social supremacy between the Brahmans and the Kshatriyas. In Judea the Israelitic Kingdom had already seen its heyday and was gravely threatened by the rising power of Mesopotamia while, finally, in Greece the little city states were maintaining a precarious existence in relation both to each other and to the terrifying power of Persia to the east. It was an age of turmoil in some respects comparable to our own across the whole civilized world.

It was in this age that, largely from religious sources, the great cultural systems of values which have guided civilization ever since took their shape. Confucianism, Hinduism and Buddhism have provided the main frameworks of the way of life of the great civilizations of the Orient, with the one major exception of Islam, which came later but was in many ways intimately related to Prophetic Judaism. The Hebrew Prophets were the authors of the world's first universalistic ethical monotheism who dared to say contrary to *all* previous religious tradition that all mankind is subject to the will of a single God and that their history has meaning in terms of His great plan for the development of the world He created. Greek society created the analytical and speculative intellect of Western civilization. Christianity came some centuries later, but in many respects may be treated as a great synthesis of the Hebrew and the Greek traditions. Without the background of Prophetic Judaism there would have been no universalistic ethical monotheism. But without Greek philosophy there almost certainly would have been no rational theology in the Christian sense. Indeed some of the most distinctive features of our Western culture undoubtedly stem from these sources.

Christianity itself arose in a similar situation in which society and human values were in flux. The Jewish people were undergoing, after many experiences in foreign rule, the difficult adjustment of absorption in the Roman Empire. That the adjustment was not easy is attested by the outbreak of the Jewish wars only a generation after the crucifixion of Jesus. The prevention of the absorption of the Christian movement in the community of the Jewish people, which was only settled by St. Paul, was one of the most decisive events of the history of civilization. But this could hardly have happened without the peculiar character of Roman imperial society with its extraordinary range of individualism and tolerance.

It was thus the great religious movements of the creative age of the seventh to fifth centuries B.C. which laid the foundation for the fundamental differentiations of the great civilizations for the next two thousand years, as Max Weber so clearly demonstrated in his remarkable comparative studies in the sociology of religion. Without taking the space to delineate the features of Confucianism, Hinduism and Buddhism which differentiate them and the civilizations they have influenced from Christianity and the West, perhaps a few of the distinctive features of the latter may be noted.

The pre-eminent place should, in these terms, undoubtedly go to two fundamental patterns which run through the whole history of Christianity, namely what may be called "universalism" and "activism." Both are deeply involved in the special way in which Christianity conceived the transcendental character of its God, as Creator and Ruler of the world, standing outside and above it, not as an immanent principle of order in the universe, a conception which, with variations, underlies all the great oriental religions.

Activism means essentially that man's goals and values are conceived not primarily as concerned with adaptation to or escape from a given set of physical and social conditions, but with mastery over them. The prototype of the first attitude is found in Confucianism, with its orientation of the organization of a stable social order, sanctioned by a completely stable religion; that of the second is the great mystical religious orientation, the mystical absorption in "nature" of the Taoist, the escape from the Wheel of Karma of the Hindu mystic, or the Nirvana of the Buddhist.

In Christianity, on the other hand, the keynote through all its various forms is doing the will of God in spite of the obstacles presented in the situation, by *overcoming* the obstacles. This may mean, as in early Christian asceticism and of course later, mastery over the flesh without further reference to life on this earth. But this drastic individualism soon gave way to the conception of a more extensive Christian ideal. The mediaeval conception still retained the view that the Christian society existed to prepare souls for the after life; but with what Weber called the "ascetic" branches of Protestantism, notably Calvinism and its derivatives, there emerged the direct conception of the Kingdom of God on Earth, which it was the duty of man to create by Divine ordinance. This whole idea of mastery, then, has oriented man to the control of the world in which he lives as distinct from a fatalistic "acceptance" of things as they are. Such acceptance has of course appeared from time to time in Christian societies and groups, but has never been the dominant keynote to anything like the extent it has been in the Orient. Furthermore, though we have undergone a high degree of secularization, even our secularism is active rather than passive. It is not "floating along on the stream of life," but is an attempt to make over the world by active intervention, in the service of human goals, it is an attempt to create the "good society."

Universalism, as the second dominant strain, is closely connected with activism. Its roots lie in the conception of the universal and only true God of the Prophets and the intelligible world as conceived by the Greek intellect. Neither ideas nor morality can be relative to the particular time and place and social group. There must be universal truths, which are as true for the "heathen Chinee" as they are for any Christian group. And the moral good cannot be defined in terms only of what is good for others, as distinguished from good for me, but the same principles must apply impartially to all men, with allowance for difference of circumstance of course, but nevertheless in principle to all. The enormous significance of this universalistic strain in Western civilization is one of the principal themes of the modern social sciences. And there can be little doubt that without Christianity it could scarcely have developed.

Three fields of application of these two major strains of the Christian tradition may be mentioned. First is the very notable fact that, in spite of the prominence of the "warfare of science and religion," it is only in the Western world that science itself has developed to a really high degree. Beginnings there are elsewhere, but in no case, except for a few specialties, beyond the level attained by the classical Greeks. Many Christians certainly have grave misgivings about where the development of science is leading us. But science is most assuredly a fully legitimate child of Christianity (which, however, is only *one* of its "parents"). It is the *active* and not merely the receptive search for truth. Nature is not merely observed, it is *investigated,* nature is "forced to give up her secrets," not merely contemplated. Man, precisely because he is conceived to be made "in the image of God" is endowed with reason which he is meant to use actively to understand. In Puritanism this strain reached a high culmination in giving direct religious sanction to the great development of physical science of the 17th century. The key-note was that the scientist could come to know God through His Works.[1] The place of universalism in science is too fundamental and obvious to need special comment.

A second fundamental direction of Christian influence is in the field of the universalism of law. This of course was foreshadowed by the great development of Roman law, in part a child of Greek thought, notably that of the Stoics. But after the decline of Rome law in the Western World

---

[1] Cf. R. K. Merton, *Science and Society in 17th Century England.*

had sunk to the level of a completely tribal pluralism; there was one law for Goth and another for Frank and so on. It is no matter of chance that it was in the Canon Law of the Church that Roman Law was preserved, and that the great development of mediaeval civilization as a whole soon came to include the revival of Roman Civil Law and the gradual creation of universalistic systems of law. Had a particularistic rather than a universalistic religion dominated Mediaeval Europe there is little doubt that Roman Law would never have been revived and English Common Law never created.

Finally, we are all aware that there is a fundamental strain of universalistic individualism in Christianity. Each human being has an immortal soul, all of the same religious worth. Though many branches of Christianity have made drastic concessions to social inequality reaching far beyond the minimum needs of a functioning society, generally on the plea that equality applied only to the spiritual realm, there is little doubt of the fundamental character of the contribution of Christianity to the egalitarian strain of modern Western civilization; the most dramatic contrast of course is the religious sanction of caste in Hinduism, the most radical conception of human inequality to be found anywhere. The relation to the conception of the dignity of the human individual, and his right to a fair chance to make his contribution to the life of society and to live his own life independently, is patent.

It should not be assumed that the above argument about the very great influence of religious traditions constitutes a theory of "religious determinism" set over against some version of "economic determinism." There seems to us to be no justification for any simple "single dominant factor" theory of social change. The religious movements we have spoken of were not "immaculately conceived" without roots in all the complex social and psychological forces which influence human action. *Of course* the emergence of Christianity was *in part* economically determined; for example, it is well known that most of its early adherents were the "little men" of the urban communities. That it appealed neither to the rural populations (the "pagans") nor to the upper classes, is partly a function of the economic interests of those groups. It was also dependent for peace and order, and for its opportunity to spread on the political and legal structure of the Roman Empire which was in no sense predominantly a "religious factor." But demonstration of the importance of these things in no way refutes the claim of the importance of creative innovation in the sphere of religious orientation itself. Economic and other "conditions" limit the incidence of a religious movement, for example, they favor or hinder it, but that is a very different matter from "creating" it. Similarly in the course of its very complex history the various developments within Christianity have been intimately dependent on non-religious features of the situation of the time. It seems to be well attested that Luther's success could not have occurred without support from the secular interests of the German Princes on whom he relied. And could the branches of Protestantism which have flourished in America have had their enormous influence if the little colonies had not had a continent over which to spread? Suppose the French had wrested the control of the seas from Britain a hundred and fifty years ago? With North America under French control from the Alleghanies west, what would the religious complexion of this continent have been? A glance at the Province of Quebec is of some significance to the answer.

35. A Comparative Study of the Role of Values in Social Action in Two Southwestern Communities
EVON Z. VOGT AND THOMAS F. O'DEA *

ONE MIGHT LOOK UPON THIS STUDY AS A SPECIFIC TEST, ON THE COMMUNITY LEVEL, OF THE QUESTION RAISED BY PARSONS IN THE PRECEDING SELECTION: HOW DOES THE RANGE OF VALUES ASSOCIATED WITH A RELIGIOUS COMPLEX AFFECT THE STYLE OF LIFE, THE DECISIONS, THE GOALS OF ITS ADHERENTS? VOGT AND O'DEA DISCOVERED THAT MORMONISM AND WHAT MIGHT BE CALLED A GENERAL PROTESTANT ORIENTATION INFLUENCED THE DEVELOPMENT OF "TWO QUITE DIFFERENT COMMUNITY TYPES."

It is one of the central hypotheses of the Values Study Project † that value-orientations play an important part in the shaping of social institutions and in influencing the forms of observed social action. By value-orientations are understood those views of the world, often implicitly held, which define the meaning of human life or the "life situation of man" and

* From American Sociological Review, December, 1953, pp. 645–654.

† The authors are indebted to the Rockefeller Foundation (Social Science Division) for the financial support of the research reported in this paper as part of the Comparative Study of Values in Five Cultures Project of the Laboratory of Social Relations at Harvard University. We also wish to express our appreciation to Ethel M. Albert, Wilfrid C. Bailey, Clyde Kluckhohn, Anne Parsons, and John M. Roberts for criticisms and suggestions in the preparation of the paper.

thereby provide the context in which day-to-day problems are solved.[1] The present article is an outgrowth of one phase of the field research carried out in western New Mexico. It presents the record of two communities composed of people with a similar cultural background and living in the same general ecological setting.

The responses of these two communities to similar problems were found to be quite different. Since the physical setting of the two villages is remarkably similar, the explanation for the differences was sought in the manner in which each group viewed the situation and the kind of social relationships and legitimate expectations which each felt appropriate in meeting situational challenges. In this sphere of value-orientations a marked difference was found. Moreover, the differences in response to situation in the two cases were found to be related to the differences between the value-orientations central to these communities.

We do not deny the importance of situational factors. Nor do we intend to disparage the importance of historical convergence of value-orientations with concrete situations in explaining the centrality of some values as against others and in leading to the deep internalization of the values we discuss. But the importance of value-orientations as an element in understanding the situation of action is inescapably clear. All the elements of what Parsons has called the action frame of reference —the actors, the means and conditions which comprise the situation, and the value-orientations of the actors enter into the act.[2] The primacy of any one in any individual case does not permit generalization. Yet the present study testifies to the great importance of the third element—the value-orientations—in shaping the final action which ensues.

FOCUS OF THE INQUIRY

The inquiry is focused upon a comparison of the Mormon community of *Rimrock* [3] with the Texan community of *Homestead,* both having populations of approximately 250 and both located (forty miles apart) on the southern portion of the Colorado Plateau in western New Mexico. The natural environmental setting is virtually the same for the two villages:

[1] Clyde Kluckhohn, "Values and Value-Orientations in the Theory of Action: an Exploration in Definition and Classification," *Toward a General Theory of Action,* edited by Talcott Parsons and E. A. Shils, Cambridge: Harvard University Press, 1951, p. 410.

[2] Talcott Parsons, *The Structure of Social Action,* Glencoe: Free Press, 1949, pp. 43–86; *Essays in Sociological Theory,* Glencoe: Free Press, 1949, pp. 32–40; *The Social System,* Glencoe: Free Press, 1951, pp. 3–24.

[3] "Rimrock" and "Homestead" are pseudonyms used to protect the anonymity of our informants.

the prevailing elevations stand at 7,000 feet; the landscapes are character-ized by mesa and canyon country; the flora and fauna are typical of the Upper Sonoran Life Zone with stands of pinyon, juniper, sagebrush, and blue gramma grass and some intrusions of Ponderosa pine, Douglas fir, Englemann spruce and Gambel oak from a higher life zone; the region has a steppe climate with an average annual precipitation of 14 inches (which varies greatly from year to year) and with killing frosts occurring late in the spring and early in the autumn.[4] The single important environ-mental difference between the two communities is that Rimrock is located near the base of a mountain range which has elevations rising to 9,000 feet, and a storage reservoir (fed by melting snow packs from these higher elevations) has made irrigation agriculture possible in Rimrock, while in Homestead there is only dry-land farming. Today both villages have subsistence patterns based upon combinations of farming (mainly irrigated crops of alfalfa and wheat in Rimrock, and dry-land crops of pinto beans in Homestead) and livestock raising (mainly Hereford beef cattle in both villages).

Rimrock was settled by Mormon missionaries in the 1870's as part of a larger project to plant settlements in the area of northern Arizona. Rim-rock itself, unlike the Arizona sites, was established as a missionary out-post and the intention of the settlers was the conversion of the Indians, a task conceived in terms of the *Book of Mormon*, which defines the Ameri-can Indian as "a remnant of Israel."

The early settlers were "called" by the Church, that is, they were selected and sent out by the Church authorities. The early years were exceedingly difficult and only the discipline of the Church and the loyalty of the settlers to its gospel kept them at the task. Drought, crop diseases, and the breaking of the earth and rock dam which they had constructed for the storage of irrigation water added to their difficulties, as did the fact that they had merely squatted on the land and were forced to pur-chase it at an exorbitant price to avoid eviction. The purchase money was given by the Church authorities in Salt Lake City, who also supplied 5,000 pounds of seed wheat in another period of dearth. The original settlers were largely from northern Utah although there were also some converts from the southern states who had been involved in unsuccessful Arizona settlements a few years earlier.

As the emphasis shifted from missionary activities to farming, Rimrock

[4] For additional ecological details on the region see Evon Z. Vogt, *Navaho Veterans: A Study of Changing Values*, Peabody Museum of Harvard University, Papers, Vol. XLI, No. 1, 1951, pp. 11–12; and John Landgraf, *Land-Use in the Rimrock Area of New Mexico: An Anthropological Approach to Areal Study*, Peabody Museum of Harvard University, Papers, forthcoming, 1953.

developed into a not unusual Mormon village, despite its peripheral position to the rest of Mormondom. Irrigation farming was supplemented by cattle raising on the open range. In the early 1930's the Mormons began to buy range land, and Rimrock's economy shifted to a focus upon cattle raising. Today villagers own a total of 149 sections of range land and about four sections of irrigated or irrigable land devoted to gardens and some irrigated pastures in the immediate vicinity of the village. The family farm is still the basic economic unit, although partnerships formed upon a kinship basis and devoted to cattle raising have been important in raising the economic level of the village as a whole. In recent years some of the villagers—also on the basis of a kinship partnership—purchased the local trading post which is engaged in trading with the Indians as well as local village business. In addition to 12 family partnerships which own 111 sections of land, there is a village cooperative which owns 38 sections. Privately-owned commercial facilities in the village include two stores, a boarding house, two garages, a saddle and leather shop, and a small restaurant. With this economic variety there is considerable difference in the distribution of wealth.

The Church is the central core of the village and its complex hierarchical structure, including the auxiliary organizations which activate women, youth, and young children, involves a large portion of the villagers in active participation. The church structure is backed up and impenetrated by the kinship structure. Moreover, church organization and kinship not only unify Rimrock into a social unit, they also integrate it into the larger structure of the Mormon Church and relate it by affinity and consanguinity to the rest of Mormondom.

Rimrock has been less affected by secularization than most Mormon villages in Utah and is less assimilated into generalized American patterns.[5] Its relative isolation has both kept such pressures from impinging upon it with full force and enhanced its formal and informal ties with the Church, preserving many of the characteristics of a Mormon village of a generation ago.

Homestead was settled by migrants from the South Plains area of western Texas and Oklahoma in the early 1930's. The migration represented a small aspect of that vast movement of people westward to California which was popularized in Steinbeck's *Grapes of Wrath* and which was the subject of investigation by many governmental agencies in the 1930's and 1940's.[6] Instead of going on to California, these homesteaders settled

[5] Lowry Nelson, *The Mormon Village*. Salt Lake City: University of Utah Press, 1952, pp. 275–85.

[6] See especially the reports of the Tolan Committee, U. S. Congress, "House Committee to Investigate the Interstate Migration of Destitute Citizens," 76th Congress, 3rd Session, Volume 6, Part 6, 1940.

in a number of semi-arid farming areas in northern and western New Mexico and proceeded to develop an economy centered around the production of pinto beans. The migration coincided with the period of national depression and was due in part to severe economic conditions on the South Plains which forced families to leave their Texas and Oklahoma communities, in part to the attraction of land available for homesteading which held out the promise of family-owned farms for families who had previously owned little or no land or who had lost their land during the depression. The land base controlled by the homesteaders comprises approximately 100 sections. Each farm unit is operated by a nuclear family; there are no partnerships. Farms now average two sections in size and are scattered as far as twenty miles from the crossroads center of the community which contains the two stores, the school, the post office, two garages, a filling station, a small restaurant, a bean warehouse, a small bar, and two church buildings. Through the years, farming technology has shifted almost completely from horse-drawn implements to mechanized equipment.

With the hazardous farming conditions (periodic droughts and early killing frosts) out-migration from Homestead has been relatively high. A few of these families have gone on to California, but more of them have moved to irrigated farms in the middle Rio Grande Valley and entered an agricultural situation which in its physical environmental aspects is similar to the situation in the Mormon community of Rimrock.

THE MORMON CASE

In broad perspective these two villages present local variations of generalized American culture. They share the common American value-orientations which emphasize the importance of achievement and success, progress and optimism, and rational mastery over nature. In the Mormon case, these were taken over from the 19th century American milieu in western New York where the Church was founded, and reinterpreted in terms of an elaborate theological conception of the universe as a dynamic process in which God and men are active collaborators in an eternal progression to greater power through increasing mastery.[7] The present life was and is conceived as a single episode in an infinity of work and mastery. The result was the heightening for the Mormons of convictions shared with most other Americans. Moreover, this conception was closely

[7] The data from Rimrock are based upon seven months field experience in the community during 1950–51. Additional data on this community will be provided in O'Dea's forthcoming monograph on *Mormon Values: The Significance of a Religious Outlook for Social Action.*

related to the belief in the reopening of divine revelation through the agency first of Joseph Smith, the original Mormon prophet, and later through the institutionalized channels of the Mormon Church. The Mormons conceived of themselves as a covenant people especially chosen for a divine task. This task was the building of the kingdom of God on earth and in this project—attempted four times unsuccessfully before the eventual migration to the west—much of the religious and secular socialism of the early 19th century found a profound reflection. The Mormon prophet proposed the "Law of Consecration" in an attempt to reconcile private initiative with cooperative endeavor. Contention led to its abandonment in 1838 after some five years of unsuccessful experiment. Yet this withdrawal did not limit, but indeed rather enhanced, its future influence in Mormon settlement. The "Law of Consecration" was no longer interpreted as a blueprint prescribing social institutions of a definite sort, but its values lent a strong cooperative bias to much of later Mormon activity.[8] In the context of the notion of peculiarity and reinforced by outgroup antagonism and persecution, these values became deeply embedded in Mormon orientations. The preference for agriculture combined with an emphasis upon community and lay participation in church activities resulted in the formation of compact villages rather than isolated family farmsteads as the typical Mormon settlement pattern.[9]

While Rimrock and Homestead share most of the central value-orientations of general American culture, they differ significantly in the values governing social relationships. Rimrock, with a stress upon community cooperation, an ethnocentrism resulting from the notion of their own peculiarity, and a village pattern of settlement, is more like the other Mormon villages of the West than it is like Homestead.

The stress upon *community cooperation* in Rimrock contrasts markedly with the stress upon *individual independence* found in Homestead. This contrast is one of emphasis, for individual initiative is important in Rimrock, especially in family farming and cattle raising, whereas cooperative activity does occur in Homestead. In Rimrock, however, the expectations are such that one must show his fellows or at least convince himself that he has good cause for *not* committing his time and resources to community efforts while in Homestead cooperative action takes place *only* after certainty has been reached that the claims of other individuals upon one's time and resources are legitimate.

    [8] The "Law of Consecration" became the basis of the Mormon pattern of cooperative activity also known as "The United Order of Enoch." Cf. Joseph A. Geddes, *The United Order Among the Mormons*, Salt Lake City: Deseret News Press, 1924; Edward J. Allen, *The Second United Order Among the Mormons*, New York: Columbia University Press, 1936.
    [9] Nelson, *op. cit.*, pp. 25–54.

Rimrock was a cooperative venture from the start, and very early the irrigation company, a mutual non-profit corporation chartered under state law, emerged from the early water association informally developed around—and in a sense within—the Church. In all situations which transcend the capacities of individual families or family combinations, Rimrock Mormons have recourse to cooperative techniques. Let us examine four examples.

The "tight" land situation. Rimrock Mormons, feeling themselves "gathered," dislike having to migrate to non-Mormon areas. However, after World War II the 32 returned veterans faced a choice between poverty and under-employment or leaving the community. This situation became the concern of the Church and was discussed in its upper lay priesthood bodies in the village. It was decided to buy land to enable the veterans to remain. The possibilities of land purchase in the area were almost nonexistent and it appeared that nothing could be done, when unexpectedly the opportunity to buy some 38 sections presented itself. At the time, the village did not have the needed 10,000 dollars for the down payment, so the sum was borrowed from the Cooperative Security Corporation, a Church Welfare Plan agency, and the land was purchased. The patterns revealed here—community concern over a community problem, and appeal to and reception of aid from the general authorities of the Church—are typically Mormon. However, Mormon cooperation did not end here. Instead of breaking up the purchased land into plots to be individually owned and farmed, the parcel was kept as a unit, and a cooperative Rimrock Land and Cattle Company was formed. The company copied and adapted the form of the mutual irrigation company. Shares were sold in the village, each member being limited to two. A quota of cattle per share per year to be run on the land and a quota of bulls relative to cows were established. The cattle are privately owned, but the land is owned and managed cooperatively. The calves are the property of the owners of the cows. The project, which has not been limited to veterans, supplements other earnings sufficiently to keep most of the veterans in the village.

The graveling of the village streets. The streets of Rimrock were in bad repair in the fall of 1950. That summer a construction company had brought much large equipment into the area to build and gravel a section of a state highway which runs through the village. Before this company left, taking its equipment with it, villagers, again acting through the Church organization, decided that the village should avail itself of the opportunity and have the town's streets graveled. This was discussed in the Sunday priesthood meeting and announced at the Sunday sacrament meeting. A meeting was called for Monday evening, and each household was asked to send a representative. The meeting was well attended, and although not every family had a member present, practically all were represented at least by proxy. There was considerable discussion, and it was finally decided to pay 800 dollars for the job which meant a 20 dollar donation from each family. The local trader paid a larger amount, and, within a few days after the meeting, the total amount was collected. Only one villager raised objections to the proceedings. Although he was a man of importance locally, he was soon silenced by a much poorer man who invoked Mormon values of progress and cooperation and pledged to give 25 dollars which was 5 dollars above the norm.

The construction of a high school gymnasium. In 1951 a plan for the construction of a high school gymnasium was presented to the Rimrock villagers. Funds for materials and for certain skilled labor would be provided from state school appropriations, providing that the local residents would contribute the labor for construction. The plan was discussed in a Sunday priesthood meeting in the church, and later meetings were held both in the church and in the schoolhouse. Under the leadership of the principal of the school (who is also a member of the higher priesthood), arrangements were made whereby each able-bodied man in the community would either contribute at least 50 hours of labor or 50 dollars (the latter to be used to hire outside laborers) toward the construction. The original blueprint was extended to include a row of classrooms for the high school around the large central gymnasium.

Work on the new building began in late 1951, continued through 1952, and is now (in 1953) nearing completion. The enterprise was not carried through without difficulties. A few families were sympathetic at first but failed to contribute full amounts of either labor or cash, and some were unsympathetic toward the operation from the start. The high school principal had to keep reminding the villagers about their pledges to support the enterprise. But in the end the project was successful, and it represented an important cooperative effort on the part of the majority.

The community dances. The Mormons have always considered dancing to be an important form of recreation—in fact a particularly Mormon form of recreation. Almost every Friday evening a dance is held in the village church house. These dances are family affairs and are opened and closed with prayer. They are part of the general Church recreation program and are paid for by what is called locally "the budget." The budget refers to the plan under which villagers pay 15 dollars per family per year to cover a large number of entertainments, all sponsored by the Church auxiliary organization for youth, the Young Men's Mutual Improvement Association, and the Young Women's Mutual Improvement Association. The budget payment admits all members of the family to such entertainments.

Observation of these dances over a six months period did not reveal any tension or fighting. Smoking and drinking are forbidden to loyal Mormons, and those who smoked did so outside and away from the building. At dances held in the local school there has been evidence of drinking, and at times fighting has resulted from the presence of non-villagers. But on the whole the Rimrock dances are peaceful family affairs.

Rimrock reveals itself responding to group problems *as a group*. The economic ethic set forth by Joseph Smith in the Law of Consecration is seen in the dual commitment to private individual initiative (family farms and family partnerships in business and agriculture) and to cooperative endeavor in larger communal problems (irrigation company, land and cattle company, graveling the streets, and construction of school gymnasium). For the Mormons, cooperation has become second nature. It has become part of the institutionalized structure of expectations, reinforced by religious conviction and social control.

THE HOMESTEADER CASE

The value-stress upon individual independence of action has deep roots in the history of the homesteader group.[10] The homesteaders were part of the westward migration from the hill country of the Southern Appalachians to the Panhandle country of Texas and Oklahoma and from there to the Southwest and California. Throughout their historical experience there has been an emphasis upon a rough and ready self-reliance and individualism, the Jacksonianism of the frontier West. The move to western New Mexico from the South Plains was made predominately by isolated nuclear families, and Homestead became a community of scattered, individually-owned farmsteads—a geographical situation and a settlement pattern which reinforced the stress upon individualism.

Let us now examine the influence of this individualistic value-orientation upon a series of situations comparable to those that were described for Rimrock.

The "tight" land situation. In 1934 the Federal Security Administration, working in conjunction with the Land Use Division of the Department of Agriculture, proposed a "unit re-organization plan." This plan would have enabled the homesteaders to acquire additional tracts of land and

---

[10] The data from Homestead are based upon a year's field work in the community during 1949–50. Additional data on this community will be provided in Vogt's forthcoming monograph on *The Homesteaders: A Study of Values in a Frontier Community*. See also Vogt, "Water Witching: An Interpretation of a Ritual Pattern in a Rural American Community," *Scientific Monthly*, LXXV (September, 1952).

permit them to run more livestock and hence depend less upon the more hazardous economic pursuit of dry-land pinto bean farming. It called for the use of government funds to purchase large ranches near the Homestead area which would be managed cooperatively by a board of directors selected by the community. The scheme collapsed while it was still in the planning stages, because it was clear that each family expected to acquire its own private holdings on the range and that a cooperative would not work in Homestead.

The graveling of the village streets. During the winter of 1949–50 the construction company which was building the highway through Rimrock was also building a small section of highway north of Homestead. The construction company offered to gravel the streets of Homestead center if the residents who lived in the village would cooperatively contribute enough funds for the purpose. This community plan was rejected by the homesteaders, and an alternative plan was followed. Each of the operators of several of the service institutions—including the two stores, the bar, and the post office—independently hired the construction company truck drivers to haul a few loads of gravel to be placed in front of his own place of business, which still left the rest of the village streets a sea of mud in rainy weather.

The construction of a high school gymnasium. In 1950 the same plan for the construction of a new gymnasium was presented to the homesteaders as was presented to the Mormon village of Rimrock. As noted above, this plan was accepted by the community of Rimrock, and the new building is now nearing completion. But the plan was rejected by the residents of Homestead at a meeting in the summer of 1950, and there were long speeches to the effect that "I've got to look after my own farm and my own family first; I can't be up here in town building a gymnasium." Later in the summer additional funds were provided for labor; and with these funds adobe bricks were made, the foundation was dug, and construction was started—the homesteaders being willing to work on the gymnasium on a purely business basis at a dollar an hour. But as soon as the funds were exhausted, construction stopped. Today a partially completed gymnasium, and stacks of some 10,000 adobe bricks disintegrating slowly with the rains, stand as monuments to the individualism of the homesteaders.

The community dances. As in Rimrock, the village dances in Homestead are important focal points for community activity. These affairs take place several times a year in the schoolhouse and are always well-attended. But while the dances in Rimrock are well-coordinated activities which carry through the evening, the dances in Homestead often end when tensions between rival families result in fist-fights. And there is always the expectation in Homestead that a dance (or other cooperative activity such as a picnic or rodeo) may end at any moment and the level of activity reduced to the component nuclear families which form the only solid core of social organization within the community.

The individualistic value-orientation of the homesteaders also has important functional relationships to the religious organization of the community. With the exception of two men who are professed atheists, all of the homesteaders define themselves as Christians. But denominationalism is rife, there being ten different denominations represented in the village: Baptist, Presbyterian, Methodist, Nazarene, Campbellite, Holiness, 7th Day Adventist, Mormon, Catholic, and Present Day Disciples.

In the most general terms, this religious differentiation in Homestead can be interpreted as a function of the individualistic and factionalizing tendencies in the social system. In a culture with a value-stress upon independent individual action combined with a "freedom of religion" ideology, adhering to one's own denomination becomes an important means of expressing individualism and of focusing factional disputes around a doctrine and a concrete institutional framework. In turn, the doctrinal differences promote additional factionalizing tendencies, with the result that competing churches become the battleground for a cumulative and circularly reinforcing struggle between rival small factions within the community.[11]

To sum up, we may say that the strong commitment to an individualistic value-orientation has resulted in a social system in which inter-personal relations are strongly colored by a kind of factionalism and in which persons and groups become related to one another in a competitive, feuding relationship. The homesteaders do not live on their widely separated farms and ignore one another, as it might be possible to do. On the other hand, they do not cooperate in community affairs as closely as does a hive of bees. They interact, but a constant feuding tone permeates the economic, social and religious structure of the community.

RELATIONSHIP BETWEEN THE TWO COMMUNITIES

Although there is some trading in livestock, feed, and other crops, the most important contacts between the two communities are not economic

---

[11] This relationship between churches and factionalizing tendencies has also been observed by Bailey in his unpublished study of a community in west Texas, in the heart of the ancestral home region of the present residents of Homestead. Cf. Wilfrid C. Bailey, "A Study of a Texas Panhandle Community; A Preliminary Report on Cotton Center, Texas," Values Study Files, Harvard University.

but are social and recreational. The village baseball teams have scheduled games with one another for the past two decades, and there is almost always joint participation in the community dances and in the summer rodeos in the two communities. Despite Mormon objections to close associations with "gentiles," there is also considerable inter-dating between the two communities among the teen-age groups, and three intermarriages have taken place.

In general, the homesteaders envy and admire the Mormons' economic organization, their irrigated land, and more promising prospects for good crops each year. On the other hand, they regard the Mormons as cliquish and unfriendly and fail completely to understand why anyone "wants to live all bunched up the way the Mormons do." They feel that the Mormons are inbred and think they should be glad to get "new blood" from inter-marriages with homesteaders. They add, "That Mormon religion is something we can't understand at all." Finally, the homesteaders say that Mormons "used to have more than one wife, and some probably still do; they dance in the church, they're against liquor, coffee, and tobacco, and they always talk about Joseph Smith and the *Book of Mormon.*"

The Mormons consider their own way of life distinctly superior to that of the homesteaders in every way. Some will admit that the homesteaders have the virtue of being more friendly and of "mixing more with others," and their efforts in the face of farming hazards are admired, but Homestead is generally regarded as a rough and in some ways immoral community, especially because of the drinking, smoking, and fighting (particularly at dances) that takes place. They also feel that Homestead is disorganized and that the churches are not doing what they should for the community. For the past few years they have been making regular missionary trips to Homestead, but to date they have made no conversions.

COMPARISONS AND CONCLUSIONS

In the case of Rimrock and Homestead, we are dealing with two communities which are comparable in population, in ecological setting, and which are variants of the same general culture. The two outstanding differences are: (a) irrigation versus dry-land farming and associated differences in settlement pattern, compact village versus isolated farmstead type; [12] (b) a value stress upon cooperative community action versus a stress upon individual action. The important question here involves the relationship (if any) between these two sets of variables. Is the coopera-

[12] Cf. Nelson, *op. cit.,* p. 4.

tion in Rimrock directly a function of an irrigation agriculture situation with a compact village settlement pattern, the rugged individualism in Homestead, a function of a dry-land farming situation with a scattered settlement pattern? Or did these value-orientations arise out of earlier historical experience in each case, influence the types of communities which were established in western New Mexico, and later persist in the face of changed economic situations? We shall attempt to demonstrate that the second proposition is more in accord with the historical facts as we now know them.

Nelson has recently shown that the general pattern of the Mormon village is neither a direct function (in its beginnings) of the requirements of irrigation agriculture, nor of the need for protection against Indians on the frontier. Rather, the basic pattern was a social invention of the Mormons, motivated by a sense of urgent need to prepare a dwelling place for the "Savior" at "His Second Coming." The "Plat of the City of Zion" was invented by Joseph Smith, Sidney Rigdon, and Frederick G. Williams in 1833 and has formed the basis for the laying out of most Mormon villages, even those established in the Middle West before the Mormons migrated to Utah.[13]

It is very clear that both the compact village pattern and the cooperative social arrangements centered around the church existed before the Mormons engaged in irrigation agriculture and had a strong influence upon the development of community structure not only in Utah but in the Mormon settlements like Rimrock on the periphery of the Mormon culture area. There is no objective reason in the Rimrock ecological and cultural setting (the local Navahos and Zunis did not pose a threat to pioneer settlements in the 1880's) why the Mormons could not have set up a community which conformed more to the isolated farmstead type with a greater stress upon individualistic social relations. Once the Mormon community was established, it is clear that the cooperation required by irrigation agriculture of the Mormon type and the general organization of the church strongly reinforced the value stress upon communal social action.

It is of further significance that as the population expanded and the Rimrock Mormons shifted from irrigation agricultural pursuits to dry-land ranching in the region outside of the Rimrock valley, the earlier cooperative patterns modeled on the mutual irrigation company were applied to the solution of economic problems that are identical to those faced by the homesteaders. Moreover, in midwestern and eastern cities to which Mormons have recently moved, church wards have purchased and cooperatively worked church welfare plan farms.

[13] Nelson, *op. cit.*, pp. 28–38.

In Homestead, on the other hand, our evidence indicates that the first settlers were drawn from a westward-moving population which stressed a frontier-type of self-reliance and individualism. They were searching for a place where each man could "own his own farm and be his own boss." Each family settled on its isolated homestead claim, and there emerged from the beginning an isolated farmstead type of settlement pattern in which the nuclear family was the solidary unit. The service center which was built up later simply occupied lots that were sold to storekeepers, filling station operators, the bartender, and others, by the four families who owned the four sections which joined at a crossroads. Only two of these four family homes were located near the service center at the crossroads. The other two families continued to maintain their homes in other quarters of their sections and lived almost a mile from "town." In 1952 one of the former families built a new home located over a mile from the center of town, and commented that they had always looked forward to "getting out of town."

There is no objective reason in the Homestead ecological setting why there could not be more clustering of houses into a compact village and more community cooperation than actually exists. One would not expect those farmers whose farms are located 15 or 20 miles from the service center to live in "town" and travel out to work each day. But there is no reason why those families living within 2 or 3 miles of the village center could not live in town and work their fields from there. In typical Mormon villages a large percentage of the farms are located more than three miles from the farm homes. For example, in Rimrock over 31 per cent, in Escalante over 38 per cent, and in Ephriam over 30 per cent of the farms are located from three to eight or more miles from the center of the villages.[14]

It is clear that the homesteaders were operating with a set of individualistic property arrangements (drawn, of course, from our generalized American culture) and that their strong stress upon individualism led to a quite different utilization of these property patterns (than was the case with the Mormons) and to establishment of a highly scattered type of community. Once Homestead was established, the individualism permitted by the scattered dry-land farming pattern, and encouraged by the emphasis upon the small nuclear family unit and upon multi-denominationalism in church affiliation reacted on and strongly reinforced the value stress upon individual independence. It is evident that the homesteaders continue to prefer this way of life, as shown by their remarks concerning

[14] See Nelson, *op. cit.*, pp. 99 and 144 for data on Escalante and Ephriam.

the "bunched up" character of a Mormon village and the fact that a number of families have recently moved "out of town" when they built new houses.

Of further interest is the fact that when homesteader families move to irrigated farms in the middle Rio Grande Valley, the stress upon individual action tends to persist strongly. They do not readily develop cooperative patterns to deal with this new setting which is similar to the situation in the irrigated valley of the Mormons at Rimrock. Indeed, one of the principal innovations they have been promoting in one region along the Rio Grande where they are replacing Spanish-Americans on the irrigated farming land is a system of meters on irrigation ditches. These meters will measure the water flowing into each individual farmer's ditches, and effectively eliminate the need for more highly organized cooperative arrangements for distributing the available supply of water.

In conclusion, we should like to reiterate that we are strongly cognizant of situational factors. If the Rimrock Mormons had not been able to settle in a valley which was watered by melting snow packs from a nearby mountain and which provided the possibilities for the construction of storage reservoir, they certainly could not have developed an irrigation agricultural system at all. In the case of Rimrock, however, the actual site of settlement was selected from among several possible sites in a larger situation. The selection was largely influenced by Mormon preconceptions of the type of village they wished to establish. In fact, Mormons chose the irrigable valleys throughout the inter-montane west. On the other hand, the physical environmental features for the development of irrigation were simply not present in the Homestead setting, and the people had no alternative to dry-land farming. There is no evidence to suggest that had they found an irrigable valley, they would have developed it along Mormon lines. In fact, the homesteaders' activities in the Rio Grande Valley suggest just the opposite. It is clear that the situational facts did not *determine* in any simple sense the contrasting community structures which emerged. Rather, the situations set certain limits, but within these limits contrasting value-orientations influenced the development of two quite different community types. It would appear that solutions to problems of community settlement pattern and the type of concrete social action which ensues are set within a value framework which importantly influences the selections made with the range of possibilities existing within an objective situation.

36. Socio-Cultural Sources of Messiahs

WILSON D. WALLIS *

The yearning for a messiah is almost as old as written records. The messianic hope of the Old Testament stimulated the Jewish sect that developed into Christianity, and inspired many other groups. Mohammedanism harbored the messianic concept soon after the faithful embarked upon a conquest of the world in the seventh century. In the aboriginal New World, messianic movements were led by native prophets influenced by Christianity or tribal concept; there have been aboriginal messiahs in South Africa, New Zealand, New Guinea, and Fiji.

The genesis of the messianic urge lies in man's search for salvation. When human aid fails and the present offers no surcease, man turns to the past for inspiration and envisages a messianic future. In his humdrum existence he is often desperately discontented; vague fears alternate with longings for the impossible. Even when he knows that the forces which encompass him are mightier than he, he refuses to accept his earthly lot. If he cannot remake the world after his heart's desire, he looks to some supernatural, or at least superhuman, being to accomplish the transformation for which he yearns. . . .

In all ages, the messiah has been a divine apostle of hope. He has infused old dreams with new vitality, promising a regenerated world to those who accepted him. Emphasizing tribal values and virtues, he has, of necessity, been faithful to his culture; he has responded to its demands, even while imparting to it a fresh meaning.

Hope has always been basic in messianic doctrine. The beasts might anticipate, but man alone has been capable of faith and hope. Man has yearned not merely for his own salvation; he has perceived that his greater good was bound up with that of his fellows. Underlying the messianic doctrine has been man's knowledge that the potential was greater than the actual, that the world has more things in it than he has ever dreamed of, that society has been influenced by dreamers and by men of vision.

Man has recognized a realm of the everyday and commonplace made up of matter-of-fact happenings, but he has recognized also a realm of the supernatural, in which events have other-worldly determinants. When

* From *Messiahs, Their Role in Civilization*, pp. 1 ff. and pp. 180 ff.

earthly agencies have been inadequate, man has sought help from the supernatural. Frequently, when man's appeal to the gods was fruitless, he has become convinced that a messiah with a promise of deliverance was a new agency of divinity. A proclaimed messiah presupposed a conscious demand for social salvation, accompanied by fairly definite ideas as to how the demand should be met. Belief has pointed the way to performance, and hope has urged man forward. Many peoples have recognized messiahs in times of cultural disintegration when despair cleared the way for hope.

Not all groups have responded to the claims of the messiah. Often, where response was expected, it was not given; and it was sometimes given when least anticipated. Messiahs have been numerous in Judaism, Mohammedanism, and Christianity; they have been rare in Shintoism, Taoism, Confucianism, and many other religious sects. Everywhere, as preliterate and historic civilizations have abundantly illustrated, special needs have been the preconditions of messianism. The messianic hope has been a culture manifestation as truly as it has been an individual response.

No culture has existed in a watertight compartment; each has been influenced by others. The story of messiahs and messianic movements, therefore, has been in part a story of the diffusion of concepts from one culture to another. Some twentieth century expressions of messianism may be attributed to ideas entertained in the Mediterranean world twenty-five hundred years ago. . . .

There were three types of messianism in Israel. One, centering around the king and the nation, expressed hope for a glorious national future under the house of David. The second type has been apocalyptic and frequently catastrophic, implying a divine warrior who should overthrow the heathen and establish the kingdom of Israel. The third type of messianism has been ethical, spiritual, and universal, almost the antithesis of the first. It has portrayed an ideal state in which love and service actuate ruler and ruled, and the will of Jahweh is realized.

Some scholars believed that Zerubbabel returned to Jerusalem to establish the messianic kingdom, and others have held that the messianic concept was not active among the Jews before the Maccabean period. . . .

In *Zechariah* (1:7–17), Jahweh assured his people that he would return to Jerusalem and that the temple would be rebuilt; yet the divine chariots and horses which traveled over the world, by Jahweh's order, returned with the report that there was no indication of a messianic crisis. The foreign tyrants were gone, Assyria and Egypt were no longer masters, and the autonomy and military power of Israel were restored. But the Jews who returned under Zerubbabel were disillusioned. The commonplaces and hardships in the actual Jerusalem dispelled the glamor that surround the Holy City of their dreams while they were captives in a foreign land. They had not successfully established national autonomy, nor attained the position among the nations demanded by pride and ambition. Out of mingled disappointment and hope there developed the concept of an ideal and distant messiah, rather than an immediate and practical one capable of fulfilling national ambitions. During the reigns of Saul and David the king was the messiah, the "Lord's Anointed." The prophets preached social regeneration and promised, especially during periods of national stress, a messiah who would cleanse the nation and exalt it above all others. Perhaps "the hour in which Isaiah parted from Ahaz gave to the world the thought of the Messiah." Certainly the aggression of Assyria, and later of Babylonia, stimulated messianic hopes.

The Babylonian exile led to a fundamental social, political, and religious transformation in Israel. Destruction of the ancient state cleared the way for the building of the new. Religion and ritual were revised to conform to political changes. In *Isaiah* and *Jeremiah* messianic expectation involves punishment of foreign nations, restoration of Israel, a new convenant, and rule by a king of David's line. The political coloring varied greatly. Some of the prophets ardently longed for supremacy over other nations; others stressed religious regeneration. *Isaiah's* post-exilic prediction of the child to be born—whose name, Emmanuel, signified deliverance of Jerusalem—was a rapturous description of the Coming One as a hero prince, who would perform many godlike deeds. In order to inspire faith and convert the Jews through disaster, Jahweh allowed Assyria to conquer them, "that they may know from the rising of the sun, and from the west, that there is no God beside me." (*Isaiah*, 45.) And post-exilic *Isaiah* (40:1–2) pleaded:

> Comfort ye,
> Comfort ye, my people
> Saith your God.
> Speak ye comfortably to Jerusalem,
> And cry unto her,
> That her warfare is accomplished,
> That her iniquity is pardoned:
> For she hath received of the Lord's hand
> Double for all her sins.

During the lifetime of Isaiah and through the ensuing century, Assyria was a persistent threat to Israel and Judah, and most of Isaiah's prophecies were motivated by a consciousness of the Assyrian threat. Isaiah declared that Jahweh would reign on earth; righteousness would prevail among his people and vengeance would be visited upon his enemies. Another post-exilic messianic faith centered in Cyrus, conqueror of Israel's foes: "Thus saith Cyrus, king of Persia, the Lord God of Heaven hath given me all the kingdoms of the earth, and He hath charged me to build Him a house at Jerusalem, which is Judah." (II *Chronicles*, 36:23.)

The views of the prophets reflected contemporary political conditions and needs. Amos (about 770), Hosea (about 750–730), Isaiah (740–700), and Micah, a younger contemporary of Isaiah, anticipated deliverance from Assyria, and a continuation of the existing political structure. Jeremiah and Ezekiel shared the hope for deliverance from enemies, but insisted that the new era demanded a new heart. Later prophets hoped for the restoration of Canaan and the triumph of Israel's God over other gods. Zechariah and post-exilic prophets were absorbed in the hard realities of their world, rebuilding the Temple and restoring the Promised Land. The expectation of national triumph varied with fluctuations in national fortune. In the fifth century, after the Temple had been built, but nothing more accomplished, Ezra and Nehemiah were concerned with the legal-religious organization of the nation and glowing prophecies were forgotten. Later, during the time of Ben-Sirach, the teaching regarding the messiah was indefinite. If the dream of *Daniel* had been realized and dominion over the nations had fallen to the saints of the Maccabean period, perhaps "the king of Israel would have been worshipped as a God, and Jerusalem rather than Rome would have become the seat of imperial cult." When national prosperity flourished, messianic hope waned. There was no messiah while the Maccabean prince Simon ruled, and the Jews, for the most part, were content with their lot. Nor did a messiah appear during the rule of Hyrcanus (135–105), when an almost Davidic splendor prevailed. Not until Israel again fell upon evil days did messianism revive. . . .

There was little interest in the messiah after the period of the post-exilic prophets and no messianic note pervaded later Old Testament writings. It came to the fore again only after the Helenistic conquest and, more emphatically, after the Roman conquest. In the second century B.C., *Sirach* voiced the hopes of a people oppressed by the foreigner. They longed for deliverance and vengeance, and were encouraged by prophecies of an end to their tribulations; the portion of the book which reflected messianic hope was, however, manifestly an interpolation. The Jewish *Sibylline Oracles* predicted that the coming messianic period was not to be expected in the near future, but many events would precede it. God would send a king who would banish war from every land; "some he shall slay and to others he shall consecrate faithful vows." During the second century B.C., the influence of messianism was negligible, though in the Hasmonian period, about 130 B.C., the belief prevailed that the messiah, in conformity with Jewish prophecy, would establish on earth a glorious terrestrial kingdom. Later, in the first half of the first century B.C., when the nation was ruthlessly oppressed, hope again centered on divine aid. The *Parables of Enoch* conceived the messiah as a supernatural Son of Man enjoying universal dominion and executing judgment on men and angels. Other writers revived expectation of the prophetic messiah from the line of David. Henceforth the messiah became the key figure in the messianic kingdom, and interest centered upon him rather than upon the people. . . .

Under the prosperous rule of the Maccabees the prophetic hope for a messiah-king of the line of David was dormant or became an expectation of a great Maccabean priest-king of the House of Levi. When the Pharisees became convinced that their oppression emanated from the king of the Jews, their messianic hope revived. As the New Testament discloses, however, at the time of Jesus, the messianic hope was not stereotyped; its expression took many forms. The reception given Jesus' messiahship varied with the demands of factions and classes. The messianic faith of the Maccabeans was interwoven with hope for national and political redemption, whereas the Pharisees sought to bring the sanctions of religion into vital touch with life. The aim of the Pharisaic school was reflected in its messianic doctrine, which it impressed upon the synagogue liturgy. Its messiah was a human son of David.

A human messiah was implied also in the doctrine of the Zealots, followers of the rebel Judas of Galilee. Among Graeco-Roman Jews messianism was raised to a high pitch by the edict against the Jews proclaimed by Tiberius and Sejanus, and messianism then became prevalent among Palestinian Jews. Expectation of the messiah was, however, not a doctrine of the Hillelites.

Enoch described the messiah as the Chosen One, Son of God and Son of Man. The pre-existent messiah, said *Enoch,* would establish a kingdom of righteousness and execute judgment upon all. The Elect One, the Son of Man, would sit on the Throne of his glory and would judge the world. The dead Jews would be resurrected, and the righteous would become angels in heaven. Prevailing ethical ideas were reflected in the messianic hope, which attached great importance to the personality of the messiah. Earlier parts of the Ethiopic version, a surviving fragment of literature that once circulated under the title *Enoch,* declared that "the Holy and Great One will come forth from His dwelling, the God of the world, and going from thence He will tread on Mount Sinai and appear with His hosts, and in the strength of His might appear from heaven." All except the elect will be destroyed. Sinning angels will be hurled into "the abyss of fire." The elect—who were the Jews, or perhaps only the Essenes— would enjoy material millennial blessings and universal peace. *Enoch* (94:6) prophesied the overthrow of the wicked and the exaltation of the righteous:

> Woe to those who build unrighteousness and oppression
> And lay deceit as a foundation;
> For they shall be suddenly overthrown,
> And they shall have no peace.

This interpretation of the millennium, apparently an Essene inspiration, was probably written before the Maccabean struggles. After these struggles, the Jews—for the last time in their history—set up an independent kingdom. Military successes and political independence led to overconfidence. "When the congregation of the righteous will appear, then will the kings and the mighty perish and be given into the hand of the righteous and holy." The Essenes shared with the Pharisees and other Jewish enthusiasts a hope for Jewish supremacy over all nations. Contemporary with the Essenes in Palestine and with the Therapeutae in Egypt, was an unnamed sect near Damascus, which expected the coming of the messiah as a Teacher of Righteousness, sprung from Aaron and Israel.

With the exception of *Daniel*, the *Psalms of Solomon* (63–48 B.C.) contained the first recorded expectation of the messiah as a person. He was heralded as belonging to the House of David, with the titles of "King," "King of Israel," "King of the Jews," "Son of David," "Christ," "Saviour." For deliverance one should look to heaven; but the blessings of the messianic advent would be wholly material. . . .

Most messiahs have claimed supernatural powers and, generally, their followers have believed in such powers. Supernaturalism was an attribute of many kings and illustrious men. The appellation "Son of God" was applied to rulers in Egypt and Babylonia a millennium before messianism appeared among the Jews. It was used also in Assyria. The *Odyssey* states that Minos, king of Knossos, "from his ninth year talked familiarly with great Zeus." Appolonius of Tyana, a contemporary of Jesus, was commonly regarded as a descendant of the Egyptian god Proteus. At his birth swans sported in the meadow about his mother, and a thunderbolt descended from heaven and then went aloft. These happenings presaged the wonderful accomplishments which later distinguished Appolonius. Divine Augustus, ruler of Rome when Jesus was born, bore the title Dei Filius, "Son of God," and many wonders, wrote Suetonius, preceded and followed his supernatural birth. . . .

Although messianism has been widespread, it has not appeared in all cultures, and it has not been of equal importance at all times in any given culture. The number of known messiahs, excluding Negroes, has been very nearly equal in Judaism, Mohammedanism, and Christianity. Inasmuch as the Jews have been a much smaller group than the Mohammedans or the Christians, it follows that messiahs have appeared with much greater relative frequency in Judaism than in either of the other two religious sects. There was a high frequency of messiahs in Judaism in the first and twelfth centuries A.D., and in the sixteenth, seventeenth, and early eighteenth centuries. The period between the ninth and twelfth centuries furnished many Mohammedan mahdis, but the peak was reached in the nineteenth and twentieth centuries. Christian messiahs have continued to appear from the sixteenth century to the present time. In each of these religious sects, probably messiahs have appeared of whom there are no extant records; and certainly some of the existing records have escaped the writer's search. . . .

The *Koran* showed much Jewish and some Christian influence; indeed Mohammedans regarded Jesus as a great and holy prophet, second only to Mohammed in importance. Mohammedanism from its inception encountered the messianic concepts of other cultures and was influenced by them. Diffusion of belief in the mahdi, the Mohammedan messiah, accompanied the spread of Mohammedanism. The cult has carried the doctrine to every land into which it has gone, from Iberia to the Malay Peninsula, and possibly to the Philippines. Many Negro tribes and other preliterate peoples who have come under the spell of Islam have produced messiahs or mahdis. In almost every Christian land there have been several messiahs. In European countries the messianic concept is first evident in the expectation of the return of the national hero, Arthur, Friedrich Barbarossa, Olaf Trygvason, or Charlemagne.

The influence of Christianity in aboriginal American messianic movements was considerable. The Hopi, who produced the first known messiah north of Mexico, had been under the influence of Christian missionaries for many years, but Hopi messianic concepts seem to be thoroughly aboriginal. The Indians of the eastern United States, among whom messianism flourished before and after the War of 1812, had previously been directly or indirectly under missionary influence; but it has not been possible to assess the stimulus of Christianity in their messianism. Soon after the organization of a messianic cult, the movement spread to neighboring tribes; so, too, did the Ghost Dance religion which originated about 1870 and was resuscitated about 1889. In each instance there had been Christian contacts, yet in the main the concepts were aboriginal. The Paviotso (Paiute) Ghost Dance of 1870 and 1890 was probably inspired by the Prophet Dance of the Northwest Coast and Plateau area, which flourished in the 1820's. The Prophet Dance complex as found, for example, among the Southern Okanagon, of Washington, involved three concepts which were prominent in the Ghost Dance: supernatural events (falling stars, earthquakes, and other portents) which herald the destruction of the world; the prophets' communication with God in dreams or by visits to the land of the dead, and—upon their return—preaching a righteous and God-fearing life; and performance of special dances and singing of special songs designed to ensure the salvation of adherents. An additional element was introduced by the arrival of the white man and the ensuing collapse of Indian culture. . . .

Through the centuries the weft of the messianic idea has crossed the warp of political, social, religious, and ethical life, with much repetition of pattern, and even of details. In each culture the messianic concept and the messianic movements have had unique expression. They have conformed to the prevailing culture patterns and have varied with time and with place. Even in the same land concurrent movements within different sects have been to some extent distinct in character. Despite this, however, there have been many interpenetrations of messianic concepts and many syncretisms. In the first century A.D., Jewish expectation of the near advent of the messianic era was widely reflected in Roman messianism. Both movements were influenced by the Christian belief that Jesus would return in the immediate future. Frequently revival of messianic hope among a people has occasioned its revival in another culture. As a result, messianic resurgences in two cultures have often been synchronous, or nearly so; "a mahdi in Islam was often accompanied by a messiah in Judaism." The Christian concept of the return of Jesus has been an inspiration to Mohammedans, Jews, Hindus, Buddhists, and several preliterate peoples. Some Mohammedan mahdis have claimed to be Jesus; and at various times belief in the return of Jesus has been cited by Mohammedan theologians in India or in Mediterranean lands to support the claim that a designated mahdi would return in the flesh to save his people. During the seventeenth century, when Europe was restive with millennial expectation, the Jewish Sabbathaian movement flourished.

This, in turn, created much interest in messianism throughout Christendom and Islam, and stimulated at least one mahdi. . . .

In the early Mediterranean world messianism was linked with political aspirations and a profound desire for social reform. Political oppression stimulated messiahs, who, in turn, fanned patriotic ardor.

The threat of Assyria inspired the words of *Amos*. *Isaiah* declared Persia a scourge in the hands of the Lord to punish Israel and Assyria for their wickedness. The belief that an ideal king would rule in Jerusalem was perhaps inspired by the political situation at the end of Hezekiah's reign. Jesus was condemned and executed on a political charge involving the question of messiahship. Jewish messiahs were involved in political movements. In the third century A.D., however, Jewish teachers declared the messiah would not come until the haughty had disappeared from Israel.

Mohammedan mahdis have occasioned much political disturbance. The Wahabis sought emancipation from the shams, ceremonials, and elaborate superstitions of Islam, revolted against their political oppressors, and fought for freedom from Turkish tyranny. The first rebellion in Andalusia after the death of Abd-el Rahman was fomented by devout theological students at Cordova. Throughout Mohammedan history, the more the masses felt themselves oppressed and humiliated by rulers of their own faith or by infidels, the more fervent was their longing for the restorer of Islam and the conquest of the world. The mahdist movement in the Sudan was inspired mainly by political oppression. The Baggara, the first and most ardent followers of the mahdi, believed that he would free them from Egyptian rule—for he was the true and only commander of the faithful—and would conquer the whole world. As a matter of fact, the mahdi liberated them from the extortions of Egyptians, and, when death overtook him, was planning a campaign against Egypt. . . .

37. Role Conflicts of Military Chaplains
WALDO W. BURCHARD *,†

THIS PAPER MIGHT WELL BE READ IN CONNECTION WITH CHAPTER 9, AS A STUDY OF SOME OF THE CONFLICTS INVOLVED IN THE INTERACTION OF RELIGIOUS BELIEF AND CITIZENSHIP. IT IS PLACED IN THIS SECTION, HOWEVER, BECAUSE OF ITS EMPHASIS ON THE DILEMMA OF RELIGIOUS LEADERS. BURCHARD'S RESEARCH

* From *American Sociological Review*, October, 1954, pp. 528–535.
† Revised version of paper read at the annual meeting of the Midwest Sociological

RAISES A NUMBER OF QUESTIONS: WILL THE OBSERVATIONS "STAND UP" WITH A LARGER SAMPLE AND IN DIFFERENT SETTINGS? WHAT KINDS OF PERSONS ENTER, AND STAY IN, THE CHAPLAINCY; IF THERE IS SELECTIVITY INVOLVED, DOES THIS AFFECT THE NATURE OF THE DILEMMA? ARE THE CONFLICTS DESCRIBED A FUNCTION OF THE AUTHOR'S DEFINITION OF RELIGION (PRIMARILY IN IDEOLOGICAL, NOT FUNCTIONAL, TERMS) AND THEREFORE PERHAPS NOT ENTIRELY RELEVANT TO THE CHAPLAINS THEMSELVES?

In a complex society many institutions are required to satisfy the manifold needs and wants of man. This means that any given individual will play many social roles in the course of his lifetime, and at any given time will be playing a number of roles simultaneously. Each person has a "hierarchy of role obligations," [1] the relative positions of which are determined by the strength of the claims made upon him by the various institutions which compete for his loyalty. Therefore, his roles may not necessarily be in harmony with each other, and in some instances, where two or more institutions demand the first loyalty of a person, they may be directly antithetical.

Assuming a "drive toward consistency of self" on the part of human actors in social situations, the person who finds himself playing two such divergent roles will seek some means of resolving the conflict between them. In the writer's estimation, the types of solutions available can be reduced to three: (1) abandonment of one of the conflicting roles, (2) rationalization, which may assume many different forms, or (3) compartmentalization of role behaviors.[2] If and when these techniques fail, the individual will invent new patterns of behavior which are usually thought of as neurotic, aberrant or psychotic, depending upon the severity of the conflict and the social definition of the given situation.

In the summer of 1952 a small-scale study was undertaken in the San Francisco Bay area in an attempt to determine the applicability of the theory in a concrete situation. A population was chosen in which the conflict in roles is extremely severe, since the ends specified by the two major institutions which define their social roles are in some respects

---

Society, April, 1954. The material for this article has been taken from the writer's unpublished doctoral dissertation, "The Role of the Military Chaplain," University of California, 1953.

[1] The writer is indebted to Jackson Toby for this terminology. See his "Some Variables in Role Conflict Analysis," in *Social Forces*, 30 (March, 1952).

[2] The reader will note both similarities and differences between these concepts and those used by other investigators. See Jackson Toby, *op. cit.*, and J. W. Getzels and E. G. Guba, "Role, Role Conflict, and Effectiveness," in *American Sociological Review*, 19 (April, 1954), pp. 164–175.

mutually exclusive. These were military chaplains.[3] Chaplains not only share the dilemma of the Christian in war time; [4] they also function as officers in both ecclesiastical and military organizations. As officers, they are responsible, in part, for the achievement of the ends specified. It was assumed that chaplains, being highly educated and much concerned with consistency of behavior, would have been acutely aware of the conflicts between military and religious ideology, and would have sought some equitable solution.

METHODOLOGY

The sample was small, consisting of thirty-six chaplains and thirty-five ex-chaplains (who had seen service in World War II)—seventy-one in all. (The Chief of Navy Chaplains and the Chief of Army Chaplains were also interviewed, although they are not included in the sample.) In order to avoid bias in the selection of the sample, an effort was made to include every chaplain and ex-chaplain in the San Francisco Bay area. Such a sampling method, while it successfully excludes the bias of the researcher, does not necessarily guarantee a truly representative sample of the population being studied. Headquarters of the Sixth Army and the Twelfth Naval District are located in San Francisco, which means that there is a heavy concentration of high ranking officers there. Consequently, the sample of chaplains is somewhat biased in favor of the higher ranks, with over half of them holding the rank of major or lieutenant commander or above. Rank is more equitably distributed in the sample of ex-chaplains, with three-fifths of them in the two lower ranks. Moreover, it was not actually possible to interview every chaplain and ex-chaplain in the area. Although only one person refused outright to be interviewed, many of them found reasons to postpone the interview until the time limit for the research had expired. It would be safe to estimate that not more than three-fourths to four-fifths of the chaplains and ex-chaplains in the area were actually interviewed.

In spite of the difficulties encountered, the coverage appears to be quite

[3] In an effort to compare the chaplains' concepts of their roles with the informal expectations of some of their "audiences," questionnaires were distributed to veterans and enlisted men. The data thus obtained will form the basis of a subsequent paper.

[4] Jewish chaplains share the same dilemma, at least to some extent, as is indicated by the statement of David de Sola Pool ("Religion's Answer to a Troubled World," in *The Military Chaplain,* official publication of the Military Chaplains Association of the United States, Inc., Summer, 1951): "We may with utter sincerity proclaim the purpose of our taking up arms as a righteous one, but the bitter unescapable fact remains that war as an instrument even of man's noblest purposes is and ever will be irreconcilable with religion."

broad. All the gradations of rank from first lieutenant to brigadier general are covered; members of nineteen religious denominations, including thirteen Catholics, three Jews and fifty-five Protestants, were included in the sample (Table 1); and by coincidence the sample of chaplains includes twelve members each of the Army, the Air Force and the Navy. Nevertheless, because the sample was small and because the study was confined to a limited area, it must be regarded as exploratory in nature, and any conclusions must remain tentative until they are corroborated by further study.

TABLE 1. RELIGIOUS AFFILIATION OF CHAPLAINS AND EX-CHAPLAINS IN THE SAMPLE

Denomination	Chaplains	Ex-Chaplains
Catholic	7	6
Jewish	2	1
Protestant		
African Methodist Episcopal		1
Assembly of God	2	
Baptist (American)	4	1
Baptist (Southern)	4	
Christian Scientist	1	2
Congregational	2	1
Disciples of Christ (Christian)		1
Episcopalian	1	4
Latter Day Saints (Mormon)	2	1
Lutheran (Missouri Synod)	1	3
Lutheran (United)		2
Methodist	6	5
Mission Covenant	1	
Presbyterian *		3
Presbyterian (USA)	3	2
Reformed Church in America		1
Salvation Army		1
Total	36	35

* Not otherwise identified.

The schedule consisted of fifty-seven questions, twenty-nine of which were "open-end." The remainder called for categorical replies. Questions were designed to bring the respondent face to face with the proposition that the role of military officer conflicts with that of minister of the gospel, and to elicit his self-concept with reference to various situations which chaplains regularly face or might conceivably be called upon to face.

There are some five major items in Christian philosophy from which role conflict for the military clergyman derives. These are the doctrines of love, of universal brotherhood, of peace, and of non-resistance to evil, and the commandment, "You shall not kill." These doctrines (or ideals, if the word doctrine seems too strong) are manifestly incompatible with the aims of a nation at war. Therefore it is impossible for the Christian in military service to put them into practice. Moreover, the age-old problem of the relationship between church and state is at issue here—whether the state or the church shall demand the first loyalty of its followers. With these items in mind, the respondent was asked to express his conception of his role in various situations.

Hypotheses to be tested included the following: (1) that the position of the chaplain does lead to a conflict in roles for the incumbent of that office; (2) that the chaplain seeks to reconcile this conflict either through rationalization or through compartmentalization of role behaviors; (3) that rationalization of conflict in roles tends to strengthen the chaplain's role of military officer at the expense of his role of minister of the gospel; (4) that the chaplain serves as interpreter of the values of the military organization, helps resolve value-dilemmas of individual service men, and helps promote smooth operation of the military organization.

ROLE CONCEPTS RELATING TO MILITARY DUTY

Chaplain's conceptions of self with relation to military duty. An attempt was made to discover the factors which motivated the individual respondent in joining the military service. Most of the replies (75 per cent) indicated that motives were mixed, but assuming that the first motive mentioned is the primary one, 25 per cent were influenced primarily by patriotic motives, while only 10 per cent were influenced primarily by religious motives. Another 25 per cent had not analyzed their motives beyond a "desire to be of service." The remainder gave replies that were in general non-committal. These replies indicate that, for those clergymen who join the military service, the claims of the state are likely to take precedence over the claims of religion at the outset.

Over 85 per cent of the respondents said that they had enjoyed military service. The aspect most frequently mentioned as being enjoyable was, for ex-chaplains, fellowship with men in the service, mentioned 17 times, and for chaplains, freedom, mentioned 9 times. "Freedom" included freedom from the cares and difficulties of a civilian parish, freedom from financial cares, and from the controls exercised by a congregation with its boards of deacons, Ladies' Aid groups, and the like, and freedom to act, preach and live as one chooses. It is no doubt significant that of the nine chaplains who mentioned freedom as the most enjoyable aspect of military life, only one stated that he did not intend to make a career of the chaplaincy.

This fact suggests an interesting possibility for research in personality. It raises the question whether or not the desire to escape from the relatively circumscribed area, dogmatically speaking, of the local congregation into the relatively free atmosphere, dogmatically speaking, of the armed forces plays a large part in the decision of a clergyman to make a career of military service. The foregoing may be stated in the form of a hypothesis, although the instrument used in this study was not designed to discover data bearing on such a hypothesis. Such data as are available do not, in fact, support the hypothesis. Exactly half of the chaplains said that they intended to remain permanently in the military service. None of them, however, gave freedom as a reason for making such a decision. Instead, the reasons mentioned were security, the opportunity to render a service, the challenge offered by the military situation, personal satisfaction, the existence of a need, and a missionary call. When ex-chaplains were asked to give their reasons for not remaining in the military service nearly 40 per cent of them expressed skepticism as to the necessity or propriety of a military chaplaincy in times of peace. In view of the difference in attitudes expressed by chaplains and ex-chaplains the foregoing hypothesis appears to be tenable in spite of the lack of evidence.

Chaplains' conceptions of self with reference to other officers. Over 90 per cent of the respondents reported that they had not felt out of place as military officers, and a like percentage believed they had been accepted as equals by their fellow officers. Only a few expressed reservations concerning their acceptance, although there appeared to be a good deal of uncertainty on the part of chaplains as to what was expected of them by their fellow officers. For instance, some felt that having a few drinks "with the boys" helped to establish rapport; others felt that they would lose esteem if they indulged. The drinking party presents a good test of the loyalties of a clergyman belonging to an anti-liquor denomination. (Many denominations, including Catholics, Jews, Episcopalians and Lutherans do not forbid social drinking, even for the clergy.) Three chaplains who were members of anti-liquor denominations reported that they did drink at parties. All three, incidentally, avowed their intention to make a career of the chaplaincy.

Chaplains' conceptions of self with reference to military authorities. With respect to military authorities, personal and impersonal, 72 per cent of the respondents reported at the outset that they had the full cooperation of their commanding officers. A closer analysis of the replies reveals, however, that at least 50 per cent of the chaplains and 40 per cent of the ex-chaplains had had experience with a non-cooperative commanding officer. There was considerable hesitancy and some attempts at evasion occurred when questions were asked concerning relations with commanding officers. There is good reason for such caution. Chaplains have been historically regarded by commanding officers as appendages to the military organization, not as integral parts. During World War II and subsequently, however, they have been urging their claims to recognition with increasingly greater success. At the present time chaplains participate actively in recruit training programs and in the disposition of conscientious objectors. Requests for transfer or discharge for reasons of hardship are reviewed by a chaplain, and chaplains participate in courts-martial and other disciplinary procedures with varying frequency. All of these activities might conceivably be resented by commanding officers as infringements on their prerogatives.[5] Chaplains appear to be optimistic about such relations, and no chaplain interviewed reported that his present commanding officer was uncooperative.

The practice of "going over the head" of a commanding officer is reserved for extreme cases, although the possibility (and sometimes the threat) of doing so serves as an effective weapon in the hands of chaplains for securing cooperation. Nineteen per cent of the chaplains interviewed reported that they had actually gone over the head of a commanding officer at some time or other.

Reactions to regulations, channels, and red tape, were mixed. Eighty-six per cent of the respondents said that they had been successful in circumventing red tape on some occasions, and 72 per cent said that they regarded it as their duty to accomplish things in the most expedient manner, yet 31 per cent of the chaplains and 66 per cent of the ex-chaplains said that red tape had not interfered with their ministry. Over half of the respondents denied that any conflict exists between military regulations and religious ideology, and three of them denied that military regulations involve any moral values. The technique of compartmentalization is involved in these situations. It appears that the chaplain regards himself as operating in a moral context while he is conducting religious services or performing other tasks which are associated in his mind with the work of a clergyman, and which are not covered by military regulations, but not while dealing with commanding officers, fellow officers,

---

[5] There is some evidence that such resentment does exist, but it is rarely expressed overtly. Instances of covert opposition, generally expressed in the planning of training exercises, do occasionally crop up.

channels of communication, and in other non-religious situations which are covered by the regulations. In religious situations he is guided by religious values; in other situations by other values.

There was evidence of ambivalence concerning the question of military discipline. Eighty-three per cent of the respondents said that at some time or other they had tried to intercede for the defendant in disciplinary cases. There were, however, a great many unsolicited comments concerning such activity, as though the respondents were trying to disabuse the interviewer of any erroneous ideas he might have concerning the functions of a chaplain as the champion of enlisted men opposed to officers. Fourteen respondents specifically stated that they had interceded only rarely and in cases of extreme injustice, and the majority indicated that in general they identified themselves with the military hierarchy on the question of discipline. Only two respondents appeared to fit the popular stereotype of the chaplain as the champion of enlisted men. Chaplains in general do not regard it as their duty to mitigate the harshness of military justice. Most of them would prefer to do nothing until after sentence is passed, then attempt to rehabilitate the prisoner by persuading him that justice had been done, that it was for his own good, and that he should profit by the experience.

On the other hand, when the question of enforcing the regulation concerning saluting arose, most of the respondents sided with enlisted men. When asked what they would do if an enlisted man failed to show deference to their rank, only 10 per cent replied that they would remind him of his status. The explanation for this is not far to seek. The salute is regarded by chaplains as extraneous—an area of indifference—and the failure of an enlisted man to salute is not perceived as a threat to his status as an officer. The court-martial, on the other hand, has traditionally been a sort of battle ground of enlisted men versus officers. If the chaplain were to sympathize too openly with enlisted personnel on such occasions he might lose caste with his fellow officers.

Chaplains' conceptions of self with reference to enlisted personnel. Relations with enlisted men are of great concern to chaplains, since enlisted men form the largest single audience toward which chaplains direct their behavior. All chaplains are aware that the fact that they are officers poses a barrier to primary relations with enlisted men.[6] By and large,

---

[6] The higher the rank the higher the barrier. More than one field grade chaplain (major or lieutenant commander and above) reported that prior to their attainment of the higher rank they had made a practice of looking the other way when an enlisted man approached, in order to avoid noticing his failure to salute. At their present rank, however, it was not necessary to cultivate such a blind spot, for the salute was always forthcoming as a matter of course.

chaplains are probably more conscious of rank than any other group of officers in the armed forces, mainly because of their ambivalent attitude toward it. The desire to become an integral part of the military hierarchy, to become accepted as one of the "fellows," is very strong.[7] On the other hand, a priest, minister or pastor is one who is set apart from the group —a leader of the flock, not just one of them. But a good leader must be accessible; he must not be too distant from his flock; he must be on good personal relations with those he is leading. A military officer, however, must not be familiar with his men. His ability as a leader is presumed to depend, in part, on his ability to keep at a distance from his men. The chaplain, being both a military officer and a clergyman, must somehow come to grips with the problem of carrying on an effective religious ministry for enlisted personnel and at the same time of retaining his status as an officer.

In an effort to minimize the difference between chaplains and enlisted men, numerous devices have been officially adopted, chief of which are: (1) the practice of addressing all chaplains by the title "Chaplain" rather than by rank, thus de-emphasizing the military status and emphasizing the clerical status of the chaplain; (2) waiving the rule against fraternization between officers and enlisted personnel in the case of chaplains, thus de-emphasizing the social distance between them; and (3) specifically stating that chaplains do not have command of troops, thus making it possible to argue that the chaplain is not really an officer after all, although the command of troops is not the usual function of any staff officer. A rationalization frequently used by the respondents in this study was that they held their rank for purposes of pay only. It is not generally known, even by chaplains, that chaplains were granted equal rank with other officers some years before they were granted equal pay and that the struggle for rank centered on such questions as the wearing of the uniform or who should occupy which stateroom on a battle ship.[8]

Nearly all of the respondents felt that if the individual chaplain were adequate he could overcome the barrier posed by rank. Only twenty-one per cent felt that they could have done an effective job as chaplains if they had not had military rank, and no respondent believed that an enlisted chaplain could perform effectively. Three major reasons were advanced for such skepticism: (1) that without military rank it would be impossible to demand concessions for enlisted men from the military

[7] Only one respondent, when asked the question, "Do you believe that your fellow officers accept you as one of them?" replied, "I am not 'one of them.' I am a priest and an extremist. Catholic personnel regard me as 'Father.' "

[8] Clifford M. Drury, *The History of the Chaplain Corps, U. S. Navy,* Vol. I (NavPers 15807), U. S. Government Printing Office, Chapters 10 and 11.

hierarchy, (2) that it would be impossible to minister to officers unless the chaplain were one of them, and (3) that if the chaplain were not an officer he could not command the respect of either enlisted men or officers. In spite of this, the usual response to questions suggesting a conflict between the demands of the chaplain's military office and those of his ecclesiastical office was to deny the existence of conflict by disclaiming the reality of his status as an officer.

ROLE CONFLICTS RELATING TO RELIGIOUS BELIEFS AND PRACTICES

Chaplains' conceptions of self with reference to religious life in the armed forces. Most chaplains curtail certain of their religious activities when they enter the military service. The prescribed duties of a chaplain do not include evangelism, and by a sort of gentlemen's agreement he is expected not to proselytize. Since the efficiency of a chaplain is not measured by the addition of members to his congregation, and since the line between evangelism and proselytism is ill-defined, many chaplains prefer not to emphasize this phase of religious activity. Conversions do occur, however. Only 10 per cent reported that they had never baptized military personnel.

Seventy-nine per cent of the respondents believed that a man with good religious training would make a better soldier than one who lacked such training, although only 30 per cent thought that an appeal to the religious motives of men was more effective in securing military efficiency than an appeal to patriotic motives. There appears to be some evidence of ambivalence here—on the one hand there is a tendency to urge the advantages of religious training (which, incidentally, reinforces the chaplains' claim to a permanent position in the military hierarchy), and on the other hand a reluctance to admit that religion can be so readily used in the pursuit of non-religious ends. All recognize the function of religion in the maintenance of morale, but they prefer to regard morale as a by-product of their spiritual ministrations rather than its major object.

Chaplains' conceptions of self with reference to the relations between church and state. In spite of the traditional American ideology of the strict separation of church and state, military chaplaincy is a state supported religious institution—not actually an official religion, but a form of state established church. It represents an odd situation, since the government specifically disclaims any interest in controlling religious beliefs, and permits individual chaplains or denominations to prescribe rituals, dogmas, and other religious matters. The only religious qualification demanded of an applicant for the chaplaincy is the recommendation of his denomination (or of an officially recognized ecclesiastical agency which reviews applications for the chaplaincy). There are, however, some rather strict educational requirements which the military services impose for reasons of their own. These requirements have the effect of defining orthodoxy, for they exclude from participation a great number of clergy-men who are considered by their denominations sufficiently qualified to carry on the ministry of the church. When asked for their reactions to the statement that the chaplaincy is a form of state established church, 68 per cent of the respondents disagreed, more or less violently. A greater proportion of chaplains than of ex-chaplains disagreed (81 per cent as opposed to 54 per cent), and with greater vehemence, arguing that the presence of many denominations and the failure of the state to recognize any denomination as official preclude a state establishment of religion.

Chaplains' conceptions of self with reference to the question of religion and war. The question of religion and war offers to chaplains even greater difficulty than the question of rank. Various passages in the Bible appear to forbid the use of violence in the pursuit of ends. However, 45 per cent of the respondents believed that the killing of an enemy soldier was a righteous act and the remainder called it a justifiable act. None felt that the individual soldier had any moral responsibility in the matter except to serve his country—a duty which in time of war takes precedence over all others. Only 7 per cent ascribed any moral content to the act of killing in war time, and these would distribute the guilt over the entire nation. The assumption of a "just" war (or even of a "holy" war) was the argu-ment most frequently used in defense of war-time killing, followed closely by the plea of self-defense. It was argued further that the commandment "You shall not kill" has been corrupted in translation (a matter concern-ing which Bible translators appear to disagree) and that when it is read according to the ancient Hebrew tribalistic interpretation, "You shall not murder," no moral wrong is involved in war-time killing.

When asked to reconcile the "turn the other cheek" philosophy with war, one-fifth of the respondents felt that the conflict was so great that it could not be reconciled; with a few exceptions the remainder felt that there was no conflict since: (1) the individual and nation are different, (2) the necessity for self-defense obviates any anti-violence teachings of Jesus, (3) "turn the other cheek" needs interpretation, and (4) this philosophy does not apply in this day and age. There were three re-spondents who said that they had never faced the question and who refused to face it during the interview.

The practice of giving theoretical adherence to a doctrine while violating it in practice is as old as religion itself, and it poses a major problem for moralists in every age. It accounts, in part, for the Christian's continuing sense of guilt or unworthiness. For the Christian to deny the relevance of the admonition to turn the other cheek is to question the value of the ethical teachings of Jesus; to admit it makes the Christian in military service a violator of his own moral precepts. The position actually taken on this question by most of the respondents was that of moral relativism.

None of the respondents would of his own volition raise questions concerning the morality of killing, or of war in general, or of turning the other cheek, or any question concerning the relationship between religion and war. If such questions came up in the course of a discussion, the majority would attempt to reason them out on a common-sense basis rather than on a religious basis. Many respondents had not attempted to answer such questions even in their own minds prior to the interview—a fact which violated one of the assumptions made at the outset of the study, namely, that chaplains, being educated men and philosophers who are concerned with the consistency of self, would have sought solutions to such a dilemma. Instead, it appears that the greater the dilemma, the greater the tendency to withdraw from it—to compartmentalize role behaviors and to refuse to recognize conflicting elements.

CONCLUSIONS

The foregoing report gives only a bare outline of a portion of the data actually collected. These data tend to support the hypotheses advanced, in some respects strongly, in other respects less strongly. The first hypothesis, that the position of the chaplain does lead to a conflict in roles for the incumbent of that position is supported in two ways: (1) by a philosophical analysis of the two social roles of clergyman and military officer and (2) by the responses to questions in the interview schedule, particularly those questions dealing with rank and those dealing with the relationship between religion and war.

The second hypothesis, that the chaplain seeks to reconcile his role conflict either through rationalization or through compartmentalization of role behaviors, appears to be well substantiated. The sample chosen did not include any member who had sought to escape the conflict by abandoning one of the roles (although one ex-chaplain had abandoned the ministry after he had returned to civilian life). Therefore, only two escapes were open. Compartmentalization appeared to be the more successful of the two techniques, and more frequently used. Rationalization requires facing the dilemma and arguing away the conflicting elements. Compartmentalization involves refusing to recognize the conflict. Perhaps one respondent was speaking for more than himself when he said that, although he had been a strong pacifist prior to World War II, when he saw the great need of men in the military service, he forgot about philosophy and resolved to help as best he could in an unfortunate situation.

Concerning the third hypothesis, that rationalization of conflict in roles tends to strengthen the chaplain's role of military officer at the expense of his role of minister of the gospel, it needs only to be pointed out that every argument cited tends to assert the military claim and de-emphasize the religious claim.

The fourth hypothesis, that the chaplain serves as interpreter of the values of the military organization, helps resolve value-dilemmas of individual service men, and helps promote smooth operation of the military organization, is less strongly supported than the others, partly, perhaps, because of a lack of data bearing on the subject. However, such data as are available indicate that the hypothesis is tenable. If a service man were in doubt about the morality of military activity, a majority of the respondents would endeavor to assure him that his relationship with God would not suffer thereby. The recently instituted "Character Guidance Program" [9] is a direct attempt on the part of chaplains to "sell" military life to service men. Moreover, all the chaplains' welfare activities are designed to help the service man adjust more smoothly to the military situation.

It would be over-hasty to generalize on the basis of the data in this study. However, two hypotheses may be suggested: (1) that the role which provides for the individual his primary identification takes first place in his hierarchy of role obligations and (2) that for the chaplain the role of military officer provides his primary identification. Further study along this line would no doubt reveal much concerning techniques of resolving role conflicts.

The role of the military chaplain offers an interesting subject for the student of role conflict. The chaplaincy is still in its formative stage, and

[9] The Character Guidance Program is a program of instruction in "godly patriotism," which attempts to equate the values of patriotism and religion by giving patriotism a religious basis. Recruits are required to attend a certain number of Character Guidance lectures during their basic training. All three services have adopted the program, and the ultimate aim is to require every enlisted person in the armed services to attend one Character Guidance lecture per month throughout his (or her) tour of duty. The lectures are "canned." They are prepared by a special Board of chaplains, and prior to being distributed to chaplains in the field, they are approved and pronounced official state policy by the Secretary of Defense.

we are witnessing here the emergence of a new social role in which the ideological clash between church and state is assuming what is, for the United States, a new form. The role of the military chaplain also offers an interesting subject for the student of personality. The instrument used in this study was not designed to reveal the individual personality characteristics of the subjects. Nevertheless, the replies to some of the items in the interview schedule (for instance, the question concerning the enjoyable aspects of military service, discussed above) suggest the existence of basic personality differences between those clergymen who choose the military chaplaincy as a career and those who do not. The hypothesis that a career in the military chaplaincy appeals more strongly to those possessing the characteristics of the "authoritarian" personality than to other types would be in order here. The student of institutional history and of the processes of social change should also find much of value in the study of the role of the military chaplain. The history of military chaplaincy, as an institution, covers several centuries, but its origin can be dated, and the various steps in its development can be located in time and space.

38. Values, Positivism, and the Functional Theory of Religion: The Growth of a Moral Dilemma *

WILLIAM L. KOLB †

IN THIS PAPER, KOLB DECLARES THAT SOCIAL SCIENTISTS CANNOT AFFORD TO BE INDIFFERENT TO THE VALUE CONSEQUENCES OF THEIR OWN PRESUPPOSITIONS AND RESEARCH. THIS IS A VALUE WITH WHICH THE PRESENT WRITER READILY AGREES; BUT HE IS NOT PERSUADED THAT A REAFFIRMATION OF THE ONTIC STATUS OR OBJECTIVE EXISTENCE OF VALUES WILL RESOLVE THE MORAL DILEMMA WHICH KOLB DISCUSSES. IN A WORLD OF CONTINUOUSLY CONTRADICTORY

* The meanings of the word "moral" used here to qualify the word "dilemma" are, of course, exceedingly complex. However, several of the simpler meanings are fully adequate in this context: When the sociologist holds a positivist view of values and a functional theory of religion the dilemma presented is moral because (1) it is difficult if not impossible to determine the *right* and *proper* behavior under the circumstances described; (2) *principles* of *right* and *wrong* (ethical principles) are involved; (3) the problem of *conformity* to a standard of moral right and wrong is presented; (4) and, finally, the dilemma is a dilemma of conscience.

The dilemma can be stated briefly as follows: A sociologist who believes that people must believe in the validity of values (functional theory of religion) but that such values actually have no validity (moral and ethical positivism) must either

REVELATIONS AND INTUITIONS, EACH PERSON BELIEVES THAT HIS VALUES ARE
THE ONES THAT TRULY HAVE OBJECTIVE EXISTENCE—A SITUATION THAT IN-
EVITABLY BRINGS RELATIVITY INTO THE PURSUIT OF UNIVERSAL VALUES. THE
OTHER PERSONS'S "ONTIC VALUES" ARE OBVIOUSLY RELATIVE—IF I DISAGREE
WITH THEM. ALTHOUGH ONE MAY DISAGREE WITH THE PERSPECTIVE OF THIS
PAPER, THERE IS LIKELY TO BE VERY WIDE AGREEMENT ON THE SIGNIFICANCE
OF THE QUESTIONS WHICH IT RAISES.

American sociology, like other American social sciences, has its roots deep
in the nineteenth century moral concern for the welfare of man. Many
of its early methods of data gathering were simply an effort to be "scientific" in securing practical knowledge for solving "social problems."
Many of its first practitioners were men of the gospel. Even those who
were rationalistic critics of religion had no doubts that moral values were
real and possessed their own validity. The builders of theoretical systems, Giddings, Ward, and even Sumner, included concepts of good and
evil in their "scientific" theories. All sociologists looked on sociology as
a means of discriminating among values.

The first serious blow to the moral certainty of the new science came
with the diffusion of German sociological theory into American universities. In particular Max Weber's claim that science must be value-free
forced a new humility in moral matters upon those who grasped his
argument. For Weber, science is only one possible mode of cognition and
it is extremely limited in the type of problems that it can solve. For any
scientist to believe that his science provides a basis for choosing among
ultimate value spheres is the sheerest arrogance. Yet there is nothing in
Weber to indicate that moral choices are not real choices or that it is
impossible to believe that in some sense there exists in the structure of
the universe a genuine and real realm of values. Men can and must make
moral choices in the realm of value, but they cannot claim scientific warrant for their choices. In Weber's thinking, ultimate values are still ultimate, and choice among them is still a matter for great seriousness and the
utmost exercise of responsibility. Weber has been attacked many times in
recent years for being a root source of value relativism, yet there is nothing in his theory to substantiate the charge.[1]

---

deceive his public or help in dissolving the forces which hold society together. The
choices involve a dilemma because neither is morally satisfactory. The demonstration
that such a dilemma is involved constitutes the body of the paper.

† From *Social Forces*, May, 1953, pp. 305–311.

[1] One of the clearest analyses of the implications of Weber's value theory is Howard
Becker's "Supreme Values and the Sociologist, or, Our Roles and Their Loyalties,"
in his *Through Values to Social Interpretation* (Durham: Duke University Press,
1950), pp. 281–305. Here there is no indication that value-judgments are simple
personal preferences or only group-induced beliefs ungrounded in reality.

At the same time that the results of Weber's impact became manifest, trouble for ethically oriented sociologists came from two other quarters: anthropology and philosophical positivism. Anthropologists introduced the concept of culture to the sociologists and in so doing convinced the sociologists that different people had different value systems and that apparently man could live happily under many different systems of social organization. Further they put the dread term ethnocentrism into the sociologists' vocabulary in such a way that most of the professors of sociology avoided evaluative discussions of culture so far as it was humanly possible.[2] Although the use of the concepts of cultural variability and ethnocentrism does not logically compel one to renounce his belief in the existence of a realm of real values, there can be little doubt but that such renunciation was the psychological effect of their use.

Philosophical positivism has probably had a much greater effect than cultural relativism in bringing most theoretically sophisticated sociologists to accept the view that value-judgments have no basis of validity in reality and are simply expressions of personal and group preference. Positivism transforms Weber's attitude of humility before values into one of arrogance. The syllogism is simple. Science is the only valid mode of cognition. The validity of values and other superempirical ideas cannot be demonstrated by science. Therefore values have no ontic status.[3] The conclusion takes two forms, one moderate, the other radical. The first

[2] Though it is true that cultures vary and that men can live under different systems of value-ideas, this fact is not a real challenge to the belief in the ontic status of values. There is no reason to believe that the good cannot take different forms, that systems of value-ideas are not imperfect conceptions of the ontic values, or that a variety of good eliminates the possibility of real evil. The whole question of cultural variability and ethnocentrism needs to be reexamined. As many writers have pointed out there seem to be certain universal moral patterns as well as relative patterns. Development of moral patterns toward greater universality is also possible. Proximate values must be distinguished from ultimate values. Thus it may be wrong for a society to say that monogamy is an ultimate value, but correct for them to say that love is an ultimate value. In such a case to be ethnocentric about monogamy is stupid, but to be ethnocentric about the value of love is one of the conditions for the belief in its ultimate nature. This task of distinguishing genuine ultimates from pseudo-ultimates is not one that can be performed by science, if it is possible at all; but science cannot disprove the possibility of performing the task, and the existence of cultural variability and ethnocentrism cannot be used as a means of denying this possibility.

[3] There is an extreme variant of positivism which holds that not even science is a valid mode of cognition, since what the scientist studies is his own responses to an unknown something. Thus science is valid only within the framework of its own axioms and objectivity becomes a matter of agreement among trained observers. If one does not wish to accept these axioms he can quite legitimately turn to a religious or metaphysical frame of reference. Only, he is warned, he must expect to pay the price in the form of maladaptation. The outstanding exponent of this form of positivism in sociology is George A. Lundberg. See especially the first chapter of his *Foundations of Sociology* (New York: Macmillan, 1939).

conclusion states that one must of necessity be agnostic concerning the ontic status of values. Since science is the *only* mode of knowing reality, any reality which cannot be known scientifically is unknowable and therefore we can say nothing about it. The second conclusion presses its logical attack harder and simply categorizes all statements about value and other superempirical ideas as nonsense.[4]

There has been some effort on the part of sociologists to cling to Weber's position of agnosticism and humility concerning values in *scientific* endeavor, and hence to make no statements concerning the possible ontic status of values. Yet even in the most careful works, we find sociologists making the positivistic metaphysical leap into complete agnosticism or complete value-subjectivism. Thus in two recent highly intelligent discussions of value one finds the conception that expressions of value are merely "acts of will and sentiment," and that ultimate ends have a "subjective and a transcendent quality—an existence only in the indoctrinated mind." [5] These two ideas go far beyond what we scientifically know about values. Philosophers who believe that values have ontic status hold that value expressions are acts of reason and intuition as well as of will and sentiment, and they also hold that values have existence independent of the indoctrinated mind. Such thinkers cannot be proved wrong by science, but only by the presuppositions of the postivistic metaphysics.

For the purposes at hand, however, we are more interested in the influence that the positivistic orientation toward values has had on sociologists as active members of the Western European community than as pure scientists. It has been stated above that it is possible to hold to Weberian neutrality as a scientist and at the same time to believe passionately in the reality of the value sphere. From the work of sociologists in applied fields, from their discussions of such work, and from conversa-

---

[4] To avoid possible confusion it is necessary to state what a belief in the ontic status of values implies and what it does not imply. To believe in the ontic status of values implies that somehow in the structure of the universe values objectively exist independent of their apprehension and espousal by man. Thus if it is objectively wrong to commit murder it is wrong even though no man knows it and no man espouses it. Such a belief does not imply that an idea which a man or a group of men have about values is correct. Thus if a society maintains that it is ultimately evil to have more than one wife, this value-idea may be wrong or right. If there is an ontic realm of values such an idea cannot be nonsense in the positivistic meaning of the term, since it is an idea, correct or incorrect, about something. The metaphysical problem is, of course, how men can bring their ideas of good and evil into a close and closer approximation of the objective reality of good and evil. The modes of cognition usually recommended are the use of reason, conscience, intuition, revelation, and, for proximate and instrumental values, careful use of the scientific knowledge of the consequences of certain value commitments.

[5] William J. Goode, *Religion Among the Primitives* (Glencoe: The Free Press, 1951), p. 23; Kingsley Davis, *Human Society* (New York: Macmillan, 1949), p. 526.

tions with many of them, I am convinced that few sociologists who have been subjected to the doctrines of cultural relativity and positivism have such an intellectual orientation toward values in their non-scientific lives. Most well trained sociologists have transformed Weber's neutrality in science into the positivist position that values are expressions of personal and social preference and have no ontic status that can be apprehended by reason and intuition.

It is an empirical fact, however, that some men can continue to act morally under such conditions—at least for a time. It is probable that most sociologists, while they do not believe that the values of freedom and human dignity have ontic status, still prefer these values to totalitarian values. They are still democrats and men of good will, even though they must always preface their statements with the dictum that these attitudes simply express their own preferences and the preferences of the society in which they have grown up. There may be some few sociologists who have used value subjectivism as a rationalization for becoming experts in human manipulation without commitment to policy; there may be others who have rationalized their failure to inquire into the ethical limitations of narrow values which they have espoused by such value relativism. But it is probably safe to say that most members of the profession still adhere to the values of human freedom and dignity.

I shall attempt to show in this paper that the recent development of the functional theory of religion, if sound, forces these men into a position where they can no longer adhere to a purely subjective theory of value validity and still believe in the possibility of human freedom and a democratic social structure. They may, perhaps, continue to be men of good will but they cannot continue to believe that it is possible for all men to have equal access to knowledge and truth. The reason is simple. Sociologists have believed for some time that in order for a society to exist the members of that society must share a system of values. If the ultimate significance of the functional theory of religion is to indicate that at least most men in a society must not only share values but must also believe that these value-ideas are connected with a realm of values which has ontic status, the positivistic sociologist who prefers a free society is placed in an intolerable dilemma. It is a prime postulate of the theory of freedom that knowledge of the truth will make men free and that in a democratic society all men must have access to the truth. Yet if the idea that values have ontic status is false but necessary for the existence of society, the sociologist cannot spread such truth. To give all men access to this truth would be to destroy society, for men cannot know to be false what they must believe to be true. To refrain from spreading the truth is to deny men their freedom and dignity, for the sociologist would then be placing a lie at the center of their social existence and would be making himself a member of an elite who know the truth but must conceal it from the mass.[6]

The existence of this dilemma depends upon the validity of the functional theory of religion with its ultimate implication that the members of a society must believe in the objective existence of values independent of the apprehension and the wishes of men. Prior to the full development of this theory in the last few years, it was possible for the moral positivist to believe that consensus could be developed without this condition. Many sociologists "knew" that they believed the values of our society to be desirable even though there was no real goodness in such values; they therefore believed that through education others could accept values on the same basis. Those who inquired further perhaps accepted the pragmatist's doctrine that most value conflicts can be decided by examining the relationship of the values in conflict to those concerning which there is agreement and that if reasonable men get together they can reach the conclusion that everyone ultimately has the same preferences. It is almost certain that they did not ask whether their present acceptance of values was not dependent either upon their own earlier acceptance of the idea that values have ontic status or upon their parents' acceptance of the same idea. They did not inquire into the significance of the empirical fact that what most people seem to want to know is not what their final preferences are but what they finally *ought* to prefer. It is precisely to these neglected facets of man's value oriented behavior that the functional theory of religion points and through which it indicates the necessity for a belief in the ontic status of values as a condition of social cohesion and personal stability.

The functional analysis of religion at the societal level begins with the question of the significance of the universality of religion. If religion makes no contribution to society, how is it that it has not long since disap-

---

[6] If the functional theory of religion is valid, I am making an assumption here that is probably false, namely that the sociologists themselves are not subject to the sociological and psychological necessity to believe in the ontic status of values. I am assuming in other words that the positivists can retain their good will and their psychological balance even though they reject what is to other people a necessity. I am making the assumption because my imagination does not have the capacity to envision what would happen in the personalities of those who try to cling to the positivistic view of values and yet at the same time are under intense psychological and sociological pressure to believe in the ontic status of values. I am inclined to believe that in many cases a sudden outcome would be a completely irrational embracing of some rigid set of value-ideas with the complete assumption that these value-ideas are a perfect reflection of the ontic realm of values, but this is largely speculative.

peared? [7] In order to get at the functions which religion performs it is necessary to understand its structural principles and its interrelations with other areas of social life.[8] In every society there is a distinction drawn between the sacred and the profane. The sacred is set apart by attitudes of respect and awe, and is partly composed of material objects toward which these attitudes are directed. One cannot find the source of sacredness in the sacred objects as such, but can find it in perceiving that sacred objects are symbols. They are almost always found to be symbols of values, social forms, or supernatural beings. Thus religious symbols and the rites and beliefs surrounding them are directed toward a super-empirical world.

The answer to what sacred objects symbolize and toward what religious beliefs and practices are oriented poses two new questions. First, why should men be concerned about a superempirical world? Second, why should their attitudes be those of respect and awe? The answer is to be found in the fact that members of a society must share a system of ulti-mate ends if the society is to endure. These ends may be divided into two categories: those which are achievable on this earth and those which are not. Those ends which cannot be achieved in this world must have their locus in a superempirical world. Further the superempirical world can appear as the source of the existence and moral validity of those ultimate ends which can be attained in this world. Thus if goodness of action is something that can be achieved in the world, the definition of what is good and the validity of this definition must be derived from the other

[7] Kingsley Davis's "Introduction" to William J. Goode, *op. cit.*, p. 15. As Davis points out, this question does not assume that religion is entirely adaptive, that all its functions will be the same in all societies, or that if it does perform some necessary universal function, such function cannot at some future time be performed by different institutions.

[8] The following functional account of religion is drawn almost wholly from the extremely clear analysis by Kingsley Davis in his *Human Society*, pp. 520–545. He, in turn, has drawn from Durkheim, William Robertson Smith, Radcliffe-Brown, Malinowski, Weber and Parsons, and not only has made a synthesis notable for its clarity but has added new hypotheses of his own. Goode, in the work cited above, has utilized this frame of reference for a careful analysis of religion in a small number of primitive societies. He also has added some new hypotheses, some careful quali-fications of functional theory, and considerable substantiating evidence.

I have used the statements of Davis and Goode because these statements, taken separately or combined, constitute the most up-to-date and complete accounts of the functional theory of religion available in the literature. They have been quoted at length because the full import of the functional theory of religion must be grasped, if the point of this paper is to be established. The theoretical positions of these two men has been well worked out, and constitutes an improvement on the earlier state-ments of Parsons and of those who developed the theory in the late nineteenth and early twentieth centuries. It is true, of course, that even today not all sociologists accept this theoretical account of religion and hence are not faced with the dilemma. But Davis is and Goode is, and so are almost all of the functional theorists among whom I include myself.

world. Further, if there are supernatural entities they function to support man's belief in the validity of ultimate ends. This super-world must appear real to the actors, even though its existence cannot be demonstrated scientifically.[9]

Thus religion may promote social unity and conformity in four ways. It offers an explanation of the origin and validity of group ends. It provides ritual reaffirmation of these ends. Through sacred objects it offers a concrete reference for the values. And finally it is a source of rewards and punishments. Although, according to Davis, this superempirical realm is "illusory" it becomes very real to the members of the society. In other words not only do realizable ultimate group ends assume ontic status, but so also do other-worldly ends, supernatural beings, and divine rewards and punishments. It is clear, however, that to Davis this ontic status is spurious, since it cannot be verified by scientific inquiry.

Now the functional theory of religion has been built up on the basis of data gathered primarily from primitive religions. There still remains the question as to the future of religion in civilized society. Both Goode and Davis show admirable scientific caution in the ideas that they advance, but there does seem to be agreement on a few central issues. Central to their theory is the idea that rational thought can supplant religion only to a certain point. There will always be the need for ultimate values and the validity of these values must always rest on a superempirical foundation. The gods may become less anthropomorphic, many of the factual statements of religion may be disproved, superempirical entities may become vaguer and more remote, religious practices may become segmental to the society, religious homogeneity may tend to diminish, and finally religious systems may become fragmented and some of their functions taken over by other agencies. But secularization can only go so far. Even though the gods disappear and other anthropomorphic entities vanish, there must still be the belief that ultimate values have an objective source and some degree of objective validity. Whatever happens, men must believe that their ends are good ends, that there is meaning in the universe, and that in some way good must triumph in the end. Men to exist must believe in the ontic status of the superempirical.[10]

---

[9] Davis's positivistic bias toward values and the superempirical is shown by his statement that "The unseen world is of course *fictitious,* but it must appear real to the actor. . . ." *Ibid.,* p. 527. My italics.

[10] *Ibid.,* pp. 541–544; Goode, *op. cit.,* pp. 219–226. One point should be made here for later reference. Neither Davis nor Goode, nor any of the other functionalists for that matter, have explored the possibility of a society believing in the existence of a real superempirical world and yet also believing that their own value-ideas are only greater or lesser approximations of the values of this world. Yet it is characteristic of certain types of civilized societies that this approach is taken to values. In our

This is not the place to concern ourselves about the scientific validity of the functional theory of religion. It can be said, I believe, that it rings truer than older rationalistic theories, that it is supported by considerable evidence, and that Davis and Goode have successfully answered many of the objections that have been made to it. But if we assume its fundamental validity, it does create the moral dilemma I have indicated. To spread the idea that a belief in ultimate validity of values is necessary but illusory would be to destroy society through destroying or confusing this belief. Yet to urge people to accept the idea that there is an ontic realm of values while believing oneself that such an idea is false is deliberately to deprive people of the knowledge necessary for their freedom and dignity.

What then is the positivistic sociologist to do in his role as a member of a democratic community? As is usual in the case of dilemmas, close examination indicates more than two paths of possible action. If the sociologist cannot find it possible to change his metaphysical hypothesis concerning the subjective quality of assigning moral validity to values, there are at least three courses open to him. First, he can value his integrity to such a degree that while he will not spread abroad his doctrine of moral subjectivism, neither will he urge people to believe in what he thinks is basically an illusion. Deeply pessimistic concerning the future of the human race, he will stand aside in a darkly splendid aloofness, bearing in his own mind what he knows is the doom of the human species. According to Irving Kristol this is the position that Freud took when in the later years of his life he came to believe that man would never discard religion even though it was a mass obsessional neurosis.[11] There is a dignity and honesty in this position that must be respected, even though one disagrees with it.

Except in times of extreme crisis most men, even intellectual men, seldom have the courage to accept the loneliness and isolation that the position just described entails. More likely is an extreme retreat in another direction, a retreat into the shelter of the expert. Sociological knowl-

---

own societies there are some religious denominations which hold that their image of the superempirical truth is only proximate, and certainly many realist philosophers of modern times have taken the position that though an objective realm of value exists we can know it only imperfectly.

[11] Irving Kristol, "God and the Psychoanalysts," *Commentary*, VIII (1949), 434–443. Kristol's article parallels this one in many respects in showing that the psychoanalyst, if he follows Freud's theory of religion, is placed in the dilemma of knowing that religion is necessary to personality but an illusion none the less. It is interesting that this cycle of thought in psychoanalysis occurred within the life work of Freud himself.

Kristol errs, I believe, in placing religious truth solely in the past and identifying the value-ideas of the religious past with the ontic realm of values.

edge will be sold to the highest bidder and the sociological expert, isolated from policy making positions, will plead lack of responsibility. *He* will not tell the people to believe in an illusory superempirical world, but his knowledge of the necessity of this belief and of the means of securing and manipulating it will be at the service of those who are not so wary of accepting responsibility. It is doubtful that in the long run the mass of people can be successfully manipulated by the expert and his leader, but there may be a bitter short run price to pay for accepting the premise that men must have a myth but that the myth is an illusion.

Finally, if the positivist clings to his humanism and refuses to isolate himself or to become an irresponsible expert, he may take upon himself the task of using his knowledge to make men a little happier and a little more adjusted. He can, of course, no longer hope to make men free, but by lowering his aspirations perhaps he can make life in the cage more endurable by giving them a myth in which they can believe, a sense of participation, even though the channels of power be far removed, and a feeling of freedom by asking of them no more than he has taught them to do. Here again it is doubtful that in the long run men can be so manipulated, but in the short run the price for adjustment would be freedom. Further, it is somewhat unlikely that such power would continue to be used for the prime purpose of adjustment and happiness. The kindly expert in power can become as brutalized as any man, and *1984* can come under the guidance of either politician or scientist. Whether it can endure is another question.

But perhaps the positivist can forsake his positivism. There is nothing in science that compels one to assert the subjective character of values. It is possible to return to the position of Weber, to recognize that the sphere of science is limited, but that beyond that sphere there are other modes of knowledge and responsibility. Such a return cannot and should not be dictated by a recognition of the consequences of not returning. If a belief in the ontic status of values has the consequence of permitting human beings to be free, the consequence is a result of the truth of the belief, not the truth of the belief a result or an image of the consequence. A knowledge of the consequences of returning and not returning to a belief in the objectivity of values can, however, be used as *one* source of evidence supporting the belief. Although it may be false, it is a reasonable assumption that what man must universally believe to be true is true. At least it makes little sense for man to take the opposite position, although non-man might be perfectly justified in doing so. In any event the sociologist can use his own reason, intuition, ethical inclinations, and conscience in renouncing a position that makes human existence meaningless.

To renounce positivism, however, is not fully to solve the problem.

Ethical skepticism, rationalism, pragmatism, and finally positivism were in large measure the intellectual result of a revolt against authoritarianism in religion and ethics. To agree that their final implication is to deny human freedom, is not to deny that in their inception they were designed to make men free. An acceptance of the belief that values have ontic status and that our own system of value-ideas represents an exact perception of the objective value structure of the universe is to return to authoritarian realism and to lose all that the intellectual revolt has gained. Human freedom lies in part in the very discrepancy between values as they exist and values as they are perceived and conceived by men. The path must be left open so that men are free to modify their conception of value; in this lies the possibility of progress and at the same time of disaster. Within this frame of reference the better life lies in the future if men have the patience and tolerance to act tentatively on the basis of our value-knowledge now and to continue searching for greater truth in the value sphere just as they have learned to do in science. Negatively we can define some aspects of evil on the basis of our experience in the last fifty years and by a study of history; but we can say very little about the realm of the good. Some things we know about love, beauty, honesty, etc., but the greatest potentialities for good, both for its definition and for its actualization, lie in the future. When the sociologist restores his belief in the objectivity of values while, at the same time, remaining humble about their final content, he rejoins the human race in its eternal quest.

39. Union of the Ideal and the Actual
JOHN DEWEY *

IN A SENSE, THIS BRIEF EXCERPT IS AN ANSWER TO KOLB'S PROPOSITION, IN THE PREVIOUS SELECTION, THAT A FUNCTIONAL THEORY LEADS INEVITABLY TO THE BELIEF THAT RELIGION, ALTHOUGH NECESSARY, IS ILLUSORY. DEWEY STATES SIMPLY THAT RELIGIOUS BELIEFS ARE NOT STATEMENTS OF FACT, BUT ARE ASPIRATIONS—AND THEY ARE FAR FROM ILLUSORY. THEY EXIST, AND IN THEIR INTERACTION WITH THE ACTUAL CONDITIONS OF LIFE, THEY HAVE CONSEQUENCES; THEY ARE REAL.

The aims and ideals that move us are generated through imagination. But they are not made out of imaginary stuff. They are made out of the hard stuff of the world of physical and social experience. The locomotive

* From *A Common Faith*, pp. 49–52.

did not exist before Stevenson, nor the telegraph before the time of Morse. But the conditions for their existence were there in physical material and energies and in human capacity. Imagination seized hold upon the idea of a rearrangement of existing things that would evolve new objects. The same thing is true of a painter, a musician, a poet, a philanthropist, a moral prophet. The new vision does not arise out of nothing, but emerges through seeing, in terms of possibilities, that is, of imagination, old things in new relations serving a new end which the new end aids in creating.

Moreover the process of creation is experimental and continuous. The artist, scientific man, or good citizen, depends upon what others have done before him and are doing around him. The sense of new values that become ends to be realized arises first in dim and uncertain form. As the values are dwelt upon and carried forward in action they grow in definiteness and coherence. Interaction between aim and existent conditions improves and tests the ideal; and conditions are at the same time modified. Ideals change as they are applied in existent conditions. The process endures and advances with the life of humanity. What one person and one group accomplish becomes the standing ground and starting point of those who succeed them. When the vital factors in this natural process are generally acknowledged in emotion, thought and action, the process will be both accelerated and purified through elimination of that irrelevant element that culminates in the idea of the supernatural. When the vital factors attain the religious force that has been drafted into supernatural religions, the resulting reinforcement will be incalculable.

These considerations may be applied to the idea of God, or, to avoid misleading conceptions, to the idea of the divine. This idea is, as I have said, one of ideal possibilities unified through imaginative realization and projection. But this idea of God, or of the divine, is also connected with all the natural forces and conditions—including man and human association—that promote the growth of the ideal and that further its realization. We are in the presence neither of ideals completely embodied in existence nor yet of ideals that are mere rootless ideals, fantasies, utopias. For there are forces in nature and society that generate and support the ideals. They are further unified by the action that gives them coherence and solidity. It is this *active* relation between ideal and actual to which I would give the name "God." I would not insist that the name *must* be given. There are those who hold that the associations of the term with the supernatural are so numerous and close that any use of the word "God" is sure to give rise to misconception and be taken as a concession to traditional ideas.

They may be correct in this view. But the facts to which I have referred are there, and they need to be brought out with all possible clearness and force. There exist concretely and experimentally goods—the values of art in all its forms, of knowledge, of effort and of rest after striving, of education and fellowship, of friendship and love, of growth in mind and body. These goods are there and yet they are relatively embryonic. Many persons are shut out from generous participation in them; there are forces at work that threaten and sap existent goods as well as prevent their expansion. A clear and intense conception of a union of ideal ends with actual conditions is capable of arousing steady emotion. It may be fed by every experience, no matter what its material.

In a distracted age, the need for such an idea is urgent. It can unify interests and energies now dispersed; it can direct action and generate the heat of emotion and the light of intelligence. Whether one gives the name "God" to this union, operative in thought and action, is a matter for individual decision. But the *function* of such a working union of the ideal and actual seems to me to be identical with the force that has in fact been attached to the conception of God in all the religions that have a spiritual content; and a clear idea of that function seems to me urgently needed at the present time.

Bibliography

Abel, Theodore. *Systematic Sociology in Germany.* New York: Columbia Univ. Press, 1929.

Abell, Aaron I. *The Urban Impact on American Protestantism, 1865–1900.* Cambridge: Harvard Univ. Press, 1943.

Aberle, David, Cohen, A., Davis, A., Levy, M., and Sutton, F. "The Functional Prerequisites of Society," *Ethics,* vol. LX, no. 2 (1950), 100–111.

Abrams, Ray H. *Preachers Present Arms.* Philadelphia: Round Table Press, 1933.

————, ed. "Organized Religion in the United States," *Annals of the American Academy of Political and Social Science,* March, 1948.

Acton, H. B. "Religion, Culture, and Class," *Ethics,* Jan., 1950, 120–130.

Alexander, Frank D. "Religion in a Rural Community of the South," *American Sociological Review,* April, 1941, 241–251.

Alexander, W. W. *Racial Segregation in the American Protestant Church.* New York: Friendship Press, 1946.

Allport, Gordon W. *The Individual and His Religion.* New York: The Macmillan Co., 1950.

Allport, Gordon W., Gillespie, James M., and Young, Jacqueline. "The

Religion of the Post-War College Student," *The Journal of Psychology,* Jan., 1948, 3–33.

Almond, Gabriel A. *The Appeals of Communism.* Princeton: Princeton Univ. Press, 1954.

Alpert, Harry. *Emile Durkheim and His Sociology.* New York: Columbia Univ. Press, 1939.

American Civil Liberties Union. *Conscience and the War.* A Report on the Treatment of Conscientious Objectors in World War II. New York: American Civil Liberties Union, Sept., 1943.

American Friends Service Committee. *The Experience of the American Friends Service Committee in Civilian Public Service,* 1945.

Ames, Edward S. *The Psychology of Religious Experience.* Boston: Houghton Mifflin Co., 1910.

Bainton, Roland H. "The Churches Shift on War," *Religion in Life,* Summer, 1943, 323–335.

———. "The Left Wing of the Reformation," *Journal of Religion,* Jan., 1941, 124–134.

———. "The Sectarian Theory of the Church," *Christendom,* Summer, 1946, 382–387.

Ballou, Robert O. *Shinto, The Unconquered Enemy.* New York: The Viking Press, 1945.

Barber, Bernard. "Acculturation and Messianic Movements," *American Sociological Review,* Oct., 1941, 663–669.

———. "A Socio-Cultural Interpretation of the Peyote Cult," *American Anthropologist,* Oct.–Dec., 1941, 673–675.

Barnes, Harry E. *The Twilight of Christianity.* New York: Richard R. Smith, Inc., 1931.

Barnes, Harry E., ed. *An Introduction to the History of Sociology.* Chicago: Univ. of Chicago Press, 1948.

Barnes, Harry E. and Becker, Howard. *Social Thought From Lore to Science.* 2 vols. Boston: D. C. Heath & Co., 1938.

Barnes, Harry E., Becker, Howard, and Becker, F. B., eds. *Contemporary Social Theory.* New York: D. Appleton-Century Co., 1940.

Barnett, James H. "The Easter Festival—A Study in Cultural Change," *American Sociological Review,* Feb., 1949, 62–70.

Baron, Salo W. "Impact of Wars on Religion," *Political Science Quarterly,* Dec., 1952, 534–572.

———. *Modern Nationalism and Religion.* New York: Harper & Bros., 1947.

———. *A Social and Religious History of the Jews.* Second edition, revised and enlarged. New York: Columbia Univ. Press, 1952.

Baron, Salo W. and Blau, Joseph L. *Judaism, Postbiblical and Talmudic Period.* New York: The Liberal Arts Press, 1954.

Bascom, W. R. "Acculturation Among the Gullah Negroes," *American Anthropologist,* Jan.–March, 1941, 43–50.

Bates, Ernest S. *American Faith.* New York: W. W. Norton & Co., 1940.

Baxter, Richard. *Practical Works.* 23 vols. Edited by William Orme. London: James Duncan, 1830.

Beaven, Albert W. "The Meaning for Religions of the Trend Toward Nationalism," *Annals of the American Academy of Political and Social Science,* July, 1934, 65–75.

Becker, Howard. "Supreme Values and the Sociologist," *American Sociological Review,* April, 1941, 155–172.

———. *Systematic Sociology,* on the basis of the *Beziehungslehre* and *Gebildelehre* of Leopold von Wiese (see also Wiese). New York: John Wiley & Sons, 1932.

———. *Through Values to Social Interpretation.* Durham: Duke Univ. Press, 1950.

Benedict, Ruth. *Patterns of Culture.* Boston: Houghton-Mifflin, 1934. Reprinted by Penguin Books, 1946.

Bennett, John C. *Christian Ethics and Social Policy.* New York: Charles Scribner's Sons, 1946.

Bennett, John C., Bowen, Howard R., Brown, William A., Jr., and Oxnam, G. Bromley. *Christian Values and Economic Life.* New York: Harper & Bros., 1954.

Bennion, Lowell L. *Max Weber's Methodology.* Paris: Les Presses Modernes, 1933.

Benyon, Erdmann D. "The Voodoo Cult Among Negro Migrants to Detroit," *American Journal of Sociology,* May, 1938, 894–907.

Bergson, Henri. *The Two Sources of Morality and Religion.* Translated by R. Ashley Audra and Cloudesley Brereton, with the assistance of W. Horsfall Carter. New York: Henry Holt & Co., 1935.

Bernard, L. L. *Social Control in Its Sociological Aspects.* New York: The Macmillan Co., 1939.

———. "The Sociological Interpretation of Religion," *The Journal of Religion,* Jan., 1938, 1–18.

Bidney, David. "The Ethnology of Religion and the Problem of Human Evolution," *American Anthropologist,* Feb., 1954, 1–18.

Birnbaum, N. "Conflicting Interpretations of the Rise of Capitalism: Marx and Weber," *British Journal of Sociology,* June, 1953, 125–141.

Blanshard, Paul. *American Freedom and Catholic Power.* Boston: The Beacon Press, 1949.

————. *Communism, Democracy, and Catholic Power.* Boston: The Beacon Press, 1951.

Blau, Joseph L., ed. *Cornerstones of Religious Freedom in America.* Boston: The Beacon Press, 1949.

Blizzard, Samuel W. "The Roles of the Rural Parish Minister, The Protestant Seminaries, and the Sciences of Social Behavior," *Religious Education,* Nov.–Dec., 1955, 1–10.

Boas, Franz, ed., *General Anthropology.* Boston: D. C. Heath & Co., 1938.

Boisen, Anton T. "Economic Distress and Religious Experience," *Psychiatry,* May, 1939, 185–194.

————. *The Exploration of the Inner World. A Study of Mental Disorder and Religious Experience.* New York: Harper & Bros., 1936.

————. "Religion and Hard Times. A Study of the Holy Rollers," *Social Action,* March 15, 1939, 8–35.

Braden, Charles S. "The Sects," *Annals of the American Academy of Political and Social Science,* March, 1948, 53–62.

————. *These Also Believe. A Study of Modern American Cults and Minority Religious Movements.* New York: The Macmillan Co., 1949.

————. *War, Communism and World Religions.* New York: Harper & Bros., 1953.

————. "Why Are The Cults Growing," *Christian Century,* Jan. 12, 1944, 45–47; Jan. 19, 1944, 78–80; Jan. 26, 1944, 108–110; Feb. 2, 1944, 137–140.

Brant, Charles. "Peyotism Among the Kiowa-Apache and Neighboring Tribes," *Southwestern Journal of Anthropology,* vol. 6 (1950), 212–222.

Breasted, James H. *The Dawn of Conscience.* New York: Charles Scribner's Sons, 1933.

————. *Development of Religion and Thought in Ancient Egypt.* New York: Charles Scribner's Sons, 1912.

Bredemeier, Harry C. "The Methodology of Functionalism," *American Sociological Review,* April, 1955, 173–180.

Brewer, Earl D. C. "Sect and Church in Methodism," *Social Forces,* May, 1952, 400–408.

Broderick, James. *The Economic Morals of the Jesuits.* London: Oxford Univ. Press, 1934.

Brown, Daniel G. and Lowe, Warner L. "Religious Beliefs and Personality Characteristics of College Students," *Journal of Social Psychology,* Feb., 1951, 103–129.

Brunner, Heinrich E. *Christianity and Civilization.* 2 vols. New York: Charles Scribner's Sons, 1948 and 1949.

Bryce, James. *The American Commonwealth.* New edition. New York: The Macmillan Co., 1917.

Buber, Martin. *I and Thou.* Translated by Ronald G. Smith. Edinburgh: T. and T. Clark, 1944.

Buck, Peter H. *Anthropology and Religion.* New Haven: Yale Univ. Press, 1939.

Burchard, Waldo W. "Role Conflicts of Military Chaplains," *American Sociological Review,* Oct., 1954, 528–535.

Burrows, Millar. *The Dead Sea Scrolls.* New York: The Viking Press, 1955.

Burrows, Millar, *et al.* "The Dead Sea Scrolls," *The New Republic,* April 9, 1956, 12–25.

Calvin, John. *Institutes of the Christian Religion.* 2 vols. Translated by John Allen. Sixth American edition. Revised and corrected. Philadelphia: Presbyterian Board of Publication, 1921.

Cantril, Hadley. "Educational and Economic Composition of Religious Groups: An Analysis of Poll Data," *American Journal of Sociology,* March, 1943, 574–579.

———. *The Psychology of Social Movements.* New York: John Wiley & Sons, 1941.

Cavert, Samuel M. "Rethinking the Social Function of the Church," *Religion in Life,* Summer, 1943, 344–355.

Chan, Wing-tsit. *Religious Trends in Modern China.* New York: Columbia Univ. Press, 1953.

Childs, Marquis W. and Cater, Douglass. *Ethics in a Business Society.* New York: Mentor Books, 1954.

The Christian Century, Sept. 22, 1954, "Evanston, 1954. The Second Assembly of the World Council of Churches."

Clark, Elmer T. "Non-Theological Factors in Church Diversity," *Ecumenical Review,* July 1951, 347–356.

———. *The Small Sects in America.* Revised and enlarged edition. New York: Abingdon-Cokesbury Press, 1949.

Clark, S. D. *Church and Sect in Canada.* Toronto: Univ. of Toronto Press, 1948.

Clark, Walter H. *The Oxford Group. Its History and Significance.* New York: Bookman Associates, 1951.

Comhaire, Jean L. "Religious Trends in African and Afro-American Urban Societies," *Anthropological Quarterly,* Oct., 1953, 95–108.

Conference on Science, Philosophy and Religion. *Perspectives on a Troubled Decade: Science, Philosophy and Religion, 1939–1949.* Bryson, Lyman, Finklestein, Louis, and MacIver, R. M., eds. New York: Harper & Bros., 1950.

Conference on Science, Philosophy and Religion. *Symbols and Values: An Initial Study.* Edited by Bryson, Lyman, Finklestein, Louis, Mac-Iver, R. M., and McKeon, Richard. New York: Harper & Bros., 1954.

Cornford, Francis M. *From Religion to Philosophy.* New York: Longmans, Green & Co., 1912.

Coughenour, C. M. "An Application of Scale Analysis to the Study of Religious Groups," *Rural Sociology,* Sept.–Dec., 1955, 197–211.

Coulton, G. G. *Five Centuries of Religion.* 4 vols. Cambridge: Cambridge Univ. Press, 1923–1936.

Cragg, G. R. "Disunities Created by Differing Patterns of Church Life," *Ecumenical Review,* April, 1952, 276–281.

Crossman, Richard, ed. *The God that Failed.* New York: Harper & Bros., 1949.

Culver, Dwight W. *Negro Segregation in the Methodist Church.* New Haven: Yale Univ. Press, 1953.

Curti, Merle. *Peace or War, The American Struggle, 1636–1936.* New York: W. W. Norton & Co., 1936.

Curtiss, John S. *Church and State in Russia, The Last Years of the Empire, 1900–1917.* New York: Columbia Univ. Press, 1940.

———. *The Russian Church and the Soviet State, 1917–1950.* Boston: Little, Brown & Co., 1953.

Daniel, Vattel E. "Ritual and Stratification in Chicago Negro Churches," *American Sociological Review,* June, 1942, 352–361.

Davis, Allison W., Gardner, B. B., and Gardner, M. R. *Deep South.* Chicago: Univ. of Chicago Press, 1941.

Davis, Jerome, ed. *Labor Speaks for Itself on Religion.* New York: The Macmillan Co., 1929.

Davis, Jerome. "The Social Action Pattern of the Protestant Religious Leader," *American Sociological Review,* Feb., 1936, 105–114.

———. "A Study of Protestant Church Boards of Control," *American Journal of Sociology,* Nov., 1932, 418–431.

Davis, Kingsley. *Human Society.* New York: The Macmillan Co., 1949.

Dawson, Joseph M. *America's Way in Church, State, and Society.* New York: The Macmillan Co., 1953.

Deren, Maya. *Divine Horsemen. The Living Gods of Haiti.* London: Thames and Hudson, 1953.

Desroche, Henri. "Areas and Methods of a Sociology of Religion. The Work of G. LeBras." Translated by E. L. Sheppard. *Journal of Religion,* Jan., 1955, 34–47.

Dewey, John. *A Common Faith*. New Haven: Yale Univ. Press, 1934.

———. *Intelligence in the Modern World*. Edited by Joseph Ratner. New York: The Modern Library, 1939.

Dewey, John and Tufts, James H. *Ethics*. New York: Henry Holt & Co., 1908.

Doll, Eugene E. "Social and Economic Organization in Two Pennsylvania German Religious Communities," *American Journal of Sociology*, Sept., 1951, 168–177.

Dollard, John. *Caste and Class in a Southern Town*. New Haven: Yale Univ. Press, 1937.

Douglass, H. Paul. *The Church in the Changing City*. New York: Harper & Bros., 1927.

———. "Cultural Differences and Recent Religious Divisions," *Christendom*, Winter, 1945, 89–105.

———. *The Springfield Church Survey*. New York: George H. Doran Co., 1926.

Douglass, H. Paul and Brunner, Edmund de S. *The Protestant Church as a Social Institution*. New York: Harper & Bros., 1935.

Drake, St. Clair and Cayton, Horace R. *Black Metropolis*. New York: Harcourt, Brace & Co., 1945.

Dreger, Ralph M. "Some Personality Correlates of Religious Attitudes as Determined by Projective Techniques," *Psychological Monographs*, vol. 66, no. 3 (1952).

Ducasse, C. J. *A Philosophical Scrutiny of Religion*. New York: The Ronald Press Co., 1953.

Dunlap, Knight. *Religion. Its Functions in Human Life*. New York: McGraw-Hill Book Co., 1946.

Durkheim, Emile. *The Division of Labor in Society*. Translated by George Simpson. Glencoe: The Free Press, 1947.

———. *The Elementary Forms of the Religious Life*. Translated by Joseph W. Swain. London: George Allen and Unwin, Ltd., 1915. Reprinted by The Free Press, 1947.

———. *The Rules of Sociological Method*. Eighth edition. Chicago: Univ. of Chicago Press, 1938.

———. *Sociology and Philosophy*. Translated by D. F. Pocock, with an Introduction by J. G. Peristiany. Glencoe: The Free Press, 1953.

Dynes, Russell R. "Church-Sect Typology and Socio-Economic Status," *American Sociological Review*, Oct., 1955, 555–560.

———. "Toward the Sociology of Religion," *Sociology and Social Research*, March–April, 1954, 227–232.

Ebersole, Luke E. *Church Lobbying in the Nation's Capitol.* New York: The Macmillan Co., 1951.

Eckardt, A. Roy. "The New Look in American Piety," *Christian Century,* Nov. 17, 1954, 1395–1397.

Eckhardt, Carl C. *The Papacy and World Affairs.* Chicago: Univ. of Chicago Press, 1937.

Eddy, Mary Baker G. *Science and Health With Key to the Scriptures.* Nineteenth edition, revised. Boston: Published by the Author, 1886.

Edel, Abraham. *Ethical Judgment. The Use of Science in Ethics.* Glencoe: The Free Press, 1955.

Eister, Allan W. *Drawing Room Conversion. A Sociological Account of the Oxford Group Movement.* Durham: Duke Univ. Press, 1950.

Ellis, John T. "Church and State: An American Catholic Tradition," *Harper's,* Nov., 1953, 63–67.

Ellsworth, Clayton S. "The American Churches and the Mexican War," *American Historical Review,* Jan., 1940, 301–326.

Ellul, Jacque. "On the Cultural and Social Factors Influencing Church Division," *Ecumenical Review,* April, 1952, 269–275.

Ellwood, Charles A. *The Reconstruction of Religion. A Sociological View.* New York: The Macmillan Co., 1922.

———. "The Social Function of Religion," *American Journal of Sociology,* Nov., 1913, 289–307.

England, R. W. "Some Aspects of Christian Science as Reflected in Letters of Testimony," *American Journal of Sociology,* March, 1954, 448–453.

Ernst, Morris L. and Loth, David. *Report on the American Communist.* New York: Henry Holt & Co., 1952.

Fairchild, Hoxie N. "Religious Faith and Loyalty," *New Republic,* Oct. 11, 1954, 11–13.

Fanfani, Amintore. *Catholicism, Protestantism, and Capitalism.* London: Sheed and Ward, 1935.

Fauset, Arthur H. *Black Gods of the Metropolis.* Vol. III of Pub. of Philadelphia Anthropological Society. Philadelphia: Univ. of Pennsylvania Press, 1944.

Federal Council of Churches of Christ in America. "The Malvern Conference Report—Official Version," *Information Service,* May 31, 1941.

———. *A Message From the National Study Conference on the Churches and a Just and Durable Peace,* March 3–5, 1942.

———. *Report of the First Meeting* (Philadelphia, 1908). New York: Revell Press, 1909.

———. "Social-Economic Status and Outlook of Religious Groups in America," *Information Service,* May 15, 1948.

Fichter, Joseph H. *Dynamics of a City Church*. Chicago: Univ. of Chicago Press, 1951.

———. "The Marginal Catholic: An Institutional Approach," *Social Forces*, Dec., 1953, 167–173.

———. *Social Relations in the Urban Parish*. Chicago: Univ. of Chicago Press, 1954.

Finkelstein, Louis. *The Jews, Their History, Culture, and Religion*. 2 vols. Harper & Bros., 1949.

———. *The Pharisees: The Sociological Background of Their Faith*. 2 vols. Philadelphia: The Jewish Publication Society of America, 1938.

Fortune, editorial. "War and Peace," Jan., 1940, 26–27.

Fortune, R. F. *Manus Religion*. Philadelphia: Memoirs of the American Philosophical Society, vol. 3 (1935).

Francis, E. K. "The Russian Mennonites: From Religion to Ethnic Group," *American Journal of Sociology*, Sept., 1948, 101–107.

Frankfort, Henri. *Ancient Egyptian Religion*. New York: Columbia Univ. Press, 1948.

Frazer, James G. *The Golden Bough*. New York: The Macmillan Co., 1922.

Frazier, E. F. *Negro Youth at the Crossways*. Washington: American Council on Education, 1940.

Freud, Sigmund. *Civilization and Its Discontents*. Translated by Joan Riviere. New York: Jonathan Cape and Harrison Smith, 1930.

———. *The Future of an Illusion*. Translated by W. D. Robson-Scott. Horace Liveright and The Institute of Psycho-Analysis, 1928.

———. *Moses and Monotheism*. Translated by Katherine Jones. New York: Vintage Books, 1955.

———. *Totem and Taboo*. Translated by A. A. Brill. New York: Moffat, Yard & Co., 1918.

Friedman, Robert. "Conception of the Anabaptists," *Church History*, Dec., 1940, 341–365.

Friedrich, Carl J., ed. *Totalitarianism*. Cambridge: Harvard Univ. Press, 1954.

Fromm, Erich. *Escape from Freedom*. New York: Rinehart & Co., 1941.

———. *Man For Himself*. New York: Rinehart & Co., 1947.

———. *Psychoanalysis and Religion*. New Haven: Yale Univ. Press, 1950.

Fry, C. Luther. "The Religious Affiliations of American Leaders," *Scientific Monthly*, March, 1933, 241–249.

Gallagher, Buell G. *Color and Conscience: The Irrepressible Conflict*. New York: Harper & Bros., 1946.

Gans, Herbert J. "American Jewry: Present and Future," *Commentary,* May, 1956, 422–430.

——. "The Future of American Jewry," *Commentary,* June, 1956, 555–563.

Garbett, Cyril. *Church and State in England.* London: Hoddes and Stoughton, 1950.

Garrison, Winfred E. "Characteristics of American Organized Religion," *Annals of the American Academy of Political and Social Science,* March, 1948, 14–24.

——. "Social and Cultural Factors in Our Divisions," *Ecumenical Review,* Oct., 1952, 43–51.

Geffcken, Heinrich. *Church and State.* 2 vols. London: Longmans, Green & Co., 1877.

Gerth, Hans and Gerth, Hedwig I. "Bibliography on Max Weber," *Social Research,* March, 1949, 70–89.

Gerth, Hans H. and Mills, Charles W. *Character and Social Structure.* New York: Harcourt, Brace & Co., 1953.

Gibb, H. A. R. *Modern Trends in Islam.* Chicago: Univ. of Chicago Press, 1947.

Gilliland, A. R. "Changes in Religious Beliefs of College Students," *Journal of Social Psychology,* Feb., 1953, 113–116.

Giordani, Igino. *The Social Message of Jesus.* Translated by A. I. Zizzamia. Patterson, New Jersey: St. Anthony Guild Press, 1943.

Gladden, Washington. *Applied Christianity.* Sixth edition. Boston: Houghton, Mifflin & Co., 1886.

Glazer, Nathan. "The Jewish Revival in America," *Commentary,* Dec., 1955, 493–499, and Jan., 1956, 17–24.

Glick, Paul C. and Young, Kimball. "Justifications for Religious Attitudes and Habits," *Journal of Social Psychology,* Feb., 1943, 45–68.

Glock, Charles Y. and Ringer, Benjamin B. "Church Polity and the Attitudes of Ministers and Parishioners on Social Issues," *American Sociological Review,* April, 1956, 148–156.

Gloyn, Cyril K. *The Church in the Social Order. A Study of Anglican Social Theory from Coleridge to Maurice.* Forest Grove, Oregon: Pacific Univ., 1942.

Goldenweiser, Alexander. *Anthropology. An Introduction to Primitive Culture.* New York: F. S. Crofts & Co., 1937.

Goldschmidt, Walter R. "Class Denominationalism in Rural California Churches," *American Journal of Sociology,* Jan., 1944, 348–355.

Gooch, G. P. *English Democratic Ideas in the Seventeenth Century.*

Second edition, with supplementary notes and appendices by H. J. Laski. Cambridge: Cambridge Univ. Press, 1927.

Goode, William J. *Religion Among the Primitives*. Glencoe: The Free Press, 1951.

Gordon-Walker, P. C. "Capitalism and the Reformation," *The Economic History Review*, Nov., 1937.

Grafton, Thomas H. "Religious Origins and Sociological Theory," *American Sociological Review*, Dec., 1945, 726–739.

Granet, Marcel. *Chinese Civilization*. Translated by Kathleen Innes and Mabel Brailsford. London: Routledge and Kegan Paul, 1950.

Greenslade, S. L. *Schism in the Early Church*. New York: Harper & Bros., 1953.

Gregory, W. E. "The Psychology of Religion. Some Suggested Areas of Research of Significance to Psychology," *Journal of Abnormal and Social Psychology*, April, 1952, 256–258.

Grunebaum, G. E. von. "Studies in Islamic Cultural History." "Comparative Studies of Cultures and Civilizations, No. 2." Robert Redfield and Milton Singer, eds. *American Anthropologist*, April, 1954.

Gurvitch, Georges, and Moore, Wilbert E., eds. *Twentieth Century Sociology*. New York: The Philosophical Library, 1945.

Hales, E. E. Y. *Pio Nono. A Study in European Politics and Religion in the Nineteenth Century*. London: Eyre and Spottiswoode, 1954.

Hall, Thomas C. *The Religious Background of American Culture*. Boston: Little, Brown, and Co., 1930.

Haller, William. *The Rise of Puritanism*. New York: Columbia Univ. Press, 1938.

Hamilton, Thomas. "Social Optimism and Pessimism in American Protestantism," *Public Opinion Quarterly*, Summer, 1942, 280–283.

Hammond, J. L. and Hammond, Barbara. *The Town Labourer, 1760–1832. The New Civilisation*. New York: Longmans, Green & Co., 1928.

Handlin, Oscar. *Adventures in Freedom: Three Hundred Years of Jewish Life in America*. New York: McGraw-Hill Book Co., 1954.

Harrison, Jane E. *Themis. A Study of the Social Origins of Greek Religion*. Cambridge: Cambridge Univ. Press, 1912.

Haydon, A. Eustace. *Biography of the Gods*. New York: The Macmillan Co., 1941.

Herberg, Will. *Protestant-Catholic-Jew. An Essay in American Religious Sociology*. Garden City, New York: Doubleday & Co., 1955.

Herskovits, Melville J. *Man and His Works*. New York: Alfred A. Knopf, 1951.

Hertzler, J. O. "Religious Institutions," *Annals of the American Academy of Political and Social Science*, March, 1948, 1–13.

Hicks, Granville. "The Parsons and the War," *American Mercury*, Feb., 1927, 129–142.

High, Stanley. "The Church Unmilitant," *New Republic*, June 22, 1942, 850–852.

Highet, John. "Scottish Religious Adherence," *British Journal of Sociology*, June, 1953, 142–159.

Hobhouse, Leonard T. *Morals in Evolution.* Sixth edition. New York: Henry Holt & Co., Inc., 1929.

Hobson, J. A. *God and Mammon.* New York: The Macmillan Co., 1931.

Hoffer, Eric. *The True Believer.* New York: Harper & Bros., 1951.

Hollingshead, August B. *Elmtown's Youth.* New York: John Wiley & Sons, Inc., 1949.

Holloway, Vernon H. "Power Politics and the Christian Conscience," *Social Action*, Feb. 15, 1950, 5–35.

Holt, Arthur E. "Organized Religion as a Pressure Group," *Annals of the American Academy of Political and Social Science*, May, 1935, 42–49.

———. "Social Changes: Religion," *American Journal of Sociology*, July, 1928, 172–176; and May, 1929, 1116–1128.

Holt, John B. "Holiness Religion: Cultural Shock and Social Reorganization," *American Sociological Review*, Oct., 1940, 740–747.

Holtom, D. C. *Modern Japan and Shinto Nationalism.* Chicago: The Univ. of Chicago Press, 1947.

Hooft, W. A. Visser 'T and Oldham, J. H. *The Church and Its Function in Society.* Chicago: Willett, Clark & Co., 1937.

Hook, Sidney. "The New Failure of Nerve," *Partisan Review*, Jan.–Feb., 1943, 2–23.

Hopkins, Charles H. *The Rise of the Social Gospel in American Protestantism 1865–1915.* New Haven: Yale Univ. Press, 1940.

Howard, Peter. *The World Rebuilt. The True Story of Frank Buchman and the Achievements of Moral Re-Armament.* New York: Duell, Sloan and Pearce, 1951.

Howells, William W. *The Heathens, Primitive Man and His Religions.* New York: Doubleday & Co., 1948.

Hromadka, Josef. "Social and Cultural Factors in our Divisions," *Ecumenical Review*, Oct., 1952, 52–58.

Hsu, Francis L. K. *Americans and Chinese: Two Ways of Life.* New York: Henry Schuman, 1953.

———. *Religion, Science and Human Crises.* London: Routledge and Kegan Paul, 1952.

Hudson, Winthrop S. "Puritanism and the Spirit of Capitalism," *Church History*, March, 1949, 3–17.

Hughley, J. Neal. *Trends in Protestant Social Idealism*. New York: King's Crown Press, 1948.

Hutchison, John A., ed. *Christian Faith and Social Action*. New York: Charles Scribner's Sons, 1953.

Hutchinson, Paul. "Have We a 'New' Religion?" *Life*, April 11, 1955, 138–158.

Huxley, Julian S. *Man Stands Alone*. New York: Harper & Bros., 1941.

Hyma, Albert. *Christianity, Captialism and Communism*. Ann Arbor: Published by the author, 1937.

Jackson, Elmore. *Meeting of Minds*. New York: McGraw-Hill Book Co., 1952.

James, Earle K. "Church and State in Mexico," *Annals of the American Academy of Political and Social Science*, March, 1940, 112–120.

James, William. *The Varieties of Religious Experience*. New York: The Modern Library. Originally published by Longmans, Green & Co., 1902.

Johnson, Charles S. *Growing Up in the Black Belt*. Washington: American Council on Education, 1941.

Johnson, F. Ernest, ed. *American Education and Religion. The Problem of Religion in the Schools*. New York: Harper & Bros., for the Institute for Religious and Social Studies, 1952.

Johnston, Ruby F. *The Development of Negro Religion*. New York: Philosophical Library, 1954.

Jonassen, Christen T. "The Protestant Ethic and the Spirit of Capitalism in Norway," *American Sociological Review*, Dec., 1947, 676–686.

Jones, W. Lawson. "Some Psychological Conditions of the Development of Methodism Up to 1850," *British Journal of Psychology*, Nov., 1951, 345–354.

Jung, Carl G. *Modern Man in Search of a Soul*. Translated by W. S. Dell and C. F. Boynes. New York: Harcourt, Brace & Co., 1933.

———. *Psychology and Religion*. New Haven: Yale Univ. Press, 1938.

Kaufmann, Walter A. *Nietzsche: Philosopher, Psychologist, Antichrist*. Princeton: Princeton Univ. Press, 1950.

Kennedy, R. C. "Why Churches Do Not Unite," *Christian Century*, July 16, 1952, 825–827.

Kidd, Benjamin. *Social Evolution*. New York: G. P. Putnam's Sons, 1920.

Kierkegaard, Soren. *Fear and Trembling* and *The Sickness Unto Death*. Translated with Introduction and Notes by Walter Lowrie. New York: Doubleday & Co., 1954.

Kincheloe, Samuel C. *The American City and Its Church.* New York: Friendship Press, 1938.

King, Irving. *The Development of Religion. A Study in Anthropology and Social Psychology.* New York: The Macmillan Co., 1910.

King, Winston L. *Introduction to Religion.* New York: Harper & Bros., 1954.

————. "Millennialism as a Social Ferment," *Religion in Life*, Winter, 1951–1952, 33–44.

Kirkpatrick, Clifford. *Religion in Human Affairs.* New York: John Wiley & Sons, Inc., 1929.

Kluckhohn, Clyde. *Navaho Witchcraft.* Cambridge: Papers of the Peabody Museum of American Archaeology and Ethnology, Harvard Univ., vol. XXII, no. 2 (1944).

Kolb, William L. "Values, Positivism, and the Functional Theory of Religion: The Growth of a Moral Dilemma," *Social Forces*, May, 1953, 305–311.

Kraemer, Hendrik and Abrecht, Paul. "Can Sociology Help the Church?" *Ecumenical Review*, July, 1951, 388–393.

Krikorian, Yervant H., ed. *Naturalism and the Human Spirit.* New York: Columbia Univ. Press, 1944.

Kroeber, A. L. *Anthropology.* New edition, revised. New York: Harcourt, Brace & Co., 1948.

LaBarre, Weston. *The Peyote Cult.* Yale Univ. Publ. in Anthropology, no. 19. New Haven: Yale Univ. Press, 1938.

————. "Primitive Psychotherapy in Native American Cultures: Peyotism and Confession," *Journal of Abnormal and Social Psychology*, July, 1947, 294–309.

Lang, Andrew. *Magic and Religion.* London: Longmans, Green & Co., 1901.

————. *The Making of Religion.* London: Longmans, Green & Co., 1898.

Laski, Harold J. *The American Democracy.* New York: The Viking Press, 1948.

Latourette, Kenneth S. *A History of Christianity.* New York: Harper & Bros., 1953.

Latreille, André and Siegfried, André. *Les Forces Religieuses et la Vie Politique.* Paris: Librairie Armand Colin, 1951.

Learsi, Rufus. *The Jews in America.* Cleveland: The World Publishing Co., 1954.

LeBras, Gabriel. *Etudes de sociologie religieuse.* 2 vols. Paris: Presses Universitaires, 1954.

LeBras, Gabriel, *et al.* "Sociologie Religieuse," *L'Année Sociologique*, 3ᵉ serie, 1940–1948, 405–461; 1948–1949, 287–332; 1949–1950, 299–330; 1951, 262–323.

Lee, Dorothy D. *Religious Perspectives in College Teaching in Anthropology.* New Haven: The Edward W. Hazen Foundation.

Leiper, Henry S. "Religion Confronts Caesarism," *Annals of the American Academy of Political and Social Science,* July, 1935, 176–182.

Lenin, V. I. *Religion.* New York: International Publishers, 1933.

Lenski, Gerhard E. "Social Correlates of Religious Interest," *American Sociological Review,* Oct., 1953, 533–544.

Leo XIII, Pope. *The Great Encyclical Letters of Pope Leo XIII.* Second edition. New York: Benziger Bros., 1903.

Lesser, Alexander. "Cultural Significance of the Ghost Dance," *American Anthropologist,* Jan.–March, 1933, 108–115.

Leuba, James H. *The Belief in God and Immortality.* Second edition. Chicago: Open Court Publishing Co., 1921.

——. *A Psychological Study of Religion. Its Origin, Function, and Future.* New York: The Macmillan Co., 1912.

——. *The Reformation of the Churches.* Boston: The Beacon Press, 1950.

Lewis, Bernard. "Islamic Revival in Turkey," *International Affairs,* Jan., 1952, 38–48.

Lewis, John, Polanyi, Karl, and Kitchin, Donald K., eds. *Christianity and the Social Revolution,* London: Victor Gollancz, 1935.

Liebman, Joshua L. *Peace of Mind.* New York: Simon and Schuster, 1946.

Lindsay, Thomas M. *A History of the Reformation.* 2 vols. New York: Charles Scribner's Sons, 1928.

Linton, Ralph. "Nativistic Movements," *American Anthropologist,* April–June, 1943, 230–240.

Lippmann, Walter. *A Preface to Morals.* New York: The Macmillan Co., 1929.

Loescher, F. S. *The Protestant Church and the Negro.* New York: Association Press, 1948.

Loos, A. William, ed. *Religious Faith and World Culture.* New York: Prentice-Hall, 1951.

Loewenstein, Karl. *Hitler's Germany.* New York: The Macmillan Co., 1939.

Lowenthal, Leo and Guterman, Norbert. *Prophets of Deceit. A Study in the Techniques of the American Agitator.* New York: Harper & Bros., 1949.

Lowie, Robert H. *Primitive Religion.* New York: Boni & Liveright, 1924.

Luther, Martin. *Luther's Primary Works.* Edited by Henry Wace and C. A. Buckhein. London, 1896.

Lynd, Robert S. and Lynd, Helen M. *Middletown*. New York: Harcourt, Brace & Co., 1929.

———. *Middletown in Transition*. New York: Harcourt, Brace & Co., 1937.

MacArthur, Kathleen W. *The Economic Ethics of John Wesley*. New York: The Abingdon Press, 1936.

MacBeath, Alexander. *The Relationship of Primitive Morality and Religion*. Glascow: Jackson, Son & Co., 1949.

McCown, Chester C. *The Genesis of the Social Gospel*. New York: Alfred A. Knopf, 1929.

MacFarland, Charles S. *Chaos in Mexico; The Conflict of Church and State*. New York: Harper & Bros., 1935.

———. *The New Church and the New Germany*. New York: The Macmillan Co., 1934.

McGiffert, Arthur C. *Martin Luther. The Man and His Work*. New York: The Century Co., 1910.

———. *Protestant Thought Before Kant*. New York: Charles Scribner's Sons, 1913.

MacIver, R. M. *Social Causation*. Boston: Ginn & Co., 1942.

MacIver, R. M. and Page, Charles H. *Society. An Introductory Analysis*. New York: Rinehart & Co., 1949.

Mack, Raymond W., Murphy, Raymond J. and Yellin, Seymour. "The Protestant Ethic, Level of Aspiration, and Social Mobility: An Empirical Test," *American Sociological Review*, June, 1956, 295–300.

Mackinson, James. *Calvin and the Reformation*. London: Longmans, Green & Co., 1936.

MacMurray, John. *The Clue to History*. London: Student Christian Movement Press, 1938.

———. *Creative Society. A Study of the Relation of Christianity to Communism*. New York: Association Press, 1936.

Malinowski, Bronislaw. *Argonauts of the Western Pacific*. London: George Routledge & Sons, 1932.

———. *Coral Gardens and Their Magic*. 2 vols. London: George Allen and Unwin, Ltd., 1935.

———. *The Foundations of Faith and Morals*. London: Oxford Univ. Press, 1936.

———. "Magic, Science, and Religion," in *Science Religion and Reality*, Joseph Needham, ed. New York: The Macmillan Co., 1925, 19–84.

———. *A Scientific Theory of Culture and Other Essays*. Chapel Hill: The Univ. of North Carolina Press, 1944.

Mannheim, Karl. *Diagnosis of Our Time*. London: Kegan Paul, Trench, Trubner & Co., 1943.

————. *Essays on the Sociology of Knowledge*. Edited by Paul Kecskemeti. New York: Oxford Univ. Press, 1952.

————. *Freedom, Power, and Democratic Planning*. New York: Oxford Univ. Press, 1950.

————. *Ideology and Utopia*. Translated by Louis Wirth and Edward Shils. New York: Harcourt, Brace & Co., 1936.

Maquet, Jacques J. *The Sociology of Knowledge*. Boston: The Beacon Press, 1951.

Marett, R. R. *The Threshold of Religion*. Second edition. London: Methuen, 1914.

————. *Faith, Hope and Charity in Primitive Religion*. Oxford: The Clarendon Press, 1932.

Maritain, Jacques. *True Humanism*. Translated by M. R. Adamson. London: Geoffrey Bles: The Centenary Press, 1938.

Marmorstein, Emile. "Religious Opposition to Nationalism in the Middle East," *International Affairs*, July, 1952, 344–359.

Marx, Karl and Engels, Frederick. *Communist Manifesto*. Chicago: Charles H. Kerr & Co., 1940.

————. *The German Ideology*. New York: International Publishers, 1939.

Mather, Richard. "The Conflict of Buddhism with Native Chinese Ideologies," *The Review of Religion*, Nov., 1955, 25–37.

Maurer, Heinrich H. "Studies in the Sociology of Religion," *American Journal of Sociology*, Nov., 1924, 257–286; Jan., 1925, 408–438; March, 1925, 534–550; May, 1925, 665–682; July, 1925, 39–57; Jan., 1926, 485–506.

May, Henry F. *Protestant Churches and Industrial America*. New York: Harper & Bros., 1949.

Mayer, Carl. "The Problem of a Sociology of Religion," *Social Research*, Aug., 1936, 337–347.

Mays, Benjamin E. and Nicholson, Joseph W. *The Negro's Church*. New York: Institute of Social and Religious Research, 1933.

Means, Paul B. *Things that are Caesar's: The Genesis of the German Church Conflict*. New York: The Round Table Press, 1935.

Mecklin, John M. *The Story of American Dissent*. New York: Harcourt, Brace & Co., 1934.

Melish, William H. "Religious Developments in the Soviet Union," *American Sociological Review*, June, 1944, 279–286.

Mensching, Gustav. *Soziologie der Religion*. Bonn: Ludwig Rohrscheid Veslag Bonn, 1947.

Merton, Robert K. *Social Theory and Social Structure. Toward the Codification of Theory and Research*. Glencoe: The Free Press, 1949.

Michels, Roberto. *First Lectures in Political Sociology*. Translated, with Introduction by Alfred De Grazia. Minneapolis: Univ. of Minnesota Press, 1949.

Micklem, Nathaniel. *National Socialism and the Roman Catholic*. London: Oxford Univ. Press, 1939.

Miller, Perry, Calhoun, Robert L., Pusey, Nathan M., and Niebuhr, Reinhold. *Religion and Freedom of Thought*. New York: Doubleday & Co., 1954.

Miller, Randolph C., ed. *The Church and Organized Movements*. The Interseminary Series, vol. 2. New York: Harper & Bros., 1946.

Miller, William L. "Piety Along the Potomac," *The Reporter*, Aug. 17, 1954, 25–28.

——. "Some Negative Thinking About Norman Vincent Peale," *The Reporter*, Jan. 13, 1955, 19–24.

Misiak, Henry. "Psychosomatic Medicine and Religion," *Catholic World*, Feb., 1953, 342–345.

Moehlman, Conrad H. *The Wall of Separation Between Church and State*. Boston: The Beacon Press, 1951.

Moody, Joseph N., ed. *Church and Society: Catholic Social and Political Thought and Movements, 1789–1950*. New York: Arts, Inc., 1953.

Moore, John M. *Theories of Religious Experience, With Special Reference to James, Otto and Bergson*. New York: Round Table Press, 1938.

Morgan, Kenneth W., ed. *The Religion of the Hindus*. New York: The Ronald Press, 1953.

Muelder, Walter G. "From Sect to Church," *Christendom*, Autumn, 1945, 450–462.

——. *Religion and Economic Responsibility*. New York: Charles Scribner's Sons, 1953.

Murray, Gilbert. *Five Stages of Greek Religion*. Second edition. New York: Columbia Univ. Press, 1925.

Murphy, John. *The Origins and History of Religions*. Manchester: Univ. of Manchester Press, 1949.

Nadel, S. F. *Nupe Religion*. London: Routledge and Kegan Paul, 1954.

Nash, Philleo. "The Place of Religious Revivalism in the Formation of the Intercultural Community on Klamath Reservation," *Social Anthropology of North American Tribes*. Eggan, Fred, ed., 375–442. Chicago: Univ. of Chicago Press, 1937.

National Council of the Churches of Christ in the U.S.A. *Yearbook of*

American Churches. 1953 edition. Benson Y. Landis, ed. New York: National Council, 1953.

Needham, Joseph, ed. *Science Religion and Reality.* New York: The Macmillan Co., 1925.

Nelson, Lowry. *The Mormon Village.* Salt Lake City: Univ. of Utah Press, 1952.

Nichols, James H. *Democracy and the Churches.* Philadelphia: Westminster Press, 1951.

Niebuhr, H. Richard. *The Kingdom of God in America.* Chicago: Willett, Clark & Co., 1937.

———. *The Social Sources of Denominationalism.* New York: Henry Holt & Co., 1929. Reprinted by the Shoestring Press, 1954.

Niebuhr, Reinhold. *Christianity and Power Politics.* New York: Charles Scribner's Sons, 1940.

———. "Co-Existence or Total War?" *Christian Century,* Aug. 18, 1954, 971–973.

———. *Moral Man and Immoral Society.* New York: Charles Scribner's Sons, 1932.

———. *The Nature and Destiny of Man.* One volume edition. New York: Charles Scribner's Sons, 1946.

———. *Reflections on the End of an Era.* New York: Charles Scribner's Sons, 1934.

———. *The Self and the Dramas of History.* New York: Charles Scribner's Sons, 1955.

———. *Why the Christian Church is Not Pacifist.* London: Student Christian Movement Press, 1940.

Nisbet, Robert A. "Conservatism and Sociology," *The American Journal of Sociology,* Sept., 1952, 167–175.

Nottingham, Elizabeth K. *Methodism and the Frontier. Indiana Proving Ground.* New York: Columbia Univ. Press, 1941.

———. *Religion and Society.* New York: Doubleday & Co., 1954.

Nuesse, C. J. and Harte, Thomas J., eds. *The Sociology of the Parish.* Milwaukee: The Bruce Publishing Co., 1951.

O'Dea, Thomas F. "Mormonism and the Avoidance of Sectarian Stagnation: A Study of Church, Sect, and Incipient Nationality," *American Journal of Sociology,* Nov., 1954, 285–293.

Otto, Rudolf. *The Idea of the Holy.* Revised edition. Translated by John W. Harvey. London: Oxford Univ. Press, 1923.

Outler, Albert C. *Psychotherapy and the Christian Message.* New York: Harper & Bros., 1954.

Page, C. H. "Bureaucracy and the Liberal Church," *Review of Religion,* March, 1952, 137–150.

Parrinder, E. Geoffrey. *African Traditional Religion.* London: Hutchinson House, 1954.

Parsons, Talcott. *Essays in Sociological Theory Pure and Applied.* Glencoe: The Free Press, 1949.

————. "H. M. Robertson on Max Weber and His School," *Journal of Political Economy,* Oct., 1935, 688–696.

————. *Religious Perspectives of College Teaching in Sociology and Social Psychology.* New Haven: The Edward W. Hazen Foundation.

————. *The Social System.* Glencoe: The Free Press, 1951.

————. *Structure of Social Action.* New York: McGraw-Hill Book Co., Inc., 1937.

Parsons, Talcott and Shils, Edward A., eds. *Toward a General Theory of Action.* Cambridge: Harvard Univ. Press, 1951.

Partisan Review. "Religion and the Intellectuals," Feb., 1950, 103–142; March, 1950, 216–256; April, 1950, 313–339; May–June, 1950, 456–483.

Pauck, Wilhelm. *The Heritage of the Reformation.* Glencoe: The Free Press, 1950.

Peale, Norman V. *A Guide to Confident Living.* New York: Prentice-Hall, Inc., 1948.

Perry, Ralph B. *Puritanism and Democracy.* New York: The Vanguard Press, 1944.

The Persecution of the Catholic Church in the Third Reich. Facts and Documents translated from the German. London: Burns Oates, 1940.

Petegorsky, David W. *Left-Wing Democracy in the English Civil War. A Study of the Social Philosophy of Gerrard Winstanley.* London: Victor Gollancz, Ltd., 1940.

Pfautz, Harold W. "Christian Science: A Case Study of the Social Psychological Aspect of Secularization," *Social Forces,* March, 1956, 246–251.

————. "The Sociology of Secularization: Religious Groups," *American Journal of Sociology,* Sept., 1955, 121–128.

Pfeffer, Leo. *Church, State, and Freedom.* Boston: The Beacon Press, 1953.

————. "The Supreme Court as Protector of Civil Rights: Freedom of Religion," *Annals of the American Academy of Political and Social Science,* May, 1951, 75–85.

Pfuetze, Paul E. *The Social Self.* New York: Bookman Associates, 1954.

Pike, Royston. *Jehovah's Witnesses.* New York: Philosophical Library, 1954.

Pittenger, W. Norman. "Religion and Morality," *Christendom*, Autumn, 1946, 509–514.

Pope, Liston. *Millhands and Preachers*. New Haven: Yale Univ. Press, 1942.

———. "Religion and the Class Structure," *Annals of the American Academy of Political and Social Science*, March, 1948, 84–91.

———. "Religion as a Social Force in America," *Social Action*, May, 1953, 2–15.

Powdermaker, Hortense. *After Freedom. A Cultural Study in the Deep South*. New York: The Viking Press, 1939.

Radcliffe-Brown, Alfred R. *The Andaman Islanders*. Cambridge: Cambridge Univ. Press, 1922.

———. *Religion and Society*. London: Royal Anthropological Institute of Great Britain and Ireland, 1945.

Radin, Paul. *Primitive Religion. Its Nature and Origin*. New York: The Viking Press, 1937.

Randall, John H. and Randall, John H., Jr. *Religion and the Modern World*. New York: Frederick A. Stokes Co., 1929.

Randall, John H., Jr. *The Making of the Modern Mind*. Revised edition. Boston: Houghton Mifflin Co., 1940.

Ranke, Leopold von. *History of the Reformation in Germany*. Translated by Sarah Austin. Edited by R. A. Johnson. London: George Routledge & Sons, 1905.

Rapoport, Robert N. *Changing Navaho Religious Values. A Study of Christian Missions to the Rimrock Navahos*. Papers of the Peabody Museum of American Archaeology and Ethnology, Harvard University, vol. XLI, no. 2. Cambridge: The Peabody Museum, 1954.

Rauschenbush, Walter. *Christianity and the Social Crisis*. New York: The Macmillan Co., 1907.

———. *Christianizing the Social Order*. New York: The Macmillan Co., 1912.

Redfield, Robert. *The Primitive World and Its Transformations*. Ithaca: Cornell Univ. Press, 1953.

Review of Religion. Horace L. Friess, ed. Whole issue, May, 1946. "Religion and Health."

Review of Religion. Horace L. Friess, ed. Whole issue, March, 1949. "Religion and Health."

Rieff, Philip. "The Meaning of History and Religion in Freud's Thought," *Journal of Religion*, April, 1951, 114–131.

Riesman, David. *Individualism Reconsidered*. Glencoe: The Free Press, 1954.

Riesman, David in collaboration with Reuel Denney and Nathan Glazer. *The Lonely Crowd. A Study of the Changing American Character.* New Haven: Yale Univ. Press, 1950.

Rivers, W. H. R. *The Todas.* London: Macmillan & Co., 1906.

Roberts, David E. *Psychotherapy and a Christian View of Man.* New York: Charles Scribner's Sons, 1950.

Roberts, William H., *et al.* "Analysis and Faith," *New Republic,* May 16, 1955, 16–22.

Robertson, H. M. *Aspects of the Rise of Economic Individualism. A Criticism of Max Weber and His School.* Cambridge: Cambridge Univ. Press, 1933.

Roll, Erich. *A History of Economic Thought.* New York: Prentice-Hall, Inc., 1940.

Rosenthal, Henry M. "On the Function of Religion in Culture," *Review of Religion,* Jan., 1941, 148–171; March, 1941, 290–309.

Ross, E. A. *Social Control.* New York: The Macmillan Co., 1901.

Roy, Ralph L. *Apostles of Discord. A Study of Organized Bigotry and Disruption on the Fringes of Protestantism.* Boston: The Beacon Press, 1953.

Ryan, John A. and Husslein, Joseph, eds. *The Church and Labor.* New York: The Macmillan Co., 1924.

Salisbury, W. Seward. "Faith, Ritualism, Charismatic Leadership and Religious Behavior," *Social Forces,* March, 1956, 241–245.

Sanderson, Ross W. *The Church Serves the Changing City.* New York: Harper & Bros., 1955.

Sapir, Edward. "The Meaning of Religion," *American Mercury,* Sept., 1928, 72–79.

Schenk, Wilhelm. *The Concern for Social Justice in the Puritan Revolution.* New York: Longmans, Green & Co., 1948.

Scheuer, Joseph F., Schuyler, Joseph B. and Santopolo, Frank A. "Parish Sociology," *Thought,* Summer, 1955, 243–259.

Schlatter, R. B. "The Problem of Historical Causation in Some Recent Studies of the English Revolution," *Journal of the History of Ideas,* June, 1943, 349–367.

———. *The Social Ideas of Religious Leaders, 1660–1688.* London: Humphrey Milford, 1940.

Schmidt, Paul W. *The Origin and Growth of Religion.* New York: The Dial Press, 1931.

Schneider, Herbert W. *Religion in 20th Century America.* Cambridge: Harvard Univ. Press, 1952.

Schwer, Wilhelm. *Catholic Social Theory*. Translated by Bartholomew Landheer. Preface by Franz Mueller. St. Louis: B. Herder Book Co., 1940.

See, Henri. "Dans quelle mesure puritains et juifs ont-ils contribue aux progres du capitalisme moderne?" *Revue Historique,* vol. CLV (1927).

———. *Modern Capitalism*. Translated by H. B. Vanderblue and G. F. Doriot. New York: Adelphi Co., 1928.

Seldes, Gilbert. *The Stammering Century*. New York: The John Day Co., 1928.

Sheen, Fulton J. *Peace of Soul*. New York: Whittlesey House, 1949.

Shires, Henry M. "The Conflict Between Queen Elizabeth and Roman Catholicism," *Church History,* Dec., 1947, 221–233.

Shotwell, James T. *The Religious Revolution of Today*. Boston: Houghton Mifflin Co., 1913.

Sibley, Mulford Q. and Jacob, Philip E. *Conscription of Conscience*. Ithaca: Cornell Univ. Press, 1952.

Simmel, Georg. "A Contribution to the Sociology of Religion." Translated by W. W. Elwang. *American Journal of Sociology,* Nov., 1905. Reprinted May, 1955.

Simpson, George E. "Jamaican Revivalist Cults," *Social and Economic Studies,* Dec., 1956, whole issue.

———. "The Ras Tafari Movement in Jamaica: A Study of Race and Class Conflict," *Social Forces,* Dec., 1955, 167–170.

Simpson, George E. and Yinger, J. Milton. *Racial and Cultural Minorities: An Analysis of Prejudice and Discrimination*. New York: Harper & Bros., 1953.

Sklare, Marshall. *Conservative Judaism: An American Religious Movement*. Glencoe: The Free Press, 1955.

Slotkin, J. S. *Menomini Peyotism*. Philadelphia: American Philosophical Society *Transactions,* vol. 42, part 4, Dec., 1952.

Smith, Homer W. *Man and His Gods*. Boston: Little, Brown & Co., 1952.

Smith, Luke M. "The Clergy: Authority Structure, Ideology, Migration," *American Sociological Review,* June, 1953, 242–248.

Smith, Preserved. *The Age of the Reformation*. New York: Henry Holt & Co., 1920.

Smith, Rockwell C. *The Church in Our Town*. New York: Abingdon-Cokesbury Press, 1945.

Smith, William R. *Lectures on The Religion of The Semites*. Third edition. London: A. & C. Black Ltd., 1927.

Sociology Club, University of Hawaii. *Social Process in Hawaii,* vol. 16, "Sociology of Religion in Hawaii." Honolulu: Sociology Club, Univ. of Hawaii, 1952.

Sombart, Werner. *The Jews and Modern Capitalism.* Translated, with notes, by M. Epstein. London: F. Fisher Unwin, Ltd., 1913.

————. *The Quintessence of Capitalism.* Translated and edited by M. Epstein. London: F. Fisher Unwin, Ltd., 1915.

Sorokin, Pitirim A., ed. *Forms and Techniques of Altruistic and Spiritual Growth: A Symposium.* Boston: The Beacon Press, 1954.

————. *Social and Cultural Dynamics.* 4 vols. New York: American Book Co., 1937–1941.

Sorokin, Pitirim A. *The Ways and Power of Love: Types, Factors, and Techniques of Moral Transformation.* Boston: The Beacon Press, 1954.

Spann, J. Richard, ed. *The Church and Social Responsibility.* New York: Abingdon-Cokesbury Press, 1953.

Spencer, Herbert. *The Principles of Sociology.* Third edition. New York: D. Appleton & Co., 1896.

Sperry, Willard L. *Religion in America.* New York: The Macmillan Co., 1946.

Stelzle, Charles. *The Church and Labor.* Boston: Houghton Mifflin Co., 1910.

Stokes, Anson P. *Church and State in the United States.* 3 vols. New York: Harper & Bros., 1950.

Stoops, Dashiell J. "Religion and Social Institutions," *American Journal of Sociology,* May, 1913, 796–807.

Strauss, Leo. *Natural Right and History.* Chicago: Univ. of Chicago Press, 1953.

Stroup, Herbert H. *The Jehovah's Witnesses.* New York: Columbia Univ. Press, 1945.

Sturzo, Luigi. *Church and State.* New York: Longmans, Green & Co., 1939.

Sundkler, Bengt G. M. *Bantu Prophets in South Africa.* London: Lutterworth Press, 1948.

Sweet, William W. *The American Churches. An Interpretation.* New York: Abingdon-Cokesbury Press, 1947.

————. "The Protestant Churches," *Annals of the American Academy,* March, 1948, 43–52.

————. *The Story of Religion in America.* Revised edition. New York: Harper & Bros., 1939.

Swift, Arthur L., Jr. *New Frontiers of Religion.* New York: The Macmillan Co., 1938.

Swift, Arthur L., Jr., ed. *Religion Today, A Challenging Enigma*. New York: McGraw-Hill Book Co., Inc., 1933.

Tawney, R. H. *The Acquisitive Society*. New York: Harcourt, Brace & Co., 1920.

——. *Religion and the Rise of Capitalism*. New York: Harcourt, Brace & Co., 1926.

——. "Religious Thought on Social and Economic Questions in the Sixteenth and Seventeenth Centuries," *The Journal of Political Economy*, vol. 31 (1923), 461–493, 637–674, and 804–825.

Temple, William. *Christianity and Social Order*. New York: Penguin Books, Inc., 1942.

——. *Nature, Man and God*. New York: The Macmillan Co., 1934.

Thomas, Norman. *The Conscientious Objector in America*. New York: B. W. Huebsch, Inc., 1923.

Thomte, Reidar. *Kierkegaard's Philosophy of Religion*. Princeton: Princeton Univ. Press, 1948.

Tillich, Paul. *The Interpretation of History*. Translated by N. A. Rasetzki and E. L. Talmey. New York: Charles Scribner's Sons, 1938.

——. "Protestantism in the Present World Situation," *American Journal of Sociology*, Sept., 1937, 236–248.

——. *The Shaking of the Foundations*. New York: Charles Scribner's Sons, 1948.

——. "The Social Functions of the Churches in Europe and America," *Social Research*, vol. 3 (1936), 90–104.

——. *Systematic Theology*. Vol. 1. Chicago: Univ. of Chicago Press, 1951.

——. "The Totalitarian State and the Claims of the Church," *Social Research*, vol. 1 (1934), 405–433.

Timasheff, N. S. *Religion in Soviet Russia*. New York: Sheed and Ward, 1942.

Toynbee, Arnold J. *A Study of History*. Vol. V. *The Disintegration of Civilizations*. London: Oxford Univ. Press, 1939.

——. *A Study of History*. Vol. VII. *Universal States and Universal Churches*. London: Oxford Univ. Press, 1954.

Troeltsch, Ernst. *Gesammelte Schriften*. Zweiter Band, *Zur religiösen Lage, Religionsphilosophie und Ethik* (1922). Vierter Band, *Aufsätze zur Geistesgeschichte und Religionssoziologie* (1925). Tübingen: J. C. B. Mohr (Paul Siebeck).

——. *Protestantism and Progress. A Historical Study of the Relation of Protestantism to the Modern World*. Translated by W. Montgomery. New York: G. P. Putnam's Sons, 1912.

————. *The Social Teaching of the Christian Churches.* 2 vols. Translated by Olive Wyon. New York: The Macmillan Co., 1931.

Trott, Norman L. and Sanderson, Ross W. *What Church People Think About Social and Economic Issues.* New York: Association Press, 1938.

Trueblood, Elton. "Vocational Christian Pacifism," *Christianity and Crisis,* Nov. 3, 1941, 2–5.

Tumin, Melvin M. and Arnold S. Feldman. "The Miracle at Sabana Grande," *Public Opinion Quarterly,* Summer, 1955, 125–139.

Tylor, Edward B. *Primitive Culture.* Seventh edition. New York: Brentano's, 1924.

Underhill, Ruth M. *Papago Indian Religion.* New York: Columbia Univ. Press, 1946.

United Nations Educational, Scientific and Cultural Organization, "Sociology of Religions. A Trend Report and Bibliography." *Current Sociology,* vol. V (1956).

United States Department of Commerce. Bureau of the Census. *Religious Bodies: 1936.* 2 vols. Washington: Government Printing Office, 1941.

Van der Veldt, James H. and Odenwald, R. P. *Psychiatry and Catholicism.* New York: McGraw-Hill Book Co., 1952.

Van Vleck, Joseph, Jr. *Our Changing Churches. A Study of Church Leadership.* New York: Association Press, 1937.

Vernon, Glenn M. "Background Factors Related to Church Orthodoxy," *Social Forces,* March, 1956, 252–254.

Vidal, F. S. "Religious Brotherhoods in Moroccan Politics," *Middle East Journal,* Oct., 1950, 427–446.

Vogt, Evon Z. and O'Dea, Thomas F. "A Comparative Study of the Role of Values in Social Action in Two Southwestern Communities," *American Sociological Review,* Dec., 1953, 645–654.

Wach, Joachim. *Sociology of Religion.* Chicago: Univ. of Chicago Press, 1944.

————. *Types of Religious Experience, Christian and Non-Christian.* Chicago: Univ. of Chicago Press, 1951.

Wagner, Donald O. *The Church of England and Social Reform Since 1854.* New York: Columbia Univ. Press, 1930.

Walker, Williston. *A History of the Christian Church.* New York: Charles Scribner's Sons, 1920.

Wallis, Louis. "Sociological Significance of the Bible," *American Journal of Sociology,* Jan., 1907, 532–552.

————. *Sociological Study of the Bible.* Chicago: Univ. of Chicago Press, 1912.

Wallis, Wilson D. *Messiahs, Their Role in Civilization.* American Council on Public Affairs, Washington, D. C., 1943.

———. *Religion in Primitive Society.* New York: F. S. Crofts & Co., 1939.

Ward, Harry F. *Democracy and Social Change.* New York: Modern Age Books, 1940.

———. *Our Economic Morality and the Ethic of Jesus.* New York: The Macmillan Co., 1929.

———. *Which Way Religion?* New York: The Macmillan Co., 1931.

Warner, W. Lloyd. *American Life. Dream and Reality.* Chicago: Univ. of Chicago Press, 1953.

———. *A Black Civilization.* New York: Harper & Bros., 1937.

Warner, Wellman J. *The Wesleyan Movement in the Industrial Revolution.* London: Longmans, Green & Co., 1930.

Warren, Roland L. "Fascism and the Church," *American Sociological Review,* Feb., 1941, 45–51.

Wax, Rosalie and Wax, Murray. "The Vikings and the Rise of Capitalism," *American Journal of Sociology,* July, 1955, 1–10.

Wearmouth, Robert F. *Methodism and the Working-Class Movements of England, 1800–1850.* London: The Epworth Press, 1937.

Weber, Max. *Ancient Judaism.* Translated and edited by Hans H. Gerth and Don Martindale. Glencoe: The Free Press, 1952.

———. *From Max Weber: Essays in Sociology.* Edited and translated by H. H. Gerth and C. Wright Mills. New York: Oxford Univ. Press, 1946.

———. *General Economic History.* Translated by Frank Knight. New York: Greenburg, Publisher, 1927.

———. *Gesammelte Aufsätze zur Religionssoziologie.* 3 vols. Tübingen: J. C. B. Mohr (Paul Siebeck), 1922–1923.

———. *The Hindu Social System.* Translated by Hans Gerth and Don Martindale. Minneapolis: Univ. of Minnesota Sociology Club, 1950.

———. *The Protestant Ethic and the Spirit of Capitalism.* Translated by Talcott Parsons. London: George Allen and Unwin, Ltd., 1930.

———. *The Religion of China.* Translated by Hans H. Gerth. Glencoe: The Free Press, 1951.

———. *The Theory of Social and Economic Organization.* Translated by A. M. Henderson and Talcott Parsons, edited with an Introduction by Talcott Parsons. New York: Oxford Univ. Press, 1947.

———. *Wirtschaft und Gesellschaft.* Tübingen: J. C. B. Mohr (Paul Siebeck), 1922.

Welford, A. T. "Is Religious Behavior Dependent on Affect or Frustration?" *Journal of Abnormal and Social Psychology,* July, 1947, 310–319.

Wesley, John. *Sermons.* New York, 1868.

White, Andrew D. *A History of the Warfare of Science with Theology in Christendom.* 2 vols. New York: D. Appleton & Co., 1896.

Whitehead, Alfred N. *Religion in the Making.* New York: The Macmillan Co., 1926.

———. *Science and the Modern World.* New York: The New American Library (Mentor Books), 1948. First published by Macmillan, 1925.

Whitley, Oliver R. "The Sect-to-Denomination Process in an American Religious Movement: The Disciples of Christ," *The Southwestern Social Science Quarterly,* Dec., 1955, 275–281.

Wiese, Leopold von. *Systematic Sociology.* Adapted and amplified by Howard Becker. New York: John Wiley & Sons, Inc., 1932.

Williams, Melvin J. *Catholic Social Thought.* New York: The Ronald Press, 1950.

Williams, Robin M., Jr. *American Society.* New York: Alfred A. Knopf, 1951.

Wilson, Charles L. "A Social Picture of a Congregation," *American Sociological Review,* June, 1945, 418–422.

Wilson, Edmund. *The Scrolls from the Dead Sea.* New York: Oxford Univ. Press, 1955.

Woodhouse, A. S. P. *Puritanism and Liberty.* Being the Army Debates, 1647–1649, from the Clarke Manuscripts with Supplementary Documents. Selected and edited by Woodhouse. London: J. M. Dent & Sons, 1938.

Workman, Herbert B. *The Dawn of the Reformation.* London: The Epworth Press, 1901.

World Council of Churches. *Six Ecumenical Surveys.* Preparatory material for the Second Assembly of the World Council of Churches, 1954. New York: Harper & Bros., 1954.

Wright, Arthur F., ed. "Studies in Chinese Thought." Comparative Studies of Cultures and Civilizations, no. 1. Robert Redfield and Milton Singer, eds. *The American Anthropologist,* Dec., 1953.

Yinger, J. Milton. "Present Status of the Sociology of Religion," *The Journal of Religion,* July, 1951, 194–210.

———. *Religion in the Struggle for Power. A Study in the Sociology of Religion.* Durham: Duke Univ. Press, 1946.

Young, Pauline V. *The Pilgrims of Russian-Town.* Chicago: Univ. of Chicago Press, 1932.

Younger, George. "Protestant Piety and the Right Wing," *Social Action,* May 15, 1951, 5–35.

Zeitlin, Joseph. *Disciples of the Wise.* New York: Bureau of Publications, Teachers College, Columbia Univ., 1945.

Znaniecki, Florian. *Social Actions.* New York: Farrar & Rinehart, Inc., 1936.

SUBJECT INDEX